Charles M Eames

Historic Morgan and Classic Jacksonville

Charles M Eames

Historic Morgan and Classic Jacksonville

ISBN/EAN: 9783337179489

Printed in Europe, USA, Canada, Australia, Japan

Cover: Foto ©Andreas Hilbeck / pixelio.de

More available books at **www.hansebooks.com**

AND

CLASSIC JACKSONVILLE.

COMPILED IN 1884-'85 BY

CHARLES M. EAMES,

(Editor and Proprietor of the Daily and Weekly Journal.)

WITH INTRODUCTION BY

PROF. HARVEY W. MILLIGAN, A. M., M. D.,

OF ILLINOIS COLLEGE.

ILLUSTRATED.

JACKSONVILLE, ILL.:
PRINTED AT THE DAILY JOURNAL STEAM JOB PRINTING OFFICE.
1885.

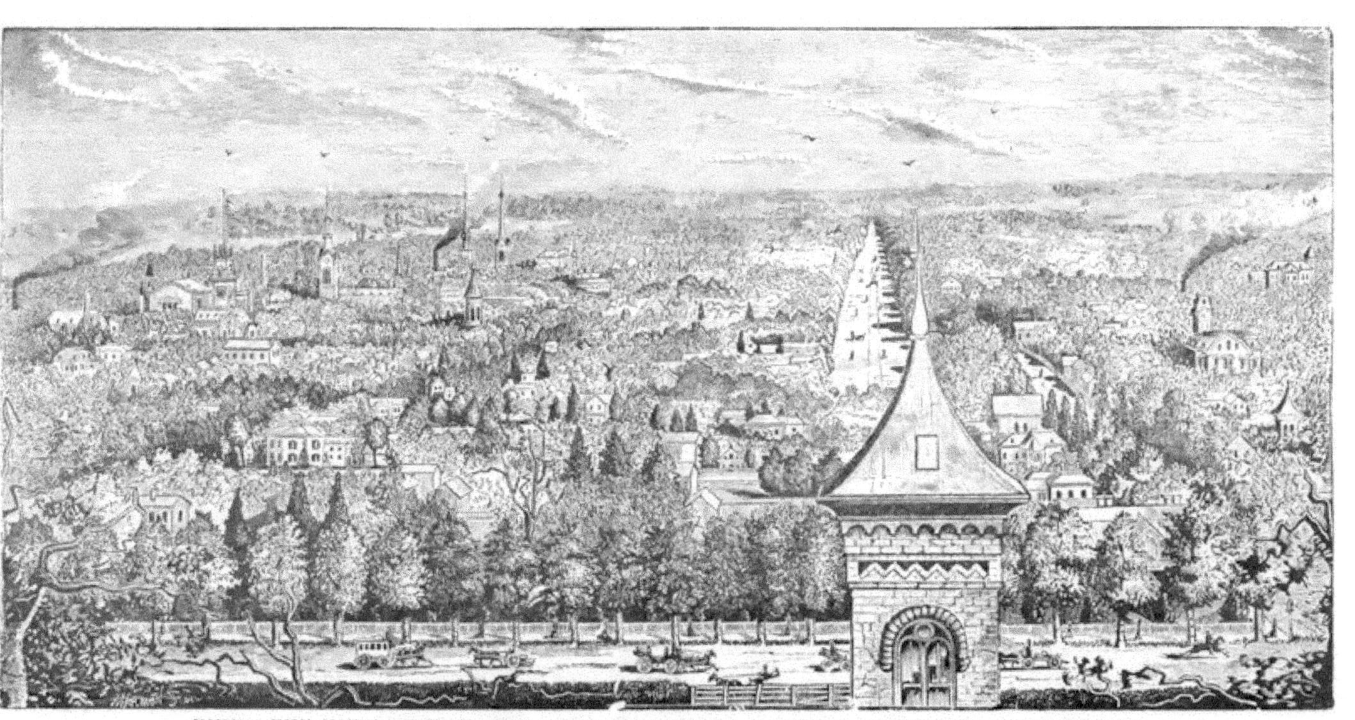

BIRD'S EYE VIEW OF THE CITY OF JACKSONVILLE, LOOKING EAST FROM COLLEGE HILL.

THIS BOOK

IS

RESPECTFULLY DEDICATED

TO THE MEMORY OF

THE OLD SETTLERS OF MORGAN COUNTY.

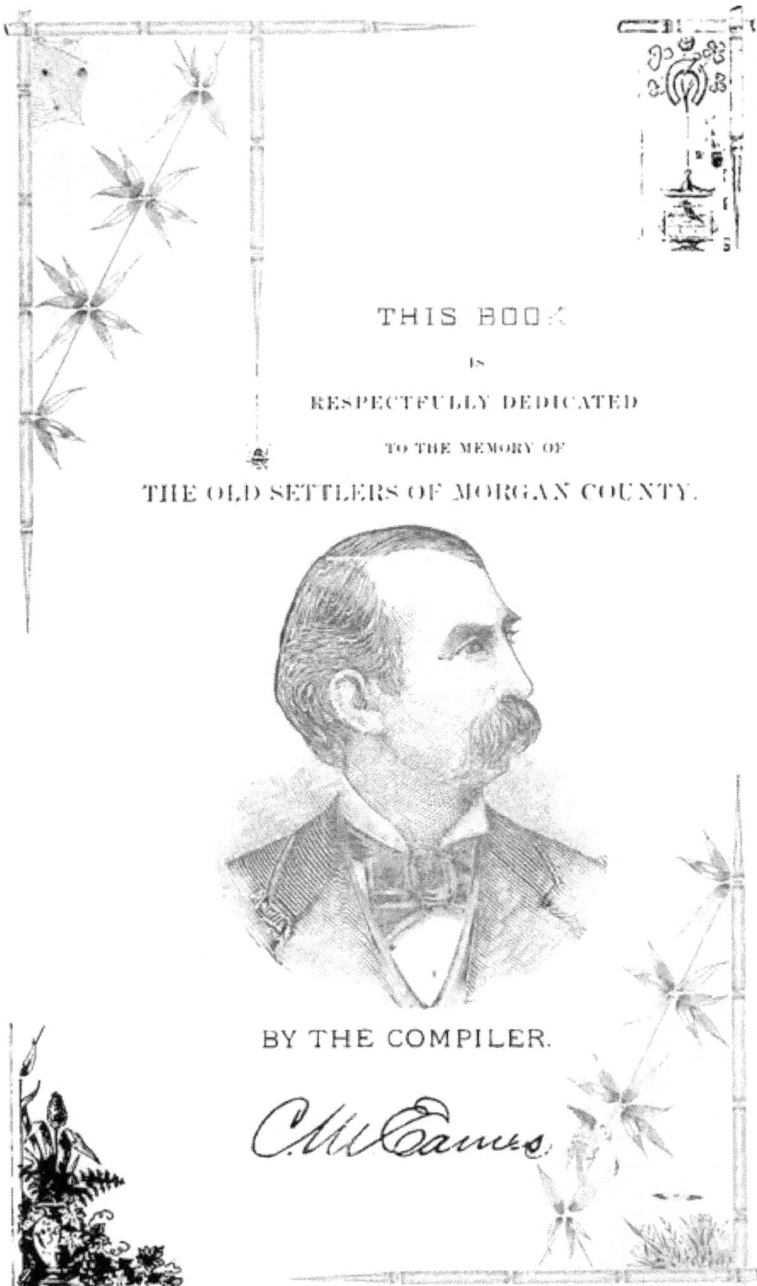

BY THE COMPILER.

PREFACE.

I am reminded by the date of these final words, as the last form of "Historic Morgan" goes to press, that just a year has passed since, in a quiet way, I began the pleasant, self-imposed task of gathering material to supply, of course, "a long-felt want." The *Journal* files, extending back a quarter-of-century—not quite one-half the time, I wished to cover by an unpretentious historic compilation—occupied attention for months, and then came researches into other newspapers, stray copies of old-time *Patriots, Sentinels*, etc., records of societies and public meetings, interviews with the few surviving rescuers of this fair portion of Illinois, from aboriginal owners, rudeness and wild, unbroken prairie condition. Written recollections of early times claimed due consideration next. Encouragement came from the "Old Settlers' Associations" of Morgan and Cass and the "Jacksonville Historical Society." The material accumulated rapidly, for the field was fruitful, and the work grew more fascinating as it progressed. The size of the volume does not, to a casual observer, indicate extensive contents; but when the size of type used and the "solid" character of many pages are properly considered, even without perusal, the examiner will realize that a vast amount of information is contained in its fourteen chapters. There has been no attempt at ornate writing, no space wasted in opinion-giving, and we lay no claim and take no credit for authorship. The honor of painstaking in research and collecting, and faithfulness in chronicling all the noteworthy steps in the sixty years' progressive history of "my own, my native" city and county, the credit of publishing the most complete and accurate compilation of historical notes pertaining to "Old Morgan," is all that I ask of the present or future readers of the volume, if the work should have more than a transient existence.

One fact will, I hope, be evident, viz., that there is nothing of a money-making or advertising character to the editing or publishing of the book. Of course many enterprises and individuals have been complimented, but no pecuniary consideration has biased a single line or sentence. Even the illustrations of business houses were inserted gratuitously, that there might be no charge of "paid puff" connected with the book. I am well aware, too, there must have been some omissions and possible misstatements, as it is absolutely impossible to furnish a perfect history of long past times with meager resources at command. My original plan, of strict chronological order from first to last, had to be abandoned, on account of the late securing of material bearing upon early times.

Due acknowledgement is made elsewhere of my indebtedness to various persons and papers for valuable aid.

It will be observed that I have made no attempt to follow up the history of the towns of the county, except Jacksonville, since the date of the incorporation of that place. I have not had access to the necessary information.

"My task is done."
"The torch shall be extinguished which has lit"
"The midnight lamp; and what is writ is writ."
"Would it were worthier!"

JACKSONVILLE, March 31, 1885. THE COMPILER.

INTRODUCTION.

Every community is born into an inheritance. This inheritance may be one of virtue or one of vice, of prudence or of folly, of health or of disease, of wealth or of poverty. The possession of wealth, health, prudence or virtue, or of an inherited tendency to secure those blessings, involves an obligation to those from whom such inclination comes; while poverty, or vice, or folly, or disease, or even a tendency to those conditions, connects us no less intimately with our predecessors.

How may we cancel this obligation which has come down to us from the past? Our ancestors are not here. If they were they would need no pay from us. But they are careless alike of praise or blame, of profit or of loss. It only remains to us to pay their heirs, who, fortunately, are also our heirs.

By what means shall we pay this debt to posterity?

We may do this by informing those who are to come of the causes of present and past prosperity. We may show them that man in his political and social relations is subject to laws which are as imperative as the laws of the physical world. We may tell them that the greatest individual liberty which is consistent with the good of society must be allowed. We may prove to them that individual production of wealth must not be checked. We may declare that intelligence is one of the greatest causes of prosperity, and that morality and piety exalt any people. To enforce and illustrate such teachings we may refer to the contents of this volume.

We should also tell of the mistakes of the fathers to the end that similar errors may be avoided. Show that neglect of education postpones prosperity, that intemperance increases taxation, that natural obstructions to trade diminish profits, that unprofitable industries destroy wealth, that debt discourages enterprise. By such teachings, both in the way of encouragement and of warning, in things industrial, social, political, intellectual, moral and religious, we may, perhaps, cancel the debt we owe to our ancestors by conferring a favor on posterity. To this end," Historic Morgan" is a means.

The following pages also have the advantage of teaching these principles by example, which is the most effective method of conveying truth. When we read that the Morganian Society, founded in 1823, and consisting of one hundred and twenty-five persons, adopted a constitution containing these words: "It is the declared design and intention of this society to promote the public good by using all honorable means to prevent the introduction of slavery in this state," we feel little surprise that, forty years later, a citizen of Illinois, from the National office in Washington, should have signed the Emancipation Proclamation. What reform of political methods, or what attainment of political good is impossible to a community which organized a Morganian society, and sustained an Abraham Lincoln?

As we read in these pages the romantic and thrilling story of the "Regulators of the Valley," we are reminded that justice is the end of society, and law is but one of its means; and that, in the emergencies of a new country, a short cut to the end may be both allowable and advisable.

It is hard for us, who order through a telephone, from a mile away, flour of the finest of wheat, to realize that sixty-five years ago, the nearest flour-mill was eighty-five long miles away. It is just as difficult to conceive of Huram Reeve's blacksmith-shop, or of Roe & Webster's grist-mill, or of the substitutes for cassimeres and broadcloth, which, only three generations ago, our fathers and mothers made and wore.

It is bewildering to compare our present methods in agriculture with those described in this book. Our planters, our cultivators, our reapers are not only sources of wealth, but their invention constitutes our titles of nobility. But the log cabins, the linsey garments and the hand grist-mills were for our fathers as clear a title to as proud a nobility. Their industry and frugality, as herein portrayed, laid the foundation of our wealth and leisure and culture.

There are economical lessons to be learned from "Historic Morgan" concerning the development of manufactures among us. From the data given we may learn the following principles: 1st, That a successful industry must have unsurpassed facilities for obtaining raw materials. 2nd, It must command a market second to none, for its manufactured goods. 3rd, It must be able to compete successfully with all other places in cheapness of labor. If, in the aggregate of these three elements of production, Morgan should fall behind other counties, it is inevitable that manufactures should fail here, and that the money invested should be lost. Unless we wish to be continually heaving our money into bottomless coal-holes, or wasting our wealth upon moribund car-works, we must heed these principles, and their illustrations as found in this volume.

And here also the record comes to our aid to show us what enterprises are profitable,—for that there are profitable industries here, five flourishing banks bear witness.

As we are living history, day by day; so also must we daily record that history for the benefit of posterity. "Historic Morgan" as it now appears, should be but the beginning of a series of recorded events to which some future historian, with a broader horizon than we behold, shall furnish the key. Without this record, enlarged and continued as it will be, a true history, showing the relation of causes and effects, would be impossible, and to a great degree past and present generations would have lived in vain. With it, posterity can profit both by our successes and by our mistakes. With it as data

> "They may discern—unseen before—
> "A path to higher destinies."

Let us greet then "Historic Morgan" as a means of utilizing the past for the benefit of the future. H. W. MILLIGAN.

TABLE OF CONTENTS.

CHAPTER VIII.

CHAPTER IX.—1858–'65.

CHAPTER X.—1866–'73.

CHAPTER XI.—1874–'80.

CHAPTER XII.—1881–'84.

CHAPTER XIII.

CHAPTER XIV.

CHAPTER XV.

HISTORIC MORGAN

AND

CLASSIC JACKSONVILLE.

COMPILED IN 1884 BY

CHARLES M. EAMES,

EDITOR AND PROPRIETOR OF THE DAILY AND WEEKLY JOURNAL.

CHAPTER I.—1819–'24.

The First White Settlers—The Original Log-Cabins—The Explorers from New York—First Ground Broken—Birthplace of Methodism in Morgan—Sixty Miles to Mill—An Anti-Slavery Society in 1825—Its Constitution and Signers—The County Created—The First Birth and First Death, First Sermon and First Sunday-School—The First Courts and Elections According to Judge Thomas and Gen. McConnel—Old Time Justices—Judge Lockwood, Col. Joseph Morton, Judge Solomon, Uncle Johnny Jordan—Recollections of Old Settlers—Beardstown and Meredosia Founded.

"Should auld acquaintance be forgot
And never brought to mind?
Should old acquaintance be forgot
And days o' lang syne?"

AS early as 1818, when the now great commonwealth of Illinois was admitted into the Union, most of the white inhabitants of this then emphatically Prairie State lived south of a line between the mouths of the Wabash and Illinois Rivers. That year Seymour Kellogg—who was born on the 21st of March, 1779, and died April 13th, 1827—moved from New York State to Illinois. He had been in the war of 1812, and was familiarly known as Col. Kellogg. In the fall of 1819, with his brother Elisha, he moved to near the head of the Mauvaisterre, and thus, to the best of the knowledge of any living "oldest inhabitant," the Kellogg brothers became the first white settlers of Morgan. They built their log-cabin—the pioneer home in this county—on the land later owned by Col. Samuel T. Matthews, in township 15 N., range 9 W. A grand-son of Elisha Kellogg afterwards married Mary Chamberlain and is now living at Santa Barbara, California. Another grand-son married Fannie Foster of this city.

Mrs. Asenath K. Mundy, daughter of Seymour Kellogg, writing from Brighton in 1879, says of her father and their frontier home:

"He then built a log cabin, clapboard roof and ground floor and no doors or windows, and twenty miles to any neighbors. Indians, wolves, wild turkeys and hogs were all around us. He stayed there one winter and came near freezing to death, having gone with two yoke of oxen twenty miles for a load of corn. A severe snow storm came and losing his way he lay out one night, and turned his oxen loose. They found their way home. Search was made at once by an uncle, who came out with us and my brother then 13 years old. They found my father with his feet frozen and had hard work getting him home, where he laid for months unable to walk. That spring we moved west of Jacksonville, near the creek. We caught fish from the Mauvaisterre, that ran over the prairie out near the high mound, where Mr. Strawn located a beautiful place. My father was appointed State surveyor, and he laid out the towns of Jacksonville, Exeter, Naples, Beardstown, Meredosia, Perry, Griggsville and many other places. He kept the first store of Exeter, was P. M., J. P., and held other positions. While living at Exeter he went to St. Louis for goods, going in a wagon, for there was no rail in those days. One week after arriving there he was buried from the residence of Mr. Charles Collins, his son-in-law. * * * * * * * The first preaching in Morgan county was at our house. The first school taught was by my sister in a log cabin without any doors or windows, in 1821."

In January, 1820, the Kelloggs entertained three explorers from New York, David Berdan, (father of Judge James Berdan,) George Nixon, and Isaac Fort Roe; and sold them corn for their horses, which had been wagoned from Madison county. Then there were neither churches or schools. People lived in tents and cabins. There were no roads or bridges, and most of the land was held by the general government. The man who settled on it did so at his peril of being tried for trespass. People risked considerable in those days, but no jury would find for the government in such a suit because they thought the government should sell the land. The army was small then, and couldn't be sent to remove settlers.

On the 12th of October, 1819, an emigration society, organized in the city of New York, had appointed the three pioneers named above, a committee to explore the western states and select homesteads for its members. They left that city on the 15th of October, crossed the Wabash at Vincennes on the 26th of December and arrived at St. Louis January 1st, 1820, passed and named Diamond Grove, January 23d, in which Mr. Roe selected a place of residence, and in February he built a log cabin, in which he resided until his death, October 12, 1821, aged forty-eight years. He was the son of the Rev. Doctor Ozel Roe, of Woodbridge, N. J., and was never married. The county of Morgan has since removed the remains of Mr. Roe, as the first person who died in the county, to the Diamond Grove Cemetery, and placed a monument on the grave. The city of Jacksonville donated a suitable lot.

The venerable Judge Thomas, of our city, says that he has "often heard Jeddediah Webster, a soldier in the war of 1812, who had passed up the Illinois River to the mouth of the Mauvaisterre in the keel boat with his family, say, that he assisted in building the first log cabin in the county, (referring to this built by Roe.) Whilst at Kellogg's these three pioneers learned that a man named Stephen Olmstead was engaged building a shanty at the point of timber, afterwards called Swinnerton's Point. They employed him to pilot them to the mouth of the Mauvaisterre—there was a deep snow then on the ground—then passed from Kellogg's around the head of Mauvaisterre Creek to Diamond Grove, thence to Swinnerton's Point, and then following their pilot they set out for the Illinois River. After reaching the timber and hills south of the Mauvaisterre, their pilot said he was lost, that he could not recognize the locations around him—they then returned to the shanty, where they remained until the next day, and from thence returned, by way of Kellogg to the head of Lick Creek, and from thence to Edwardsville."

The ranks of those who date back their residence in Morgan county "before the deep snow" are sadly thinned. Still fewer in number are those who can celebrate the "golden" anniversary of their location upon these prairies. Remarkable, then, was that social reunion, in 1877, of the Reeve family, the dining together of six out of a family of nine, who came to this "neck of the woods" in 1820, fifty-seven years previous. The party consisted of Messrs. Lazarus, John, Isaac and Huram, and Miss Keren Reeve and their sister, Mrs. Martha Reeve Crain. It was at the house of the latter that they met and recalled the days gone by. Only three of the family now are living.

One of the little company tells us that in 1820, when Isaac Reeve, Sr., came to this locality with his wife and nine children, the county boundaries covered what is now Madison and all that lies between that county and this, and was called Madison. In coming, the party followed an Indian trail, they being about the first white people to track the prairies between what is now Alton and Jacksonville. They drove ahead of them, all the way, a sow and her shoats and two cows having bells upon them that they might not be lost in the wild woods. Reaching here a halt was made, their property dumped upon the ground, while Mr. Reeve, Sr., started at once to return to Edwardsville for provisions. With the second load he brought a blacksmith's bellows, anvil and hammer. The former was swung between two saplings, a tree was felled and an anvil block made of the stump, logs were rolled up for the furnace and thus they began life in "Old Morgan." This first blacksmith shop was of great service to the emigrants, who began to settle in this region, for the sharpening of the plows with which the virgin sod of the "Prairie State" was to be upheaved. All provisions then had to be hauled one hundred miles.

Of Mr. Reeve's place of business, Rev. N. P. Heath has said in an historical address:

"It was a mammoth structure, as big as all out doors. Talk about your modern watch factories, and reaper factories, why the outside walls of Reeve's blacksmith shop extended as far as the lines of creation, to say nothing of the interior arrangements. This shop was the first for some time, and the only one in the county, in fact, it embraced all the county and more too. This soon became the headquarters of the county. Here, like the Athenians of old, the settlers would meet from all parts, in order to tell and hear the news, and I have been informed that the first post-office was opened at or near this place. And, from all that I can learn, they only lacked one thing of having a full grown town out on Sandy, and that was a doggery. However, the size of the blacksmith shop may account for that deficiency."

The first ground broken in the county for purposes of cultivation was in the spring of 1820. We have been furnished with the following names of persons who settled in the county during that spring: John Wyatt, William Wyatt, Isaac F. Roe, Jedediah Webster, Isaac Reeve, James B. Crum, Isaac Dial, Thomas Smith, James Deaton, Robert James, Jesse Ruble, Ancil Cox, Joseph Buchanan, Samuel Scott, Isaac Edwards, Archibald Job, Stephen Olmstead, Michael Arthur, James Buckley, Aaron Wilson, Isaac Smith.

Mr. Olmstead settled at a point now known as Allison's Mound. A settlement was made the same year on the north fork of the Mauvaisterre by Samuel Scott, and James Kerr. General McConnel came into the county the same year.

In 1819, when the Kelloggs located their humble and now historic cabin on the banks of the Mauvaisterre, their nearest white neighbors were thirty miles distant, where Illinois' capital city is now growing so vigorously.

In the spring of 1820, James Deaton, Isaac Reeve, Sr., and family, Robert R. James and others settled north-west of the present site of Jacksonville. In the fall of the same year John Bradshaw, Joseph Morton, Joseph Buchanan, Ancil Cox and Michael Antyl settled south and east of the same. In 1821, Lott Luttrell, Johnston Shelton and Francis Petree became residents within the present bounds of Morgan county. In 1822, William. C. Verry, Thomas Wiswall, Adam Allison and a few others were added to the sparsely inhabited settlement. From this time emigration poured into this golden land of promise. The wild prairies were fenced, plowed and sown, rank wild grass yielded to corn, wheat, oats, etc. Homes were established, fruit trees planted, live stock imported and the savages' hunting ground converted into as charming a farming region as beautifies this earth.

The act of Congress reducing the price of the public lands from $2.00 to $1.25 per acre, was passed on the 24th day of April 1820, and took effect on the first day of July thereafter. Very little land, if any, had been sold in Morgan county before this time.

Levi Deaton, one of the first settlers in Morgan county, has, in answer to an inquiry, written the following about the introduction of Methodism into this county:

"The first sermon preached in the county, so far as I know, was by Rev. John Glanville, at my father's house, in 1822. A class was then and there organized, consisting of my father and mother, and a brother named Johnson and his wife. The first quarterly meeting was held the same year at Father Jordan's—father of John and Wm. Jordan, in the east part of Jacksonville. The first camp meeting in the county was held on Walnut Creek, near Lynnville, by Peter Cartwright."

The statement is undisputed that the first Morgan county church was organized in 1822 by a few persons who held their meetings for worship in this famous large log cabin of "Father" Jordan. It stood just back of the old Berean College building and was erected before Morgan county was created. Its members were scattered over the country, many of them coming many miles to attend service. The Methodists continued to hold meetings in this cabin until the completion of the school house in which Judge Thomas held the first school in Jacksonville. They worshiped here until 1833 when they erected a brick church on East Morgan street, which was the first brick church in the county.

It was in 1822 that "Uncle John" Jordan, now living in Jacksonville, removed with his father to this county, but he went back to Missouri and did not finally settle here until 1833. That year cholera prevailed, and he and his brother spent nearly their whole time during the season in caring for the sick. They settled on the Hardin farm, in the east part of town and the first Methodist meetings were held at their house, as stated above, and since that time the home of the Jordan's has been the place of religion. He has been married three times and has survived all. Considering his age he is still very strong and hardly a day passes but that he is seen upon our streets. He does all his work, even to sawing the wood. During his whole life he has been a staunch Christian and one of the most honored members of Grace M. E. church. Ever since there was a *Journal*, or an ancestor to the *Journal*, published in Jacksonville, he has been a subscriber and now reads his *Daily Journal* thoroughly and regularly. Mr. Jordan is one of the few men now living who took part in the war of 1812 which forever decided the strength of our claims. He was in the most disagreeable part of that war, because those troops who went out against the Indians experienced unspeakable hardsnips and many died from exposure. After the treaty was made they moved back to Buffalo creek and engaged in the more peaceful pursuits of farming. The principal crop was corn and not much wheat was planted. At that early day Uncle John tells us he went sixty miles to mill, and that many people used the hand-mills to keep from going so great a distance. They had plenty of meat, corn-bread, butter, wild honey and milk, but coffee, sugar, etc., were very scarce. Coffee 75c per lb.

In a book entitled the "Annals of the West" we learn that there were in 1823 in Morgan county about seventy-two families. In 1821 there were but twenty families in (now) Morgan, Cass and Scott.

One of the most valuable historical documents of these earliest Morganian days is the constitution of a political society "to prevent the introduction of slavery into this state." Its supposed date is A. D. 1823. For, in February 1823, the Legislature passed an act authorizing the people to vote at the next election for and against calling a convention to adopt a new constitution, the object being to create the institution of slavery. The election was held in August 1824. A society in Morgan county was organized against the call, and of the one hundred and forty signers or members of this society, so far as is known, Lazarus Reeve and Alfred Mills, are the only survivors. Honor to the memory of their colleagues! And all honor to the living, who rejoice with us to-day in being citizens of a country that is free—the asylum of all the oppressed!

CONSTITUTION OF THE MORGANIAN SOCIETY.—Under a free government, public opinion gives energy to the laws, happiness and security of the community being the legitimate end. Every good citizen thereof has an interest in its support. Under its fostering wing his moral, his religious and his political rights are maintained. Virtue and intelligence should be its bond of union.

But as man is naturally prone to abuse power, it is rendered necessary for the security of the whole, that this dangerous propensity should be guarded against.

Therefore, we, citizens of Morgan county, have thought it advisable to form a society for the purpose of concentrating public opinion, and by a frequent interchange thereof, to enlighten and direct each other.

When entering into association it becomes an indispensable duty to adopt a regular system of establishing order. It is the declared design and intention of this society to promote the public good, by using all honorable means *to prevent the introduction of slavery into this State*, by maintaining the purity of elections; by cherishing political harmony, and by restraining vice and immorality.

The better to secure these objects, we, the undersigned, citizens of Morgan county, agree to the following constitution:

Art. 1. The style of this society shall be *The Morganian Society* for the dissemination of political knowledge and the maintenance of the unalienable rights of man.

Art. 2. No person shall be admitted a member of this society unless he has attained the age of eighteen years, is averse to slavery and is a citizen of this county.

Art. 3. The officers of this society shall be a president, vice-president, treasurer, a corresponding and a recording secretary, and a standing committee of twelve members.

Art. 4. The President shall preside at all regular meetings, preserve order repeat the question proposed by any member and perform such other duties as from time to time the society may require of him.

Art. 5. The Vice-President shall preside at the committee meetings and he shall in case of a tie have a casting vote; moreover, in the event of a vacancy, perform such duties as may be annexed to the fourth article.

Art. 6. The duties of the Treasurer shall be to receive and account for all moneys paid in by the society.

Art. 7. The secretaries shall keep a register of the transactions of this society and correspond with any others that may be formed in this state for similar purposes; they shall, moreover, exhibit the records at any regular or call meeting when requested by the President.

Art. 8. The standing committee shall individually and collectively promote the views of this society, by procuring qualified subscribers to this constitution, by using efforts to disseminate the principles of liberty, by striving to expose the views of those who are hostile to the natural and political rights of man; and by using all lawful means to prevent the introduction of slavery into this State.

Art. 9. There shall be neither local or political distinction of parties in the selection of candidates for office, save one, which requireth that he shall be decidedly opposed to slavery; nevertheless, it is expected that he shall inherit morality, integrity and capacity.

Art. 10. There shall be four regular meetings annually, viz: on the last Saturday in July, at the county seat, the last Saturday in October at the house of Col. Kellogg, on Plumb Creek, the last Saturday in January at the house of ——— ———, on Mauvaisterre, on the last Saturday of April at the house of ——— ———, on Indian.

Art. 11. All officers of the society shall be elected for one year and by ballot, subject to removal by the concurrent vote of four-fifths of the members present at any of the quarterly meetings.

Art. 12. On the first meeting after the adoption of this constitution there shall be a code of by-laws framed, which to enact or amend shall require a majority of votes at a quarterly meeting.

Art. 13. On the application and previous to the admission of new members, the president, or in his absence, the vice-president shall exact the following pledge:

"You, A B., do solemnly pledge your word and sacred honor that you are friendly to the natural and political rights of man and will use all honorable means to prevent the introduction of slavery into this state."

Art. 14. This constitution may be altered or amended at any quarterly meeting, provided two-thirds of the members present agree to the same.

Archibald Job, Moses Nash, Peter Conover, Thomas Arnett, Stephen W. Spencer, Elisha Kellogg, Elijah Wiswall, Eli Redding, Moses Keelock, Page Blake, David C. Blair, Robert Henry, Israel Robertson, Abram Johnson, Peleg Sweet, Robert Sweet, Charles W Horrell, David Beebe, Andrew Reed, Wm. C. Verry, Joseph Sweet, David Shelby, Constant Claxton, Wm. B. Burritt, Peter Smith, ALFRED MILLS, Elisha Henry, Wm. S Jordan, Andrew V. Patter, H. G. Taylor, Curtis Cadwell, John Weatherman, Joseph T. Leonard, Zachariah Cockburne, Bennett Smart, Robert Eckler, G. Cadwell, John Adams, Alford Carpenter, Samuel Bristow, Dennis Rockwell, Roswell Parmerlee, Lewis Allen Thomas Blair, Timothy Harris, Alex Blair Nathan Eels, John Box, Martin Dyer, Simeon Herron, James Hills, Stephen Langworthy, James Arnett, Wm.

L. Morse, Daniel Lieb, James Gillham, Wiley Green, Samuel Bogart, Aaron Robertson, Charles Self, Orris McCartney, Obadiah Waddell, Nelson McDowell, Timothy Demars, Phillip Mallett, Abram S Bergen, Rowland Shepherd, Ephraim Lisles, Henry Robley, John P. Tefft, Wm Robertson, Forrest Fisher, Aquilla Clarkston, William Samples, Horatio Eddy, Abram B Dewitt, Jonathan C. Bergen, Jesse Bellamy, Noah Wiswall, Stephen Olmstedt, Anthony Thomas, Levi Newman, James Jenkins, John Edwards, Isaac B. Reeve, LAZARUS REEVE, David Casebar, Myron Bronson, Joel Reeve, Levi Conover, Guinn Porter, John Angelo, James Deaton, Sr., James Deaton, Jr, George Hackett, Samuel Shepherd, Isaac Dial, Alexander Robertson, Robert James, Joseph I Basey, Stephen Nash, Baxter Broadwell, Patrick Lynch, Olney Ticknor, Seymour Kellogg, Charles Troy, Hiram Duff, Henry H. Snow, Joseph Stanley, Andrew Arnett, Joseph Carter, Thomas B. Arnett, Levi Deaton, Patrick Mullett, Thomas Kinnett, Benj Schmitz, Nicholas Jones, Joseph Milstead, Henry Kettner, Robert Bowen, James Redmond, Andrew Bowen, Levi Scott, Samuel Matthews, Richard Matthews, Sr., Richard Matthews, Jr., Robert Morgan, George Bristow, John Rusk, Armsted Cox

In January, A. D. 1823, when Morgan county was established, not a human being lived where now are the hundreds of handsome residences of our city—the homes of thousands of happy hearts; elegant business blocks—the every day haunt of enterprising and energetic merchants—and scores of schools, churches and charitable institutions—elevating the mind, ennobling the heart and kindly caring for the dependent—comprising what has endeared itself to the hearts of all her citizens, under the comprehensive name of Jacksonville.

The county was created by an act of the Legislature of date of January 31st, 1823, and named after the revolutionary general. The territory then included what is now Morgan, Cass and Scott counties, and was attached to the senatorial district composed of the counties of Greene and Pike, and of the representative district composed of Greene county. Dr. George Cadwell was elected to the Senate and Archibald Job to the House.

Of Mr. Job his friend Judge Thomas writes to the *Daily Journal*:

"Though humble and retiring in his pretensions, yet his mind—well stored with information upon all questions relating to the history of the country, the powers and practical operations of the government, the rights and duties of citizens, and above all, his stern integrity and persistent advocacy of the right, in connection with sound practical judgment—constituted him in the early settlement of the Sangamon country and for years afterwards a man of mark. He settled in the grove, which he called Sylvan Grove*, near the present site of Virginia, in Cass county, in the year 1820. In 1822 he was elected to the Legislature from the district composed of the county of Greene and the territory afterward included in the county of Morgan."

In 1821 Greene county was formed from Madison, in 1823 Morgan came from Greene, in 1837 Cass from Morgan, in 1839 Scott was set off.

In 1822, and the years following, the brave and hardy hunters, trappers, and pioneers gathered together, one by one, for mutual protection and for the cultivation of the fertile soil. There fortunately happened to be a higher culture among them than was usual for that class of men, in those days. Both the north and south contributed in about equal proportions their sons and daughters to form the society of the embryo city, and Jacksonville may owe, to some extent, her honorable and influential position in the state to this fact, since she avoided the vices and clung to the virtues of both sections. To the energy and enterprise of the Yankee she joined the generosity and hospitality of the Southron; and her sons and daughters grew up an educated, industrious and open-hearted race. To come more slowly up the plane of time we find the virgin sod of the prairie where Jacksonville now stands first furrowed in 1824, and the man who planted the first crop of corn lived in the county until 1881—Mr. John Reeve. Mr. "Jacky" Smith, deceased, is another claimant of the honor of breaking the sod here. At this time the county was much larger than at present, and the location of the county seat had not been decided upon, and the sessions of the circuit court were held temporarily at the house of James G. Swinnerton, some six miles west of the city, at Swinnerton's Point. The discussion as to the permanent location of the seat of justice came up in the autumn of 1824, and the geographical centre of the county was found to be on the

* Surrounded by Kickapoo and Pottawatomie Indians.

"Mound," about three miles west of the present site of the court house. This land, however, was already "entered," while the present site of Jacksonville was what was then called "congress land," and on account of its cheapness was accordingly purchased. The first court was held on the level prairie in the open air.

In a paper prepared for the Old Settlers' Meeting in 1873, and subsequently published in the *Daily Journal*, Judge Thomas says:

"The county of Morgan was created with the following boundary:

Beginning at the northwest corner of Greene county, thence east to the range line between seven and eight west of the third principal meridian, thence northerly along the middle of the prairie that divides the waters of the Sangamon from those of Apple Creek, Mauvaisterre and Indian Creek, until it arrives at the middle of range eight, thence north to the middle of the main channel of the Illinois river, thence down said last mentioned channel to the place of beginning.

An election of county officers was required to be held on the first Monday in March, 1823, at the house of James G. Swinnerton. Joseph Klein, John Clark and Daniel Lieb were appointed judges of the election. Samuel Bristow, John Clark and Henry Fahnestock were appointed commissioners to fix on a place for a temporary seat of justice. Milton Ladd, a member of the legislature from Johnson county, was elected judge of the court of probate, and was appointed clerk of the circuit court. Dennis Rockwell was appointed recorder. I believe Ladd made one visit to the county, and declined accepting the offices to which he had been elected and appointed. Dennis Rockwell was then appointed clerk, and Aaron Wilson, judge.

The county was attached to the first judicial circuit of which John Reynolds (elected governor in 1830) was judge—and was made to constitute a part of the senatorial and representative district with Greene county.

Jonathan Piper, Stephen Pierce, James Deaton, John Clark, Daniel Lieb, Thomas Arnett, Samuel Bristow, Aquilla Hall, David Blain, John Green, Joseph Buchanan, and Seymour Kellogg were appointed justices of the peace; Johnston Shelton, surveyor—all deceased.

At the election of county officers Daniel Lieb, Peter Conover, and Samuel Bristow were elected county commissioners, and Wiley B. Green, sheriff. Dennis Rockwell was subsequently appointed clerk of the county commissioners' court—all of whom are dead.

The commissioners appointed for that purpose agreed upon the house of James G. Swinnerton as the temporary seat of justice.

The first circuit court was held by Judge John Reynolds on the third Monday of April, 1823, in a log cabin owned by Dr. Cadwell, near Swinnerton's house.

At the election in 1824, Daniel Lieb, Peter Conover, and Seymour Kellogg were elected county commissioners, and Joseph M. Fairfield, sheriff.

Thomas Carlin, (elected Governor in 1836,) and Isaac N. Piggott, (now a resident of St. Louis, over ninety years old,) were candidates for the Senate, Carlin obtained the certificate of election, but Piggott contested his right to the seat, and upon investigation the question was referred back to the people, when Carlin was elected. Mr. Job was re-elected to the House from the counties of Morgan and Greene."

Gen. Murray McConnel's account of these first courts and elections varies a little from Judge Thomas'. In May '68 Gen. McConnel said in a speech at the laying of the corner stone of the present Court House:

In January, 1823, the legislature by law created Morgan county, and included therein all the country before described as attached to Greene county for judicial and political purposes, now composing the counties of Morgan, Scott and Cass. This, the attached parts of Greene county, then included about fifteen hundred inhabitants. The county was organized on the first Monday of March, 1823, and on that day the first election was held therein, at a place called Swinnerton's Point, a mile and a half north-east of where the town of Lynnville now stands. At that election, Joseph Klein, John Clark and Daniel Leib, acted as judges, and Dennis Rockwell and Joseph M. Fairfield were the clerks. Seymour Kellogg, Thomas Arnett and Peter Conover, were elected county commissioners, and Wiley B. Green, sheriff.

Three persons—Samuel Bristow, John Clark and Henry Fahnestock, had been appointed by the legislature to fix the county seat of the county, and, on the third Monday of March, 1823, they located the same at a place called Olmstead Mound, now called Allison's Mound, about one and a half miles north of the present town of Lynnville, and now near the eastern boundary of Scott county. In the fall of 1823, the first circuit court was held at that place. John Reynolds, afterwards governor, was the judge. Milton Ladd was the clerk, Wiley B. Green, the sheriff, and James Turney, then of Carrollton, Greene county, was state's attorney. The persons present claiming to be lawyers, in addition to James Turney, were Alfred W. Caverly, then of Greene county; Murray McConnel, of Morgan county; Benjamin Mills, of Vandalia; Jonathan H Pugh, and William S. Hamilton, then of Sangamon county

There was but one building at the place, that was made of round logs, a single room of about sixteen feet each way, with an addition, leaned up against one side of it, about half as big as the main building. This was the dwelling-house of Mr. Olmstead and family, who turned out, lived in a camp, and gave up his house to the court. In that camp, by a big log-heap fire, the females of Mr Olmstead's family cooked for the judge and lawyers, and other attendants upon the court, and set the table, barbecue fashion, between the camp and the house, and all slept on a bed made on the floor in the room where the court was held. This was called field-bed—the sleepers laid across the bed, not lengthwise. There was about room enough in this house for the court, clerk, sheriff and lawyers, and one jury at a time—the grand jury was called in, and sworn, and sent out to deliberate under some forest trees near by. The by-standers gathered around the jury and all hands took part in the proceeding. The travis jury, when trying a case, was accommodated with seats, made of split logs, inside the house, and when the trial closed, they were sent out into the grove, under the charge of a constable, to make up their verdict, and the constable often had much trouble to prevent the parties and witnesses from participating in the deliberations. In one instance he entirely failed, and the contending parties got into a rough and tumble fight, and the constable called on the jury to aid in keeping the peace, and in their attempting to do so, all parties, jury, bystanders and constables, got into a general row, the lawyers and people left the court, and the grand jury left their shade trees, and all ran to the scene of action; several fights were going on at the same time, and all this increased the confusion, which grew hotter and louder, until the judge himself and the sheriff also, repaired to the jury room, alias, the field of battle, and by an effort quelled the fray. The idea of imprisoning the offenders was out of the question, as there was no prison within eighty miles, and to punish them by a fine would have been fully as useless, as in nine cases out of ten, the offenders had no property but a gun, and as the law then was, that could not be taken for debt or fine any more than you could lawfully take a piece of the owner's ear for the same purpose.

During this court a newly made justice of the peace, claiming the right to call upon the judge to advise him in the line of his duty as a squire, came bolting into the court room, saying, "Mr Judge, I am a squire, and I want to *ax* you a question about the law." The judge said to him, "why sir, you had better enquire of some of those lawyers, or Mr. Turney, who is the state's attorney." "Oh! shaw, now judge," said the squire, "I know about as much law as any of them ar fellows, and I begin to find out that I don't know much, and now, I want you, old feller, to tell me if a squire can divorce a couple?" "Why no," said the judge, "a justice of the peace has no jurisdiction over such a case" The newly made justice then stretched out his big fist towards the judge, and with a stentorian voice said, "now look here, old feller, I know better nor that myself, I know a squire can divorce a couple, for I done did it yesterday, and the *ooman* has gone back to her mammy, and the fellow started to Packinsack this morning, so he did." The judge at once submitted to the superior experience of the squire, and admitted that he must be wrong in his law, and the squire right.

There was but one more court held at Olmstead's Mound.

Of the funny things done by the squires of this county in an early day, we are told the following: Esquire Fanning had been justice of the peace for several years and he kept his docket on separate pieces of paper, which were stuck up over the laps of the board roof of his cabin. Each case was carefully kept by itself, and a strange mass of summonses, warrants, estray notices, etc., and docket entries could be found there. Manning Mayfield was elected his successor and, according to law, Esquire Fanning prepared to turn over his docket. He carefully put all these papers into and filled a two bushel sack and took them over to Mayfield. "Now," says he, "here is my docket all made up and in good shape, except an execution which I believe, is not quite paid up." They looked through the lot and finally found it, and Mayfield sat down and made a calculation of the credits and reported that he had been overpaid by some $15. "Is that so? All right, then, let it go with the balance," and Mayfield tossed the sack up into the loft of his cabin.

Rev. J. E. Roach, of Virginia, Cass county, once said at an Old Settlers' Reunion:

"I do not feel fully prepared for the work of representing Cass county. I will speak about what the country was then and now. When Cass, Morgan and Scott counties were first formed they blossomed then, but they were wild, and now they are tamed. The people who then occupied the county were just the ones to hand down the country in its present condition. Mr. Job was among the first. He settled about 1822, when there was nothing but wild flowers. In one respect we are all kin and come here to have what may be called a family reunion. It is not necessary to describe the people that settled these counties and are here to-day, because we all know them. In the olden days we came very near having nothing but a grand and glorious country.

The first man that built a mill was a Mr. Sweet, and we have a man (Mr. Gatton) that was at that mill waiting to get his grain ground when the deep snow began to fall. The first mill was built on a stump. Now we have a different kind of milling business. The first place of business in Cass county was in a log cabin, now near Little Indian, and was kept by Mr. Gatton. Soon after this Beardstown became a place of considerable business, and even competed with Chicago, and for a long time we held it at arm's length in the packing business. Ashland is on the other end of the county, and was named for Henry Clay."

In the west part of the county, situated on the east bank of the Illinois River, is the thriving town of Meredosia. In 1819 Gen. Murray McConnel, in passing up the river, found one man residing near the present site of the town. This is the earliest mention that we have of the town. This man was a priest by the name of Antoine D'Osia, and the town was named from the circumstance of a man by this name living on a lake (Mere). In 1833 Mr. Pickett opened the first school in that town.

Col. Joseph Morton, recently deceased, was once called upon and gave a lengthy and interesting account of his experience in the days of the first settlement of this county—coming to the neighborhood of Alton in 1819, and raising a corn crop the first year in Madison county. In 1821, in company with Mr. Bradshaw, he came to the new settlement in Morgan county, or what was afterwards called Morgan county. Here he made rails to enclose thirty acres—quite a farm in those days. They went seventy-five miles to mill, and hauled wheat to St. Louis and sold it at fifty cents per bushel, which was thought a good price.

Judge Lewis Solomon, of Macoupin county, in 1874, gave a history of the queer old plow which his father brought from Kentucky in 1824, and which was placed on the table before him. The speaker had used that plow many a day. It was drawn by a horse named Pace, (a voice, "Where is the horse?") "He has gone where all good horses go. There were ten children, besides, father and mother, and the old plow, and they all moved from Kentucky in a cart." He asked them to look at this plow and compare it with what they now used, and they would have an idea of the progress made since then. He told the difficulties they had in carrying their grain two days' journey to mill, sometimes getting entirely out of provisions and nearly starving, and illustrated the hospitality of the settlers to each other. Flies, wolves, panthers and everything of the kind obstructed their path, and almost every fall they had to look for at least twenty-five shakes of ague. The country was entirely destitute of the arts and sciences, and had to do without them. They endeavored to make all the corn and pork they could, and that was their salvation. It took from three to five yoke of cattle to break the tough sod so that they could cultivate the soil. They had to labor hard to secure homes and every dollar went to the land office to pay for them. The young men of to-day ought to cut wheat with the sickle as they did. He bore one of the marks of the sickle on his hand now. Several in the audience showed scars obtained in the same way. And one said, "I'd rather have the hook now."

After they got the wheat cut they had to thrash it on the ground, and then hold it up in the air so that the winds would take the chaff out. Finally they got a horse-mill started, and he never knew it to stop as long as the team could keep going. The young folks don't know anything about it now.

When they got to raising more wheat than they could consume they had to carry it off, and he had hauled it to Alton and got twenty-five cents a bushel. "And now you grumble when you get a dollar." It just about took a load of wheat to get a bolt of domestic. They were a set of energetic, industrious men, who brought us to where we are now. They had no bridges; they crossed the streams by fording or in canoes.

To-day within the limits of this county, nearly all agricultural products are raised with profit. Corn is one of the principal crops, although wheat, oats, rye and barley are raised. In the days of Strawn and Alexander cattle raising was followed very extensively and grazing was one of the principal uses to which the land was put.

The Hon. Samuel D. Lockwood, in January, 1821, was elected, by the Legislature, Attorney General of the State, which office he resigned in December, 1822 having been nominated by Gov. Coles for Secretary of State, and confirmed by the unanimous vote of the Senate. This office he resigned during the same or succeeding year, and accepted the office of Receiver of public monies at the land office at Edwardsville. In 1825 he was elected by the Legislature, Associate-justice of the Supreme court, which office he held until after the election of judges under the constitution of 1847, when he resigned before his term expired.

By the act incorporating the Illinois Central Railroad Company, he was appointed one of the trustees of the road, and continued in that position until his death. He resided in Jacksonville more than twenty years, during which time he served as trustee of each of the State institutions located here.

According to Elder D. Pat Henderson:

The first death in Morgan county was Isaac Fort Roe.

The first death in Jacksonville was David Ditson.

The first marriage in Jacksonville was John Smith and Deborah Thornton.

The first sermon preached in Morgan county was by Rev. Jos. Basey a minister of the Methodist Episcopal Church.

The first Sunday-school in the county was organized in Jersey Prairie, at or near Princeton, by a Mr. Leonard, whose widow is still living, having married a gentleman of the name of Rucker.

The Methodists and Baptists held meetings at different places in the county in 1821. The house of James Deaton was one of the places where the Methodists held their worship.

The Baptists held meetings for worship at the house of Major Peter Conover, in Jersey Prairie, and at one or two more places in that part of the county. All of these meetings were held in private houses, after the apostolic example, there being no public houses erected for that purpose.

Peter Conover was the first President of the Morgan County Bible Society. He was a native of New Jersey, removed to the neighborhood of Lexington, Ky., and from there to this State. He was a man of more than ordinary information and intelligence, and an active member of the Baptist church.

Other authorities inform us that:

The mother of the first white female child born in the county was Mrs. Crain, the wife of James Crain, who settled near Diamond Grove in 1820. Sarah Crain was the name.

The first physician was Dr. Ero Chandler.

The first preacher was Rev. Joseph Basey, of the M. E. Church; the next was Rev. N. Pickett, who is now living in St. Louis. Joseph Basey is living in Pittsville, Wis., a worthy man.

The first bridge was built in 1821.

The first tavern was opened by a Mr. Brown.

The first mill was put up in 1821, by Rowland Shepherd.

According to Mr. Anderson Foreman:

Rev. Wm. Drinkwater was the first Baptist minister- about the year 1822.

Rev. John Glanville was the first Methodist preacher who travelled this circuit— about 1822.

Rev. Thomas J. Starr was the first Methodist pastor to be stationed in Jacksonville. He came from North Carolina.

Rev. Mr. Brich was the first Presbyterian sermonizer, coming in 1824.

Mrs. Martha Davenport and Mrs. Charles Chappell are the only living members of the Methodist church, now living here, that were here when the first M. E. society was organized.

Joseph Coddington was the father of the first white male child born in the county. Its birth occurred in a tent in Diamond Grove.

Of the Wyatt's mentioned in the first part of this chapter, John was the father of Col Wm. J. Wyatt, now of Franklin and William the parental ancestor of Col. W. D. Wyatt, of Lincoln, Logan county, Illinois, who was born near Diamond Grove September 1821.

There seems to be no certainty as to the exact year in which Gen. McConnel came to Morgan as a settler. His account as given in this chapter of the first court and the jury deliberations is, of course, quite entertaining, but is quite indignantly denied by the only settler of '20 that is now living here—Mr. Huram Reeve, whose brother Lazarus, still living but not in this county, was on the first jury impannelled.

Florentine E. Kellogg, who came to this county in 1818 with his father Elisha, one of the original Kellogg brothers, lived in that pioneer log cabin with him a year and then moved some three miles northwest of Jacksonville, where he resided seven years. He and his father moved to Rushville, Schuyler county, and built the second house in that place. They lived there one year when they returned to Morgan county. In 1832 they moved to Galena where the younger man married in 1837. In 1846 he moved to California where he resided twenty-five years, engaged in raising fruit, grain and stock and carrying on a machine shop. In 1871 a second time he returned to Morgan where he now resides.

Of those whose arrival in the county dates between 1820 and '24 and whose names have not been already mentioned are Wm. H. Broadwell, '23, Mrs. Catherine F. Barton, '27, W. S. McPherson, '22, Mrs. Minerva J. Rector, '24, John Robertson, '23, B. B. Richardson, '21, Charles Sample, '23, C. R. Wilson, '20, Thomas and Joseph P. Deaton, '20, S. B. Smith, '24, John Smith, '24, Patterson Hall, '21, S. J. Mattingly, '24, J. M. Wilson, '24, Clayborn Coker, '23, George Curts, '22, H. R. Green, '24, Michael Huffaker, '23, Samuel Magill, '21, A. K. Barber, now living here, '24. The Bartons, three families, came together; also, Verian Daniels and wife, the latter a Barton—in all twenty persons.

CHAPTER II. 1819-'24.—*Continued.*

"The Regulators of the Valley"—A Tragedy in Real Life—A Chapter of the Dark Side of Pioneer Days in the Mauvaisterre Country—Captain Pistol—The Wild Hunter—The First Grave on the Banks of Mayer's Creek—The First Settlers of Cass (then Morgan) County—Sales of Public Lands in 1823—Venison, Blackberries and Milk.

"Across the stretching scene, where years had died,
The spirit of the past swept to my side;
Silent and sad and haggard, for to him
Earth's visage had been dark and cold and grim."

"The good and bad he kindly laid away
In one dark fold to wait the judgment day;
And spread the turf, and with paternal care,
Wept o'er the dead and planted flowers there."

IN view of the commendable and continually increasing desire to rake up from among the ashes of the dead past all the incidents and legends of the early settlement of this county manifesting itself everywhere in our midst, we are encouraged to give to our readers a sketch of a thrilling scene which occurred in our county at a very early date, and although it may read much like a fictitious narrative of border life, yet we are assured that every part of the following narrative is a literal fact. The whole story in much fuller details than we have room for was once before made public; in February, 1832, a communication appeared in the *Illinois Patriot*, chronicling at considerable length these stirring events. The article was signed "J. G. R." but was from the pen of Gen. Murray McConnel, who was himself cognizant of many of the doings of these "regulators."

At that time it was not prudent or discreet to reveal the true names of any of the parties, hence false ones were used throughout the article, but now, as none of the relatives of any concerned are living hereabout, we give their proper appellations, and the facts, as given by the general.

The hero of this story was one of a gang of desperadoes and renegades from good society, which infested our county at a very early period of its existence.

The persons who now emigrate to Illinois have but a faint idea of the hardships, privations and troubles of the first settlers. Few have been the years which have rolled away since the county of Morgan, now so populous and flourishing, was a frontier county. The settlers were few and far between; many of them were without dwellings to shelter them and their families from the storms, and none of them had more than a cabin of round logs thrown together in the rudest manner. Provisions of every kind were scarce and very dear; the means of the inhabitants were small and their wants great. The county was infested by a set of unprincipled renegades from a more civilized society, who equally disregarded the rights of the citizens and the laws of the land.

We, who are living now in a county teaming with life, and under codes of laws, (executed by multitudinous officers,) which guarantee protection to our lives and property, can have but a faint idea of the hardships and privations of the first settlers in Morgan. Yet comparatively few have been the years since ours was one of the frontier counties with inhabitants few and far between. Many were without a sheltering roof of any kind, and society was troubled by unprincipled men.

Of one of these uneasy spirits we propose to unfold a "tale," his name was Abraham Williams Keller, but for reasons best known to himself, he dropped his proper surname before he came to our county and was known here as Abe Williams. In the fall of the year 1820, a small cart bearing this man and his family pushed forward into the wilds of the valley of the Illinois. Then all was wild and dreary here, the site of our flourishing and beautiful city was surrounded and inhabited only by the wild beasts. "Westward, ho!" was this traveler's cry until he reached a romantically beautiful grove in a small prairie at the extreme west end of what is now Morgan county. There was his first "squatting ground," that was the first sod breaking in the valley of our little Mauvaisterre. Williams' trail was soon followed, until, within a year, a settlement of six families was made, all choice spirits for frontier life, ready for cabin raising, bear hunting, or Indian fighting. All was then peace and quietness in the colonies.

The next season brought other families, until enough were living within helping distance to rear up new cabins with ease. This mutual help was a great blessing, but we have "no rose without a thorn," so this blessing brought evil in its train. Among the new comers came "certain lewd fellows of the baser sort" as St. Paul says. With only three of these will we deal particularly, John Cotrill, Henry Percifield and his brother Jerry, were of the very worst of men, and settling near Williams, (south of the Mauvaisterre,) in a short time became his intimate friends and associates. During that autumn Jerry Percifield, the eldest and by far the worst of the lot, brought up to the little settlement two barrels of whisky, the first of the cursed stuff brought to the county after its settlement by the whites. Williams', the depot of the liquor, soon became the headquarters of the male portion of the colony, and from this date the downfall of Williams and others began. Robberies occured in this and neighboring counties, and the goods from plundered stores were by rumor said to be secreted near or in Williams' grove, and he and his trio of cronies were suspected. The law-abiding citizens were anxious to have their settlement retain a fair name for honesty and good order, hence warrants were issued, the suspected parties searched and some stolen goods were found. Upon examination by the magistrate however, they were allowed to testify in each other's favor, so all were acquitted.

Soon after, horse theft, house breaking, store robbing, and other depredations began to multiply. Williams became suddenly rich, having horses, cattle, and household goods in abundance. To his house came all the idle and profligate of the region. Their daily occupations were drinking, gambling, horse racing, pocket picking and horse stealing, with all their concomitants.

At this time two new characters appeared upon the scene of action, one a respectably wealthy old gentleman, who settled near the mouth of the Mauvaisterre. As his house was said to contain much money, it was soon visited by Williams and his crew who laid plans to ascertain how much money the owner of the house had, where it was concealed, when he would be absent from home, when he would return, &c.

The other emigrated here from Kentucky, whence Williams had come, a singular sort of a man, yet a good type of the daring backwoods scouts of those days. He was clad in a leather hunting shirt which trailed almost to his knees, (decorated with fringes of various lengths,) and in pantaloons of the same material. Deer skin moccasins were on his feet, and an enormous catamount skin upon his head. His weapons were an unerring Kentucky rifle and a knife of a frightful length. The "wild hunter of the prairie," was the only name by which he was known. His movements were mysterious; one day he would be seen in one part of the settlement, the next in another. He visited every house in the little colony except Williams'.

Our characters being introduced, we proceed:

One evening as Williams and Percifield were returning from a visit at the house of this wealthy and aged gentleman, (whose name was Lewis G. Newell,) they perceived by the aid of the moon's bright rays which were adding beauty to the already charming Illinois prairies the form of a man moving towards them.

"There," said Jerry, "is the wild hunter—did you ever see him?"

Before Williams could reply, the mysterious man stepped up, exclaiming, "Abraham, do you know me?"

The stern glance and thrilling voice chilled the very heart of the cowardly Williams; his cheek paled, his knees smote together, and he trembled like a leaf. "What's the matter?" asked Jerry, "do you know the man? If so, come forward and speak for yourself." No reply was needed, for the stranger continued to address the scoundrel, using these words:

"Abraham, you know me well; you know, too, that I am acquainted with your unnatural deeds; your ill-gotten wealth shall avail you little. Before many days pass by I will see you again, when circumstances are different, and times more favorable than now." Immediately he was out of sight, having fled to an adjoining grove.

Percifield was astonished, and Williams trembled, especially by the threat "I will see you again," but the latter obstinately refused to impart any information as to the stranger, moreover immediately began to dispose of his property, and shortly removed with his family to the west side of the Illinois River, not far from the spot where his bones were shortly laid to moulder back to their native dust.

A few days before Williams moved away, Newell, who was supposed to have so much money, also left his home on business, leaving his wife and a small boy to guard their treasures. A few nights after this man's departure, the roof of his house was broken open, and the dwelling robbed of all the money and valuables that could be found. This glaring robbery alarmed and aroused the citizens of the whole settlement. "Something must be done," was the cry. A public meeting was held, and among other things, a company was formed, consisting of ten law-abiding men of well known courage, who bound themselves together, under the name of the Regulators of the Valley, to rid the country of horse thieves and robbers, and not to cease their operations until they had accomplished that great object. A regular constitution was drawn up and subscribed to, and this paper is still in existence.

There was another man in the community at this time, who needs introducing. By his vain boasting and braggadocio, he had induced his fellow-citizens to believe that he was a man of great courage, a daring warrior. He lived, at that time, near the place where now is built the town of Exeter, in Scott county. By his own bold-facedness he was chosen the captain of this little band who were taking the law into their own hands. He was dubbed Captain Pistol. (James H. Pistol was his ordinary appellation.) Organization being completed, the party resolved to perform their first operations on Williams himself.

The plan agreed upon was to go to his house in disguise, seize him by force, tie him to a tree and scourge him with whips, until he should surrender the money and goods which they believed were in his possession unlawfully, and also disclose to them his associates and accomplices, but by no means or under any circumstances to take his life. This arrangement was known to none but this little band of associated law preservers. The little band proceeded immediately to the Illinois River for the purpose of commencing the work of reform with Williams, but before they proceeded far, Captain Pistol became very sick; it was totally impossible for him to proceed any further on this enterprise, and down he laid himself on the prairie. He entreated his soldiers, however, to go on and not wait for him. He instructed them that if he did not overtake them before they crossed the river, to appoint some one as leader in his stead. They were no sooner beyond his sight than he rapidly recovered, and with 2:40 speed made for his home, and within an hour he was by his wife's side, armed with a spoon and filling his empty stomach with hominy. Thus ended the valorous feats of this "twilight glory" hero of ye olden times. Would that such men were confined to those days.

The band of regulators marched on—crossing the Illinois River near the mouth of the Mauvaisterre, and having arrived in the vicinity of Williams' house, halted to make further arrangements. Several fruitless efforts were made to elect another captain, but no one seemed to wish to take this responsibility upon himself. While thus debating and waiting their sentinel gave the warning cry, "Who is there?" "A friend!" was the answer, and the Wild Hunter appeared upon the scene. Grant-like, his speech was short and to the point, as follows: "My friends, I know all your intentions. I have overheard your conversation. There is nothing hid from me Williams is my enemy —I am his. Why it is so, is not material for you to know, suffice it to say that he has years gone by planted a dagger in the heart of my domestic peace, and did me an injury I am bound to avenge. You, I have discovered, are without a leader, will you accept the services of a true soldier?"

The animated words and prepossessing manner of the speaker gained for him immediately the coveted command. They chose him their captain, and under him marched directly to Williams' house, which they surrounded. They selected two of the band to force their way into the cabin, with the hunter captain, and seize their victim. Before the encircling lines could be formed, however, and the outposts stationed, the family became alarmed by the noise, and the fierce barking of the dogs. One of the household cautiously opened the door, and by means of the light proceeding from the room, discovered one of the attacking party. The immediate cry was, "Indians! Indians!" supposing that the house was surrounded by the savages. Williams, seizing his rifle, rushed out of the house, and the first object that met his eye was the mysterious captain. He immediately exclaimed, "Thomas G——, stand back, or I will blow you down," and presenting his rifle, attempted to suit his actions to his words. By some unaccountable accident, the weapon snapped but missed fire. He was again making ready, when, from all sides came the shouts, "fire! fire!" One single report was heard, and Williams fell, exclaiming, "I am a dead man, Thomas G——. You have taken my life." The regulators gathered around their leader and his victim, and stood in speechless astonishment gazing at the convulsed limbs and twinging muscles of the dying man. It was an unexpected event, but they did not remain long in this silence. Their reveries were interrupted by the screams of a woman, who, running from the house in her night dress, with disheveled hair, and crying piteously, exclaimed at the top of her voice, "Oh, you devils! you devils!—you have killed my husband. I knew it would come to this. It all comes by associating with them drunken thieves, Henry and Jerry. Murder! murder! Stand back, you black-looking monsters. I *will* see my husband. O, dear, O, dear." Two of the party, in order to frighten her back into the house, discharged their guns near her head, but all in vain. She pressed on until arrested by the strong arm of the hunter (it seems she had seen him before); he forced her back into the house and closed the door upon her. Now, the question arose quickly, what was to be done? Many asked, but none answered. Williams' rifle was picked up, and the adjoining hills echoed back the sharp, keen crack, for so near were the preparations completed for a second shot at the revenging hunter. "Retreat, retreat," was now the reply of all to the query, "What shall be done?"

Quickly the line of march for the higher lands was taken. As soon as the place of blood was fairly out of sight, upon a hillside overlooking an extensive plain, they called a halt. The captain again addressed them as follows: "My friends, the deed is done. We cannot now recall it. I did it in self-defense. I have rid the world of a monster and myself of an inveterate foe. My conscience acquits me; so I regret not the act. My advice to each of you is to go your way and I will mine. You never will see me again; let every man guard well his secret, and none other will know you were here." In the language of the sensation novelist, we might now say that, "then with the elastic bound of a buck, he darted down the hill, was in a moment out of sight, and has never been heard from in this country since." We suppose that, his object accomplished, he retraced his steps to Kentucky, where some of his descendants may still be residing, and for this reason we think it best to still preserve the mystery, as to name and motive.

(for of this we have been apprised,) which in those days hung about the "Wild Hunter of the Prairie."

The news of the murder of Williams was speedily noised about. It went like the wind, but found each one of that little band safe in his respective home as innocent and ignorant as you please. Cotrill and the Pereifield left the county with haste, and Morgan county has never been troubled with such desperadoes since. Friends and neighbors performed the last services of burial for Williams. Near the spot where he was shot the body was laid, and there was the grave of "the first man that ever settled in the valley of the Mauvaisterre." As near as we can learn, the site of the grave was on the left bank of Magee's Creek, in the county of Pike. Around that grave the weeds and grass grow in rich profusion. The winds of heaven sweep over it, and the wolf, unconscious of its existence, sets up his midnight howl by its side. No gaudy pillar or flattering epitaph points out to the traveler the spot of earth where lie the bones of the pioneer of the Mauvaisterre. This man was dreaded by the people of the county in which he lived, and was feared by his family, and was also a terror to his enemies. His death was attended by circumstances of a truly tragical and very singular nature, a detail of which has been given above.

Before taking up again the regular thread of our historic narrative we append to this tragic picture of pioneer life a quotation from Judge J. Henry Shaw's "Historical Sketch of Cass county," an oration delivered July 4, 1876, as it covers a period when that region was included in the bounds of Morgan county.

In 1821, there were but twenty families within the present limits of Morgan, Cass and Scott counties.

In the early years of the white settlements here, wheat was unknown, and Indian corn, the only breadstuff, was exceedingly hard to obtain, as mills were scarce. Jarvoe's Mill, on Cahokia Creek, was for a long time the only one accessible to our pioneers. In 1821, a small horse-mill was erected on Indian Creek by one Richard Shepard. Then a horse-mill was put up at Clary's Grove, Menard county. To these mills the boys of the families had to make frequent and tedious journeys to procure corn meal for bread.

The public lands were first offered for sale in November, 1823; so that all those who settled here previous to that time were only squatters on the public lands, and could hardly be termed permanent settlers. In fact, Thomas Beard, and his friends who lived with the Indians at Kickapoo village, were merely squatters, dependent upon the Indians for the privilege of erecting their huts.

The first land entry was made by Thomas Beard and Enoch C. March, jointly, who entered the northeast quarter of 15, 18, 12, September 23, 1826. It was upon this quarter section that Mr. Beard's cabin was built. On the 28th day of October, 1827, Beard and March entered the northwest quarter of 15, 18, 12, which extended their river front down below the mound. Thomas Beard individually entered the west half, southwest, 15, 18, 12, October 10, 1827; and John Knight entered the east half, southwest 15, 18, 12, July 17, 1828. Thus there were three men who entered the entire section upon which the original town of Beardstown was located, in the years 1826, 1827 and 1828. So you will see that the stories current that Beardstown was laid out in 1824, and that the site was bought by Beard and March for twenty-five dollars, are not founded on record evidence.

The fact is, that the original town of Beardstown consisting of twenty-three blocks, fronting on the river, three blocks deep, reaching from Clay to Jackson Street, of which block ten, lying between the Park and Main Street, is the centre one, was laid out and platted by Enoch C. March and Thomas Beard, and acknowledged before Thomas B. Arnett, a justice of the peace of Jacksonville, September 9, 1829, and is recorded on page 228 of Book B of the Morgan county records.

Among the first settlers in Beardstown, after it became a town site, were Francis Arenz and Nathaniel Ware, who purchased an interest and became joint landed proprietors with Beard and March. The town was named after Thomas Beard.

The very first deed from March and Beard upon record, of lands within the present limits of Beardstown, was made before the town was laid out, and is dated August 21, 1828, to "Charles Robinson, of New Orleans," for the consideration of $100, being for a "part of the fractional part of the northwest quarter of section 15, in town 18, 12; beginning at a forked birch tree on the Illinois River bank, marked as a corner, running thence down the river meanders thereof, so as to make two hundred yards on a straight line, and from thence running out from the river at both ends of the above line by two parallel lines, until they strike the north line to the east half of the southwest quarter of section 15, 18, 12, supposed to contain 12 acres."

And immediately following this deed upon the record is this singular "deed of defeasance," executed by Charles Robinson.

DEED OF DEFEASANCE.—"I having this day bought of Enoch C. Marchand Thomas Beard and his wife Sarah a piece of land on the river below the ferry of the above Beard and having this day received from them a deed for the same I hereby declare that it is my intention to do a public business on the said land between this date and the first day of October next year and if I have not upon the land by that date persons and property to effect the same, or actually upon the way to do so, I will return the above deed and transfer back the land to them upon receiving the consideration given them for the same. The above public business means, a steam mill, distillery, rope walk or store. Witness my hand and seal this 21 day of August 1828

(Signed) "CHARLES ROBINSON. [SEAL.]"

Acknowledged August 21, 1828, before Dennis Rockwell, Clerk of Morgan Circuit Court; recorded June 29, 1829, Book B, deeds 180. This land is part of the original town of Beardstown.

Mr Charles Robinson, party to these deeds, still lives in this county, near Arenzville. On the 8th of February, 1872, he wrote a letter to the Chicago *Journal*, from which I make this extract:

"Fifty years ago, or in the summer of 1821, there was not a bushel of corn to be had in Central Illinois My father settled in that year twenty-three miles west of Springfield. We had to live for a time on venison, blackberries and milk, while the men were gone to Egypt to harvest and procure breadstuffs The land we improved was surveyed that summer, and afterwards bought of the government, the money being raised by sending beeswax down the Illinois River to St. Louis in an Indian canoe Dressed deer skins and tanned hides were then in use, and we made one piece of cloth out of nettles instead of flax. Cotton matured well for a decade, until the deep snow of 1830."

The southern part of the State, referred to by Mr. Robinson as Egypt, received this appellation, as here indicated because, being older, better settled and cultivated, it "gathered corn as the sand of the sea," and the immigrants of the central part of the State, after the manner of the children of Israel, in their wants, went "thither to buy and bring from thence that they might live and not die."

The section of country drained by streams heading in the Grand Prairie, and emptying into the Illinois River between Alton and Peoria, was known as the Sangamo country. By this name it was known in the south and east, and at the time of the settlement of the part comprised in Morgan county, it was the destination of all emigrants to the central or southern part of the State.

Emigration was great to the Sangamo country during the intervening years between 1822 and the "Deep Snow." To give the names of all who located during that time is impossible. The principal families, however, were those of Jonathan Atherton, Thornton Shepherd, Rev. John Brich, James Mears, George Hackett, Elijah Wiswall and sons Noah, Thomas and Henry, Jacob Deeds, Daniel Daniels, William Jackson, Elijah Bacon, Jacob Redding, Montgomery Pitner, William C. Posey, John Redfern, Aaron Wilson, Daniel Richardson, William Hays, Jacob Huffaker, Sr., Mr. Buckingham, William Scott, Mr. Scroggin, Sr., Abner Vanwinkle, James Evans, Sr., James Green, Andrew Karns, Elder Sweet, and Peleg Sweet.

The settlers of 1819, '20, '21 and '22 have now been mentioned. Some further account of their privations should be given, and the difficulties they encountered in founding their homes. For this see next chapter.

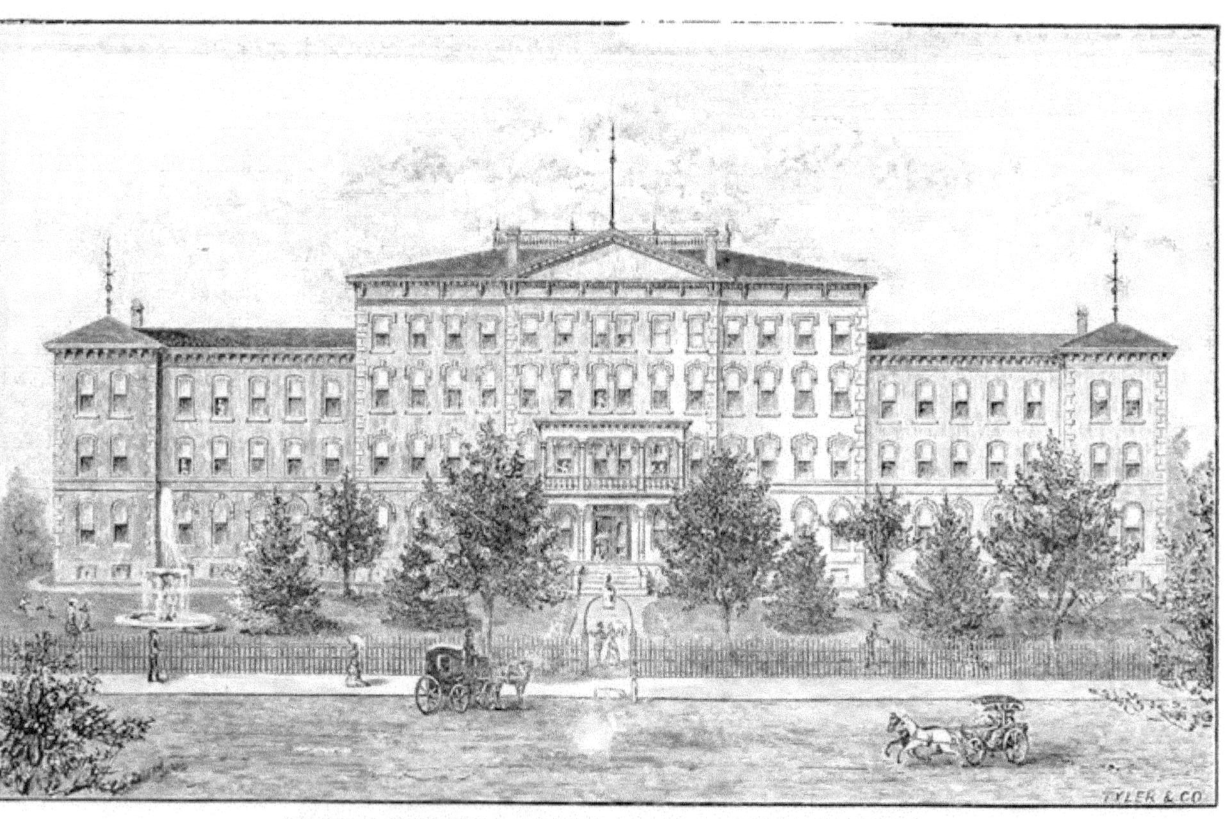

ILLINOIS INSTITUTION FOR THE BLIND AT JACKSONVILLE.

CHAPTER III.—1819–'24. *Concluded.*

Covering the same period as chapters I and II, but with greater detail. Annals of the earliest years in Morgan, as published in the Illinois Sentinel in 1867, by J. R. Bailey, now deceased, and vouched for in 1884 by Huram Reeve, Esq., the oldest male resident of the county now living therein—Log Cabin Raising—Meal Grinding in Hand-mills—Honey Hunters—The First Tavern, Bridge and Steamboat—Greene and Sangamon County Settlements.

Few are the men who live to-day
And by experience know
The toils and ills of frontier life
Of sixty years ago.
The hunt, the shot, the glorious chase
And the captured elk and deer.
The camps, the big bright fire, and then
The rich and wholesome cheer.
How sound is our sleep at dead of night,
By our camp fire blazing high,
Unbroken by the wolf's low growl,
And the panther's ringing cry.
And so merrily pass the time, despite
Our wary Indian foe;
In the days when we were pioneers,
Sixty years ago.

WHILE the early general history of the state of Illinois, comprising its first exploration by the French, the settlements of Kaskaskia and Peoria, and its subsequent organization as a territory and settlement by the hardy pioneers from Kentucky and other states; while these incidents of the early history of our state are familiar to the reading public, there is yet much historical detail connected with the first settlement, organization and growth of each county of the state that is unwritten, existing only in the memory of the remaining pioneers, or in the traditions preserved by their descendants.

Each county has had its local history, spiced with interesting detail and varied incident, the collection of which in the shape of local historical annals, would afford valuable and correct data to the future historian, and prove an interesting bequest to the generations to come after us in the possession of this beautiful and fertile land, the vast wealth and future resources of which are now just beginning to be developed.

To this end, in part, a meeting of the early settlers of the county was held in this city on the last Saturday of the month of May, 1867, for social re-union, organization, and to take steps for the collection of statistics, historical details and local incidents as data from which correct annals of the county might be compiled for preservation and transmission to posterity.

In aid of this object we have been courteously furnished by Mr. Huram Reeve and others, with a correct account, based upon the personal knowledge of our informant, of the first settlement made by white men in this county, with the leading incidents connected with such settlement during the first season.

At that early day the face of the country, although attractive in its wild beauty, presented an appearance different from that which now strikes the eye under its condition of cultivation and improvement. The surface of the country, prairie and timber, was covered with a luxuriant and rank vegetation. On low grounds and flat prairie the wild grass grew to a considerable height. The "hazel roughs" that crept out on the dry prairie knolls near the timber, and the young timber skirting the prairies, had a hard struggle for life with the autumnal fires, lighted by the Indians for hunting purposes, and, after the passage of such fires in the fall, presented a blackened and stunted appearance; and among this timber, already fire-girdled to his hand, the settler subsequently opened up his first five acre field, and planted his first patch of corn.

The traveler exploring the country found the grassy surface unbroken except by a rarely met Indian trail, and in skirting the timber of the Mauvaisterre, Sandy or Apple Creek, he saw attractive points of timber, and enticing locations for settlement, but no smoke was rising where the house should stand; no bark of dog or low of cattle to be heard; naught but nature clothed in the grand robes of her virginity, breathing solemn silence.

During the spring of 1820 the first settlement of white men (after the Kelloggs') was made in Morgan county, in the vicinity of where Jacksonville now stands. This settlement was made by Mr. Roe, who located his claim and commenced work on what is now known as the Becraft place, west of Diamond Grove.

Next came Messrs. John Wyatt and Wm. Wyatt, who commenced their improvement on the farm later owned and occupied by Cyrus Matthews, Esq., formerly sheriff of Morgan county. These settlements were made about the 1st of March, 1820, and soon after, during the same month, Isaac Reeve, Joel Reeve, Lazarus Reeve Jno. Reeve, James B. Crain, Martin Dial, James Deaton and his son Levi, and Robert James pitched their tents and selected their claims.

Mr. Reeve settled on Sandy, southwest of the Diamond Grove on what has since been known as the Deed's farm. Being a blacksmith he brought with him his anvil, hammers and bellows. As the season advanced and the plows of the infant settlement began to need sharpening, Mr. Reeve extemporized the first blacksmith shop in the open air, the interlocking stumps of two saplings being his anvil block, the bellows rigged to stakes driven in the ground, the fire place of the most primeval construction. This airy shop became at once a public institution, and from far and near the settlers trudged there through the high grass, to get their little jobs of smithing done.

The persons above named made their settlements in the immediate vicinity of the present location of Jacksonville, scattered around as attractive locations had caught their fancy. Mr. Deaton and his son made their claim about four miles west, on what is now called the McCormack place, on the Meredosia road, and Mr. James also settled in the same neighborhood.

During the same spring, 1820, but somewhat later, settlements were made in two other neighborhoods. Mr. Swinnerton, Mr. Olmstead and Mr. Pierce fixed their location and commenced improvements at Olmstead's Mound, since known as Allison's Mound; and on the north fork of the Mauvaisterre settlement was made by Samuel Scott. The Messrs. Kellogg were on the north side of the creek, and the first improvement was commenced on what is known as the Huffaker place, by Isaac Edwards. Mr. Buchanan settled on the head of south fork of the Mauvaisterre the same spring; also Mr. Roberts and sons at Island Grove.

Thus the first settlements of white men made in Morgan county in the spring of 1820, were in three distinct neighborhoods, the pioneers who first attacked the primeval forests with the all conquering axe and turned the first furrow in the virgin soil, having chiefly emigrated from Madison, St. Clair and other southern counties.

The little band of pioneers during this first spring, comprised, with a single exception, only males—the pioneers and their sons; the women and smaller children not being removed to their new homes until late in the fall. Jas. B. Crain, however, brought his family with him, and Mrs. Crain was the only white woman in the settlement during the first summer, being, it is claimed, also, the mother of the first white child born in the county.

The first steps and subsequent proceedings of the pioneers in making their settlement, are well worthy of record. After selecting a location suited to his fancy, the first act of the settler was to pitch his camp. For this a site was selected under shelter of the timber, near a spring or running branch. The team was unhitched from the wagon, and after being carefully belled, was turned out to browse upon the swelling buds. The next care was to provide a camp for protection from the weather during the season. The ringing sound of the axe then awoke the forest echoes, and rails were split for the erection of a rail cabin. A "board tree" was selected, felled, and in the absence of a cross cut saw, butted off with the axe into four feet cuts. These being opened and hearted with the maul and wedge, were rived into clapboards for covering the rail pen cabin, the boards being held to their place by weight poles laid on them as each layer was placed, the eave pole being pinned fast and each succeeding weight pole, up to the comb, being kept from slipping toward the eaves by blocks placed at each end and in the centre between them.

The rail cabin being raised and covered, a door was cut out, jams pinned on and a clapboard door made and hung with wooden or leather hinges, to be fastened when closed, with a wooden pin. Dry grass was then collected for underbedding, clapboards nailed over the cracks between the rails, or bed quilts hung up over the walls to keep out the driving rain. The summer camp was then completed.

The settler next proceeded to mark off the boundaries of his claim, each settler being entitled to claim, under the rules of the frontier, three hundred and twenty acres. The claim lines were marked by blazing the trees with an axe through the timber, and driving stakes into the ground at short distances through the prairie. The lines thus established were respected by new comers, and if they did not happen to correspond with the government surveys when made, the claim title of the settler, to parcels cut off or divided was not affected, and transfers were often made between neighbors after the land had been entered, in order to make the old claim lines good to each particular owner.

The next step was to mark out five or ten acres of ground, as the help of the settler might justify, in the young timber skirting the prairie, as a patch for the first crop of corn. The timber land was selected as being better fitted for immediate cultivation and more easily broken than the tough, wild prairie sod. The work of making rails for fencing was now commenced, to be followed by the clearing, grubbing and breaking of the ground, and planting of the crop. The corn having been planted in the fresh soil required but little further attention for some time, enabling the settler to finish his fencing, which was usually done at this period and during the intervals of working the crop. This was the experience of the pioneer settlers of Morgan during the first season.

The provisions brought with them by the settlers were intended to last till fall when the corn crop would be made; but it happened that Mr. Deaton and his son exhausted their supply of corn-meal and bacon sometime about the first of June, compelling them to leave their partly made crop and travel a distance of eighty-five miles, to Edwardsville, to renew their supply. The journey had to be made chiefly in the night to avoid the green-head flies of the prairie, which at this season would in the day time almost bleed a team to death. Shaping their course by the stars, and without a road or trail, they started on the trip, provisionless and hungry. Their first camping place was on Apple Creek. The country had been pretty well cleared of game by Indians, but here they were fortunate enough to kill a squirrel, which they roasted at their camp fire. During the next day they succeeded in killing a deer near where the town of Jerseyville now stands, and thus they were enabled to reach Edwardsville in excellent time and good spirits.

Although at this period game was exceedingly scarce, having been killed out or driven off by Indians, bees were abundant, and in the fall after the corn crop had been made, the first settlers reaped a rich harvest in honey and wax, the latter constituting at that time, in connection with furs, the circulating currency of the frontier. An average of from six to eight bee trees a day was considered ordinary luck by the bee hunters, and the Messrs. Wyatt, who appear to have excelled in this line of woodcraft, were known to have found as many as twelve bee trees in a day. Diamond Grove was a favorite haunt of the wild bee, the surrounding prairies blooming with a succession of wild flowers, affording them a rich field for the collection of wax and honey. If the land did not literally flow with honey, it afforded a convenient and welcome source of revenue to the pioneer settlers.

As the fall approached, house logs were chopped, clapboards rived, puncheons for flooring split, and preparations made for erecting log cabins to shelter the families of the settlers during the coming winter. In raising the cabins the entire force of the little colony would be assembled, thus lightening the work of "raising," and each settler soon found himself the proud possessor of a log cabin prepared to shelter his wife and little ones in their new wilderness home.

The patch of corn having been safely "laid by," the cabin built and a good supply of honey and wax collected —the latter to be bartered at Edwardsville for necessaries, the team was hitched up, the trackless prairies and unbridged streams again traversed and the family safely landed at their new home.

As the new corn began to harden it was made into coarse meal for family use by rubbing the ear on a tin grater until the grains were rasped off close to the cob. This meal made a bread very sweet and palatable, but the work of grating was very laborious When the new corn became hard enough to grind, a small hand mill was put up at Diamond Grove, by Isaac Fort Roe and Jedediah Webster, and upon this "mill privilege" the surrounding neighbors depended mainly for grinding their meal during the first winter, the nearest regular mill being eighty-five miles. The hand mill was primitive in construction and its manipulation was tiresome work, as some of the youngsters of that day, now grown gray-headed, will doubtless remember. Two stones of the kind known as "lost stone," some two feet in diameter, were procured. These were dressed into millstone shape and a hole drilled through the centre of the one intended for the upper stone. With a simple contrivance by which to regulate the grinding space between the two stones the upper stone was made to revolve on a pivot. A hole was drilled on the top side and near the outer circle of the upper stone and in this hole a wooden peg was driven.

This was the handle by which the stone was revolved, being thus turned exactly like an ordinary millstone with the right hand, while the left hand managed the shelled corn and represented the hopper, dropping the grains slowly into the hole in the centre of the stone, to be ground into meal. The labor involved in grinding a bushel of meal by the above manual process can only be correctly appreciated by those who have tried it.

We have already described the first hand-mill. We might add that it could be changed into a horse mill by fixing it firmly between two posts and attaching a sweep to it. Another contrivance for making meal was the mortar; this was made by burning or excavating the end of a stump or log. As the hole in the stump or log became deeper, it was narrowed until it came to a point. A pestle was made to fit closely into this aperture; in the end of the pestle an iron wedge was fixed. When the pestles were made of great weight they were attached to a sweep, made like a well sweep; by this means they could be raised and dropped into mortars. Meal was made in this manner by simply breaking or pounding the corn until it was thoroughly pulverized. The mortar in this country was probably the invention of the Indians, as it was in use when discovered by the white men. The hand-mill is spoken of in the Bible, and is probably as old as the world.

After the hand-mill and mortar came the horse-mill, made after various plans which, in its day, was considered a great improvement on its primitive predecessors. During the first years of the settlement of Morgan county, the pioneers of that time, did they desire better accommodations than that furnished at Diamond Grove, were compelled to go to Edwardsville, eighty-five miles away. The settlers were greatly dependent on each other during this period, and were noted for their hospitality and kindness toward one another and to strangers. Their latch-strings were always out, and though frugal their fare and humble their accommodations no one was allowed to go away hungry or uncared for. During this early period the settlers were much dependent on each other, in illustration of which it is related that one of them during the first summer, trudged eighteen miles in the tall prairie grass to borrow an iron wedge of his neighbor. Long journeys would have to be made to procure tools to use in their daily avocations. It was not uncommon for men to go fifteen or twenty miles for an ax, a chain, or any such article when needed.

During the fall of 1820, sometime in December, Mr. John Bradshaw visited the settlement and marked out his claim on what was known later as the Warner farm, and still later as the Chestnut place, adjoining this city on the southeast. He did not, however, remain during the winter or make any improvements until the following spring.

Gen. Murray McConnel, a gentleman who has since occupied no mean position among the noted men of the state, also paid his first visit to Morgan county during the fall of 1820. He made his settlement on the place now owned and occupied by Mr. Riggs, in what is at present known as the Gilham neighborhood, within the present limits of Scott county, but did not commence improvements or remove his family to his claim until the following spring.

Thus the early annals of Morgan county have been opened up, and details of its history given, based upon the personal knowledge of persons who were upon the spot and themselves witnessed what has been described, the facts given covering the period of the first year of the settlement of the country within the present limit of the county. Some of the first settlers of that period yet remain, and numerous descendants of others of them who have passed away, yet live in the county, some of them on the very spot first settled by their father or grandfather.

The Kerr place was settled in 1820 by Mr. Jesse Ruble. He sold his first improvement and claim to Mr. Kerr, who came the following year. Mr. Bailey says:

"The delineation of the early western frontier character has become hackneyed, yet many of the writers upon this subject have picked up their information in every possible way, except that afforded by a long personal experience and observation. Hence much of error has naturally crept into published descriptions of pioneer character and its early primitive surrounding.

"This fact is illustrated in a recent article of considerable length in the *Atlantic Monthly*, giving a descriptive account of the early settlement of Sangamon county, Illinois, purporting to be from the pen of an eastern guest of Wm. H. Herndon, of Springfield, upon whose authority many of the incidents embodied are given. While the article referred to gives some true descriptions, there is also interwoven much that the early pioneer will recognize as exaggeration and absurdity; and the writer's deductions and conclusions in reference to the pioneer character as a class, are in some particulars little short of positive slander. For instance, he pictures the early settlers of Illinois as characterized by looseness of morals in the relations and intercourse of the sexes, ascribing the cause to the absence of the enlightened social refinement of a more advanced civilization.

"Never were the pioneers of Illinois more grossly misrepresented. In honesty and purity of morals they were the peers of the men of Massachusetts, and in openness of character, kindly hospitality, neighborly fraternity and some other noble qualities, their superiors; because uncontaminated with the vices of a refined and advanced eastern civilization. Female purity was a marked social feature among the early settlers. A majority of them were newly married people who came to establish homes. Of the unmarried the young men outnumbered the young women, and as the girls grew to maturity they were early sought in marriage, few remaining single to the age of twenty years. Incentives to vice that are incident to densely populated communities in the east, were not to be found in the scattered settlements of a new country; hence purity in the social and domestic relations was a ruling characteristic among the pioneers.

"The early settlers were especially noted for kindly fraternity of feeling. They were much dependent upon each other, having to borrow and lend and the strong bonds of fellowship were cemented by mutual interests and necessities. The visit of a neighbor always awakened pleasurable emotions, and the stranger was welcomed to the homely cabin with an open hospitality unknown and unfelt amid the surroundings of an old settled country. The settler would cheerfully leave his own work and walk five, ten or fifteen miles to assist his neighbor in rearing his cabin or the performance of any heavy labor requiring help, regarding it as a pleasant duty which his neighbor would, if required, perform for him with equal cheerfulness.

"There was no law in those days, nor need for any, the rule of kindly fellowship governing in the intercourse and business relations of the settlers, while politics as a disturbing element was unknown. It was several years later when disreputable characters began to straggle into the settlements, rendering the organization of "regulators" necessary.

"As the supply of clothing which the settlers brought with them began to wear out, they were driven to shift in the best way they could to supply that want. Many of them had brought with them their spinning wheels, and those who were so fortunate as to own a few head of sheep were in a measure independent, the women being able to spin and weave linsey and jeans for the family wear, the weaving being done on home-made wooden looms. The game beginning to multiply after the first season, the rifle was brought into requisition and the skins of the deer were dressed and converted into warm and comfortable clothing.

"The Corrington farm on the Mauvaisterre, was settled in 1821, by Mr. W. Miller. Stephen Jones settled the Cassell place, and Joseph Slattern made the first improvements on the O'rear place.

"Billy Robinson, an old, white-haired hunter, made an improvement north of Antioch Church, on which Bennett Jones afterward settled. Isaac Edwards and Mr. Scott located north of the Curts and Reeve places.

"John Anderson settled on the Layton place; James Taylor taking the farm west of the Stephen Dunlap place, on the northern side of the north fork. Mr. Murray was the first settler on the Dunlap farm, and Mr. S. Berey took possession of the quarter section east of it.

"Mr. Olmstead settled on the quarter-section east of Colonel Matthews. All of the above settlements were made in 1821.

"Rev. Peter R. Boranan was one of the early Methodist preachers in the county: he became a noted revivalist, and died in Chicago, some forty years ago."

"Martin Lindley settled at Camp Hollow, since known as the Fisher Place, near Beardstown; and Timothy Harris and John Catrough accompanied him. Harris settled on the north side of the creek opposite the Bluff House; but Catrough remained with Lindley for some time afterward, and during a prairie fire came near losing his life, his jeans clothing being burned to a crisp. On December 20, 1820, Julia A Lindley, daughter of Martin Lindley, was born; supposed to be the first white child born in the county. In 1821 Mr. Lindley moved to Peoria, where he remained one season, then proceeded down the river and stopped for a time at the mouth of the Mauvaisterre, from thence returning to Camp Hollow. He was killed by the caving in of a well in the year 1830; his family remained at Camp Hollow until 1855.

"Mr Thomas Beard came to Beardstown in 1820, but did not commence improving until 1822 It is related that he built his cabin over a den of snakes, and for some time the inmates were annoyed by the reptiles crawling through the crevices of the puncheon floor. In 1826 he married Miss Sarah Bell, I. R. Bennett, Esq., of Emerald Point performing the ceremony. After the location of the seat of justice at Beardstown, it became an important shipping point, and Mr. Beard became wealthy Elisha Lenn, Mr. Waggoner, Simeon Lenn, Solomon Bery, John Baker and Nathaniel Herring were among the earliest citizens of Beardstown.

"The first steamboat ascended the Illinois River in 1826, the river being navigated, prior to that time, only by keel-boats, flat-boats and canoes.

"Bees were very plenty, and two of the settlers, Messrs. Buckleman and Robinson, collected in 1827 fourteen barrels of honey, selling the wax for money enough to enter their claims.

"Mauvaisterre Creek is said to have been named by the early French voyagers on the Illinois River. Indian Creek is supposed to have been named by the early rangers under General Whitesides, from the fact that while pursuing a marauding band they killed an Indian on that stream, in 1814. Archibald Job, subsequently, for many years a noted public man, settled on Job Creek, in Cass county, in 1820. With his family he left Pittsburg on a keel boat, on the 30th of October, 1819, and landed at St. Louis early in February, 1820, having been detained some time by ice. Leaving the keel-boat in charge of his wife and children, Mr. Job came up the river located his claim and built a cabin. He broke twelve acres the first season, fencing it by felling saplings with their tops interlocked. About the 12th of May, 1820, David and Thomas Blair settled in Mr. Job's neighborhood, and during the same season went for their families. On the authority of Mr Job, it is understood that the first Baptist preacher was Rev Samuel Bristow; Rev. William Sims and Rev William Crow being next in order.

When Hon. Archibald Job came to Morgan county, as mentioned above, he left his wife on the west side of the Illinois River, alone in camp by a log fire, while he came over into the Sangamo country to meet a brother-in-law. During his absence twelve Indians came to Mrs. Job's tent and demanded whiskey. She told them her husband had taken it all away with him, but they refused to believe her or to leave and she had to remain there all night alone, with those savages lying upon the ground on the opposite side of the camp-fire. How few matrons of the present day could stand such a trial of nerve!

"Alexander Wells, James Gillham and Alexander Bell were the first settlers in the 'Gillham neighborhood.'

"Mr. Keller was one of the settlers of 1821, and was killed by the Regulators.

"In the year 1820, Mr. Thomas Arnett settled near the present reservoir for the Insane; he was the first justice of the peace in the county, and one of the proprietors of Jacksonville. He sold his first claim to John Leeper and moved to the Loar place.

"Col. Joseph Morton and John Bradshaw came to Morgan county in 1820, and located claims, but did not remain. They returned the next season and commenced improvements. Col. Morton used a wooden cart—in which there was no iron to be found—when hauling his rails and doing farm work. They fenced eighteen acres the first season. Mrs Minnie Conover settled on Indian Creek about 1821. The public lands in this section were surveyed in 1821 and brought into market in 1823. Mr. Charles Robinson settled at the head of the southern fork of Mauvaisterre Creek in 1820; his money capital was twenty-five cents, and he invested that in whisky to make bitters for curing the ague. He hunted bees for a time, and sold wax enough to enter the first eighty acres. He afterwards became wealthy.

"Miles Wood settled the Posey place, adjoining Jacksonville on the east.

"The first school taught regularly in the county was held at Isaac Edwards' farm, on the Springfield road—now owned by John Shuff—Mr. Palmer being its teacher.

"After Rev. Joseph Basey, Rev. John Miller was the first local Methodist preacher, but Rev. Newton Pickett rode the first Methodist circuit established in the county. Rev. Levi Springer traveled from Indiana to Morgan county, Illinois, in company with his wife, each on horseback, in the fall of 1823. From Paris they started on the 'lost trace,' crossing the Grand Prairie to the head of the Sangamon River. They were two nights on the prairie, sleeping on the grass, with no protection save the blankets which they carried, the wolves howling all about them. Reaching Springfield they found only a few cabins, and thence proceeded to Crow's Point, on Indian Creek, near which place they settled.

"Abel Richardson, and his sons Daniel and Benjamin, settled on the Mauvaisterre in 1821, on the place now owned by Benjamin Richardson, three miles east of Jacksonville. During the same year Judge I. R. Bennett located at Emerald Point. He was one of the early justices, and performed the ceremony between Mr Beard and his first wife. He afterward served in the legislature, and as associate county judge.

"Joseph Slattern settled in 1821, on the Orear place. In the year 1823 Enoch C. March came, and afterward built the Exeter mills, being one of the proprietors of Exeter, and held the first sale of lots, in the fall of 1828.

"Roland Shepherd came to the county about 1821, and in 1823 built a band-mill, which was run by horse or ox power. It was located on what is now the William Taylor farm, situated on Indian Creek.

"Deaton's mill was the next built, and Magill's mill was afterward erected on the northern fork of the Mauvaisterre. John Wyatt afterward built a horse-mill.

"Rev. John Brich came to the county at a very early day, and left it many years ago. He perished in a winter storm in the wilds of one of the northern countries, while pursuing his missionary labors. Finding himself overcome by the cold, he took his will from his saddle-bags, signed it, and hung the saddle-bags on a bush. He was afterward found dead near the bush, the saddle-bags leading to the discovery.

"The first census of Morgan county was taken by General Murray McConnel, in 1824; but the returns were lost with other county records by the burning of the first court-house. At that time, in a northeasterly direction from Crow's Point, the country was wilderness. Led by the barking of a dog in that direction, General McConnel found a family encamped; but upon inquiry, and examination of a blazed line and witness-tree, he found he was on the line of Sangamon county, and that the camp was in Sangamon."

The Cumberland Presbyterians were also among the pioneers in religious organizations in the settlements. They had a camp-ground and church six or eight miles northeast of Jacksonville, and here they maintained regular religious services for many years. No records of their organization can now be found, nor can any one now living remember the year when this church was founded. Mr. Huram Reeve remembers they were holding camp-meetings in 1824, and thinks their organization had been in existence but a short time. Others concur in this view, although some maintain that this church is as old as any in the county. The latter view is in all probability incorrect, for had such a church existed in 1821 or 1822, it would have been well remembered by the settlers of that time. This church was probably organized about the year 1823, and though it does not exist at present was one of the oldest in the county.

About the same time that Col. Morton and Mr. Bradshaw settled on their claims in this county, the Rev. Samuel Bristow, a Baptist minister, brought a colony, composed of the Box, Reid, Curlock and Boyer families. These were organized into a church, which was in all probability, the second religious organization in what afterward became Morgan county. This little colony settled about three miles northwest of the present city of Jacksonville, in the vicinity of Box Creek, which derived its name from one of the families who settled near its banks, on what now is known as the McDonald farm. This Baptist Church continued in existence for many years, but the organization has for some time been disbanded. The preaching of the Rev. Samuel Bristow was probably the first religious services of this kind, held in that settlement. The Methodist ministers are generally found with the advent of settlements, and are almost always among the pioneers, proclaiming the good news of salvation. It is not definitely known whether any were here during the years of 1820 or 1821. Mr. Huram Reeve, says, that the first Methodist preacher that he remembers being in the settlement, was the Rev. Joseph Basey. Rev. Samuel Thompson was the first presiding elder here, and held a camp meeting on Walnut Creek, within the present limits of Scott county, in 1822 or 1823. Mr. Reeve remembers attending this camp-meeting and thinks his recollection is correct.

The season of 1820 is remembered as being remarkably dry. One of the settlers remembers that no considerable fall of rain occurred from April, 1820, to the same date the following year. A good crop of corn and other field products, owing to the richness of the soil, and the heavy dews, was however grown. The next season considerable cotton was raised, and a cotton gin erected by Mr. Johnson, on the farm later owned by C. M. Dewey, Esq., on the Meredosia road. To this gin the neighbors from far and near brought their raw cotton to have it ginned. Esquire Sears, who with Mr. Johnson and some others settled early this year, is reported to have raised one thousand pounds of cotton on four acres. The cotton when woven with hemp or flax made an excellent article of clothing. Until cotton and flax were raised the clothing of the settlers in some cases gave out, and they were compelled to supply the deficiency as best they could. Deer skins, when properly tanned, made a good article of clothing, much worn by the early pioneers. As soon as cotton and flax could be raised they were spun and woven into cloth by the women, who used the spinning wheels, often brought from their former homes, and the old-fashioned wooden loom.

During the spring of 1821, a storm occurred, in which a tree was blown down upon the roof of the cabin of James Crain. The roof was crushed in, and John Reeve killed. Mrs. Crain was badly injured. One of her arms was broken and one shoulder was put out of place. The broken arm was set by a man named Langworthy, but his limited medical knowledge did not lead him to discover that the shoulder was out of place, and in consequence Mrs. Crain remained ever afterward a cripple.

It was during the summer of 1821, that Dr. Ero Chandler located and began his practice. He erected his house and office on the ground now occupied by the Grace M. E. Church, in Jacksonville. He proved a useful man in his profession, and in after years accumulated considerable property. It is related of him that he came into the settlement on a broken down horse, and with but the single suit of clothes he was wearing. When in his pedestrian visits to his patients his clothes were rent by underbrush or briars, he was accustomed to borrow a needle and thread and repair the damage himself. His medical fees would be regarded as exceeding moderate these times, his charge for a visit made on foot and not occupying a whole day being seventy-five cents. When the visit occupied a day, and he had to borrow a horse to accomplish the distance, his charge was a dollar. But the doctor prospered with the growth of the country, and he afterward owned the eighty acres of ground in Jacksonville on which the Academy stands, and on which Chandler's Addition, now occupied by many of the most valuable residences in the city, was platted; and by him the Rockwell house was built. His memory is warmly cherished, and his usefulness remembered by the early settlers.

"Point or Turn-round" Brown built the first tavern in the county in 1821, at a place about seven miles south of the present county seat, on what was then the St. Louis road, afterward the upper road. The accommodations afforded by this tavern would not compare favorably with those furnished by the hotels of to-day. The sleeping arrangements consisted of two beds, one of which was occupied by Mr. and Mrs. Brown, and the other a large square bedstead, in which the children slept. The children were placed with their feet to the center and their heads out on the four sides, thus enabling them to economize sleeping space. Travelers of that day usually carried a few bed quilts with which they "turned in" on the floor; but when a bed was called for at the tavern, the old folks gave up their bed and crowded in with the children.

The first bridge in the county was built this summer (1821) over the Mauvaisterre Creek, at a place east of the city on the Springfield road, where Rock bridge now stands, by Col. Joseph Morton, Mr. Levi Deaton and a few others. The long sills intended to span the creek, were drawn to the bank by cattle, and the work of getting them to their place was accomplished by splicing together a sufficient length of log chain to reach across the creek, one end being attached to the sill and the other stretched to the opposite bank, where the oxen were hitched to it and the sill drawn over to its place. Split puncheons were then pinned on the sills for flooring, and the bridge was finished to be used until the next flood carried it off, when the work had to be repeated.

When the Robertson family came to Morgan county, in 1821, and struck the northern fork of the Mauvaisterre, where they settled, the only white men living on Indian Creek, were Roland Shepherd, who was settled at Taylor's Point, and his son, Peter Shepherd, who had made an improvement at Adams' Point. The Kelloggs had built two cabins in the neighborhood, in 1820, one on what is now known as the Roach place, and the other on the place settled by Alexander Robertson. They vacated these cabins and claims, for a location further west, in the Gilham neighborhood.

During the period between 1823 and 1827, there was a constant increase of emigration to Morgan county, principally from the southern counties of the state.

But little trouble with the Indians was experienced by the early settlers of Morgan county. There were none in its limits, after the white men entered, save straggling hunters or small roving bands who came to some parts, especially those near the rivers to fish and hunt. The western part of the county contains several Indian mounds of great antiquity. Just above Meredosia, on the east bank of the river, is a beautiful level plateau containing about fifteen acres. This was the village home of a tribe of Indians, and it was here that Antoine D'Osia, a French priest from whom the lake and present town of Meredosia received its name, labored for the good of these sons of the forest. The Indian village and its dusky inhabitants have long since gone, but the name of D'Osia will live as long as Meredosia and its lake remain. During a visit of some Indians to Washington City, not many years ago, they stopped at Meredosia while on their way, where one of them, nearly ninety years of age, related how he had roamed over various parts of the county, and pointed out many objects of interest to his companions. He also related to one of the citizens of Jacksonville, while they were encamped at the fair grounds, many interesting stories of his youthful days. He had hunted and fished in the woods and streams near the present city, when no thoughts of the white man existed in his mind, and when he and his comrades were sovereigns of this country.

No depredations by the Indians were ever committed among the settlers of Morgan county, and no record of the killing of any white men, after the settling of the county, is known to have occurred. The settlers north of the Illinois River were, however, not so fortunate.

The Kelloggs with their families, being the first permanent settlers within what is now Morgan county, deserve a more extended notice. When the erection of the monument to the memory of Isaac Fort Roe, took place, in 1869, it was supposed that he was one of the first three settlers in the territory of which we are writing. He was one of the first three explorers passing through this region, as narrated, and was the third settler in the present limits of the county. Mrs. Minerva Richards, now living in Jacksonville, a daughter of Ambrose Collins, distinctly remembers the settlement of the Kelloggs. She states that in the Summer of 1818, her father, a native of Ontario county, New York, left his home with his family, a few articles of household furniture and provisions enough to last some time, came with two wagons to the Alleghany River, above its junction with the Susquehanna, where he procured a flat-boat on which he embarked his possessions, and proceeded down the Ohio River. His destination was the southern part of Illinois. On the way down the river he fell in with Seymour and Elisha Kellogg, who with their families were proceeding in a similar conveyance to the same destination. Mr. Collins and Seymour Kellogg had been acquainted in their native state. The latter had been a Colonel in the war of 1812, and was known by that title. At Shawneetown they disembarked and proceeded in their wagons to Carmi, on the little Wabash River. They remained here during the winter and the following summer. Early in the autumn of 1819 they loaded their effects again into their wagons, and went on westward to Edwardsville. Here Mr. Collins was taken sick and was compelled to remain through the winter. The Messrs. Kellogg with their families and Charles Collins, a son of Ambrose Collins, with their teams, some cattle and provisions for the winter, started for the Sangamo country. They followed a more northern route than that generally adopted by emigrants. Their only guide was the compass and a few indistinct trails, made by roving Indians or adventurous bee hunters. Late in the Fall of 1819, they arrived near the head of Mauvaisterre Creek, erected two cabins and made provisions for the winter, now rapidly approaching. The country lay about them in all its native wildness. No signs of life were seen, save foot-prints in the brown paths, worn by Indian feet; and the shy, frightened birds, squirrels, or deer, that darted away into the wildwood, at the approach of the emigrants. No foot of white men save that of the adventurous scout, or wandering hunter, had pressed the sod of these wild prairies, or roamed through the trackless forests. Mauvaisterre Creek had not known the abode of a white man. Anxious to build homes where they could rest secure, and where they could gather the fruits of a life-time, these pioneers braved the dangers of a frontier life and founded their homes where now are:

"—— spacious mansions firm and strong,
In place of forests dark and dense:
And now instead of underbrush
Runs many a line of even fence.

"But times will change! The verdant hills
Are covered o'er with growing grain;
And white men till the fertile soil,
Where once the red man used to reign.

"The Indian's voice is hushed and still;
Existing but in Mem'ry's hall,
Where now with echoes of the Past
We hear his *war-whoop* rise and fall!"

The winter of 1819 and '20 proved to be an unusually severe one. The long grass of the prairies had been destroyed by fires lighted by the Indians or hunters, and much of the undergrowth in the woods was destroyed by the same element. Before the close of the winter, the provisions gathered by them for their stock, from places where it had escaped the ravages of the fire gave out and they were compelled to cut down trees, from the boughs of which the cattle and horses could procure a scanty supply of food. Many of these wandered away and were lost, while several of them died from the effects of cold and hunger. The supply of food for themselves and families proved to be sufficient, yet their suffering from the cold was often intense.

Early in the spring Charles Collins returned to Edwardsville with his wagon and team, to aid his father, should he be sufficiently recovered, in bringing his family to the new settlement. It was just before his start to Edwardsville, that the three explorers, whose names and exploration we have already recorded, came, and one of them, Mr. Roe, settled at the place to which he gave the name "Diamond Grove." Mr. Collins with his family started on their journey about the first of March. On the way they were compelled to camp out two nights, there being no settlers between Edwardsville and their destination. On their arrival, they remained one night with Seymour Kellogg, and then went to an unfinished cabin, erected by Mr. Olmstead who had been exploring this country, and had built the cabin entered temporarily by Mr. Collins. The location not being a desirable one, Mr. Collins selected his claim, erected a cabin thereon as soon as possible, and moved his family to it. When Mr. Olmstead returned with his family, he was not satisfied with the claim he had selected, and chose another, afterwards known as "Olmstead Mound," where he made his permanent home.

In 1820 Dr. George Cadwell, the first physician located in the county.

We have now fully described the earliest settlement in what is now Morgan county We have also stated the names of others who came here during the spring of 1820, and noted the places of their settlement. We have described at some length the settlement of the Kelloggs (Charles Collins being then a young man, not making a claim or founding a home for himself, can hardly be termed one of the early settlers) because they were the first settlers of the county, and deserve more than a passing notice. The information can be relied on as correct, as Mrs. Richards distinctly remembers the emigration and settlement of these families.

These and the other pioneers came from the southern part of the state, generally about Edwardsville, where some had remained but a short time on their journey to a western home. They came in emigrant wagons over the unbroken prairies, through the wild forests, fording unbridged streams, and encamping wherever the shades of night overtook them. They were seeking a home that in old age would afford them protection and comfort. Upon reaching their destination, their first care was the erection of a cabin in which to shelter themselves and their families. As these primitive abodes were generally built alike by all pioneers, we will give an old writer's account of their construction, in addition to what we have written already about them.

The cabins of the pioneers were of various sizes, and generally made of round logs. Some of the more favored ones, however, had hewed log cabins, and were regarded by their neighbors as more fortunate than themselves. These round-log cabins were made by taking two logs, generally about one foot in diameter, and, we will suppose, thirty and twenty feet long. This length of logs would build a tolerably sized cabin. The logs were notched in near the ends, the shorter laid upon the longer, forming the first round, and leaving a small space between the first tier and the second, which was laid in the same manner on these. In this way round after round was laid, until the sides of the cabin were ten or twelve rounds high, as the owner might desire. The last two end logs laid were made long enough to project over the corner three or four feet, thereby forming eaves to carry the water, during a rain, that distance from the cabin. This projection also afforded a diminutive porch, and in the summer kept the hot rays of the sun from the side of the house. After these logs were laid on, completing the walls of the cabin, two logs, cut slanting at the ends, and just long enough to fit between the notches, were laid on at each end of the cabin; two more, cut in the same manner, and shorter than the first, were laid on these, and so on until an apex was reached. On the last one, generally about one foot in length, a long log, smaller than those laid in the sides of the building, was placed from one to the other, and also projecting over each some three or four feet. To secure these short, slant pieces, forming the apex of the cabin, a cleft of a small tree was placed on the outside and securely pegged on, and also fastened to the last mentioned log or pole. One or two poles of the same length as that forming the "comb of the roof," as it was called, were generally laid between the eaves and the comb, supplying the place of rafters. On these, clapboards—split boards about four feet in length—were laid nearly double, so as to cover the joints; the boards at the top of the cabin projecting a little over those on the other side. When the roof is thus covered, some poles were laid along the building to keep the shingles on. These poles were kept at about three feet distance from each other by pieces of wood laid on the roof between them These poles were called weight poles, and sometimes stones were used in their stead. When all this was complete, the cabin was "raised," and where several neighbors joined in a day's work for some new comer, or some newly married persons, such a cabin would be constructed in one day. It was simply now a pen without any openings, save the cracks between the logs. A door was made by sawing out a section in the logs to the lower one, which was generally sawn about half through and cut out to form a door-step. The top of the door was made in the same manner, and secured closeness. A stout piece of wood was pegged on each side, forming a jam, as it was termed, wooden hinges were made, and a door, made of split puncheon, hung thereon. A wooden latch, with a leathern string hung outside, fastened it. This old fashioned latch string was always out, and owing to the known hospitality of the pioneer, has given rise to a very suggestive aphorism. A door was often made on each side of the cabin. Windows, after glass came into use, were made in the same manner, though smaller, and instead of being capable of raising and lowering, as in modern times, were hung on hinges, made to slide, or taken entirely out in warm weather. The floors were made of split puncheon, in most cases joined neatly and closely together, and laid on the ground, or on cross pieces. The chimney was generally placed at the end of the building, and made as follows: first, four or five logs were cut out, as for a door or window place, of whatever width the occupant chose. It was generally four or five feet in width, and often wider Then some logs were cleft and placed so that the ends came just inside the cabin wall, and projecting outward formed a square pen. These were placed one on the other until they rose as high as the opening in the wall The chimney was carried up, as was the cabin, until it reached the top, when it was drawn in and constructed of sticks It was drawn in gradually from the bottom upwards, until the top was generally about one foot square. It was then thoroughly chunked and "daubed;" often stones were placed at the bottom and some distance up the sides, so as to effectually prevent the action of fire. Next the cabin itself was chunked and daubed—that is, the cracks between the logs were filled with split pieces of wood, held in with pegs, and securely closed by daubing with mud It was also plastered with loam or clay, and sometimes the inside was covered with well made split boards, pegged on. It was often whitewashed where lime could be obtained. A ceiling was made by taking stout poles and laying them on the upper tier of logs, their ends projecting through under the eaves, and being placed from two to four feet apart. On these split boards were laid, forming a floor. Sometimes the chimneys were walled several feet in height, and were always so carefully constructed that fires seldom occurred.

This completed the cabin. It was now ready for occupancy, and in it, many who now live in opulence, the fruit of years of labor, stoutly affirm they passed their happiest days. One room served all purposes, and when friends or travelers came, a bed was made on the floor, and every convenience offered in their power. Two cabins were often built near together, between them a space of ten or twelve feet was left, covered with a roof, and under this cover the pioneer stored many articles One side of it was generally walled up, leaving the front open A covered porch was also often seen in front of the cabins. Here the farmer could rest at noontide, and a common sight was the busy house-wife spinning under this porch on a warm summer's day.

These cabins are yet used in many parts of the state, especially in the southern and western portion. Some have more modern conveniences, and are equal to many frame dwellings now built. But in the early days of the country, none other could be made. There were no mills for sawing lumber; the pioneer was almost always poor, and was compelled to endure many privations. Yet these dwellings were comfortable, and healthy, such diseases as consumption and bronchial affections being entirely unknown.

Building for stock and for the protection of farming machinery were the result of after days. Says an old writer: "When pigs are shut up for fattening, it is common to make a fence for them of rails, in the same manner as for fields; sometimes one corner is covered over to make a lodging for them, but it is more common for them to be left to the mercy of the winds and weather; but as they are hardy animals, and accustomed to hard living and lodging, it does not appear to hurt them. There are but few cattle yards and sheds. The cattle are most left abroad in the winter, and no other shelter but what the leafless trees afford. There were few granaries, except corn cribs, and a few poultry houses, built generally the same as cabins, as were the stables also. The stables were often carried higher, to provide for a hay-loft; some had a rack made out of a hollow log, which answered for a manger. These out-houses were built in the forest—as well as were all the cabins—and were sheltered from the blasts of the winter thereby." As the country improved, the buildings were made better, and after the advent of the railroads good substantial buildings were erected, which now appear on every hand. It is doubtful if many counties in the state excel Morgan in the fine dwellings and barns scattered over her prairies.

Before we leave this epoch, so fruitful of pioneer settlements in Morgan, we may be pardoned for glancing at our county neighbors upon the east, within whose bounds towers up the great State House, of which, although unfinished, Illinois is so justly proud. A Springfield "Visitor's Guide" says:

"In 1818, there were no white inhabitants north of Edwardsville. In the same year an old bachelor, named Elisha Kelly, a hunter from North Carolina, emigrated to this locality, and was much pleased with the country and the abundance of game.

He returned to his native state and induced his brothers to move with their families to this point. In 1819 his brother, John Kelly, built a log cabin north of the town branch, near what is now the corner of Jefferson and Klein streets. Another brother, William Kelly, built his cabin further north, on the grounds where the beautiful residence of C. A. Gehrmann now stands. Other families settled around them on the edge of the timber, as all early settlers thought the prairie lands would never be settled, but would remain free pasture for those along their edge for all time.

In 1821 the county of Sangamon was formed by an act of the legislature, including what now comprises the counties of Sangamon, Logan, Mason, Menard, Tazewell, Cass and parts of Morgan, Christian, McLean, Marshall, Woodford and Putnam. The same act provided for the appointment of three commissioners to select a temporary seat of justice for the new county. After thorough investigation they learned that besides the Kelly settlement, no other neighborhood contained a sufficient number of inhabitants to board and lodge the members of the court, and those who would attend its sessions. At a meeting held in John Kelly's cabin, the proper action was taken settling the question of a temporary county seat, and on account of its proximity to Spring Creek it was named 'Springfield.' Notwithstanding the efforts made at different times to change its name to Calhoun, Sangamo and Illini the name of Springfield has clung to the settlement, village and city through all its hardships and successes, until it is now a name at the mention of which its citizens feel a thrill of worthy pride, and which has achieved not only a local and state, but also a national and world-wide reputation.

The first court in the new county was held in John Kelly's cabin in May, 1821. A log court house and jail were built in the latter part of the year, at corner of Second and Jefferson streets. In 1825 the county seat was permanently located in Springfield, and a frame court house was built corner Sixth and Adams street, where the clothing house of Hall & Herrick now stands. This was in turn abandoned upon the building of a brick court house in the center of the present square in 1831. This was demolished in 1837 to give place to the State Capitol, which was that year located here and for which the citizens donated the ground and $50,000. The court was held in the Edwards building, at 109 North Fifth street, now occupied by Thomas DePleaux, until 1845 when the court house was built on the corner of Sixth and Washington streets, which was used until the county offices were moved into the old state house, which had been purchased from the State for $200,000 and interest for eight years. Upon the site of the old court house a beautiful three story stone front block of four stores was erected, an ornament to the city.

We have given the different steps taken in building of court houses as showing the rapid and steady growth of wealth and cultivation in the community, from the simple log court house costing $84 to the substantial stone structure costing over $300,000. Springfield obtained a village charter in 1832, and, prospering under its village organization, secured a city charter in 1840.

Few cities have been honored as the home of so many illustrious men—Abraham Lincoln, Stephen A. Douglas, E. D. Baker, Stephen T. Logan, James Shields and many others whose names have been inscribed high on the roll of fame and will be handed down as undying legacies to generations yet unborn. While Springfield has been maligned and misrepresented on all sides, and burdened almost beyond endurance by a municipal indebtedness, she has ever, Job-like, retained her integrity, and now, re-organized under the general law, her bonds refunded at low interest, her streets paved, business blocks and comfortable homes building in every direction, new manufacturing enterprises clustering about her, she can proudly point to her past record, of obligations honestly met and her garments free from even the slightest taint of repudiation

In these days of railroad progress, when towns spring up as if by magic, we fail to realize the difficulties under which our fathers labored and the obstacles an inland town had to contend with in early days.

High hopes were raised and much excitement was created in Springfield in 1832 when it was announced that the *Steamer Talisman*, would leave Cincinnati for Springfield, Ill., and intermediate points. The arrival of the boat was anxiously awaited and in due time arrived in the Sangamon River near Springfield, but the problem of cheaper freights was not yet solved, as owing to the narrow channel the boat had to back down stream, and the inhabitants still had to rely on hauling their goods and produce until relieved by the building of railroads

Richard Matthews, Sr., and his sons Samuel, Cyrus, John and Richard, his wife, his daughter and Samuel's family, came to this county in 1821, settling on what is still known as the Matthews farm some eight miles northeast of Jacksonville, and his descendants are still living there and in other parts of the county.

Mr. Edward Harvey, one of the old settlers of this county, is still living in Lynnville precinct and claims that he went to school to Mr. A. K. Barber in 1821.

From a historical sketch of Jersey county, delivered at Jerseyville, July 4, 1876, by Elder B. B. Hamilton, postmaster of White Hall, we learn as to Greene county, which was organized by act of legislature in 1821, that

The first session of the county commissioner's court was held in Carrollton on the first day of May, 1821, and there were present John Allen, John Brown and Seymour Kellogg as commissioners, and Samuel Lee, Jr., was appointed clerk At this session the commissioners to locate the seat of justice reported, under date of February 20, 1821. This report was signed by Thomas Carlin, John Allen, Thomas Rattan and John Huitt. Of these, John Huitt is the sole survivor. The county-seat was located at Carrollton, on land donated to the new county by Thomas Carlin At this session John Wilkins was licensed to keep a tavern on the Piasa, about one mile south of Delhi. In later times Mr. Wilkins was known to many of the citizens of this county as the father-in-law of Perley Silloway, one of our early sheriffs. Twenty lots owned by the county in the town of Carrollton were ordered to be sold. * * * * *

Hon. Joseph Philips was judge of the circuit court at the spring term of 1822 At the October term of that year Thomas Reynolds was judge, and again at the spring term of 1823. In the September term of 1823, and then until the May term of 1825, John Reynolds was judge. From the latter date until the April term of 1827, John York Sawyer was judge. From this date until Jersey county was organized, Samuel D. Lockwood was judge. John G. Lofton was the first probate judge, as I find an allowance made him of $20.12½, in full for his service as judge of probate until he went out of office, and $5 for recording deeds. This was at the December term of the county court in 1822. He had been in that year a candidate for lieutenant-governor.

Elder Hamilton tells us that Greene county records show that Seymour Kellogg, when commissioner was allowed $1 extra pay because of having to travel so far—from Apple Creek to Carrollton.

The spot where the town of Manchester now is was first settled in 1821 by Mr. Marks. The place was called at that time; "Burnt Hay Stack Spring," from the charred remains of a stack of prairie hay that was burned by the side of the passing trail, and was afterwards known as Marsh's Point.

CHAPTER IV.—1825-'29.

The Infant Town of Jacksonville—Locating the County Seat—The Early Settlers Arriving—Churches, Schools and Colleges Founded—Judge Thomas' Arrival and Experiences—The Winnebago War—County Officers—Liquor in the Harvest Field—The First License—Recollections of early times by Dr. Sturtevant, Anderson Foreman, John R. Harney, Murray McConnel and Judge Samuel Woods—First Court House, Jail and Poor Farm—John J. Hardin's Death.

"The world moves on,
The years roll slowly by;
Youth comes of age,
The aged droop and die.
New faces crowd the ever bustling scene,
And tell to me what I have been."

LOOKING back with justifiable pride over a life covering more than half a century Jacksonville may well be thought to have forgotten not only her appearance, but many of her deeds during the infantile period of her history. For the benefit of the Present and the Future let us recall all that we can of those days of small beginnings.

In 1825, two years after the creation of Morgan county, by Legislature, and five years later than the arrival in this region of some—two at least, Mr. Huram and Miss Keren Reeve—who are still here, after 64 years of residence, the town of Jacksonville was duly laid out. To the great disappointment of a rival town, older in years, the embryo city was selected as the seat of justice instead of Naples, Scott county, then in Morgan.

Our city, the county seat of one of the wealthiest, and most fertile counties of the noblest state of the Union, has not been in a hurry to climb the hill of fame: the increase in her population has been slow until within a year or two. Her citizens have been attracted to the place by beautiful rolling prairies adjacent, and later by the unusually good school privileges of the town. Thus the villagers were gradually increased by the addition of such as came to educate their children, and who, allured by its attractions, remained: others came to enjoy and dwell in the midst of the growing circle of *literati* which was gathering in the embryo "Athens." Speculators, with no settling intentions, sordid business men, and the riff-raff of society, on the contrary, found no attractions in the place. A truly fortunate fact.

We say that the growth of Jacksonville was slow, we mean slow in comparison with the cities, which, like Jonah's gourd, have arisen in a night, for although now numbering over twelve thousand inhabitants it is yet young in history. The time does not seem far distant when the Indian chose his hunting grounds upon the banks of the Mauvaisterre, and the rich soil of the county furnished a tempting pasture to the roaming herds of deer and buffalo. Not being near a navigable river the present site of the city was not early chosen as a home by the hardy pioneers of the great west. Many towns were in full vigor, and Illinois had entered the sisterhood of states while yet the twang of the bow by day and howl of the wolf by night were the only sounds heard here. Only a few years have passed away since the aboriginal chieftains paid their adoration to the rising "orb of light," where now on every Sabbath so many church bells summon Christians to the worship of the true God.

It was in January, 1825, that the legislature passed the act appointing John Howard, John Lusk and Abraham Pickett commissioners to select a permanent seat of justice for Morgan. The government then owned the land selected—now the site of Jacksonville, but two shrewd gentlemen, learning of the commissioners' decision, immediately purchased the land from the government, and were at once ready to lay out the new town. The act providing for the location of the permanent seat of justice stipulated that the owners of the land selected should donate not less than twenty acres to be laid out into lots and sold for the erection of the necessary county buildings.

On the 10th of March, Mr. Johnston Shelton, the county surveyor, began the survey by laying out a public square of little more than five acres, directly in the centre of the site, partly on the land of Isaac Dial, partly on land owned by Jacky Anderson, and partly on the land of Thomas Arnett, the three who had bought in the "quarter" selected by the commissioners.

Previous to that time there had been a public road laid out from Springfield, the then recently located county seat of Sangamon county, to the town of Naples, on the Illinois River, in Morgan county. This road, by way of eminence and distinction, was called the State road. This State road passed east and west on top of the ridge of land directly over the spot selected for said county seat. The surveyor began the survey by laying out the square directly in the center of the said one hundred and sixty acre tract, the State road running through the square. Upon this State road he located a street, sixty feet wide, intending it to run due east and west across said one hundred and sixty acres, and on the north line of the land belonging to the proprietors. Thus locating one-half of said square and one-half of the width of the street on the land of said private owners, and the other half on the land of the county. This street was called State street.

A street was then laid out running north and south through the center of said land and said central square, of the same width, and it was called Main street. Taking those two streets as base lines, the town was laid out into square blocks, of one hundred and eighty feet nine inches on each side, which blocks were divided into three lots, each of equal size. All other streets, except those two, were made forty feet wide, and the alleys twenty feet wide, all running at right angles with each other.

There are several stories as to the origin of the name of our city, but the most generally accepted one is, that it was named after, and in honor of "Old Hickory"—Gen. Andrew Jackson—the hero of that day. The other generally circulated tale is that it was named directly after a colored boy, the first negro ever seen in the county—a slave at the time, of Thomas P. Clark. This boy is living here to-day and preaching the Gospel, being no other than the venerable Rev. A. W. Jackson who informs us that when a boy he was living with a man named Clark, about ten miles west of the city, and was sent to some parties located near Diamond Grove to get some seed corn. Losing his way he wandered across the unbroken prairie until he reached a spot about where the Dunlap House now stands. Here he saw some men, evidently surveyors, driving stakes among the grass and inquired of them the way. They gave him the desired information and then asked him how he, a colored boy, happened to be there. He told them, whereupon they inquired his name and being told it was A. W. Jackson they remarked that Jackson, or Jacksonville, would be a good name for the place they were laying out. They said to him: "Young man, we have entered this land and are staking off lots for a town which we are going to name after you; do you understand?" He replied that he did, little thinking that he would live here sixty years after and see such great changes.

The streets thus and then laid out were afterwards abundantly lined with the shade-trees which make them now the crowning glory of an unsurpassably handsome residence city.

The only human habitation on the selected town site was that of a man named Alexander Cox, a hatter by trade. It was located near where Trinity (Episcopal) church now stands, though just over the eastern boundary of the town was the double log cabin of Father Jordan, within the walls of which was formed the first class of Methodists—the germ from which the Centenary, Grace and Brooklyn M. E. churches have since sprung. The site having been decided upon, houses and occupants soon made their appearance. Joseph Fairfield and George Hackett were the first merchants in the new town, though George Rearick, whose widow is still living here, followed them so closely that he may be said to co-equal with them, all locating nearly at the same time in the summer of 1825. The first tavern in the town was under the supervision of Thomas Carson, who bought the log cabin formerly occupied by Mr. Cox, for tavern purposes, and to which before a year he made a large addition. His wife, for many years known as "Mother Carson," carried the frames for the doors and windows on her arm, from Jersey Prairie, where they were made, making the journey on horse back.

As the county was incorporated in a municipal capacity, Carson was required to procure a license. In all licenses to keep public houses, or ferries, at that date, the rates of charges were established. By the destruction of the court-house and records in the Autumn of 1827, all such records were destroyed, and we have no means of determining such charges save by those prescribed after that event. It is probably correct to suppose that the prices allowed for entertainment did not change much in that short interval, and we can very safely assume that Mr. Carson received for rum, brandy gin, and wine twenty-five cents per half pint; for whisky, half that sum for the same quantity; for a meal of victuals or keeping a horse over night, twenty-five cents; for lodging twelve and one-half cents, and for feeding a horse six and one-fourth cents. Mr. Huram Reeve and some others think that Mr. David Tefft opened a tavern in a small building sixteen feet square, erected by him on the east side of the square previous to the opening of Mr. Carsen's. Mrs. Carson, however, once stated to Mr. J. R. Bailey that her husband procured his license first, and was the first tavern-keeper in the town. This opinion was confirmed by Mr. Dennis Rockwell, the first county clerk, and is probably correct.

The cabin tavern of Mr. Carson was removed to East Morgan street to give place for the erection of the Congregational church, which was afterward known as the "Union Hall." The old building is partly standing at this time.

Mr. Carson has the honor of being also at the same time the first jailor. He was the custodian of that supposedly safe institution whose new and strong doors were hung upon common wrought hinges, which fact the inmates were not slow to discover, and Sampson-like, lifted them up, and went off with them—at least so the old legend runs.

Mr. Carson remained in Jacksonville during his life-time, and was always an excellent citizen, doing much toward the prosperity of the city. His old log jail, though uncouth in appearance, was probably as safe a repository for criminals as its more pretentious successors. Mrs. Carson was more widely known than any woman in the county. "Mother" Carson, as she was called, was known in St. Louis, Springfield, and equally distant places. She followed the profession of mid-wife, and so extensive was her practice, and so remarkable her success, that she was often called to these and equally distant places in the practice of her profession. She seldom lost a patient, and it has been confidently asserted by many that she was present at the birth of fully three thousand children. She died while court was in session, and so respected was she by all, that, upon motion of Judge William Thomas, court adjourned to attend her funeral. The immediate descendants of this pioneer family are located in Jacksonville today (1884.) It is said that the Carson log cabin hotel was eighteen feet square and consisted of two rooms.

Mr. Michael Huffaker, deceased, is another of Morgan county's pioneer settlers. He reached Illinois in 1823 and located in Mauvaisterre precinct in the spring of 1824 Land could then be purchased for $1.25 per acre—the choicest pieces only bringing that amount at private or public sale. Jacksonville had no existence and the hunter roamed over the present site of the city for deer and other game. Wolves prowled around the sheep-fold and greatly disturbed Mr. H. by preying upon his stock and rendering the night hideous with their barking. Here and there upon the prairie huge piles of buffalo bones could be perceived. Now and then a black bear would make its appearance, and the hunters would gather together and have a jolly and long hunt after Bruin. The hunting stories of those days cause the modern tales of sport to sink into insignificance. As to produce prices, he reports that the very best wheat brought only twenty-five cents per bushel; corn from eight to ten cents, and pork one dollar per one hundred pounds. Even at these low prices very little could be sold. There was a very limited amount of gold in the country, and this was controlled for purposes of circulation by a very few men.

In those days, substantiality rather than elegance, comfort rather than fashion was looked after in the construction of the settler's cabin homes. When Jacksonville was laid out it became the point to which all arrivals came, and Mother Carson's hostelry, over which she presided with satisfaction to all, was generally filled by the immigrants. Springfield was then but a small village where they kept the land office, Vandalia being the state capital. For nearly fifty years Mr. Huffaker exercised a great influence upon the surrounding country. He was a type of those sterling characters of the past generation. Through weal and woe he kept the even tenor of his way and won a solid reputation for honesty, industry and public spirit. When he came to Illinois, his property consisted of $200.25 and what household goods could be packed upon the back of a horse. He rode one horse and his wife another. His $200 was all invested in land, leaving the twenty-five cents for food and other necessities—an illustration of the poverty of our early citizens, and a marked contrast to the wealth, refinement and luxuries possessed by the farming community of to-day. Mr. Huffaker died in 1883.

The laying out of the city, and its selection as the seat of justice, brought immediately a number of families thither. Dennis Rockwell, the first recorder, clerk of court, and the first post-master here, was without doubt among the first settlers.

Mr. Rockwell was a native of Vermont. He resided for some time at Edwardsville, Illinois, and when Morgan county was organized, he was appointed clerk of the Circuit and County Commissioner, Court, and recorder, and, upon the location of the county seat at Jacksonville, post-master. In 1854 he removed to Chicago, where he was engaged in the lumber business until 1867, when, his health failing, he returned to Jacksonville. He was one of the first directors of the Institution for the Deaf and Dumb, and, with Colonel Geo. M. Chambers, superintended the erection of that building. He was also one of the trustees of the Institution for the Blind. For a time he held a position as cashier in the Branch of the State Bank, located in Jacksonville. He donated to the Episcopal church, of which he was a member, the block of ground on which that church now stands, and gave largely toward the erection of the house and support of the minister. After his return from Chicago, in 1867, his health failed him and he died shortly thereafter.

The first store in the county was opened soon after the town was laid out, by Hackett & Fairfield. Before opening this store in town, they peddled through the settlements, exchanging goods for furs, beeswax, and honey, the only money found in the settlements at that time. Town property, for the first three or four years of the growth of the town, was very low. A lot on the southwest corner of the square, was offered to Mr. Dennis Rockwell for a cow and calf, worth at that time ten dollars, and Mr. Rockwell sold at one time eight acres of land, just north and west of the square, now in the heart of the city, for eighty dollars—to be paid in blacksmithing.

The first improvements on the west side of the square were a row of small frame houses. In one of these houses the first barber shop was opened, by a colored man named Ball, and in one of these buildings Colonel John J. Hardin held his office.

General Hardin, one of the most prominent men in Morgan county, was born in Frankfort, Kentucky, on the 6th day of June, 1810. He came to this part of Illinois at an early day, and at once entered actively into the practice of his profession the law. He was a member of different legislative bodies, and held other and various offices of trust. He was elected a general of militia, and, on the breaking out of the Mexican war, was the first one in the county to enlist. He was immediately chosen captain of a company raised here. After leaving for the seat of war, he was chosen colonel of a regiment; and, while gallantly leading his men at the battle of Buena Vista, on the 23d of February, 1847, received a death wound. In July, his body was brought home, and deposited in the old cemetery. His funeral was one of the largest ever held in this city, being attended by many state officials and others from abroad.

At the time of the building of Illinois College, all the large tract of land lying between that institution and the public square, was in its primitive condition, or cultivated as a farm. Where now are the finest residences, the most beautiful yards, and the best shaded streets, was then open prairie, or used for farm purposes. What changes time produces! Then all buildings in town were small, almost entirely frame or built of logs, the former being pointed out to the traveler as the home of elegance and wealth. The business of the time was proportionate to the residences. No large stores graced the public square, or stood as monuments of the industry of the owners, in other streets. The houses of that day are succeeded now by more elegant affairs, though no more homelike than their predecessors. Their owners have grown with the town, and can look over the scenes of their labors with feelings of pride at the results obtained, and know that the passing years have been those of care and toil, though sweetened by the thoughts of the rest and comfort sure to follow.

The early log stores speedily gave way to frame buildings, which in their time became too small and insecure, and were replaced by more substantial brick structures. The first of these was erected in 1828, by John P. Wilkinson, Esq., and occupied the lot of ground where is now the store of Hoffman Bros. Another was built on the south side of the square, and one on the north, by Cornelius Hook, Esq., and in 1831 or '32, the late bank building of M. P. Ayers & Co. Like its population, the business of Jacksonville was growing. New and more substantial stores were appearing about the public square, while in the residence portion, better dwellings were being erected. Streets were accurately defined; pavements took the place of mud sidewalks; fences were built before the door-yards, and a finer and more elegant life was becoming manifest.

During the summer of 1825 and 1826, building progressed rapidly in the new town. Mr. Carson's tavern was always full, and more than once the traveler was glad of a chance to shelter himself and enjoy the luxury of a bed on the puncheon floor, with his traveling cloak for a covering. Hospitality was a reigning virtue among the early pioneers of Illinois, and no one in search of a home on these western prairies went unsheltered or hungry.

In the fall of 1826 Jacksonville had a mail from St. Louis, *via* Alton and Carrollton, once in two weeks, and also a like mail from Springfield; so arranged as to give a weekly mail.

One of the few survivors of this foundation age is our honored fellow citizen, Hon. William Thomas. From his recollections and contributions to the *Journal*, from time to time in later years, has been gleaned much of the information compiled in this unpretentious history. The judge came to this county from Bowling Green, Ky., in the fall of 1826, traveling on horseback (the only way of journeying at that time) and visiting on the route some of the settlements which had been made at that time in various sections of the country, although they were very small. The judge gives as his reason for settling in Jacksonville in preference to other places, that he had traveled about as far as his money and horse would take him, and there is no one that would not consider that a sufficient reason for stopping. But besides this reason he says that he was pleased with this section of country and with the location of the town, and taking all these reasons together, he consented to make this his home, which was no doubt a very wise choice, both for his own personal welfare and for that of the town. He reports that the population of the town consisted of the families of Dennis Rockwell, Murray McConnel, Thos. Carson, John Handy, David Tefft, Samuel Blair, George M. Richards, George Rearick, Joseph M. Fairfield, John Laughrey, John P. Tefft, and the brothers, Savage. The men without families were George Hackett, John Turney, Benjamin Cox, Samuel C. Richards, Moses Atwood (?) Orson Cobb, Rice Dunbar and Joseph Coddington. John Handy was the "Buckeye" carpenter; Fairfield, Rearick and Moses Atwood were merchants; Richards was deputy county surveyor; Blair and Dunbar were carpenters; Laughrey was a brickmaker. John P. Tefft was a plasterer. Rockwell was clerk of the two courts, postmaster and notary public; McConnel, Turney and Cox were attorneys; John Savage was a carpenter; Peter Savage was a teamster; and was a tailor as was Orson Cobb. This shows something of the occupations of our forefathers in the early days when it was necessary for one man to follow several trades.

The judge himself soon after landing in this county began attending the courts and got his start in law practice in this section, and from these beginnings rose to the high position he afterwards occupied and the estimation in which he is now held by his fellow-townsmen. His active practice extended over forty-five years.

We quote as follows from Judge Thomas' "Recollections of Early Times," as contributed to the *Journal*:

"In September, 1826, I started from my home in Kentucky for Peoria, but after reaching this state I changed my destination to this place, where I landed on the 12th of October thereafter. The first court that I attended was held in Jacksonville by the Hon. John York Sawyer, circuit judge, in November, 1826.

There were about forty cases on the docket, all told. The attorneys present were James Tracy, attorney general of the state, and Alfred W. Caverly, of Carrollton, Thomas W. Neely, Isaac W. Steele and Jonathan H. Pugh, of Springfield, John Reynolds, of Kankakee, William H. Brown, Benjamin Mills and George Farqueir, of Vandalia; Murray McConnel, John Turney, Benjamin Cox and myself, of Jacksonville—of whom Mr. Caverly and myself are the only survivors, this 12th of October 1883; he eighty-one years old, and I near seventy-two.

In November, 1826, I first saw the Illinois river. The state of the water was too low for the navigation of loaded flat-boats. Grass had grown up from the bottom so thick and strong that ferry-boats could not be used without mowing the grass and opening the way. Except in a channel, occupying a narrow space, I could not discover any current.

A short time after I reached Jacksonville I heard of the time of the sales of the personal property of Rev. Mr Byrne, who had died in January previous. I went to that sale expecting to meet some acquaintances from Kentucky. I met Mr. Thomas Gatton and went home with him, and by him I was introduced to most of the settlers in that prairie. The log buildings and unfinished frames, were at that day, as houses of worship, few and far between. I am confident that during the winter of 1826-7 there was not a comfortable meeting house in the county. Religious meetings were held in log and unplastered frames, school houses and private dwellings. In warm weather such meetings were often held in barns and under arbours in the woods. The first sermon that I ever heard in Jacksonville was in the fall of 1826, in the frame court house (subsequently burnt), preached by a Baptist minister named Kenney, prepared for mothers, when the only female in attendance was Mrs. Joseph Fairfield, who had no child. During the winter of 1826-7 and previous, as well as subsequently to that time, the meetings of the Methodist Society were held at Mr. John Jordan's, who was well-known as Father Jordan. He occupied a double log cabin east of town, where now stands the building formerly called "Berean College." During the service the females occupied one room and the males the other, the beds being used for seats. During that winter the society of Presbyterians, with Rev. John Brich, as their minister, met in the log school house occupied by me during the week in the south side of the town. I acted as sexton, sweeping the house in the morning and building fires.

Father Brich, as he was called, though a bachelor, was an educated Scotchman, but like many others was never able to make his learning avail him much as a public speaker, but he was a devoted Christian.

Among the public improvements in the county designed for public benefit and convenience, was the grist and saw mill at Exeter, owned by Enoch C. March; a band horse mill for grinding corn, owned by Capt. John Wyatt; also one owned by Mr Reeder, and one tread wheel mill, owned by James Overton, Esq.; a grist and saw mill on

Indian Creek, owned by William Harrison and James Dinwiddie; a horse mill, owned by Mr. A. Hall, near the head of Indian Creek; a saw mill, owned by Mr. James McGill, on the Mauvaisterre Mr. Abraham Johnson owned a cotton gin north of town.

I soon found two classes in society. Those from the north and east were called "yankees" and those from the south and west "white people." The political division was between the supporters of John Quincy Adams and General Andrew Jackson, the yankees supporting Adams and the white people, Jackson. Most of those who had voted for Mr. Clay supported Mr. Adams. The election of August, 1826, had been warmly contested between Gov. Edwards and Mr. Sloo for governor, and Daniel P. Cook and Joseph Duncan for Congress. Edwards and Duncan were elected by a small majority, though differing in politics. Duncan was one of the few public men who never had credit for what he was worth.

In the summer of 1826, a young man named Carson, had been employed to teach school in the court house, but not meeting with such encouragement as he thought would pay, abandoned his employers and left that neighborhood.

In July, 1827, Gov. Edwards received information on which he relied and acted, that the Indians of the north-west, led by the Winnbagos intended to make war upon the settlers and miners in the vicinity of Galena. He therefore authorized Col. Thomas Neely, of Springfield, to accept of the services of any number of mounted volunteers, not exceeding six hundred, who would equip themselves and find their own substance and continue in service thirty days, unless sooner discharged. Upon this call upwards of three hundred volunteers were obtained in the counties of Sangamon and Morgan, among whom I was one When the volunteers from Morgan reached Peoria, the place of rendezvous, I was appointed quartermaster sergeant. I accompanied the regiment to White Oak Springs, some ten or twelve miles from Galena, where I remained several days, when the Colonel being satisfied that the further service of the regiment was not required, ordered the return home.

The regiment, composed of independent farmers and mechanics, was raised, organized, marched to the White Oak Springs, and returned home in not exceeding thirty days. Two of our Morgan County men were drowned in a branch of Crooked Creek returning home. We had no baggage wagon from this county. My mess had a very good tent, which very few of the other messes had. Having no baggage wagons, and having to carry our provisions, arms, and equipments on horseback, we had but little room for tents, even if they had been supplied We slept on saddle-blankets, with our heads on saddles, and for covering had overcoats and blankets; but during that season of the year we had but little use for covering other than overcoats.

* * * "The question of pay was not considered of much consequence; it was well understood that this depended on the action of Congress, and no fears were entertained of the success of General Duncan, our representative in Congress, in obtaining the necessary appropriation. We were not disappointed, for appropriations were made by the Congress of 1827-'28, and we were paid in the Spring of 1828, the following rates: Each sergeant major and quartermaster-sergeant, $9 per month; each drum and fife major, $8.33 per month; sergeants, $8; each corporal, drummer, fifer and teamster, $7.33; each farrier, saddler and artificer included as a private, $8; each gunner, bombardier, and private, $6.66 In addition to which we were paid for the use of horses, arms and accoutrements, and for the risk thereof, except for horses killed in action, ten cents per day. For rations, twenty-five cents per day, and one day's pay for fifteen miles travel to the place of rendezvous and returning home." * * * *

Three companies were raised in this county, one commanded by Wiley B. Green, then sheriff of the county, numbering nearly one hundred, with John Wyatt first, and James Evans second lieutenant. Jesse Ruble was orderly sergeant. The second company was commanded by William Gordon, and numbered not more than forty. Nathan Winter was first lieutenant. Captain Rodgers' command numbered the same as Captain Gordon's. The names of the other officers I do not now remember I was a volunteer in Captain Green's company. My messmates were Doct. H. G. Taylor, McHenry Johnson, Enoch C. March, Samuel Blair, and a man named Biggs, a visitor from Kentucky Of these I am the only survivor. We were required to take ten days' provisions, during which time it was expected we would make Galena, where additional supplies could be obtained. During our preparations to start we had constant, heavy rains, which raised the rivers, creeks, and branches to an unusual height. The companies from this county made their way to Peoria in messes and squads, swimming the streams not bridged. Upon the arrival of all the companies at Peoria, Colonel Samuel T. Matthews was elected lieutenant-colonel, and Elijah Iles, of Springfield, major, who, because he rode a mule, was called the 'mule major.' So soon as organized we left Peoria. James D. Henry (afterward General Henry), was appointed adjutant, Dr. G. Jayne, of Springfield, surgeon, and Dr Taylor assistant.

By the action of the Legislature in 1826-'27, the State was divided into four circuits. To the first circuit, composed of counties bordering on the Illinois and Mississippi, the Hon. Samuel D. Lockwood, of Jacksonville, was assigned. In the spring of 1827, I attended all the counties in this circuit, Greene, Morgan, Sangamon, Peoria, Fulton,

Schuyler, Adams, Pike and Calhoun. The judges and lawyers traveled on horseback and visited all the county seats After leaving Peoria we either took our dinners in our saddle-bags or traveled all day without dinner. This circuit included all the organized counties in the northwestern part of the State, including Jo Daviess.

I continued to attend the courts in this circuit until additional circuits were created. The rides were rather sources of pleasure and amusement than labor. Our libraries consisted of Digests, Chitty's Pleading and Blackstone. I could relate many incidents of trials, of travels, of swimming creeks, and the like.

Through the exertions of Mr. Thomas, coupled with those of other enterprising citizens, an unfinished log cabin, originally intended for such a purpose, was so far completed, and furnished in a primitive style, that it could be occupied as a school house, and in it he taught the first school in the town. This identical one-story log school house, located in the southeast part of the town, thus was the legitimate predecessor of all the halls of learning that Jacksonville can now boast of and Judge Thomas the veritable professional ancestor of all the more than three hundred school teachers of "the Athens of the West."

This cabin was also used as a place of worship by the Methodists; and other denominations occasionally sent ministers to preach within its walls.

Mr. Atwood, already referred to, in July, 1883, when in his 79th year, wrote to the postmaster of Jacksonville in regard to his arrival in this place, as follows:

"I removed from St Louis in June, 1825, and located myself in a corner of a double log cabin on the east side of the common with a stock of goods for a variety store; at that time there were but eleven buildings in the place, a court house in the center of the common, two taverns, three stores and a hall, all built of logs. I built the first frame with a brick chimney inside of the house, located on the northeast corner of the common. I assisted in forming the Lodge of Free Masons, in a small hall on the northwest side of the common, by singing, and at that time I assisted in singing for the congregation at their communion season, although I was not a member of the church. Father Brich was the minster at that time My first partner was E. C. March, of Exeter, sixteen miles west of you; my next partner was H. G. Taylor; his wife and a daughter, Louisa, then about two years old, was living at Jacksonville. I remember the names of Hackett, Fairfield, Nicely, Rockwell (clerk of the county. I went to his house to board at first.) McConnel, Cobb, Wiswall and others."

We here will quote the following record of county affairs as given in Donnelly, Loyd & Co's. History:

The care of the poor, review of roads, justices' districts, and such matters, engaged the attention of the county court at its first sessions. As the county increased in population, its division into smaller road and justice's districts was made The first jury lists are now lost. The first one preserved is that drawn for the April term of court in 1828. The grand jury was composed of the following gentlemen: William Wood, William Rodgers Frederick Bolinger Samuel B. Jones, David Marks George M. Richards, Allen B. Hughes, Larkin Brown, Matthew Elder, Nathan Compton, Joshua Crow, Solomon Penny, William Miller, George Camp, William Sharon Ira A Hooker, William B. Schott, Thomas Cowhick, Martin Humphries, and Thomas Allen Those composing the "travers" jury, as it was called, were Richard Beall, Samuel Holloway, Charles W. Horrell, Samuel Berry, Elias Williams, James Martin, Stephen Burrows, James D. Morrison, William Jarrod, Benjamin Shartzer, Peter Dew, Samuel White, David Hibbard, Thomas Wiswall, Richard P. Carter, John Box, John Wilson, Andrew Armstrong, James Taylor, Benjamin Case, William Wyatt, Solomon Perkins, Samuel Matthews, and James Redman.

At the meeting of the county court on March 4, 1828, the county was divided into seven road districts, which number was shortly greatly increased, so rapidly did the county fill with settlers. On the 6th of the same month, the court ordered the clerk to give notice that on the 10th of April following, the building of a court house would be let to responsible bidders. At first the plan was to construct a brick building, two stories high, forty feet square. On the 22d a special meeting of the commissioners was called, and the plan altered, making the building fifty feet long and forty feet wide. None of the bids offered for its construction were accepted, and no contracts made that year. The next year the county commissioners were Joseph M Fairfield John Wyatt, and Samuel Rogers, and at a meeting of this court on January 31, 1829, it was decided to let the work in separate bids, and these were accordingly advertised. On the 14th of March, the contracts for its construction were let; the brick and stone work to Garrison W. Berry and Henry Robley, for $1,720; the carpenter work to Rice Dunbar and Henry Robley, for $1,350, and a few minor contracts to other individuals. On March 5, 1830, contracts for finishing the court house, putting in windows, placing window-shutters in place, with many other articles needed, was let to Rice Dunbar and Henry Blandford, for $1,250; for lathing and plastering to Henry Robley and Isham Dalton, for $326.62½; for painting to John Challon, for $389, and to James Hurst, for the floors $41. The court house was accepted by the county commissioners at their meeting on September 8, 1830. The contractors and builders were paid in installments, as had been agreed. The total cost, when complete, was about $4,000. The building was the first brick house in the county, and occupied the central square of land on the south side of State street and west of Main street. To meet the expense in the erection of this edifice, and for the county revenue, a tax was ordered levied at the meeting of March 4th, 1829, on all slaves, indentured or registered, negro or mulatto servants, on pleasure carriages, on distilleries, on stock in trade, on live stock, and on all personal property, except household furniture—the ratio being one-half per cent. One per cent. was also established for the erection of public buildings, in accordance with an act passed by the General Assembly.

This court house remained in use until it was superseded by the present commodious structure, completed in 1868. It had served the county thirty-eight years, and then gave way to its handsome successor. It had for some time been the desire of the citizens generally that it should be removed from its position, and the square left for an ornament to the town. The "old court house," as it was called, was also inadequate to the increasing demands of the county, and was, when the "new court house" was erected, pulled down and the material used elsewhere. The present structure is one of the finest in the West, and is unusually safe from fire. It is constructed almost entirely of stone and iron; the first named material being obtained from the quarries at Joliet.

The old jail was built of hewed timbers, each was about one foot square, and every wall was made double. Between these double walls, upright pieces of timber, of the same dimensions as that used in the wall, were placed, so that if a criminal attempted to escape by cutting through the wall, these inner pieces would, when a section was cut out of one of them, drop down, and thus the process would have to be repeated until the whole would be cut away. This would take more time than any criminal could use without being detected, and it is doubtful if the process was ever attempted. At the meeting of the county court, on March 9, 1832, it was decided to erect a new jail, and the clerk of that court was ordered to advertise in the *Illinois Patriot*, for sealed proposals from builders for its construction. It was determined it should be built of brick and stone, and the contract for that part of the construction was, at a subsequent meeting, awarded to Abram DeWitt, for about eighteen hundred dollars. The carpenter work to Ebenezer Miller, for nearly fifteen hundred dollars. The jail was completed in 1833, its entire cost being about thirty-five hundred dollars.

This jail was the stronghold of detaining criminals many years. It, in turn, also became unsafe through the lapse of years, and was declared unfit for use. In the spring of 1864 steps were taken for the erection of a more substantial jail. The old one was pronounced unsafe and uncomfortable by the county commissioners, who decided to erect a new one. After mature deliberation, it was decided to construct the building with iron cells, and Hon. Stephen Dunlap, a member of the court, was instructed to proceed to Cincinnati, Ohio, with a competent mechanic, and make arrangements for its construction.

Mr. Jesse T. Newman had offered $3,000 for the old lot and jail. It was decided to accept this offer, and purchase another site. After examining various offered sites, a lot owned by Mr. John Trabue was selected and he was paid for the same $3,500. Work on the jail was soon after begun, and prosecuted until its completion. The building cost $27,500, and is yet in use.

The keeping of the county poor has always been a serious question in the management of county affairs. At first they were "farmed out," as it was termed, that is given to suitable persons to keep. These were obligated to provide a reasonable maintenance. In case the person kept was able to work, the one keeping him could obtain a partial recompense in that manner, and in addition was given an allowance from the county treasury. Minors were bound out until of age, and the person to whom they were given was required to provide for them schooling a reasonable length of time during the year. These and various methods were tried in the early days of the West, but did not at all times prove satisfactory. With all due diligence, in some cases the poor would fall into the hands of those who only desired gain by their labors, and who cared nothing for their moral advancement. Minors would often be mistreated and unprovided with the means of education, and the moral training wholly neglected.

The earliest attempts to keep this class of people by the county were made about 1840. A poor-farm was established a few miles north of Jacksonville, and many of them sent there for keeping. The house was not built expressly for this purpose, having been a residence, but was used. Additions were made to it in 1847, when Joseph Heslop was superintendent, as the accommodations were not such as were desired. At this time insane persons were kept by the county. Miss Dix, a woman who devoted her life to this unfortunate class of humanity, and whose history is given in connection with that of the

Insane Asylum, elsewhere in this volume, came about this time to Morgan county and visited the poor-house. Finding all classes of the poor kept together, and no provision for the insane, she vigorously set to work to remedy the evil. She visited the county commissioners and urgently importuned them to sell the property and purchase elsewhere. She selected a site just east of the city, and succeeded in her purpose. On July 12, 1847, James H. Lurton was appointed agent, on behalf of the county, to purchase fourteen acres at a price not to exceed fifty dollars per acre. Before the purchase was made the number of acres was increased to thirty. On September 10th the old poor-house, and property belonging thereto, was ordered to be sold. An addition to the new location was purchased of W. B. Warren, in 1854, for four thousand dollars. In accordance with the views of Miss Dix, a building for the use and care of the insane was erected, in addition to the building intended for the paupers, and new and improved methods adopted in the treatment of all.

The farm was occupied until 1867. The city's growth had reached the grounds, and advantageous offers were made to the county for the property. As the population of the county had increased, the number of poor augmented until more land and more accommodations were necessary. Land adjoining the farm was too valuable for such purposes, and the county commissioners decided to sell the property, and, by going farther from the city, purchase more land. On January 27, 1866, in accordance with an order of this court, the county farm, and all property therewith, was sold at public sale to Joseph R Askew and John T. Springer for $13,375. These persons soon after laid the farm out in town lots, and as such it is now known as Askew and Springer's addition to Jacksonville. This sale necessitated a new location. The most eligible site, offering timber for fuel, was the farm of Cornelius Goltra, about three miles northwest of the city. This farm, of two hundred acres, was purchased for about $13,000, and the present poor-house built thereon. It is a good structure, capable of accommodating all those who may call upon the county for keeping, and is excellently managed. In ordinary years the farm bears a large share of the expense, and furnishes employment to all inmates able to work.

The erection of the several county buildings has now been conclusively stated, and it will be well before closing this chapter to note the various divisions of the county. From its earliest existence, as settlements increased, the justices' and road districts were set off, and their boundaries determined. On June 30, 1828, the county was divided into five election precincts, known as Jacksonville, Exeter, Sandy, Apple Creek, and Clay Creek precincts. The judges appointed for each district were: Joseph Klein, John Leeper, Aaron Wilson, Jacksonville; Daniel Lieb, Baxter Broadwell, and Daniel Burbank, Exeter. James Hatchin, Alexander Walls, and Alvin Coe, Sandy; John Lappington, John Williams, and Thomas Luttrell, Apple Creek; Thomas Gatton, William Summers, Joshua Crow, Clay Creek. Indian Creek precinct was not long after added, and William Lager, Isaac R. Bennett, and Aquilla Hall appointed judges of election. All those named were to serve two years from the dates of the appointments. On the next day after the division of the county into election precincts, the trustees for the school sections were appointed. On June 8, 1831, William Thomas was appointed school agent on behalf of the county to sell these sections, and thereby create a school fund. His bond was $12,000, and he, with his characteristic honesty, discharged his duties faithfully. It is doubtful if the National Congress ever passed an act, which resulted in equal benefit to the people, as this one. Three years before Judge Thomas' appointment, on Sept. 2, 1828, the Mound school district was established; probably the first school district, at least the first on record, in the county. At this time no bridges were built for the accommodation of travelers. All crossing of streams was done by ferries, the owners of which were allowed to charge a fee, regulated, like tavern licenses, by the county court. On the day the trustees for the school sections were appointed, the rates of ferriage over the Illinois River were established as follows:

"For each four-horse or ox team and carriage, seventy-five cents; for each two-horse or ox team and carriage, fifty cents; for each one-horse and carriage, thirty-seven and one-half cents; for each man and horse, twelve and a half cents; for each footman, six and a fourth cents; for each head of loose horses or cattle, six and a fourth cents; for each head of hogs, sheep or goats, three cents." These were the common rates charged. The price of license was according to the location. At Beard's ferry it was four dollars; at Green's, two dollars, and at Philips', three. Others were charged like amounts.

Enough has now been told to give an intelligent idea of the acts of the county as a corporate body. At every meeting of the county court new tavern and ferry licenses were issued. Prominent among the names appearing on the records are those of Joseph Beutly, Nathan H. Gest, Abraham Vance, Abraham DeWitt, and Thomas Bently, all of whom were licensed to "keep tavern" in the county seat, and the majority of whom paid five dollars fee. Ira Kelley was licensed to open a house of entertainment in Exeter, Thomas Beard at his ferry, Archibald J. Hite at a mill on Sandy Creek, Jacob Ekelburner at Naples, and others at different places, as the county filled with settlers, and the needs of the country required. These persons' rates of charges were all fixed, and, as will be seen by the reader in those quoted elsewhere, included wine, gin, rum, cordial and whisky.

The increase in population also demanded new road districts, which from time to time were made. New polling places were also established, and we find as early as 1830, Jacksonville had so increased in inhabitants, that on June 8th of that year an additional voting place was made therein. The next year Stephen R. Bartlett and Isaac Negus were licensed to sell clocks. The former, being a non-resident, was charged twenty-five dollars for the privilege, while the latter, a resident, was charged half that sum. Knapp & Pogue, B. Ayers and Francis Arenz paid ten dollars for the privilege of opening a store and doing business in the county seat. At the meeting of the commissioners' court on March 9, 1831, the following firms were licensed to sell goods in the county. From the number the reader will readily perceive the increase in population and commerce a lapse of five years had produced in Morgan county. The list with the rates of charges for the license is herewith appended as given on that day:

Alexander T. Douglas, five dollars; James Dunlap & Co., twelve dollars and fifty cents; Nathan H. Gest, seven dollars and fifty cents; N. and N. H. Johnson and Joshua D. Austin, five dollars each; John P. Wilkinson, the same as James Dunlap & Co.; Archibald T Hite, Joseph M Fairfield, William Hunter, and Davenport & Henderson, each five dollars; Hook & Wiswall and James P. Coddington & Co., seven dollars and fifty cents each, and Gillett & Gordon, fifteen dollars, making a total amount received that day from this source, ninety seven dollars and fifty cents. Tavern licenses had by this time raised, as we find F. C. Maupin was charged eleven dollars to open such a house on Apple Creek, and five dollars to "vend merchandise therein."

By an act of the legislature, approved April 23, 1831, James Green, John Henderson, and Joseph Cloud were appointed commissioners "to survey and lay out" a state road from Henderson's Grove in Montgomery county to Jacksonville, and afterward John Green and Abraham Vance were appointed to lay out this road through the county to Naples on the river. This road was reviewed from Jacksonville to Naples by Abraham Vance, John Green and Alexander Wells, and thereby finally established. Throughout the county's existence its several acts as a corporate body have be similar to those narrated, being changed as the exigencies required, and as the increase in population, wealth and commerce demanded. The county is yet under the old form of government, the township form not being adopted. Three commissioners comprise the county court, and attend to all business relating to the commonwealth.

Gen. Murray McConnel, in a historical address delivered at the laying of the corner stone of the present Morgan county court house, May 12, 1868, (see cut next page) made the following reference to the first seat of justice, its successor and the leading lawyers of those early days:

"The first court house was built in Jacksonville, in the year 1826, and in that day it was as good a court house as the state of the county finances could afford. It was a frame building set on blocks sawed from a round log, and of course, we laid no corner stone under it, as we are now doing with this great building. That house was located on the northwest corner of the public square in Jacksonville, and cost about four hundred and fifty dollars, and although it was a cheap court house, I have no doubt but that as pure justice was administered therein as ever will be in this great, costly and magnificent building.

In connection with this low priced court house, it should be remembered, that our people were new settlers and poor, and that our county revenue that year was but $758 00, and out of that we had to pay $35.75 collector's fees, and to lose a pretty large delinquent list, as our inhabitants were constantly on the move, and, as I told you, generally poor people. We should remember, too, that a good horse in those days in this county, was only worth about thirty dollars in trade. A good cow was worth four or five dollars. Pork from sixty to seventy-five cents per hundred, and beef was not generally sold at all. Corn, where it was sold at all, brought five cents per bushel, seller delivering it in the purchaser's crib. Wheat about thirty cents per bushel. Potatoes were worth from five to ten cents per bushel, and everything raised by the farmers bore about such prices, and this was not generally paid in money, but in other property called trade, such as honey, beeswax, furs, &c., &c. The truth is that there was no market for anything the farmer raised, nearly everybody raised their own provisions and only a few had anything to sell, and if they had, there was nobody to purchase it. Every dollar that was brought to the country was paid into the land office for land, and thereby the country was constantly kept drained of money, and if any one had more money than they wanted to lay out in land, it could be loaned at one hundred to one hundred and fifty per cent. per annum. I loaned a part of the money to enter the land at one dollar and twenty-five cents per acre whereon this city is laid out, at one hundred and twenty-five per cent. per annum.

MORGAN COUNTY COURT HOUSE, ERECTED 1868.

But to return to the subject of the court houses, about which I was speaking—the first court house was burned on the sixth of December, 1827, and with it was destroyed all the records of the circuit and county courts of the county, and some deeds for lands belonging to citizens in the recorder's office. To supply its place another court house was built in 1829, of brick, and costing about four thousand dollars. In this house, the people of Morgan county have met and held court, discussed public matters and nominated candidates for nearly forty years. In it some of the great men of the nation made their first *debut*. There one of our greatest statesmen and orators, Stephen A. Douglas, made his first law-argument, and presided as one of the judges of the supreme and circuit courts of this state, and in that house, by a meeting of his friends, he was first nominated for congress, where he did honor to the state that elected him, and by his powerful talent rose to be an equal to the greatest man of the nation.

In that court house the energetic and talented John J. Hardin commenced his brilliant career. There he, too, was first nominated to congress, where, by his energy, tact, and talent in an uncommonly short space of time, he rose to eminence in the councils of the nation. His bright and promising future was brought to an untimely end on the bloody field of Buena Vista in Mexico. There he fell with McKee, Clay, and other brave men, bravely fighting the battles of his country.

In that old court house, also did the kind-hearted and polished gentleman, the highly talented statesman, and profound lawyer, James A. McDougal, late senator in congress from California, but now deceased, commence his career as a practicing lawyer.

In that house, too, the young man of brilliant mind, a good lawyer and a polished writer, John L McConnel, born and educated in Morgan county, made his maiden speech as an attorney at the bar, but like the memorable Hardin, he, too, fought and was wounded at the battle of Buena Vista, and although he was not, like Hardin, left dead upon the field, yet, that most painful wound brought him to an untimely grave, in the midst of his youth and usefulness.

In addition to these, I could mention Governor Joseph Duncan, Judge John Turney, John W. Evans, Josiah Lamborn, Myron Leslie, Waller Jones, Jesse B. Thomas, Governor Thomas Ford, and ABRAHAM LINCOLN, and many others whose names are intimately connected in memory with the old and crumbling walls of that old court house, but whose bones are now mouldering in the dust and whose names are written among the dead. But I will not pursue the mournful subject further. I will only ask that the dust of the falling edifice may be respected for the good it has done, and for the noble and honorable heads it has sheltered in by-gone years.

Since that court house was built, there have been two powerful and wealthy counties made out of Morgan county, and the people of the county as the same is now curtailed, have risen from a few hundred in number to many thousands, and from an annual county revenue of six or seven hundred dollars to near eighty-four thousand, and our county collector, instead of getting fifty or sixty dollars, as then, when the three counties were all Morgan county, now receives over five thousand dollars in fees per annum from the county with its present boundaries, for collecting the revenue including the school fund. Notwithstanding all this great advancement and increase of wealth, our county is yet comparatively new, there not being one-half the tillable land in the county in useful and profitable cultivation, and, I assert the fact here now, that more improvements are being made in this county than in any former period.

I will read to you a list of the various judges who have presided in the circuit courts of this county, and also a list of the names of the lawyers who have resided in this county from its organization to the year 1845. I do this to put their names on record if anyone should desire to refer to the list:

JUDGES—John Reynolds, John York Sawyer, Samuel D. Lockwood, Stephen T. Logan, Jesse B Thomas, Thomas Ford, Stephen A Douglas, William Thomas, William Brown, David M Woodson, Charles D Hodges.

LAWYERS—John Turney, Murray McConnel, J. Quimby, Benjamin Cox, William Thomas, James Berdan, P M Irwin, John J Hardin, Waller Jones, David Evans, John W. Evans, Josiah Lamborn, James A. McDougal, Stephen A Douglas, A. H. Buckner, Myron Leslie, Henry B McClure, William Brown, S. G. Anderson, A. S. Manning, T. J. Deumus, C. J. Drake, Charles Jones.

Of the first school teaching in this city, Judge Thomas has said:

Not being able to obtain other employment, out of which to pay for board, and being out of funds, I engaged to teach school for three months, upon the old plan of obtaining subscribers for scholars. A log building had been erected, and used for a school house, in the south part of town, having no floor, chimney, doors, windows or loft, which I was to occupy. In the month of November the house was finished, with an unjointed floor and loft, a sod and stick chimney, one window in the east and two in the north, with slabs for seats and wide plank for writing tables, and on the first Monday in December my school was opened in due form. About twenty-five scholars had been subscribed, with the understanding that each subscriber might send all the children that he could spare from service at home. I agreed to teach reading, writing, and the ground rules of arithmetic. I had scholars to learn A, B, C's, spelling, reading, writing and arithmetic, and two only to study English grammar. I attended punctually every morning by seven o'clock, made a fire and had the room warm by the time the children arrived. Very soon I found that the Kentucky lawyer was giving general satisfaction, and the house was filled with children from the town and neighborhood, several families sending their children in the winter. I was to receive my pay in cash or produce, pork, cattle or hogs at cash prices. I bargained with Mr. Bentley with whom I boarded to receive the pay from my subscribers for my board, and my three months school enabled me to pay for a year's board, besides furnishing money to pay postage and immediate expenses. My board cost me only $1.00 per week, including washing, food and lights. Mr. Bentley had two log cabins, one was given up to Dr. Chandler and myself, and the other was occupied by his family. The winter was cold, in the east rain, but here more snow than has been usual since. I often had as many as fifty children in the school, and scarce ever less than thirty. It required about 10 hours any day to hear the routine of lessons and frequently 12.

As an illustration of manners, customs, food, etc., at this time we are tempted to give a traditional report of a double wedding in the county, in the year 1825.

It was, it is said, a double affair. Nancy Cole and Joe Cole were married to Joe Porter and Nancy Porter respectively. The first day Joe Cole and Nancy Porter were married. On the next day Joe Porter and Nancy Cole were married. On the third day an "infare" was given by Guinn Porter, who lived at what is now known as the Dr. Lurton place, in Arcadia township, Morgan county, at his residence (consisting of a cabin of one room). A puncheon-table groaned beneath the weight of the good things that day. The *menu* was: Lye hominy, dried venison, boiled venison, fried venison, wild turkey, prairie chickens, pork in every style, wild honey, dried pumpkin, turnips boiled and raw, the latter being a substitute for apples, of which they had none, hickory nuts, walnuts, pecans, and whisky, (brought from Naples on horseback.) All were invited for miles around, and nobody sent their regrets, but turned out *en masse* to the number of twenty or thirty. Sam Bristow, a "forty gallon Baptist," performed the marriage rites at the weddings and was on hand at the "infare."

Before we pass beyond the year 1826, we must note the arrival of Samuel Woods afterwards a member of the legislature and judge of the county court of commissioners, and in 1884 one of the largest land owners and heaviest tax-payers in Morgan. In an address at one of the annual meetings of the "Old Settlers' Association," he said:

"We came to this county in 1826, and settled nearly in the same place that we now live. There was only one business building in town and that was a small log cabin with a door so low that a man had to stoop to enter. There was neither school house nor church in the county. But we always managed to go to church. We nearly always had to go in ox carts. We had no nails, pins or needles. There were four families that only had one needle between them. Thorns were used for pins and pieces of gourds covered with cloth for buttons. Now we have everything that man can desire, and if we are not happy it is our own fault. We had to go to St. Louis to do our trading, and it took two weeks to make the trip one way and now I can go to St. Louis and back in one day, and do more business than I could do then.

I never had a great deal of schooling. I graduated at Sulphur Springs. My mother and father went once a month to the head of Indian Creek to church."

Another settler of '26, but one who passed away in 1882. Mr. David G. Henderson came from Apple Creek, Greene county, to Jersey prairie in Morgan, in April of that year. He purchased a cabin giving in payment a cow valued at $10. He rented some land but his first corn crop proved a failure. At harvest time he returned to Apple Creek, a distance of over forty miles, with a sickle in his hand to reap a patch of wheat. Said wheat was threshed the old way, and carried to a tread mill near Alton, where it was ground, and then taken home, where it delighted the family, who had been so long without good bread, and "Uncle Davie" was wont to say "it was delicious, and tasted better than any sweet cake that he had ever eaten since that time." Mr. Henderson held the office of constable for eight years, justice of the peace for sixteen years, and township treasurer for twenty-eight years, without a single doubt as to his honor and integrity as a public official. In 1847 we notice his name as county commissioner, which position brought him in contact with many of the leading citizens of the county.

In fact nearly all the time from his arrival in '26 to the end of his long and successful career, he served the people in some official capacity.

An arrival in the family of Mr. Dennis Rockwell the county clerk, during the same eventful year made William Rockwell, of this city, the oldest native resident of Jacksonville. Baker Daniels another present resident, was born a little later, making them the first two males born in the village and now living in it. The first child, however, born in Jacksonville, was a daughter in the family of Mr. and Mrs. George Hearick.

Mrs. Catherine Carson was the mother of the first male child born in Jacksonville. She named him Alexander Wolfendall. He was born December 21, '25, and died August 10, '33.

A history of Jacksonville with the rise and progress of her institutions of learning omitted, would indeed be like the great play of Shakespeare with the title role omitted. So in this chapter we must chronicle the founding of both Illinois College and Jacksonville Female Academy—twin sisters in a bright galaxy of mind-training stars. The thought from which both sprang may be ascribed to Rev. John M. Ellis, of whom it has been well said "he "came to Illinois a messenger inspired and sent of God to cry throughout the land 'prepare the way to build churches and schools for the incoming population that will flood these rich prairies.'"

The late Dr. L. M. Glover, in an historical address, described him as

"A man not at all distinguished except with a wise foresight of the needs of forming society, and a singular zeal in projecting educational schemes with which he had no thought of sustaining any personal relation whatever. He had the genius which proposes good things and successfully invites co-operation in realizing them. His thoughts were not seemingly great, but they were such as might not occur to others, and they proved to be seed thoughts in not a few instances. His mission was that of a fore-runner; his specific work was not with superstructures, but with foundations; when he had staked out one enterprise and assured himself that it would go forward, he passed on to another; and his life was fruitful in suggestions that did not vanish with the breath that uttered them, but took form and have become incorporated among the influences which will prove a permanent blessing to society, the land, and world."

Mr. Ellis came to Illinois to labor as a minister under the direction of the American Home Missionary Society. For two years, amid other duties, he was maturing a plan for a seminary of learning, and was exploring the counties of Randolph, Bond, Madison, Greene and other counties for the best location.

At Edwardsville, at Kaskaskia, everywhere his constant effort was to awaken in the hearts of others an interest in the subject like that which glowed in his own. Nor did he allow the indifference or the incredulity which he often met, to cool his zeal or hinder his efforts. Through the press, in the pulpit, at the fireside, with unflagging zeal he pressed the question, "how shall the means of education be furnished to meet the wants of this growing state?" In Bond county, where the first Presbyterian church organized in the state was located, he found sympathy and awakened interest, and efforts were made for the location of a seminary there, but before any decisive steps were taken Judge Lockwood, of Jacksonville, and Dr. Todd, of Springfield, dining with Rev. T. Lippincott, the friend and helper of Mr. Ellis, suggested that the new counties of Morgan and Sangamon should be visited before a location for the school should be finally decided upon. From this hint resulted a visit to Jacksonville from Messrs. Ellis and Lippincott and the selection of College Hill in our city, where, soon after, the first building was erected, and within five or six years after the walls of the south half of what is now known as the "library building" were lifted up, all the land within three miles of Jacksonville rose in value at least a thousand per cent., and has never since depreciated. Previous to closing the contract securing the college site, an association of young men in New Haven, Conn., bound themselves together for an effort to build a college in the opening West. Correspondence with Mr. Ellis decided them to operate in Jacksonville. Pledges to the amount of nearly $2,000 and two valuable tracts of land had been secured here, and Rev. Julian M. Sturtevant came from New Haven with assurances of $1,000 more.

Those young men, then studying theology at Yale College, were Mason Grosvenor, Theron Baldwin, John F. Brooks, Elisha Jenney, William Kirby, Asa Turner and J. M. Sturtevant. They were planning to go west, as home missionaries, and to establish a christian college wherever their lot was cast, and to-day, nearly sixty years later, one of them—ex-president Sturtevant—is in the faculty of Illinois College, which, since its foundation, by him and his fellow students, has sent forth its hundreds of graduates to adorn the highest places in the religious, political and intellectual kingdoms of this great country and to carry the Gospel of Jesus Christ into the remotest corners of the globe.

According to Dr. Sturtevant in his quarter-century celebration discourse in 1855, Messrs. John M. Ellis and Thomas Lippincott were acting as a committee of the Presbytery of Missouri (which, by a stretch of territorial jurisdiction which now looks rather grasping, then embraced the whole state of Illinois as well as Missouri) when they selected the site now owned and occupied by Illinois College. The next spring (1828) they reported their plan to that presbytery, and that body rejected their report, and refused to give the scheme any support or countenance.

Their "outline of a plan for the institution of a seminary in Illinois" was circulated through Bond, Sangamon, Morgan and other counties; also a subscription paper in which the articles solicited in subscription, etc., were, besides cash, building materials, land, stock, wheat, books, bedding, furniture, etc. The subscribers promised to pay to Samuel D. Lockwood, John Leeper, Hector G. Taylor, Ero Chandler, Dennis Rockwell, William C. Posey, Enoch C. March, Archibald Job, Nathan Compton, Morgan county—John Allen, Greene county—James McClung, Bond county—John Tilson, Jr., Montgomery county—John Todd, Sangamon county, and William Collins, Madison county, the Trustees of said Seminary, or their agent, the sums set opposite their names respectively, in aid of the institution. This instrument was dated May 1st, 1828.

To this plan about $3,000, was subscribed. Then the Yale students heretofore mentioned, says one of them, (Dr. Sturtevant:)

"Offered to furnish the proposed institution the sum of $1,000, provided the previous subscribers would consent to certain modifications of their plans, deemed by the New Haven men necessary to the permanent prosperity of the institution." The subscribers were seen personally, and the written consent of every one of them obtained to the proposed modifications of the plan to which they subscribed, on certain conditions.

On the 18th of December, 1829, in the south half of the old college building now standing, and known in 1884 as Phi Alpha Hall, at that time in process of erection, amid carpenter's benches, shavings and piles of lumber, a meeting was held of the original subscribers, and two gentlemen, Theron Baldwin and J. M. Sturtevant, representing the young men at Yale College. The conditions on which the proposed modifications of the plan had been agreed to were formally fulfilled.

A board of trust was organized, and the institution was christened "Illinois College." The first Monday of the following January saw nine students assembled, with J. M. Sturtevant the only instructor.

Of the origin of the name "Illinois College," and Mr. Ellis' connection, Dr. Sturtevant says:

"On motion of Hon. James Hall, of Vandalia, well known in the literary world both before and since that time, it has unanimously resolved that the institution be called Illinois College.

* * * The proposed institution had up to that time always been called the seminary at Jacksonville, or the Jacksonville seminary, or as it was generally pronounced in the speech of the time, "siminery." It was never called the college, much less Illinois College. To me, and I think to all present, Judge Hall's motion was a surprise. I saw no objection to it and it passed unanimously without any discussion. * * * * Mr Ellis did not first conceive the idea of founding a college at Jacksonville. That idea originated with the association. It was distinctly in their minds to found a college before they ever heard of Mr Ellis. Their attention was turned to Illinois and to Jacksonville by correspondence with him. * * * * * * * The reason that Mr Ellis was not conspicuously associated with the management of Illinois College in after years was, that he soon after these events ceased to be the pastor of the First Presbyterian church of Jacksonville, and for that reason left the place and State."

Turning now to the founding of the Female Academy, we quote from the semi-centennial address of Dr. Glover:

"Almost every enterprise begins somewhat before the recorded beginning; begins in the original thought, the incipient suggestion, the pregnant inquiry, from which at length it starts into form and becomes fact Somewhere, in some single mind, by some unknown process, in some moment of solitary reflection, or in some season of earnest prayer, there springs the idea of a project which seems worthy, and, with the idea, a desire to realize it. Thus secretly and silently, divine providence often plants the seed of something valuable in the mind of an humble person not intent upon ambitious ends except as ambition is worthily related to the best interests of the human race and the glory of God. This seminary is no exception to such an origin. The thought from which it sprang is confidently ascribed to Rev. John M. Ellis, the first Presbyterian pastor in this place."

One of the first meeting houses erected for the worship of Almighty God was about eight miles east of Jacksonville, near Col. Samuel T. Matthews', by the Cumberland Presbyterians, and Needham Roach was the preacher. In 1829 the Presbyterians erected the first meeting house or church in Jacksonville, on the corner of West State and Church streets, and Rev. John M. Ellis was the preacher. He was installed in 1828.

In 1828 John P. Wilkinson built the first brick house or store in Jacksonville, on the southeast corner of East State street (then called Springfield street), which, with slight changes stands there to-day. The Carson tavern, already referred to, was a two story log house on the east quarter of the public square, and now stands on East Morgan street and is occupied as a dwelling house by his daughter, Mrs. Vail.

In another portion of this chapter will be found Judge William Thomas' experience as a teacher, during the winter of 1826 and '27. He states that at that time there was an unfinished log house, situated in the south part of town, which had been built for what had always been known as the "West District School." The building was used as a school house, the upper story being used by the Masonic fraternity as a lodge room. When the growth of the district demanded more school room, the Masons withdrew from the room occupied by them, and it was used for school purposes.

A few years after the erection of this building, the east district, or that part of the town lying east of the public square, built two school houses, in which school was at once opened. Under the formation of these two districts the schools of Jacksonville were maintained until the adoption of the city charter in 1867. When the buildings already mentioned became too small for the school populatian of the growing town, rooms were rented in various parts of the town, so that all who desired the benefit of a free school could be accommodated. Private schools were also opened at different times and were generally well patronized.

On January 22, 1829, the General Assembly passed an act providing for a Commissioner in each county to sell each sixteenth section therein, that funds for common school purposes might be established. In accordance with the provisions of this act, Judge Thomas was appointed Commissioner for Morgan county. This duty the Judge faithfully discharged. About 1833 or '34, a public meeting of the citizens of Jacksonville was held to take action in regard to the establishment of a school in their midst. This being prior to the act of 1839, and no provision being made for township organization, it was decided to support the school by private subscription. This method of support was used for some time.

Returning again to political matters, we learn from Judge Thomas, that in 1826, Archibald Job, who died in 1874, after passing his 90th year, was elected to the senate from this district then composed of the counties of Morgan, Pike, Adams, Schuyler, Fulton and Peoria. During a service of eight years, his constituents never had cause to regret his election, nor to complain of his want of devotion to their interest. He maintained the character of an honest, fearless, intelligent and industrious representative. In 1820 he was again a candidate for the senate, but was defeated, not because of any complaint of his previous action, or any want of confidence in his ability and integrity, but because the Whig party, with which he was identified, was in the minority. Upon the passage of the law providing for the building of the State house at Springfield, because of his known integrity and intelligence, he was appointed one of the State house commissioners.

A new court house was erected in 1829-'30, and was the second brick building in the county. The early records having been destroyed by fire, we can give no list of county officers earlier than 1828, viz:

Representative in Congress, Joseph Duncan; Representatives in State Legislature, William L. May, Wiley B. Green, William Thomas; County Commissioners, Joseph M. Fairfield, Samuel Rogers, John Wyatt; Sheriff, Samuel T. Matthews; Coroner, William Jarred.

As to taxes in these primeval days, one of our old settlers, D. G. Henderson, writes to the *Journal* in 1875, that his tax receipts show as follows:

1826 50 cents; 1827 50 cents, J. M. Fairfield, sheriff; 1828 55 cents, Wiley B. Green sheriff; 1829, $3, Cyrus Matthews, sheriff; 1830, 87½ cents, Samuel T. Matthews, sheriff; 1832 $1, 1833 $2.20, 1834 $2.40, 1835 $2.40, William Orear, sheriff; 1836 $2.40, Alexander Dunlap sheriff.

He adds: Now I could go on for forty years more, for I have every one neatly filed away. No other man could have kept the first receipts, for they are written on old newspaper not more than two or three inches square. Since paying these *heavy* tax bills, the real estate that I have accumulated and given to my children is now worth $80,000 or more, all being in Morgan county except one farm, which is in Menard county.

The entire amount paid in for taxes in the then county of Morgan, in 1827, was $753.20, the population was then 7,000. Fifty years later in the same territory it was 45,000.

In view of these latter day discussions of the dram-shop and license question we here copy a document which is preserved in record in the county clerk's office—the third tavern and liquor license ever issued by our county commissioners. The date is 1827.

George M. Richards having this day applied to this court for a license to keep a tavern: It is ordered that said Richards be licensed to keep a tavern in the town of Jacksonville for the term of one year, from the date hereof, upon paying to the county $5.00.

Whereupon he executed his bond, with Chas. Luttrell as his security, and the court established his rates for selling as follows, to wit:

For rum, brandy, gin, wine and whisky 25 cents per half pint; for meal of victuals 25 cents; for lodging 6¼ cents; for horse feed, corn or oats 12½ cents; keeping horse over night, 25 cents.

As will be readily seen lodging, feed and drinks in the ancient days when Jacksonville was but a hamlet upon the prairies cost considerably less money than they do now.

As to the use of intoxicating liquor in harvest fields, Mr. J. Gorham, father of Josiah Gorham, now of Champaign county, claims the credit of being the first farmer in this county who refused to furnish ardent spirits to laborers employed in the harvest field and in raising a barn; he furnished as a substitute ginger beer and butter milk.

Mr. Silas Massey, who bought land here in 1826 and lived here from 1832, was another farmer, if not the first in Morgan county, who succeeded in having his harvesting done without whisky, and when the men declined to work without it, told teem he could just turn in his hogs, and they would take care of the wheat, and not say *whisky* once; but they thought better of it, and the wheat was harvested in good condition, and from that time no liquor was allowed in his field.

In 1833 Mr. Timothy Chamberlain refused to give his farm hands liquor, substituting ginger beer and coffee.

We cannot give a better description of the appearance of the place in 1827 than by quoting from the *Journal* a report of a speech made to the old settlers of Morgan county at one of their annual love feasts, by Hon. Newton Cloud, since deceased:

He said he located here in 1827, three years before the great snow. When he settled here the great prairies were covered with flowers, in their native luxuriance, and were untrodden by the foot of the white man. They were but a vast bone-yard, in which thousands of buffaloes killed by the Indians lay bleaching in the sun. He far from realized then the developments which would be made in this country, and remembered to have told a visitor from Kentucky that he could give him a deed to all that vast arm of prairie which they were viewing, but that it was so far from market as to be without value. He did not forsee the change which a few years would bring about. Then, deer could be seen in herds on the prairie, so tame that they were evidently unacquainted with the murderous rifle of the white man. Wolves would come up to the cabins seeking food. He said that on his arrival he pitched his tent on the same quarter section where he then lived, and his circumstances had not materially altered since, as he was as poor now as then. But he was glad that he had come to this county, where food and raiment had always been provided in plenty, and thanked God that he was permitted to see such a day. Friends had differed with friends in politics and religion; yet warm friendships had ever marked the way, and he was glad to take them all by the hand and wish them, if may be, long lives, and joy even in their decline. It might now seem that shadows would come upon them, but the clear sunlight always shines upon the virtuous life. Ours was indeed a good country and never was there a better promise for crops. Egypt, in her palmiest days of plenty, did not excel it; perhaps it is to protect us by its bounty against some approaching contingency. The young of the present day would be astonished to know of the hardships endured by the pioneers of Morgan county. When they wanted flour or meal they were obliged to travel over bad roads, or no roads at all, twenty miles to Allen's mill on Apple Creek. Sometimes they were obliged to crack or grate the grain themselves, and subsist on such food as Armstrong's mill, which was a very primitive machine indeed, could provide.

"The little patches of a few acres have given way to wide-spreading fields of growing corn, and golden harvest. The rail pens and log cabins have now moldered away, and splendid mansions like kings' palaces have taken their places.

The hand-mill, the mortar, and the old graters, which some of you remember, have all gone by the board. Steam has taken the place of elbow power, and the smoke of a thousand chimneys point out the spots where bread stuffs are manufactured from the finest wheat in abundance for home consumption, and to feed the nations beyond the seas. The hum of the spinning wheel, the clatter of the hand-loom have disappeared, and ten thousand noiseless spindles have come instead. The single shuttle, thrown by the fair hand of a mother or loving sister, is superseded by a thousand shuttles that fly by steam. The development and prosperity of this beautiful country is owing in a great measure to the *noble men* and *women* who first settled here."

He made a very happy allusion, by way of contrast with the present, to the sociability of the early settlers; their readiness to assist one another, &c., enumerating many of his early day experiences, and closing his remarks with the admonition to the young present to imitate the example of their ancestors.

The Jacksonville of to-day, is as emphatically a city of churches as of schools. The religious element has been prominent in her population from the first. The christianizing idea has been in the mind of the founders of all her institutions—educational and eleemosynary, as well as strictly religious. The existence of two church societies and two educational institutions before 1830, proves that the old settlers thought with solemn earnestness, of laying the foundation of a christian civilization among those rude beginnings; that there were prayers and hopes, and endeavors, which looked towards a great destiny for this place in the near future. In Morgan county, churches and seminaries of learning, are not recent novelties. They hold by pre-emption right.

Looking back to the little flocks that were first gathered together under care of faithful pastors, we find that the first Presbyterian church organized, was by Rev. John Brich, in Judge John Leeper's barn, which stood until July 1887, about a mile east of the present Illinois Central Hospital for the Insane. Seven men and five women constituted this little church, and from this small beginning have grown three large Presbyterian churches in the town besides several in the county. Like their Methodist brethren, the Presbyterians at first occupied private houses or the log school house, until 1831.

At the founding of this church, officially known as "The Presbyterian Church of Jacksonville," the following persons presented their certificates: John Leeper and Fidelia, his wife, Edwin A. Mears and Sarah, his wife, James Mears and Polly, his wife, Hervey McClung—all from Shoal Creek church; James Kerr and Janet, his wife, from Reformed church in the city of New York; William C. Posey and Sarah, his wife, from Winchester and Paris churches in Kentucky; and Hector G. Taylor from Kingsbury, Vt.

This church being duly constituted, William C. Posey and John Leeper were elected elders, James Kerr and Hector G. Taylor trustees for one year. John M. Ellis, moderator. On July 28, 1827 and July 26, 1828, there were additions by certificate and profession that made up the total membership to twenty-two. February 29, 1830, there were forty-seven members, March 29, 1831, there were eighty-seven, October 29, 1831, there were one hundred and twenty-five, August 19, 1832, there were one hundred and sixty-six.

Of the piety and principle of the early settlers of this vicinity, Dr. Sturtevant on one occasion well said:

"We began to build the church of God when we began to build our own houses And we have generally tried to build as well for the Lord as for ourselves. There have always been those here in the midst of us, and in the darkest times, who regarded the privileges of christian institutions and worship as among the necessaries of life, and to be provided for as they provided shelter and food and clothing for their children. Such men were John Leeper and James Deaton and Wm. C. Posey, and the two Hedenbergs, (Peter and James V.,) and James Kerr, and David B. Ayers, Elihu Wolcott, Hector G. Taylor, and many more whom we cannot name. Such men could not dwell in their ceiled houses while the house of God was lying waste. They must plan and act for the moral and spiritual wants of themselves and their fellows, and even of distant posterity. Wherever such men make their homes in any wilderness there the church of Christ will be."

Of this period and the first churches and preaching here the same authority said in an historical address delivered in 1871.

"Before the deep snow!" What was Jacksonville—what was old Morgan then?

For the most part old Morgan was covered by primeval forests, or else the primeval prairie grass waved in its breezes. I have not the means of making exact statements, probably the data are not in existence; but it is my opinion that at least nineteen-twentieths, probably a much larger proportion of the soil of this country, was then unmodified by the hand of cultivation. I could have traveled from the spot where Illinois College now is, seven or eight miles to the southeast without being obstructed by a single fence or a single acre of cultivated land. Cultivation was confied to a very narrow belt along the groves of timber, Human dwellings were but the rudest structure of logs, designed only for the most temporary purposes. School-houses and churches can scarcely be said to have had any existence. In Jacksonville there was one log school-house about twenty or twenty-five feet square. That was generally used as a place of worship on the Sabbath. No other church or school-house existed. The Methodist society generally worshipped at a private house, John Jordan's double log cabin, but sometimes at the old court house, which, a few months ago, disappeared from the public square. The Presbyterians generally met at the log school-house just referred to.

In that house I preached my first sermon in Illinois, on the 15th day of November 1829. It was without pulpit, table, or stand of any description. The only distinction enjoyed by the preacher was that he had a split bottomed chair while the rest of the people sat for the most part on fence rails. You may be sure that this did not seem a very satisfactory arrangement to one who felt that he must depend on reading his sermon from a manuscript. I was not satisfied. I think the people were still less so. The next Sabbath things were still worse. The chimney of sticks had been pulled down for the purpose of arranging to warm the house with a stove, and a hole in the logs some eight feet by six, marked the place where the chimney had been. The chair had disappeared, and I might sit on a rail and lay my book on the rail by my side. A little such experience cured me of reading sermons from a manuscript, for a log time. Such were the rude beginnings of things in Jacksonville before the deep snow. And yet two of our churches and two of our institutions of education are old settlers. They antedate the deep snow.

A Methodist church was here, now the Centenary church, and the First Presbyterian church, now Dr. Glover's, though neither of them had houses of worship.

The first church to be started by the Baptists, was in 1824 or 25 in Diamond Grove, but it was short lived.

Mr. Anderson Foreman, one of the few survivors of the period covered by this chapter, writes to the *Illinois Courier* as follows:

On the 8th of November 1828, I arrived in Morgan county and stopped with Mr. Humphrey, about a mile south of the town of Winchester, his residence being near what was then known as Rattlesnake Springs. Here I made my first acquaintance in "old Morgan," embracing at that early day the territory or slips of land now known as Scott and Cass counties. In this neighborhood there were no public houses in which to worship Almighty God or "teach the young ideas how to shoot." Two weeks after my arrival, in company with Mr. Humphrey I visited the little village of Exeter where there were several dwelling houses, a shoe shop and a grist mill, the latter owned by Enoch C. March. Being here introduced to Mr. Mills I was by him invited to settle there, but anxious to see the country, I left on the 19th of November, 1828, and reached the town (now city) of Jacksonville; put up at a tavern on the northeast corner of the public square kept by Mr. Hull and his father-in-law, Bentley. Soon thereafter I formed the acquaintance of nearly every one in the town.

Many of the citizens were not intellectual giants, still there were among them some moral heroes—good and true men, who gave tone and direction to the moral and religious sentiments of the community. Here brother John Eads lived, a man of great moral worth, loved and respected by all; being a preacher of the Christian denomination, he was in the habit of calling on the boys in the stores and shops saying, "come, boys, this is prayer meeting night," and the boys attended the meeting out of respect for the man of God, and in that way the moral and religious sentiments of the people were built up and extended. This godly man lived to be 85 years old, and joyfully entered into rest" having been born in Snowhill, Delaware. About that time Rev. Mr. Brich (a Presbyterian minister), born in Scotland, spent the greater part of his life preaching to the people and doing good as opportunity offered; traveling a circuit from Edwardsville to Galena, and when well stricken in years was found on the prairie in the northwestern part of the state, frozen to death. Here, also, Mr. Drinkwater (a Wesleyan Methodist), devoted his life to preaching the gospel and doing good; whose example and good life were long remembered by the old settlers; he had his residence in a hole on the bank of Indian Creek about a mile and a half above Bath & Horn's mill. Afterwards for many years he lived below the mill, and on his way to the distant territory of Oregon died, and sleeps with the early pioneer preachers.

Rev. Wm. Crow, also a preacher of the Baptist (regular) church, lived here, whom many knew and kindly remember. His life and character, striking and proverbially good, and his power and fame as a man and preacher extended far and near, and having achieved a grand, good work, at a ripe age was gathered to his fathers, and "his good works follow him." Here, too, lived the venerable Thomas White (member of the Presbyterian church), whose good example and pure life were known and loved by all, having wrought a good work in the community where he resided, he departed this life, full of years and the respect of the people of the county, having been born in North Carolina. The Rev. John Green (a preacher of the Christian denomination), some of whose children live here, lived and spent his life, like the other old veterans of the cross, in teaching his neighbors and friends to live good and useful lives, and when, like the grain fully ripe, was gathered into God's granary above, loved and esteemed by all. Elder Matthew Elder, a compeer of Fathers Eads and Green, settled in Jersey Prairie (a strip of territory cut off from old Morgan in 1839, when Scott also became separated and formed a county), and after a long life of usefulness and kindness to his many friends and neighbors, joined the silent throng to that bourne whence no traveler returns! Pausing here to drop a tear for the good old men long dead and gone to their reward, let me turn aside and mention one who sat in justice and dispensed the law in solid chunks to his neighbors—Father James Deaton, who, born in old Virginia ("the mother of presidents") settled not far from Jacksonville in 1819. The first class meeting was organized and held in his house, and it is said of him that, during forty years as justice of the peace, he never gave judgment against any of his neighbors. Being a man of peace, he settled all his disputes and suits by compromise; and falling from one of his apple trees, full of years, honors and the good-will of all, he fell asleep. At the beginning I said there were no giants then! I forgot the venerable man of God, the Rev. Peter Cartwright—the hero of "the battle-axe and saddle-bags"—the grandest pioneer, the well-known Methodist minister and elder of the west and south. Wherever Methodism has gone, the wide world over, the fame, eccentricities and wonderful preaching of Cartwright will be known and remembered. He was to Methodism, everywhere, what Daniel Boone was to Kentucky and the great Northwest! His field of operations was the world, his great heart, pluck and unflagging zeal in his Master's cause, having reached four score years of hardships and self-sacrifices, battle-scarred and his soul made happy and radiant with numberless human souls borne to God by his herculean labors in the Lord's vineyard. He died as he had lived, with his face to the foe of humanity, and his faith in God and the salvation of sinners clear and unshaken. In this county lived and died my good old friend, Thornton Shepherd (regular Baptist or Hardshell), who, after preaching every Sunday fifty-five years, told me, not long since, ' that he had not, for all his services as a preacher, received so much as $5 from any of his brethren." And yet the Lord blessed and prospered him; and having done what he could to serve and honor God, far advanced in years fell asleep, and the quaint old man and preacher will be remembered by his neighbors as faithful and true to God and humanity. Who in old Morgan will forget that good little old man eloquent, Elder Harrison W. Osborn. with a manner so meek, a voice so gentle and loving; who, for nearly three-quarters of a century, broke to thousands in this and other states, the bread of eternal life. The compeer of the venerable and saintly Barton W. Stone (the leader and founder of the people known as "New Lights" in Kentucky), he was active in forming the union of the New Lights or followers of Stone, and Campbellites or Christians, and these united in Jacksonville in 1831 formed one body of disciples known and called the Church of Christ or Christian Church. He continued actively in his Master's work until a little while ago he fell asleep in Jesus, and his memory and life work none will ever forget to love and honor.

Of these grand old heroes I might fill a book, but time flies, my space and the reader's patience all admonish me to hasten to the end. Having said so much of the dead, both good and great, what shall I say of even great men still living? Rev. Peter Akers, LL. D., who, in his younger days, lacked only one vote of being knighted a bishop of the M. E. Church. He is the Boanerges of Methodism in the nineteenth century. Who shall sketch this grand life or compass his colossal intellect? Although a nonogenarian, he still walks our streets, and at times the old time fire and force of fifty years ago lights up his face—flashes from his eagle eyes and rings in his stentorian voice like thunder, or the roar of Niagara! His life work is about done. What pen so trenchant or historian so truthful can tell of his power and usefulness, or even do justice to the grand old man, learned and eloquent, by writing his wonderful life, the most remarkable in the history of Methodism in the great Northwest?

Then, too, there is the Christian statesman (if that can be), the Rev. Newton Cloud. No man in this community stood higher in the state and church than he. Nature and grace combined to make him good and great.

His wise counsels in the organic laws of church and state will live and keep his name and memory bright and honored as long as time shall last or civil and religious government endures. Having reached that serene and honorable round in life's fair temple and Christian exaltation, he passed gently down the steps of time, and now sleeps with the pure, noble, honored and loved of earth.

I shall speak only too briefly of my friend and neighbor, John P. Wilkinson. He was a gentleman in the highest sense, the young man's friend and the widow's hope in time of need. Few, if any, knew him but to love and praise. He has gone to his reward, and his precious memory and good deeds will follow on.

What shall I say of old Father Scott Riggs, that good old man? He was an earnest, active Christian, and contributed to unite the two bodies of Christians in the old court house in Jacksonville in 1831. Father Riggs, octogenarian though he was, achieved much good and lived a useful life, and, dying, left a grand, rich legacy, a Christian life, for his children and friends to imitate and cherish his memory.

"What visions of the inhabitants of Jacksonville forty-eight years ago. Where are they now? Why some have risen high, aiming their arrows even at the sky. Some have been wayward and gone astray, some hold the even tenor of their way. Some are recording an immortal name, with gilded letters on the scroll of fame. Many have departed hence, and some remain of forty-eight years since. I will give the names of all the heads of families, and the young men that were then living and doing for themselves in the then town of Jacksonville. In giving names and business followed by each family and person, I may not be able to give all their given names correctly, but their surnames I can. I hope some citizens now living may recall their names and give a more correct list.

"Dennis Rockwell, circuit clerk and county clerk; Mrs. Kellogg; John Handy, carpenter; Mr. Bunnell, carpenter; Samuel Titus, teamster, first colored man; Murray McConnel, lawyer; Matthew Stacy, saddler and harness maker; Geo. Rearick, merchant; Joseph Fairfield, merchant; Abram Vance, merchant; Nathan Gest, merchant, Thomas Carson, hatter and hotel keeper; George Nicely, hatter; Mr. Robinson, school teacher; Verien Daniels, gunsmith; S. H. Henderson, grocer; John P. Wilkinson, merchant; Rice Dunbar, carpenter. Thomas Church, farmer; John Buckingham, brick mason and plasterer; Ero Chandler, doctor; Doctor Allen, old practice; Bazaleel Gillett, doctor and merchant; Ranson Cordell, constable; Mr. Shull, hotel keeper; Mrs. Palmer; Wm.

S. Jordan, farmer; Mr. Robley, farmer and brick maker; Hervey McClung, tanner and currier; E. T. Miller, carpenter; George Graves, cabinet workman; John Savage, carpenter; Edward Durant, carpenter; James Martin Eads, blacksmith; John Eads, Jr., blacksmith; John Eads, Sr., blacksmith; Simeon McCullough, tailor; Levi Church, tailor. John Laughrey, laborer. David Tefft, carpenter; Joseph Coddington, merchant; Enoch C. March, miller and merchant; Thomas Arnett; William L. May, Representative in the Legislature; Mrs. Joiner; Josiah Gorham, Sr., carpenter; Samuel Rixford, no employment; John Henry, cabinet maker; Dr. H. G. Taylor, merchant and postmaster; James Parkinson, wood-cording machine; William Thomas, lawyer; Jacob W. Barton, farmer; James Blair, dry goods clerk; James Leeper, dry goods clerk; Joseph Robinson, dry goods clerk; James Buckingham, plasterer; Daniel Busey, saddler and harness maker; Thomas Carson, Jr., brick mason; James Carson, cabinet workman; John Carson, brick mason; Rev. J. M. Ellis, Presbyterian preacher; Aquilla Hutchins, farmer; George Richards, surveyor; Emanuel Metcalf, chair maker; Mrs. Buckingham; Phillip Haines; Darius Ingalls; Wm. Conn; Garrison W. Berry, brick maker; McHenry Johnson, blacksmith; Mr. Grimsly, blacksmith; Nelson Johnson, dry goods clerk; Enos Hobbs, mail carrier; Mrs. George Rearick, Mrs George Richards, Mrs. John P. Wilkinson, Mrs. Simeon McCullough, Mrs. Martin Eads, Mrs. John Eads, Mrs Verien Daniels, Mrs. Doctor Taylor, Mrs George Nicely, Mrs Matthew Stacy, Mrs. Handy, Mrs. Bunnell, Mrs. Emanuel Metcalf, Mrs. Robley, Mrs. Garrison W Berry, Mrs. James Parkinson, Mrs. E. T. Miller, Mrs. Thomas Church, Mrs. Charles Chappell, Miss Ann Robison, Miss Hester Kellogg, Mrs. Thomas Carson, Mrs. Nathan Gest, Mrs. Abram Vance, Mrs. William L. May, Mrs. Conn, Mrs. Ero Chandler, Mrs. Jacob Barton, Mr. John Savage, Mrs. John Henry, Mrs. Dennis Rockwell, Mrs. McClung, Mrs. Ranson Cordell, Mrs. Joseph Fairfield, Mrs John Buckingham, Mrs. Dr Allen, Mrs. John Laughrey, Mrs. Samuel Titus, (colored,) Mrs. Grimsley, Mrs. McHenry Johnson, Mrs. Aquilla Hutchins, Mrs. Darius Ingals, Mrs. Phillip Haines, Mrs. Thomas Arnett.

In 1829 John R. Harney, now living in Woodson, came with his family to the then new state of Illinois and located near Jacksonville, Morgan county, where he has ever since resided. Coming to the state at so early a period he tasted of the contents of the pioneer cup of tribulation; and being a man of but moderate means has often been compelled to drink deep draughts from its unpropitious ebullitions. As for instance, going to mill thirty miles away through the most inclement weather and over roads blockaded with almost insurmountable depths of snow; through interminable prairies and dense forests whose wild depths were rendered still more frightful and hideous by the howling winter blasts and the distant and ominous yelp of the wolf; breaking the stubborn glebe, as yet untamed by the kindly hand of agriculture, and all the while bracing against the miasmatic poisons infesting all the land and resulting in low fevers and chills. But why in this biographical sketch need we speak of these trials; the abiding friendships formed and never to be broken only by death; the bitter adversities and the unsophisticated manners of those times, since they were the common experience of all who lived in those never to be forgotten pioneer days.

John R. Harney has been married sixty years the 13th day of next February. Perhaps but few of the old settlers are ahead of him in this particular. He has reared ten children all of whom are still living in Morgan county

When Mr. Harney came to Jacksonville, in 1829, there were but two brick building in the town—the old court house and Wilkinson's and no houses more than one story high, except two log houses, which were story and a half buildings, occupied by Mr. Church and Thomas Carson. John P. Wilkinson was the first man who built a brick dwelling house. The first dry goods merchant remembered was James McAllister, and among the first grocers Chambers, Rearick, Taggart and Israel, the last of whom was a brother of Miss Hettie Israel, who died but recently. Some of the above grocers also kept a saloon in connection with the grocery store. So we see we are making some advance steps after all. The first tavern keepers were Wm. Miller and Thomas Church. The first cabinet maker was Capt. John Henry. The first harness makers were Mat Stacy and Peter Hedenburg. The first school was kept by the late Mr. Spalding in the southeastern part of the town. The first doctors were Drs. Prosser and Chandler. The first lawyers, Judge Thomas, Murray McConnel, John J. Hardin, Stephen A. Douglas, etc

The first postmaster was Dennis Rockwell, who used to go over the town delivering letters which he carried in his hat, and in those primitive days the receiver paid 25 cents for each letter received. The first druggist was David B. Ayers, father of the bankers, and the first blacksmith was Seth Weatherby, father-in-law of Mr. A. C. Wadsworth, the hardware man.

Among the old and cherished friends and acquaintances of Mr. Harney were Dr. Reed, Mr. Milburn, Mr. Ayers, the Stevensons, Coffmans, Humphreys, David Cole, T. D. Eames, the Rockwells, David A. Smith, Richard Yates, Jacob Strawn, the Masseys, Thomas Wiswall and many others. Some have passed over the stream and some yet linger on this side.

The following account of the earliest known destructive cyclone in this county was obtained by the editor from the venerable A. K. Barber:

It is stated, on page 40, that Mr. Edward Harvey went to school to Mr. Barber in 1821. Mr. Barber is still living in Jacksonville, although he has not been here all of the time since he came to Morgan in 1824. He taught school before as well as after coming here and it was probably in Greene county that Mr. Harvey was his pupil. Mr. Barber tells us that upon first locating here he rented land a few miles west of town; did not raise a profitable crop the first year, and footing it to Bond county taught school there in the winter of 1825. In the spring he was teaching in Morgan, in a log cabin school house on the Johnson farm, a few miles west of where stakes were being set for the future Jacksonville.

He described to us a cyclone, or as they called it then "hurrycane," which burst upon this vicinity in April, 1825. The school-house had a puncheon floor, and underneath an excavation which had been used for mixing mortar. There was a terrible rain, hail and wind storm, so that everything in the cabin was wet. The books were put away where they could be best protected, and teacher and scholars went outdoors to gather up hail and watch the storm. Mr. Barber looked south towards Lynn Grove, now Lynnville, and saw a funnel-shaped cloud approaching. He had read enough of such to know what it meant to all in its path, so they re-entered the house and he and his one big scholar put all the little ones down into the mortar hole *under the floor*. The cyclone struck the neighborhood with great force, but not the schoolhouse. Among the houses unroofed of their clapboard coverings were those of Abraham Johnson (owner of the cotton gin, whose farm is now owned by Cortez M. Dewey) Robert James and Father Deaton. The cotton gin of Mr. Johnson and the cabin of Stephen Gorham —one and a half miles due west of the Mound—were blown down, Dr. Cadwell's house near Swinnerton's Point, the only one in the vicinity with a shingle roof, lost one-half its roof, and a house standing about where the county poor house now is was demolished. Many fences and trees were levelled to the ground, especially on the Johnson farm and the storm cloud went on north and west until finally scattered. No lives were lost that Mr. Barber knows of.

The following is a partial list of the early settlers of "Old Morgan" that located in that part which is now Cass county, with the date of their coming into the county:

Mrs. Elizabeth Hopkins, 1826; Mrs. Mahala Brady, 1827; Mrs. Maria Cunningham, 1824; John S. Clark,* 1826; Arthur Loughary, 1828; J. E. Roach, 1828; W. T. Treadway, 1829; W. S. Huffaker, 1830; Franklin Bridgeman, 1830; Francis Ryan, 1825; Mrs. M. A. F. Carpenter, 1828; Mrs. D. B. Hunt, 1830; Mrs. A. Cox, 1830; Alexander Pitner, 1827; Mrs. G. Shirrill, 1830; Mrs. H. McClure, 1828; Mrs. M. J. Tureman, 1830; Charles Cox, 1828; Mrs. Elizabeth Davis, 1822; J. A. Davis, 1824; S. B. Jones, 1828; R. D. Thompson, 1829; Jacob Epler, 1829; John Yaple, 1824; Levi Dick, 1829; Wm. Clark, 1826; Jas. A. Dick, 1829; Mrs. Mary Dick, 1829; Mrs. S. H. Petefish, 1827; Zack Hash, 1822; Dr. J. M. Wilson, 1828; Mrs. John E. Haskell, 1828.

The following are the names of others who were there previous to 1830, but the ex-

* Mr. Clark freighted salt to Beardstown, on the "Mechanic"—the first boat that came up the river. Salt shipped from Washington county, Ohio.

act year of their coming we do not know: Zack W. Gatton, Mrs. C. H. Oliver, Mrs. Mark Buckley, Mrs. Andrew Gale.

Among the mercantile and other licenses issued by the county commissioners in 1831, besides those given on page 51, might have been named those to George F. Bristow, Stephen Malloy, Erasmus Elliott, Zeph Judson, A. and M. Collins ($7.50.)

Judge Thomas says, that in 1826, when he came to Jacksonville there were but twelve or fourteen families here, none of them had a separate room for him to occupy; the entire family slept together in one room. The country was quite naked, yet still beautiful. In Morgan, Scott, and Cass there were then perhaps 1,000 voters, all told. The county did not fill up rapidly between 1820 and 1826, but after that people commenced to roll in, but were forced to live in tents and rail pens. In 1827 was the Winnebago war, a war few remember or know anything about, because it did not amount to much. In 1826 most of the milling was done in Greene county, though there was a mill in Exeter which, however, had no water part of the year to run it. They were dependant on ox or horse mills, and Allen's, on Apple Creek, was the most prominent. One man would go for the neighborhood, and stay a week.

Col. W. D. Wyatt, of Lincoln, master in chancery for Logan county, was born in Morgan county September 1st, 1821, his father was a Virginian, and moved to Nashville, Tenn., and afterward to Kentucky, and settled on the Ohio River. He relates how his father and many other men of his neighborhood were brought to Illinois to fight the Indians, and in this way were brought to settle in this state and in this county.

Before passing into the 1830's we will add a few names of settlers of 1819 to '29 not already mentioned John Gorham, '24; M. R. Foster, '23; Mary Smith, '23; Minerva Smith, '28; Aaron Phillips, '29; Amanda Reeve, '24; Mary Humphrey, '28; Mrs. P. W. Vail, '25; Amanda M. Harney, '21; G. L. Gilham, '23; Eliza W. Foreman, '29; Jacob Stout, '25; Mrs. Sarah J. Turley, '29; Wm. H. Markley, '29; Capt. Wm. Patterson, '29; Mrs. Edward Harney, '19; J. R. Clark, '28; Mrs. Mary Hinrichsen, '25; John F. Jordan, '24; W. W. Riggs, '25; Elizabeth Smith, '29; Elizabeth Freeman, '29; Matilda Willhoit, '22; Rachel King, '29; J. G. Babbitt, '29; Stephen Shepard, '29; Mahala Turley, '28; James Edmonson, '28; G. W. Smith, '25; William James, '22; Palmer Holmes, '21; J. M. Filson, '29; Mrs. Sarah Fay, '29; William Clark, '25; Eliza Clark, '23; Elizabeth Moss, '21; J. D. Jaywood, '22; W. C. Johnson, '29; A. C. Woods, '27; Mrs. A. C. Woods, '24; Charles Rockwell, '25; William Rockwell, '27; John T. Robertson, '23; Wm. C. Stevenson, '29; Edward Scott, '29; John Carter, '27; Joseph Cooley, '25; Wm. H. Broadwell, '23.

ERRATA.

The amount of money offered by the Yale students for the founding of Illinois College, see pages 55 and 56, was $10,000 not $1,000 as stated a typographic error.

Mrs. Emma F., widow of George D. Rearick, and sister of Mrs. Joseph Coddington, informs us since the first chapter was put into type that her sister's child was not born "in a tent in Diamond Grove," (see page 19) but in a log cabin. Mr. Coddington was postmaster at one time. She states further that "Mr. Roe built the first *hewed* log cabin that was built here, there were other rough log cabins before his. Mr. and Mrs. Coddington lived in this cabin, Mr. Roe boarding with them and it was in this log cabin Mr. Roe died."

Michael Antyl and Michael Arthur mentioned on page 11, are probably the same persons, but which is the correct name the compiler cannot decide.

JACKSONVILLE FEMALE ACADEMY. FOUNDED 1830.

ILLINOIS COLLEGE. FOUNDED 1830.

CHAPTER V.—1830-'36.

"College" and "Academy" Chartered and in Full Blast—Faculty and Graduate—Weddings in Ye Olden Tyme—The Black Hawk War—Methodist, Presbyterian and Episcopal Church Growth—Old Settler's Testimony as to Business, Transportation, Crime, &c.—The Deep Snow and the Quick Freeze.

THE interesting period of which we propose to write in this chapter, begins with the actual opening of those two educational institutions, the foundations of which were laid in the previous year—Illinois College and the Female Academy, pioneer schools of the modern Athens—the Western New Haven. As we have recorded, the place was laid out in 1825. It was incorporated as a town in 1826, and made the county seat of Morgan, then embracing the territory now included in several counties, viz: Cass, Scott, Greene.

The population had slowly increased until in 1830, it is said to have numbered 446.

The board of trust for Illinois College had been organized in December, 1829, among the carpenters' benches and shavings of its unfinished building; and on the 4th of January 1830, nine students assembled to receive instruction.

Dr. Sturtevant says: "It was said that morning, 'We are met to-day to open a fountain for future generations to drink at. May God prosper the omen.' The deep snow fell upon and around the building, now known as the library building. I remember as though it was but yesterday, how the snow lay around it An area of a few feet in breadth all around the building was blown quite bare. Beyond that stood the frowning wall of snow three feet high, as if forbidding our escape to the outside world. That building is by many years the oldest brick building now standing in this town.

There are names among the early founders and friends of this college that ought to be held in lasting remembrance. Among them are the names of William Collins, the donor of $500 on its original subscription list, John Tilson, Thomas Lippincott, John M. Ellis and Theron Baldwin. In the mind of Mr. Ellis the idea originated, and the site on which it stands was selected by him and Thomas Lippincott, after an extensive tour of exploration for the best place; both of them poor in this world, but rich in faith, and caring for the welfare of this great people with self-sacrificing solicitude for generations yet to be. Such men are the true founders of states and empires.

More than half a century has passed since those consecrating prayers dedicated that school. Clouds have gathered, winds have shifted, tempests have beaten, supplies have been uncertain at times, frowning rocks have threatened a wreck, but through all he has stood erect in his place, and with a firm, faithful hand guided the craft he then launched. After the school was in actual operation funds were procured, students were gathered, and an able faculty secured. Families looking to the best advantages for the mental and moral training of their children, came in increasing numbers from the east and south, and our village in the prairie became the nucleus, around which was to gather, not only many other schools of learning, but also three of the great eleemosynary institutions of a state holding a proud place in the union.

The erection in 1832 of the large dormitory building, which was burned in 1852, involved the institution in a heavy debt. To relieve that, and to provide for a more numerous faculty, subscriptions amounting to more than $100,000 were obtained, chiefly in this state, in 1835 and 1836.

The first application for a charter was unsuccessful, on account of the prejudice then existing against such institutions. But at the session of 1834-35, by a combined effort, Illinois, McKendree, Jonesboro and Shurtleff colleges were each granted a charter and upon the same day, February 9, 1835. Illinois College was founded as a college proper, and as such is the oldest in the state. Its first president, Edward Beecher, D. D., was appointed in 1832, holding the position until 1844. The year of the granting of the charter was also that of the sending forth of the first graduate—Richard Yates, in later years the brilliant orator, the patriotic war governor of Illinois, and the state's representative in the House and Senate of the Congress of the United States. Since that graduation in 1835, four hundred and ten have been added to the alumni of "Old Illinois," and three hundred and forty are still in the land of the living.

The school's founders were undoubtedly wholly influenced in their efforts in its behalf by motives of patriotism, philanthropy and piety. They recognized liberal learning as indispensable to national and general prosperity, to the maintenance of civil and religious liberty and the highest influence of christianity, over the minds and hearts of men. They meant, in the infancy of this State, the future greatness of which was already foreseen, to found an institution which should be a fountain of generous culture to the mighty people that should soon inhabit these fertile plains, and to millions that are yet unborn. They had no religious ends to subserve except to promote the kingdom of God among men; and no political ambitions except to extend the dominion of liberty over a vast and fertile region, then a wilderness. The ends and aims of the institution are still the same; and the ends will be strictly pursued by the men who now have it in charge, and by them will be transmitted in sacred trust to their successors.

In the courses of instruction provided, the trustees and faculty always aim at thoroughness. They seek to extend the course over as wide a field as practicable. But they believe it is better to know a few things well, than many things superficially.

Turning to the sister institution, now known as the Jacksonville Female Academy, we find the origin due to the same Christian pioneer and Presbyterian preacher, Rev. Jno. M. Ellis. The seminary was organized the same year (1830), and simultaneously chartered by the Legislature (1835.)

The earliest proceedings with reference to the Academy, took place September 29th, 1830, when "a meeting of gentlemen favorable to the establishment of a Female Seminary in the town of Jacksonville, was held at the house of Mr. John P. Wilkinson." The record does not give the names of those who were present, but it states that "Hon. Samuel D. Lockwood was called to the chair and Rev. J. M. Sturtevant appointed clerk." What the spirit of the occasion was may be inferred from the fact that a committee was appointed to report upon the subject at a subsequent meeting. That committee consisted of Judge Lockwood, Rev. Mr. Ellis, and Professor Sturtevant. The adjourned meeting was at the same place, three days afterwards, *i. e.*, October 2d, 1830, when the committee reported the following preamble and resolution, which appears to have been unanimously adopted, viz:

"WHEREAS, The vast importance and urgent necessity of extending the blessing of education to all classes of American citizens are felt and acknowledged by all enlightened patriots and christians, and

"WHEREAS, The power of female influence over the intellectual and moral character of the community must ever be too great for any or all other causes entirely to counteract, commencing as it does with the first dawn of infant intelligence, and forming perhaps the most important, certainly the most desirable part of that character before any other causes can begin to act upon it, and accompanying it through all the subsequent stages of its developments; considering too that in the present important crisis of our beloved republic not one effort ought to be withheld which can tend to give permanency to its foundations—the intelligence and virtue of the people; wherefore

"*Resolved*, That an Academy ought to be immediately established in this State, to be devoted to female education; and that Jacksonville, in Morgan county, is, in our opinion, a situation highly favorable for the successful operation of such an institution."

In the language of Dr. L. M. Glover (1880), we can but mark and admire the breadth of these views, the patriotic and christian sentiments they embody, the directness and energy of purpose they exhibit; and it is impossible to overestimate the value of the record containing them, occupying the place it does at the very outset of an important educational movement, and so clearly outlining the motives to such a work and the objects it was designed to subserve. That record will be to the friends of this institution, in all the future, a reminder of the principles on which it was founded, and a covenant against its perversion to bad or unworthy purposes.

At the same meeting, and in immediate connection with the action just referred to, an organization was effected by choosing a board of trust, consisting of thirteen members, whose names are as follows:

"Bazaleel Gillett, Joseph Duncan, David B Ayers Dennis Rockwell, John M. Ellis Elihu Wolcott, Ero Chandler, Joseph M. Fairfield, James G Edwards, John P. Wilkinson, Samuel D Lockwood, Ignatus R Simms, and Julian M Sturtevant," all of whom, except two, have passed away from earth—Dr. Chandler, of Warsaw, Ill., and Dr. Sturtevant, who is permitted in his fresh old age to witness with satisfaction so much good fruit of educational enterprises to which his early and later life has been wholly devoted.

It would be difficult to find in any community, large or small, especially in one just forming, a body of men more intelligent, cultured, and wise, than those to whom this important interest was first committed. Taken together, they were persons of mark in the professional, business, and social circles in which they moved. All of them were well educated, and some of them liberally educated; several of them belonged to the learned professions and reached high rank in them. As religiously distributed, two of them were Episcopalians, two Baptists, while the remaining nine were by profession or sympathy, at that time connected with the Presbyterian church. Other denominations were afterwards represented in the board; but though the institution was designed to be broad in principle and unsectarian in spirit, its principal management was always without question and without jealousy conceded to those who took the leading part in founding and rearing it. No denominational name found a place in its legal title, it was and is simply the "Jacksonville Female Academy," though in common speech designated as the "Presbyterian Academy."

It is a noticeable fact that no sooner had the enterprise been organized by the appointment of Trustees, than a piece of ground was donated upon which to locate the new institution, and to be forever consecrated to the sacred purpose of female education. This was the gift of Dr. Ero Chandler, and is the magnificent block on which the Academy now stands. * * * * * * This ground, when thus donated, was of small comparative value, being then some distance from the business centre and the platted limits of the town, and embraced in fields that were used for farming purposes. Here grew the tall corn, here cattle grazed, rude fences enclosed these outlying prairie regions and not a tree was seen, as one looked westward from where we stand, nearer than Wilson's grove in the rear of Illinois College, almost a mile away But what shall we say of its value now, near the heart of a beautiful and thriving city, surrounded by costly residences and by public buildings that are regarded as fortunate because of their proximity to it; charming too in itself, with its fascination of venerable trees and shaded lawn; nature and art vying in the effort to clothe it with attractions and to bring it into complete harmony with the purpose to which it is devoted. * * * * * * An act of incorporation was secured in January, 1835, and it received approval on the 27th of that month. It was prepared by Hon. James Berdan and introduced into the Legislature by Hon. John Henry and advocated by Hon. Wm. Thomas. The corporators were the original Trustees with the exception of John M Ellis, Joseph M. Fairfield, Ignatus R. Simms and James G. Edwards, whose names disappear and are supplied by new appointments as follows: Benjamin Godfrey, Ebenezer T. Miller, Matthew Stacy and William Brown. The provisions of the act were for the most part liberal and wise, though exhibiting a rather unnecessary fear of monied monopolies as appears in Section 6th, which limits the amount of land to be held in perpetuity for the uses of the Institution to twelve acres, and requires that lands donated to it at any time "shall be sold within three years from the date of such donation," and "in failure whereof, the lands so given shall revert to the donor;" further, the trustees were forbidden "to lease or rent out any lands so held in trust." The charter, however, was gladly accepted and it was entirely acceptable with the exception of the following rider which was attached to it: "That all the real and personal property of each of the trustees shall be bound for the payment of all contracts which they shall enter into for the said institution," a proviso which was subsequently repealed on motion of the late Col. John J. Hardin. Among the good things in the charter which there can never be a motive or desire to change, is the provision of section 2d, that the trustees "shall hold the property of the institution solely for the purposes of female education and not as stock for the individual benefit of themselves or of any contributor to the endowment of the same, and no particular religious faith shall be required of those who become trustees or students of the institution."

It is worthy of notice that this seminary is the first of the kind established in this State, and the first of any kind to be chartered by the Legislature, though three colleges Illinois, Shurtleff and McKendree, were subsequently incorporated by that body, during the same session. It is a still more interesting fact that in all the vast territory covered by the ordinance of 1787, excepting only the State of Ohio, this is the earliest school of high grade having exclusive reference to the education of woman. This circumstance may be mentioned in honor of our commonwealth, and it confers a precedence upon this seminary of which it may justly be proud. In the wide region referred to, many institutions now share in the work begun here, but Jacksonville Female Academy antedates most of them by many years, and in the generous sense of the words, it will be admitted that she is the mother of them all.

The trustees were no sooner organized than they began to agitate the subject of building. They had suitable ground, but there was no structure of any kind upon it. The plan of an edifice was soon projected and adopted, though by no means with the hope of realizing it in full except in the course of years. The plan contemplated a centre building 40x50 feet on the ground, with wings 30x40 feet each, respectively two stories and one and one-half stories above the basement, all fronting the north, the main entrance covered with a lofty portico supported by heavy columns. It was calculated that the building when completed would cost something more than twenty thousand dollars, but what it actually did cost we have no means of ascertaining. The first thing undertaken was the erection of the east wing and subscriptions for that purpose were at once taken.

It should be noted here that the actual founding of the Academy was due, in great measure, to the efforts of Mrs. John M. Ellis, who had been preceptress of a boarding school for young ladies for some years, the church parsonage being used for that purpose, as well as that of home for the pastor and his family.

It was owing to the prejudice then existing in the popular mind against institutions with educational, charitable or religious aims that the Legislature refused to grant any charters until the session of 1834-'35, when this feeling was measurably overcome. No regular classes were graduated until the year 1844; but that year Catherine Murdock and Juliana Wolcott, (afterwards Mrs. Prof. James B. Smith and Mrs. W. Chauncey Carter, both living in Jacksonville at the present writing,) received the first diplomas of the institution, and from that time there has not been a year without a class ranging from three to twenty-six graduates, the whole number now (1884) in the alumnæ being about 400.

The history of the Academy speaks for itself—a history of constant growth, advancing reputation and prosperity. Over three thousand young ladies have been connected with the school since its establishment. It is and always has been the aim to make its course of study equal to the best. It already requires four years, or three for the scientific, not including the preparatory course. The system of classification is that usually adopted in American institutions. It ranks first in age among the now numerous schools of high grades for young ladies in the west, and is second to none in point of excellence. But to resume our extracts from Dr Glover's remarkably complete and able historical address upon the occasion of the celebration of the Academy's semi-centennial in June 1880:

There is still in existence the original subscription paper containing the names of those who first contributed to this object and the respective amounts contributed by them. The heading is printed and embodies the preamble and resolution previously adopted by the board and already referred to. * * * * Dr Ero Chandler leads with $150, and others follow in smaller amounts, but with marked liberality for the times and circumstances when the effort was undertaken. The wing went slowly up, for the necessary funds came slowly. But there was an unflagging zeal in the work. As might be supposed, the women of Jacksonville heartily shared in it. At length, after much struggling, that part of the building was ready for use, probably during the year 1835. Meantime the school was kept in rooms elsewhere, rented for the purpose. It was not until 1843 that the original plan was carried out and the entire building completed. Since then, various changes have been made and but few features remain by which one who only remembers it as it was twenty or thirty years ago could recognize it now. The chapel is much as it was and the columns at its front are just as they were, but a pupil of the early time would not be able without help to find the old east wing which was all there was of the Academy for several years.

The Academy was not opened to the reception of pupils until two years and a half after the organization of the board. A private school for young ladies, however, had for several years been kept by Mrs. Ellis, wife of Rev. John M. Ellis, which measurably supplied the needs of the community, and though never having any organic connection with the Academy, may properly be regarded as a precursor of it, and as having had not a little to do with stimulating the enterprise and moulding public sentiment in its favor. Mrs. Ellis was a woman of high character and culture, zealously devoted, as was her husband, to the cause of education, and eminently qualified to give instruction and in other respects to manage a boarding school. Some who were under her care still survive and they uniformly speak with enthusiasm of her as a teacher, a friend, and a christian woman, nor can they forget the sorrow by which they and the whole community were stricken when she fell a victim to the cholera in 1833, the year of its first visitation in this country when few places escaped and Jacksonville lost sixty of its six hundred inhabitants. Among these were Mrs Ellis and her two children, all three being laid in the grave at the same time.

On the 22d of May, 1833, the board made arrangements for the formal opening of the Academy. A room was procured and fitted up with suitable furniture and apparatus for school purposes, with a view of accommodating day pupils, such as might come from abroad, securing board in private families The location during the first year was on the lot now (1880) occupied by the First Presbyterian Church; then it was removed to West Court Street, just east of Church Street, in a house then owned by Mr. Ebenezer T Miller, afterwards and for a long time a trustee of the institution, and still living among us at an advanced age since deceased.

The first teacher and principal of the Academy was Miss Sarah C. Crocker, from New Hampshire She had been preceptress of the Academy at Boscawen, in that state, and was recommended by the celebrated Miss Lyon, of South Hadley, as a suitable person to take charge of this institution Fortunately, the roll of the school during her term of service and during part of that of her successor is preserved, with the amount of tuition received for each pupil. The scholars enrolled for the first term of about ten weeks, beginning May 22d, 1833, were thirty-one in number, and for a manifold reason, their names are worthy of a place in this historical discourse. I therefore give them just as they are preserved in the hand writing of Miss Crocker, as follows: E. C. Bill, Jane E. Clark, F. E. Dulaney, Mary Haskins, A. E. Johnston, M Leeper, Cordelia Parkinson, Laura Parkinson, H. M. Ross, H. Spencer, S. Spencer, R Spencer, M. Spencer, M. Street, L Street, P. Scott, M Collins, S. Graves, J. Graves, H. Alears, J. Symms, E. White, S. J. Israel, M. S Stites, E. A. Conn, S. Conwell, M. McConnel, Minerva McConnel, Louisa Taylor, H. P. Melendy, M. E. Melendy. With these the fountain started, and it has been flowing ever since with a widening, deepening current, quietly refreshing in its course. Miss Crocker proved a very successful teacher and manager, the school continuing to increase under her care, so much so that during her last term, ending in April, 1835 forty nine pupils enrolled Her services would no doubt have been gladly retained, but they were required in another relation and she was married to Mr. Elihu Wolcott, one of the trustees of the Academy, and who as special superintendent of the school, had opportunity for observing her good qualities, and was so favorably impressed by them that he deemed it a pleasure to call her up higher, and she became his wife, performing the duties of that position well until her death, August 4th, 1844.

The next preceptress was Miss Emily P. Price, of Boscawen, New Hampshire, who was recommended for the position by Miss Z. P. Grant, (afterwards Mrs. Bannister), herself a distinguished educator, and at that time in charge of the Female Seminary at Ipswich, Mass. During her first term, commencing May 25th, 1835, twenty-two pupils were enrolled and no further record of the kind has reached us while the school was under her care. We know, however, that her services were satisfactory to the patrons of the institution and much appreciated by the trustees, who upon receiving her resignation recorded a vote of thanks "for the fidelity with which she had discharged her duties." Having completed two years as preceptress, she retired and was subsequently married to Rev. Z. K. Hawley, a Congregational minister, to whom she was a helper indeed in the various offices of christian work as well as in those of wife and mother. Her death occurred in 1878.

During Miss Price's administration the school was brought into the Academy building, the old east wing, and a boarding department was organized. Then first appeared the domestic feature of the institution, and pupils who were beginning to come from abroad found there a home, and it is worthy of remark that the school room and dormitory rooms were to a considerable extent provided with needed furniture, desks, tables, bedsteads, &c., from the workshops of Illinois College, and we have a bill for the same amounting to $112 25, and receipted January 26, 1836, by Joel Catlin, then college agent. Those workshops are things of the past, but they established friendly relations between the two seminaries which have ever since been cultivated, and were never more demonstrative than in our day; may they never be less sincere and timid than they now are.

The record of the assistant teachers is rich in goodly names and characters, and yet the record is so largely traditional and unwritten it would be impossible to produce it in full, and so to characterize any part as not to run the risk of doing injustice to the rest. The earliest item in regard to helping in the school room is dated August 15th, 1835, and is a receipt in full of Miss Sarah Camp, "for services as assistant teacher in the Academy." This was in the time of the second preceptress, Miss Price

The subject of female education as illustrated in the history of the Academy, brings us naturally to another organization of Jacksonville identified from its inception with this and other schools. A recently published annual report of the Secretary, Mrs.

Joseph H. Bancroft, daughter of one of the earliest principals of the Academy, contains the following record:

In 1832, a few ladies, who had come from various parts of the country to reside, with hearts full of love, and wishing to be helpers in the cause of truth and knowledge, held preliminary meetings for the purpose of organizing in some benevolent enterprise. They were oppressed with thoughts of the future destiny of this Western Valley, and of the millions of souls to occupy it, and of the future influence of present exertion; also that upon the moral and intellectual character of the rising generation, depended the decision of the momentous question: Shall our civil and religious liberty be perpetuated, or shall this Land of Promise become the stronghold of error?

The first year, five were aided, receiving tuition and books, assisting in some family as part compensation for board. The third year, forty-five were assisted in different parts of the State. The association met with favor wherever known. It was a common object, the emancipation of the female mind, which ignorance had too long bound. Friends and means were raised up, not bounded by rivers, or hemmed in by mountains. Auxiliaries were formed in New York City, Rochester, New York; Madison, Wisconsin; Davenport, Iowa; Chicago, Galesburg, Springfield, Canton, Peoria and Waverly, Illinois. Sewing circles in New Haven, Connecticut; Brooklyn, New York, and in various other places, contributed to the treasury.

Feeble and insignificant the effort they might put forth, yet they rejoiced in adding to the influences which would decide the future destiny of this country. With these thoughts burning in their souls, they assembled October 4th, 1833, in the school room occupied by Miss Crocker, afterwards Mrs. Wolcott, on the spot where the First Presbyterian Church now stands in ruins. Mrs. Ellis who taught the first school for girls, and was deeply interested in anything pertaining to their welfare, had fallen a victim to the cholera, which swept over this prairie during the summer.

At this meeting a constitution was adopted. Article 1st reads thus: This Association shall be called, "The Ladies' Association for Educating Females," the principal object of which shall be to encourage and assist young ladies to qualify themselves for teaching, and to aid in supporting teachers in those places, where they cannot otherwise be sustained.

These young women after receiving instruction, were to return to their homes, gather the children together, teaching them to read, for in some homes not *one* could read. Often in a settlement, *parents* were found unable to read and indifferent to the improvement of their children. * * * * *

The first money received by the society was October 1833, being a donation from Mrs. Duncan of	$ 5 00
Total receipts the first year	246 40
" " " fiftieth year	280 00
Expended in the education of five young ladies the first year	29 58
" " " " " six " " " fiftieth year	138 00

* * * In 1853 the name was changed, and now bears the title "*Ladies' Education Society of Jacksonville, Illinois.*"

In July, 1872, it was incorporated, thereby enabling it to hold bequests in a legal manner. Several legacies have since been given, which, with all financial matters will be presented by the treasurer. The business is transacted by twelve managers who meet each month.

Passing from educational chronicles to the history of the churches of Jacksonville from 1830 to '36 inclusive, we find that in 1831 the Presbyterians erected a frame building, in place of the famous log cabin, their pastor, the Rev. John M. Ellis, laboring earnestly to accomplish this desirable end.

The following is the pastoral call given to Mr. Ellis and the subscription list of his supporters in the year 1830:

"The congregation of the Jacksonville church being on sufficient grounds well satisfied of the qualifications of you—*John M. Ellis*—and having good reasons from our experience of your labors, that your ministrations in the Gospel will be justifiable to our spiritual interests do earnestly call and desire you to undertake the pastoral office in said congregation, promising you in the discharge of your duty all proper support, encouragement and obedience in the Lord. And that you may be free from worldly cares and avocations, we hereby promise and oblige ourselves to pay to you the sum of *four hundred dollars*, and rely upon the Home Missionary Society to pay one hundred and fifty of the same, promising to relieve the said society in whole or in part as soon as our circumstances will admit, in yearly payments, during the time of your being and continuing the regular pastor of this church. In testimony whereof we have respectively subscribed our names this 15th day of March, 1830."

SUBSCRIPTION.	Cash.	Wheat.	Pork.	Corn.	Wood.	Flour.	Potatoes.	Chickens.	Total.
William C. Stevenson	10 00								10 00
J. G. Edwards	10 00								10 00
Bedford Brown	5 00								5 00
James Kerr		5	2	3	2				12 00
John Leeper	10 00				10				20 00
James Mears			4	3			1		8 00
Edwin A. Mears	8 00								8 00
Robert Smith				8					8 00
John Scrogin	5 00								5 00
Elliot Stevenson	5 00								5 00
Hervey McClung	5 00								5 00
Thomas White	5 00			5					10 00
To rent of house and lot									60 00
W. C. Posey	2 00	8		3			8	1	12 00
Thomas Prentice	5 00			5					10 00
Joseph M. Fairfield						5 00			5 00
Walter Jones	2 50								2 50
S. T. Matthews						2 50			2 50
Dennis Rockwell	5 00								5 00
John Ayers	2 50								2 50
Henry Blanford	2 50								2 50
J. P. Wilkinson	5 00								5 00
J. R. Browning	2 50								2 50
C. Hook	2 50								2 50
Miller & Thomas	5 00								5 00
Samuel D. Lockwood	12 00								12 00
Bazaleel Gillett (in store goods)	5 00								5 00
Ero Chandler	10 00								10 00

Making a total in rent, cash and produce of $250.00.

"And here is another subscription list dated 1831."

We, the undersigned, being desirous that the worship of God should be maintained in this town, and placing implicit confidence in the Rev. J. M. Ellis, as a faithful minister of the Gospel, do agree to pay the sum set opposite our respective names, towards his support, for the year commencing March 15th, 1831:

James Kerr, $12.00; Jas. G. Edwards, $12.00; David B. Ayers, $20.00; Edwin A. Mears, 5.00; Alex. Robertson, $10.00; John Leeper, $20.00; Wm. Sewall, $10.00; James Mears, $8.00; Elihu Wolcott, $25.00; Hervey McClung, $5.00; B. Brown, $8.00; Maro M. L. Reed, $5.00; Elliot Stevenson, $5.00; Ero Chandler, $10.00; H. C. Wiswall, $2.00; Thos. White, $5.00; C. H. Perry, $2.00; C. Hook, $2.50; L. W. Graham, $3.00; A. M. Clark, $5.00; Jacob Barton, $3.00; Wm. C. Posey, $12.00; J. M. Sturtevant, $3.00; W. C. Stevenson, $10.00; Lancelot Clark, $5.00; John Hill, $3.00; Jno. J. Hardin, $5.00; Thos. B. Prentice, $10.00; B. Gillett, $8.00; Jos. Duncan, $15.00; Jer. Graves, $5.00; S. D. Lockwood, $12.00.

And to show that this congregation were not unmindful of those less able to provide for regular Gospel ministration, we append a home mission collection taken up in 1832.

J. P. Wilkinson, $10.00; J. M. Sturtevant, $10.00; Elihu Wolcott, $15.00; M. A. Wilkinson, $10.00; Jas. G. Edwards, $12.00; M. M. L. Reed, $6.00; C. H. Leonard, $5.00; L. Hardin, $5.00; Joel Catlin, $5.00; Bedford Brown, $5.00; Mary B. January, $1.00; Joseph S. Graves, $1.00; R. McCormick, $1.00; P. W. January, $1.00; M. Turner, $1.00; E. Sewall, $1.00; Eliza Town, $1.00; Annie Ellis, $2.00; Alvin M. Dickson, $3.25; Edward Beecher, $13.00; Ero and E. Chandler, $16.00; David B. Ayers, $10.00; Mary Lockwood, $10.00; Tim. Chamberlain, $10.00; Coleman Gibson, $6.50; James Mears, $5.00; B. Gillett, $5.00; T. Beecher, $5.00; Salem Town, $2.00; H. C. Wiswall, $2.50; Martha Hackett, $2.50; Allen Hitchcock, $2.00; Ralph Perry, $2.00; Stephen Nash, $2.00; C. E. Blood, $2.50; Lancelot Clark, $2.00; Eleanor Edwards, $2.00; total $195.75 all in cash; also Wm. Sewall one-third part of the production of three acres in wheat.

Rev. Alfred H. Dashiel was installed as pastor in December 1835.

The Congregationalists of Jacksonville, like others of their faith in the west, worshipped with the Presbyterians up to the last of the year 1833, under the arrangement entered into by the highest judicatories of the two denominations in 1801 known as "The Plan of Union."

The Jacksonville Congregational Church was organized in the Methodist Episcopal Church, then located on East Morgan Street, on Sunday, December 15, 1833. "The sermon was preached by Rev. Wm. Carter, a young licentiate, who was already engaged to be their pastor, but who was not yet ordained" says Rev. J. M. Sturtevant, in his historical discourse delivered December 15, 1883, on the fiftieth anniversary of the church. Prof. Sturtevant propounded the creed and covenant to the members of the new church and now gives their names as follows:

Timothy Chamberlain, Abraham Clark, Melicent Clark, Elihu Wolcott, Jeremiah Graves, Mary Ann Graves Benjamin Allyn, Cynthia M. Allyn, Edwin A. Mears, Sarah Mears, Maro M. L. Reed, Elizabeth L. Reed, Daniel Mann, Benjamin B. Chamberlain, Asa Talcott, Maria Talcott, Salem Town, Joseph Town, Eliza Town, Jesse B. Clark, Ralph Perry, Robert B. Lord, James K. Morse, Edwin Scofield, George B. Hitchcock, Elizabeth Scott, Mary Chamberlain, Abigail Chenery, Eliza Hart, Lucy Town, Frances J. Wolcott, Abigail Graves; three days afterwards the following names were added: George T. Purkitt, Calvin S. Beach.

In September 1835, less than two years after the organization, its first house for worship—the first Congregational church in Illinois—was dedicated. At the request of the beloved pastor, Rev. William Carter, Prof. Sturtevant preached the sermon, and he says, forty-eight years later—"It was then much the most commodious religious edifice in the place. It was on the east side of the square, a few doors south of East State Street." Previous to building this wooden structure, the society occupied for a time a house where the Athenæum now stands, and then one on West State Street, where Williamson's store now is.

In 1883 at the "Golden" anniversary of the church, the venerable Dr. Post, of St. Louis, is his sermon referred to the organization as follows:

"The year 1833, the birth year of this church, calls up the landscape under the skies of the far-away morning; the morning of this land and its people, of its settlements, its institutions, its churches, its schools, its colleges and of my own life also. It was morning with the freshness and hope, the ideals and possibilities that hover over it like the many hued cloud around the sunrise; the morning that comes but once to a land or to a human life, and then drifts away into the Eternal past to return no more. The personages of that far off morning have most of them drifted with it into climes beyond our mortal horizon. Of the few that remain, the faces remembered as once so smooth and fair, are written over now with the legend of life's history, and the prophecies of the transfiguration; themselves changed and in a changed world, and with look toward the setting sun. The hour calls up my own first coming to this place, then a frontier settlement, toward the great northwestern wilderness. My coming from St. Louis here, most of the way by a walk through a lone blazed or bridle path, through solitary wilds, where the red man had gone and the pale face had not yet entered. It calls up my first entrance and early career here, my first public solemn confession of Christ, with visible union and communion with His people, in the presence of a little band of disciples gathered in the upper chamber of a small printing office not far from the place where we are now assembled. So far had I come from the cities and churches of the east and from the companionship of my early life, to make my first formal public christian confession in these wilds in the ends of the earth, and with a little band of believers far away from the knowledge of the great world and with postal communication with it measured by moons rather than days, separate from its thought and care, and to the extent that they were known in their purpose to establish a Congregational Church, largely regarded with coldness and positive disapproval rather than sympathy, by the eastern churches, to whose principles of church order they adhered. * * * * * * *

The little band which gathered in that upper chamber contained elements of strong character for the enterprise it had undertaken. It numbered among its members, earnest, intelligent, true hearted, devoted, stalwart men, some bringing much of the granite of the Old Rock, some with something of the metal of the Cromwellian Ironsides in their veins, to blend with the charm of gentle, cultivated, brave and saintly womanhood, in the composition of the infant church. Their names are this moment on my lips, as their memory is in my heart, but time forbids my beginning with names, when I shall not know where to stop, only let me record my grateful remembrance as due from me to the

Rev. William Carter, to whose christian intelligence and good sense I owe it that I was able to unite with the church with no false commitments in the form and terms of my acceptance of its creed."

According to a copy of a memorandum made by the Rev. John Batchelder in 1834, and by him deposited in the corner stone of the church, laid the same year. "The parish of Trinity Church, Jacksonville, was organized by a few individuals, on the 11th of August, 1832." This was the first parish belonging to the Protestant Episcopal church, that was organized in the state of Illinois. Previous to the organization of this parish, no Episcopal clergyman had labored within the limits of the state, and so far as can be ascertained, but few sermons had ever been preached by Episcopal clergymen in the state. As it may be a matter of interest to know something more of the early history of a parish which, in this land of yesterday, has already become venerable for antiquity, we venture to make a few extracts from the record, carefully preserved, of those feeble beginnings.

"Trinity Church was destitute of a minister, till the summer of the year 1833, when the Rev. John Batchelder, from Providence, R. I., took charge of it. In the autumn of this year, 1833, the wardens and vestry of the parish determined to take immediate measures for the erection of a house of public worship. The following spring, the erection of the church was commenced, Ebenezer T. Miller being the architect. On the 7th of June the corner stone was laid with suitable religious exercises by the Rt. Rev. Bishop Smith, of Kentucky, he being then on a visit to Illinois. At the time of laying the corner stone of this church Andrew Jackson was president of the United States, and John Reynolds was governor of the state of Illinois. Jeremiah Barker and Bazaleel Gillett were the wardens of Trinity Church, and Joseph Coddington, Ebenezer T. Miller, Samuel M. Prosser, Dennis Rockwell, Ignatus R. Simms, Richard W. Dummer, Aylet H. Buckner, and Austin Brockenbrough were the vestry. At the time when this parish was organized the number of families of which it was composed was about twelve. The year after the rector commenced his labors among them, more than one-half of this membership was separated from the parish by death or removals.

The number of the families now (August 1834) attached to the society is fourteen. In addition to this, the English settlement at Lynnville is included within the rector's charge. The number of communicants has never exceeded five; that is the present number. During the first year of the present (then) rector's labors the sacrament of the Lord's Supper was administered but once. Two children were baptized by him. There were four burials and one marriage.

January 9th, 1836, the church being completed, it was consecrated to the worship and service of Almighty God, by the Rt. Rev. Jackson Kemper, D. D., missionary bishop of the Protestant Episcopal Church in the states of Indiana and Missouri, and having in charge the diocese of Illinois, in absence of its bishop, the Rt. Rev. Philander Chase, D. D."

It ought to be added to the foregoing statement of the Rev. John Batchelder, that the church was erected on land donated by Dennis Rockwell, Esq. Revs. Messrs. Batchelder, Hyer, Darken, Worthington, and Morrison, were successively in charge of the parish in its earlier years. The last named gentleman, now of Chicago, remained true to his charge during fifteen years of patient, unobtrusive usefulness, and it must be exceedingly gratifying to him to contemplate the elegant and tasteful result of his long and faithful labor in the now flourishing parish, worshiping (1884) regularly in a neat and commodious church, under the care of the Rev. Dr. Easter.

When the city was platted, in 1825, the Methodists were holding meetings in a cabin, and continued to occupy it until the completion of the log school house in which Judge Thomas taught the first school in Jacksonville. They worshiped in this log structure when not occupied by other denominations, until about 1830, when they erected a brick church, which stood on East Morgan Street, near East Street. This was the first brick church in the county.

The successive M. E. preachers of this period, at "Jacksonville Station," were as follows:

1831, Wm. Askins and J. T. Mitchell; 1832, W. S. Crissy; 1833, Thomas J. Starr, (dead); 1834, S. T. Robinson, (dead); 1835, J. T. Berger, (dead); 1836, J. T. Mitchell, (dead.)

The presiding elders were:

1831, Peter Cartwright; 1832-'34, Simon Peter; 1835, J. Sinclair.

In 1883 the semi-centennial of Jacksonville Methodism was celebrated in the spacious M. E. Church. Among the speakers was the venerable Dr. Sturtevant, who had then lived in the city fifty-four years. He said:

I am glad to remember that the city of Jacksonville did not have its origin in the horse race, gambling hell, or other rascality. It was in the church. When I came here (in 1829) there were two churches—the First Presbyterian and the Methodist, and in less than four hours after my arrival in this city, I was preaching in the former one of these two churches. Clear back to the beginning of this town there was a religious atmosphere. The foundation of this church is entitled to a glorious record with the first. This town has always been a sort of a Jerusalem where great things were to be done for the christian cause. This is the cause of the peculiar past history of the place, and the reason that the Institutions for the Blind, Deaf andDumb and Insane are here, and that so many institutions of learning are located in this city.

There is far more christian kindred in this town now than there was in those early days. Let the same improvement go on and on still. I want to say before I sit down that the work which I have been connected with owes a debt of gratitude to this church for its kindness and accommodation in the past, and I desire to return my most hearty thanks for past favors.

Among the pioneer Methodist preachers of that day and this vicinity was Father Dickens, lately deceased, who was at the time of his death the oldest effective pastor in the old Illinois Conference—the mother and grand-mother of all the other conferences. Mr. Dickens tells of himself and those times, as follows:

"I was raised in the old Tennessee state, right under the shadow of General Jackson's hermitage; in 1829 concluded could do better: took rib from the south and came north, in 1830, just before that ever memorable great snow; lived within two miles of Jacksonville that hard winter. We had eaten all the potatoes, and had drawn heavily on old hog and hominy, and thought we must have some meal. A long journey was made to find a mill that had not been frozen up, and a terrible time had in getting through the snow in the bitter cold, nearly freezing to death.

He told also about ferrying a bride over a swollen stream in a hog trough, about eight feet long and fourteen inches wide. They got him to do it because they said he was the best prepared to die, Once he attended a camp meeting in a log building, when a dog was disturbed by one of the congregation. This dog howled and every dog about —and there were about a hundred of them—set up a howling and fighting, and it seemed as if pandemonium was let loose. The congregation rushed out and drove them off, and the rest of the services were sadly interrupted. He says:

"Those days were such as tried men's souls, their mettle, their nature. I would like to take some of the young preachers around some of those circuits—one of them was 300 miles round—flies terrible; mud bottomless; no bridges, no ferries, no canoes; sometimes they would swim; sometimes swim their horses; and in winter cross on the ice. Those were times of trial, but some of them were the happiest days I ever spent. They thought they were laying the foundation for some grand future, but they never expected to see what we see to-day."

At an "Old Settlers' Picnic"—an annual feature of modern Morgan county life Mr. Larkin was called out and said:

"I came to Morgan county in 1836. The county was entirely new. The first time I was ever in Jacksonville I came in town, stayed over night, and in the morning I took breakfast at the mound. The jail when I first came to this state stood about where the Park House now is, and any man could go through it with a jack knife."

Mr. John File, of the northwestern part of the county, was called on and contributed some remarks of which we give a few:

"I came to this state in 1831 and was in a store. They thought I was about sharp enough to make a peddler. I followed that business two years with several others, now citizens of this city. In those days if you would go to a house and ask to put up they would say certainly, if you can put up with what we have. The hospitality at every house was almost always very warm. One of the questions that was always asked in buying a horse was 'will he carry double;' because we always took the girls on behind us on the horse. Things are very different now-a-days, and young people enjoy themselves in different ways."

Mr. T. Shepherd bought a farm of Levi Fanning, and moved to it March 8th, 1831.

He made his first well bucket, by chopping off a section of a log, boring an auger hole through it, and lengthening and enlarging the hole with a chisel until nothing remained of the block but a thin rim. He then fitted in a bottom. A split appearing in the side he was compelled to take his bucket to Fielding Grimsley, the nearest blacksmith, to get it ironed. That individual, when questioned as to what he was doing, dryly replied that he was "hooping Shepherd's folly." Mr. Shepherd was a "*hardshell*" Baptist preacher, and was highly esteemed for noble traits of character and strict rectitude. He remained on Big Sandy until his death, a few years since, and left a large family.

In 1830 a meeting of the citizens of Jacksonville, was held in the cabinet shop of John Henry, in pursuance of a public call, to make arrangements for the celebration of the Fourth of July. The usual committee was appointed with the venerable John Eads as chairman. The committee met in Henry's cabin to make the necessary arrangements. It turned out to be a successful observance of the day, and the first celebration in this county of the Nation's birth that there is any account or recollection of.

It is worthy of mention here that in 1833 Stephen Arnold Douglas, afterwards of state and national reputation as statesman and patriot, came to Illinois. He was born April 23, 1813, at Brandon, Vermont. He landed at Meredosia in 1833, and tried to secure a school to teach, but was unsuccessful, so he went on foot to Naples and from there to Jacksonville. At both these places he was unable to get a school. He then went to Winchester, where he succeeded in getting a school of forty pupils at a salary of $3 per quarter.

In 1834 Mr. Isaac D. Rawlings opened shop in the tailoring business in this city. Subsequently he abandoned custom work and devoted himself to ready made clothing exclusively. Steadily but constantly the business grew on his hands, through the strictest adherence to his upright business principles. In the year 1863, his sons Isaac and Daniel were taken into the firm but the business continued under the old name. In 1868, however, the senior member retired but is still living as one of our honored citizens, represented in our business circles by his two merchant sons.

As indicative of merchandise prices here in olden times, the following document is of interest. Mr. Stevenson thinks this was about the first credit he ever had in a store in Jacksonville:

MR. ELLIOT STEVENSON,

To HOOK & WISWALL, *Dr.*

March 2d, 1832,	for 1 Curry Comb	$ 38
" " "	for 1 pair Cards	50
Sept. 29th, "	for 12 lbs. Iron, at 8½	1.02
Oct. 13th, "	for 5 lbs. Coffee	1.00
		$2.90

The following were the trustees of the town of Jacksonville during these years:

1834. A. Brockenbrough, Jas. Dunlap, William Thomas, T. Thornton, Jno. T. Cassell.

1835. John Hurst, Jacob Cassell, Thos. T. January, James J. Tilton, John J. Hardin.

1836. William Brown, William W. Happy, Thomas W. Melendy, William P. Warren, Murray McConnel.

The county officials, Representatives, Congressmen, &c., were as follows:

1830-'32. Sheriff, Samuel T. Mathews; Coroner, Wm. Jarred; County Commissioners, Wm. Gillham, Jas. Green, Wm. Woods; Representatives, N. Cloud, J. M. Fairfield; State Senator, James Evans.

1832-'34. Congressman, Joseph Duncan; State Senator, Waller Jones; Representatives, Murray McConnel, Samuel T. Matthews, John Henry, John Wyatt; Sheriff, Wm. Orear; County Commissioners, William Gillham, Wm. Woods, James Green; Coroner, Jacob Redding.

1834-'36. Congressman, Wm. L. May; State Senator, Wm. Thomas; Representatives, Newton Cloud, John Henry, Wm. Gordon, John Wyatt; Sheriff, William Orear; Coroner, Anthony Arnold; County Commissioners, Jacob Redding, Jacob Ward, James Green.

1836–'38.—Sheriff, Alexander Dunlap; Coroner, Anthony Arnold; County Commissioners, Jacob Redding, Jacob Ward, James Ethel; Representatives, Stephen A. Douglas, W. W. Happy, John J. Hardin; State Senator, William Orear.

L. F. Stoddard, now of Ramsey, Ill., wrote in 1883, to a friend in Jacksonville, of these times, thus:

"Fifty years ago, when you and I were young men, these prairies were sparsely settled, in fact but few farms were found except along the edges of the timber. Then houses were of logs, covered with boards and floored with puncheons, chimneys of sticks and mortar, inhabited by as whole-souled, hospitable set of people as ever lived. The benighted stranger was never turned away. The entertainment was primitive but generous—corn dodger, jerked venison and coffee the staple diet; the scaffold bedstead or a pallet upon the floor, was the couch.

Our mode of transportation was in the saddle, or if by wheels it was in a wagon drawn by oxen. During the summer if we crossed the prairies we necessarily traveled by night, on account of the flies (green heads). Now how changed! The cabins are all gone, and with them, I fear, much of the sociability. The prairies are all in cultivation, railroads and telegraph lines crossing them in every direction. Villages and various industries have sprung up on every hand * * * *

Camp meetings are conducted so different from what they used to be when you and I were boys.

Then we had no young man to gather and report a synopsis of all that passed—arrivals, departures; who preached and his discourse, and who was to lead the meeting the following day, nor had we a *Journal* to publish his reports.

As already noted, Judge Thomas of our city, served as quartermaster-sergeant, in the Winnebago War under Col. Neale. From 1828 he served two years by appointment of Gov. Edwards, as State's Attorney for the (then) fifth circuit. He was one of a commission to inquire into the relations of the government and Black Hawk, and served as quartermaster under Gov. Duncan in the Black Hawk War.

He was twice elected to the State Senate—in 1834 and '38 and then elected as judge of the first circuit. He was the author of the first bill which became a law about 1839, to authorize free public schools.

The Church of Christ was organized in January, 1832, with seventeen members, prominent among whom were Josephus Hewett, John T. Jones, Jacob Cassell, and Peter Hedenberg. Of these Mr. Hewett became the first preacher. In October, Mr. Stone was instrumental in effecting a union of this and a similar organization which had been organized some time previously. In 1835, Elder Gates, of Louisville, became pastor.

But no glimpses of "auld lang syne" are quite so vivid as those gained from the weekly newspaper of the time. From copies of *The Illinois Patriot*, James G. Edwards, editor, issued in January and February 1832, we glean the following facts:

Among those who were in business and who advertised, were John Ament, Joseph McKee, cabinet makers; James Fally, N. H. Gest, butchers; Gillian & Long, merchants, Upper Alton; Knapp & Pogue hardware merchants, Beardstown; Drs. Chandler and Jones, Jacksonville; Gillett & Gordon, who "want all accounts settled either in pork, wheat or cash;" Wm. Manning, jr., cooper, &c., &c.

Among the agents of the *Patriot* announced are Gershom Jayne, M. D., Springfield; Wm. R. Smith, Esq., Naples; C. H. Perry, Exeter; F. Arenz, P. M., Beardstown; H. Fellows, P. M., Rushville; Postmaster, Quincy; B. W. Holliday P. M., White Hall; Justus Rider, Esq., Carrollton; Wm. H. Brown, Esq., Vandalia; W. Manning, jr., Alton; Levi Harlan, Winchester, and a score of others in the region between St. Louis and Galena.

The issue of January 7th opens with a grand New Year's address, knocking the kings and queens of the old world right and left, and, in dealing with domestic affairs, hits "Old Hickory" a severe blow in these lines:

"He has his failings, which we think
Should not be passed without a wink—
His wicked system of reform
Has gather'd o'er him a dark storm."

Of the cabinet of that time, the poet says:

"The cabinet, of late turned out,
Have kicked up a confounded rout."

He laudeth Henry Clay, at the expense of "Old Hickory," in this style:

"Old Hickory, in our estimation,
Has lost the people's approbation—
His brightest laurels fade away
Before the blaze of Henry Clay.

It is an elegant effusion, and we wonder why Cheever overlooked it in his "Poets and Poetry of America."

Next comes a long memorial to congress, gotten up at Quincy, "to locate and construct a railroad from Buffalo in the state of New York, to the Mississippi River." Stories and miscellaneous items follow: A letter from Joseph Duncan, at Washington, to Col. John J. Hardin, concerning the pay due "Capt. Edmonson's company." The proposals of Benjamin McCary, to publish the "*Beardstown Chronicle.*" A long "list of letters," signed by Dennis Rockwell, postmaster. Then come numerous advertisements—among the names we notice Gillett & Gordon; William Thomas, school commissioner, the same as attorney at law; Jesse Barber, and Alton and Beardstown business cards.

In another copy of this same paper—one of the issues of October, 1833—we find at the head of the editorial columns the name of the same James G. Edwards, once of the Burlington *Hawkeye*. *The Patriot* was published weekly, and as in 1832,at $2.50 in advance, $3.00 if not paid within six months, and $3.50 if not paid within a year. And yet it was a four page paper, and to-day men are unreasonable enough to grumble at $1.50 for a ten page paper. From the advertisements we learn that John S. Clark "wishes to sell his farm lying seven miles north of Jacksonville, and one-half mile east of New Lexington in the Jersey Prairie."

Gillett & Gordon advertise that they "will pay fifty cents per bushel, of sixty pounds, in goods, for good, clean, dry, merchantable wheat delivered at the Exeter Mills."

A large cutting from a *Sentinel* of August, 1835, gives us the name of William H. Coyle as editor and proprietor, and the name of Hugh Lawson White as "the people's candidate" for president. In the advertising columns R. William Dummer's card appears as attorney at law, Frederick Collins prints a notice as executor of Anson Collins' estate, Carleton H. Perry as administrator of the estate of David Dinsmore, and John White as administrator of Thomas Smith. The leading editorial is in relation to the Jacksonville Female Academy, of which Miss E. P. Price was then "superintendent." The writer says: "The Academy is yet in its infancy, having only been incorporated at the last session of the legislature, and this being its first chartered term. The present number of pupils is from twenty to thirty," etc., etc. "A superior seminary for the instruction of young ladies in a sound and refined education we may safely say exists not in our state."

Among the memorable personages of those days we must not forget "Grandma Conn." She was born in one of the West India Islands, educated in New York. She married Mr. Conn and afterward emigrated to Cincinnati, thence to the vicinity of Kaskaskia, but later removed to Jacksonville in 1829, with Rev. Mr. Ellis, who married her half sister. Mrs. Ellis died with cholera in June 1833. Mrs. Elizabeth Conn was the mother of eight children, Richard, Matilda, Julia, William, Curtis, Eliza, Samuel and Eunice. She was always cheerful and as full of life as many, much her junior.

Mrs. Conn was raised a Catholic, and after removing to Kaskaskia she formed the acquaintance of the leading Protestant families there, among others an intelligent Protestant lady. They had frequent discussions upon the subject of their faith, and ultimately agreed to discuss the various points. Says a friend: In relating this to me she asked me what I thought was the result. I replied that I supposed she was made a Protestant, as she was then a very zealous one. She replied "Yes, but the other became as zealous a Catholic."

From a "Gazetteer of Illinois" written by J. M. Peck, and published at Jacksonville by R. Goudy, 1834, a copy of which is in the Free Library, we learn that then "Jacksonville has sixteen stores, six groceries, (?) two druggists shops, two taverns or hotels, one baker, two saddlers, three hatters, one silversmith, one watchmaker, two tinners, three cabinet makers, one machinist, one house and sign painter, six tailors, two cordwainers, four blacksmiths, three chair makers, one coach maker, one wagon maker, one wheelwright, eleven lawyers and ten physicians. It has one steam flour and one saw mill, a manufactory for cotton yarn, a distillery, two oil mills, two carding factories, a tannery, and three brickyards, with a proportion of various mechanics in the building line to other trades.

The public houses are, a spacious Court House, of brick, a neat frame building for the Presbyterian house of worship, a large brick building for the Methodist society, and a handsome edifice, also of brick, for the Episcopalian denomination; a female academy, a brick market house, and a county jail.

The college edifices are one mile west of town. There are two printing offices that publish weekly papers, the "*Patriot*" and the "*Gazette*," and also a book and job printing office, with a book bindery attached.

The present population is about 1,800, exclusive of the college students. Situated near the center of the county, and in the midst of one of the finest tracts of land, densely populated with industrious and enterprising farmers, with the advantages of good water, health and good society. Jacksonville must continue to prosper, and doubtless will attract many emigrants, who are seeking an agreeable home in the far West."

Of those then engaged in trade or business in this town, how many and who are still so engaged? The watch-maker was Mr. Nolan. Of the lawyers, probably Judge Thomas is the only one now living here. And of the physicians, Dr. Henry Jones. So many lawyers were credited to the town, we presume some must have been enumerated who did not reside, but only practiced here.

In an appendix is a table giving the counties in the State (60,) "vote in 1834," and estimated population—Morgan is credited with a population of 22,950, being 1,350 more than Sangamon, and the largest in the State. This was before Scott and Cass were sliced off. Cook county is credited with 3,265.

Of Illinois College it is stated that the buildings consist of a brick edifice 104 feet in length, 40 feet wide, five stories high including the basement. To this are attached two wings, each 38 feet long and 28 feet wide, three stories high, including basement, The chapel is a separate building, 65 feet long, and 36 feet wide, two stories high. There are also upon the premises a farm house, barn, bake-house, workshops for students who wish to perform manual labor, and other buildings. The farm consists of 300 acres of land all under fence.

Students who choose are allowed to employ a portion of each day in manual labor, either upon the farm or in the work-shop. Some individuals earned each $150 during the year. The library consists of about 1,500 volumes. There are 16 students connected with the college classes, and 60 students in the preparatory department. The faculty consisted of Rev. Edward Beecher. Rev. J. M. Sturtevant, Truman M. Post, J. B. Turner, Erastus Colton, and Dr. Henry Jones, lecturer on chemistry.

Other places in the near vicinity of Jacksonville are "Deaton's Mill," one of the first settlements in Morgan county, on the Mauvaisterre, three miles northwest from Jacksonville. Here is a mill and a large and flourishing settlement.

"English Settlement" is in Morgan county, west of Jacksonville, on Cadwell, Walnut and Plum Creeks. There are about one hundred families, mostly from Yorkshire England, and farmers. They appear to be well pleased with the country, and to be accumulating property.

Of the Mauvaisterre it is said, "for beauty of situation, fertility of soil, salubrity of climate, a due proportion of timber and prairie, good water, and almost every other advantage for agricultural purposes, no country in the widespread valley of the west excels this; and yet, by a most singular misnomer, the French, who explored the Illinois River, called it the '*Mauvaise-terre*'—poor land."

The year 1834 witnessed the arrival of Cleveland J. Salter whose death nearly fifty years later was a sore loss not only to Waverly, but to our county. The year after his first visit to Jacksonville, Mr. Salter invested largely in Morgan county lands, purchasing some 5,000 acres in the southeastern portion. In 1836 the town of Waverly was laid out by him and Messrs. D. B. Salter, A. C. Twining and J. A. Tanner. They donated the land for the public square and also 640 acres for educational purposes. A $5,000 building was put up and a flourishing high school established.

Crime was not unknown or unpunished in these primeval days, although churches had been planted and a God-fearing sentiment prevailed. In an old and time-worn book in the Morgan county court house "A," p. 243, Law Record) can still be found the following recorded as a proceeding of the September term of court, 1831, Samuel D. Lockwood, judge, Samuel T. Matthews, sheriff.

The People of Illinois vs. Charles King. } Upon indictment for forgery.

The said Charles King being brought to the bar in custody of the sheriff and being inquired of whether he had anything to say why the court should not now proceed to pronounce sentence of the law against him, and replied that he had not, whereupon it is ordered by the court that defendant be fined in the sum of fifty dollars, that he be imprisoned for the term of four months in the jail of the county of Morgan, that he receive *on his bare back twenty-five lashes* for the offense of forgery, whereof he stands convicted by the verdict of the jury. And it is ordered that the sheriff inflict the punishment of stripes on the defendant on the first day of December, next, between the hours of ten o'clock and two o'clock, of that day, on the public square of Jacksonville. It is further ordered that the defendant pay the costs of this prosecution and be imprisoned until the fine and costs be paid and the costs of imprisonment.

There are citizens now living who saw the sentence of the court carried out. The man, King, was soundly flogged. An old citizen asserts, however, that the report that in this public flogging blood was drawn is incorrect. He states that the whipping was administered in the mildest degree consistent with the carrying out of the sentence, and that the kind-hearted sheriff was moved to tears when he was ordered to administer the punishment. There are other instances of public flogging: one of Benjamin Crisp, for larceny, and others.

Mr. J. W. Lathrop writes to the *Courier:* "It seems too that some rascality went unpunished. In 1822, and previous to that time, a man named Holmes lived on what is known as the Claybourne Coker farm, a few miles east of this city. Holmes had an excellent wife, and though a hard worker himself, he was looked upon with suspicion by many of his neighbors as a man not to be trusted, and altogether as "slippery" in his dealings with other men—ever ready to make a dollar, no matter by what way. It was at length thought by some that he was regularly making counterfeit Mexican dollars, and he was closely watched. His wife was not in sympathy with his wicked ways, and protested strongly against his pursuit of them. At length he became alarmed lest she should expose more than he would have the public know, and he decided to circumvent arrest should exposure be made. On the 3d of July, 1832, he went to Naples, taking his wife, to spend the Fourth. Next day he disappeared, and was never seen in this part of the country afterward.

In 1875, Mr. Atterbury, who now lives on the same farm occupied by Holmes at the time given above, was plowing a field near the site of the old house, when his plow turned up an iron concern, that at once invited his scrutiny. It proved to be a pair of *iron moulds for Mexican dollars.* The iron was, of course, rusted and eaten from long burial in the ground, but the inside of the moulds was as bright as though new, and stamps were perfect. Mr. Atterbury now has the moulds in his possession, and they have been examined by persons among whom were many old residents who knew Holmes well, and remember the cirumstances surrounding his disappearance, and furthermore, they are re-assured in their belief, by this last indisputable evidence, of Holmes' guilt.

On the first Sabbath in April, 1830, Rev. John M. Ellis was installed pastor of the First Presbyterian Church of Jacksonville.

Mr. Ellis resigned his pastorate about 1832, but his family remained in this village until the terrible cholera year of 1833, when they all died during his absence from home, and he learned of the fate of all at the same moment, *en route* homeward.

Of Mr. and Mrs. Ellis, Father Lippincott writes in 1859:

To those of us who knew the worth of the extraordinary woman whom the Lord thus snatched from him and the strength and tenderness of his affections, there was in his behavior a delightful proof of the supporting power of faith. My first acquaintance with him was made as they stopped at my house when removing to Jacksonville. With the politeness of a French lady, she combined the sobriety of the serious christian. If I misjudged not, her intellect was more carefully cultivated than her manners, elegant as they were. Her influence over her pupils was gentle but powerful. I have never known any one who could unite so perfectly the mild and the firm in the training of the young.

Mr. James S. Anderson, of our city, now believed to be the oldest undertaker in America, having begun business in that line in 1832, gives his recollections of the cholera period of 1833 as follows:

"The first case made its appearance in May or June of the year 1833. A mover traveling by wagon through the country stopped here and his wife was taken sick. The citizens went to his assistance and the woman's disease was pronounced a case of genuine Asiatic cholera. The citizens conveyed the sick woman and the others to a log cabin outside of town, so as not to spread the infection. This cabin was on the ground now owned by George Mauzy, and where he lives at present. The woman died and the people burned the clothing, &c., supplied the man with money and sent him on. I saw this woman just before she died. Myself and several companions went to see her out of curiosity. Two weeks afterward the second case appeared, being that of a young man from Exeter, who was visiting relatives who kept a boarding house where Marble Block now stands. He died, and the disease began to spread rapidly. The town at that time contained about 500 inhabitants, fully half of whom fled to the country. Of those who remained about seventy-five were attacked with the epidemic, of whom about fifty-five died. It was very malignant. Besides these quite a number who fled to the country died; some of them, I actually believe, were scared to death. When the disease first appeared my brother Robert, my partner Ross and myself were all working together. Robert became alarmed, and went to father's, on the farm near Murrayville. The next day he returned for Ross and I, but we concluded to take our chances and stay in town. We were both young, unmarried men, and we left our shop and commenced to nurse the sick, and we were almost the only ones who devoted our time to it. We went from house to house, sitting up night after night and day after day, waiting on the sick, preparing the dead for burial and doing what we could. The whole community seemed paralyzed, and but little business was done. I don't believe that a man would have picked up a dollar if he had seen it in the street. We had a hard time getting anything to eat. Our boarding house was broken up, and no one could take us regularly, as all were either afflicted or waiting on those who were; but we were always welcome to a meal wherever we could find it. The scourge lasted six weeks, and was the most terrible that ever visited Jacksonville. The disease usually lasted from six to twenty-four hours before the sufferer died. Some curious cures were effected. Occasionally, after the doctors had given a patient up, one of what they called steam doctors would come in and cure him."

"What about coffins?"

"Well, coffins are usually made to order. We never thought of keeping a stock on hand; when a person died the measure of the body was sent us and we made the coffin out of cherry wood and lined it with domestic, but it was very seldom that any attempt at any ornamentation was made."

"Were funerals as expensive in those days as now?"

"You can judge for yourself; a good cherry coffin for a first class funeral cost from $9 to $12. I kept a hearse myself and the charge for it was a dollar a funeral and sometimes nothing. It was not customary to provide a string of carriages for the use of the public. My hearse was my own invention. It was a kind of buggy with a long bed and movable seat with a truck to hold the coffin. I used to hire it to the boys to drive around in when not in use at a funeral. It costs more to bury a pauper now than it did in those days to bury the owner of a thousand acres of land."

From 1824 to 1835 paupers were sold in the county, and some time in 1835 a poor-house was built.

In 1834, near Middle Creek, in Cass county, now, but in Morgan, then, a religious society of fanatics was organized, who not only believed in witchcraft, but actually made offerings of themselves, and were burned at the stake, to appease and propitiate, as they believed, their offended Deity, and cast lots who of their members should be burned at the stake. Once the lot fell to an old lady, whom the others tied and bound to the stake, and when she began to burn she screamed so loud and pitifully that Mr. Elmore, hunting near by, broke the door open with a fence rail, released the burning woman from the stake, broke up the meetings, and the grand jury of Morgan county indicted many of the members, and the religious fanatics left the country.

Nothing of interest occurred in the history of the county from the close of the

Winnebago war until the fall of the "deep snow," which happened in the winter of 1830-'31. Quite a number of persons had settled in the county during this interval, and population and improvements had largely increased. This fall of snow was indeed a remarkable event. Nothing like it had ever occurred in the annals of the northwest. The Indians relate that years before the discovery of the Mississippi River, a great snow fell to the depth of a man's waist. Wild animals perished in great numbers, and the suffering among the Indians, which followed the loss of so much game, was severely felt. In the early days of Kentucky a snow fell to a depth of more than a foot, causing great privation among the settlers; it however did not equal the "deep snow" of 1830-'31.

No meteorological events of this century are so deeply fixed in the memories of "the oldest inhabitants" as "the deep snow" of 1831, and "the quick freeze" of 1836. Dr. Sturtevant says of the first named:

In the interval between Christmas, 1830 and new year, 1831, snow fell over all Central Illinois to the depth of fully three feet on a level. Then came a rain, with weather so cold that it froze as it fell, forming a crust of ice over this three feet of snow, nearly, but not quite, strong enough to bear a man, and finally over this crust of ice there was a few inches of very light snow. The clouds passed away and the wind came down from the northwest with extraordinary ferocity. For weeks, certainly for not less than two weeks, the mercury in the thermometer tube was not, on any one morning, higher than twelve degrees below zero. The wind was a steady, fierce gale from the northwest, day and night. The air was filled with flying snow, which blinded the eyes and almost stopped the breath of any one who attempted to face it. No man could, for any considerable length of time, make his way on foot against it.

The story of such a winter may be pleasant enough to hear, to one who hopes never to experience it; but the situation of the inhabitants of this county was certainly rather alarming. The people were almost wholly from regions more southern than this, and knew nothing by experience of dealing with such a depth of snow, and such cold. Indeed I had then had some experience of New England winter, and have had some since, but I have to this day never seen any other which bore any comparison with that. Jacksonville had then about four hundred people. We were dependent chiefly for keeping warm on having plenty of wood, for our houses were certainly far enough from being warmly built; and yet our supply of fuel for the winter was not, as is more commonly the case now, piled at our doors before the beginning of winter. It was in the forest, and must be brought us, through that snow, and by people who were quite unaccustomed to it. Could it be done? It was at first not quite apparent that it could. Our corn was in the fields over which this covering of snow was spread, and to a great extent the wheat for our bread was in stacks in like condition. Snow paths could not be broken after the New England fashion. There, a few hours of wind blows all the snow from exposed places, and deposits it in valleys and behind hills where the wind cannot reach it. A little energy with ox teams and sleds will break out a road and there will be no more trouble till the next snow storm. There is no truer picture than that given by Whittier in his "Snow Bound" of the frolic of breaking the roads after a great snow storm. But nothing of the sort would have been of much use in our case. In this level country there is no end to the drifting as long as the snow lasts, and the wind blows. There are no covered places into which the snow can be driven, consequently the path would fill behind a team, or any number of teams, in a few minutes, so that the track could not be seen. The only way in which snow paths were made was by going as nearly as we could in the same place till the snow was finally trodden hard and rounded up like a turn pike. This snow-fall produced constant sleighing for nine weeks, and when at last warm rains and sunshine prevailed, about the first of March, melting the snow from fields and untrodden places, the roads remained as lines of ice which disappeared but gradually. The New Englander has scarcely any such experience of winter as this, certainly not unless it be quite in northern New England. We had no railways then, nor indeed any dream of having them. But our mail communications with the rest of the world were interrupted for several weeks continuously. We, in those days, had only one mail a week, and that on horseback from Springfield, and to bring that through that snow required more energy than mail boys in those days were masters of. * * * * *

I cannot say, after all, that in town there was any very serious amount of suffering—we did get food and fuel, and a good deal of fun and frolic out of the deep snow; though at the expense of not a few frozen ears, noses and faces. But the loss to the farms in stock and crops are very considerable. Some varieties of wild game were nearly exterminated. Deer were entirely unable to protect themselves from the dogs and the huntsmen.

Mr. Anderson Foreman another living resident of Jacksonville at that time writes to the *Courier*, as follows:

The famous historic "deep snow" occured in the winter of 1830-'31. On the 20th of December, 1830, sleeting and snowing began and continued throughout December. Through January and February, 1831, snow fell and in many places drifted to the depth of six feet and more. The snow, on an average all over the country, was three feet deep. It was indeed a season of great hardships and suffering to men and beasts and birds throughout the country.

In 1836 the cold wave and quick freeze occurred. The cold wave traveled at the rate of 70 miles an hour. Before the wave came it had been thawing and raining, and the geese and ducks, swimming and bathing in the ponds and puddles of water, when struck by the cold wave, froze, and were taken into the house and their wings, feet and feathers relieved of the icicles. The wagon wheels, when they ceased to roll, froze to the ground; and all the animals, and birds of all kinds froze to death far and near. Men killed their horses, and after disemboweling them crawled in and thus saved their own lives.

Mr. John W. Lathrop describes the sudden freeze thusly:

I was, at the time, boarding with Prof. Turner, who lived in a one-story frame dwelling on the lot where now stands the fine brick dwelling of Mr. Henry Hall, on College Avenue.

During the previous night snow fell to the depth of about eight inches, and at sunrise the next morning it was raining and very warm and foggy, and continued raining until nearly noon. I spent the forenoon in writing, and after dinner started to the postoffice, which was then in the old brick court house situated on the public square. The snow was completely saturated with the rain, so that in walking my feet went to the bottom of the snow until I passed the Female Academy; then the cold wave struck me, and as I drew my feet up the ice would form on my boots until I made a track that looked more like that of a Jumbo than a No. 7 boot. When I reached the square the ice bore me up, and when I returned to Mr. Turner's, a half hour afterwards, I saw his chickens and ducks frozen into the ice—some on one leg and some on both.

Two young men who were traveling for Philadelphia merchants were frozen to death not far from Rushville. One of them was found sitting with his back against a tree with his horse's bridle over his arm and his horse frozen in front of him. The other young man was partly in a kneeling position, with a tinder box in one hand and a flint in the other—with both eyes open, as though attempting to light the tinder in the box—that being the usual mode of lighting a fire before the days of friction matches. These young men were here only a few days before, calling on the merchants, and, as was the custom then, traveled on horseback.

The only other person who was frozen to death, who was known here, I think was a minister known as Father Brich, then living near Galena.

According to Mr. Ensley Moore's epitome of local affairs in 1830: The State of Illinois had a population of 155,447, and Morgan county then included what is now Cass and Scott counties, making about 1,114 square miles.

In 1821, Morgan county contained only 21 families; in 1825, its population was 4,052; in 1830, it was 13,281.

Dr. J. T. Cassell made his first tour to Jacksonville in 1830,and bought two lots on the west side of the square, for $100 each. One of them is now occupied by T. J. Hook & Co.'s store.

In the county there are "thirty mills for sawing and grinding, propelled by animal or water power. Seven large steam mills are in operation, and two more have been commenced and will be finished the present year," wrote Peck, in 1834.

Land was worth about $3 to $15 per acre, and villages were about to spring up all around Jacksonville.

The *Western Observer* was published every Saturday, by James G. Edwards; terms $2.50 a year, if paid in advance.

"Mrs. Ellis' school re-opened on Monday, the 20th day of September; tuition per quarter, elementary branches $3.00, higher branches $4.00, boarding per week $1.00, washing 25 cents. Needle work is carefully taught; the French language is spoken in the family. Members of the school will have access to an excellent library without additional charge," says an advertisement in the *Western Observer*, the advertisement bearing the date of Sept. 17, 1830.

David B. Ayers says: "The subscriber has just received, principally from Philadelphia, the following articles, viz." (Then follows a list of paints, glass, drugs and patent medicines, at wholesale and retail.)

The Jacksonville School Association having gone to pieces, William Sewall advertises his school to open under his own direction; terms $2.50 per quarter.

"An apprentice is wanted at this office."

Capt. John Wyatt was a prominent citizen, who farmed about six miles south-east of town. He was the father of Col. Wm. J. Wyatt, now also a prominent citizen.

Col. Joseph Morton took the census of Morgan county this year, 1830.

The Court House, which was taken out of the southwest corner of the city park in 1870, was accepted from the contractors September 8, 1830. It cost about $4,000 dollars; our present Court House cost about $201,000 - a slight difference.

The contracts for the "old court house" were made March 14th, 1829, by Joseph M. Fairfield, John Wyatt and Samuel Rogers, county commissioners. Garrison W. Barry and Henry Robley took the brick work for $1,720, Rice Dunbar and Henry Robley the carpentering for 1,350, besides minor contracts to others. Henry Blanford, Isham Dalton, John Challon and Jas. Hurst, were also employed in constructing the building. It was the first "brick" in the county, as at present bounded. To meet the expense of this improvement, and for county revenue, a tax was levied on all slaves, indentured or registered, negro or mullatto servants, on pleasure carriages, distilleries, or stock in trade, on live stock, and all personal property except furniture.

The "old jail" was built of hewed timbers, each about one foot square, and every wall was made double. This jail was followed by another, built in 1833, succeeded in time by the present one on South Main street.

Minors were "bound out" until of age, when thrown upon the county for support, and in 1830 there was neither a "poor farm" nor "poor house."

William Gilham, James Green and William Woods were elected county commissioners in this year.

Venison was a favorite article of food, and, during the "deep snow" one man captured thirteen deer in one day- to the best of our remembrance.

Marshall P. Ayers came to Morgan county in 1830 and Augustus E. Ayers was in the same party.

Samuel Bateman came the same year as did Robt. L. Caldwell, Edward Craig, James Craig, J. R. Chambers, Jesse Gunn, A. S. Gunn, Elijah Henry, George Loar, Harrison Osborn, A. C. Patterson, F. H. Patterson, Preston Spates, John Spires, J. J. Shepherd, W. D. R. Trotter, S. Turner, Elizur Wolcott, Dudley Young, and Wesley Mathers.

No trouble with Indians is known of as occurring in Morgan county, but in 1829 '30 the trouble began along the Rock River, which culminated in the Black Hawk War, to which many of our citizens went in 1831.

One of the Jacksonville volunteers in that war has recently narrated briefly his experience in the following language:

"My experience was not a very exciting one. There had been a call for troops, the first term of service having expired, but it was in the spring of the year and the farmers would not volunteer. The town boys were ready to go, but the order was for cavalry and they had no money to buy horses. James Deaton, who was the chief military man of this neighborhood, called out every able-bodied citizen and the first draft we had ever experienced occurred. Somehow the thing did not work right, and a compromise was make by which we agreed to furnish a company of infantry instead of cavalry. Cyrus Matthews was our captain and Col. Samuel Matthews was commander of the regiment. We marched to Beardstown and went by boat from there to Fort Welburn, opposite La Salle on the Illinois River, where we were mustered into the service by General Gaines, of the regular army. Our regiment, by reason of its being partly infantry, was stationed at this fort, which was the base of supplies for the expedition. We stayed there until the war was over (seventy-two days) and then came home, having never had a scratch. If the bill to pension the survivors of the Black Hawk war is passed our regiment ought to be excepted, for not one of us ever received a wound or contracted any disease while in the service, although some of us were badly scared by the report of the cholera amongst Gen. Scott's troops at Chicago.

Among those from Morgan in this war, with their age in 1879 when a "Reunion" was held, were the following:

Anderson Foreman, 70, Jacksonville; Thomas Wright, 74, Franklin; A. W. Stice, —, Jacksonville; Arch. P. Riggs, 69, Franklin; Richard Seymour, 71, Franklin; William Wright, 72, Waverly; Lee T. Morris, 69, Jacksonville; James Morrison, 80, Jacksonville. Governor Duncan, then major general of militia, was in command of the mounted brigade sent by Governor Reynolds to this "war." Judge Thomas went as quartermaster of the brigade.

Commencing May 1st, 1831, there were frosts and freezes for ten consecutive nights killing all vegetation. Even forest trees were injured so as to soon die.

"The marriage ceremony, in those days, was a very unceremonious affair," says John McConnel, whose excellent description in his "Western Sketches" we quote in full:

"The parents never made a 'parade' about anything—marriage, least of all. They usually gave the bride—not the 'blushing' bride—a bed, a lean horse, and some good advice; and, having thus discharged their duty in the premises, returned to their work, and the business was done. The parade and drill which now attend it, would have been as ridiculous as a Chinese dance; and the finery and ornament, at present understood to be indispensable on such occasions, then bore no sway in fashion. Bridal wreaths and dresses were not known, and white kid gloves and satin slippers never heard of. Orange blossoms—natural and artificial—were as pretty then as now; but the people were more occupied with substance than with emblem.

"The ancients decked *their* victims for the sacrifice with gaudy colors flags and streamers; the moderns do the same, and the offerings are sometimes made to quite as barbarous deities. But the bride of the pioneer was clothed in linsey-wolsey, with hose of woolen yarn; and moccasins of deer skin—or, as an extra piece of finery, high-quartered shoes of calf-skin—preceded satin slippers. The bride-groom came in copperas colored jeans—domestic manufacture—as a holiday suit; or, perhaps, a hunting shirt of buck-skin, all fringed around the skirt and cape, a 'coon-skin' cap, with moccasins. Instead of a dainty walking stick, with an opera dancer's leg, in ivory, for a head, he always brought his rifle, with a solid maple stock; and often, during the whole ceremony, he did not divest himself of powder-horn and bullet-pouch.

"Ministers of the gospel were few in those days, and the words of form were usually spoken by a missionary. Or, if the pioneer had no objections to Catholicism—as many had—his place was supplied by some justice of the peace, of doubtful powers and mythical appointment. If neither of these could be procured, the father of the bride, himself, sometimes assumed the functions *pro hac vice*, or *pro tempore*, of minister or justice. It was always understood, however, that such left-handed marriages were to be confirmed by the first minister who wandered to the frontier; and, even when the opportunity did not offer for several months, no scandal ever arose—the marriage vow was never broken. The pioneers were simple people; the refinements of high cultivation had not yet penetrated the forests or crossed the prairies, and good faith and virtue were as common as courage and sagacity.

"When the brief, but all sufficient ceremony was over, the bride-groom resumed his rifle, helped the bride into the saddle—or, more frequently, to the pillion behind him—and they calmly rode away together.

"On some pleasant spot—surrounded by a shady grove, or point of timber—a new log cabin has been built; its rough logs notched across each other at the corners, a roof of oaken clapboards, held firmly down by long poles along each course, its floor of heavy 'puncheons,' its broad, cheerful fire-place, large as a modern bed-room—all are in the style of the frontier architecture. Within—excepting some anomalies, such as putting the skillet and tea-kettle in the little cupboard, along with the blue-edged plates and yellow-figured tea-cups—for the whole has been arranged by the hands of the bride-groom himself—everything is neatly and properly disposed. The oaken bedstead, with low, square posts, stands in one corner, and the bed is covered with a pure white counterpane, with fringe—an heir-loom in the family of the bride. At the foot of this is seen a large, heavy chest—like a camp-chest—to serve for bureau, safe, and dressing-case.

"In the middle of the floor—directly above the trap-door which leads to a 'potato hole' beneath, stands a ponderous walnut table, and on it sits a nest of wooden trays, while, flanking these, on one side, is a nicely folded tablecloth, and, on the other, a wooden handled butcher knife and a well worn bible. Around the room are ranged a few 'split-bottomed' chairs, exclusively for use, not ornament In the chimney corners, or under the table, are several three-legged stools, made for the children, who—as the bride-groom laughingly insinuates, while he points to the uncouth specimens of his handiwork—'will be coming in due time.' The wife laughs in her turn—replies 'no doubt' —and, taking one of the graceful tripods in her hand, carries it forth to sit upon while she milks the cow—for she understands what she is expected to do, and does it without delay. In one corner near the fire-place, the aforesaid cupboard is erected—being a few oaken shelves neatly pinned to the legs with hickory forks—and in this arranged the plates and cups; not as the honest pride of the housewife would arrange them, to display them to the best advantage, but piled away one within another, without reference to show. As yet there is no sign of female taste or presence.

"But now the house receives its mistress. The 'happy couples' ride up to the low rail fence in front, the bride springs off without assistance, affectation, or delay. The husband leads away the horse, or horses, and the wife enters the dominion where, thenceforward, she is queen."

In August, 1884, the Park family had a pleasant reunion in Jacksonville after a separation of many years. Of six brothers and one sister, the youngest born in 1828, all were living and most of them in good health. Altogether they made an interesting group of substantial citizens of whom any county might well be proud. Five of them lived in this county and two at a distance. Thomas Park, the father, came to the state in 1828, and with a wife, six boys and one girl, moved to Morgan county in the spring of 1831. He died in 1852 and Mrs. Park died in 1873. This year the seven children are still living and met in this city and were photographed in a group. Their ages were as follows: John J., 69; H. M., 67; J. A., 65; Elijah H., 63; Wm. R., 60; Robt. Y., 56 and Sarah J., 54. They all met at the Old Settlers' Reunion, August 7th, 1884, and ate dinner together, and on the next Thursday they had a reunion at the old Park, homestead, eight miles northwest of the city, and now the residence of J. A. Park. This is probably one of the most remarkable reunions which was ever held in this county. They were all born as early as 1828 and have lived to meet at the end of fifty-three years residence in the county, a complete family of children, the father and mother both having died.

As to the first printing, publishing and book-binding in this city and county, we extract as follows from the scrap-book of Capt. John Henry, deceased, preserved in the Free Reading Room of the Jacksonville Y. M. C. A.:

"The first editor was an old gentleman by the name of Robert Goudy. He was a book-binder by trade and his office was in a little frame building in the west part of the city. He established a printing office in connection with his bindery. His was the first book-bindery established in Illinois, but owing to his advanced age he did not succeed well in business. He had three sons, all of whom were good business men, and one is now living in Chicago and is a leading lawyer and politician of the democratic party. This bindery and printing office was established about 1830. The next paper established in Jacksonville was by James G. Edwards in the same year. He came to Illinois as one of the company to establish the Illinois College at Jacksonville but soon after he opened in a wider field, becoming tired of being confined to one organization. He soon adapted himself to the western people and their customs, and launched out boldly for himself (with the assistance of his wife) in the printing business and his paper soon had a respectable circulation. He continued to publish the paper for about eighteen months or two years, and then moved to Iowa, and there established the Burlington *Hawkeye*. By his ability, energy and pluck his paper soon became the leading one of the state, and still retains its popularity. He proved himself to be a valuable citizen, but he died young, leaving no heir. His paper was published in the interest of the old whig party.

"The next paper in Jacksonville was published by Samuel S. Brooks, a man of much independence. He was quiet and pleasant in his manners and an able writer and possessed of great determination. He published one of the ablest democratic papers in the state and advocated the claims of Gen. Jackson for the presidency. He labored hard to bring Stephen A. Douglas before the people of Illinois and he was a great favorite with Douglas in the great contest between Lincoln and Douglas in 1858. No man that I know figured so largely as an editor as did Brooks. He was at different times connected with several papers, among which were the Quincy *Whig* and the *State Register*. He died between the age of 65 to 70 years after leading a busy and useful life.

Mr. Josiah M. Lucas emigrated from Maryland to Illinois and settled in Jacksonville in 1830 and after being here a short time he conceived the idea of establishing a weekly paper. He was a single man. He ventured out west on his own hook without friends, but it was only a short time before he comprehended the situation of the country and people. He was well calculated to adapt himself to a mixed community and soon brought warm friends to his aid. He established his paper in the interest of the old Whig flag and rallied for Henry Clay for president. He ranked among such men as J. J. Hardin, Wm. Thomas, Richard Yates and others of the same class. He proved himself equal to the task of conducting his paper in the proper manner, always keeping in sight of it himself and never allowing anything to enter its columns which was mean or disrespectful. They were always open to friend or foe for fair and honorable debate. Mr. Lucas retired from newspaper life and went to Washington where he was elected postmaster of the House of Representatives. He filled many positions, both civil and military, and was a United States Consul for several years. Those positions he filled with credit to himself, the government, and those whom he served.

We have been told that the first straw bonnet for ladies wear ever brought to town for sale was by Mr. T. D. Eames, who began mercantile life here in 1835.

In illustration of the difficulty of obtaining news promptly in olden times, we quote as follows from the editorial columns of *The Illinois Patriot*, predecessor of *The Journal*, of date of Thursday, February 23d, 1832, and flying the name of Henry Clay for president.

THE OLD STORY.—The mail, which was due on Tuesday, arrived yesterday, bringing us no news east of Springfield. We learn by the Springfield papers that a gentleman who arrived at that place from St. Louis, informed the editors that the nomination of Mr. Van Buren had been *rejected*. We await with great anxiety for some official news which will confirm this statement.

That the protection of American industries was then as now a question of political discussion is shown by the following editorial:

"With nothing on hand but old papers, we are glad to have it in our power to lay Mr. Clay's speech on the tariff before the public this week. We have seen Mr. Hayne's reply—it is an eloquent speech, but the doctrines it inculcates aim a death blow at the American system, and would, if adopted, prostrate the energies of the manufacturer, choke the avenues by which our farmers are to realize a compensation for their labors and throw out of employment many industrious citizens."

We have already made frequent reference to the Rev. John M. Ellis and his pioneer work here as preacher and founder of educational institutions, but feel that all the readers of "Historic Morgan" will be glad to know more of this saintly man and his early labors. Hence we extract as follows from the *Presbytery Reporter*, Dr. A. T. Norton, editor, of September 1859: "Furnished with a hundred dollars as an outfit, the young minister made his way in six weeks (for the Ohio was low) to Illinois. There were then but three Presbyterian ministers in the state, Rev. John Brich, who resided near Jacksonville, and who perished by cold a few years after; Rev. Stephen Bliss in the southeast part of the state, and Rev. B. F. Spillman in the southwest part of the state, who lived until the present year." * * * * * "Mr. Ellis was that type of mind and from that stock of mankind, with whom it is an instinct to build colleges. From Elias Cornelius he had received the charge 'to build up an institution of learning which should bless the West for all time.' He gave instruction himself to a select class near his residence, and in all journeys and intercourse it was a prominent subject of his conversation. In Presbytery he obtained the appointment of a committee to advise on the subject. Of this committee Mr. Giddings was removed by death. Mr. Chamberlain was averse to the movement and Elder (now Rev.) Thomas Lippincott gave his cordial aid to Mr. Ellis." * * * * * * "The earliest considerable subscription was $400, made by Deacon William Collins, Sr., of Collinsville."

"In January 1828, Mr. Ellis and Mr. Lippincott went on a tour of inquiry and observation to the Sangamon country, the latter having an extensive acquaintance with the public men in that region. At Jacksonville so charming was the landscape, so rich the soil around and so enterprising the people who settled there that Mr. Ellis appears to have concluded at once that this was the place for a seminary in preference to other towns he visited. Within a few days with characteristic promptitude, he purchased eighty acres of land and set the stakes for a building. It remained to secure the approbation of Presbytery (Missouri) to this location, and the sanction of those who had subscribed money. The latter point alone was obtained. Mr. Ellis appears to have determined to remove to Jacksonville and in the summer he took up his residence there. The following extracts from his letters to the A. H. M. S., will be read with interest:"

JANUARY 6, CARROLLTON.—This is in Greene, one of the three most important counties in the state. A few Presbyterians, perhaps twenty, are in a church, weak and faint. I told the people of the Home Missionary Society, and gave them what encouragement I could, and this relieved their spirits a little; but they must have something more.

JANUARY 13.—Preached in Jacksonville Sabbath and week-day, as in Greene county. Morgan is an interesting county. There is a little church in it, trying to do what they can, and with good prospects.

JANUARY 20, SPRINGFIELD, Sangamon county.—Audiences full and attentive. When I inquired whether any Presbyterian Church existed here, no one could tell me. During the two weeks spent here, however, a church of twenty members was formed, to which additions have since been made.

In passing from Springfield to Hillsboro, I swam two creeks with my horse in the winter season. But this should be no terror to the missionary coming from the east. This and other like trials and exposures are no more than lawyers, judges, and all men of business are occasionally exposed to; and if one cannot do as much for the *souls of men*, how can he be called a missionary of the cross. Still as the country improves these hardships disappear.

Mr. Lippincott accompanied him on this journey, and his recollections of it are recorded in a letter which follows. The meeting of Presbytery was one in which a vote passed adverse to Mr. Ellis' plans. It is no wonder that a Presbytery in Missouri should think Jacksonville out of the center. His visits to Shoal Creek and Collinsville were necessary to secure their ratification of his purchase and confirmation of their subscriptions. His marriage occurred the day following the date of the letter preceding:

AUGUST 1, 1828.—The church at Jacksonville, on the last Lord's day, received an accession equal to the whole number of members, making now twenty-eight. There seems to be a rich blessing in store for this section of the state, if we can obtain laborers. These counties, Morgan, Sangamon and Greene, are populating with unexampled rapidity, having doubled their inhabitants in three years. The market on the Illinois River was opened this year by team, and eight or ten steamboats have visited the Morgan landing this spring, and more expected.

SEPTEMBER, 25, 1828.—The church here are engaged in building a parsonage, and is perfectly unanimous in all its proceedings. Nothing can exceed the kind attention paid to me and my family. The sum engaged for my support is $150 or more, principally in produce. Building the house is a heavy burden.

In the engagement made with the people I have reserved one Sabbath in four to preach occasionally in other parts of the county, and to visit churches abroad. In compliance with repeated solicitations, I went on the 8th of September to Canton, Fulton county, seventy-five miles northwest of Springfield, and returned in seventeen days, during which I rode in all 234 miles, preached thirteen sermons, constituted a church in Fulton of nine members, administered the sacrament three times, baptized six adults and five children, and attended six prayer meetings. The anxiety to obtain preaching of our denomination is expressed in language of earnest entreaty. In Fulton county two men are ready to engage $50 each for the first year. It is a desirable place. Half the people are from New England and New York, and the health is excellent. At least five or six missionaries are imperiously needed in Illinois.

A seminary of learning is projected to go into operation next fall. The subscription now stands at $2,000 or $3,000. The site is in this county. The half-quarter section purchased for it is certainly the most delightful spot I have ever seen. It is about one mile north of the celebrated Diamond Grove, and overlooks the town and country for miles around. The object of the seminary is popular, and it is my deliberate opinion that there never was in our country a more promising opportunity to bestow a few thousand dollars in the cause of education and of missions.

FEBRUARY 16, 1829.—We have occupied for several weeks the house built for us by the church here; a convenient frame house with three rooms. They are now adding out buildings. Everything goes on harmoniously. What is most needed now is a suitable meeting house. Preaching is held in a school house, but on common occasions it is usual to see numbers going home unable to gain admittance. Few towns have risen as rapidly as Jacksonville. About a dozen frame buildings finished in good style have gone up the last year. I have not counted the temporary log buildings going up daily almost.

God is sending forth laborers in answer to prayer. Another young man, licensed October 8th, by our Presbytery, now offers his services to your society. In January a Presbytery was organized in this state, having been set off from Missouri by Synod of Indiana last October. We have eight ministers and two licentiates.

(The ministers were John G. Bergen, Springfield; Solomon Hardy, Greenville; John Matthews, Kaskaskia; John Brich, Jacksonville; Stephen Bliss, Centreville; B. F. Spillman, Shawneetown; J. A. Spillman, Hillsboro; and Mr. Ellis. The lecutiates, C. L. Watson and Thomas Lippincott.)

As the result of the correspondence between Mr. Ellis and the young gentlemen at Yale College, having been sent commissioner to General Assembly he spent the summer of 1829 at the east, aiding them in raising a fund of $10,000 for the college and in maturing their plans. Two of them Rev. Messrs. Sturtevant and Baldwin arrived in Jacksonville in November, and the instruction in the college began the first of January. The original stockholders passed resolutions of thanks to the young men of Yale College who had aided in their enterprise, and placed them in the Board of Trustees; of thanks also to Mr. Ellis, and to donors to the college.

MARCH 8, 1830.—With no small degree of satisfaction I again address you from "my home in the west." The object of my late tour to the eastern states has been accomplished beyond what we had dared to anticipate. And since we returned Providence has accommodated every occurrence so as to promote and not to hinder its interests by conciliating prejudice, disarming opposition and securing public favor. The number of students is seventeen; others are expected, and we fear we shall not have sufficient accommodations. The present building contains, besides school room, only four rooms for students.

On the last week in January, I aided in the formation of a church in Schuyler county of twelve members. A year ago last July the church in Jacksonville consisted of fourteen members; now there are more than fifty.

JUNE 1830.—The pastoral charge of this church was committed to me by installation on the first Sabbath in April. We have a very promising Sunday School. There is a good spirit in relation to the Bible cause. I hope to have something interesting to state concerning temperance. On the last Sabbath in April a church of fourteen members was formed in Jersey Prairie, ten miles from here, to which we dismissed six members, leaving our number fifty-one. We had received at the two preceding communions eighteen members.

JULY 1831.—I am happy to state that our meeting house (30 feet by 40) is completed, and was dedicated June 19. No other Protestant church is finished with pews in the state. For more than one-third of the means of erecting this house we are indebted to friends in Philadelphia, New York and Boston. On common occasions it is filled to overflowing. Our meetings are solemn, and the church is increasing. At our next communion we expect to receive additions which will make our number exceed one hundred. I preach every week from three to six miles from town to interesting audiences.

OCTOBER (?) 1831.—A new church has recently organized six miles east of this place, consisting of thirty members, mostly from our church, with prospect of great good. We have had several four days' meetings in this part of the state, but have not realized all the permanent good effects which we had fondly hoped. There are circumstances in a newly settled country doubtless less favorable to a continued revival than in the older states.

This brings down his history till the close of 1831, when his pastorate in Jacksonville ended. He had projected the college and procured it real estate. The designs which resulted in the Female Seminary at Jacksonville and procured its beautiful grounds were formed in his house. This institution continues to be a monument in honor of him and his accomplished wife. He entered at once upon the service of the American Education Society in Illinois. In a short time he wrote as follows: "I have been engaged for two months (February and March, 1832) as agent for the American Education Society, and as I am about to engage in the Indiana Branch of the Presbyterian Education Society at New York, I report the result of these two months, viz:

an addition of more than one hundred members to the State Society, ten of whom are life members at $10; the rest pay one dollar annually. I have collected money in the following places, viz: Bond County, $27; Montgomery, $34; Vandalia, $35. Madison County, $76; Greenville, $16; Jacksonville, $70; Collinsville, $38. The winter has been severe, traveling difficult, meetings small.

The next year 1833, he was prosecuting his agency in Indiana, his family residing meantime at Jacksonville. The town was visited during July and August by the cholera; and Mrs. Ellis and their two children were swept away at once. The husband and father, constantly traveling, had not heard from them for two months. Having heard that the pestilence had reached Jacksonville he started homeward at once, alone and on horseback, his anxiety increasing every hour. He was just setting forward one day after dinner, when a man rode up whom he recognized as a townsman. "How long have you been from home?" inquired Mr. E. "About two days." "Do you know anything of my family, sir?" "Mr. Ellis, your wife and children are all dead and buried!"

Years after, in relating it, the stricken man said, "Oh, I can never express the loneliness, the unearthly abstractedness, and finally the sweet submissiveness of that afternoon. At first I was staggered and stunned, but before night God seemed nearer to me and Christ dearer than ever before." Such a crushing calamity might well break down the strongest man. Those who saw him then seem to have been divided between sympathy for his unspeakable sorrow, and wonder at the faith and fortitude which he exhibited under it.

Among these coming to Jacksonville in 1831, was a promising boy of fifteen named Robert T. Cassell. He came with his father's family and here pursued a common-school education for five years and then was married to Miss Nancy Butler of Sangamon County. After his father's death that year, 1835, he lived in Woodford County until 1868, acquiring as well as inheriting much property and gaining quite a reputation as a lawyer. In 1866 he was elected to the Illinois House of Representatives, and in 1868 received the appointment of United States special agent, making his home in Chicago and Philadelphia.

CHAPTER VI.—1837–'43.

The First Secret Societies—Prospering Schools and Churches—Crime and Criminals—The Earliest Railroading in the West—The Incipient Wabash—County and Town Officers—The First State Charitable Institutions.

"Gather up each foot-fall of the trodden way
All the tender lispings of the by-gone day."

"I hear the tread of pioneers,
Of nations yet to be,
The first low wash of waves, where soon
Shall roll a human sea."

THE first ramification of any secret order in Jacksonville was established in July, 1837, Illini Lodge, No. 4, I. O. O. F., being then founded, before there was any Grand Lodge in the State, by Thomas Wildey, Past Grand Sire of the United States, from whom a dispensation was received, and by whom, in person, the lodge was instituted.

Thus "Illini" is one of the oldest and has since become one of the largest Odd Fellows' lodges in the State of Illinois. The charter members were George Hamilton, George Darlington, Josiah M. Lucas, Matthew McBride, Wm. Davis, Mike Rapp, J. Burns and Sam Michael. This lodge was instituted in the old jail building on North Main street, where it met for some three years.

From the old jail the lodge was removed to a room over what was then known as Wilkinson & Bancroft's store, on the north side of the square. Before the year was out some trouble arose, the charter was surrendered, and meetings suspended. July 1st, 1839, the lodge was revived, a new charter being granted, dated August 1st, to the same parties. Then the members moved to the third story of the building now occupied by Wm. Russel on the west side of the square. From there it was removed to the old Coffman building, now occupied by F. H. Stebbins. The next change was to Chambers' building, on the north side of the square. In 1863 they took possession of a fine large third story hall in the Adams-Smith building. Lastly, all the Odd Fellows societies moved into their new hall in the McDonald Block, north side of the square, which is one of the finest, largest and best furnished lodge rooms in the State. This new hall is rented and furnished jointly by all the bodies, and is leased for a period of fifteen years.

Since its organization, Illini lodge has expended for charities (sick benefits, and death benefits for widows and orphans) about $40,000. During this time the lodge has lost only forty-seven members by death. From its organization over 800 candidates have been initiated, and there are at present over 240 active members. The members embrace many leading and reputable citizens, some of whom have been honored with high positions both in the order and in the State.

Harmony Lodge, No. 3, A. F. and A. M., was the second secret organization formed in Jacksonville, and from its birth to the present time has had a pleasant and prosperous career. It was instituted October 4, 1841, the first officers being as follows: John Gregory, Master; Matthew Stacy, Senior Warden, and George Hackett, Junior Warden. In giving the places of meeting of this lodge the other Masonic bodies are included from their organization—all using the same hall.

The first lodge room was the third story of Goltra's building, on the southwest corner of the square, occupying the same from 1841 to 1850. This lodge then joined with the town and placed the third story on what is now the second ward school house. This hall they continued to occupy for eight or ten years, when they sold their interest in said third story to the city and moved their hall to the third story of the building now occupied by Eppinger & Lehman. From there, in 1868, they removed to Gallaher's Block, on West State street, which they occupied ten years. In 1879 they changed their hall to Broadwell's Block, on South Main street. There they are now located, and have one of the best, most convenient and handsomely furnished lodge rooms in the state. This lodge has now an active membership of 100.

At the Jacksonville Female Academy Miss Price was succeeded, as principal, by Mr. John Adams, afterwards LL. D., who had had a long and successful career as a teacher at the east, first for fifteen years in the Academies of Canterbury, Plainfield and Colchester, Connecticut, his native State, and then for twenty-two years as head of Phillips' Academy, at Andover, Mass., an institution of high grade, designed to give preparation for the colleges of New England and even for advanced standing in them, therefore requiring the best scholarship; and, as well, the highest qualities of a cultured Christian manhood; likewise rendering necessary the utmost skill and prudence in the exercise of government and discipline. All these qualifications Mr. Adams had, in an unusual degree. The great work of his life was done at Andover. While connected with that school he had under his care an aggregate of more than eleven hundred pupils, of whom about one-half afterwards graduated from colleges; and, to say nothing of other learned professions, more than two hundred of that number entered the ministry. Mr. Adams came west, preceded by a great reputation as an educator of youth.

Dr. Glover says of him: Already advanced beyond the age of threescore, it is presumable that he thought his work nearly done, and was meditating only what might concern the welfare of his family in the coming evening of his days; but on his arrival in Illinois he found that he was still in demand, and that opportunities of special usefulness and of giving to his life-work a more rounded fulness, were by no means wanting. The principalship of this Academy was offered him. He accepted it in February, 1837, and his school opened May 17th, with twenty-three pupils. He entered upon the work with much of the enthusiasm of his youth, being assisted in it by his cultured daughters, Emily and Phebe, teachers brought up under his hand, and readily seconding his views and methods. Mr. Adams had a long experience in educating, but he had no experience of the sort that was dawning upon him. He had taught in male, but not in female Academies. Girls direct from the prairie, the timber, and the creeks, and about as wild as any of the creatures which in the early days had their homes in those haunts crowded about him. Their manners were ungainly, their provincialisms were barbarous, and it was a question whether the venerable pedagogue from the neighborhood of Boston would understand such material or be able to make anything of it. But he saw the situation at once, and, unlike some in their profession, had the good sense and grace to adapt himself to it. He perceived no difference between the youth of the east and of the west, but such as resulted from circumstantial causes, and he well knew that the work upon which he was entering was the very work by which alone the scale could be re-adjusted and the equal balance restored. His policy in dealing with wild girls was first of all to win their hearts, then he had them secure and could mould them to any form he pleased. Love was the power by which he subdued them; this was his only threat, this his only penalty; he had no occasion to call in parents or trustees to help enforce authority. Often the wrong-doer was melted by his tender manner and tearful eye, often she threw her arms about his neck in token of unqualified and happy submission. His will was like iron, but his heart had all the soft tenderness of childhood. His law was like that of the Medes and Persians, but it was law in the hands of a mediator.

The school greatly flourished under his care, but as catalogues were not published and records are missing, it is impossible to give any exact statistics of that part of our history. But it is known that the numbers in attendance were such as rendered the completion of the building necessary, and it was accordingly completed and made ready for use toward the close of Mr. Adams' administration. The Academy under him was still in its forming period; struggling toward shape, and order, and classification; aiming at a regular curriculum, and a higher standard; also beginning to venture in the direction of artistic and ornamental branches; but the transition was slow, and Mr. Adams had the honor of laboring at the problem where its difficulties were greatest. His term of service continued six years, or until the spring of 1843, when he retired from the work of teaching in which he had been almost continuously engaged for forty-eight years. But even then his work was not done, but for ten years he traveled and labored incessantly in an agency for the American Sunday School Union, accomplishing what would have been marvellous had he been in his prime, and not already past the boundary of human life. It is meet that they who live thus should live long, and we cannot be surprised that where there was such wisdom there should have been such length of days. Mr. Adams died in the 91st year of his age, April 24th, 1863.

Rev. W. H. Williams, A. M., succeeded to the principalship of the Academy in 1843. He had been for a short time pastor of the First Presbyterian church and was a gentleman of liberal culture and finished manners, and, aided by his accomplished wife, he did much, during his five years of service, by way of promoting classification with reference to required courses of study looking to graduation, thus stimulating the ambition of pupils and encouraging them in the pursuit of a more lengthened, systematic and thorough training. Primary and advanced departments were organized, the latter including junior, middle and senior classes with distinct lines of study running through three years, with the promise of honorable testimonials at the end of that period. Painting and music were more formally introduced than before. Daily records of scholarship, manners, deportment, were kept and the result disclosed at the end of each term. Regular study hours were appointed and enjoined. Catalogues were published and scattered abroad; public examinations were held.

Mr. Adams was aided by his two daughers, one of whom, Mrs. J. H. Bancroft, survives. Mr Williams was aided by his wife, Mrs. Abby L. Williams, Miss Lucretia H. Kimball, Miss Catherine Murdock and Miss Marie P. Fitch.

At the Academy semi-centennial celebration in June, 1880, Mrs. Emily Adams Bancroft, who came in 1837 and is still spared to a life of usefulness and honor among us, gave some interesting reminiscences from which we quote as far as they relate to the period considered in this chapter:

As one of the early settlers, and a witness to the many trials through which pioneers are called to pass, you will permit me to pay a tribute of love and affection to that noble band of men and women, who stood so firmly for truth and battled for the right—persons of enlarged views and generous with their means, laying the foundations of society broad and deep. A few of these are still spared and are with us to-day: their children and other residents are enjoying the benefits of their labors. The thousands who now live in this city do not and cannot realize the struggles of the few hundred, who came to this place to establish institutitions of learning and build our churches. They laid their plans not on the narrow scale of that age and this world, but with a wise reference to all coming time. They were thinking of the millions of immortal souls who were to occupy this western valley, of the future influence of their exertions, and that other generations would soon sit in judgment upon their works. I am thankful that I am present on this occasion, and can testify to the earnest, self-denying efforts of those to whom we owe so much.

Many of the customs, habits and fashions have passed away, and of some of these we are glad. We shall never forget our feelings as we approached this building forty-three years ago. It was standing solitary and alone, with but one house between it and Illinois College. No trees, or grass, or shadows. Our parlor was in the basement. The second story was the school and recitation rooms; the third sleeping apartments; the fourth the attic. We could roam and ride over this prairie with not a house or fence to obstruct our passage. We were homesick and sad, but as we had been four weeks traveling day and night, we did not care to retrace our steps. Our mirrors (in whose face we had often gazed) were crushed, our tables and chairs broken; all for a few days seemed desolate. Soon the furniture was mended, the Brussels carpet (the third brought to this town), was spread, and happiness and cheerfulness filled the place. We are glad to-day that the old east wing has given place to this large and commodious building. We never passed this spot without admiring it; for the taste and neatness displayed, for the beautiful lawn, and the dear old trees, but dearer than all is the old basement. It was there, morning and evening, we gathered around the family altar, while the dear old father read from the book he loved so much. There, we spent our evenings in social chat with the young gentlemen, (now the grey-headed men of our city). There, in her youth and beauty, my sister was married. There the farewell word was spoken. Though all else be removed, let not the tender associations connected with the old basement ever pass away. We found here some educated, refined persons. The people generally were hospitable, free, easy, sociable; in some localities a fear was expressed at the importation of so many Yankees. All were on an equality as to houses. Log cabins, basements, smoke houses, were occupied; anything, which would afford a shelter. Some of the most pleasant parties were in those good old times. Friendships were formed, which have continued, cemented by age, severed only by death.

The style of the dress of the western people was peculiar, in size shape, quality, etc. Six yards of calico were ample for a dress, no trails or overskirts were worn. The *old* fashion has given place to the *new*, the plain skirt to the polonaise, with its ruffles and plaits, its hoops and bows and fringes, its beads and bugles and jets, its velvet and passimentary trimmings, until we lose sight of the wearer and gaze upon what is worn.

The sun bonnet, so universally worn, was made of calico or gingham, with pieces of pasteboard, in size and shape like a lath, removed at pleasure. This has given place to the turban, or to the crown, with a front turned up at one side, or both, worn either on the front or the back of the head, or sideways, or to the almost invisible hat. *Surely* "the *fashion* of this world passeth away."

It was very difficult to arrange or organize a school, there was such a diversity as to *what* and *when* certain studies should be pursued; a restlessness and uneasiness for fear of too much or too little taught. One instance on this point will suffice. A man called one morning, saying to my father as he entered the room, I *have came* to see if you are qualified to teach my daughter. "What do you wish her to study?" "I don't want no arithmetic, I don't want no grammar, I want geometry, geology, philosophy, and rhetoric." "Well," says my father, "I will examine her, and see *what* she is prepared to study." "I don't want *her* examined," he said, "I have *came* to examine you." "Well, please proceed." After asking a few questions and receiving ready replies, he said, "I think *upon the whole*, you will do." About two weeks after, two ladies called. "We hear you are about to form a class in Natural Philosophy?" "Yes," was the reply. "We do not think young ladies should study the sciences; if they can read and spell, write and count, it is all they need to know." We thought the examination of teachers had passed away, but we hear that in the public schools of our city, they are examined and re-examined quite frequently.

We take pride in the musical taste and the appreciation of art, *high* art in our city, and justly too; but this is not all *new*. We had music and drawing in those old times. When we came here there were six pianos in the place. Dr. Beecher brought the first. The one rented by the Academy was from London, small, having five octaves. Its legs resembled in size and general appearance, a modern stick of candy. It gave forth uncertain sounds, sometimes discordant but never in harmony. With all our tuning, we could not get it up to concert pitch without snapping first one, then another of the strings. I say *we*, for we then did our own tuning. The first music teacher was a young lady from Philadelphia, Miss Dwight, now Mrs Wolcott, who is with us to-day. She taught classical music, too. Mozart, Beethoven, Mendelssohn and other music so popular at the present time. My sister gave some lessons in drawing, but the first one who organized a class was Mrs. B. F. Stevenson, who, with some of its members, is present. The first geranium brought here adorned the basement window of the old building. This can be proved by Mrs. Wadsworth, who has since shown her fondness for flowers. A slip was given her, with the injunction to watch it, and see it put forth little tendrils. She was faithful and pulled it up each night to see how much it had grown through the day. The first calla lily was brought by Mr. J. O. King. The musical circles, the Art Association and Horticultural Society, must remember that they are enjoying what was commenced years ago in this Academy.

The subject of female education was agitating the public mind then as now. We have neither time or inclination to dwell upon this theme only as it relates to the establishment of this Academy and the formation of the Ladies' Education Society. That we may fully appreciate the motives, which brought them into being, we must invert the telescope and take a view of this town and surrounding as it then stood. These prairies, covered with flowers which bloomed and faded, had but recently been trodden by the foot of civilization. Five years before, the logs were drawn to erect the first building in this place. Illinois College was in its infancy. Small communities, which could not boast the name of villages, were found here and there in different parts of the sate. Influenced by social feelings, they had brought their houses near together, while their farms were scattered far and wide. Moral dearth was visible amid the luxuriance of an earthly paradise. No Sabbath, no sanctuary, no school. Families were found with four and five adults; not one could read. There were in the Southern and Western States not less than 1,400,000 children destitute of common school instruction: forty-six counties in one of our Western States, in which there was not a single female teacher. It needed no prophetic eye, as they glanced over those boundless fields and saw the tide of emigration pouring in to see the rise of towns and cities, and to imagine the time when they would be surrounded by a dense and still increasing population. With the exception of Carrollton, an unbroken prairie lay between this place and St. Louis—the northern part of the State was then the home of the Indian. The Catholics were selecting places where to establish institutions. A few benevolent ladies were aroused to action, resolved to labor 'till the cloud of mental darkness was rolled away.

In Illinois College new teachers were employed and new hopes were entertained. Then followed the financial crash of 1837, ruining most of the subscribers and making their paper worthless. For ten years the struggle continued, the college became more and more involved financially, until, in 1848, it cleared itself from debt, by giving up the larger part of its property. Rev. Edward Beecher, D. D., served as president from 1831 to 1844.

This panic of 1837 was the greatest money panic that ever occurred. The banks all suspended, and until 1840 there was no money seen. But they lived through it, and we honor the energy and enterprise which survived it all. It yet remains with the younger men of to-day to occupy the land with equal energy. They should say that they are chips off the old block, and determined to do as well as their fathers did.

By 1840, according to the United States census, and notwithstanding serious drawbacks the population of Jacksonville numbered 1900.

The town trustees during this period 1837-'43 inclusive, were:

William Miller, 1837; Wm. P. Warren, 1837; George McHenry, 1837-'38; Garrison W. Berry, 1837-'38; James Dunlap, 1837; Samuel W. Prosser, 1838; Philip Coffman, 1838; Nathan Gest, 1838; Matthew Stacy, 1839-'40-'41; John Hurst, 1839-'40-'41-'42; E. T. Miller, 1839-'40-'41-'42-'43; *Wm. Branson, 1839; Robert T. McNeely, 1839; *Isaac D. Rawlings, 1840-'41-'42-'43; Cornelius Hook, 1840-'41-'42-'43; Peter Hedenberg, 1843; John Henry, 1843.

The result of the elections during the period embraced in this chapter was as follows:

1837.—For creating Cass county, 300; against creating Cass county, 479. For Representative to fill the vacancy caused by the resignation of Stephen A. Douglas—John Wyatt.

1838-'40.—For Congress, John T. Stuart beats Stephen A. Douglas 115 votes. For State Senator, *Wm. Thomas. For Representatives, John Henry, John J. Hardin, Wm. Gilham, N. Cloud, W. W. Happy. For Sheriff, A. Dunlap. Coroner, Anthony Arnold. County Commissioners, W. L. Sergeant, John White, Wm. Woods.

1839.—For Probate Justice, D. Pat Henderson; County Recorder, James McKinney; County Clerk, Joseph Heslep; County Treasurer, John Green; County Surveyor, H. Saunderson; County Commissioner, Isaac Ward.

1840-'42.—For State Senator, John Henry; Representatives, Jeremiah Cox, J. Parkinson, J. J. Hardin; Sheriff, Ira Davenport; Coroner, Robert Saunderson; County Commissioner, George Engelbach.

1841.—Congress, John T. Stuart, re-elected; County Commissioner, Harvey Roatt.

1842-'44.—State Senator John Henry; Representatives, Newton Cloud, Wm Weatherford, David Epler, Richard Yates; Sheriff, A. Dunlap; Coroner, Samuel Reaugh; County Commissioner Jacob Ward.

1843.—County Recorder, Josiah M. Lucas.

Newspapers and periodicals have not been supported with the degree of patronage that we would naturally expect from such an educated centre. It was not until long after the population was large enough to need a local press that the first attempt to establish a weekly newspaper was made. Afterwards quite a number of efforts were made, and proved failures. But the first paper of which we can hear that continued any length of time was the *Illinois Patriot*, with J. G. Edwards as editor and proprietor. In the latter relationship he was succeeded by Geo. Duncan. In 1838 Josiah M. Lucas became the owner. He changed the name of the sheet to the *Illinoisan*, and for a while Buckner & Hardin (Col. John J.) were the editors, afterwards Lucas himself. Contemporaneous with the *Illinoisan* was the *Jacksonville Standard*, a democratic sheet, published and edited by S. S. Brooks, of the *Quincy Herald*. It ran a course of two years and fainted away for want of circulation, but afterwards revived for a spell only to soon die *sine die*.

Mr. Lucas continued in control of the *Illinoisan* until about 1843, when he was elected recorder of Morgan county, which office he resigned. He was re-elected that same year and retired from the *Illinoisan*.

Major Lucas, later in life, became the representative of his government in Foreign lands as United States Consul at Tunstall, England, and to-day is a resident of St. Louis, Missouri.

*Now living here.

As giving an insight into affairs in 1838 we will quote from an issue of his paper, of November 10th, when A. H. Buckner, was associated with him as editor. The first editorial is to the familiar tune of "Pay Up." The patrons are informed that it takes no small amount of cash to buy paper, ink, etc., and "*to pay our journeymen*." It seems that the paper then had a weekly circulation of 1,200.

A quotation is made from the Springfield *Journal* announcing "the departure of the postmaster at Pekin for Texas," with $600 of the people's money.

"Is not this," says the *Illinoian*, "carrying out the sub treasury scheme? What a glorious band of fellow laborers against the bank will be found in the young republic of Texas; all boasting how they have profited by this experiment of the 'powers that are!'"

And is it at all surprising that such fellows should be warm in the support of Van Buren, etc. There is also considerable denunciation of "Loco foco" leaders and presses.

In State news we find that Mr. Gong has been elected to the Lower House from Macon county, vice Dr. Reddick, deceased; that Gen. James Turney, of Greene county, has been appointed to the Galena land office, vice H. B. Truett, resigned; that Bishop Chase has located a college on the Vermillion river, LaSalle county, near Ottawa, styled the "Jubilee College;" and that a branch of the State bank has been located at Belleville.

Reference is made editorially to "a rencontre at Burlington, *Iowa Territory*," to the election of Hon. S. S. Phelps as United States Senator from Vermont, and of Jennison, the Whig candidate, for Governor by 5,507 majority.

Nathaniel Coffin has a column communication in regard to Illinois College, in reply to an article previously published, with manifest tendency to injure the College in its pecuniary concerns as well as its general character." He gives this scrap of history:

"This seminary was opened January, 1830. It was then a mere school for young men and boys and was opened for all, without regard to age, and almost without regard to qualifications. It began with nine and gradually increased in numbers till 1835; it then had become a college," etc., etc. He says also that "Catalogues have been yearly published in the month of January, commencing in 1835, and on examination of them I find the number of regular college students, commencing with that year and ending in 1838, to have been eight, sixteen, twenty-six, thirty, thirty-three, and thirty-seven."

It might properly be mentioned that Major Lucas is the only man now living who was an eye-witness of the alleged duel Mr. Lincoln and J. W. Shields, across the Mississippi River, at Alton, in 1842. Details of that now almost forgotten "affair of honor" are still present to his mind, although he is rather reluctant to call it up out of the past, where, as he says, it is as well it should be buried. The idea of Abraham Lincoln going to the field armed with a broadsword to fight a duel seems to those who knew him in his later days, so inconsistent with his pacific character, that many have doubted the authenticity of the story. But it verily did occur, says Major Lucas, who rode down to the spot, and was there when the affair was amicably adjusted.

The challenge of Shields arose out of a quizzical newspaper article, which was written by the sister of Mrs. Lincoln, who yielded a peppery pen. This gave such offense to Mr. Shields that he went to the editor and demanded to know who the writer was. The editor of the paper was in a quandary, and, meeting Lincoln on the street, asked him what he had better do. "O," said Lincoln, "just tell Shields that it was me." The editor sent a challenge to Lincoln, who had just gone to Tazewell county to attend a lawsuit.

Lincoln accepted the challenge, and the weapons selected were broadswords, which Uncle Abe knew well how to handle, having been thoroughly drilled in its use by Maj. Duncan, a brother-in-law of Maj. Lucas. The field selected for the combat was near Alton.

Major Lucas possesses a great many letters of Lincoln, written in a free, off hand spirit, and full of spirit and anecdote, which would be quite interesting to read now, only they are of a private nature, and the major would not be induced to give them publicity.

Before we leave the political field we should note the fact that Jacksonville was peopled by many who were in conscientious and hearty sympathy with the earliest efforts to rid this land of the curse of human bondage. An anti-slavery society was in existence in the county in 1822, and the "underground railroad" had an oft used station in this vicinity. At the famous Lovejoy convention held in upper Alton, October 26-28, 1837, among the members enrolled were the following from Morgan county: Edward Beecher, Elihu Wolcott, Wm. Carter, E. Jenney, A. B. Whitlock, and J. B. Turner. The convention was broken up by a mob of outsiders, but next day a State anti-slavery society was formed. In the election of officers Mr. Elihu Wolcott was chosen as president. An "address" to the people of the State was issued, prepared by Messrs. Wolcott, Beecher and Carter, all of Morgan county.

In regard to the first day's proceedings, with charming innocence the newspaper report, at the time, reads:

"In consequence of a number of disorderly persons, the convention did not duly organize until the afternoon." There is nothing more about martyrdom than this, which seems to have been a full enough statement that the rioters broke up the meeting at one time. The call for the convention, signed by Elijah P. Lovejoy, touched on the fact that the *Observer* press had been three times destroyed in Alton in the space of a little more than a year, calling thus to the mind the history of that series of abuses which culminated in the tragical death of Lovejoy.

In May, 1842, Rev. Wm. H. Williams was installed as pastor of the First Presbyterian church, succeeding Rev. Ralph W. Gridley who had been installed April 25, 1837.

The Methodist churches during these years were under the care of the eccentric but consecrated backwoods preacher Peter Cartwright, who was presiding elder from 1836 to '43. The pastors in charge of Jacksonville station were: 1837, J. T. Mitchell; 1838, John P. Richmond; 1839, W. D. R. Trotter; 1840, Thomas W. Chandler; 1841-'42; W. M. Grubbs; 1843, Chauncey Hobart.

They worshiped in their first brick church until 1838 or '39, when they sold it to be used as a chair factory and erected a more commodious church on the south side of East State street, where the marble front now stands. This church was dedicated by Peter Akers, D. D., who preached the dedication sermon from the words, "This is the house of God, this is the gate of heaven." This house they occupied until the centennial year of Methodism in America, 1866, when they dedicated their present house of worship, at a cost of $35,000.

The congregation, small at first, grew in numbers during all these years, and it was known as the Methodist church of Jacksonville. When the Grace church was organized, being on the west side of the city, it was called the West Charge, and the church of which we are writing was called the East Charge. By this name it was known until the erection of the present church, when it was, in commemoration of the year of its erection, called the "Centenary Methodist Church."

In 1836, for the Church of Christ, a house of worship was erected, and from this date until 1850 some of the prominent ministers were D. P. Henderson, John T. Jones Jerry Lancaster, Bryson Pyatt and Elder Trimble. In 1850, a larger house of worship was erected on North Main street. The first pastor there was Elder A. J. Kane, now at Springfield. His successors were Elder Jonathan Atkinson, W. S. Russell, John Underwood, Dr. Cox, and Enos Campbell. The congregation began to hold meetings in its present church, on East State street, under Elder Campbell, who remained until 1873, when he was succeeded by Rev. J. W. Allen, and he by J. Mad Williams, L. W. Welch and A. N. Gilbert. The membership is now four hundred and fifty, and the Sunday-school two hundred and fifty.

In 1838 occurred the division in the Presbyterian church in the United States resulting in what was known as the "Old School" and "New School" organizations. The Jacksonville Presbyterian church, like many others throughout the land, was rent in twain by this division. There were three elders in the church at the time of the division: Wm. C. Posey, David B. Ayers and Daniel C. Pierson. Mr. Posey and a minority in the church sympathising strongly with the Old School Assembly, adhered to that body, and carried their cause before the Synod of Illinois, which met in Peoria that year

We learn from the Rev. Dr. Harsha's historical discourse delivered April 26, 1874, that "this church was found, after the division, to embrace forty-two members, only three of whom are living, viz: Huram Reeve, Jane Branson (Mrs. Wm.) and Eleanor E. Chambers (Mrs. George M.) The church secured the services of Rev. Andrew Todd, (who died in 1850) of Flemingsburg, Kentucky, who entered upon his labors in the autumn of 1838." They worshiped first, for a few months, in a frame building which stood on the north end of the lot on the square on which the Park House now stands, the use of which was given by Gov. Duncan without charge, afterward the Congregational church edifice was secured at a nominal rent. This edifice then formed the rear portion of the building on the east side of the square, used by Messrs. Johnson & Son as a furniture store, afterwards known as Union Hall and finally destroyed by fire. In the mean time preparations were made for the erection of a sanctuary for themselves.

In the year 1840, about two years after the division of the church, a frame building on West State street was completed—the lot having been donated by Colonel John J. Hardin, as his subscription at a cost of eighteen hundred dollars. In this sanctuary the congregation worshiped for nearly thirty years, leaving it only a few months before entering the lecture room of the present building, in 1871.

Dr. Harsha summed up in 1874, as to the church's growth: "In the thirty-eight years that this church has maintained its separate existence, 688 persons have connected themselves with it, and enjoyed its privileges and fellowship. Of these, 342 have been brought to Christ through its instrumentality."

Since the division in 1838, this church has had four settled pastors. Rev. Andrew Todd, labored with great zeal, earnestness and self-denial, from November, 1838, until failing health compelled him, in the autumn of 1849 to seek a warmer climate. The hopes of his greatly attached people, of his immediate family, and of his wide circle of friends and admirers, were not, however, to be realized. He continued to fail, until on the 2d day of September, 1850, in the 51st year of his age, he fell asleep in Jesus, at Casa Bianca, near Monticello, Florida.

Rev. Truman M. Post, D. D., was pastor of the Congregational church from 1840-'47, as well as professor in Illinois College. He was their second pastor succeeding Rev. Wm. Carter.

Before we leave the year of grace, 1838, we must give a pen picture by "Father" James Hussey, to the *Journal:*

In the fall of the year 1838, as I was standing between the then court house and the market house, a young man put his hand on my shoulder and said; "Old man, we want you to go to old man ——— and splice a couple." He led me to a log cabin; an elderly lady met me at the door and said: "You will lose no time, for supper is now ready." I took a look at the room, and saw an elderly couple, and three young ladies, and as many young gentlemen Each lady had a dress made partly of wool, and partly of cotton, home manufactured; the gentlemen were dressed in a similar way. The room was furnished with a table and three benches, (home made,) an iron spoon (filled with lard and a shred of cotton) that was stuck in a crack in one of the logs, supplied the place of a lamp.

I took off my hat and said: "You that wish to be joined in wedlock, stand up and join your right hands." One of the ladies and gentlemen arose. The splicing and kissing were soon over, we then sat down to supper. We had a nice corn cake baked in the skillet, ham and eggs nicely fried, coffee make of corn, no sugar, plenty of nice sweet cream, a clean cloth on the table We had a merry time; and I think I never enjoyed a supper better. As I was retiring the young bridegroom followed me to the door, and in a whisper said: "I cannot pay you to-night, it took all the money I had to pay for the license; but I will pay you as soon as I can." In a few days I met him; he smiled and gave me a dollar, and said: "I got this with chopping." Thus, the bridegroom went on his wedding tour chopping, and the bride went playing music, on that musical instrument, the spinning wheel.

I lost all trace of them from 1838 until 1873. As I was traveling on the road I met a splendid carriage, a fine pair of horses A gentleman and lady and a pretty girl sat in the carriage. I was gazing at the carriage, thinking what a pretty turn out it was, when lo! it stopped. The man spoke to me; I got out of my buggy, took the slate from my pocket and said, "I am quite deaf." He wrote on my slate, "What is your name?" I told him my name; he then wrote, "I thought it was you, but you look old." We had ten or fifteen minutes' chat. He gave me to understand that they were the couple that were spliced in the log cabin in 1838. I said, "Is that your daughter?" He said, "No, she is a grand-daughter." He gave me a present and we parted. I have not seen him since, but I have often thought since I saw him how truly did Dr. Franklin say, "He that by the plow would thrive, himself must either hold or drive."

As to his coming to Morgan county, Mr. Hussey writes:

In the year 1838, I with five other Englishmen, saw Jacksonville for the first time. We all traveled from the north of Jacksonville twelve miles in a wagon, we got into the square, we tied up our horses, my companions looked around, and began to laugh and said "Is this Jacksonville? Why it's nearly as small as a village." They went into the grog-shop and I into the market house. It was empty at the time, and with my pencil I wrote these lines while sitting on a bench in the market house. When they came out of the hell hole I let them see the lines. They said I was a softy

Here are the lines:

Just pause a moment when you look at me,
And think what I was thirty years ago;
Can you imagine what I then must be,
Known only as hunting ground for who?
Savage tribes then only tread my plain,
Or howling wolf and wild beasts of prey—
Now look and think what you can find to say.

View me when thirty more years are gone;
I then may stand a monument of wonder,
Like some great city I may become
Loaded with wealth, but not with plunder,
Even I may then be called a city.

At present, 1884, there are living in Jacksonville seven persons who have been residents of the city since 1828, and in October 1883 one of their number, Mr. Foreman, published the following lines entitled: "Reminiscences of 54 Years and 10 Months."

The world moves on
The years roll slowly by;
Youth comes of age,
The aged droop and die.
New faces crowd the ever bustling scene
And tell to one what I have been.
My old friends are wrinkled, bald and grey,
And I advancing grow old as they.
Yet my thoughts oft backward flow,
To memories of 54 years 10 months ago.
Ah, oft when busy recollection plays,
Mid by gone scenes,
What fancies rise familiar to the call?
What memories all my faculties enthrall?
What various visions of Jacksonville 54 years, 10 months ago?
Where are they now?
Some have risen high.
Aiming their arrows even at the sky;
Some have been wayward and gone astray;
Some hold the even tenor of their way.
Some are recorded with immortal name,
With gilded letters on the scroll of fame,
Many have departed; a few remain, of 54 years, 10 months ago.

The names of the seven referred to are Matthew Stacy, William Thomas, Smiley Henderson, Anderson Foreman, Mrs. George Richards, Mrs. Charlotte Chappel, Mrs. E. T. Miller.

Writing of old settlers we should refer to Philip Stringham, born 1794. He came to Ohio from New York in 1836, and two years later reached Jacksonville, and found lodging in one part of a house occupied by Mr. James Cooper, who was postmaster then. Joseph McCaslin was the first man he became acquainted with. Mr. McCaslin was one of Jacksonville's oldest citizens and a fine, genial man. His second acquaintance was the late Dr. Reed, whose life still stands out grandly in our midst. Murdock, Coffman, Milburn, Bancroft and, we might mention a score of others, were also among his old and highly esteemed friends and acquaintances. Some of his old friends still survive, while most of them have gone to the echoless shore of great Eternity. He became afflicted with asthma about the year 1845, and continued to grow worse until 1856. Dr. Reed, his physician, advised him to go over the "plains," which he did the same year. He reached Salt Lake City with his family in September and found himself perfectly free from his old trouble, asthma, but environed by such a state of things as soon resolved him to return to the states again. He landed again in Jacksonville early in September, 1859, where he is now residing in 1884.

The first indictment for murder in Morgan county was found in 1839, at the June term of the circuit court. It was against John A. Hall for killing Robert Denny, by stabbing him in the left breast with a large pair of shears. He was tried in November, 1839 and found "not guilty." Wm. Brown was State's Attorney, Wm. Thomas, Judge, and Josiah Lamborn, Attorney for the defendant.

The second murder case tried in the county was George Gardner indicted in Scott county in May, 1841, for killing Philip W. Nash by shooting him in the heart with a shot gun. The case came to this county by a change of venue. John S. Greathouse was state's attorney and the defendant had John P. Jordan as his attorney. The case was tried in July, 1841, and the defendant was found guilty by a jury and sentenced by Judge S. A. Douglas to be "hung by the neck until dead," on the 23rd day of July, 1841, between the hours of twelve o'clock noon and three o'clock p. m. This is the only person ever sentenced to be hung in this county. The execution did not take place, however, as the prisoner escaped from jail a few days before the time of his execution and has never been heard of since.

Among "old settlers" reminiscences we might quote Mr. A. J. Thompson, as follows:

There has been a great improvement in many things in this country. I was not here in the earliest times, but I was here in time to have seen many and great changes in this country. I have been almost persuaded to believe that this part of the country has been more highly favored than other sections, but it is probably because I am more intimately acquainted here. In the olden times a man would rig out a plow, harness and all necessary rigging to go to work, and the only iron used was the bridle bits and the plowshare, and sometimes they used rope for bridle bits. One of the greatest meetings that was ever held in this county was that assembled to consider the propriety of putting through a railroad in this county. In the olden times there was everything to encourage us if it was rude.

Mr. Thompson, as noted above, refers to the railroad meeting, a subject which we must now consider at some length, because the laying of those rails was indeed an historic occurrence of much more than local interest.

Mr. Thompson came to Morgan in 1834, and says:

They had no wagon roads, no railroads, except those they made by taking some of Uncle Sam's timber to lay in the mud. There was a little railroad laid before that from Jacksonville to Meredosia. It was built in 1836, about a mile out from Naples, and there was a tremendous ado made about it. He supposed it could make that mile out and back in less than half an hour! It was about that time that the first steamboat came up the Illinois River to Naples, and when she blowed off her steam every horse all over this country broke loose and ran, and it was three weeks before some of them got back.

Of this railroad the four men taking prominent part in the laying of the first rail were Col. James Dunlap, Prof. J. B. Turner and Senator Richard Yates, of Jacksonville, and George B. Plants, of St. Louis. Mr. Plants and of the Jacksonville gentlemen drove the first spike, and Senator Yates made an address upon that occasion.

Rev. Levi Crawford, of Bloomington, formerly an Illinois College student, in 1881 contributed to the Lincoln (Ill.) *Herald*, the following about this and connected occurrences:

In the year 1836-'37, one Charles Collins, an enterprising but somewhat visionary citizen of St. Louis, took in hand to build a railroad from Naples on the Illinois River to Jacksonville. I am not sure but his plan took in Springfield as the terminus.

Well, the survey was made and the forces gathered to build the road. We began at Naples, threw up a road bed as far as the slough, about two miles east of town, then we put down ties and laid upon them rails of white oak, six inches square. These were fastened to the ties by oak or hickory pins. *Not a particle of iron was used* in the construction. In this way the road was built until we reached the slough; and that is as far as it ever went, under the corporation of Charles Collins.

Upon this railroad there ran but one car, and it was not a locomotive, but a simple four wheeler, drawn by gray horses. Poor fellows, they are dead and gone long ago! Well, the road was finished, as I have said, to the slough, and was in readiness for the grand Fourth July celebration in 1837. Let me tell you something about that celebration. It was a grand affair The celebration was held in a grove of "black jacks" up on a sand ridge in the northeast part of the town. The stage was built under one of the trees, the tree being used as a support.

Early in the morning, the people began to gather from all quarters, making a great crowd. There was a cavalry company, I believe from Jacksonville, I am not sure, but think John J. Hardin was the captain. Well do I remember their gay appearance as they came prancing out upon the green where stood the old church, built by the Collins brothers. They came at the call of a bugle blown by a little man dressed in a red suit and mounted upon a bay horse. After the company had galloped around for awhile, the little man in red with the bugle, got off his horse and came and stood on the platform where the band was. Then they gave us "Hail Columbia" in grand style. Then some one got up and read the Declaration of Independence Then the band gave another tune. Then the orator of the day was introduced. I remember just how he looked—a slender boy without beard, blushing like a girl and with his knees smiting together like that old Babylonian king's.

Well, I did not know much about oratory then and have learned but little since; but I made up my mind that he had done "first rate," for a boy; and I think all the people thought so, too, for they swung their hats and yelled like Indians. Some of the men on the stage took him by the hand and congratulated him on his success. I remember of hearing some one ask who that boy was. The answer was, "Dick Yates, a young chap from Jacksonville."

After the speech the great ones went down to the hotel where dinner was prepared for the select few. After dinner there was music, speeches and toasts. I was outside, but remember one toast given by Gen. Hardin: "Naples—the great commercial emporium of Illinois The time is not distant when she will cover the plain to the Bluffs, which will not be able to confine her; but she will burst the bounds and unite with Jacksonville and they shall become, in fact, what they are to-day in heart." I do not give the exact words, but such was the sentiment. Alas! the prophecy was never fulfilled. Naples had reached her pinnacle of glory on that day.

In the afternoon the grays were put to the car, upon which had been constructed a frame work for seating the magnates The band was put aboard and also the president of the road—I believe—and the orator and a few others and away they sped across the prairie for two whole miles with banners flying and music filling the air. As I walked home through the dust, I met the returning excursionists, and it was a grand sight—such as Illinois had never before seen. And I venture the assertion that it was the first railroad excursion ever given in Illinois, made on Illinois' first railroad. As I have said, the railroad was never built further than the slough, under the Collins management; for that same year the company, which was made up of one man, failed and left the laborers in the lurch. Sure am I that I am one of the creditors of the concern still; the last pay I received was twenty pounds of soap grease, weighed out to me by the boss after the laborers had all left. This I turned over to my mother, and quit railroading.

The Hannibal branch of the Wabash uses the old Collins road bed. If that corporation wishes to confer any favors upon the laborers who built that first road and never got their pay, or if they feel that they inherited the obligations with the property, I would say, "Gentlemen, please send me a ticket for a free ride over your road, and you shall have a receipt in full!"

Mr. Editor I have some very distinct recollections about that other road, built after the same pattern with a strap on top of the oak rail. Well do I remember seeing the first locomotive ever brought to Illinois make its trial trip from Meredosia to "Dickinson Lake," as it was then called; filling the tender with a hand pump. * * * * * *

Almost every one whom I have heard speak of this matter "the first railroad in the west" has insisted that it was the old road, built by the state from Meredosia, on the Illinois River, to Springfield, and that it was built in 1839. In fact I have just read an account of the arrival of the first train to Jacksonvile, furnished by some of the old residents of that city. * * * * *

That was not the first railroad in this Sucker state. I claim the honor of having helped build the first railroad that was laid down or thrown up, in this great state.

The following is probably some such account as Mr. C. refers to, which went the rounds of the press:

"The first railroad train ever run in Illinois made its appearance on the first railroad in the state, which extended from Jacksonville to Meredosia. This was in the fall of

1839, and the day was a memorable one. Nearly all Morgan County had, according to accounts, assembled in the public square to witness the arrival of that wonderful first train. School children had been given a holiday and the daily labor was everywhere neglected except in the shops in the town.

The public square was filled with teams, and when the engine steamed into the square making all the noise possible, there was such a stampede of horses as was never before heard of, nearly every team breaking loose, and at least one-third of the vehicles in the county were broken, and many of the people were as much scared as the horses at the steaming monster as it came rushing up into the square."

There were then 23 miles of railroad in Illinois. Now the county is crossed by the Chicago & Alton, the Wabash, St. Louis & Pacific with the Peoria branch, the Jacksonville Southeastern and the C. B. & Q., which goes through Chapin. Two have their termini in Jacksonville, and there are several trains run for the accommodation of this city.

But of this old road, the track took its course down what is now known as West State Street, and directly through the center of our public square. Those who have made Jacksonville their home for many years remember well the sensation which was created when the iron horse first came puffing and blowing down State Street. Not such a locomotive, to be sure, as we have now, but for all that a novelty, and the same persons doubtless remember when the engine was discarded and mules took its place, and also, when the road was abandoned, and the rails extending through town were torn up. Many of the ties, which were left in their places and covered with dirt were unearthed by the men who were digging the trench for the sewer, on State Street in 1880. They were but a short distance below the surface of the earth, and were, of course, so badly decayed that they fell to pieces when struck by the pick-axe. They were arranged in as regular order as when first laid down, and for some distance not one was missing.

An eye witness reports that when the Jacksonville & Meredosia road was first completed, an excursion was planned from this place to Meredosia, the railroad men promising to return the train by sundown. The train, by the way, consisted of two common passenger cars and several sand cars. The excursionists had a merry time at the river, and in fact were enjoying themselves so much that they did not get started on the return *voyage* until about sundown. Then came the tug of war—the engine was by no means a powerful one, the grade was rather steep, and in the language of our informant, "every time they came to a leaf or a twig on the track, the engine couldn't pull them over, and all hands were obliged to get out and *push*." Of course they made but little headway, and when midnight came they had accomplished but half the distance At this juncture the conductor slyly unfastened the coupling which joined the cars, and away went the engine with the two passenger cars, leaving a terribly enraged crowd upon the platform cars. The engine and favored few arrived in Jacksonville about daylight, and then it started back after the remainder of the load. When they reached the place where the remaining cars had been left, the engineer found that they had all been pried off the track, and thrown into a ditch by the maddened passengers, who were, in consequence, obliged to walk home.

Gov. Duncan, in his message to the general assembly in 1835, uttered this significant thought: "It is yet to be determined whether railroads will be more benefit to the state than the Illinois and Michigan Canal."

At that session Wm. J. Gatewood, a state senator from Gallatin County, and a man of eminent ability, was one of many who earnestly opposed legislation in favor of railroads, but, nevertheless, the agitation continued, and in 1839 the completion of the first railroad in the state, known as the Northern Cross Railroad, was celebrated. It extended from Jacksonville to Meredosia, a distance of twenty-four miles; it was built by the state and laid with flat iron. In 1841 it was extended from Jacksonville to Springfield. In 1847, or later, the road was changed from the square to its present location.

As to the construction and operation of this incipient Wabash system, known first as the Northern Cross Railroad. The contractors to whom were awarded the bids for the construction of. this road were Miron Leslie, T. T. January, Charles Collins and James Dunlap. Ground was first broken in Meredosia in 1837, with great ceremony and in the presence of a vast concourse of citizens. Speeches were made by Mr. J. E. Waldo and Hon. O. M. Long. Mr Daniel Waldo was selected to dig the first shovel ful of dirt, which he did amidst the shouts of the multitude. This labor so exhausted himself and the multitude that no more work was done that day. On the 9th of May 1838, the first rail was laid at Meredosia, and the first engine was put on in October, set up and on the 8th of November the first puff of a locomotive was heard in the great Mississippi Valley, and the first turn of a wheel made, eight miles of the track were completed, and the first train ran to the extent of the completed track and back, carrying Daniel Waldo, Joseph E. Thompson, Engineer Fields and Joseph Higgins. This trip greatly delighted those interested in the road and as greatly astonished the dwellers along the line and all day wondering crowds of gaping rustics, stood and gazed on the "thing" and wondered what made "ze wheels go wound." Among the first engineers was the late Verien Daniels, whose encounter with a belligerent Taurus, is quite amusing. In February 1842, the first train of cars from here went into Springfield, and the Sangamo *Journal* of March 11th, of that year, boasts of the immense utility to its citizens and the traveling community of getting from Springfield to St. Louis in a day and a night! Wagons were a thing of the past, so far as speed of travel was concerned. The route to St. Louis was from Springfield to Meredosia by the train and from Meredosia by steamer to St. Louis. The road, though accommodating, would not pay and when at one time the engineer ran the engine off the track, east of Jacksonville, it was abandoned and lay there nearly a year. It was afterward bought by Gen. Semples, of Alton, and a new set of wheels, with tires about two feet wide placed thereon, and it made one trip from Alton to Springfield as a steam road wagon. The two broad parallel tracks over the prairies were thought to be the tracks of some huge serpent and two men actually followed it to Springfield to see "what kind of a critter it might be."

Mr. J. W. Lathrop relates of this road:

The first engine used on this road was called the "Pioneer," and was about as powerful as a good-sized tea-kettle, and frequently got stalled with one freight and one passenger car. The road was finished only from Meredosia to Jacksonville, and sometimes they made a round trip in twenty-four hours and sometimes in forty eight hours.

Many of the country people called it the "bullgine." I never knew the reason why unless it was because a two year-old bull, owned by a family who lived about three miles west of town, would some times dispute the right of the way, but was finally overpowered and killed, which so exasperated its owner and his wife that they put soft soap on the track, which effectually stopped the train.

After the abandonment of the engine, mule power was brought into requisition to haul the cars, but the travel on stage line surpassed the "mule railroad," and the road bed went unrepaired, the strap rails were stolen for sled soles, and in 1847 the road was sold, at the door of the State Capitol, to Col. T.Mather, N. H. Ridgely, James Dunlap and ex-Gov. Joel Matteson for $100,000—one-tenth its original cost. The purchase money was paid in state bonds issued in aid of its construction, which the state was obliged to accept, though not worth twenty cents on the dollar. The new organization went vigorously to work, repaired the road-bed, put down the "U" rail, purchased three new engines, new and better cars, removed the track from our public square and State Street to the present site, north of the city, and by the autumn of 1849 daily trips were made between Meredosia and Springfield. From this primitive beginning, the different sections of the now Wabash road started, and finally came the mergement of them all into the great Gould system, one of the main thoroughfares of the commerce of the nation.

A railroad incident of those days now under consideration is as follows:

At one time the Great Western Railroad wished to pay off its hands on the section west of Jacksonville. Early one fine morning the pay car was furnished with funds and started on its mission. Soon after its departure the morning mail was opened at the office and the "detector" at once sent for. It revealed the rather startling fact that nearly all the funds in the pay car were worthless. Nothing remained but to telegraph to Jacksonville, stop the car and order its return to Springfield, and the workmen went without their pay, that time at least.

The people who live in this day of greenbacks and National bank notes, have little idea of the trials and tribulations of the unfortunates who existed during the reign of wild cat banks. A business man was required to keep his "detector" at his elbow, and frequent editions of this book were required to keep pace with the failures. It frequently happened that a farmer would board a train at a way station, offer his fare to the conductor, who, on consulting his book, found that the bill was worthless, and the unfortunate agriculturist, having no other funds, had to be carried free.

Elder E. G. Rice, still living a few miles west of our city, once said in a public address:

Fifty years ago, and I for the first time gazed on the tall wild grass of our prairies. In the olden times if a man got three or four miles from the timber he thought he had an everlasting fortune, but how is it to-day? I saw the first engine that was plied between Springfield and Naples. They started it with the crow-bar, before they would try the strength of the steam on the machinery. If in the short space of forty-five years so much has been accomplished, what may we expect in the next fifty years? I dreamed last night that I was standing with some friends when I saw a huge eagle pass far above us and smoke was coming from the top of its head. I asked my friend what that was and they said that there were three men in that machine. It was an aerial conveyance. This was only a dream, but such a thing in the next fifty years would be no more wonderful than what has been done in the last fifty.

Col. George M. Chambers, one of the few earliest settlers of the city still living here, said, in 1884, to an interviewer of the *Illinois Courier:*

"In 1837-'38 real estate in and near the city was about as follows: Farm from $20 to $40 per acre; after the crash, owners still held on in hopes of better times. The same lands sold in from 1840 to near 1848 for whatever was offered. The Bradshaw estate was sold in 1846, from $7 to $15 per acre; Chestnut farm is part of it, and the Rector homestead is also part of it. The estate of Smedley was sold about 1848. The homestead, now the Insane, brought about $20 per acre. I had offered him $40, he wanting $50. His other lands, on Sandy, brought from seventy-five cents to $1 per acre. Vacant lots, and lots with small houses, nearly worthless, owners leaving them vacant and they were destroyed by others. One instance; a house and lot on East Street sold for about $45. The buyer afterwards burned up the flooring and joists, and left it. One more; the eighty acres north of town, adjoining Capps's old factory, was mortgaged to the State Bank for $8,000. After the bank's failure the certificates were worth, first, about twelve and one-half cents; went up to forty cents; I was offered it for $80 per acre in certificates; tried to get my father-in-law to buy it; he declined. Well, you ask, why did you not buy it? Because I had all I could do to pay my own indebtedness. As for other things, being in business, we put out our bill of prices in 1841: $1.75 for hogs weighing 250 lbs.; $1.50 for 225 lbs.; $1.25 for 200 lbs.; $1 for 150 lbs. It being a bad crop year many small ones were bought as low as seventy-five cents per 100; these, if we had thrown them into the river when weighed, would have made us money. Dewees, west, the Cassell neighborhood, east, and the Routt neighborhood, south, refused the offer, and drove to Alton and sold at our offer there, and even at these prices, all lost heavily."

Question.—"What was the general condition of business here when you came to the country?"

"Everything was flush and on a boom, every man bought all the land he could get hold of, and many of them did in this way: At that time the State Bank was permitted to loan money on land, at, say, one-half its value. A man would enter land at $1.25 per acre, handle the appraisers so that they would call it worth $5, and then take the money borrowed, and enter more lands. Of course this kind of business assisted in the destruction of the bank. The crash commenced in the east in 1837, and soon came west, and was the result of over trading. Everything soon became flat. Unimproved lands dropped from $15 per acre to nothing, and other things in proportion. For several years money was very scarce and people had a very hard time. Everything was done by barter and a silver dollar looked as big as a grindstone, and it was, too. People had enough to eat and wear, such as it was, but the man who was in debt had a hard time."

Mr. J. W. Lathrop has also contributed to the local press recollections of those days from which we extract as follows:

When I came to Illinois game was quite plenty. Deer were often seen grazing with the cattle south of the mound, where Mr. Rice and Mr. Samuel Killam now live, their range being in the timber of Sandy Creek south, and the Mauvaisterre and Indian Creek north. At one time—I think in 1838 or '39—I was riding with J. O. King to Manchester, our horses walking leisurely along in Sandy timber, when within gunshot at our right, we counted fourteen fine deer feeding quietly upon the early spring grass. On our return in the afternoon they were still feeding nearer the road, and a part of them crossed the road just before us. Venison was sold at seventy-five cents to one dollar for the loin and two hind quarters; wild turkeys, twenty five cents each; prairie chickens, fifty to seventy-five cents per dozen; quails were usually sold at twenty-five cents per dozen, although I have known them sold three dozen for fifty cents, and wild pigeons the same price. Potatoes, twelve and one-half cents; turnips, ten cents; corn, ten cents; pork, two cents; eggs, three cents; butter, eight to ten cents.

For many years prairie chickens were very abundant quite near town. I have been out to where the Insane Hospital now is located and shot as many as three or four birds, and got back to seven o'clock breakfast. I usually shot from my horse and never killed more than three at a shot. In the winter of 1836 and '37 they used to come from what was then called "Duncan's big field," northwest of town, to the College Grove, and to Elm Grove (as Gov. Duncan then called his residence) to roost. Gov. Duncan, who was a good shot, once saw a lot of prairie chickens sitting on a rail fence, and returning to his house, took his shotgun and killed fourteen at a single shot.

In 1843 we bought wheat at thirty-five to thirty-seven and one-half cents delivered in Jacksonville; forty cents delivered at Naples, Meredosia, Beardstown, Bath and Havana. We bought one thousand barrels of flour of Ira Davenport and C. Mathews, at $2.25 per barrel, delivered at Naples. We also bought quite a lot of pecan nuts, all of which we shipped to New York, having chartered a steamboat which we loaded on the Illinois River for New Orleans, where we re-shipped on vessel for New York, where we sold the entire cargo, and, counting our exchange at ten per cent. premium, we made $22 profit on the entire lot, and considered ourselves lucky, as we had paid our debts east previously, paying twenty-five per cent premium for exchange. At that time we could get no sacks to ship our grain in; there was no railroad with grain cars as now, and we had to get barrels to ship in. I think we bought one thousand from Mr. Hinrichsen and one thousand from a Mr. Arnold, of Exeter, recently deceased. Some years we bought hemp and wool, to make our payments in New York and Philadelphia with, and even up to the time of the Mexican war, at which time Mr. J. H. Bancroft and I were in business together, we bought hemp and wool to ship to meet our payments, which we always did, one hundred cents per dollar, though we sometimes lost money on what we shipped.

As an incident of these times it is narrated that:

In the year 1843 a Mr. H. A. Crittenden came here and lectured on Millerism, and quite a number were made to believe that the world would be destroyed by fire that year.

A man by the name of Phillip Haynes, who lived just northwest of town, heard about it and, as his reputation was not above reproach, he was very much worried about his prospects in the hereafter. About that time a large bell had been placed in the tower of the Congregational Church, and on Saturday night it was all ready to be rung. Several of those present tried it, but no one but J. O. King could "set the bell," and of course a terrible clatter followed, as one after another tried to set it as King had done.

Haynes heard the bell and, with his family, was terribly frightened, so much so that he could not sleep.

The next morning at nine, King rang the bell again for Sabbath School and just at that time, Haynes was mounting his horse to go out deer hunting. He was frightened worse than before, dropped his rifle, ran his horse to the nearest neighbor, by the name of Darius Ingalls, and asked him if he heard the strange noises in the air, and if so, what it meant?

Ingalls, who was something of a joker, told him the day of judgment had come, and the sound was to wake up the dead.

Haynes believed it, and early Monday morning was in town trying to sell his farm, but would take nothing but gold or silver. He sold out and moved to St Joseph, Mo., then a new settlement, squatted on Congress land, and in a few years the town had become so large that churches were built and bells placed upon them.

The Sigma Pi Society of Illinois College, has the honor of being the first literary society to be organized not only in that institution, but in "the Athens of the West," since then so prolific of such associations.

Samuel Willard and Henry Wing entered college in 1840 and became room-mates.

Their apartment became the centre of spontaneous conversational gatherings of members of classes of '42 to '46, wherein topics of literature, theology, politics, philosophy, &c., were discussed. These informal meetings led to the formation of "Sigma Pi" just at the close of the school year '42-'43. The constitution was a paper originally prepared by Willard and Wing. From its official catalogue issued in 1882, we learn that its membership to that date, 663, includes 87 of the then alumni of the college. Its roll of patriot dead during the war for the union, numbered 10, out of the 104 that were in the volunteer service of their country.

The following items of the "Tip and Tyler" year, were compiled for the *Journal* by Mr. Ensley Moore, of our city.

Wm. Hamilton kept a bakery, Joseph Capps had recently established himself in the wool-carding business, E. T. Miller was a prominent carpenter, David Cole and James Cosgrove were blacksmiths, B. F. Gass was a carpenter, J. S. Anderson was a cabinet maker as was Wm. Branson, D. B. Ayers kept a drug store, Robert Hockenhull was clerking for Reed & King (J. O.) druggists, Thos. W. Melendy was a carpenter, Matthew Stacy sold harness, Talma Smith came to town with his father, Thomas Smith, who was a shoemaker, James Buckingham was a plasterer, David C. Creamer, Samuel Hunt and William Lewis were tailors, Cornelius Hook was a merchant, Israel, Taggart & Smith were another firm, Col. Jas. Dunlap, of the firm of January & Dunlap, was building the railroad, as contractor, Jonathan Neely was in the same line, Edward Scott was farming near town, and Wm. H. Broadwell was learning his trade as blacksmith.

Josiah M. Lucas was editor of the *Illinoisian* and the Goudy's had a job office.

Rev. T. M. Post was in charge of the Congregational Church; Rev. R W. Gridley was pastor, (and succeeded by Rev. Wm. H. Williams,) of the First Presbyterian Church, and Rev. Andrew Todd, of the Second Presbyterian, which finished its church building this year, (1840.)

The First Baptist Church was organized in 1841, by Rev. Alvin Bailey.

John T. Jones was, probably, elder in charge of the Christian Church.

The Methodist society worshipped in a brick church on Morgan Street, near East Street.

Rev. W. G. Heyer was rector of the Episcopal Church.

John Cooper was postmaster, and charged 12½ cents per quarter year for box rent.

A. F. and A. M., Harmony Lodge, No. 3, was chartered.

The Jacksonville Mechanics Union loaned money at 12 per cent. per annum in 1841.

E. T. Goudy and Miss Catherine McMackin were united in marriage, July 1st, 1840, by Rev. L. Lyons.

Drs. M. M. L. Reed, Nathaniel English, Thomas Munroe, Archimedes Smith and Henry Jones were prominent physicians.

Reed & King's store was in Goltra & Stryker's building, southwest corner of the square.

Hard times were very fashionable. One house and lot purchased in 1840 depreciated one half in value during next two years.

John Adams, LL. D., since known as "Father Adams," was principal of the Female Academy.

The following boys entered Illinois College, in September: D. S. Baker, Rochester; N. Bateman, College Hill; T. K. Beecher, Walnut Hills, O; Wm. C. Merrit, Winchester; John T. Morton, Quincy; Wickliffe Price, and W. H. Sigler, Jacksonville; H. W. Starr, Alton; C. F. Thayer, Springfield.

Board was furnished students at from $1 to $2 per week. Those who desired it could "get plainer board at a cheaper rate." Washing cost 50 cents per dozen. The total annual expense of a student was estimated at $103, excluding clothes and books.

John T. Pierce offered his services in preparing young men for college, terms $5 per quarter. His vacations were to be six weeks from August 1, one from February 14, and one week from May 11.

Jacksonville luxuriated in a daily mail, and people paid 25 cents postage on a letter from Philadelphia, and 12 cents from Quincy. Postage was paid by sender, or recipient, according to the sender's notion or pocket.

There was a branch of the State Bank of Illinois situated in Jacksonville, of which Henry D. Town was teller. In 1840 Mr. Town was married to an estimable young lady of this place.

Imperial tea sold at $1.50 per lb., butter 12½ cents per lb, molasses 50 cents per gallon, candles 19 cents a lb., flour $4 per bbl., in 1840.

In 1841, oak wood was cut for house use at 62 cents per cord, white lead sold at 12½ cents per lb., chickens 13 cents each, domestic at 12½ cents per yard, a horse was used three days for $1.60, calico cost 31 cents per yard, sugar 12½ cents per lb., one venison ham, cured, cost 75 cents, spool cotton 8 cents, black satin ribbon 19 cents per yard, pearl buttons 10 cents per dozen, bleached shirting 25 cents per yard, cotton velvet 75 cents per yard, eggs 6 cents der dozen, "1 dozen bunches Loco Focos 63 cents," bacon 6¼ cents per lb., coffee 20 cents per lb, brown Holland 38 cents per yard, black bombazine $1 per yard, figured bobinet 76 cents per yard, skein silk 12 cents, 1 pair boot lacings 6 cents, starch 19 cents per lb., Seidlitz powders 50 cents per box, linseed oil $1 per gallon, arrow root 74 cents per lb., British lustre 13 cents, castile soap 38 cents per lb., 1 corn broom 25 cents, whisky 40 cents per gallon, sperm candles 62 cents per lb., eggs 5 cents per dozen.

"The Morgan House" was what is called the Park now, and it was a "stage office" The Western House, corner West State Street and the square, on Central Bank location, was also a favorite stopping place

Dennis Rockwell's residence, now occupied by his son Charles, was the only noticeable house between the Ellis House now Mrs C. McDonald's, and Governor Duncan's "seat." Duncan's house, Mrs. McDonald's and Mrs. Dr. Cassell's, were all built about 1836.

John B. A. Reid's father owned most of the land between Rockwell's and Caldwell Street, and there was a "run" across State Street between L. W. Chambers' and W. S. Hook's houses.

Boys going to college from town had to climb the fence to get into the college lot, opposite O. D. Fitzsimmons' house.

Wm. C. Swett had a printing office in the town.

August 13th, Ira Davenport was elected sheriff and Robert S. Anderson, coroner. This was at the general election, which occurred earlier in the year than now.

Before the building of the present admirable system of water works, Jacksonville was without an adequate supply of this most necessary article in case of an extensive conflagration. Volunteer firemen and other citizens promptly turned out when a fire alarm was given, and generally subdued the flames and saved their homes from destruction. The legislative act of 1835 for the incorporation of fire companies led to the formation of the first regularly organized fire company, on the 23d of April, 1840.

The names of its members show that its numbers were composed of some of the best citizens of the place. The buildings were generally of wood, mostly of a small size, and but few disastrous fires occurred. Their equipment consisted of a double-decked hand-engine. It was a very heavy "machine," and required quite a number of hands to work it. The same engine, with some improvements, is still used when occasion require. In addition to the old "Union" engine, the company had several hundred feet of hose, buckets, ladders, axes, and other necessary equipments. As the list of members comprising this company will be of interest to the readers of these pages, it is here inserted. Since that company was organized one of its members has been a United States Senator, another a member of Congress, several mayors, two judges, several town trustees and aldermen, two postmasters, one sheriff, several county assessors or clerks, one United States consul-general, several trustees of state and educational institutions, while nearly, if not all, have been prominent and useful citizens. We doubt whether any community ever had a better fire company. Those marked * are now numbered with the great company in the Silent Land:

James Berdan,* Morris Collins,* J. D. Stone, A. V. Putman,* Stafford Smith, Jos. O. King, James H. Lurton, B. B. Chamberlain,* Robert Hockenhull, Thomas Anderson,* James Stark, William French,* William Branson, John Hurst,* D. P. Palmer, Orlando C. Cole, John Fisher, J. A. McDougall,* Nicholas Milburn,* Patrick Cresap,* J. Johnson, Samuel Galbraith,* F. Campbell, J. McAlister,* John W. Goltra,* C. B. Clarke, I. D. Rawlings, Timothy D. Eames,* Henry Keener, J. Harris, Morton Mallory, F. Stevenson,* I. S. Hicks,* William S. Hurst,* G. A. Dunlap,* J. S. Anderson, Benjamin F. Gass, B. F. Stevenson, D. A. Bulkley,* A. C. Dickson, B. R. Houghton,* S. Hunt,* James Hurst,* William G. Wilson, Geo. Henry,* S. H. Henderson, Moore C. Goltra,* Phillip Coffman,* R. S. Anderson,* John Mathers,* J. W. McAlister, R. Bibb,* Michael Rapp,* Geo. M. Chambers, William H. Corcoran,* J. A. Graves, L. Berry, John W. Chambers, H. S. Carson,* J. Harkness,* David Smalley, M. A. J. Hunter, A. Smith, William Smalley, W. W. Happy,* J. T. Jones,* Cornelius Goltra, Stephen Sutton,* W. Patterson,* F. C. Sutton, A. Lohr,* J. Cosgrove,* William C. Gwin, W. Akins,* E. T. Miller,* John Henry,* John Gregory,* L. Filson, Eli Harp,* W. B. Warren,* W. Braidwood,* A. W.

Tilford,* J. M. Lucas, J. J. Cassell,* C. Ogle,* J. B. McKinney, W. C. Swett,* W. B. Lewis,* Joseph Gledhill.* W. C. Scott, A. B. Hathaway, M. Dulany, John Freeman.*

The earliest facilities of Jacksonville were quite meager compared with those of to-day. When the town was created, and a few families had established themselves therein, a postoffice was of necessity required, for people loved to write then as well as now, and were only deterred in the number of letters by the rates of postage and the facilities for transmission. The postage on a letter was twenty-five cents, and generally paid by the receiver. Money was a scarcer article then than now. The United States Government did not receive "coon skins" or beeswax" in payment for postage, and it was not an uncommon affair for a letter to lie several months in the office before the person to whom it was addressed could raise the required twenty-five cents. When the express companies came into existence, they began to carry letters for a less rate than the United States mails, which department lowered the price of postage gradually until it reached ten cents per letter. This was thought to be a great reduction by the people, and the number of letters began to increase very rapidly. Jacksonville received, at first, a mail from St. Louis, brought by stages once in two weeks. Another route was established from Springfield west through Jacksonville to Meredosia, and thence on to Quincy. By the alternation of these mails, a weekly budget of letters and papers was received in town, and the people thought themselves well provided for in this way.

The postoffice in town was kept in various stores, shops, or offices, removed from time to time, as a change in administration and postmasters occurred. As time passed on, a semi-weekly mail was secured, then a tri-weekly, and, finally, by the time the first railroad was built, a daily mail had been firmly established. The number of daily mails increased as facilities for transportation were furnished.

With one more topic we close this chapter. It is a subject vitally connected with the history of the city, the location here of the state charitable institutions of Illinois, which to-day add more than 1,000 to our population.

In 1838-'39 the representatives from Morgan county in the legislature consisted of William Thomas, William Weatherford, and William Orear, senators, and J. J. Hardin, Newton Cloud, John Henry, John Wyatt, William Gilham, R. Walker, representatives.

Judge Thomas says:

Hon. O. H. Browning, senator from Adams County, having prepared a bill for the establishment of a *Deaf and Dumb Asylum*, leaving a blank for the place of location, presented it to me for examination, and to secure my assistance in its passage. Approving of the object as well as the bill, I proposed filling the blank with "Jacksonville," assuring Mr. Browning that all the delegation from Morgan would give the measure a hearty support; relying on members and supposed influence, he consented to my proposition.

The bill required as a condition to the location, "a donation of five acres of ground suitable for the use of the institution." It appropriated, in aid of the institution, one per cent. annually on the interest of the school, college and seminary funds, amounting then to about $6,000. The bill was introduced by Mr. Browning and read at length (not by the title) on three days, and passed the Senate without one word of debate or discussion, or even the calling of the yeas and nays.

In the House it met with considerable opposition. The appropriation was reduced three-fourths, making it equal to about $1,500. And, out of abundant caution, a clause was inserted that the legislature might repeal the section making the appropriation.

Thomas Carlin, Daniel G. Whitney and Thomas Cole, of Adams County; Ottawa Wilkinson, Samuel D. Lockwood, Joseph Duncan, Dennis Rockwell, William Thomas, Julian M. Sturtevant, George M. Chambers, Samuel M. Prosser, Porter Clay and Matthew Stacy of Morgan County; Richard F. Barrett and Samuel H. Trent, of Sangamon County; Cyrus Walker, of McDonough; B. F. Morris, of Hancock; William E. Withrow and James M. McCutchen, of Schuyler County; and Thomas Worthington, of Pike County, were appointed directors.

The citizens of Morgan County purchased and donated to the institution about six acres of ground, on which the building now stands, at a cost of about eleven hundred dollars. Subsequent to the organization of the board of directors and the election of officers, all the directors residing out of Morgan County resigned. The annual appropriations being too small to justify the contracting for a building, the money as received from the state treasurer was deposited in the branch of the State Bank of Illinois at this place, until it accumulated to a sum deemed sufficient to justify the commencement of a building. In 1843 a contract was made for the erection and enclosure of what is now the south wing of the building.

The nucleus of the Illinois Institution for the Education of the Blind, was a school for the sightless unfortunates, organized by a few citizens of Jacksonville, and supported by private donations for one year, when the state legislature placed it on a permanent basis by an act of incorporation, approved January 13, 1843.

Mr. Samuel Bacon was the first principal; though blind himself, he was engaged to teach the blind in this city.

Dr. Joshua Rhoads was elected superintendent in August, 1850, and continued in office until his resignation, in August, 1874, a period of twenty-four years. He was succeeded by the present superintendent, Dr. F. W. Phillips.

The school was first opened in the house of Col. J. Dunlap, which was rented for that purpose until the buildings for which the legislature had made provisions could be erected. This building was placed on ground purchased by Col. Hardin; it was burned, however, in April, 1869. A new building was immediately erected by Messrs. Bruce & Loar, contractors. The present building will accommodate one hundred and fifty pupils, but the present number in attendance is 130.

Dr. Phillips, the present superintendent, has been well chosen for his present position, and from the flourishing condition of the school, it speaks well of his management.

Stephen A. Douglas, of this city, was secretary of state of Illinois from November 30th, 1840, until his resignation February 27th, 1841; was appointed judge of the supreme court of the state of Illinois February 15th, 1841, resigned June 28th, 1843; was elected member of Congress that year and served through that term (the 28th); was elected for the 29th term, and resigned his seat April 7th, 1847, and was elected to the United States Senate that year to succeed James Semple, and served in the Senate by re-elections till 1860. He died June 3, 1861. He never was in the Illinois State Legislature but once and that was 1836-'38.

"The little giant," was one of our best known citizens for several years. Having attended academy and studied law in Canandaigua, N. Y., until in 1833 the mighty west with all its vast opportunities opened out on his vision. On his journey westward, he stopped at Cincinnati, Louisville and St. Louis then on to Jacksonville. Casting about for occupation, he received and accepted a call to teach school at Winchester, obtaining forty pupils for a three months tutelage at $3.00 each per quarter. He devoted his evenings and spare time to perfecting his law knowledge, and at the close of the school term he was admitted to practice by the supreme court of the state and opened his law office in Jacksonville. In 1834, when not quite 22 years old, he was elected Attorney General of the state by the Illinois Legislature, and in 1836 was elected to a seat in that body from Morgan County and first met president-to-be Lincoln at the opening of the session in Vandalia in December of that year. After the adjournment of the Legislature in 1837, he was appointed register of the land office in Springfield, and removing there he and Abraham Lincoln became neighbors.

In preparing matter for this volume, we have endeavored to strictly follow chronological order, but have found it impossible, because after the opening chapters were in type and advance or proof sheets read, much additional information came to us, which we insert at the close of a chapter regardless of date in order not to have it omitted.

Mrs. Frederick King, now of Austin, Minn., who formerly resided here as Miss Julia M. Eddy, daughter of the pastor of the First Presbyterian Church, writes to us of 1844-'46 as follows:

"My father came in 1844—he mowed a path from our house back of church to the church. W. C. Goudy, Talmage Collins and J. B. Shaw graduated in 1846."

And Mrs. B. F. Stevenson, formerly of our city, writes as follows from York, Neb.:

"I would say I had the *first sewing machine* in a private family brought to the place. Mr. Goodrick, the tailor, had one in his shop but did not like it, and I believe did not use it long. He told my husband sewing machines were of no account, and in a short time mine would be thrown away with the rubbish. But he proved a false prophet, as I used it for many years and have never since been without; am now using the third one. I think I brought the first *collection* of house plants, but of this am not sure. Unfortunately they were short lived.

"The firm of F. & B. F. Stevenson was established some five years before Mr. Eames sold goods. They sold *all sorts*; dry goods groceries, hardware, boots and shoes, &c., &c. They brought the *first piece of alpaca dress goods*. There are many things that might be interesting to future generations, if he were with you to speak about them. His recollections of the cholera are very vivid as he was one of a number that bound themselves together to stay in town and nurse the sick should the scourge visit the place. Since coming to York he has found one who often watched with him and helped bury many victims."

Not later than the fall of 1835, M. Stephen Gorham with four horses and a wagon and his oldest brother, J. Harvey Gorham with a wagon and five horses went to Chicago from Jacksonville and brought from there a load of cooking stoves for our citizens—the first that has been brought here. The Gorham's kept one apiece and delivered the rest to those that had ordered the new fangled things. Among them Matthew Stacy and Seth Weatherbee.

Joel Headington, D. W. Osborne and Phil Coffman, bought cooking stoves in the year 1837 brought by Phil Coffman at a cost $75 apiece.

Included in the "Springfield Baptist Association" are not only the Baptist churches of Jacksonville, Waverly and Berlin, of this vicinity, but the Diamond Grove Society—one of the oldest organizations in Illinois. It was constituted April 26, 1823, with twelve members. It is the oldest church connected with the Springfield Baptist Association and was one of the constituent churches of that organization. Among its earliest pastors were Rev. Jonathan Sweet and Rev. Joel Sweet, the former having been the first moderator of the association, and the latter one of its earliest missionaries, as early as 1839. Rev. Thomas Taylor was pastor in 1848 and the two years following.

From 1848 to 1856 the church was supplied with preaching irregularly.

In 1856 the Diamond Grove Baptist Church completed the erection of a house of worship.

In 1859 Rev. D. Lewis was engaged to preach one-half of the time, and served two years. These were years of more than usual progress in the church.

In 1862 Daniel D. Holmes was licensed by the church to preach, and was not long afterward ordained to the work of the ministry. He has served the church as pastor with great acceptance, and without interruption from 1865 to the present time, at which time the membership has reached the number of fifty.

ILLINOIS FEMALE COLLEGE. FOUNDED 1846.

CHAPTER VII.—1844-'57.

Illinois Provides for her Deaf and Dumb, Blind and Insane—Illinois College Fire.—Illinois Female College Founded—Arrival of Portuguese Colonists from Madeira—"The Forty-Niners" Start for California—City and County Officers—Church and Secret Society News—The Mexican War Volunteers—Death of Col. John J. Hardin—"Phi Alpha" founded—The Northern Cross Railroad.

But this—is present! On the fargone past,
Time's iron fingers pinned the curtains fast,
Shutting all human tracery from the page
Which mortals gaze on, in the present age.

Backward we turn us, with a timid look,
But the hand of ages had locked the book,
And laid the key in eternity's urn.

THE next six years—1844 to 1850—were marked with such an increase of business and population as might be expected of a place with its *railroad connections*, State Institutions and growing school reputation. At their close the census showed a population of 2,745. During the period town affairs were managed by the following named, as trustees:

Philip Coffman, 1844-'45-'46; Wm. Branson, 1846-'47-'48-'49; George A. Dunlap, 1844-'45; John W. Lathrop, 1846 and 1849; Michael Rapp, 1844 and 1850; Benjamin F. Gass, 1846; Richard Bibb, 1844; J. R. Simms, 1847; William G. Johnson, 1844, '46 '48-'49; Benjamin Pyatt, 1847; David A. Smith, 1845; John W. Goltra, 1847; Andrew Newcomb, 1845; James Hurst, 1847-'48; Joseph O. King, 1845-'48; Wm. N. Ross, 1848; Joseph H. Bancroft, 1849-'50; Andrew F. Wilson, 1849; Martin H. Cassell, 1850; Jonathan Neely, 1850; William Ratekin, 1850.

The results of the county elections are shown in the following:

1844-'46—Congress, E. D. Baker; State Senator, John Henry; Representatives, Francis Arenz; Richard Yates, Samuel T. Matthews, Isaac D. Rawlings; Sheriff, Wm. Green; Coroner, James Holmes; County Commissioners, H. Saunderson, Wm. Crow.

1845—Sheriff, Ira Davenport; Coroner, D. C. Creamer; Surveyor, Wm. B. Warren; County Commissioners, John Samples, D. G. Henderson.

1846-'48—Congress, Abraham Lincoln; Representatives, Newton Cloud, Wm. H. Long, Joseph Morton, Wm. Thomas; Sheriff, Ira Davenport; Coroner, D. C. Creamer; County Commissioner, A. Becraft.

1847—Probate Justice, Matthew Stacy; County Commissioner, Henry Saunderson; County Clerk, Joseph Heslep; County Recorder, Josiah M. Lucas; Assessor, James H. Lurton; Surveyor, George M. Richards.

1848-'50—Congress, Thomas L. Harris; Senator, Newton Cloud; Representatives, George Waller, Richard Yates; Sheriff, Ira Davenport; Coroner, David C. Creamer; County Commissioner, David L. Hodges.

1850-'52—Congress, Richard Yates; Representatives, Wm. Thomas, B. F. Bristow; Sheriff, Jonathan Neely; Coroner, Timothy Chamberlain; School Commissioner, H Spaulding.

In 1844 Dr. Edward Beecher resigned the presidency of Illinois College to Prof. Julian M. Sturtevant, identified with it from the very incipiency, and a member of its faculty to this day—forty years later. He served with the greatest acceptability as president for thirty-two years, that is from 1844 to 1876 and since then has been connected with the institution as professor of Mental Science and Science of Government.

In the autumn of 1846 the first steps were taken for the founding of the third educational institution of Jacksonville of high rank—the seminary for young ladies now known as Illinois Female College. It was established and is still successfully conducted under the auspices of the Methodist Episcopal Conference of this State. A committee composed of Revs. Peter Cartwright, Peter Akers, W. D. R. Trotter, Messrs. Matthew Stacy, Nicholas Milburn, Sr., Wm. Brown and Wm. Thomas, (previously appointed by the Conference,) met for the purpose of superintending the "establishment of a Female Academy," on the 10th day of October, 1846, and selected as a location a piece of ground on the south side of East State Street, in Jacksonville. The work of securing the necessary funds by donation and subscription had progressed so successfully that, in the fall of the following year, the contracts for erecting the college building were let. About the same time the school was opened in the basement of the Methodist Church, with N. S. Bastion, M. D., as principal. He filled the position until August, 1848. The building was completed in 1850; it was built of stone and brick, substantial and commodious—one hundred feet in length, fifty feet in width, and four stories in height. The "Female Academy" was opened for scholars in the fall of 1848, with Rev. J. F. Jacquess as principal, he filling this position for some years. The original charter being for an "academy" simply, it was decided, on account of the growth of the school, to apply for more extended powers, and accordingly, in 1863 a charter for the Illinois Female College was obtained, with full college powers.

The institution has suffered many times and severely from the effects of fire, the whole building having been at one time or another virtually destroyed in this way. The many friends of the college came promptly forward, however, and in each instance the damages were fully repaired.

The courses of study, classical, scientific and in music, vocal and instrumental, the fine arts, etc., are arranged and pursued with special reference to the wants of young ladies, and are equal to the same in similar institutions elsewhere. The domestic regime is on the home plan, the president and his family, and teachers living in the College and having charge, not merely of the intellectual, but the social and religious instruction of the students. Marked success has attended the operations of this institution from the first.

Over the sister female seminary, the Jacksonville Female Academy, the Rev. W. H. Williams, A. M., was Principal from 1843 to 1848. In 1845 the regular graduation of classes began; and never, for a single year, has failed from that time to this, a period of thirty-nine years. Mr. Williams died but a few years since at a good old age.

"Miss Lucretia H. Kimball, who had taught under Mr. Williams, succeeded him at his retirement in 1848, and had charge of the school two years, 1848–'49 and 1850–'51, the intervening year 1849–'50, being supplied by Miss Elizabeth Mead, as preceptress, during which, nothing special occurred, but the Academy moved prosperously on. Miss Kimball was equal to the place, exhibiting marked ability as well in managing as in teaching. She gave entire satisfaction to her employers, and was universally beloved by her pupils. All things prospered under her oversight, and she would doubtless have been continued in charge for many years but for the fact that personal charms so commended her to a young professor in Illinois College, Rev. Reuben S. Kendall, that he took her to himself, thus completing the good understanding of the two institutions which was begun in the days of the workshops, as above referred to. Prof. Kendall, as a kind of Prince Consort, for a time assisted his wife in the management of the school."

The above are the words of Dr. L. M. Glover, the Academy's life long friend, benefactor, chaplain, trustee, historian and President of Board of Trust for many years. In July 1848 the First Presbyterian society, which in the previous year had superceded its frame meeting-house with a more commodious brick structure, invited young Glover to visit them as a pulpit candidate. He was then preaching in Michigan, but came in October and began his ministry, being installed in November.

In 1873 he said of his coming: The journey hither, occupying the best part of a week, accomplished partly by rail, partly by coach, partly by canal packet and partly by steamer is quite in contrast to the journey now between the same points, all by rail, and occupying only twenty-four hours. At that time there was not a foot of railroad in active operation in this State, which now may boast from three to four thousand miles. In going to the meeting of Illinois Synod in the fall of 1849, which was held that year in the extreme eastern part of the State, the route lay across what seemed an almost interminable and uncultivated prairie, and the time occupied in going and returning was three days each, or a full week of working days; the same region is now traversed by numerous lines of steam travel, sprinkled over with fine farms and villages, and rapidly receiving its quota of a thriving and happy population. The State then had some eight hundred thousand inhabitants. Chicago, then as now, the gateway of the west, had a population of about forty thousand. Numerous little villages have become large towns and some of them respectable cities. Jacksonville, now numbering twelve thousand, then had about two. I will tell you how the place appeared to me at first sight. It appeared a very pleasant but a very unpretentious village. Among the public buildings there was not one that had any claims to architectural attractions. The old Court House, the old College, and the old Academy were very ill-looking as compared with the structures which have replaced them. The houses of worship were models of unstudied art, built to serve all needs but those of cultured taste, except our own, then new, which made some pretensions to style, but which, a dozen years after, the fire swept away. At present, however, we have to say that no town of the size east or west can boast of more spacious or beautiful church edifices than our own. Twenty five years ago the private residences of the place were with few exceptions small, low, unplanned, without the ornament even of a cornice, creations of necessity not of wealth or fancy, and yet many of them were really beautiful with the attractions of tree, and vine, and flowers, and green-sward without, and of neatness, comfort, intelligence, industry, good taste, and Christian hospitality within, the recollection of which in the midst of growing splendor with the usual decadence of early simplicity makes us almost sigh for what we have lost rather than boast of what we have gained. Jacksonville was called an Athens twenty-five years ago, and yet its whole stock of literary institutions consisted of Illinois College, Jacksonville Female Academy and one public school. * * * * * * * Twenty-five years ago this church had a nominal membership of about one hundred and fifty persons, one-third males and two-third females, which is about the usual proportion in the churches generally.

The Presbyterians of the "New School" Church had the ministerial services of Rev. L. M. Glover. In the "Old School" organization, after the death of their gifted pastor, Dr. Andrew Todd, who, under God, laid such a good foundation for their spiritual edifice, the Rev. J. V. Dodge was called to the pastorate. Mr. Dodge continued his labors but four years and a half; from the autumn of 1850 until the spring of 1855, when wholly at his own desire, the pastoral relation was disolved, greatly to the grief of the church. Mr. Dodge's ministry was efficient and faithful, and highly appreciated by the church and community. He still lives at Evansville, Indiana, a highly respected minister of the gospel in connection with the Presbyterian Church.

After the resignation of Mr. Dodge, the Rev. John H. Brown, D. D., afterward pastor for some years of the First Presbyterian Church, Springfield, Ill., acted as stated supply for one year. From September 1856, until the following spring, the pulpit was supplied by different persons, chiefly by Rev. Dr. Bergen of Springfield. In 1857 Rev. R. W. Allen, formerly pastor of the Pisgah Presbyterian Church of Kentucky, took charge of the church as stated supply. Having received a unanimous call to the pastorate, Mr. Allen was installed December 5th, 1858, and continued his efficient and faithful labors until May, 1867, when he resigned. It will be seen that Bro. Allen's pastorate embraced the period covered by the late civil war—a period most distracting and highly unfavorable.

Passing from Presbyterians to Methodists, we can only record names of the shepherds of their fast growing flock. The honored and venerable Peter Akers still living with us and still able to preach his annual sermon, although 94 years of age, was presiding elder from 1844 to '47, succeeding Dr. Peter Cartwright and being followed by Rev. W. D. R. Trotter, now gone to his Heavenly charge.

The preachers for Jacksonville station were:

1844, Chauncy Hobart; 1845, W. J. Rutledge; 1846, W. J. Rutledge; 1847, J. B. Corrington; 1848, W. A. Bastain; 1849, C. M. Holiday.

EAST CHARGE.—1850, B. C. Woods; 1851, Harvey Brown; 1852, R. E. Guthrie;

1853, C. D. James; 1854, C. D. James; 1855, Wm. Stevenson; 1856, Wm. Stevenson; 1857, S. Elliott, (dead.)

WEST CHARGE.—1850-'51, J. L. Crane; 1855, S. Elliott; 1853-'54, R. W. Travis; 1855, J. E. Wilson; 1856, W. S. Prentice; 1857-'58, J. R. Locke.

PRESIDING ELDERS. 1851-'53, John S. Barger; 1854-'57, Geo. Rutledge.

The German M. E. Church was constituted in 1856, with thirty-two members. They met in the Grace M. E. Church, where they had divine services about six months, when they purchased a church of the Baptists, which they now occupy. They have now about forty members.

The Grace M. E. Church, first called M. E. Church of West Jacksonville, was organized in the fall of 1850, with five classes; James L. Crane was appointed first preacher. Rev. W. D. R. Trotter was the first presiding elder, Joseph Capps and William Thomas, stewards. First rented the old frame church built by the Presbyterians, on the northwest corner of Church and West State Streets, building afterward owned by Universalist Society. Central Presbyterian Church now stands upon the spot. Removed to the southwest corner of same streets when the brick church was completed, which cost $6,000. While undergoing repairs, six years ago, a strong gale of wind blew down the west gable and damaged the building so much that it was taken to the ground and an entire new edifice was erected, at a cost of about $17,000. The new church is built in form of a cross, and is finely frescoed and is provided with handsome stained glass windows.

The Rev. Edwin Johnson served the Congregational Church as the pastor from 1851-'58.

The Catholic Church of our Saviour—Roman Catholic—has at present a very large membership. In 1851 the Rev. Gifford, the priest at Springfield, came to Jacksonville and finding four or five families professing that faith, held divine service, and appointed George Eberhard, Edward Keyes and Henry McDonnell as collectors to raise funds and assist in the establishment of a church here. The meetings for services were held in a private house at first, but soon the increase of the congregation demanded more room and the old court house was occupied. Murray McConnel donated the society a lot near the railroad depot, on which a house of worship was erected. This, however, became too small, and during the war the present fine structure was commenced.

As to the benevolent fraternities, Jacksonville Chapter, No. 3, Royal Arch Masons was instituted July 25, 1845. The charter members were as follows: Wm. B. Warren, Philip Coffman, John T. Jones, Horace Spalding, Levi Lusk, E. M. M. Clark, Nath. Coffin, C. W. Chatterton and A. R. Robinson. The first officers were W. B. Warren, H. P.; Philip Coffman, K., and John T. Jones, Scribe. In 1882 this body had 138 active men here and was one of the most flourishing chapters in the state. The fees for membership were $42 for the degrees and $2.00 yearly dues. Meetings were held on the second and fourth Monday evenings of each month. Stephen Ellis was H. P., Dr. C. G. Brown, secretary and C. M. Eames treasurer.

In the great mining excitement of 1848 and '49, the city and county contributed its quota to the host that hurried to California to seek their fortunes in the gold fields. There were some forty-five from Morgan, and among them were Cyrus Epler, William Rockwell, A. C. Patterson, E. M. Rees, Wash. Graff, Joseph Heslep (who led one company across the plains,) John Hill, Abram Grimsley.

From a copy of the *Morgan Journal*, a four page weekly paper, of February 28, 1845, then in its first volume, under that name, "edited by an association" and published by Wm. C. Swett, we learn that among the lawyers of the town that year (but now sleeping in the silent city,) were Gen. E. D. Baker, Senator Richard Yates, Judge William Brown, John L. McConnel, Esq., Col. John J. Hardin and Hon. David A. Smith. In the advertising columns are the following named business and professional men that were still residents of Jacksonville in 1878—thirty-three years later:

William Thomas, James Berdan, *Robert Hockenhull*, T. D. Eames, Michael Rapp, *J. H. Bancroft*, Jos. W. King, *William N. Ross*, *David Prince* and John W. Goltra.

Those italicized are living with us at this writing—six years later.

For the Mexican War, under Gov. Ford's call, a company was raised in Jacksonville by J. S. Roberts, editor of the Jacksonville *Standard*. Jacob Zabriski was elected first lieutenant, J. L. McConnel, second lieutenant, and James Dunlap, third lieutenant. Another company was raised at Waverly, Morgan County, by Col. Wm. Weatherford, who had figured in the Black Hawk War. Jacob Brooks was organizing a company at Bethel. Neither this company nor Capt. Roberts' was quite up to the minimum when the day arrived to start to Alton, the place of rendezvous, and it was decided that the company that was full should be accepted and go. Both companies were marched around the square in Jacksonville with an understanding that a part at least of one of the companies would break and go with the other. The wagons which were to take them to Alton were drawn up in South St. Louis Street. The companies started from thence to march around the square. After in motion Lieut. McConnel passed back along the line and asked the men to preserve their organization, and when back to South St. Louis Street to make a break and take possession of the wagons. The other company preserved its organization, not a man faltered, but when Roberts' company reached the wagons and made a break and climbed into them, they stood for a minute in a dazed sort of a way, when about one-third of them broke ranks and joined Roberts' and moved off with them in triumph for Alton.

The first night the boys stayed at White Hall. They received an address of welcome at Carrollton, and reached Alton at the end of the second day, and were quartered for night in an old stone packing house on front row by the wharf or levee. The next morning they were marched out to Frytown, where they were incorporated into the first regiment Illinois volunteers, Colonel J. J. Hardin commanding. Roberts' company being designated as D. The drill, both company and regimental, began in earnest. Captain Roberts was compelled to resign in consequence of a diseased limb, and Lieut. Zabriski was elected captain. The other lieutenants went up one step, and S. Black was elected third lieutenant.

By copies of the same paper dated in April and May, 1847, we find extracts from letters written by Maj. Warren, detailing the incidents of the bloody battle of Buena Vista, at which Col. Hardin, Capt. Zabriski and privates Emerson and Connaught, of Jacksonville, were killed, also a report of a meeting held in Alton "for the purpose of adopting measures expressive of their gratification on account of the *recent victory of American arms* on the field of Buena Vista. Also a statement that the population of the world is 812,553,721; that Jersey City has elected the Whig ticket by 283 majority; that the fashionable color in Paris is *amaranth*; that the Camden (N. J.) *Phœnix*, an administration paper, has declared for General Taylor as the democratic candidate for the presidency, and another paper for Hon. John Sergeant for vice president on the same ticket with him. The *Journal*, by the way, has the name of Gen. Zachary Taylor at its mast-head, to which N. M. Knapp, in a communication, objects as "premature." In another column are election returns, and among other things these show that N. M. Knapp and his Whig colleague, Daniel Dinsmore, were elected in Scott County over their "Locofoco" antagonists; that A. R. Knapp (Whig) carried Jersey; W. A. Grimshaw (Whig) Pike; J. M. Palmer (Loco) Macoupin; Col. Singleton (Whig) Brown, and B. F. Northcutt (Whig) Menard. Editorially the *Journal* declares that "everything looks favorably for the Whigs," the Whig gains since the gubernatorial election being remarkable.

"Details of the battle of Buena Vista," from the New Orleans *Delta*, occupy three and a half columns. On the editorial page we find the names of S. D. Lockwood, Wm. Thomas, Jas. Dunlap and Jas. Gordon on the "Union Ticket" for the convention. Below is a card from "A Whig," who seems to bolt the nomination of the Union candidates, and set up the names of Newton Cloud and J. W. Evans in opposition to Dunlap and Gordon. Then follows a few editorial squibs, something about the "Virginia Academy."

As items of local news, we notice the dedication of "the new Presbyterian meeting house," on May 11th, 1847; a public meeting with speeches and resolutions in respect for the late Col. John Hardin; a call for mounted volunteers by Capt. Joseph Heslep, also a call for a Sunday School convention, signed by John Adams, president of the association, and the following superintendents: H. Spaulding, Wm. Ratekin, Wm. Storer, J. W. Goltra, W. H. Holland, E. T. Doane and D. B. Ayers. It seems, too, that the Illinois College catalogue is just out and the *Journal* is pleased to announce 111 students—29 medical, 38 collegiate, 12 irregular, and 22 preparatory. But a comparison of the advertising columns with the *Journal's* of today shows the ravages of time. To be sure W. H. Broadwell sells "ploughs," Robert Hockenhull is in the drug business, B. & J. Pyatt are in the tobacco trade and William Thomas is land commissioner, but no other modern signs appear.

H. Spalding advertises "photographic miniature;" Rev. Chauncey Eddy has lost a pair of spectacles; Cheeseman and Lucas are blacksmiths; D. Robb is a liberal advertiser of his store, (dry good, boots and shoes, nails, salt, school books, bonnets, furs, whips, carpets, &c., &c.,) Kibbe & Lathrop (groceries and dry goods) hold forth under the Morgan House, afterwards Mansion and now Park Hotel); J. W. King has gold pens at his jewelry establishment; E. & W. Hamilton have a bakery and confectionery; Scott & McDonald are also in the dry goods and notion field, as are Jackson & Gillett, P. Coffman & Son, T. D. Eames, R. Bibb, Ottawa Wilkinson and Cornelius Hook. Nathaniel Coffin is agent for the Northeastern Mutual Life Insurance Company and William A. Conn is pork and beef packer.

Wm. R. Williams has a daguerreotype gallery, McDonald & Chambers deal in cloths, satinets and jeans; J. B. C. Smith has "new goods and a new store"—sign of the "Beehive;" D. B. Ayers & Co. are druggists and booksellers; David Prince, Nathaniel English, G. Y. Shirley and O. M. Long are the M. D's.; Hardin & Smith, Brown & Yates, Wm. Thomas, H. B. McClure, James Berdan, John W. Evans and Wm. H. Sigler are the lawyers; W. Catlin sells watches, clocks and jewelry; E. Corcoran sells books, stationery, *quills*, &c.; Conn & Chambers are commission and forwarding merchants; Matthew Stacy, Michael Rapp and Thomas Ford are saddle and harness men; C. P. Dunbaugh keeps the Morgan House, and J. H. Finch announces his stage routes—three times a week to Alton, via Athensville, and three times a week to Quincy, via Meredosia.

The *Morgan Journal* was then (May 21st, 1847,) in its third volume. The paper was then a six column quarto weekly sheet, two columns to a page smaller than the present *Daily Journal*, "published every Saturday morning, in the building over O. Wilkinson's store, on the southwest corner of the square." The editors and publishers were W. C. Sweet and J. B. Shaw." "Terms, $1.50 in advance, $2.50 at the end of the year."

Wm. C. Sweet in 1848 had succeeded the retiring publisher and changed the name of the paper to the *Morgan Journal*, with Wm. H. Sigler, editor. John B. Shaw also edited the paper for a short period in 1847. It should have been remarked before that the paper was an advocate of the Whig party.

We find in this paper the resolutions adopted at a mass meeting of citizens on receipt of the news of the battle and death of Col. Hardin. Also the proceedings of a meeting of the Scott county bar on receipt of similar news. Army operations take up two-thirds of the paper, and but little space is given to home or local matters except reports of meetings.

In the proceedings of a "Union mass meeting" to nominate candidates to the constitutional convention, regardless of party and of politics, we find the following parliamentary fillibustering on the part of the old wheel horse of democracy, Gen. Murray McConnel, Esq., who offered the following resolution, viz:

Resolved, That in the opinion of this meeting we, now present, have not the right to select the candidates for the whole county, and that we have no power to sell out the votes of the free voters of Morgan County, be they Whigs or Democrats.

To which resolution, N. Coffin, Esq., offered the following amendment, viz:

"But that we have a right to make our own selection, and recommend that selection to our fellow citizens, which is all this meeting intends to do."

Which amendment was accepted by Mr. McConnel, who then moved further to amend said resolution by the following: "But nobody is bound by our actions, not even ourselves; which last amendment being put to the meeting by the chair, was by vote laid upon the table, and the original resolution as offered by Mr. McConnel and amended by Mr. Coffin, was adopted.

On the evening of September 30, 1845, in the room of G. R. Henry, then a student of Illinois College was born the Phi Alpha Society. The founders were only eight in number. The object of the organization was the improvement of their literary tastes and the acquirement of readiness in debate and extempore speaking. The founders were (Dr.) Wm. Jayne, Springfield, Ill., (Congressman) H. S. Van Eaton, Woodville, Miss., (State Senator) Eugene Baldwin, ——— , Minn., Robert Wilkinson, ———, Colo., (Dr.) G. R. Henry, Burlington, Iowa. (Dr.) P. C. Ross, Fulton county, Ill., (Prof.) Robt. D. Wilson, ——— , Cal., (Dr.) N. Wright, Springfield, Ill.

In the first 25 years of its history 500 members were enrolled.

In 1848 two State eleemosynary institutions were "on their feet," established by the State or by private munificence and enterprise. The institution for the Deaf and Dumb had just been opened on a small scale, the foundation of the Hospital for the Insane were being laid, and a class of blind was being taught by a blind man.

The building for the Deaf and Dumb was so far completed as to be open for the reception of pupils January 1846. Committees of the board of directors superintended the building in person without charge to the State. In December, 1846, there were thirteen pupils in the school. Since that time, as the number of pupils has increased, additions have been made to the buildings, and improvements, until now about two hundred and fifty can be accommodated. The trustees residing in Morgan county have always served without compensation. Those from other counties are paid their traveling and personal expenses in attending the meetings of the board. The treasurer makes no charge for his services.

Mr. Thomas Officer, formerly of the Ohio institution, was appointed superintendent and the school continued under his efficient management until 1855.

By the act of incorporation indigent pupils alone are allowed to be educated at the expense of the State. By an act passed in 1847 the board and education of all of suitable age is made free. After the establishment of this institution, General Hardin and Judge Thomas, consulting about future action in the Legislature, agreed to next endeavor to secure a hospital for insane; but in March, Thomas was elected circuit judge, and left the Senate, and before another session of the Legislature the State, for the time being, became bankrupt, so that Gen. Hardin, though remaining a member of the House, never moved in the matter.

During the winter of 1845-'46, several public meetings were held in this place at the instance of Dr. Meade, then connected with Illinois College, who made speeches on the subject to secure action on the part of the people and the establishment of a hospital. The doctor had collected information from almost every county in the State as to the number and condition of the insane. Gen. Hardin also took part in the discussion. The result was that a committee was appointed consisting of Samuel D. Lockwood, Dennis Rockwell, James Dunlap, Nathaniel English, William Thomas, David Prince, John J. Hardin, Samuel Adams and Edward Meade, to take charge of the subject and to inquire and ascertain what could be done. It was supposed to be possible to obtain by donation a tract of land on which to place a hospital, and that by private contributions sufficient funds could be obtained to erect buildings for those having means to pay for care and support.

These gentlemen subsequently met as a board of trustees and appointed Dr. N. English president, William Thomas secretary, and Dennis Rockwell treasurer.

James Dunlap, John J. Hardin, Dr. N. English and Dr. D. Prince were appointed a committee to select a location for the institution. Dr. Samuel Adams was appointed to obtain information in regard to the construction of buildings, laying out of grounds, the treatment of the insane, and the general management of such institutions.

The committees had several meetings, made divisions of labors, assigning to each division specific duties. This was a time of great pecuniary embarrassment throughout the State; the State government was being supported on credit; auditor's warrants selling at 74 to 80 cents on the dollar; property and produce selling at great sacrifices, and the people acting under fearful apprehensions of the future. This committee soon found that the people, though willing to aid in such an enterprise, were unable to contribute sufficient means even to purchase 160 acres of land. If they had been asked for corn or pork, or cattle or hogs, which could not be sold for much more than the cost of transportation to market, they would have given liberally in kind.

In the spring of 1846 Miss Dix, upon the earnest solicitation of a citizen of Jacksonville, Mr J. O. King, changed her intended programme for that season and visited this place, and after several conferences with our citizens agreed to traverse the State, visit the penitentiary, the county poor houses and jails, and make an appeal to the succeeding Legislature in behalf of the insane. She made a trip through several counties north of the Illinois River and returned. She then visited some parts of Missouri, and then went into the counties south to Belleville, and probably to Nashville, and from thence in pursuance of some previous engagement she went across the State to Indiana and from thence to Columbus, Ohio, where she was taken sick and remained until December. Our State Legislature met the first Monday in December—Morgan county had one Senator (Hon. John Henry) and four Representatives, Newton Cloud, (who was elected speaker of the House) Joseph Morton, William H. Long and William Thomas. Soon after the organization of the House the latter introduced a bill to establish a retreat for the insane, with no provision for any appropriation; it passed the House, went to the Senate and was referred to a committee, and before it was reported Miss Dix arrived in Springfield, in very feeble health; by special invitation she made the house of Col. Thomas Mather her home during the session of the Legislature. Wm. Thomas was the only member of the Legislature with whom she was acquainted. He introduced her to Senator Henry who had charge of the bill, and he introduced all the senators who were willing to see her, after which Thomas introduced all the members of the House, by companies of from ten to twelve.

She thus had the opportunity of presenting the object of her mission. She very soon presented a memorial to the Legislature asking for the establishment of a hospital for insane. The Senate committee instead of reporting the bill which had passed the House, reported a new bill, prepared by the late Judge Constable, under the direction and supervision of Miss Dix, entitled "An act to establish the Illinois State Hospital for the Insane," accompanied by a report prepared by Dr. Meade. About this time Senator Henry was elected to Congress to fill a vacancy and left the Senate. The bill provided for levying a special tax of one-fifth of a mill on the dollar for three years for the purposes of the institution. It passed the Senate, 23 to 8, locating the hospital at Peoria. When it came up for consideration in the House, on motion "Peoria" was stricken out and "Jacksonville" was inserted. The rules were dispensed with and the bill passed. The Senate on the same day concurred in the amendments.

The trustees purchased 160 acres of land at about $21 per acre for the use of the institution, and during the summer and fall had the foundation of the building nearly or quite laid. Judge Thomas says: Miss Dix informed the board that the plan of the hospital building then in the process of erection in Indiana was the best in the United States, and in consequence the board obtained a copy of that plan, which upon examination was adopted. The plan of heating at that day was by furnaces with hot air.

ILLINOIS INSTITUTION FOR THE DEAF AND DUMB AT JACKSONVILLE. FOUNDED 1846.

Of the Insane Hospital the first board of trustees was composed of Judge Thomas as president, Samuel D. Lockwood, Joseph Morton, Owen M. Long, Nathaniel English, William W. Happy, James Dunlap, James Gordon and Aquila Becraft. Dr. James M. Higgins was the first medical superintendent, and served until about 1854.

The real credit for the legislation which secured the Hospital is perhaps due to a greater extent than to any body else to the venerable Judge Thomas, of Jacksonville, who prepared the original bill for the location of the Hospital for the Insane; to Richard Yates who introduced it in the House, and to the late Joseph Morton, who, as a member of the House, zealously supported it. We accord this credit to Judge Thomas because he not only framed the bill locating the first State institution at Jacksonville, but afterwards, as a member of the House, was the leading and influential champion of similar measures as to other institutions, although he was zealously aided by other citizens of Jacksonville.

Gov. French approved the Thomas bill on the 1st of March, 1847, it passed the House February 27, by a vote of 67 to 17. Jacksonville was selected as the site of the future institution the twenty-eighth in number in the country.

The bill appropriated $60,000 to erect the centre building and one section on each side. The capacity of the institution was then rated at 250 patients.

In 1847 a blind man named Bacon, visited Jacksonville and proposed the opening of a school for the blind, with a view to the location of such a school by the State. A number of the citizens of Jacksonville agreed that if he could secure and teach a small class for six months as an experiment, that they would pay the expenses, to which he assented. He secured a class of six and opened the school, during the summer of 1848, which was continued at the expense of the citizens until relieved by the State, more than a year later. The Legislature met in January, 1849, and early in the session a bill which Judge Thomas had prepared was introduced in the House by Mr. Yates, for "an act to establish the Illinois Institution for the Education of the Blind."

The six scholars were taken to Springfield and had an exhibition before the Legislature to satisfy the members that the blind could and ought to be educated. The bill appropriated the proceeds of a tax of one-tenth of a mill on the dollar to aid in the establishment of the school, and also $3,000 in advance to enable the trustees to commence building. This tax was required to be set apart as a separate fund, to be known as the fund for the blind. The last section of the act, provides "that the blind of this State, who are of suitable age and capacity, shall be raised and taught in the school, and enjoy all the benefits and privileges of the same, free of charge." Samuel D. Lockwood, Dennis Rockwell, James Dunlap, William W. Happy and Samuel Hunt were appointed trustees. The names were agreed on by the members of the Legislature from this county, and were inserted after the bill was proposed. The school was superintended chiefly by Dr. Nathaniel English and Mr. Jas. O. King, neither of whose names ever afterwards appeared in connection with the institution.

The trustees organized by electing Mr. Lockwood president, James Berdan secretary, and Mr. Rockwell treasurer. The school under their control was opened for the reception of pupils the April following, (1849).

Mr. Bacon was engaged as principal of the institution. The number of pupils, quite small at first, gradually increased. No vacation occurred in the school until the 10th of July, when the first term was closed, and the pupils, then numbering twenty-three, after a public examination, were dismissed until the first Wednesday of October. Mr. Bacon opened his first school in a building on North Main Street, now known as the John McConnel property. After the incorporation of the school, it was removed to the Wilson farm, west of the city, which place is now known as the Robb place.

Mr. Bacon having resigned at the close of the term in July, the board deputed one of their number to visit similar institutions, in other States, for the purpose of engaging a competent superintendent. The result of this visit was the selection of Dr. Joshua Rhoads, former superintendent of the Pennsylvania Institution for the Blind, as principal, and Mrs. Rosanna Rhoads as matron. Under their direction the school opened on the first Wednesday of October, 1850, with twenty-three pupils, this number being all that could be accommodated at this time.

In May and June, 1844, there was more rain and higher waters, throughout the State, than ever known by the oldest inhabitant.

In 1845 the Northern Cross R. R., was extended from Jacksonville to Naples. The State operated the road until 1847, when the Legislature passed an act, February 16th, authorizing the sale of the sale of the road between the Illinois River and Springfield, fifty-two miles in length, at public vendue. One of the peculiar features of this law was that it provided for a forty years' lien upon the road in order to secure the amount for which it might be sold. The sale took place soon after the approval of the act, and Nicholas H. Ridgely, of Springfield, became the purchaser, paying $21,100 in state indebtedness. Mr. Ridgely afterwards sold Thomas Mather, of Springfield, and James Dunlap, of Jacksonville, each an interest. They changed its name to the Sangamon & Morgan railroad. During the time the State had operated it but one engine had been obtained, and when the new owners took possession they found the engine so worn as to be unfit for use, and for nine months they were compelled to run their trains with mules. The trains consisted of two cars, drawn by two mules. There were two trains daily, one of which left Springfield in the morning for Naples, and the other Naples for Springfield.

About the close of 1847 the company received three new engines, when the services of the mules were dispensed with. The Legislature passed an act extending the charter of the road to the Indiana line, and in 1857 Mr. Mather visited New York and negotiated a sale of the road to Robert Schuyler, who was then deemed the great railroad manager of the country, for $100,000. Mather and Ridgely continued stockholders, and were elected local directors. In the same year Mr. Schuyler became the purchaser of the thirty-three miles of railway between Meredosia and Camp Point, which had been built through the influence of Gen. James W. Singleton. In 1859 the name was changed to the Great Western Railway, and the work of extending it eastward was begun in earnest. In 1865 it was consolidated with the Toledo & Wabash railway. January 6, 1877, the Wabash railway company was organized and acquired the property of the Toledo, Wabash & Western railway at foreclosure sale in February, 1877, and in 1879 the name was changed to the Wabash, St. Louis & Pacific railway.

Now that insignificant twenty-four miles of flat railroad is a part of what is known as the Gould system, which has business connections from the Atlantic to the Pacific ocean, and is one of the greatest railroad combinations in the world. The company owns in fee simple, or operates by lease, 1,598 miles of railway in Illinois.

Of the banking business in 1850-'52, Mr. Marshall P. Ayers, more than thirty years later said to a *Courier* interviewer:

"My father, David B. Ayers, was agent for John Grigg, the famous book publisher of Philadelphia, and as such agent entered 120,000 acres of land for him, and sold the same as opportunity offered a profit. My father died in 1850, and I succeeded him as agent for Mr. Grigg of such lands as remained unsold. I would say right here that the bulk of these lands sold for $3 to $5 per acre, and the same lands now will bring from $60 to $75 per acre At that time there was no bank here, the Shawneetown and State Banks having gone out of existence. Owing to the difficulty of procuring exchange with which to make my remittances, I interviewed Mr. Bacon, of Page & Bacon, St. Louis, and they placed to my credit the sum of $2,000, with the American Exchange Bank of New York, and thus opened my account with them This was on December 20th, 1852, and was the beginning of my banking. I opened an office in the rear of a wooden building where Ayers's block now stands, on about the spot where Jenkinson keeps his butter and eggs. All the money received for exchange was kept in a tin box under my bed and was sent to St. Louis by express as fast as possible."

"What was the rate of exchange in those days?"

"One-fourth of one per cent. on St Louis and one-half of one per cent. on New York on gold and one per cent. on currency."

"What was the circulating medium at that time?"

"Gold, silver, eastern Ohio and Indiana State money, and the notes of the Wisconsin Marine and Fire Insurance Company, and Page & Bacon scrip, of which there was a large amount."

From Mr. Ensley Moore's local epitomes contributed to the *Daily Journal* in 1879, we glean the following paragraphs about the city in 1840:

Hon. D. M. Woodson was circuit judge, James Berdan was county judge of Morgan, Ira Davenport sheriff, G. A. Dunlap clerk of county court, Henry Routt surveyor, David C. Creamer coroner and Charles H. Hardin circuit clerk.

Richard Yates having served in the Legislature from his twenty-fifth year, in 1842, is spoken of as a candidate for Congress.

When people referred to "the war," they meant that in Mexico, from which our soldiers had but recently returned.

An epidemic called the "California fever" was very prevalent, and carried off many of our citizens, across the Rocky Mountains to the new Eldorado.

Our Congregational brethren worshipped in a large one-story frame building with brick basement, on the east side of the square, where King's & Johnson's stores are now.

The Methodist church, east charge, was a one-story-and-basement brick, standing where R. C. Smith's marble building now is.

Rev. L. M. Glover's First Presbyterian Church occupied the site of the present edifice, and was a large one-story and basement brick building, with a high wooden steeple painted white.

The Episcopalians occupied a one-story-and-basement brick, upon the lot they now hold, but the building fronted south, to Morgan street. This church had an organ, the only one in the town at that time, we think.

A Methodist church was built and called the "West Charge," upon the present site of Grace M. E. Church, but it was a one-story-and-basement brick, devoid of steeple, fronting east on Church Street.

The present German M. E. Church was owned by the Baptists, and a building similar in appearance was occupied by the Second Presbyterian Society, situated opposite Dr. Glover's church, main entrance.

Bells called the people to meeting in the East Charge, First Presbyterian, Episcopal and Congregational churches. A Portuguese Presbyterian church was just getting itself in order.

Among the lawyers were D. A. Smith, Richard Yates, James Berdan, Wm. Thomas, Wm. Brown and Murray McConnel. D. B. Ayers and Robert Hockenhull were druggists. Jos. W. King had a one-story bow window jewelry store, where D. W. Rawlings now is.

I. D. Rawlings dealt in clothing. T. D. Eames had a dry goods store, on the east side of the square, and S. Reynolds King also sold dry goods.

A boy named "Billy" D. Crowell, clerked for J. B. C. Smith, who sold dry goods in a frame building where Dobyns & Co. now are.

Philip Price had a jewelry store on the north side, east half of the square. George W. Fox kept the Mansion House. D. C. Creamer, known as the fashionable merchant tailor, occupied the old one story frame on Hatfield's corner. Ebenezer T. Miller was postmaster.

Samuel Hunt kept the jail, in the house next south of the brick livery stable, on North Main street.

N. English, O. M. Long and Henry Jones were among the prominent physicians.

The town trustees were Wm. Branson, Jos. H. Bancroft, Wm. G. Johnson, Andrew F. Wilson and John W. Lathrop.

A one-story-and-a-half frame building, painted white, was one of the principal stores on the south side, where Huntley now is.

Next door west of it, stood a large two and a half story frame house, with a yard in front, where Johnson & Co., and King & Stebbins now ('79,) are. Two or three long one story frames occupied the site of Strawn's Opera House, and the only good brick in that block is part of Metcalf & Fell's big dry goods store now.

On the west side, south half, the buildings were better, but three or four two story frames were beginning to wear out, where the Central Bank, Fox and Rawlings now are.

The Ayers' building was most noticeable on the north half of the west side.

Two brick buildings of good size, besides the Mansion House, stood in that block.

McDonald's and two or three bricks east of it, were the ornamental part of the east half of the north side.

Henderson's corner store was built, and Bancroft's good brick (now Walsh's) stood opposite, and no other good stores till R. Hockenhull's and Eames' building, in north half of east side.

Then came Stevenson's corner, a good building, succeeded by two two-story frames, and the Congregational Church, then Branson's store, and a two-story frame on the corner.

Hamilton's corner, now Gill's, and the double Davenport building were the brick improvements on the south side, east half, with some of the frames now standing to fill up the spaces.

It need hardly be remarked that the old court house, with its cupola, stood in the southwest corner of the public square.

David Robb, Willys Catlin, J. S. Anderson, Ben. F. Stevenson, Wm. Branson, Kibbe & Lathrop, Goltra & Stryker, and Edward Lambert were dealers in their respective lines of trade.

In February, a new board of trustees was elected, consisting of Joseph H. Bancroft, Michael Rapp, M. H. Cassell, Jonathan Neely and William Ratekin.

Among the persons having titles from the Mexican War were Col. James Dunlap, Capt. J. L. McConnel, Capt. Wyatt, Col. Chambers, Major William Warren.

The old, original, Methodist Conference Female College, was completed this year.

Illinois College graduated the following persons: Wm. H. Collins, now of Quincy, and Edward Ruggles.

Jacksonville Female Academy gave diplomas to Mary A. Allison, Susan E. Church, Anna L. Holmes, Susan A. Holland, Electa M. Holland, Eliza Johnson, Malvina C. Melendy, Harriet P. Murdock, Harriet Reed and Elizabeth E. White.

Rev. J. F. Jaquess was principal of the Methodist College, and Rev. J. M. Sturtevant of Illinois College.

Mr. Thomas Officer was Superintendent of the Deaf and Dumb Institute; J. M. Higgins, M. D., of the Central Hospital for the Insane, then not completed, even on the original plan; Dr. Joshua Rhoads was principal of the Institution for the Blind, which occupied the house west of Jacksonville, known as the Robb place.

Revs. J. M. Sturtevant, Theoron Baldwin, J. F. Brooks, E. Jenny, William Kirby, John G. Bergen, Thomas Lippincott, William Carter and Albert Hale, and Messrs. S. D. Lockwood, John Tillson, Thos. Mather, Frederick Collins, David A. Smith and David B. Ayers were trustees of Illinois College.

Among the boys going to college in September, were A. C. Clayton, W. B. Cowgill, Phil Davis, A. N. Denny, Edward P. Kirby, J. A. Laurie, D. B. Nash, G. Magill, H. M. Merriam, H. M. Miller, R. A. Ritter, H. C. Stephens, J. M. Sturtevant, Jr., Paul Selby, R. M. Tunnell and A. J. Van Deren.

The first board of trustees for the Blind Institution were S. D. Lockwood, Jas. Dunlap, W. W. Happy, Dennis Rockwell and Samuel Hunt, with Lockwood as president, James Berdan secretary, and Dennis Rockwell treasurer.

Moore C. Goltra was superintendent of construction at the Central Insane Hospital.

The Christian Church building on North Main street was erected this year, Elder A. J. Kane being pastor in the new edifice.

Rev. Andrew Todd was pastor of the Second Presbyterian Church, dying at Casa Blanca, near Monticello, Florida, in September, 1850.

Urania Lodge, No. 243, I. O. O. F., was chartered, as was also Ridgely Encampment No. 9.

Joseph Capps had a small wool carding establishment.

The population was 2,745.

During the campaign of 1850, this district was badly "tore up" by the race between Col. Thos. L. Harris and Richard Yates, for congress. Mr. Yates was elected, and found himself the youngest member of the House of Representatives.

The Western House was a small hotel and boarding house, on the west side of the square, up stairs, where Rawlings & Fox now are.

Dennis Rockwell dwelt in the house now occupied by his son, Charles Rockwell, on West State street.

The first district school was built and opened in 1850, being the west district, now called second ward, and Newton Bateman was principal. The third story of the school house was occupied by Masons for lodge rooms.

At the election, November 20th, Jonathan Neely was chosen sheriff, and Timothy Chamberlain coroner.

A young man from New Jersey, named S. Henry Thompson, came to town, bringing his trowel with him, and commenced laying foundations for the mayoralty.

Joseph Morton, James Dunlap, John J. Hardin, John Henry, S. D. Lockwood, Wm. Thomas, B. Gillett, N. English and O. M. Long were first trustees of the insane, Judge Lockwood being president and Judge Thomas secretary.

Dr. E. R. Roe, U. S. Marshal for southern district of Illinois, was editor of the *Journal*, we think.

Miss Elizabeth Mead was principal of the Academy during 1850-51.

Lastly but not leastly, as to the local press: William Swett established the *Morgan Journal* in 1843, and from that time to the present it has been issued regularly as a weekly, "Jacksonville" being substituted for "Morgan" in 1870. It has passed through the vicissitudes of fire and been under many different firms. But to return, in 1850 the *Constitutionalist* was started by E. R. Roe, who sold out to T. H. Kavenaugh, and he to John M. Taggart. Under the latter's *regime* the first experiment of a daily was made, and an edition of two hundred and fifty copies was printed off for six months from a hand press, but it was found to be too unprofitable to be continued longer.

Dr. E. R. Roe, who had been a professor in Shurtleff College, succeeded Mr. Swett as owner and editor of the *Morgan Journal*. Dr. Roe has since been county or circuit clerk of McLean county; and for eight years United States marshal for the southern district of Illinois. He is now a resident of Springfield, this State.

Dr. Roe was succeeded in the proprietorship of the *Morgan Journal*, by Paul Selby, who had Mr. A. C. Clayton associated with him.

The year 1846 witnessed the arrival in this country of a band of from 300 to 500 men, women and children of Portuguese blood, exiles from the island of Madeira. They came to this country under the guidance of a missionary named Kally, who had labored among them in the island. They were comparatively poor. They had been converted, or proselyted, from Romanism by Presbyterian missionaries, Mr. Kally being the chief instrument in the work. Their Catholic neighbors on the island persecuted and maltreated them for their desertion of the Holy Mother Church, and their residence on the island was made particularly disagreeable. Under these circumstances a happy thought occurred, to bring the little church to America and their co-religionists of Springfield and Jacksonville gave them a cordial invitation to settle at these points. Money was contributed and the little colony, like the Pilgrim Fathers, embarked for America, seeking a home where they might find freedom to worship God.

They settled almost entirely in Springfield and Jacksonville. Occasionally their numbers have been recruited by accessions from the mother country, but these have not been large.

As a rule, they came here poor in purse but rich in determination. They have prospered and many of them have become wealthy. They all manage as soon as possible, to acquire a piece of ground, no matter how small, which they can call their own, and they cultivate this with all the care and diligence they formerly bestowed upon the little patches of earth between the rocks and hills of their rugged native isle. As a class, they are industrious, frugal, upright, peaceful, law-abiding citizens and may be found in all trades and professions, to which they readily adapt themselves. Many have been placed in offices of position and have faithfully discharged their trusts, and filled the duties of their office acceptably.

Many of the older class maintain the peculiarities of their native land, but the younger portion more readily than any other of our foreign born citizens, adapt themselves to the customs, manners and habits of their adopted land. They are for the most part, exemplary christians, maintaining as they now do, in our city three churches and three Sabbath schools. Their girls are for the most part sweet singers and many of them quite beautiful; their dark complexion betraying their Arab or Barber blood. Their boys are bright and active, quick to learn and many of them will make good thrifty business men.

The first bank was established in Jacksonville in 1851, by M. P. & A. E. Ayers, who, together with Mr. W. S. Hook are still carrying on the business of general exchange banking, with four other banks in successful operation—The First National, The Jacksonville National, the banking house of Hockenhull, King & Elliot, and the Savings Bank.

William Brown was indicted at the March term, 1854, of the circuit court, for the murder of Geo. Groves on November 27, 1853, by stabbing him with a knife, Cyrus Epler being State's Attorney. This case was stricken from the docket at the October term,1854. We mention this merely because we intend this history of the city to be a complete record of all trials for murder.

The sum of $6,000 was appropriated in 1851 for the completion of the building of the Hospital for Insane, and $66,666 in 1857 for additional buildings. In 1854 Dr. Higgins resigned as superintendent when he was succeeded temporarily by Dr. H. K. Jones, and then by Dr. Andrew McFarland. The latter remained until July, 1870, when he resigned.

The enlargement of the hospital by the addition of the east wing, was in accordance with the recommendation of a joint committee of the legislature, of which Dr. Boal was chairman, and who submitted the report of the committee during the session of 1857. The committee was authorized to, and did, act during the recess of the legislature, or between two sessions. The citizens of Morgan county had no agency in the subsequent enlargement of the building. This measure proceeded from the committee acting for the whole state, and not for the county of Morgan. The first appropriation tion on the report of the committee was $66,666.66, half payable in 1857, and half in 1858. With subsequent appropriations, including what was asked by the trustees, both wings were completed for the reception and use of patients. Until 1857 the majority of each of the State institution boards resided in the county of Morgan—all of them without compensation. In 1857 an act was passed reducing the number of trustees in each board except the blind, and provided that no person should be a member of more than one board, and that not more than one member of any of the boards should be appointed from any one county. Since that time Morgan has been represented by but one person in each board. This provision is considered as essential to the successful operation of the institutions.

The Blind Asylum board purchased an eligible site, comprising twenty-two acres of ground, in the eastern part of the city, where the foundation of a building suitable for the accommodation of the sightless was laid, and work on the walls progressed favorably; this building in an unfinished condition, was occupied for the first time in January, 1854; it was entirely completed January, 1855. The course of instruction was enlarged, so as to include the various trades, and some of the fine arts. The buildings completed January 1, 1855, were with various additions and improvements, occupied without interruption, until the morning of the 20th of April, 1869, when the main building with its contents, was entirely destroyed by fire.

At the close of the year 1855 the number of pupils who had been in attendance at the State Institution for the Deaf and Dumb was 162. At this time Mr. Officer presented his resignation to the board of directors, which was accepted.

The board were fortunate in securing as the successor of Mr. Officer, Phillip G. Gillett, A.M., a graduate of Asbury University, at Greencastle, Indiana. Mr. Gillett having taught for four years in the Indiana Deaf Mute Institution, came to preside over this one with an experience which was of incalculable value to the institution at that time. The board of directors who were instrumental in procuring the services of Mr. Gillett, in their report for the years 1855–'56, say: "The board of directors deem themselves fortunate in having procured the services of Mr. Gillett. He is a gentleman of strong and vigorous mind, an accomplished scholar, and experienced in teaching the sign language: Indeed he has made this his occupation for life, and with him it is as much a labor of love as duty."

The number of pupils in actual attendance at this time was one hundred. There were but two trades taught: shoe making and cabinet making. The school flourished from this time forward, new buildings were erected, more land was purchased, and needed improvements were added from time to time, as necessity required.

About 1853 or '54 the Christian denomination began the erection of a building known as the Berean College. A charter was received dated February 12, 1855, soon after which the building was completed, and the following year school was opened, with Dr. Jonathan Atkinson as president. The school was opened under very favorable auspices, and for several years was continued very successfully. The college received its name from "Berea," a place mentioned by the apostle Paul, in the seventeenth chapter of the book of Acts where the following language is used: "And the brethren immediately sent away Paul and Silas by night unto Berea: * * * these were more noble than those in Thessalonica, in that they received the word with all readiness of mind, and searched the Scriptures daily, whether those things were so." The college continued until about 1858 or '59, when a division in the church occurred, and soon after the school was discontinued. A few years after, the property was sold to Mrs. Eliza Ayers for twelve thousand dollars. Its original cost was over thirty thousand dollars. Mrs. Ayers has since deeded the property to a board of trustees, to be used as an Orphan's Home and City Hospital. The frame building immediately in the rear of the college is occupied by the orphans, while the college itself is used as the hospital. The frame building was formerly the home of Col. John J. Hardin, so well known throughout this portion of the State, and who lost his life at the battle of Beuna Vista. The home is conducted on the "Muller plan," by Rev. Dr. Passavant, who has charge of eight similar institutions in different parts of the United States.

The home and hospital are each well managed, and are institutions worthy the attention of the citizens of Jacksonville.

For all of the six years, 1851–'57, Rev. Chas. G. Selleck, A. M., had charge of the Presbyterian Academy. He brought to the position much of fitness for it, knowledge, culture, zeal in education, love for the young, and considerable experience in teaching; but in the person of the beloved Mrs. Selleck, he brought, in addition, other helpful qualities rarely so combined in a single individual. It is seldom that the law of compensation is better illustrated than in their case; seldom that a man is so fortunate in the wifely supplement as he. They were as truly counterparts as the wax and the seal. In the one was found what was essential to the completeness of the other, and after her death, which preceded his many years, old friends sympathizingly thought of him in his loneliness as a bird with a broken wing, drooping where once he soared. The union of their gifts and graces brought to the service of the Academy more of what is essential to the completeness and prosperity of a boarding school for young ladies than can ordinarily be contributed by any single individual, male or female.

Dr. Glover afterwards said:

"I do not think their administration wanting in intellectuality, but it was distinguished for realizing the spirit of family and home in an unusual degree, and yet not in such degree as to produce contempt by familiarity and thus to mar the efficiency of rules and discipline. Teachers and pupils were brought into the most intimate relations, and the truly parental regards on one side were rewarded with truly filial regards on the other, and those regards which at the time were so tender, proved also abiding. The school under Mr. and Mrs. Selleck enjoyed such increase that more room was demanded and another story was added to the main building, at a cost of about two thousand six hundred dollars.

In 1855, a large and commodious wing was added to the Illinois Female College.

The Morgan county representatives in the United States Congress, Illinois Legislature and county offices were:

1851—Treasurer, Wm. G. Johnson; Surveyor, Harvey Routt.

1852-'54—Congress, Richard Yates; Senator, Joseph Morton; Representatives, Wm. Brown, Edward Lusk; Sheriff Martin H. Cassell; Circuit Clerk, Charles Hardin; Prosecuting Attorney, Cyrus Epler; Coroner, Timothy Chamberlain.

1853—County Judge, James Berdan; County Clerk, Matthew Stacy; Treasurer, Wm. G. Johnson; Surveyor, Geo. M. Richards; School Commissioner, Willys Catlin.

1854-'56—Congress, Richard Yates; Senate, Joseph Morton; Representatives, Horace A. Brown, Isaac R. Bennet; Sheriff, Cyrus Matthews.

1855—Treasurer, Wm. G. Johnson; Surveyor, Charles Packard; For Prohibition 1,571, against 1,416.

1856-'58—Congress, John Williams; States Attorney, Albert G. Burr; Senator, Cyrus Vanderen; Representatives, Cyrus Epler, E. B. Hitt; Sheriff, Charles Sample, Coroner, James E. Mitchell; School Commissioner, Newton Bateman.

1857—County Judge, Joseph T. Cassell; County Clerk, Matthew Stacy; County Treasurer, Wm. G. Johnson; Surveyor, Wm. S. McPherson; School Commissioner, Newton Bateman.

On December 30th of the year 1852, the principal edifice of Illinois College, a building 104 by 40 feet, and four stories high, was destroyed by fire; and through the neglect either of college agents or insurance agents, or both, with only three thousand dollars insurance; and many believed that than must be the end of the institution. That it was greatly depressed could not be denied. The whole value of its endowment at that time was not much over $20,000, and all its property of all kinds could not have been estimated so high as $50,000; $30,000 would have been nearer to its real value.

Since that time the trustees have never rested many months at a time, from efforts to increase its resources. A new building was erected and finished in 1857 at an expense of more than $20,000 at a time when the cost of building was not more than half as great as now. In 1858 a subscription for the endowment of the college and discharging a debt incurred in erecting the new building was completed, amounting in round numbers to $50,000. This subscription was payable in installments running through several years; and, owing to the disasters of the times, some of it remains yet unpaid, but esteemed good. Another portion of it will never be paid. But more than $30,000 has been paid and the sum ultimately realized from it will be more than $40,000. In 1855 the college graduates numbered 130, of whom 118 were living. Over 1,000 pupils had been taught in the college during the first twenty-five years of its existence.

The following named represented their fellow citizens in the town board of trustees, during the years named. Only those italicized are living to-day (1884):

Michael Rapp, '51 to '55 and '57; William Ratekin, '51 to '54; Fleming Stevenson, '51; David A. Smith, '51; Stephen Sutton, '51 to '54 and '56 to '57; Joseph Capps, '52 and '54; William Branson, '52 and '55; Alexander McDonald, '53 and '54; Nimrod Dewees, '55; *Joel Goodrick*, '55; Benjamin Cassell, '55; Timothy D. Eames, '55; *James*

S. Anderson, '56; Edward Elliott, '56; Cyrus Matthews, '56; Edward Lambert, '57; *William H. Broadwell*, '57; *Lewis Hatfield*, '57.

In 1857 Illini Lodge, No. 4 of Odd Fellows, had a membership of 125, and certain members thereof, thinking it had growth large enough, and that there was room in this city for another similar organization concluded to withdraw and found a second lodge. This was done on the night of October 7, 1857, the lodge being instituted by R. W. Grand Secretary, Saml. Williams. It was christened Urania Lodge No 243, with the following charter members: P. B. Price, R. D. Landers, G. W. S. Callon, B. F. Bristow, W. D. Crowell, G. S. Smith, W. T. Dunlap, J. E. Dunlap, W. D. R. Trotter, Henry Rice, P. G. Gillett, Pres. Spates and S. Dewees.

The first officers elected were as follows: B. F. Bristow, N. G.; W. D. Crowell, V. G.; Henry Rice, Recording Secretary; and G. W. S. Callon, Treasurer. The best of feeling has always existed between the two lodges, and they have jointly occupied the same lodge room. For some five years Urania Lodge grew and prospered, when reverses came, and for two or three years a quorum could be got together with difficulty, and several times the members came within a few votes of surrendering their charter. New life being given the lodge by the initiation of some active and earnest men, a fresh start was taken and prosperity has since attended its existence. It now is the second lodge in size in the state, having an active membership of 220.

In Odd Fellowship a "camp" is a higher degree to which only third degree members can be admitted. It is to Odd Fellowship what the Knights Templar are to Masonry. In this city Ridgely Encampment, No. 9, was organized October 14, 1857, with Jacob McFarland, E. W. Roberts, G. W. S. Callon, M. Rapp, James H. Lurton, Wash. Allen, Lewis Hatfield, Aug. E. Ayers, Mortimer Stout and John Pyatt as charter members. This encampment has always been in flourishing and prosperous condition.

In 1855 the *Sentinel* came into existence as the organ of the Democratic party, and for many years it manfully and ably stood up for the doctrines and interests of the party. It was established by Mr. J. R. Bailey, who removed to this city from Mt. Sterling, where he had been for three years both publisher and postmaster. He continued as editor and proprietor for seventeen years.

Mr. Paul Selby conducted the *Journal* during the hot, exciting times of "Kansas-Nebraska," and other discussions preliminary to the war, and he made it a Republican newspaper.

It was during Mr. Selby's ownership, that the office was burned out of its home, over the east end of what was then B. F. Stevenson's store, now the "Standard" store. The scattered material and books were moved into one of the upper rooms nearly opposite its present stand, and the *Morgan Journal* continued at a new stand.

Mr. Selby has since been employed, editorially, upon the *State Journal*, been an editorial proprietor of the Quincy *Whig*, served on a Minnesota paper, and is now one of the proprietors of the *State Journal*, besides holding the lucrative position of postmaster at Springfield. He has fought a long fight, seen the triumph of principles that he advocated at personal risk, and deserves his success.

We get a glimpse into Jacksonville business affairs in 1855 through the columns of the Jacksonville *Constitutionalist*, (Democratic) "a weekly paper for the people, devoted to the best interests of Illinois." Under date of May 25, the editor, J. M. Taggart, says: "We have authorized Mr Wm. M. Springer (not then M. C.) to receive subscriptions and receipt for same."

Other agents of the paper are announced, among them John Gordon, Lynnville, D. C. Callon, P. M., Bethel.

Hon. S. T. Logan is advertised for a temperance speech, at the Court House. The annual session of the Grand Temple of Illinois had been meeting at "Grierson's Grove," and Rev. Jonathan Atkinson, president of Berean College, and Hon. Wm. H. Herndon, of Springfield, had made addresses. The marriage of McLean F. Wood and the death of Charles, infant son of Charles and Elizabeth Hardin, are announced. Note is made of the expedition in search of Dr. Kane—the vessels being named "The Release," and "The Arctic."

As to advertisements, G. M. Chambers is to have a sale of Short Horn Cattle, on his farm; John Selby gives notice of his fine assortment of dry goods, groceries, &c: Dr. Wm. S. Edgar is in the drug business; J. W. King and J. N. Kayser in partnership in watch-making; Alderman & Tomlinson in clothing; Bristow & Bros. in dry goods, etc., Stewarts is the leading millinery house; the law partnership of Wm. Brown & H. B. McClure is dissolved and Richard Yates (not then governor, or senator) and Mr. McClure form a co-partnership; S. A. Corneau is a candidate for clerk of the Supreme Court; Alex. McDonald sells dry goods, and A. C. Dickson & Son lumber and grain; Edward I. Eno is also a grain dealer; Edwin Clement has marble works on West State street; I. L. Morrison & M. P. Ayers are in partnership in real estate business; W. H. Hartley has imported horses; R. & J. Hockenhull as druggists dissolve partnership, and Thos. C. Routt has opened a new stock of groceries.

Among the doctors are C. K. Sawyer, G. Y. Shirley and Owen M. Long. Rivers has a daguerrean room, and Corcoran & Austin are grocers. B. F. & W. S. Ford are associated as brother harnessmakers. J. H. Lurton has carpets to sell, and E. Hamilton holiday presents. Galbraith & Cassell keep stoves and tinware, and P. B. Price advertises "time keepers." Ayers & Co. are in the hardware line, and Hamilton & Sutton are a new dry goods firm. From the secret society cards we see that Dr. N. English was W. M. of Harmony, No. 3, and W. S. Hurst of Jacksonville, No. 570. A. C. Dickson was secretary of the latter and R. D. Landers of Illini, No. 4, of which Wm. H. Bowen was N. G., Wm. Ratekin was C. P. and Lewis Hatfield Scribe of Ridgely Encampment and James Berdan W. P. of Excelsior Division Sons of Temperance, and W. B. Warren Grand Master of the Grand Lodge A. F. & A. M. of Illinois.

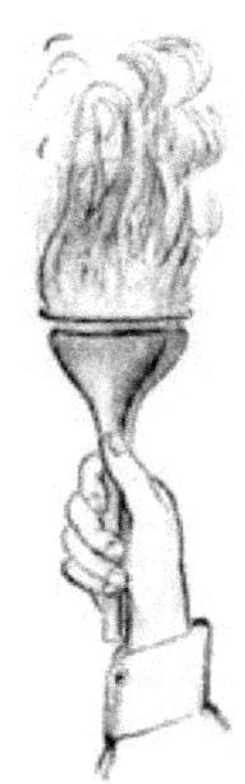

CHAPTER VIII.

Devoted to Politics in Old Morgan—The Early Political Career of Hon. Richard Yates—The Election Returns in 1856—Rocking the Cradle of Liberty in the West—Lovejoy, Beecher & Co—"The Underground Railroad" had a Station at Jacksonville, Conductors Snedeker, Irving, Henderson, Spencer, and others, Directors Wolcott, Reed, Carter, Wilberd, Melendy, et al.—Old Time Abolitionists—Formation of the First Republican Club in the Nation—The "Free Democracy" of 1853—The Missouri Compromise Discussion, Prince, McConnel, Dickens, Adams, Sturtevant, et al.

HISTORIC MORGAN and Classic Jacksonville have their political history as well as religious, social, educational, etc.

As stated in the first chapter the first election in the county was in March 1823. In August, 1824, was the election for and against a constitutional convention, and as this would settle the slavery question in this State it roused much feeling as is shown by the Morganian Society, whose constitution is recorded in that chapter. Mr. A. K. Barber, now living in Jacksonville, and who came here in 1824, well remembers the party feeling then between Whigs and Democrats and the charges of corruption made against Henry Clay. He voted then for John Quincy Adams, and voted this fall for James G. Blaine.

Rev. D. Pat Henderson insists that the first abolition newspaper (called the *Statesman*) ever published west of the mountains, even before Lovejoy's time, was published in this city, over Goltra's hat store, by himself; and edited by Prof. Turner. Of this Turner cannot himself affirm, as he does not distinctly remember the dates, as Henderson does. Turner says: "Even that tame little sheet was regarded as a menace to the church and the state and a danger to the college. I have not seen a copy of it since those days. I have no doubt I should now be heartily ashamed of its stupid conservatisms."

From 1851 to '57 the most honored political representative claimed by Jacksonville as peculiarly her own, Hon. Richard Yates, was making for himself a reputation as orator and statesman extending all over and beyond this State. In 1852 he was a candidate for congressional honors from the then sixth district on the same ticket with Gen. Winfield Scott, for President The latter was not elected as our readers know, the latter was chosen first in 1850 and re-elected in 1852 and 1854. Of his canvass of his district in 1852, the Carlinville correspondent of the Carrolton *Gazette* of that year says:

"*Triumph* is the only word in our language that will give you a full idea of the effect of Richard Yates' progress round about us, and also in Carlinville, on Monday last True, Mr. Calhoun acquitted himself with his usual ability, but Mr. Yates replied in an unusual strain of eloquence and power, and left an impression among our people, such as no man, not a member of the Democratic party, could possibly attain. While Democrats here grant to Mr. Calhoun all they can grant in ability an energy, still Dick Yates accomplished, from a cause which none of us can describe, in the HEARTS of the masses, that which will *lead to his election in November next*.

The meeting here was well attended by members of both parties, and I hear of no man who takes exception to the eloquence, the power, the ability, earnestness, energy, and honesty of Richard Yates."

In 1856 when the national Republican party was organized, upon an anti-slavery platform, Mr. Yates heartily espoused its cause and stumped the State in favor of John C. Fremont and the Republican party. During the campaign in the court house at Virginia, Cass county, he made an appeal to his old Whig friends and acquaintances and to the Democrats present to induce them to cut loose from the old parties. He urged that there was no issue between Whigs and Democrats, and that the question of human slavery was the great issue before the American people.

The Whigs present, Dr. Allard and others, were indignant, and greeted the speaker with groans and hisses, while the Democrats laughed in his face and treated the matter as a huge joke.

When Richard Yates earnestly declared to this sneering audience that the Republican party would yet be the ruling party of the nation, the statement was received with an incredulous smile of contempt.

At the close, Mr. Yates, not daunted by the unmanly and contemptible manner in which his arguments had been received, asked those in the audience who were in favor of the Republican party—opposed to the further extension of slavery—to rise to their feet. In the entire audience there w re only eight persons who had the manhood, moral courage and genuine nerve to face the sneers and scoffs of the crowd, and stand up in favor of human liberty.

Among these brave men and women who so nobly placed themselves on record, was Horace Spaulding, the well-known school teacher, Rev. Wm. Collins and the wife and daughter of Mr. Spaulding.

The Whigs who at that time called Dick Yates a "fool and fanatic," afterwards assisted in electing him governor of Illinois. The men who at that time abused Dick Yates for drawing votes from the Whig party, today abuse Prohibitionists for drawing votes from the Republican party.

Apropos of politics and Jacksonville lawyers of 1852, we will quote further from the *Gazette* letter already referred to. The writer from Carlinville says:

"We have had in connection with our court and bar several old members who have long stood by the law and its administration. There is Judge Woodson, who gets younger in good looks and intellectual strength as he advances in years; David A. Smith, of Jacksonville, belonging to an age that is past, but who nevertheless, still keeps the capacity of holding his own in corpulency; Charles D. Hodges, whom Greene county ought to be proud of, besides our own Palmer, Weer, etc. These men have long officiated in courts of justice to the advancement of equity and good order.

Both the interest manifested in hearing the returns from the election of 1856—the first national struggle by the ever since victorious republicans, and also the meagreness of the news received the day after the balloting as compared with the completeness of returns of later campaigns, is shown by a Springfield *Journal* extra, dated November 6th, 1856:

The following dispatches have been received at this office this a. m.:

CHICAGO, 9 P. M.

MESSRS. BAILHACHE & BAKER:

We shall go to Springfied with 28,000 majority for Fremont.

CHICAGO, 5th, 9½ P. M.

EDITORS JOURNAL:

Cook county gives Fremont 3,600 majority. The First and Second Congressional Districts give 18,000 majority for Fremont The counties of Cook, Carroll, Kane, Kankakee, Joe Daviess, DeKalb Boone and seventeen towns in Bureau county show 13,179 majority for Fremont; being a gain of 967 on vote of 1854. The indications are that the Republican State ticket is elected.

LOUISIANA.—Parishes show steady gains for the Democrats. The State is doubtful.

MISSISSIPPI.—Scattering reports show Democratic gains.

GEORGIA.—Meagre returns show gains for the Democrats.

ALABAMA.—Scattering returns show Democratic gains.

TENNESSEE.—Nashville —Buchanan gains on Johnson's vote

ILLINOIS.—St. Clair county reported 300 majority for Fremont. Morrison, Democrat for Congress about 800.

Kœrner, Republican, beaten for Senate.

Madison county.—About half heard from gives Fremont 705, Fillmore 908, Buchanan 1,038. Bissell 695, Richardson, 735 Morris 52.

St. Clair county.—Belleville.—Fremont 331, Fillmore 196, Buchanan 338

Rushville.—The full returns from all townships except five, are in. Buchanan's majority is about 1,100 over Fremont. This will be increased by the five townships to hear from which are all Democratic but one, which gives a small Republican majority. As far as heard from Richardson 897, Bissell 560, Morris 24.

In July 1881, Richard Yates, Jr., a talented young lawyer just entering zealously into political life and the practice of law, prepared for the *Daily Journal* of this city, an article entitled "Rocking the Cradle" and showing the difficulties contended with by local Republican party in the days of its formation, the story of Abolitionism and its agitation here and the liberty movement. It appears from the writer's interviews with Mr. J. O. King, Mr. Anderson Foreman and Mr. Henry Irving, as published in this article that Jacksonville has the honor of organizing the *first Republican club in the nation in 1853.*

Mr. Yates writes in introducing this matter as follows:

But in 1840 a party organization was effected, a national convention held and candidates nominated. Jas. G. Birney for president. The war was begun. The small party grappled with slavery and from the first the slave power winced at the force of its grip. Birney polled 7,000 votes. In 1844 he was again a candidate and polled 62,000 votes, of which Jacksonville furnished seventeen.

The year 1848 saw the organization of the "Liberty Party," composed of a combination of all anti-slavery elements. It held a National convention at Buffalo in June, 1848, and nominated Martin Van Buren for president vs. the Whig candidate, Gen. Taylor. Among the anti-slavery Whigs who supported Taylor and voted against both Van Buren, the Liberty candidate, and Cass, the Democratic candidate, were New England's great statesman Daniel Webster, New York's popular leader, Wm. H. Seward, and the West's favorite, Abraham Lincoln—not then an Abolitionist, though a sworn enemy to slavery.

Compromise measures of 1850 made California a free state, permitted slavery in New Mexico and Utah, gave Texas 90 000 square miles of free soil, abolished the slave trade in the District of Columbia and humiliated the free states by a more stringent fugitive slave law. The demise of the old Whig party followed in 1852.

The Kansas Nebraska bill repealing the Missouri compromise and establishing "squatter sovereignty" in the two new territories of Kansas and Nebraska, was forced through Congress by the slave power in 1854. Bissell, Yates and Washburne opposed it. The result was that this district refused to re-elect Yates to Congress that year and he retired to private life "to come up again later," as he said in a speech at the old court house in Jacksonville that year, "on the very same principles he then went down on." But though the slavery sentiment was thus strong in this vicinity, the people were startled and alarmed by the passage of that act, and it led to the organization of the new party, to prevent the introduction of slavery into the territories, which afterwards became known as the Republican party.

The writer is convinced that the first club or society for that purpose was organized in the city of Jacksonville. A great many clubs and societies had been organized previous to that, all over the country, for the abolition of slavery, but so far as known the first club ever organized for the same purpose that the Republican party espoused when organized, was a society of seven citizens of Jacksonville.

Mr. Foreman says it was held at Mr. King's store on the north side of the square in this city, where Chamber's & Co.'s grocery store is now located. There were only seven persons present, namely: Elihu Wolcott, Joseph O. King, Anderson Foreman, John Mathers, William Harrison, Chas. Chappel and James Johnson.

"How and by whom was the meeting called?"

"By the mutual consent of all the seven named. There was a simple understanding between them to the effect that they would meet and organize at that place."

"Had these seven men ever held any conferences together before that meeting?"

"Oh, yes, they had often talked of the necessity of making the curbing of the slave power, a political issue; but they had never formally met together or organized in any way."

"There had been a great deal of Abolition agitation all over the country, including Illinois, before that time, had there not?"

"Yes, and the feeling had aroused not a few of our citizens. Elihu Wolcott had been president of the Illinois State Anti-Slavery Society, which first met at Upper Alton, October 28, 1838, and of which Elijah P. Lovejoy was secretary. Dr. Edward Beecher drew up the preamble and declaration of sentiments of that society and it was a document of singular solemnity and force. Yes, the Abolition spirit was abroad in Illinois long before 1853."

"Well, Elihu Wolcott was called to the chair and presided. Joseph O. King was appointed clerk of the meeting. The seven men mentioned above enrolled their names as members of the organization. The prime object of the society was to use all honorable political means to prevent the extension of African slavery into states and territories, now known as free states and territories; this we continued to do as long as the institution of slavery existed."

"Did your organization grow fast?"

"No; there was too much pro slavery feeling united against for us to increase in members rapidly at first, but the time came, I tell you, when no house was large enough to hold our meetings, and our membership was immense."

"Did you make public the fact that you had organized?"

"Not right away. But in the course of a year or two we had begun to have public addresses. Richard Yates made one of our first speeches. Not long after our organization we had to meet in the old tavern hall on the east side of the square, second door south of East State street. We held a great many meetings and conferences there."

"Was there ever any violence or turbulence at these meetings of yours?"

"No violence, but the excitement was often intense."

"How long was it before you began as an organization to figure in conventions and State politics?"

"Well the anti-slavery Whigs ran a candidate for State treasurer in 1854 as an anti-Kansas-Nebraska man. From that time on the Republican party began to make itself felt."

"When was the name Republican party first used?"

"By a convention at Bloomington in 1854 The new party was formally organized in May, 1856, at Bloomington Paul Selby, of the Jacksonville *Weekly Journal*, had called a conference of anti-Kansas Nebraska editors at Decatur in February, 1856, and that conference called the Bloomington convention, of which John M Palmer was president and Richard Yates one of the vice presidents. Though Buchanan carried Illinois that year by 9,100 majority over Fremont, Bissell, the Republican candidate for governor, and the whole State ticket were elected by 4,700 majority."

"Was the Republican organization pretty strong in Morgan county in 1856?"

"Yes; we were firmly established long before that. The pro slavery element, though it abused and despised us, could no longer bring to bear the pressure that they did upon the Abolitionists."

"Did any of the charter members of your club ever hold office at the hands of the Republican party?"

"No; they were not office seekers. King and Mathers were long afterwards each elected mayor of the city of Jacksonville, but they were all content and well satisfied with the assistance they had rendered to the grand party of freedom during its earliest struggles. We were the first club in Illinois to avow the same principles afterwards championed by the national Republican party."

Mr. King was found at his office, at the Jacksonville Gas Company's works, and interrogated as follows:

"Mr. King, were you the clerk of a meeting, held at your store, in this city, in 1853, for the purpose of organizing a political agitation for the exclusion of slavery from the free territories?"

"I was."

"Were all of the seven men, spoken of above, abolitionists?"

"I think so. I am certain that Wolcott, Mathers, Foreman and myself were. Perhaps all were not so active as some of us."

"Were the active ones known by the public to be such?"

"Yes; and we were the most hated and despised of men. We were the most unpopular people in town for a long time, and were almost socially ostracised. Although there was a New England settlement here, which in the main sympathised fully with the abolition movement, still the element of southern descent and feelings predominated, and the best and otherwise worthiest people of the town united in deeming us fanatics and revolutionists. The churches were all against us with the exception of the Congregational church, of which a number of abolitionists were members. We could get no other church when we wished to have a lecture or an address by any eminent agitator like Wm. T. Allen or Owen Lovejoy."

"Will you please mention some of the Jacksonville abolitionists?"

"Well besides those already named there were Thomas Melendy, J. B. Turner, Samuel Adams, Timothy Chamberlain, William Kirby, William Carter, Julius and Samuel Willard, Azel Pierson, William Holland and Henry Irving, William H. Williams and William Strawn."

"Sometimes our opponents created disturbances at these abolition meetings. I remember once when Wm. Allen, a noted preacher, was addressing us, at the Congregational church, some malicious person threw a black rag baby straight at his head. As you may imagine we were all very indignant. The feeling against us was intense. Men came to my store—old customers—and refused to deal any longer with me because I was an abolitionist. The fact that Richard Yates, then a Whig, dined at the house of Willard, created a great commotion and was used against him. But such opposition deterred neither him nor us."

"Was there any abolition organization here?"

"No formal organization, but we were firmly united and known to be so. As I said, the New Englanders in general sympathized with us, but their cautiousness and conservatism didn't permit some of them to admit it publicly."

"Did the underground railroad run through here?"

"Well, there was an occasional passenger. One night when I went home my wife informed me there was company to be entertained, and surely enough I found them *in the barn*—three fugitive slave women from Missouri. We clothed, fed and cheered them, and while a musical party were gathered at our house, the three women (clad in the well-known garments of the three daughters of Wm. Holland, who had come to the house as invited guests) were quietly moved, escorted by Mr. Holland, Prof. Turner and myself to the house of Azel Pierson, thence to Mrs. Kirby's, whence after a stay of ten days, Benj. Henderson took them in a closed carriage to Lyman's at Pleasant Plains, and Lyman sent them on their way rejoicing. They had been tracked to Jacksonville by officials acting under the odious Fugitive Slave law, and at the time of their concealment at Mrs. Kirby's they were advertised all over town and rewards offered for them. This was the only case of fugitives I was connected with. But I have no doubt there were many others. Timothy Chamberlain was a particularly active 'underground railroad man.' As it was a penitentiary offense in those days to harbor or assist a fugitive slave, you may rest assured not very many were ever connected with the enterprise and the few that were, didn't talk much about it."

"As for Wolcott and me and the others named, we never denied the charge, and I consider it one of the greatest compliments I ever received, that when the colored people of Jacksonville held their first emancipation celebration, they chose me, a white man, to be their chairman. It was a great and a memorable honor."

"The survivors of your original band are very few in number, Mr. King?"

"Very few. They are almost all dead. Turner, Chamberlain, Irving, Henderson, Foreman and myself are all that are alive now; and of the eight, who formed that first Republican club Foreman and I alone survive."

"Tell me about that first meeting of that club."

"Well, Elihu Wolcott, a noble pioneer in that movement, presided at that meeting, and we organized such a club. We met quietly for a time in my store, and afterwards held meetings in a room in a building owned by John Mathers, on the square, two doors south of East State street, where I now own a storeroom, occupied by Phelps & Osborne, a dry goods firm."

"The object of your organization being as stated, what kind of work did you set out to do?"

"Well, we first turned our attention to the 'sinews of war' and went quietly to raising money. Our membership being so small, you can imagine that our subscriptions were not very numerous. All gave what they could. There were not many, in addition to the original eight, who contributed anything. Our next step was to purchase and disseminate literature. We procured and distributed a large number of pamphlets. They served to awaken no little feeling and prepared the way for a still more effective campaign document.—Uncle Tom's Cabin."

"Immediately upon its publication we determined to procure a number of copies of that soul stirring production and circulate them gratis in the interest of our cause."

"We had to send to Cleveland, Ohio, to get the books. Wolcott, Mathers and myself supplied the funds and we bought *five hundred copies*. We scattered them, discreetly and judiciously, far and wide. They did more to increase the hostility to slavery than any other agency, in this vicinity. They were read and re-read by man, woman and child in every neighborhood, and at the very mention of 'Uncle Tom' the blood boiled in every just man's veins."

"Several Methodist ministers and other friends helped us circulate them. The Rev. Mr. Hindall, a circuit rider, was especially active in the work. Rev. James H. Dickens was also full of enthusiasm. A German friend, too, at Beardstown, helped us in the good work."

"We had only a few real Republican addresses before the Fremont campaign. One of the first strong anti-slavery speeches made here was by Abraham Lincoln. He spoke in the court house park, and when he came out sharp and strong against slavery I threw up my hat and shouted 'Hurrah for Abe Lincoln for president of the United States'."

"Members of your organization took prominent parts, I suppose, in the first Republican conventions in this region?"

"Yes; we were many of us members of the conventions here and of the state conventions during all that period."

Mr. Henry Irving was one of the bravest men connected with the underground railroad and did good service on it from 1843 until the war. Though his principal work was that of conducting he always did what he could in the way of entertaining fugitives. Once he kept a man in the garret of his house for a week, the roads being so closely watched that it was unsafe for anyone to start away with his guest, and so cleverly did he manage the affair that he finally got away with him in spite of the vigilance of the slave catchers. He and William Strawn once took a runaway on horse-back to Pleasant Plains. Returning with the extra horse they were alarmed at meeting Judge Lockwood, who they feared would suspect what they had been doing, but if he did, he never spoke of it. The man had been steward on a steamboat and was quite valuable which caused the owner to pursue him hotly, but he was a bright active fellow and declared he would never be taken alive.

The darkest nights were chosen for the trips which Mr. Irving made, Farmington being the station to which he generally drove, and he still speaks highly of the good people in that village who were always so willing to aid the cause. One trip is especially impressed on his memory, which he undertook one very dark disagreeable night. There were something near a dozen persons aboard and the station was between thirty-five and forty miles distant. The darkness could almost be felt and the roads being none of the best, no time was to be lost. Frequently he had to get out of the wagon and feel for the track when passing over the prairie. Once the sound of approaching hoofs caused the hearts of the whole company to stand still. Stopping the team he requested perfect silence, but they were soon relieved by finding that two stray horses had caused their fright. The road was bad and they frequently strayed from the track, and nothing but the excellence of Ebenezer Carter's team brought them through. Daylight appeared when they were yet some miles from Farmington and then from behind every bush they looked for an enemy to appear and every sound seemed to be that of pursuers. Their destination was safely reached, however, and after resting the next day the fugitives went on and their brave conductor returned.

This is but one of a host of adventures through which he passed, never once being apprehended by the officers of the law though often suspected and pursued. He still vividly recalls the early abolition meetings when so much disorder was created by the enemies of freedom, causing Prof. Turner on one occasion at the court house to pound on the platform with his cane and shout, in the language of Gen. Jackson, "By the Eternal, we will have order here."

These were times in which political excitement ran high. The anti-slavery sentiment was developing and men were risking proscription, persecution and punishment for aiding fellow-beings to escape from the unrighteous slave-masters with which the nation was accursed. The laws of the State made its citizens slave catchers and against this the souls of the freedom-loving rebelled. Prof. Turner, one of the old time abolitionists of Jacksonville, narrates in the *Daily Journal* August 2, 1884, the following incident of 1846:

One bitterly cold night in December, the fall after we so nobly welcomed the Portuguese to our city, Mr. Irving came to me while in my barn feeding my horse and said that there were three colored women escaped from the St. Louis slave market which their friends had escorted and concealed in an old abandoned cabin, southwest of Negro-town in the fields. If left there they would freeze to death or be captured, as their pursuers and our police were close after them. He wished me to go to their rescue while he returned to the city to watch the police. The man was deeply in earnest, quite up to sobbing and trembling. What could I do? But one thing was possible. I at once cut me a heavy hickory bludgeon from the woodpile—which I could then wield far more fearlessly and unscrupulously than now—hid it under my camblet cloak and proceeded to the rescue, while he returned to town to attend to matters there. Arriving at the cabin door I rapped, no one stirred, I repeated my raps but all was still, and I supposed my birds had been captured or had fled from fear. I bethought me to say "I am your friend." At once there was slight rustle and soon the crack of the door was cautiously opened. I quickly reassured them and three trembling, frozen and half dead women stood around me, all, as I afterwards learned, regular members of the orthodox Methodist church in St. Louis, who had been out of doors for a week, trying to escape from a sale down south, away from all their families and friends, which they deemed far worse in those days than death. Seeing the lanterns of the police glancing about "Negro-town," as we called it, I told them to follow me, one after the other, within sight of each other as I led them out of the bright starlight under the shadows of the trees and fences; and if anything happened to me or them, to scatter and hide in the cornfields. By this time my blood was up. I was ready for business, and determined to defend my charge at all hazards. But it soon occurred to me that I had "got an elephant on my hands," and that it would be impossible to conceal them at my house, or in that of any known anti-slavery man.

Dr. Pierson then lived on the old Post place, one mile or more west of town. He was an elder in the Presbyterian church, a good Christian man, but regarded as pro-slavery in his sympathies. I resolved to take them to him. For I thought I knew the bottom of the old man's heart better than he did himself. So I proceeded to pilot them to the gate that leads to his house, and waited for them to come up. Only two of the three came. I supposed the last one had been nabbed, or from her excessively frozen feet had missed her way. I therefore hid the two under the shelter of a fence and brush, and ran back toward town at full speed for the third. I found she had fallen behind and missed her way from excessive lameness. I then took them up to Dr. Pierson's door, rapped and called for the doctor, and said to him: "Here we all are, doctor. I found these strangers so and so. You know I cannot protect them. I have brought them to you. You must either protect or betray us." "Come in, come in, Mr Turner. We won't betray you. We will do the best we can for them. Wife, these people need some hot coffee and something to eat." On went the tea kettle, open flew the larder as though the king himself had knocked at the door, as indeed he had. The Lord's children got their supper and left the devil out doors to feed on creeds, orthodoxies, conservatisms and wind, to his heart's content. They were kept and carefully nursed for a week or two in Dr. Pierson's barn, and a man took my horses and old sleigh and shot them off towards the Canada line. This is all I know about the affair. I heard they got through safely. How those women got to that old cabin I never knew till I read it in the *Journal* last week. I do not remember to have spoken with any of the parties about it since, as gassing with each other has been no part of our business. But all who really know anything about it will confirm this general statement.

The first of January after this, on another bitterly cold night, we had one of our old-fashioned annual union dress-parade prayer meetings, in the basement of the same church in which we had before welcomed the Portuguese. In these meetings all the sects united except the Campbellites, who had not then got fully on their orthodox pinafores. For, then as now, no faith was deemed orthodox that had not been salted down long enough to begin to petrify and turn to stone. Any true description of those union prayer meetings would now be resented as a caricature.

On this occasion a most excellent Christian man, now in Heaven, but then too orthodox for either Heaven or earth, quoted freely from the Assembly's catechism, to show the exceeding danger and peril of all heretics and especially of all Unitarians, or men so inclined. I stood the first round very comfortably in silence. But when he again renewed the assault so vigorously that all eyes were turned over to my corner, I could not resist the temptation to reply. I quoted from Christ's creed instead of the church creeds; narrated my experience in detail, as given above, in an effort to conform to Christ's creed, only taking care to implicate no one in it but myself; commended them for their noble reception of the Portuguese in that church but little before, who had been deprived by the tyrrany of the Portuguese of the privilege of reading only one book—the Bible. But here were American-born citizens, orthodox church members whom the tyrrany of our laws and votes and churches had deprived of the privilege of reading all books whatever, from God or man; sealed their immortal souls in total midnight darkness; denying them the right to their own wages, husbands and children, nay to their own souls and bodies; and when about to be sold from all these, fleeing from lusts more dreadful to them than death, with frozen feet and starved bodies, they appealed to me for aid, I was compelled to skulk away, through the darkness of midnight, from all our court houses and officers, our churches and creeds and orthodoxies, as though I were a whipped dog, or was perpetrating some infamous crime.

We have had enough of creeds that never were anything but the bastard and leprous progeny of the old Papists and despots of Europe. Let us Americans return to the creed of Him who alone is son of man, son of God and savior of the world, and alone competent to give us a creed.

Of course I do not remember the words of this little speech, but its spirit I can never forget: for at the time I felt that more fines than all my property was then worth and a possible term in the state's prison, in which my old and much beloved classmate Torry gloriously died, hung on every word of its utterance.

The next morning the town was of course astir. Esquire Smith, a southern man, our leading lawyer, one of our grandest old men, was at the prayer meeting and heard, all that was said. The pro-slavery party naturally went to him to get out writs for me, on my own confession.

He said to them: "You go home and keep quiet. The less you have to say about that meeting the better it will be for you and for us all."

So these poor old slaves are, I suppose, in heaven, with nearly all the others who bore any part in those transactions, while we are still here to thank God every day and every hour that even the lowest and meanest of our citizens cannot now be tempted with crimes and infamies that in those days sorely beset, if they did not overcome the wisest and the best of us, and that all other creeds are so rapidly giving way to the creed of the Christ of God.

The early days of the underground railroad were fraught with great hardship for those who conducted the enterprise. It meant for them social ostracism, great labor and expense as well as the risk of heavy fines and imprisonment; but caring for none of these things these brave souls went forward unflinchingly in the path of duty. No monument can now be reared to their memory which will begin to do them justice; their reward is the gratitude of 4,000,000 liberated slaves, and their monument the grand fact that in our country all men are really free and equal before the law.

At one time a slave girl had escaped, and it was suspected that she was hidden at

Ebenezer Carter's, two miles south of the city. Immediately a band of southern sympathizers rode out there, and driving up to the house, the leader inquired of Chauncey:

"Where's your father?"

"He's not at home just now."

"Where's your mother?"

"She's gone away, too."

"Isn't there anybody at home?"

"Yes; I'm here."

"Is that nigger girl about the place?"

"Well, really, I don't believe I can say.

"You'd better say, for we've got a warrant and are going to search the house."

"All right, if you've legal authority go ahead."

The two daughters were much alarmed, but the boy stood his ground and the crowd left without a clew and cursing the lad for his nonchalance.

At one time a citizen of this county bought a boy in the south and brought him here to work on his farm for a number of months. When his master was taking him back to the south some one in St. Louis told him he was entitled to his freedom and legal proceedings were at once instituted in his behalf. Ebenezer Carter was requested to go down and testify, but being busy sent his son Chauncey. The slaveholder met the boy on his arrival, and, shotgun in hand, said:

"What are you doing down here?"

"I came down to look around a little."

"Well, you'd better make tracks for home and that in a hurry."

"I thought I wouldn't go until I'd seen something of the city."

"Well, I tell you you'd better leave or you'll find it a very unhealthy place."

"I guess I won't go to-day, anyhow."

Nor did he go until he had given his testimony, which we are informed, resulted in the freedom of the slave.

A number of persons now living were acquainted with the history of these days. Among others Mr. Timothy Chamberlain, who says, "I had no active part in the underground road, but when Mr. Henderson or some other person would come to me for money or clothes, I knew where to go for them. A good many persons now claim always to have been avowed abolitionists who were certainly not very outspoken then. When I was living in Macoupin county a man from Jacksonville came down there to tell a slave boy who had been brought there from Missouri, that he was entitled to his freedom. He ate dinner with me, but suspecting an armed mob, I urged him to flee for his life, which he did, and none too soon. The next day the mob compelled the slave boy to swear that I had put him up to running away, and they came to my house with him. The leader drew his pistol and said, "Mr. Chamberlain, you have been putting this boy up to running away, and we are going to settle with you for it." Backing up against the house I drew a knife and said, "If you attack me I don't expect to live ten minutes, but when I go to heaven I will take several of you with me as witnesses. Your accusation is wholly false, but I now say to the boy in the presence of you all that he is entitled to his freedom and can get it in any court in the land. You came here to find an abolitionist, and there was none here, but you see one now right before you."

"Several of the company began to sympathize with me and the crowd left. When a second attack was contemplated some time later several of these same persons secreted themselves near by without my knowledge so as to be ready to help me if necessary. From that time forward my opinions were pronounced and everybody had a chance to know what they were. My friends thought it safer for me to move back to Jacksonville which I did, going into the hack business. Sometimes my hack would be missing for a day or two but I had a very good idea where it had gone."

Mr. Jos. H. Bancroft says he took no part directly in aiding fugitive slaves to escape but when he was mysteriously asked for a pair of shoes or other articles he handed them out gladly. Public attention was much aroused by a visit of E. P. Lovejoy to this place about the year 1835 or 1836. It was very detrimental to any man to be known as an Abolitionist. One old lady was looking at some black and white straw bonnets at his store and remarking that they were Abolition bonnets said she wanted none of them. A customer once called him aside very privately and wanted to know it he was an Abolitionist as he had determined to have nothing to do with any such person.

Alderman W. C. Carter being asked at what time 'underground railroad' work was systematically undertaken in this place, answered:

"About the year 1838 or '39. Though but a boy at that time the stirring scenes then enacted have left a vivid impression on my memory. Elihu Wolcott was at that time the head and front of the enterprise, bestowing his money and energies on the cause with a devotion that never wavered and a courage that never faltered. Immediately associated with him were T. W. Melendy, Ebenezer Carter, my father, Benjamin Henderson, D. B. Ayers, Dr. M. M. L. Reed, and later, Samuel Willard and his father and some others."

Mr. Carter has in his possession two documents, yellow with age, dated February 22d and 23d, 1843, which we present herewith.

NEWS—EXTRA—NOTICE.—The citizens of Jacksonville are requested to assemble at the court house on Thursday, the 23d inst. at 1 o'clock p. m., for the purpose of expressing their feeling in relation to the late outrage committed upon the property of a widow lady visiting our town by one of our citizens.

Here followed a list of thirty names of prominent citizens. The meeting was largely attended and the following resolutions unanimously adopted:

"WHEREAS, An outrage having been committed some short time since by two citizens of this place upon the property of a stranger and that stranger a widowed lady, the injury was promptly repaired so far as the lady was concerned, and time having now been given that all excitement and intemperance of action might subside, the citizens of Jacksonville believe that it is due to themselves, to the people at large and to their friends at a distance that the public mind should be disabused of all prejudice against the town by publishing to the world a full, fair and unvarnished state of facts, authorized, indorsed and accredited as the act of the town.

"Some short time since a widow lady by the name of Lisle, a resident of Louisiana, on her way home from Kentucky, came to this place to visit a couple of sisters residing here. She was accompanied by her child and nurse and a female slave about 18 years of age. Mrs Lisle was unexpectedly detained here longer than she had anticipated by the closing of the river. On Thursday night of week before last, the night before she intended starting, and did start home in the stage, the negro girl was stolen off by a certain Samuel Willard and conveyed to the house of Ebenezer Carter, two miles south of this place where she was concealed until Saturday evening, when she was run off by J. A. Willard, the father of the former. Many of the citizens promptly volunteered to look for the girl and on Saturday night made the above discovery with the addition that the elder Willard would carry the girl to a Mr. Cushing, one mile south of Greenfield, and from this place she would be conveyed by some other person toward Canada. The pursuit was so prompt that the girl was taken while in possession of Willard and both brought back to this place when the girl was sent to her mistress, and the two Willards were immediately arraigned, and after a full hearing of the case, defended by N. Coffin, they were admitted to bail in the sum of $2,500 to answer to our penal code at the next March term of our court.

These being the facts, therefore

Resolved, That although a judicial investigation will be had upon the matter, we feel it our privilege and duty to say that we do not consider this a question of slavery or anti-slavery, abolition or anti-abolition, but a flagrant and high hand infraction upon one of the penal laws of our land."

Then followed an admission of the evils of slavery, but since it is protected by laws and honored by many good men, the meeting doesn't know how it is to be put down, but certainly not in this way.

Resolved, That the citizens of Jacksonville will at all times extend the hand of friendship and hospitality to their acquaintances of the south, and will be pleased to reciprocate the friendly acquaintance of neighbors, ready at all times and on all occasions, promptly and efficiently to aid and protect them in the enjoyment of their property.

And to that end, having reason to believe that there are bands of abolitionists, organized with depots or relays of horses to run negroes through our state to Canada, and that one of them is in this town we will form an Anti Negro Stealing Society as we heretofore formed an Anti Horse Stealing Society, and that we will, in this neighborhood, break up the one as we broke up the other

Resolved, That although young Willard, who stole the negro, and young W. C. Carter, who assisted to conceal the negro, and Coleman, who pursued the men who were returning her to her mistress, are all students of Illinois College, and as yet have not been dealt with by said college; yet it may be proper for this meeting to abstain from any action in the case, leaving the college to defend its own reputation.

Resolved, That these proceedings be signed by the president and secretary, and that they be published in the *Illinoisan* and the Missouri *Republican*, and that the southern papers generally be requested to copy it.

A hand bill is still in the possession of Miss Melendy, calling attention to the wants of a slave buyer for the southern market, who desired to buy one hundred negroes. Though it was issued in Missouri it is a document of much interest.

Mr. Carter was asked: "Were there any stations of the underground railroad near here?" and answered:

"My father's house was long a stopping place on the route until it became so well known that it was impossible to avoid the slave catchers and then another place was chosen. Mrs. W. C. Verry was always ready to harbor the fugitives, and was a remarkably fearless woman. So far as I know none of the Abolitionists about here ever went from home to encourage slaves to run away, but when they knew of any already on the road they were ready to help them. Mr. Isaac Snedeker used to bring a great many fugitive slaves through here and the amount of work he did in this way, purely from a love for his fellow men, was truly wonderful. He was a total stranger to fear, though his life was repeatedly threatened, while abuse and calumny were heaped upon him without measure. Living near Jerseyville, he had to come to this place through a part of the country inhabited almost entirely by southerners, who were on the watch for him. He always went well armed, and it was by no means safe to attack him. Through all these perilous years, although very frequently on the road with his human freight, he was never once taken himself, nor did he ever lose a fugitive. Sometimes his pursuers would fire at him and sometimes they would try to overpower him, but he was both too brave and too smart for them. When closely pressed he has been known to put his passengers on the horses and leave the wagon.

"From this place Benjamin Henderson use to run the trains for some time, and more than once he has started out in the night with his freedom seekers, followed by the prayers of the lovers of freedom he left behind. C. E. Lippincott had a great deal to do in this work, and was always ready for business.

"At one time a citizen of this place brought here from Kentucky a boy and girl named Bob and Emily Logan. Coming under such circumstances they were entitled to their freedom and when they found that preparations were being made to take them back south they appealed for help to their anti-slavery friends, and so one night they were missing. They were secreted in the town for some days, but one day Bob incautiously ventured on the street, when he was caught, gagged, bound, hurried into a carriage and conveyed to the river and there shipped for the south and never heard from afterwards. Emily undertook legal proceedings to gain her liberty, Elihu Wolcott, D. B. Ayers and T. W. Melendy going on her bond. The case was fought up to the Supreme Court of the State and there decided in the girl's favor."

"How long was the underground railroad kept up in this place?"

"Until about 1855 or '57, though with intermissions, as the slave catchers would sometimes watch my father's house so closely that some other place had to be chosen for a depot for a while.

"One afternoon I saw a colored man whom I at once believed to be a runaway slave. I asked him in and in the evening started off with him on horseback. It was raining hard and was very dark with occasional vivid flashes of lightning. We soon heard steps behind us, and I told my companion to lie down on his horse and conceal himself, which he did so completely that when the next flash of lightning came I thought he had dropped off entirely. Our pursuer turned out to be a cow and we were much relieved.

"I remember after the southerners had been busy looking elsewhere for a time a large party of fugitives was brought to my father's barn about the year 1853. I shall never forget the sight; strong men and women hungering for freedom, boys and girls hardly realizing the situation, and one infant in its mother's arms, looked around in bewilderment at its strange surroundings. They were in due time successfully removed and sent on their way to the north star."

From Benjamin Henderson, (colored) some very interesting reminiscences are obtained.

"Mr. Henderson, in what year did you begin your labors in the cause of freedom?"

"I came here to live in the year 1841 and was soon at work on the underground railroad and kept it up more or less until 1857 or '58. My house was a regular stopping place for fugitives, though at intervals it had to be abandoned as it would be watched too closely by the slave catchers. I did a great deal of teaming in those days and so was called on to transport the fugitives frequently. Sometimes I made two trips a week, carrying all the way from one to sixteen."

"Where was your next depot?"

"We generally went to Springfield, Farmington and other places."

"Who were your best friends here?"

"Elihu Wolcott and Ebenezer Carter were always the main pillars of the enterprise, sparing neither trouble nor expense, always acting as though they knew nothing of fear. Next to them came T. W. Melendy, Dr. Reed and several others who have been previously mentioned. When we wanted supplies for the fugitives we always found friends in Joseph and Horace Bancroft, J. W. Lathrop, T. D. Eames, Asa Talcott, Mr. Hoyt, Mr. Burdette and others. Henry Irving was always ready to go on the road or entertain parties, and Rev. Mr. Kirby often proved himself a friend in need.

"Considerable driving was also done by Washington Price, of this place."

"Please tell me some of your adventures."

"My first experience was in a small way. A fugitive came in one Saturday evening and we carefully secreted him a short time and then put him on the road for the next station. Next, a man came to my house from Mississippi and as I was not well acquainted with the road to Springfield I tried for two days to get some one else to go but couldn't; so I got a buggy one night and started. Indications of day appeared before we reached the city and my man began to get uneasy. I lost the way and hardly knew where to go, but finally made a successful turn and found the town. Daniel Callahan and Wm. Butler were our station keepers, and without very much trouble I found the latter and left my charge with him.

"At one time a man hotly pursued came to my house. He was valuable and the main roads were closely watched. I took him by a round about way and got him through all right.

"Once two girls were brought to my house, one of them dressed in men's clothes. I kept them several days till two others came and then took all off.

"Three women and two men were left at my house when I was away from home. My wife and Mr. Price made up a team and took them on. At Berlin one of the men let the buffalo robe get tangled in the wagon wheel and the driver had to stop in front of the tavern and loosen it. Fortunately no one heard them. A few years ago I had the pleasure of meeting one of these women in Chicago and we had a pleasant time talking over those days of terror and danger.

"Walden Stewart, Mr. Snedeker and Mr. Pitman used to operate below here and for a time the fugitives they sent north to the house of a colored man whom they trusted were never heard from. One night they sent two men on to this man who received them all right and started on with them the next night. They were soon met by white men who halted them, handcuffed all three and started toward St. Louis. The man who received the fugitives was sent off by himself and the other two taken on to St. Louis and thrown into the slave pen. One was sold to a party who took him to New Orleans, but he managed to escape and return to St. Louis on the very boat which had taken him away. Meanwhile his comrade escaped from the slave pen, and the two made another start for the north. On their way up they met their old friends and told them of the treachery of the man who had been trusted and he was severely let alone. The city of St. Louis offered a reward of $100 for each fugitive returned and the owners generally gave an equal amount and for this paltry sum, or a part of it, these and others had been betrayed. We were always very much troubled by men working to secure these rewards.

"Once Stewart brought three women and one man to my house. I took the man in and sent the women to a neighbor. The next morning as we were talking over the best means of escape, a man came in boldly and arrested my guest. I went down stairs and met a comrade of the intruder who inquired for the women. Meanwhile their host had heard of what was going on and in a cowardly manner turned them out of doors as I was standing there. I engaged the attention of the man who was after them and though but a few rods away they succeeded in climbing the fence and escaping to J. O. King's barn. One of them, a large woman, broke the top rail in getting over and fell back but the next attempt was successful. The remainder of their story has been told by Mr. King. The man was taken back to St. Louis but got away for good about a year afterward.

"From that time forward my house was closely watched day and night and I had to be very cautious. Not long after I was called on one evening to shelter six runaways, but I was afraid to do so as it was not prudent. I first went to Henry Irving's, but found him away from home and his wife sick. As she had company I found it very hard to state my errand. Finally I edged up to the bedside and told her what I wanted. As Mr. Irving was away she told me to go to Rev. Mr. Kirby's which I did. He had company in one of the front rooms at the time, but when he came to the door to me he fortunately shut the door from the hall to the parlor and so I was able to speak freely. He said at once, "Bring them along." He built a fire for them up stairs and I brought them in through the hall, right by the parlor full of people without being suspected. Mr. Irving took this load away, as it was not safe for me to do it. This company consisted of a one legged man, another man who was lame, a sound man, a woman and two children. When they left Springfield they were joined by two young women who had been waiting for a chance to go on.

"Before they had gone many miles they were captured by two white men, who were after the usual reward, and brought back. On the way the one-legged man made an excuse to get out of the wagon, the drivers getting out with him. When all were on the ground, quick as thought the fugitive knocked down both his captors. The well man and the young women took to their heels and escaped, leaving the cripple on the ground to fight alone, which he did for some time, knocking both white men down as fast as they could get up, until one of them grabbed away his crutch and then he was helpless. The next morning the one-legged man said he was sick and couldn't travel, so one of the captors loaded the other cripple, the old woman and the two children into a hack to take them to St. Louis. Under the seat was a jug of whisky which the man got hold of and as the driver was getting into the hack his prisoner attacked him with it and after a vigorous fight made his escape, so that at last only the woman and two children were returned. For these the owner refused to pay more than $10 instead of the $300 as he said he didn't care a cuss for the old woman anyhow.

"A fine looking couple once asked me for shelter in great haste. The hunters were hard after them and $1,000 reward was offered for their capture and return. I was then closely watched and hardly knew what to do. Finally I made an excuse to take some hemp cradles to Springfield, so I laid some hay in the bottom of the wagon, put my passengers on it, more hay over them, and my cradles on top of it and drove leisurely through town about the middle of the afternoon and got through all right.

"There was a man named Freeman who frequently used to undertake to conduct parties of fugitives from St. Louis to Chicago, and he often passed through here. He was a brave fellow, often courting danger from a love of it. At one time he had the lines of the team he was driving shot out of his hands but he pushed right on. Once he brought a party of sixteen to this place and the next night started away with two teams he had hired. A few miles out one of the wagons broke down and so he put his whole company into the other and returned to Ebenezer Carter's. The next morning Mr. Carter came to town for me and said I must take this crowd in hand myself. I told him it would never do to take my team, and beside I very much feared to go to Springfield. Finally he said I should take his, a fine one by the way, and go to Farmington. At dark that night he put them and Freeman aboard the wagon and drove to the corner of Morton avenue and St. Louis street where I met them and took charge. I had never been to Farmington but had an idea of the route to take, but along toward morning we lost our way. Finally Freeman ventured to arouse the people in a house we were passing, and so we were righted and in time found the house of Dr. Lyman, a friend to the cause. We called him up and stated our wants. He said he was sick and couldn't possibly take us in, but directed us to the house of Mr. Burt, a quarter of a mile distant. By this time indications of day began to appear and we were quite uneasy. When we aroused Mr. Burt and stated our errand, he refused to receive us also, although Freeman begged and protested. Finally his wife called out from the bedroom,

"How many are there?"

"Sixteen, Madame," I replied.

"Bring them in."

"She at once arose, and after dressing, fixed the parlor for us and we all lay down on the carpet to get a little much needed rest. About noon I started for home, arriving safely that night.

"This was one of my later adventures: I have had many others, but these will give you an idea of the work. I became so well known to the slave catchers, who used to congregate about St. Louis, that for years I would not have visited that city for any amount of money. It is now rather a matter of pride to be reckoned among the abolitionists of those days, but it was not so then. A good many now lay claim to the title whom I never knew as such until after the war. It may be said we were law-breakers, and perhaps we were, but I am sure no one to my knowledge ever crossed the line into a slave state to advise any slaves to run away, yet who could resist the entreaties of the poor creatures struggling for liberty? To my mind it was fearing God rather than man. I think if any of the men who refused to help us had been captured by another nation and legally held as slaves they would have escaped as soon as possible and showered blessings on the heads of those who helped them get away."

Dr. M. M. L. Reed was another fearless member of that little band never afraid to avow his sentiments though it cost him daily in a financial way beside endangering his life and greatly destroying the peace of his family. Coming to this state in 1830 he had a fine opening ready for him in St. Louis, but he would not live in a slave state, no matter what inducements might be offered. While going his professional rounds he used many opportunities to learn the movements of the enemy and to assist the conductors and often he went in disguise to find out what course the slave catchers were pursuing that he might at once report it at headquarters, and frequently he would not return until two o'clock in the morning. So cordially was he hated by the pro-slavery party that for years he seldom felt safe in walking on the side-walk at night, taking the street to avoid a possible unseen enemy. His family were always startled by a knock at the door fearing it might be some one to arrest him instead of a messenger to ask his presence at the bedside of a patient. One morning while in the midst of family devotions, a furious summons was heard at the door which caused the hearts of each member of the household to beat almost audibly. Calmly finishing his supplications the doctor went to the door where he found three angry men demanding to know the whereabouts of Bob and Emily Logan. Neither threats nor persuasion were sufficient to overcome the courage which had suddenly possessed the mind of the man who was not afraid to do right, and the early callers had to go elsewhere.

One night during his absence his family had reason to believe an unsuccessful attempt was made to set his house on fire. His wife and oldest daughter became very brave through such frequent exposure to danger. One night a man under the influence of liquor called quite late and asked Mrs. Reed for the doctor, saying his child was sick. She told him the doctor was at Waverly and proceeded to shut the door. The man was not satisfied and persisted in coming in. Placing a chair in his way she called her daughter who seized a pair of tongs and brandishing them aloft told the intruder he would be a dead man if he put his head inside that door, which he very wisely concluded not to do.

David Spencer, another prominent colored citizen said: "I came to this country in 1835 and have seen much of the underground railroad. At that time or soon after, it involved a penalty of $1,000 and six months imprisonment to aid a fugitive slave. If a man freed a slave in this state he had to file a bond of $1,000 for the good behavior for the freedman. Such a document for my benefit, signed by J. T. Holmes, is at the court house in this place. I became of age in 1854 and moved to Jacksonville and then determined to help my race in bondage. From the first the prime leaders in the work were Ebenezer Carter and Elihu Wolcott. These good men seemed to fear neither man nor devil when helping a slave to his liberty. Dr. Reed, T. W. Melendy and D. B. Ayers were also pronounced abolitionists. Benj. Henderson and Henry Irving did most of the driving. There were many other good friends to the cause who helped more or less, though mostly in secret. My first exploit was in the memorable winter of 1853-54. One night a wagon drove up to Wm. Olmstead's, on Grove street, with eight runaways. The signal was given and the party unloaded and cared for. Money and supplies were raised and I was appointed to start with them on the Great Western railroad. We boarded the rear of the train just before daylight. When asked several times who my companions were I replied that they were friends from Chicago who had been here to spend the holidays. Soon after we started one of the men whispered in my ear that his old master was in the car a few seats ahead of us, no doubt on the hunt for his property. I told him not to be afraid, for I had a revolver with me and would use it if I had to do so. To our great relief the slaveholder left the train at Springfield, little thinking who had been riding with him. This is one of the experiences I had."

We have tried by diligent inquiry to do justice to all the brave men who took the lead in this work, though it is possible that some names have been omitted which should have been mentioned. We have heard the name of Mr. Lowry in connection with the work, but have been unable to obtain particulars of the part he took.

At the time of the discussion and excitement over the Missouri compromise, spirited public meetings were held in Jacksonville for consideration of this question and the place was pretty effectually waked up. The first meeting was called as a meeting of those opposed to the repeal of the compromise, by a card signed by more than 100 names, published in the papers and by a hand-bill, to take place at the court house. The court room was densely crowded at an early hour and Dr. N. English was made chairman and J. W. Galbraith secretary. Dr. David Prince presented a set of resolutions and was about to proceed with a speech, when Gen. Murray McConnel asked permission to read some resolutions which he should offer as an amendment. Immediately after the reading of these, his son Mr. John L. McConnel read another set of resolutions. Both of the latter sets were in favor of Douglas and his repeal measures, while those offered by Dr. Prince were against the repeal.

Much confusion prevailed and it was charged that the repeal party came there to break up the meeting. The chair decided that it was a meeting at which any were free to speak. Confusion grew worse and finally the repeal folks announced another free-for-all meeting for the next evening and the Anti-Repealers remained, called Dr. Russel to the chair, made J. O. King, Esq., secretary and unanimously passed the Prince resolutions also others introduced by Dr. Adams and Mr. John Mathers. The discussion upon them was participated in by Mr. Isaac D. Rawlings, Prof. J B. Turner, Pres. J. M. Sturtevant, Mr. Mathers and others.

The resolutions were as follows:

Resolved, That it is inexpedient to repeal directly or otherwise, the act admitting Missouri, known as the Missouri Compromise, which section reads as follows:

"SEC. 8. Be it further enacted, that in all that territory ceded by France to the United States, under the name of Louisiana, which is north of thirty-six degrees and thirty minutes north latitude, not included in the limits of the state contemplated in this act, *slavery and involuntary servitude* otherwise than as the punishment of crime, shall be and is hereby forever prohibited."

Resolved, That as good citizens we wish to abide by the second clause of the second Section of the fourth Article of the Constitution which says:

"Congress shall have power to dispose of and make all needful rules and regulations respecting the territory or other property belonging to the United States"

On the next evening there was "a dense crowd assembled" according to the *Morgan Journal's* report. Dr. Cassell was called to the chair and Cyrus Epler, Esq., made secretary. Mr. John McConnel re-offered his resolutions (of which we cannot procure a copy now,) of the night before and Dr. Prince offered his as a substitute. Gen. M. McConnel made a Repeal speech of an hour's length and Dr. Prince followed in opposition. Prof. J. B. Turner and John L. McConnel, Esq., also spoke, the latter for and the former against the repeal. Both sets of resolutions were voted upon amid great confusion and excitement. If sound alone could have been taken as a guide, says a "Spectator," both sets were lost, but the chair declared the McConnel ones carried, and refused to accede to a strong call for a "division of the house."

According to the reports published at the time in the *Morgan Journal*, a meeting of the "Free Democracy" was held in Jacksonville, Thursday, Feb. 10th, 1853, for the purpose of taking some steps with a view to permanent organization in this county and congressional district, Rev. James H. Dickens was called to the chair and Hon. John Mathers appointed secretary. The object of the meeting having been stated as above, the following named gentlemen were appointed a committee to prepare and submit to an adjourned meeting a plan of organization, viz: Hon. John Mathers, Prof. J. B. Turner, J. O. King, Esq., Dr. David Prince and Rev. J. H. Dickens.

After which the meeting adjourned to meet again the next Thursday evening, Feb. 17. At this adjourned meeting, the committee reported as follows and the report was unanimously adopted:

WHEREAS: Past experience has proven to use the necessity of a permanent organization of the Free Democratic party in this county in order to success, therefore,

Resolved, That we members of said party, do hereby form ourselves into such an organization for the Jacksonville precinct, and will do all we can to advance our cause for the next four years.

Resolved, That the Pittsburg platform as adopted by the Free Democratic National Convention, meets with our approbation, and by it our principles and objects must be judged and not by the false representations of our enemies.

Resolved, That an executive committee of five be appointed whose duty it shall be to raise funds for the purpose of purchasing documents, and to use their influence to have similar organizations established in each precinct in the county and to take steps with the view to a county convention of delegates from each precinct.

Resolved, That a committee of correspondence for the congressional district be appointed for the purpose of obtaining the views and feelings of the other counties as to the propriety of holding a district convention and the establishment of a district paper.

Resolved, That a notice of our organization be published in the *Western Citizen*, *National Era* and all political papers published in the Congressional District.

Resolved, That in future we will vote for no proslavery, illiberal, proscriptive Whig or Democrat for any office, if we know it.

After a full discussion this meeting also unanimously adopted the following preamble and resolutions, and then adjourned:

WHEREAS, The General Assembly of Illinois, did, on the 12th of Feb. 1853, pass an act entitled "An act to prevent the immigration of free negroes into this state, and

WHEREAS, This act is open and shameless violation of Articles II and VI of the ordinance of 1787—of the preamble and entire spirit of the constitution of the United States, especially of Art. 1 Sec. 8, clause 18, and Art. 4, Sec. 2, clause 1, and to the spirit of Articles V, VI, and VIII of the amendment, and also of that provision of the constitution of this state which "prohibits slavery or involuntary servitude, except in punishment for crime," and

WHEREAS, Said attempt to inflict upon all free citizens of this state, heavy pains and penalties by fine and imprisonment, for acts in themselves always innocent, and in some cases highly meritorious, reduces all colored persons, bond and free, (even though legal voters in this state) attempting to reside in this state to a condition of perpetual slavery, without crime, thereby making this state, in fact, a slave state, giving to petty magistrates the power of holding courts for cleaving down the liberty of free men and throwing the most shameless obstacles in the way of an appeal from their decision, when made in favor of the inalienable rights of the freeman, and taunting these magistrates themselves with accusations and impeachments for crime should they refuse to commit this greatest of all crimes against the constitution of this state and of the United States, and the laws of both God and man and thereby attempting to force them to its commission—throwing the whole powers of the state at all points against the natural and inalienable rights of the poor and oppressed and pandering with the most disgusting servility and meanness, to the viles and most corrupt despotism on earth that of the AMERICAN OPPRESSOR, and having thus extorted its price of treason from the innocent and helpless, as if in impudent derision of mockery and both God and man, it denominates this "price of blood," a "CHARITY FUND! !" for the relief of the poor! ! In other words, it enables our counties to sell the free black citizens of other states to pay their own pauper tax!!

We think such a law containing the above and many more odious features, was fitly denounced by able senators on the floor of the Senate as "making Illinois a slave state" and being in itself "monstrous, inhuman and unconstitutional."

We, therefore, unanimously resolve, That we regard it with utter loathing and detestation in whole and in all its parts, and hereby solemnly enter our indignant protest against such unrighteous, shameless and disgraceful legislation.

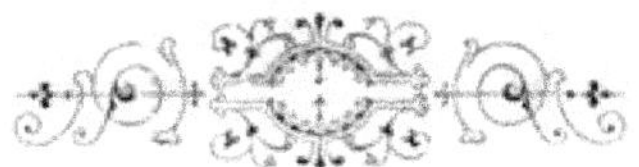

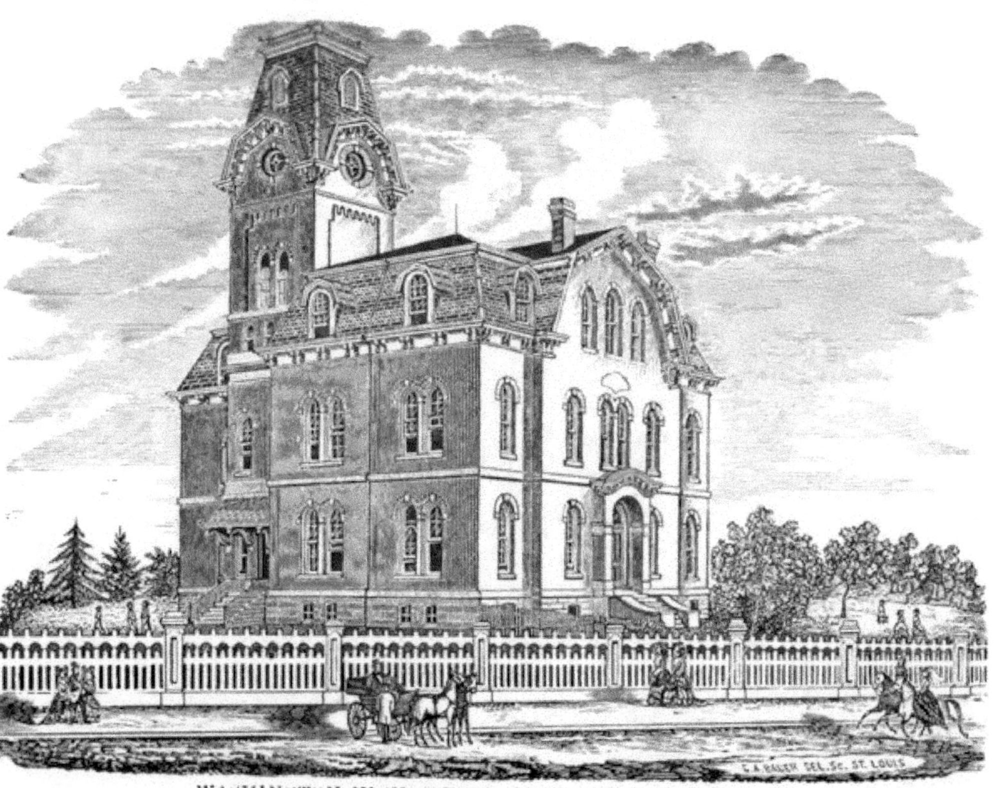

WASHINGTON HIGH SCHOOL, JACKSONVILLE, ILLINOIS.

CHAPTER IX. 1858-'65.

The Business Men—Institution Appropriations—Churches and Preachers—Colleges and Sabbath Schools—Criminal Cases—Local Journalism—Epitomes of News—"Just Before the Battle"—Grant's Regiment—Recruiting for the Union Army—The Pension Roll.

AMONG the firms doing business in our city in 1858 were Dobyns & Co., W. K. Dewey, Kaiser & Russell, Catlin & Co., Scott & Fitch, David Sterrett, F. T. Gillett, D. Robb, B. F. Stevenson, Wm. M. Mayo, Dayton & Co., Hamilton & Jones, J. W. King, A. Bulkley, J. M. Snyder & Co., Wm. H. Collins, A. & C. McDonald, J. Mitchell, W. C. Woodman, Lightfoot & Easton, E. C. Lax, Trabue & Chambers, Wm. Love, Rosenhaupt & Co., C. K. Sawyer, Flack & Risley, F. G. Farrell, Samuel Wolfe, Robert Hockenhull, Wm. H. Corcoran, John Pyatt, Myers & Knollenberg.

It will be seen that many of these have been gone from the business circle of our city a number of years, many are dead, and only a few are still among our merchants and business men.

At the opening of the session of the Illinois Institution for Deaf-Mutes in '56, repeated applications were received to admit persons who, though mute, were not deaf; their inability to articulate being the result of imbecility of mind. Dr. Gillett in his report for that year, urged the establishment of an institution where this class of children might be cared for. But it was not until 1865, that the General Assembly incorporated the "Asylum for Feeble Minded Children." A building near the Deaf and Dumb Institution—the Governor Duncan property—was rented, and placed under the supervision of Dr. Gillett. Having thoroughly organized the school, Dr. Gillett resigned the superintendency and recommended as his successor, Dr. Chas. T. Wilbur, who was accordingly appointed.

In 1859 the Legislature appropriated $75,000 for the completion of Insane Hospital buildings. The most important appropriations since then have been $84,000 for the east wing, $75,000 for the east and west extensions and the furnishing of the same, and further amounts from time to time for boilers, laundry, kitchen, chapel, amusement hall, shops, stables, and a variety of other outside buildings. The general style of the original structure has been adhered to, and both the old and new buildings to-day present as uniform and harmonious an appearance as if they had been erected at one time and by one contractor.

Recalling the churches and pastors of this period we find that during Rev. Robert Allen's pastorate of ten years, from 1857 to 1867, over the Central Presbyterian Church, including the unpropitious era of the war, 123 were admitted to membership, an average of more that 12 per year. Of these 56 were received on profession, an average of nearly six each year.

The Methodist Episcopal preachers were:

EAST CHARGE—J. R. Locke, 1858; W. J. Rutledge, 1859-'60; J. L. Crane, 1861; L. C. Pitner, 1862-'63; A. Semple, 1864-'65.

WEST CHARGE—J. H. Moore, 1859-'60; H. Buck, 1861-'62; R. E. Guthrie, 1863-'64

The presiding elders were: Peter Cartwright, 1858-'60; W. S. Prentice, 1861-'64.

The First German Lutheran Church was organized in 1858, with eight members, among whom were John Knollenberg, Fred. Walker, Edward Beyer, Henry Pecklseffel and Joseph C. Kackman. The organization was effected in the Christian Church, then situated on North Main Street. They met for divine services in various places, until 1863, when they completed their present house of worship. This was used until 1877, when they purchased their present church, selling their old one.

In 1858, the Congregational Church, on the East side of the square, was sold preparatory to erecting the commodious brick structure now occupied by them on West College Avenue. At a comparatively recent date the old church—afterwards "Union Hall"—was used as a furniture wareroom. The new church was dedicated in December, 1860. In 1860, Rev. C. H. Marshall, late of Hudson, Wis., was the pastor.

On Sunday, May 14, 1860, about forty members of the First Presbyterian Church were organized into a separate society known as the Westminster Presbyterian Church. The services were held in the Congregational Church, the sermon being preached by Rev. Cyrus L. Watson, of Farmington, in pursuance of order of Presbytery. From that day there have been six churches of this denomination—three American and three Portuguese. The Westminster congregation soon erected a substantial and comfortable brick house of worship, in the western part of the city, and their membership has been gradually increasing under the faithful ministration of Rev. Dr. David H. Hamilton, deceased and Rev. Samuel M. Morton, the present incumbent.

The first day of December, 1861, was a sad one to many a soul in Jacksonville, but especially to the First Presbyterian Church. Twenty-four hours before a large church and congregation had felt that they had a holy and beautiful house where they could worship God, and which for fourteen years had been their spiritual home. It was a a plain, but commodious structure of brick, built in 1847, just at this time, 1861, re-furnished with cushions, carpeting, paint, and a new organ. Now, nothing remained but ashes and smouldering ruins. It was awful, though grand, to see in the darkness of that first night of winter, the steeple, seemingly a fretwork of living gold, still pointing as the finger of the church to heaven; and to hear the groans (if we may so speak) of that short-lived organ as the pent-up air rushed through its pipes, while the consuming element devoured all about it.

Strawn's Hall, but recently erected, proved a needed place of refuge for the homeless people, which they occupied for some time for all Sabbath exercises, while the week-day meetings were held at the Female Academy. After waiting two years and a half for more prosperous times to come, the corner-stone of a new and still greater temple was laid, in 1864, and the work of erection proceeded steadily, though slowly, until the finishing touches of the upholsterer and painter rendered the whole fabric ready for its intended use, a goal so long waited for by so many praying, working ones, in that large churchless company.

The Sabbath-school cause in Morgan county was earnestly espoused by many zealous workers Annual county conventions of those actively engaged in the work were held, also numerous precinct meetings of similar character. We notice appended to the call for the annual county convention of 1863, the names of "Father" Stephen Paxson, the veteran S. S. organizer and missionary, Prof. B. F. Mitchell, principal of the Academy, Judge William Brown, W. W. Jones and Rev. D. D. Holmes. These conventions have been held every year since, but a new generation has arisen to take charge. The pupils of 1863 are the leaders and teachers of 1884. There are now 81 Sabbath-schools in the county and over 6,000 in attendance.

During the War for the Union the cause of the sick and suffering soldiers brought into existence that grand organization, representative of the whole church, the Christian Commission. Morgan county not only gave her citizens in defence of country, but also liberally donated of her means to relieve the wants of the wounded and sick. The magnificently liberal offer, in 1864, of Mr. Jacob Strawn, Sr., to give ten thousand dollars to the Christian Commission if the citizens of this county would give a like sum met with a most liberal and praiseworthy, response. Through the efforts of a few of our prominent citizens aided by Mr. Reynolds and Rev. McCabe, something over the ten thousand was raised. Mr. Strawn gave his check for the amount of his offer, and if nothing more was done, Morgan county is entitled to rank as the banner county of the banner State of the Union. Jacksonville gave her proportion of this generous offering.

Mrs. Phebe Thompson had charge of the Jacksonville Female Academy for one year, 1857-'58, and was succeeded by Newton Bateman, afterwards LL. D., who had already acquired a solid reputation as an educator, so that his appointment to his office gave great satisfaction, but soon after entering upon his duties in the fall of 1858, he was elected superintendent of public instruction for the State, which position he accepted and filled with great honor to himself and with great advantage to the cause of general education in Illinois. The vacancy thus occurring in the principalship of the Academy was then supplied by the appointment of Miss Hattie P. Murdock, then and for several years previously, a successful and beloved teacher in the school, a graduate of the class of 1850, and the only one of the alumnæ ever raised to the office of preceptress in this institution. That academical year, during which she was at the head, is remembered as one of unusual prosperity, and the catalogue shows a larger enrollment at any previous time, the aggregate of pupils being 171. The trustees desired to continue Miss Murdock in the position for which she had shown marked ability, but she declined, though willing still to serve as teacher, which she did for a year or two under her successor. In 1864 she was married to Mr. D. C. Whitwood, of Detroit, but the happy relation was cut short by her death which occurred September 1865. A discourse in memory of her, delivered by the Rev. Dr. Glover, and entitled "No waste in the bestowment of piety" was published and widely circulated among the alumnæ and friends of the institution.

From 1859 to 1865, Prof. B. F. Mitchell, A. M., served as principal. He was a graduate of Bowdoin College, a thorough scholar, and excellent teacher, a man of mild and gentle bearing, as humble as he was learned, and whose piety was as fervent as it was simple and child-like. His life was that of an educator and he gave to his position the benefit of much experience acquired at the east, the south and the west. His pupils remember with lively feelings his goodness of heart, the affectionate mildness of his rule, and the tenderness of his interest in their spiritual welfare. And if, as is likely, they often took advantage of his unsuspicious and yielding disposition, they uniformly found that such sinning re-acted in the way of regrets, which made it both hard and unprofitable. The period of his service covered that of the civil war, during which, by reason of the general diversion of thought and means to a great national issue, educational interests suffered much; and yet, during all that time, the academy enjoyed reasonable prosperity, regularly graduating good classes, though diminished somewhat in size. It will, however, long be remembered as a period of marked spiritual manifestations in the school, considerable numbers of the day and boarding scholars, through the personal influence of the principal being led to Christ and the formal consecration of themselves to his service.

Resigning in 1865, Prof. Mitchell went south and taught again, as he had before, in Tennessee, but was soon released from labor and went to the rest which remained and the crown which was waiting in heaven. "Blessed are the dead which die in the Lord."

Prof. Gilbert Thayer, A. M., took charge of the institution, boarding department and all, in 1865, by virtue of a lease entered into with the trustees, in which the term of ten years was named. He had just completed seven years of similar service at Bloomington, Ill., and previously had taught for some time at Keesville, N. Y. The record of his success in those places was a sufficient recommendation. He came with the repute of an accomplished instructor and of a shrewd and successful business manager. In this latter respect particularly, he was believed to be the man for the place. The trustees were prepared the more to appreciate financial talent in him, from having seen the want of it in some of his predecessors, and especially as they were anxious to resign to his hands all care and responsibility in regard to the domestic arrangements of the institution which during much of the previous time they had found it difficult to manage satisfactorily and without the annoyance of debt.

In 1865, a public spirited individual made a donation to the trustees of Illinois College in partial endowment of the professorship of Latin, of $5,000. In 1866 a few individuals contributed a fund of $25,000 for the endowment of the presidency of the college, nearly all of which is either paid in and invested, or bearing interest in the hands of the subscribers.

In the autumn of 1862, a disastrous conflagration destroyed the whole west wing of the Illinois Female College. It was promptly rebuilt and the school continued with unchecked prosperity. Dr. Charles Adams, principal.

The court records of "the war period" show that at the August term of the circuit court for the County of Greene, 1858, an indictment was found against Jacob Theby and James Markham for the murder of Cyrus Lake on July 1st, 1858, by striking him upon the head with a deadly weapon. The case was tried in this county at the October term, 1858, and the defendants found not guilty.

Patrick Waters had a "true bill" found against him at the March term, 1861, for the murder of Michael Hawkins on the 14th of January, 1861, by striking him on the head with a bar of iron. The jury found the defendant not guilty.

Wm. P. Chrisman was indicted at the October term, 1860, for the murder of Chas. Kreiger on Sept. 1st, 1860, by shooting with a shotgun. This case was stricken from the docket.

Miles Gibbons was indicted in Greene county in 1859, for the murder on the 23d of February, 1859, of William Swift by striking him on the head with a stick of wood. Change of venue to Morgan; case tried, defendant found guilty of manslaughter and sentenced to the penitentiary for five years; case taken to supreme court; reversed; brought back, and case nolle prosed.

Benjamin F. Church was indicted by the grand jury at the September term, 1864, for the murder of Hugh M. Campbell by shooting him with a pistol on July 4, 1864. Defendant found guilty of manslaughter and sent up for two years. This killing grew out of the excitement of the war and created considerable feeling. He was pardoned by the governor before being taken to Joliet.

David Hutchinson was indicted at the September term, 1864, for the murder of Hugh M. Campbell, by shooting him in the breast with a revolver. This case was stricken from the docket in 1866.

William Gordon had an indictment for murder found against him at the March term, 1863, for the killing of Frank Sherry on the 20th of January, 1863, by striking him in the breast with a knife. This case was also stricken from the docket in 1866.

Robert Pile was indicted in Brown county, in November, 1864, for the killing of John Murphy by shooting him with a shot-gun, and brought to Morgan county by a change of venue. Defendant plead guilty to manslaughter and was sentenced to the penitentiary for ten years.

Passing from bloody records to those of quiet, care and culture we record the birth of one of the most venerable and best known associations of Jacksonville *literati*—The Jacksonville Literary Union.

On April 14, 1864, the following gentlemen met at the residence of Judge William Brown to consider the propriety and practicability of forming a literary association. The late Dr. L. M. Glover, Messrs. Wm. Brown,* Elisha Brown,* William Brown, Jr., Prof. B. F. Mitchell,* Dr. C. Fisher, Prof. William Dod,* Rev. R. W. Allen,* Dr. H. K. Jones, Prof. P. G. Gillett, Prof. J. Loomis, J. H. Wood, Esq., and Prof. John H. Woods. After a free interchange of opinions as to ways and methods, a committee was appointed to prepare the necessary rules and regulations, and at a meeting held on April 21, 1864, and at the same place, the organization was perfected and the first officers were chosen as follows: Judge William Brown, president; Dr. L. M Glover, vice president;

*Deceased.

Philip G. Gillett, secretary. Thus was organized a society, which for more than twenty years has kept the even tenor of its way, and is to-day thriving and vigorous as at the start.

Although its component parts have thus been continually changing, year by year, the Union has preserved its original distinctive character throughout. This fact, while not detracting, in the least, from the reputation of the society for progressiveness, is a high compliment to the wisdom and sound judgment of its founders.

The membership is limited to twenty. A unanimous vote is necessary to an election. Meetings are held weekly, on Monday evenings, at the residences of the members. The exercises consist of essays, debates, conversations and selected readings, on alternate evenings. A leader, or leaders in debate, opens the discussion of the subject, which is then further ventilated by others, at greater or less length. Oratorical display is never cultivated and finds no favor. The conversational style is almost uniformly followed—the conversation not being promiscuous, however, but each speaker having his say and then subsiding into silence.

In 1864, the Young Ladies Athenæum was added to the roll of city educational institutions. It was founded by the Rev. Wm. D. Sanders, D. D., who for many years so successfully filled the chair of rhetoric, elocution and English literature in Illinois College. The Athenæum, early in its career, banished sectarianism. By its organic act of incorporation, not more than three of its twenty-one trustees are members of the same religious denomination. The aim of its founder, Prof. William D. Sanders, was not merely to add another to the list of schools for young ladies; but to found an institution on sounder principles, and to be conducted on a method at once more philosophical and more practical than the generally accepted principles and methods. It grew out of the conviction of the grave defects inseparable from common system and the belief that there was a better way. It was a practical protest against the cast-iron routine and superficialness of the accepted method. Among its chief peculiarities, the Athenæum, 1st, Prescribes no arbitrary and inflexible course of study, 2nd, It classifies on a new system, 3rd. It is not sectarian.

Tracing up the history of the *Morgan Journal* we find that Wm. H. Collins, a former minister, and a graduate of Illinois College, bought out Mr. Selby about September, 1858. He changed the name of the paper, then an eight column weeekly, to *Jacksonville Journal*.

Mr. Collins left the paper September 26, 1861, to accept a chaplaincy in the army. He afterwards became a captain of volunteers, went to Quincy, became a plow manufacturer, is now sound in body, witty in speech, and probably, plethoric of purse—always welcomed by his friends in this city. And now a member of Illinois Legislature.

Mr. Collins, in his valedictory, announced that he left the business management in the hands of Mr. W. C. Brown.

H. Barden soon became the publisher, and moved the concern into a room or two in the second story of McDonald's block, on North Main street. Barden continued the publication until November 17, 1864. Hon. H. J. Atkins, Mr. Wm. W. Jones, and perhaps others, acted as editors under Mr. Barden's management.

Mr. Atkins was a brilliant young lawyer from Maine, who was afterwards member of the Constitutional Convention of 1870, and died soon after.

Wm. W. Jones was a well known Jacksonville boy, son of Henry Jones, M. D., and a young man of much literary taste and promise. He edited the *Journal* during the political campaign of 1864, and was afterwards an assistant editor of the *Illinois State Journal*. He died, in that position, in September, 1867.

Ironmonger and Mendenhall bought out the establishment at the time Mr. Barden retired, and, both being practical printers, put the paper and office upon a business basis, improving the appearance of the sheet. Mr. J. J. Ironmonger had begun his typographical life in the Morgan *Journal* office with Mr. Selby, going afterward to Peoria, whence he returned with Mr. Amos H. Mendenhall, to become a proprietor. The latter had been foreman of the Peoria *Transcript* office, and was an experienced printer. He withdrew from the *Journal* in about a year, and went, eventually, to Lincoln, Nebraska, where he is now one of the proprietors of the *Nebraska State Journal.*

In the year 1860, as condensed in Moore's "Local Epitomes:"

Edward P. Kirby, was appointed Principal of the West Jacksonville District School, succeeding R. M. Tunnell, and began his duties in September.

The great State Fair began September 11th. Hon. Schuyler Colfax delivered the opening address, Mr. C. S. Goltra was Superintendent of the grounds. The hall for textile fabrics was built 40x84 feet, that for power and machinery 24x60 feet, fine arts 24x98 feet, and natural history 24x36 feet. The floral and agricultural hall in the shape of a Greek cross, was 104 feet each way, by 32 feet in width, all these halls were 18 feet between joints. In addition, the editors hall was 16x32 feet, the business office 24x80 and the president's headquarters 24x60 feet. Two large eating houses were provided and about 600 large stalls for animals, besides other preparations being made. The fair was held at our present fair grounds, which presented a beautiful appearance, the amphitheatre being estimated to have held 8,000 people at one time. A steam plow was, perhaps, the most noticeable feature of the show.

March 15th, 1860, the *Jacksonville Journal* flung the names of Lincoln and Yates, for president and governor, to the breeze, and editorially began talking up its men.

Richard Yates was nominated governor, at Decatur, May 9, by the Republicans. On the first informal ballot Yates had 183 votes, N. B. Judd 245, Len Swett 191, and Mr. Knox 12. On the fourth formal ballot Judd had 237 votes, Yates 363, and Sweet 36, giving Yates the majority. Yates was called for, then Judd and then Swett, the two latter congratulating their successful competitor.

Among the objections made by political opponents of Mr. Yates, was the statement that he was too old for governor. The fact being he was only 43 years of age and looked young.

November 6, Abraham Lincoln was elected president, and Richard Yates governor.

November 6, Sam. P. Thompson, E. L. Ryland and Ben. H. Grierson, of Meredosia, came up on the night train to proclaim Yates' election with music. The band, followed by a crowd, went up to Yates & Berdan's office, West State street, upon the awning of which Mr. Yates appeared and thanked his friends. As Yates stood uncovered the first snow fell, touching his head with the silver which ten succeeding years of public life thereafter made plentier.

Rev. C. H. Marshall was pastor at the Congregational church. Rev. Jesse H. Moore, of the West Charge M. E. church; Rev. L. M. Glover, of the First Presbyterian; Rev. R. W. Allen, of the Second Presbyterian; Rev. W. S. Russell, of a Christian church.

The Tonica & Petersburg railroad was being pushed rapidly.

"Considerable progress is being made with Mr. Strawn's building"—that meant the present Opera House.

Mr. J. J. Cassell erected four fine stores on St. Louis street, directly south of Coffman & Bruce's corner.

The early part of the year 1860 was very dry, injuring early vegetables.

Westminster church was organized, at the Congregational church, May 13. Rev. A. T. Norton, President Sturtevant, Profs. Sanders and R. Nutting, and Rev. Wm. Gallaher taking part in the exercises. About forty-five persons "entered into covenant relationship." D. A. Smith and Dr. Henry Jones were unanimously elected as elders.

Westminster Presbyterian church was dedicated in September, and Rev. D. H. Hamilton, of New Haven, Connecticut, became pastor in October.

The *Jacksonville Journal* was a weekly newspaper, published by Wm. H. Collins, now of Quincy, the office being on North Main street.

J. R. Bailey was editor of the *Sentinel*, also weekly, which was printed in the second or third story of Goltra and Stryker's building, now Goltra's.

In the Jacksonville market, Upham & Snyder quote wheat at 80@$1; flour, best, $6; oats 30c; corn 30@35c; shelled 40c; lard 10@12½c; eggs 15c; potatoes 30@50c chickens $1.50 per doz.; bacon 12½c; hams 13c; country do 10c; hay $8@10; sugar, brown, 10@11c; crushed 14@15c.

H. J. Atkins, B. Lewis and B. D. Dawson, advertise themselves as attorneys-at-law, Josiah Day as a practical watchmaker. Robt. Hockenhull was a wholesale and retail druggist, Wm. Brown succeeds Elliott & Brown as a banker, Ayers & Co., were in the same line, W. S. Edgar had a drug store, U. C. Edgerton sold dry goods, George Mader sold clothing assisted by Preston Spates, W. O. Brooks dealt in farm machinery, Flack & Risley sold dry goods, E. M. Sanford had marble works, Stevenson & Tompkins sold stoves and tinware, S. H. Hamilton had a new bakery, probably in opposition to the older one of E. Hamilton. C. H. Dunbrack kept seeds and agricultural implements, F. & E. B. Eno were grain commission merchants, David Prince, M. D., had "office and residence" on West State street, C. K. Sawyer was a surgical and mechanical dentist, Massey, King, Neely & Co., dealt in lumber and had a planing mill, Catlin & Co., were booksellers, Adams & Trover kept a news depot, and David Robb sold dry goods.

June 21st, the commencement of Illinois College was held in College Grove. The graduates were Franklin Adams, John A. Ballard, Thos. Booth, Chas. S. Brown, Robt. H. Buckley, Wm. H. Edgar, Wm. L. English, E. B. Hamilton, David B. Smith, John A. Smith, J. B. Turner and Wm. H. Turner.

J. J. Ironmonger opened a news depot in the "little brick," between Union Hall and Wm. Branson's.

A lodge of Good Templars was organized at the "Sons of Temperance Hall."

Murrayville was called Iatan.

Julia D. Jones, Louisa Long and Louisa M. Warren, were graduated from the Academy.

Deborah Cramer, Mary O. Edwards, Caroline R. Hurst, Anna Kerr, M. F. Little, M. E. Maupin, G. Martin, M. C. Moore, Emily Parker, M. G. Snyder, Anna M. Thompson, M. V. Thorp, and Mary Yates, were graduated from the Methodist Conference Female College, Rev. Charles Adams, president.

Johnson & Richards sold stoves and tinware.

June 18th, at a meeting of the Ladies Education Society, Judge Brown presided and addresses were made by Prof. Haven, of Chicago, and Dr. Edgar. The officers of the society were Mrs. Tillson, Quincy, president; Mrs. Sturtevant, vice-president; Mrs. S. Brown, secretary, and Mrs. A. E. King, treasurer. The executive committee were Mrs. Reed, Bancroft, Sturtevant, B. F. Stevenson, Brown, Moore, Gillett, A. E. King and Wadsworth.

D. A. & T. W. Smith were attorneys-at-law.

Mr. Springer reports 83 schools in the county. Highest monthly wages to males, $80, do., to females, $40. Amount raised by special district tax for all purposes, $25,792.52; whole amount received, $38,793.95.

One hundred and twenty-six persons were buried in our cemeteries in 1859, eighty-eight persons having resided in the corporation.

S. Hunt signs the letter list as postmaster.

The scarlet fever was quite prevalent.

The population of Jacksonville reached 5,528 according to the census of 1860.

Among the town trustees were: E. T. Miller, 1858, Wm. G. Gallaher, 1858, Chas. Dalton, 1858, Jonathan Neely, 1858-'61, Henry C. Coffman, 1858, I. D. Rawlings, 1859, Michael Rapp, 1859-'65, Jesse W. Galbraith, 1859, R. C. Bruce, 1859-'60, Isaac L. Morrison, 1859, William Ratekin, 1860, T. W. Wright, 1860, Wesley Mathers, 1860, Edward R. Elliott, 1860, C. H. Knight, 1861, Chas. Sample, 1861, A. G. Link, 1861, Isaac S. Slerer, 1861, Elizur Wolcott, 1862-'63, O. D. Fitzsimmons, 1862-'63-'64, Wm. Branson, 1862-'63-'64, Benj. F. Gass, 1862-'63-'64, Edward Lambert, 1862-'63, A. Edgmon, 1864, Chas. H. Howard, 1864, Chas. McDonald, 1865, Stephen Ellis, 1865, A. C. Wadsworth, 1865, Wm. C. Woodman, 1865.

COUNTY OFFICERS—1858—Congress, Thomas L. Harris; Representatives, Cyrus Epler, E. B. Hitt, Cyrus Matthews; Sheriff, Isaac S. Hicks; Coroner, John Selby.

1859—Congress, John A. McClernard; Assessor, Thomas J. Caldwell; Surveyor, Zenas F. Moody; School Commissioner, John T. Springer.

1860—Senator, Murray McConnel; Representatives, Isaiah Turney, A. G. Burr; Sheriff, Edward Scott; Circuit Clerk, Charles Hardin; Coroner, Samuel S. Davis.

1861—Treasurer, James H. Lurton; Surveyor, Wm. S. McPherson; School Commissioner, John T. Springer; County Clerk, John Trabue; County Judge, Sidney S. Duncan.

1862—Senator, Cyrus Epler; Representative, John T. Springer; Sheriff, Andrew J. Bradshaw; Coroner, Edwin C. Drew.

1863—Circuit Clerk, B. F. Bristow; Treasurer, J. H. Lurton; School Commissioner, S. M. Martin; Surveyor, W. S. McPherson.

1864—State's Attorney, Wm. Brown; Sheriff, S. M. Palmer; Circuit Clerk, Stephen Sutton; Coroner, Field Sample; Senator, Murray McConnel; Representative, J. T. Springer.

1865—County Judge, H. G. Whitlock; County Clerk, John Trabue; School Superintendent, S. M. Martin; Treasurer, J. H. Lurton; Surveyor, W. S. McPherson.

The hotel accommodations in Jacksonville were always sufficient for the demand of the traveling public or transient boarders needs. The community has always been peculiarly a settled-in-housekeeping-one. In 1850 Mr. George W. Fox, Sr., and wife became host and hostess at the "Morgan House," corner of North Main street and the square. They changed its name to "Mansion," which title afterwards became "Park Hotel." The Fox's managed the hostelry for eleven years leaving it with an unblemished record. The rival hotel on the square was the "Western" on the west side of the square, kept by the Chenery family, later of Springfield, until 1852. In 1857 Col. James Dunlap's private dwelling on West State street was remodelled into a hotel and christened "The Dunlap House," since then it has been *the hotel* of the city.

As to the local newspapers N. B. Walker attempted to publish a paper called the *Argus* in 1859, but it soon breathed its last. During the presidential contest in 1860, the Campaign *Argument* was edited by C. J. Sellon. In 1861-'62, Edward Trover, now deceased, published a weekly paper called the *Dispatch*, but it was not long-lived. From 1863 to 1867, Mr. H. L. Clay, of the Carrolton *Gazette* was in our city as chief clerk in the Provost Marshal's office, and ten years later was here as editor and part owner of the *Courier*.

Gov. Bissell died March 18th, 1860, and was succeeded by lieutenant-governor John Wood, of Quincy.

En route home from the funeral of Gov. Bissell, the Quincy Guard, under command of Capt. Morgan, stopped on the cars for a few minutes to visit the grave of Col. John J. Hardin. The company marched through our streets to the East Cemetery, where addresses were made by Capts. Morgan and Prentiss and Mr. Yates. The sash worn by Prentiss was stained by the blood of Hardin, when he with Morgan, had assisted in preparing Hardin's body for burial, at Buena Vista. Upon returning to the depot to re-embark for Quincy, Capt. McConnel (Jno. L.) presented the Guard a handsome bouquet, on behalf of some ladies. Our citizens then gave three cheers each for Morgan, Prentiss and the Guard, when the soldiers departed homeward.

As a sequence, probably, of the visit referred to above, the young men of Jacksonville began to organize some military companies. The first was called the Hardin Light Guards and chose C. H. Adams as captain. The second, or Union Guards, chose James Dunlap as captain.

The Quincy Guard was here March 22d, 1860, our companies were organized the week after. April 21, 1861, the Quincy Guard passed through Jacksonville to Springfield. April 22, our two companies, the Hardin and Union Guards, followed, and all three companies were at once sent to occupy Cairo, where, with others, they were organized into the 10th Illinois infantry, with B. M. Prentiss as colonel, Jas. D. Morgan as lieutenant-colonel, and Chas. H. Adams as major. Prentiss came home a major general, as did Morgan: Adams became lieutenant-colonel, and many others from the three companies were promoted rapidly and deservedly. Many of the boys went forth never to return, but tears still are shed at mention of the names of our heroes. God bless their memory!

The stories of the war of the Rebellion are always fresh, no matter how many times they are told. The stories of the hardships and privations which they endured for their country, and the glorious victories gained, have a charm which holds every true American and makes him wish to hear them repeated again and again.

Morgan county was by no means deficient in the number or bravery of her soldiers. And among them are many who held high rank and did splendid service for their country. The *Daily Journal* in 1883 gave its readers some extremely interesting interviews with veteran soldiers who took very prominent and interesting parts during the war, and passed through many hairbreath escapes, and only by the best of good fortune are with us to-day to do good work in civil life.

When the war first began there were six regiments mustered from this state for three months' service. The first of these in which we find the name of an officer from Morgan county is the Tenth Infantry Regiment of Illinois Volunteers, in which the name of Charles H. Adams is enrolled as Captain of Company B. He was successively promoted to Major and Lieutenant-colonel of the First Illinois Artillery. John W. King, entered Company B of the same regiment as First Lieutenant and was promoted to Captain. Thos. W. Smith entered as Second Lieutenant and was promoted to the rank of First Lieutenant. McLean F. Wood was Captain of Company G, and re-entered the three years service. James Mitchell was First Lieutenant and James F. Longley was Second Lieutenant of the same company.

The Tenth Regiment was mustered into the United States service for three years July 29, 1861, by Captain T. G. Pitcher. In Jan., 1862, it took part in a movement made by General Grant to the rear of Columbus. On January 1, 1864, the regiment re-enlisted as veterans, and left Illinois for the field again in February, 1864, under command of Col. John Tillson. They were mustered out of the United States service in July, 1865. The first Morgan county man whose name appears on the roster of the Tenth Illinois Volunteers after they were re-enlisted is that of McLean F. Wood, as Lieutenant-colonel, his term expired January 12, 1865. Following this are the names of Oliver S. Pyatt, Quartermaster, mustered out October 9, 1864; B. F. Price, of Meredosia, mustered out July 4, 1865; John W. Craig, Asst. Surgeon; Chaplains Wm. H. Collins, resigned June 21, 1862, and Wm. B. Linell, resigned July 12, 1863; Captains of Company A, James F. Longley, who was promoted to that position from First Lieutenant, and resigned Dec. 31, 1862; Charles Carpenter, of Meredosia, promoted from First Lieutenant and mustered out October 31, 1864, and Henry McGrath also promoted from First Lieutenant, and mustered out July 5, 1865; First Lieutenants Robert Cromwell, of Meredosia, promoted from Second Lieutenant and mustered out July 4, 1865; Second Lieutenants Otho D. Critzer, of Meredosia, resigned June 17, 1862, and James M. Swales, mustered out (as Sergeant) July 5, 1865.

Company B Captains, Thomas W. Smith resigned June 3, 1862, Charles P. McEnally, promoted from Second Lieutenant and mustered out October 28, 1864, and James B. Shaw mustered out July 4, 1865. First Lieutenants, Wm. D. Green appointed A. A. G. April 21, 1863; James B. Tait, promoted from Second Lieutenant and resigned September 15, 1864; James A. Shaw, promoted from Second Lieutenant to Captain; Robert Brown on detached service June 4, 1865; Second Lieutenant, James R. Graves mustered out June 4 1865.

The following extracts from a recent communication to a Springfield newspaper by a member of the 10th, gives some facts as to the first Illinois Volunteers in the War for the Union and Jacksonville's promptness in responding to the Governor's call:

On the 17th of April, 1861, the Springfield Grays' muster roll was increased from 30 men by some 70 or 75 men and the organization completed.

On the 18th, a portion of the company and quartermaster's stores were transported to Camp Yates and a detachment of Springfield Grays detailed to mount guard for the night.

On the 19th, Capt. Wyatt's company of Lincoln, (afterwards of the Seventh Regiment) arrived at Camp Yates.

On the 21st, two companies from Quincy (afterwards of the Tenth Regiment) arrived at Camp Yates.

On the 22d, two companies from Jacksonville (afterwards of the 10th regiment) arrived at Camp Yates. On the afternoon of the same day Companies A and B, Quincy Guards, the Hardin Light Guards, of Jacksonville, the Union Guards, of Jacksonville and Hopkins battery of light artillery departed for Cairo, after having been duly mustered into the state service by Adj-Gen. Mather. The Hardin Light Guards, of Jacksonville, mentioned above, Capt. Chas. H. Adams, (afterwards Co. B, 10 Ill. Infy.) every man of them enlisted on April 16, 1861, and it is within the knowledge of the undersigned that on the next day (April 17th) Capt. Adams tendered the full company to the governor.

At the time of the departure of the Quincy and Jacksonville companies and Hopkins' battery, the only troops left in Camp Yates was the company of Capt. Wyatt from Lincoln.

The companies named arrived at Cairo on the night of the 23d, and at once entered into active service—that is such active service as was demanded at the post at that time—which, however, was not very arduous, consisting principally of standing guard on the levee, making cartridges (we had left Springfield without a round of ammunition) and trying to crowd about 25 meninto an eight-man wall tent.

Within two days after we reached Cairo, a regimental organization was completed and field officers chosen, and everything was ready for muster. But Capt. Pope came to Springfield and mustered theregiments that were in camp there before going to Cairo, and so we lost the number that priority of entry into service should have given us simply because of such priority.

Wm. Cam, of Winchester, subsequently of this county, was lieutenant colonel in Fourteenth Infantry, and Jas. H. Stewart was quartermaster of the same regiment and was mustered out at consolidation. Wm. J. Rutledge was chaplain of the regiment: he is now chaplain of Joliet Penitentiary. Company I of the Fourteenth was made up at Waverly and the following are the names of the officers: Captains, Jonathan Morris, afterward promoted to major; John W. Meacham promoted from first lieutenant and dismissed November 11, 1872; E. D. Ward promoted from first lieutenant and was mustered out at consolidation; L. W. Coe was first lieutenant and was mustered out at consolidation. In Company K of the same regiment William Mason, of Exeter, was second lieutenant and was mustered out at consolidation. The regiment was first called into service for thirty days under the "Ten Regiment Bill" on May 4th, 1861. For a time it rendezvoused in this city until it was mustered into the three years' service. They afterwards proceeded to Quincy and from there to Missouri. They took an active part in the siege of Corinth. They also took an active part in the siege of Vicksburg. The regiment was finally mustered out at Fort Leavenworth, Kan., Sept. 17, 1865, arriving at Springfield, Ill., Sept. 22d, where it received final payment and discharge. The aggregate number of men who belonged to this organization was 1,980, and the aggregate mustered out at Fort Leavenworth was 480. During its four years and four months of arduous service, the regiment marched 4,490 miles, traveled by rail 2,330, and by river 4,490 miles—making an aggregate of 11,670 miles.

The Twenty-seventh Infantry was organized with only seven companies, at Camp Butler, Ill., Aug. 10, 1861, and ordered to Jacksonville as part of Brig. Gen. John A. McClernand's Brigade. Sept. 1, 1861, ordered to Cairo, where the three remaining companies joined.

Under Gen. McClernand it was engaged in the battle of Belmont, Nov. 7, 1861, where it bore quite a prominent part, and lost severely. On the evacuation of Columbus, Ky., the regiment was sent to that point. On March 14, 1862, in company with the Forty-second Illinois, Eighteenth Wisconsin, and part of the Second Illinois Light Artillery, and Second Illinois Cavalry, it formed the "Mississsppi Flotilla," and started down the Mississippi River, and remained during the siege of Island No. 10. The

Twenty-seventh was the first to land on the island. Was engaged in the siege of Corinth, and battle of Farmington, May 9, 1862.

It was with the advance from Nashville, and engaged in the battle of Stone River, where it distinguished itself.

Sept. 2, 1863, the corps crossed the Tennessee and moved down towards Rome, Georgia, below Chattanooga, and returned in time to take part in the battle of Chickamauga, where the Twenty-seventh suffered severely. Was in Chattanooga during its investment, and was engaged in storming of Mission Ridge, where it was noticed for its good conduct. From Mission Ridge, it went upon a forced march to the relief of Knoxville, then closely pressed by Longstreet's corps.

Was engaged at Rock Face Ridge, May 9th, 1864; at Resaca, May 14th; near Calhoun May 16th; Adairsville May 17th; near Dallas from May 26th to June 4th; near Pine Top Mountain from June 10th to 14th; battle of Mud Creek June 18th; in assault on Kenesaw Mountain June 27th; skirmished about the vicinity of Chattanoochie River; was in the battle of Peach Tree Creek July 20th, and in the skirmishes around Atlanta.

The regiment was relieved from duty at the front August 25, 1864, and ordered to Springfield, Ill., for muster out.

During its term of service the regiment had the following casualties: Killed or died of wounds, 102; died by disease, 80; number of wounded, 328; discharged and resigned, 209.

In Company K are the names of A. T. Bozarth and Lewis Hanback; First Lieutenants, E. S. Jones and Isaac Nash, both of Concord.

In the roster of the 29th Infantry is the name of James E. Dunlap as lieutenant colonel of the regiment. He was mustered in August 19, 1861, and resigned March 14, 1862.

The next names appear in the 33d Infantry, in Company K—Captains E. H. Twining and Franklin Adams.

The Thirty-fourth Infantry was organized at Camp Butler by Col. E. N. Kirk, September 7th, 1861, and moved to Lexington, Ky., and from there to Louisville. December 22d they were mustered as a veteran organization. July 12th, 1865, they were mustered out at Louisville, Ky. In this regiment Company G was partially composed of Morgan county men: Captains—M. G. Greenwood, killed at Murphysboro, December 31, 1862; Isaac Rawlings resigned June 19, 1863; James Hindman, of Liberty, entered as a second lieutenant and was promoted to captain and afterwards to major; James Perkins, of Arcadia, was promoted from first lieutenant to captain. The first lieutenants were John Hindman, of Cross Roads, T. J. Carney, of Jacksonville, and I. V. Moore, of Liberty. The second lieutenants were S. R. Cavender, of Arcadia, S. C. Rawlings, of Jacksonville, A. S. Crisler, of Shiloh Hill, and Henry Pratt of Monroe. In the Forty-fourth Infantry the name of Wm. H. Miner appears as second lieutenant. He was mustered out September 25th, 1865.

The 101st Illinois Infantry contained the largest number of Morgan county men. It was recruited entirely in the county under the call made in the summer of 1862; was mustered in Sept. 2, 1862, at Jacksonville; remained at Fair Grounds drilling, &c., until Oct. 6th when marching orders were received. On the 6th Cairo was reached where guard duty was performed until the 25th.

Nov. 28th, it started on its first march, and on the 30th reached Lumpkins Mills, six miles south of Holly Springs, where the regiment first heard the "clash of contending arms" from the Tallahatchie River, six miles beyond. The regiment remained at Lumpkin's Mills three days, when it received orders to return to Holly Springs, Mississippi, for provost and garrison duty.

Dec. 13th, Co. A, Capt. John B. Lesage, was sent to Cairo with rebel prisoners. Dec. 20th, Holly Springs was captured, and Companies B, C, E, F, I, and the sick men of Co. A, who had been left behind were taken prisoners and paroled. Soon after they were sent to Memphis, thence to Benton Barracks, Mo., where they remained until exchanged in June 1863.

At the Holly Springs disaster, the men of this regiment on duty did all they could under the circumstances. Another regiment was doing the picket duty, while the One Hundred and First was in the town doing provost duty, and divided about the town in squads, too small to make resistance to the overpowering numbers that surrounded them. Wherever the blame of this disaster shall rest, it surely should not attach itself to the One Hundred and First Illinois.

Sept. 24, 1863, the regiment received orders transferring it to the department of the Cumberland, and started at once for Louisville, Ky., via Cairo and Sandoval, Ill., and Mitchell and New Albany, Ind., arriving in Louisville Sept. 27th. On the 30th, it left Louisville via Nashville, and arrived at Bridgeport, Ala., Oct. 2d, and remained there until the 27th. This period of service is always referred to as a hard time, owing to the severe rains and destitution of tents. In fact, most of the regiment was tentless until the first of January following.

Oct. 27th, the regiment was temporarily assigned to the First Brigade, Third Division, Eleventh Army Corps, and started on the march to the front, arriving next day at Lookout Valley, where, on the night of its arrival, it participated in the night battle of Wauhatchie, where by singular good fortune not a man was hurt. For nearly a month following, the regiment lay encamped in the valley, exposed to a daily shelling from Lookout Mountain, which, during that time, killed one man and wounded another.

Nov. 27th the regiment received marching orders and proceeded to Chattanooga, where it participated in the battle of Chattanooga, losing one man, killed. Immediately after the battle, it was ordered to the relief of Knoxville and participated in that severe march; and finally returned to Lookout Valley. Dec. 17th. Many of the men were bare-footed, and in that condition had marched many a weary mile, over the frozen ground and sharp rocks, even as their forefathers had done in revolutionary times, leaving their blood to mark their steps.

Recruiting its strength in the valley for a few days, the regiment was then set to work building corduroy roads; after which, on the 1st of June, 1864, they were sent to Kelley's ferry, to relieve the Sixteenth Illinois, then about to return home on veteran furlough. Here the regiment remained until the last of January, when upon the completion of the railroad to Chattanooga, they were ordered to Bridgeport where they went into camp, and quietly remained there until the 2d of May, when they started for the front. May 10th it marched for Snake Creek gap, reached it next day and held it two days. On the 13th, having marched through the gap, the troops were ready for action near Resaca, but were held in reserve all day. On the 14th, were again held in reserve until 3 p. m., when they started on the double-quick for the left, which was reached just in time for the brigade to render important service in the action then progressing. During this engagement, it is said the One Hundred and First was ordered to take a hill in front of it, which it did in so gallant a style as to win the admiration of Gen. Hooker, who happened to be standing near, and who cheered the troops with the encouraging shout of "go in, my Illinois boys." The next day afternoon it was ordered forward, and at four o'clock while in column, was charged by a rebel force. Both officers and men of the regiment conducted themselves gallantly and rendered valuable services, losing one man killed, six mortally wounded, and forty wounded left. Again on the 25th it got into a heavy fight at the New Hope church. Among the wounded at this place, were Adj. Padgett, Lieut. Hardin, and Lieut. (afterward Capt.) Belt, who subsequently died of wounds.

After this the regiment bore an honorable part in the various manœuvers around Kenesaw and Pine mountains, losing one killed and five or six wounded. After the rebels evacuated Kenesaw, was engaged in the pursuit, and on the 6th of July, took possession on Chattahoochie Heights, where the regiment remained eleven days.

July 17th, crossed the river, and on the 20th just after crossing Peach Tree Creek, the rebels assailed the corps with terrible force. Forming line under fire, the enemy was held at bay, and their charges repelled until 8 p. m., when he abandoned the attack and returned to their fortifications. In this engagement five were killed and forty-five wounded. Among the killed was Capt. Thos. B. Woof. The morning report next morning, showed only one hundred and twenty effective men for duty, having left Bridgeport with three hundred and sixty-five men. August 25th, it was ordered back to Chattahoochie bridge, which the corps was to guard, while the rest of the army swung into the rear of Atlanta, Sept. 2d, the regiment was on a reconnoissance, and claims the honor of having been the first regiment that entered Atlanta, Ga., after its fall, which occurred on the second anniversary of its muster into service. It remained in Atlanta until the destruction of the place most of the time having charge of the fire department.

Nov. 15th, started on the "grand march," and participated in all its glories, its trials and its triumphs; and whether as an advance guard, driving rebel cavalry before it, or as rear guard pulling wagons out of the mud, or corduroying roads, or unfathomable mud-holes, the One Hundred and First Illinois always did its duty so well as to win high commendations from its brigade and division commanders. The story of that march is about the same for all regiments, and need hardly be repeated. The regiment reached Savannah and entered the place Dec. 22d, 1864.

Jan. 17th, 1865, crossed over into South Carolina, and went through the great campaign of the Carolinas, participating in the battles of Ayersboro and Bentonville, losing only one man, wounded. March 24th, entered Goldsboro, and on the 13th of April entered Raleigh, where the regiment remained until the final surrender of the rebel army after which, on the 30th, it started overland for Richmond, Va., which was reached May 8th; there it remained until the 11th, when it marched through Richmond and took up the line of march for Alexandria, where it arrived on the 19th.

May 24th, participated in the "grand review," and then went into camp at Bladensburg, where on the 7th of June it was mustered out, and started for Springfield, where, on the 21st of June, it was paid off and disbanded.

Morgan county furnished 2,732 soldiers for the Union Army, as shown by official records in the State Adjutant General's office.

Among the regiments in which were volunteer soldiers from Morgan were the 10th, 14th, 16th, 18th, 20th, 21st, 23d, 26th, 27th, 28th, 29th, 31st, 32d, 33d, 34th 35th, 38th, 39th, 41st, 43d, 44th, 45th, 50th, 53d, 54th, 56th, 57th, 58th, 61st, 68th, 74th, 76th, 87th, 91st, 94th, 95th, 101st, 105th, 113th, 115th, 129th, 133d, 145th, 154th, 155th, Infantry; 3d, 6th, 8th, 9th, 13th, 16th, cavalry; 1st, 2d, artillery; 29th (colored) infantry; 13th colored infantry. There were 179 volunteers from this county in Missouri regiments, and 152 in regiments of other states.

Up to March, 1864, the county had a surplus credit of 141 over all calls for volunteer defenders of the Union.

As one of the incidents of the war period, was the passage through the city of an Illinois regiment with that brave and loyal, but stern, little man at its head, who had just received his colonel's commission from Governor Yates, but who afterwards received at Appomattox the swords, whose surrender indicated the collapse of the great rebellion.

July 3d, 1861, the 21st Illinois Infantry, with Colonel Ulysses S. Grant in command, broke camp at Springfield, Illinois, and took up the line of march for Quincy, Illinois. Transportation by rail had been offered, but Colonel Grant said his men would soon have to learn to march, and the arts and sciences of camp life, etc., had also to be learned, and the sooner they were properly initiated the better, for the boys will all remember the new accoutrements and knapsacks had been issued the day before, and notwithstanding the knapsacks were large, still not one of them would contain half the accumulations of the forty-five days previous, and right well Col. Grant knew this; hence the easiest, and in fact the only way to teach the boys the first principles and proper condition of a soldier in perfect marching order was to put him on the road, when a very little experience would soon induce him to dispense with all extras, confining himself to the smallest amount of wants as a soldier, and they are few, especially on the march. How light and comfortable apparently were these knapsacks at

2 o'clock in the afternoon, and how heavy at 5 o'clock that evening, after a march of only four miles from Camp Yates, at Springfield.

Transportation wagons gathered up all over the country and driven by their owners were in abundance; and it was well, for when the regiment halted but few soldiers had their knapsacks on, but the wagons as they came in looked more like the baggage wagons of a first-class circus or menagerie than anything else. The lesson was taught All extra clothing, etc.,—and almost every soldier had a spare suit, with several changes of shirts—was bundled, labeled and sent to friends at home.

The next day was the glorious old Fourth. The boys were feeling good and marched along lively. The people along the road and far in advance, had heard of their coming. A great dinner was spread with all the delicacies of the season, fit only for the lords of creation and not for soldiers; so thought Col. Grant. A committee appointed for the purpose met the advance column and informed the colonel what had been done for the "soldier boys," but Grant thanked them kindly, and said his men might be permitted to march on either side of the long lines of tables and see what good things the kind ladies of the country had brought them, but not one mouthful should they eat. Imagine, if you please, the feelings of a thousand half-fed soldiers, who had not seen or tasted a good square meal for nearly two months. Deep and bitter curses were uttered by those new made soldiers, and at one time it was thought they would rebel and disobey their commander; but a sober second thought convinced them that their colonel was right, for as he told the committee, "If I permit these men to go to those tables they will not exercise proper discretion, but will fill themselves with the good things, and the result will be that I shall be unable to move the regiment at all to-morrow, as they will all be sick."

The regiment went into camp on our fair grounds on the evening of the Fourth. Col. Grant took a position at the entrance gate to watch the soldiers as they passed through and to see that none of them carried whisky with them. The first to be halted was old Johnny Hanks, or more familiarly known as "Uncle Johnny," who was a boon companion of ex President Lincoln in his rail splitting days. "Uncle Johnny" was seated high on one of the wagons and feeling unusually good, when Col. Grant said, "Uncle Johnny, you have a bottle of whisky up there, I want it." Uncle Johnny looked at the colonel but a moment, when he discovered that famous determination visible upon his countenance, and at once brought forth the treasured prize and handed it reluctantly to him, when he immediately dashed it against the post on the opposite side breaking it to pieces. The next to run the gauntlet was an old Mexican soldier who went by the name of "Mexico," and who had gone through the Mexican war with Grant, and was well-known by him. When he arrived at the gate he brought his gun from a "right shoulder shift arms" to a "shoulder," and saluted the colonel in the usual manner as he attempted to pass, but the colonel halted him and said: "Mexico, you have whisky; hand it over." Mexico denied the charge, but Col. Grant insisted that he had, and told to give him his gun, which he did. The colonel pulled the tampion out, turned the gun up, and sure enough it was full of Jacksonville's best. The gun was passed back by the colonel, with the remark, quietly, that the trick was an old one, and would do to play on new soldiers but not on old ones. Mexico proved a source of annoyance, and Grant summarily and without warning discharged him, at Quincy, Ill., and told him if he was ever found within the lines of the Twenty-first again he would have him arrested and confined to the end of hostilities. This was the last of Old Mexico.

On the 5th, being Saturday, they reached Naples, remaining in camp over Sunday, and on Monday crossed the river and went beyond some five miles, when orders were received to return and take the cars for Quincy, Ill., landing there on the 9th, crossing the Mississippi that evening. On the 22d, the regiment went by rail to Mexico, Mo., and remained until the 6th of August, when Col. Grant was commissioned Brig. Gen.

No better idea can be given of the part the county played in the bloody drama of the War for the Union than by the roll of pensioners the names of those who incurred disease, lost limb, or whose near relatives laid down their lives for their country. This list was furnished the *Journal* by Public Printer Rounds in October, 1883.

ALEXANDER.

Spencer, Major W., wounded left thigh $2.

Baker, Francis M., wounded left breast, $4.

Brown, Richard, wounded right foot. $18.

Ferguson, Anthony, chronic diarrhœa, $4, June, 1882.

Carter, Wm. D., pneumonia pleurisy, adhesion, $8, July, 1882.

Harris, John, wounded left shoulder, $6, August, 1879.

ARCADIA.

Diover, Joseph, wounded left foot, $6.

Angeline, Henderson, widow, $8.
Saffley, Elizabeth, dependent mother, $8, April, 1865.
Bridgeman, Virginia, widow, $8.
Rodgers, Catharine, widow, $8.

BETHEL.

Sullins, Mary L., dependent mother, $8, July, 1864.

CHAPIN

Osgood, Charles H., wounded right shoulder, $8.50.
Cunningham, James D., disorder of stomach and rheumatism, $6, January, 1882
McCormick, James, gun-shot wound left leg, $2, December, 1881.
Ayers, Theophilus, gun-shot wound left thigh, $4, June, 1882.
Vance, Nancy, dependent mother, $8, June, 1879.
West, Jane, widow, $8.
Evans, Rebecca Jane, widow, $8.
Heiser, John, gun-shot wound right thigh, $6.
Perkins, Caroline W., widow, $8.

CONCORD.

Whorton, Joseph W., wounded left shoulder, $8
Wise, Frederick, chronic rheumatism, $6.
Lewis, Joseph B., wounded right side, $4
Moss, Benjamin F., loss left leg, $24
Hatfield, William M., disorder of throat and lungs, $6, June, 1882.
Hickel, Charles, chronic diarrhœa and disorder of liver, $4, April, 1882
Ater, John J., injury to abdomen, $8, February, 1880.
Roach, Harriet, dependent mother, $8
Mulligan, Nancy C., widow $12, July, 1880.
Leonard, Levina R., widow, $8, January, 1879.

FRANKLIN.

Anderton, Margaret, widow, $8.
Duncan, Adaline G., widow, $20.
Wright, Keziah, widow, $8, March, 1879.
Weatherford, Mary A., $15, June, 1859.
McKeen, Amanda, widow, $8.
Hill, James H., chronic diarrhœa, disorder of abdomen vis., $17, November 1881.
Snyder, Geo. W., gunshot wound left shoulder, $2, April, 1882.
Wyatt, James L., chronic diarrhœa, dyspepsia, $4, August, 1880.
Jones, Curtis J., gun shot wound left clavicle, $4, June, 1882.
Roberts, James A., injury to left knee, $2, December, 1881.
Sullet, James W., disorder of eyes, $12, April, 1879.
Whitlock, Alexander, disorder of lungs, $8, May, 1881.
Bunch, Benj. H., chronic diarrhœa, rheumatism, disorder heart, $4, March, 1882.
Dougherty, James R., partial blindness, $8
Sargent, John T., loss right leg, $18.
Dougherty, John C., gun-shot wound left leg, $8, December, 1877.

JACKSONVILLE.

Gibbons, Julia A., widow, $8.
Babbitt, Sarah, dependent mother, $8, June, 1881.
Davenport, Sally, dependent mother, October, 1867.
Dalton, Mehitable, dependent mother, $8, July, 1866.
DeFrates, Josquina, dependent mother, $8, June, 1880.
Vasconcellos, Maria, widow, $8.
Seegar, Sarah A., widow, $8.

Stuart, Mary A., widow, $8.
Seaver, Charlotte, widow, $12.
Smith, Annie E. widow, $20.
Erwin, Mary A., widow, $12, October, 1882.
English, Kate W., widow, $19, January, 1878.
Sprague, Joshua, $8, June, 1878.
Samuel, Lewis, $8, May, 1881.
Jordan, John, $8, August, 1877.
Graves, Lydia F., widow, $8, January, 1879.
Denny, Phebe, widow, $8, February, 1879.
Sample, Sarah, widow, $8, March, 1879.
Rearick, Emma F., widow, $8, September, 1878.
Martin, Lucinda, widow, $10.
McElroy, Harriet, widow, $8.
Peebles, Elizabeth J., widow, $8.
Wood, Emily E., widow, $22.
Higgs, Susannah, dependent mother, $8, August, 1866.
Heimlick, Christina, widow, $8.
Bingham, John, minor of, $10.
Common, James, minor of, $12, May, 1880.
Martin, Eliza, dependent mother, $8, December, 1879.
McDaniel, Mary, dependent mother, $8, February, 1867.
Nishswonger, Louisa, dependent mother, $8, August, 1865.
Lane, Mary E., widow, $20, September, 1880.
Rodrigues, Antonia, dependent mother, $8, March, 1880.
Minnan, Ann, widow, $30, April, 1864.
Kislingbury, Annie J., widow, $8, November, 1882.
Goodrick, Elijah A., gun-shot wound left arm, ankle, $4, September, 1882.
Glen, Geo. R., gun-shot, wound left arm, right thigh, $4, July, 1882.
Angel, David, scurvy and disease of kidneys, $4, October, 1882.
Wingler, John, injury to abdomen, $6, December, 1882.
Keefe, Jeremiah O., injury right leg var. veins, $8, October, 1880
Chesney, Samuel P., gun-shot wound right thigh, $4, February, 1882.
Peake, John W., shell wound left thigh, $4, February, 1881.
Ferguson, Champion, disease of right knee, $6, April, 1879.
Fox, Chas. H., typhoid fever, spinal irritation, $30, January, 1881.
DeFrates, Emanuel, gun-shot wound right leg, $4, September, 1879.
DeFrates, Justin, wound right side, $1, June, 1880.
Bruce, Robert C., disease of abdominal viscera, $7.50, November, 1882.
Doyle, Patrick, var. veins both legs, $12, March, 1878.
Fanary, John, disease of lungs, $4, October, 1882.
King, Wm. H. H., fractured left leg, $6, June, 1881.
Mosely, Frank A., exostotis right tibia, 4, July, 1882.
Cassell, Harrison O., injury to abdomen, $8.50, July, 1878
Clay, Henry, wound left leg, $1, April, 1880.
Cline, Henry, chronic diarrhœa, $2, January, 1882.
Spelman, Byron T., chronic diarrhœa, $15, November, 1882.
Sample, Charles, chronic diarrhœa, $10, November, 1882.
Henderson, Oliver P., wound left shoulder, $6, July, 1880.
Humphrey, Wm. T., disease of bowels, $8, June, 1880.
Lyons, Chas. C., g s wd right arm and shoulder, wd left forearm, $2, Oct., 1882.
Lamb, Lafayette, wound forearm, $4, July, 1879.
Swales, James M., debility and disease of abdomen viscera, $6, May, 1882.
Sorrels, James W., injury hip, $2, June, 1878.
Brown, Daniel R., gun-shot wound right forearm and elbow, $6, October, 1882.

Boban, Dennis, wound right arm and left side of neck, $4, April, 1879.
Schoen, Egge, gun-shot wound left arm, $6, March, 1881.
Baptist, Sanders, gun-shot wound of back, part paral lower extremities, $8.
Donaldson, Richard, wound right hand, $4.
Reed, Thos. J., wound left hand, $4
May, Horace E., rheumatism right knee, $15.
Kershaw, Albert, gun-shot wound lower part spinal vertebra, $6.
Davenport, Wm. W., chronic rheumatism, $50, February, 1881.
DeSueza, Emanuel, fractured left side, $18.
DeFreitas, Gregory, wound right shoulder, $8
Fanning, Geo. W., disease of lungs, $20.
Dickens, Wash M., disease of eyes, $24
Jackson, John, wound left leg, $18.
Crain, Hiram, loss right leg, $18.
Cook, James, loss right leg, $18.
Stout, Jacob, wound right leg, $18.
Miner, wound left scalpula, injury to abdomen, $8.
Smith, Joseph, wound left leg, $4.
Barrick, Jesse, chronic diarrhœa and rheumatism, $8
Poe, Barney W., wd r arm an forearm, injury to abdomen, chronic diarrhœa, $12.
Nunes, Patrick, wound left grain and left leg, $6.
Windsor, Jesse, blindness, $72
Riggs, Taylor C., wound left side, $262½
Christian, John, total blindness, $72.
Poisal, Henry K., wound right hand, $2
Patterson, L. A., fractured left leg, $4.
Harper, John S., sunstroke and nervous debility, $14.
Hamilton, James O., chronic diarrhea, $6
Allen, Wm. H., wounded cranium, $18
Matthews, Lewis, wounded back and hip, $8
Metcalf, Marion L., wound left leg, disease of brain, result of sunstroke, $14.
Matthews, Richard T., wound left shoulder and left breast, $6.
Sampson, John W., lumbago and chronic rheumatism, $6, June 1881.
Perry, Elzra H., chronic rheumatism, $15.
Smith, Wm., gun-shot wound right hip, $12.
Bates, Edwin D., gun-shot wound left hip, $8.
Warren, Charles, injury to abdomen, $8.
Atkins, Lizzie E., widow, $18, March 1880.
Bird, Samuel W., gun-shot wound left leg, $6, August 1875.
Shoulders, Wesley, chronic bronchitis, $15, September 1882.

LITER.

Liter, George B., wound of left leg, $10.
Petefish, Aaron W., wound right thigh, $8, June 1880.
Johnson, John H., lumbago, $4, April 1880.
Coe, Alfred, gun-shot wound head and left ear and right foot, $4, December 1881.
Settle, Edward, variose veins of left leg, $4, June 1881.
Ratcliffe, Richard A., rheumatism and disorder of liver and kidneys, $6, Oct. 1882.

LYNNVILLE.

Murray, Alexander, wound left arm, $2.

MEREDOSIA.

Buckner, Charles P., gun-shot wound right shoulder blade and left arm, $6.
Luger, John C., loss left a[illegible] r $24.
Hyatt, Thomas, loss third figure left hand, $2, June 1879.
Hawksham, James, wounded in face, $6, April 1878.

Hillig, Frederick A., gun-shot wound thigh, $6, August 1882.
Watson, Lettitia, widow, $8, April 1866.
Weathers, Precious, widow $8.
Naylor, Elizabeth A., widow, $16, May 1881.
Mathews, Susannah, widow, $8, February 1879
Smith, Henry, gun-shot wound left leg, $4, May 1881.
Tanter, August, wound left leg, $6.

MURRAYVILLE.

Slaughter, Silas G., chronic diarrhea injury to abdomen, $10.
McKean, Samuel, chronic rheumatism, $8.
Bush, John G., wound left leg, $2.
McNabb, David, disabled right eye, $4, February 1881.
Wade, Isaac R., injury to right hip, $2, December 1882.
Hopper, Eliza E., dependent mother, January 1865.

NEELYVILLE.

Chapman, Christ C., wounded left forearm, $2, October 1879.
Rogers, Armilla A., widow, $8.
Lansing, Orrin, wounded right arm and breast, injured left arm, $8

ORLEANS.

Cox, Lucy H., $8, February 1879.
Cully, James, disease of lungs, $4, March 1881.

PRENTICE.

Tilford, Nancy, widow, $15, December 1864.
Williams, Edward, $8, February 1872.
Whitton, Jesse, minor of, $10.
Karney, Franklin, $4, May 1882.

SINCLAIR.

Wilson, George, disease of lungs, $12, September 1881.
Fox, Elisha T., wounded left buttock, $6.
Brown, James R., wounded right hand, $4.

WAVERLY.

Hunt, Charles, wounded right leg, $8.
Hardin, John, loss left leg, $18
Talkington, John W., wounded right thigh, $6.
Weatherford, Jonas, wounded right arm, $18
Narr, Henry, wounded left arm and left foot, $6.
Lindsay, Wm. D., wounded chest and injury to abdomen.
Church, Thomas E., chronic rheumatism, $6
Pullian, Maria, widow, $8; May 1881.
Vanhise, Catharine, widow, $8.
Brown, Cassandra, widow, $8, April 1879.
Anderson, Lucy, widow, $8, February 1879.
Cary, Lydia J., widow, $8.
Hazzard, Annette, widow, $12, May 1876.
Lybarger, Esther J., widow, $8, August, 1879.
Twiner, Isaac W., chronic diarrhea, $4, July 1881.
Holmes, George T., disease of eyes, $2, December 1880.
Harris, James M., disease of eyes, $6, June 1882.
Burnet, Moses, chronic diarrhea, $4, December 1882.
Maginn, John C., injury to left side, $8, July 1881.
Dikes, William, loss right index finger, $3, June 1878.
Henderson, John, gun-shot wound of right side head, $4, January 1882.
Ferguson, Francis M., variose veins of right leg, $12, October 1879.

Kimber, Alonzo L., chronic diarrhoea, $6 50, September 1879.
Hairgrove, Wm. J., chronic diarrhoea, $4, January 1881.
Bradway, James, chronic diarrhoea, $6, June 1882.
Van Winkle, Alexander, gun-shot wound right thigh, variose veins and dropsy, $6.
Jones, Timothy, injury to abdomen, $8.
Merwin, Issac N., loss of eye, $4.
Rice, John F., disease of spine, $12.
Miller, Joseph K., disease of eyes, $8.
Roach, James F., injury to abdomen, $4.
Coard, Frank M., chronic diarrhoea, $6.

WOODSON.

Shelton, Stephen G., chronic diarrhoea and disentery of abdominal viscera, $6.
Henry, Edwin R., wound of head, $6.
Seegar, James W., blindness, $72.
Butcher, John, gun shot wound of throat, $2, June 1882.
Self, James F., chronic diarrhoea and dis. of abdominal vis. $4, September 1880.
Clerihan, James R., chronic diarrhoea, $4, June 1882.
Sloan, Catharine, widow, $8, February 1867.

As illustrative of the home feeling in favor of the Union while the war was in progress, and of rewarding the soldier boys by election to local offices after their return from the war, we append two county tickets, (1861 and 1865):

UNCONDITIONAL UNION CANDIDATES.

(Nominated by the Unconditional Union Convention, September 28, 1861.

For Congress,
MURRAY McCONNEL.

[Subject to the decision of the Unconditional Union Convention to be held in the city of Springfield, October 16th, 1861.]

For Delegate to Convention,
ISAAC L. MORRISON.

For County Judge,
HARVEY ROUTT.

For Associate Justices,
D. C. CALLEN,
B. W. GUNN.

For County Clerk,
MATTHEW STACY.

For Assessor and Treasurer,
CHARLES SAMPLE.

For School Commissioner,
SAMUEL M. MARTIN.

For County Surveyor,
WILLIAM LYNN.

MORGAN COUNTY UNION TICKET—1865.

For Judge of County Court,
CAPTAIN H. G. WHITLOCK.

For Associate Justices,
CAPTAIN J. M. LANE.
LIEUT. JOHN HARDIN.

For County Clerk,
CAPTAIN HORACE CHAPIN.

For Assessor and Treasurer,
CAPTAIN WYLLYS MEACHAM.

For School Commissioner,
LIEUT. WM. L. ENGLISH.

For County Surveyor,
PRIVATE JOSIAH BARROWS.

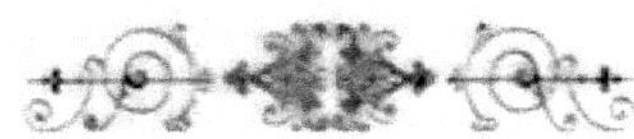

YOUNG LADIES' ATHENÆUM. FOUNDED 1864.

CHAPTER X.—1866–'73.

Jacksonville Incorporated as a City—Conservatory of Music and Oak Lawn Retreat Founded—City Waterworks Constructed—The Murder of Gen. McConnel—Murder Trials—New Societies—School for Feeble Minded.

THIS period was quite an interesting one to the churches, schools and business interests of the city. The population reached over nine thousand, and the present city charter was adopted, (1867,) the Conservatory of Music, Oak Lawn Retreat, the State Asylum for the Feeble Minded were founded and incorporated, and our splendid system of city waterworks begun and completed.

In 1857, Rev. R. W. Allen, formerly pastor of the Pisgah Presbyterian Church, of Kentucky, took charge of the Central Presbyterian church as stated supply. Having received a unanimous call to the pastorate, Mr. Allen was installed December 5, 1858, and continued his faithful labors until May, 1867, when he resigned. After Mr. Allen's resignation, the church was without a pastor for two years, during which time they were dependent upon transient supplies for preaching, with the exception of six months, when they enjoyed the very efficient labors of Rev. R. J. L. Matthews, formerly of Vandalia. Eleven persons were added to their membership in that time. The foundation of their present church edifice was laid in the autumn of 1870, and the building was enclosed the following summer. The first Sabbath of January, 1871, they entered upon the occupancy of their new lecture room.

In May 1869, Rev. W. W. Harsha, D. D., was called from the South Presbyterian Church, Chicago. He was born in West Hebron, Washington county, N. Y. He received his collegiate education in Union College, Schenectady, N. Y. He studied law, but shortly after entering upon the practice, changed his profession and entered the ministry, in connection with the Associate Presbyterian Church. Joined the Old School Church in 1854. He commenced his ministry in Galena, in 1846. His pastoral charges have been at Galena, Hanover, Savanna, Dixon, Chicago and Jacksonville. He received the degree of Doctor of Divinity in 1872, from Fulton College, Missouri, of which institution Rev. Dr. Price was at the time president. On going to Dixon, in 1855, he founded the presbyterian institution, known as the Dixon Collegiate Institute, and acted for some years as its president. He continued as pastor of the Central Church for fifteen years, resinging in June 1884 to accept the presidency of Bellevue College, Nebraska.

At the beginning of this term of years Rev. James G. Roberts was the pastor of the Congregationalists. He was succeeded, in 1869, by Rev. Wm. H. Savage, now of Boston, and he in turn, in 1875, by Rev. Eli Corwin, D. D., now in Racine, Wisconsin.

The First Presbyterian congregation lost their church edifice by fire in December, 1861. Its successor was dedicated January 5, 1867. In the interval, worship was held in Strawn's Hall. Preparations to build were commenced in the Autumn of 1863. The corner stone of the new edifice was laid with appropriate ceremonies Aug. 4, 1864. The Lecture and Sunday School rooms were set apart to their appointed use June 28, 1866. The dedication of the building, as a whole, took place as stated above. The day was propitious, and the exercises appropriate and of great interest. The pastor was aided by Rev. James G. Roberts of the Congregational Church, Rev. S. A. Kingsbury of the Baptist Church, Rev. Robert W. Allen of the Second Presbyterian Church, and Rev. W. F. Phillips of the Methodist Church. The dedicatory prayer was offered by Rev. Mr. Allen. The music was of a high order of style and adaptation.

The building was of the Romanesque style of architecture, from designs by W. W. Boyington, the masonry work and ornamental plastering were by Howard & Thompson. the carpenter work by Hugh Wilson, the painting and graining by McDonnell & Rightmire, the glazing by George A. Misch, the upholstering of seats by George W. Graves, and the gothic chair for pulpit by Jacob Braun. The entire cost of the building, including clock, (by the city) bell and furnishings (by the Ladies' Sewing Circle,) was $60,000, and the estimated value of the property, including ground. $75,000. A debt of $6,000 was provided for *before* dedication.

The new and capacious cathedral for the Roman Catholics of the county was completed about 1866, and including the school and convent property is worth about $65,000. The church was dedicated by Archbishop Purcell, of Cincinnati, Ohio. The parsonage, now used for the school, was built about two years after the completion of the church. The school is under the control of the Sisters of the Order of St. Dominic and is supported by the congregation. It is conducted ten months in the year.

In 1867, Trinity (Episcopal) Church edifice was remodeled and greatly improved, at a cost of some $16,000, by the addition of a recess chancel at the south end and an extension of thirty feet, with tower and spire to the north end, stained glass windows and heightening of roof and ceiling.

Another "Christian" church was organized in the old Court House, in 1866, by twelve persons, adherents of that denomination. Among them were Workman Cully, L. B. Ross, Charles E. Russell and Hiram Smedley and their families. Rev. J. E. Wright was the pastor, and continued to serve them until 1869 or 1870. They occupied the Court House until the completion of their house of worship, on South Main Street, in 1868. The pastors succeeding Rev. Wright were Revs. J. J. Summerbell, C. W. Garoutte and P. W. Sinks.

As is well known one of the most successful christian and philanthropic institutions of the city is the Young Men's Christian Association, whose fine building attests the estimation in which its usefulness is held by the public. Robert D. Russell tells the story of its origin, or the first attempt to inaugurate the movement for a city Y. M. C. A.:

"During the month of May, 1870, the City of Jacksonville, Illinois, was visited by Mr. Weidensall, agent of the National Young Men's Christian Association with a view to the formation of a local branch." The first meeting was held on the 29th of May, 1870. Up to December 23d, 1870, four meetings was held. So far as the record discloses, the only business transacted at these meetings was the adoption of a Constitution and By-Laws, and the election of officers. This last item of business occurred at three different meetings. First temporary officers were elected at the organization meetings, then officers to serve until November, then the annual election the first Thursday in November. On the 23d of December, 1870, the last meeting of this first association was held. The record reads as follows:

"A called meeting of the Association was held at C. M. Eames' book-store this morning. President DeMotte presiding On motion it was decided to have Prof. G. W. Brown examine the subscription list for library and reading room, and after returning the portion to subscribers which he thought best, to pay the balance of money in the treasury to the president of the Ladies Benevolent Association. On motion the Jacksonville Young Men's Christian Association adjourned *sine die*."

For the history of this society's successful successor, see next chapter.

The Soule Chapel Congregation (Methodist Episcopal South) is very small at present and does not support a regular ministry. Among its constituent members were E. B. Hitt, S. S. Spurgeon, Silas Veitch, Mrs. Becraft, James Cravan and D. C. McCoy. The congregation had a very neat house of worship on East College street which cost about $5,000.

The compiler of this volume, then "Ye Local" of the *Daily Journal*, said in April, 1867 of the churches of Jacksonville:

"Hand in hand with a love of education goes the love of worshipping God. The founders and patrons of institutions of learning are God fearing, God serving men and women. The Athens ot the West almost deserves the title of the city of churches, for her churches will attract any one's attention, from their number and prominence, seventeen houses of worship are already erected, many of them beautiful in appearance, and two more church societies are about to build sanctuaries for themselves.

Presbyterian.—This denomination has now five edifices completed. The First church, (new school) which was organized in 1827, with only a dozen members, and now has two hundred and fifty upon its rolls, with three hundred children in its Sabbath school, has just dedicated the finest church building in the state, a brick structure, built in modern style, with organ, stained glass widows, immense auditorium, &c. Rev. Dr. L. M. Glover, pastor. The Westminster church, (new school) has just been completed by the erection of a bell tower, and furnished with organ, altar, frescoed walls, &c. The society was organized in 1860, with thirty-five members, now has one hundred and forty-one, with Dr. D. H. Hamilton as pastor and a flourishing Sabbath school of one hundred scholars. The Second church, (old school) was organized in 1838, having then twenty-one members, which have since increased in number to one hundred and twenty. Their house of worship was erected in 1840. Rev. R. W. Allen is at present the pastor, with T. G. Taylor, Esq., as superintendent of the Sunday school of eighty pupils. The Portuguese colonists in Jacksonville have two Presbyterian societies, each with a neat and commodious church. The first society was organized in 1849, built its church in 1852, and now has one hundred and thirty members, with Rev. A. DeMattos, pastor. The second congregation was originally with the former, but re-organized in 1858, erecting a house in 1864. Rev. Robert Lennington is in charge. Over three hundred children are in their two Sabbath schools.

The Methodists are the next in number of churches, having four finished and one soon to be constructed. The west charge now has three hundred and thirteen members though organized only as far back as 1850. Rev. James Leaton, pastor. The east charge have not yet moved into their new buiding, which is about finished, but are worshipping in the house erected in 1839. They have two hundred and fifty members, with Rev. Dr. Phillips as pastor. The south charge are now procuring subscriptions for the building of a church. The German and African Methodists each have a meeting house, each society consisting of about sixty members, and carrying on Sabbath schools. The former society was organized in 1856, the latter in 1842.

The Baptists have two churches. The first was organized in June, 1841, dedicated their large brick edifice in 1857, and at present have over two hundred members. The Rev. S. A. Kingsbury is the pastor. One hundred and fifty scholars are in their Sunday school. The other society is the African with one hundred and three members and Rev. A. W. Jackson as pastor. Their Sabbath school consists of fifty members.

The Christian denomination have two societies, one with a commodious building, erected in 1847 and two hundred and forty communicants. The church numbered eighty when organized in 1832. Elder Enos Campbell is the present pastor. The other society has lately organized, and is under the charge of the Rev. J. E. Wright. They are now making efforts to erect a building for their Sabbath use.

The Congregationalists have a spacious church in a beautiful part of the city, well furnished. Rev. James G. Roberts is their pastor. They have a membership of one hundred and ninety, with one hundred and fifty in the Sabbath school. Their present house was dedicated in 1850. Their first place of worship (1833) was a log cabin, the first regular church was built in 1835 and since known as Union Hall.

The Episcopalians have one edifice, Trinity church. Dr. T. N. Morrison, rector. Number of members, eighty. The society was organized in 1832, and the church erected four years later. The building is to be entirely remodeled this spring.

The German Lutherans were organized into a church society eleven years ago. They now have twenty members, a neat church and fifteen Sabbath school scholars. Rev. Francis Lehman is the pastor.

The Catholic society was organized in 1856, and now numbers two thousand members. Rev. Joseph Costa is the priest and superintendent of the Sabbath school.

As to the local press, in 1866 Frank Martin published for a short time the daily *Advertiser*, with also a weekly issue. Both were short lived.

Col. George P. Smith became associated with Mr. J. J. Ironmonger, and editor of the *Journal* in 1865. Under Ironmonger & Company the *Journal* took a great step forward and became quite a political power. April 14, 1866, the firm having purchased a steam press, began the publication of the *Daily Journal*, with G. P. Smith as editor; Mr. David M. Swales being foreman of the news-room. He is now foreman of the printing office of the Institution for the Deaf and Dumb.

In its first issue the firm advertised for a local editor of the paper, and Frank Mitchell was appointed. Mr. Mitchell was a son of Prof. B. F. Mitchell, principal of the Female Academy from 1859 to 1865. Frank began work about April 17, 1866, also acting as night editor for a time.

Incidentally it may be mentioned that, at the birth of the new daily, as its first sheet came from the press, there were present, G. P. Smith J. J. Ironmonger, R. B. Mitchell, John Oliverson, pressman, John K. Lathrop and Ensley Moore.

The young daily was a small, unpretentious sheet, compared with its present size and appearance, but Jacksonville had a daily, and that daily has lived!

As before stated, Frank Mitchell became local editor, and his facile pen and keen intelligence were employed about six months, when he went to Missouri, where he became an American Sunday School Missionary, and is now a Presbyterian minister in Callaway county. Among Mr. Mitchell's special associates was Charles M. Eames. It was, perhaps, owing to this circumstance that Eames succeeded Mitchell as local editor. Mr. Eames resigned in 1867, to become city editor of the re-organized Quincy *Daily Whig*. He was succeeded by Mr. Lyman B. Glover, then about 21 years of age, as local of the *Journal*. Under Ironmonger & Co., the *Journal* increased in job work, and July 19, 1866, the *Weekly* was enlarged to nine columns. Soon after this Mr. Ironmonger retired from the *Journal* and purchased the Franklin Job Office from Franklin J. Martin.

Col. Smith was now sole proprietor of the *Journal* establishment, with L. B. Glover as local editor and Mr. Robert Bradbury in charge of the job department. Observant students of the list of income payers soon saw that the newspaper business appeared to be getting profitable, for Col. Smith reported a handsome income. It was, therefore, not difficult for the gallant Colonel to dispose of his property at a large price.

Col. Smith was a native of Virginia, an original Republican in that state, a fine public speaker and ambitious of political success. He sold Chapin & Glover the paper and emigrated to Kansas.

Capt. Horace Chapin and L. B. Glover became proprietors April 14, 1869, Mr. Glover being editor. Ensley Moore became their local editor for a short time. He was subsequently local and assistant editor of the *Jacksonville Independent*.

Mr. Glover's management was noted, perhaps, most for the development of the job office, with Mr. Bradbury, who has ever since continued in that capacity, as foreman.

Mr. Glover was but 23 years of age when he became editorial proprietor, and Capt. Chapin was then postmaster of this city. Capt. Chapin had lived at Chapin, Morgan county, before the war; he entered the army and lost a leg at Chickamauga, after which he made Jacksonville his home. Edward Dunn, afterward city attorney, succeeded Moore as local editor. He was followed in turn by Jarvis G. Shaw formerly of the Springfield (Mass.) *Republican*, and Shaw gave place to George N. Loomis, all during Chapin & Glover's ownership.

In 1872 Mr. J. R. Bailey, who for 17 years had edited and published the Jacksonville *Sentinel*, was compelled, by failing eyesight, to dispose of all his newspaper interests. He retired to farm life, remaining there in quiet retirement until his death. His successors in newspaperdom, were Fanning, Paradice & Co., who also bought the Jacksonville *Independent*, and added steam fixtures and a power press. The latter had been established April 29, 1869, by Ironmonger & Funk, Henry B. Funk being editor. During its continuance under Mr. Funk, Ensley Moore was employed as assistant editor. In 1873 the establishment was sold to Gersham Martin—W. T. Dowdall, of the Peoria *Democrat*, afterward purchasing an interest. It was conducted by Martin & Co., until purchased by T. D. Price & Co.

On a beautiful autumnal afternoon, in the month of September, 1869, a large concourse of people gathered to witness the dedication of Diamond Grove Cemetery. On reaching the cemetery, the company gathered about a fine monument standing near the entrance. It is of white Italian marble with a square base about three feet in diameter, and about three feet high above the pedestal to the shaft, which is of the same material and eight feet in height, surmounted with a wreath, making the whole height of the monument, from the foundation to the top of the shaft, thirteen feet. It is the first monument which strikes the visitor as he enters the enclosure, and its historic inscriptions at once explain the fact that the cemetery itself still bears the name given it by the first pioneers of the county. On the eastern base of the monument appears the following inscription:

ISAAC FORT ROE,

SON OF

REV. OZEL ROE, OF WOODBRIDGE, N. Y

Left New York for the West October 15, 1819, settled in

DIAMOND GROVE,

In February, 1820, Died October 12, 1821.

AGED FORTY-EIGHT YEARS.

ROE.

The inscription on the western side reads:

1869.

ERECTED BY THE COUNTY OF MORGAN,

TO THE MEMORY OF

ISAAC FORT ROE,

One of three first settlers, and the first person

who died in this county.

Facing the drive-way, on the north side of the monument, is a bas-relief representation of him who sleeps beneath, in his pioneer dress, with rifle on his left arm, and broad-ax in his right hand, while in the distance the pioneer's cabin is seen.

On the south side of the monument the following historical sketch is engraved: "An emigration society in the city of New York, October 12, 1819, appointed David Berdan, Isaac Fort Roe and George Nixon, to explore the Western States and select places of settlement for its members. They left the city October 15, 1819, crossed the Wabash at Vincennes December 26, passed and named Diamond Grove January 23, 1820, in which he selected a place of residence, and in February built a log cabin and became one of the first three settlers in the county."

Among the audience assembled were those who knew Mr. Roe, and could testify to the facts narrated. Dr. Chandler, who attended him in his last illness, and Mr. Huram Reeve, who had in his possession the nails used in making the linn-tree coffin for Mr. Roe, were there.

After appropriate exercises dedicating the cemetery and the monument, Judge William Thomas read a paper, prepared by him from facts, mostly obtained from the journal of Mr. Berdan, furnished by his son, Judge Berdan. All of especial interest have already been given in condensed form in the first chapter of this book.

The Methodist Episcopal pastors of these years were:

EAST CHARGE—1866, J. M. Lane; 1867-'68-'69, F. W. Phillips; 1870-'71-'72, N. P. Heath; 1873, F. W. Phillips; 1873, A. S. McCoy.

WEST CHARGE—1865-'67, J. Leaton; 1868-'70, W. F. Short; 1871-'73, E. Cranston.

SOUTH CHARGE—1866, J. M. Lane; 1867, J. Harshman, 1868-'69, H. Wallace; 1870, G. Barrett, 1871, W. W. Roberts; 1872-'73-'74, J. W. Sinnock.

The presiding elders were; 1865-'68, Peter Akers; 1869-'72, George Rutledge.

In 1868 the terms East, West and South Charges were changed to Centenary, Grace and Brooklyn and by these names have since been known.

The Brooklyn M. E. Church was organized in the fall of 1867, with about seventy members. First held preaching in a private house, afterward in the school-house, until the brick building now occupied by them was completed in 1868. First preacher, Rev. John M. Lane, followed by S. R. Harshman, Hardin Wallace, George Barrett, W. W.

Roberts, J. W. Simnock and W. H. H. Moore. In 1878 the membership was 120, while Grace numbered 320.

The period under consideration was more prolific of murder trials than any one of similar length in the history of the county.

John Buchin was indicted at the August term, 1871, for the murder of his son, Paul Buchin, on the 27th day of May, 1871, by shooting him in the head with a gun. His trial was had at the April term, 1872; he was found guilty of manslaughter and given five years.

Henry Henslee was indicted in Tazewell county for the murder of his wife, Caroline Henslee, by mashing her head with a flat iron. The case was brought to this county by a change of venue. He was sentenced for twenty years.

John H. Douglas had a true bill presented against him at the May term, 1872, for the murder, on May 23d, 1872, of Willis J. True, by striking him in the back with a hoe. The jury found the defendant not guilty.

George W. DeWitt was indicted in Brown county for the murder of Edward DeWitt by shooting him with a gun, on September 1st, 1870. Case brought here by a change of venue. Defendant plead guilty to manslaughter and was given eight years.

Charles Atwood was indicted for the killing of Peter Hodin on the 13th day of July, 1870, a little northeast of this city, by stabbing him with a knife. The defendant was found guilty and sentenced to the penitentiary for a term of twenty-one years.

James F. Carpenter and Wesley Jones were indicted for the murder of Richard Beatley, on July 20th, 1871. The defendants were found not guilty.

Henry R. Gillespie was indicted at the March term, 1868, for the murder of John Ruschie by knocking him in the head with a fence rail. The case was tried once with a hung jury, after which the defendant gave bail, went away and never returned, on account of which the case was stricken from the docket.

Thomas Cantrall was indicted at the November term of the circuit court, 1869, for killing Sampson Cantrall by cutting him in the stomach with a knife. He was found guilty of manslaughter and was given ten years.

John Minter had a bill found against him for the shooting of Samuel Newland on August 11th, 1870, at the August term, 1870. The jury found the defendant not guilty.

Lewis Maddox, William Maddox and William Knowles were indicted in Scott county for killing their father, William Maddox, by shooting him with a gun, on the 24th of November, 1870. A change of venue was taken to this county and the indictment nolle prossed.

Mahon Chapman had a "true bill" found against him for murder, at the August term, 1869, for killing Jephemiah Rodgers, by killing him with a shot gun, south of Neelyville. The defendant escaped to Missouri and was closely pursued by officers. Knowing that he would be arrested he killed himself with a gun. His indictment was stricken from the docket in November, 1869.

Isaac Berry *et al.* were indicted in Tazewell county for the murder of Henry Pratt, a deputy sheriff of Tazewell county, on 30th of July, 1869. This case created much excitement in Tazewell county and brought many people from there here. The jury sent Isaac Berry up for life, Emanuel Berry for fifteen years, William Berry fifteen years, Robert Britton fifteen years, Frank Daly fifteen years, and declared Simeon Berry not guilty.

Dr. Henry F. Carriel, who had been connected with the New Jersey Insane Asylum at Trenton for thirteen years previously, was secured as Dr. McFarland's successor as superintendent at the Central Hospital for the Insane, and is at the head of the institution to-day. It is the unanimous verdict of those who have watched the growth and continued success of the charity under Dr. Carriel's excellent supervision, that there could hardly have been a wiser choice. The present trustees are R. W. Willett, of Yorkville, David E. Beatty, of Jerseyville, and Judge Edward P. Kirby, of Jacksonville. Dr. Carriel's present medical assistants are Dr. Lewis A. Frost, who has charge of the female wards, and Dr. J. D. Waller, recently from the Cook county Hospital, who has charge of the male department.

Dr. Carriel's experience in the East stood him in good stead. The institution required a course of renovation and remodeling, and the doctor, who is also an expert civil engineer with the instincts and education of a first class builder, was the very man for the work. He entered at once upon a series of changes which were judiciously planned and have since been carried out both economically and well.

Although the institution to-day retains its venerable aspect throughout, the improvements are all in accordance with the more modern idea which have been utilized at Kankakee and Elgin, and an air of comfort permeates the place. The institution grounds comprise 160 acres in one tract, including 40 acres in ornamental grounds, and a detached tract of 40 acres half a mile east. The farm produces corn, potatoes and vegetables, hay from the meadow lands, and pasturage for the cows. The pasture land is insufficient, however, to feed the number of cattle requisite to supply the institution with all the milk it needs, and a considerable quantity of that article is necessarily bought outside.

The general plan of the hospital comprises a centre building and two irregular shaped wings—one on the east for the male inmates, and one on the west for the females and each containing twelve wards. Between the main and rear buildings, which are connected by a corridor, is a large open court, curving around to the roadway which separates the hospital and the outside buildings. In the rear of the extreme wards at the ends of either wing is an inclosed court in which even the more violent patients take their occasional airing.

The method of treatment at the Jacksonville asylum is the same in all respects as that at Elgin and Kankakee, save that, having no detached wards, or cottages, the patients are not accorded the same degree of freedom to roam at will which prevails at those institutions. They have their periods for exercise in the courts and on the lawn, however, and the convalescents and the better class of patients generally, enjoy fully as many privileges as those at the average hospital. Their health and general appearance compare very favorably with those of the inmates at Elgin and Kankakee.

In April, 1869, the main building of the Blind Asylum was destroyed by fire. The pupils and teachers were immediately removed to the Berean College building, situated two squares west. Through the kindness of Mrs. E. Ayers, who owned the building, school was again resumed, and continued until the institution could be rebuilt. The new building was completed and opened January 26, 1870. The school has progressed most favorably ever since.

During the fall term of 1868, two experimental classes in articulation were formed at the Deaf and Dumb Asylum, and after a fair trial, it was found to be of such great value to those for whom it was intended, that it was continued, and there are now three teachers devoting their time exclusively to that department. The General Assembly of 1869-'70, appropriated $4,000 for procuring printing presses, and the necessary equipments; since that time quite a number of the pupils have learned the trade, and after quitting school have found themselves able to be self-supporting. An art department has been added, and those of the pupils who evince talents in that direction, have the benefit of instruction from a competent teacher. Drawing, painting, wood carving, and scroll work, are taught in this department. A fine library—provided by the Legislature—is an attractive feature of the institution.

The institution was for years unable to secure a sufficient supply of water, but this difficulty was overcome in 1870, by building a reservoir on the grounds of the institution, capable of holding three and a half million gallons of water, and here the ice for the use of the household is procured in winter.

The buildings of this institution are all of brick, and are built in the most substantial manner. The number of pupils increased so rapidly that greater accommodations were needed, and the General Assembly in 1873, made an appropriation for the erection of a dining-room sufficiently large to seat five hundred pupils all at one time; this building was soon after finished and is found to be all that could be desired. It is one of the largest rooms used for this purpose in the State, being sixty-seven feet wide and ninety feet long. An appropriation was made at the same time for the erection of a school building, one of the largest detached buildings in the State used for school purposes. It contains besides the twenty-eight school rooms, a chapel, capable of holding one thousand people. The garden is under the supervision of a competent gardener, who instructs those of the pupils who may be placed under his charge in this useful employment.

Jacksonville Natural History Society was organized 1870 for the study of natural sciences. Among the earliest members were Mr. and Mrs. H. H. Hall, Prof. and Mrs. Storrs, Prof. and Mrs. Bailey, Dr. Samuel Adams, Mr. Howard Turner, Miss Mary Turner, (Mrs. Dr. Carriel) Miss S. F. Ellis, Miss Mary Selby, Prof. and Mrs. Harris and Dr. and Mrs. Milligan. The society studies subjects rather than books, drawing its knowledge from different text-books, from cyclopedias, from general literature, from newspapers and from personal experience.

Dr. Andrew McFarland having resigned the superintendency of the State Hospital for the Insane, founded a private institution for the treatment of the mentally disordered, calling it Oak Lawn Retreat. It was incorporated by charter in 1872, and is designed for the treatment of such cases of insanity as require more especial treatment than can be offered in most state institutions. It occupies a site of sixty acres fronting on Morton avenue, about one and a fourth miles from the public square, in the city of Jacksonville. The location, as regards picturesqueness, salubrity, water-supply, drainage, etc., is everything that could be desired. It has accommodations for about twenty patients, and is occupied to its full capacity, though early additions to its buildings are contemplated. It has been successfully conducted ever since its establishment. Dr. McFarland's sons, Dr's. George and Fletcher, being associated with him in the management.

Passing from private to public institutions we note, during this period, the founding of the Illinois Asylum for Feeble Minded Children. The growth of this charitable and humane enterprise was remarkable. It was not custodial as its name implies, but was designed as a school for the education and training of idiots and feeble minded children. Great good has already been accomplished by the asylum, many of its pupils having been taught to read, write and comprehend the first principles of arithmetic and geography. We were sorry to lose this charitable enterprise from our midst, but our State legislature in 1875, saw fit to locate the asylum at Lincoln, Logan county, making an appropriation of $185,000 for the construction of buildings at that place. To the late Hon. Murray McConnel, of Jacksonville, State Senator, is due the credit of introducing a nd carrying through the legislature in 1865, a bill appropriating $5,000 per annum for two years to make an experiment in the interest of this most unfortunate class for whose benefit nothing had as yet been done by the State. Mrs. L. P. Ross and Miss Walton were appointed matron and teacher, and on the 1st of June, 1865, the Institution for "Feeble Minded Children" was opened with four pupils. The number had increased to twelve on the 31st of December following. Dr. Chas. T. Wilbur was the superintendent.

In 1870 according to the census, Morgan county had 26,202 people. Of this number, 13,235 were males, and 12,576 females.

In 1868, Prof. J. B. Turner, of our city, was selected by the Republicans as their candidate for Congress from this district. Possessing abilities which his most bitter opponents have been compelled to concede, though by no means a politician in the ordinary acceptation of the term, he has ever been found in the front rank in all movements for political and educational reform. A Birney and Garrison abolitionist, a free-soiler and Wilmot proviso man in 1848 and 1852, a Republican in 1856, and an earnest supporter of the war for the Union, he has never taken any step backward, but has always been abreast of the most advanced in all the important movements of the day. To his individual and persevering efforts, more than to those of any other ten men in the nation, is the country indebted to-day, for that broad and beneficent scheme of industrial education which, by the aid of munificent grants of land by congress, has now been adopted in most of the states of the Union, and is yet destined to become general. It is to the eternal disgrace of Illinois that a man to whom, more than to any other, the state owes this grant, should not have been recognized in carrying the plan, which he was so largely instrumental in devising, into practical execution.

The famous trial of Wm. A. Robinson for the killing of Hon. Murray McConnel on the 9th of February, 1869, took place in the Opera House, at a special term of the court, held for that purpose, Judge Charles D. Hodges presiding, commencing on the 25th of May, 1869, and ending June 8th, the house being crowded during the entire time. One hundred and thirty-two jurors were examined. This was the most noted trial, and created more excitement than any that ever took place in the county. Feeling ran very high at the time against the prisoner.

William Brown, State's attorney, was assisted by I. J. Ketcham and H. J. Atkins, and Hon. James Robinson, Judge Shaw, Judge Woodson and W. H. Barnes appeared for the defendant. The jury consisted of Robert Jones, John Bracewell, William T. Spires, David Saunderson, William S. Larton, William R. Dyer, Joseph Dyer, C. P. Johnson, William Bacon, Albert Rouse, William A. Allcott and Henry Standley, and found the defendant not guilty.

The agitation of the Water Works question and discussion of various plans for the same, covered many years. Actual labor on the works began in October, 1872, but little was accomplished that season. The distributing reservoir was finished August, 1873, at a cost for excavation and embankment of $3,125, for paving, $2,175; total cost, $6,308.

The impounding reservoir was completed December 2d, 1873. Cubic yards of earth to the number of 83,850 having been excavated at a cost of $16,586. The iron pipe costing $52,000, furnished by Schickle, Harrison & Co., of St. Louis, was laid in August and September by the contractor, M. W. Quan, at an expense of $6,089. Cost of waste weir and sluice way, $2,000; cost of land for the impounding reservoir, 25 acres, $3,100; stoneware conduit pipe, 4,650 feet long, laid during November and December, cost $2,800; building pumping works $5,000; pumping engine, $3,000, from the Niagara steam pump works, Brooklyn, N. Y. The capacity of this pump is about 700 gallons per minute. Boiler made by J. M. Wilson, $2,000; 34 fire plugs, $1,000. Total expenditures for the construction of the water works $118,000.

The storage capacity of the two reservoirs is 62,500,000 gallons. And at the present time there are 5 feet 3 inches of water in the impounding reservoir, and several feet in the distributing reservoir. Of the importance of this system, it would, of course, be superfluous to speak. All the public buildings of the city and most of the private residences, are protected by the water mains. The supply of water is assured unless the ocean of lakes go dry, and the rain no longer falls.

At an election held on June 15, 1869, in pursuance of a city ordinance, the legal voters by a majority vote empowered and authorized the city council to issue bonds not exceeding $150,000, said bonds having twenty years to run and drawing ten per cent interest. The funds arising from the negotiation to be expended by the council or their agents in building the Water Works and procuring a supply of water

As to the fraternities 1866-'72 they were all flourishing like bay trees. As our city grew in size, it became evident that there was room and a necessity for two Masonic lodges here. The second one, called Jacksonville Lodge, No. 570, was organized June 12th, 1867. As charter members there were J. H. Hackett, D. W. Rawlings, J. C. Pyatt, Thomas Scott, S. M. Palmer, Thomas Turley, E. S. Gordon, J. R. Foley, J. H.

McConnell, J. C. Smith, Wm. Johnson, C. H. Howard, L. Weil, Ed. Lambert and W. S. Hurst. The officers first elected were Ed. Scott, Master; T. J. Bronson, Sen. Warden, and Ben. Pyatt, Jun. Warden. From the very first this lodge has succeeded beyond expectation.

The subordinate Masonic bodies here prospering and growing, a want was felt for a higher degree in Masonry. A Knights Templar body became a necessity. On December 30, 1868, a charter was applied for, and on November 9, 1869, one was granted, establishing Hospitaler Commandery No. 31. The charter members were P. G. Gillett, William S. Hurst, Thomas Hine, S. M. Palmer, C. M. Morse, G. W. Fanning, Charles H. Howard, L. C. Barrett, H. W. Milligan, C. W. McLain, J. M. Dunlap, C. E. Broadwell and L. W. Chambers. The Past Commanders in the order of attaining this rank in this Commandery are as follows: Philip G. Gillett, Charles M. Morse, Calvin W. McLain, Leonard W. Chambers, Samuel M. Martin, Stephen H. Thompson, Edward C. Kreider, Thomas J. Bronson, William H. Worrell, William H. Smith and W. C. Green. This Commandery ranks as one of the best in the state. Most of its members are shining lights in the order, and many of them have been chosen to positions of honor and trust in both the state and national bodies.

In 1870 the Odd Fellows thinking there should be some branch of the order where the wives and daughters of members could come together and enjoy pleasures and social evenings, organized, some fifteen years ago, what they term a Rebekah lodge. In these lodges all third degree Odd Fellows and their wives, daughters and sisters are entitled to membership. Jacksonville Rebekah Lodge, No. 13, was organized in this city October 11, 1870. As charter members we find John Rottger, J. C. Cox, J. C. McBride, Amos Henderson, J. H. Gruber, Mary E. Gruber, Mary M. Lord, Mary E. Keemer, Emma L. Rottger and Sophia Benson. This lodge meets twice a month. Has a membership of 125, and its meetings are made enjoyable social gatherings. The success of this lodge was greatly due to the exertions of the late Bro. W. D. R. Trotter, in whose death the lodge lost a valued and greatly missed member.

The Jacksonville Sorosis was organized November 30, 1868. At that date there was no literary society for women in Jacksonville. The call to organize such a society was responded to with eagerness and enthusiasm.

The membership at first was limited to twelve, but the candidates for admission were numerous and the number was soon changed to eighteen, finally to twenty-five, at which it now stands. Sorosis is governed by a constitution and by-laws similar to those used by other societies of like interests.

The literary exercises consist of essays, conversations, debates, readings and biographical and critical reviews of authors and their writings. One of these exercises is presented at each meeting.

An alphabetical list of the members is kept by the secretary who makes the appointment from this list in the order of their names. Those appointed are notified four weeks in advance. The subjects considered are of the widest range, including everything that tends to the development—mental, moral or physical—of human beings. The papers are of such length as to allow of sufficient time for a thorough discussion of the subjects presented. The meetings are held weekly—Friday afternoons from half-past two to half-past four o'clock at the houses of the different members, taken in alphabetical order. Anniversaries are held to which each member has the privilege of inviting one guest. It has been the custom at these social meetings to present annual reports, short literary exercises, music and the most esthetic viands the members are able to prepare. Sixteen fruitful years bear witness to the interests and vitality of this society. May it long live to be an honor and benefit to Jacksonville.

As a matter of record we append the names of the officials of Jacksonville, 1866-'73.

In 1866, the town trustees were Ralph Reynolds, Chas. H. Howard, Elizur Wolcott, James H. Lurton, Isaac J. Ketcham.

In 1867, city airs and titles were assumed under the incorporation act.

1867.—John Mathers, mayor; Robert T. Osborne, Charles H. Howard, David M. Simmons, Alexander Edgmon, aldermen; Harrison O. Cassell, city clerk; Ellis M. Allen, marshal; Wm. L. English, attorney; Andrew N. McDonald, collector and assessor.

1868.—William P. Barr, mayor; James Redmond, Edward Lambert, David M. Simmons, William Branson, aldermen; John C. Pyatt, city clerk; George W. Smith, marshal; Wm. G. Gallaher, Jr., attorney; William W. Happy, collector and assessor. James J. Rowen was appointed city clerk vice John C. Pyatt, resigned.

1869.—John Mathers, mayor; Irvin Dunlap, Leopold Weigand, George M. McConnel, William Knox, Ebenezer T. Miller, William Hamilton, Jr., Alexander Edgmon, Robert C. Bruce, aldermen; James H. Kellogg, city clerk; James McKay, marshal; Edward Dunn, attorney; William W. Happy, collector and assessor.

1870. William Branson, mayor; Irvin Dunlap, Daniel Redmond, Jonathan Neely, Joseph Capps, John H. Fink, William Hamilton, Jr., John W. Hall, Joseph H. Bancroft, aldermen; Andrew N. McDonald, city clerk; James M. Swales, marshal; James H. Kellogg, attorney; William G. Johnson collector and assessor.

1871.—William Ratekin, mayor; Richard M. Gregory, Ferdinand Schmalz, Jonathan Neely, Joseph Capps, James L. Montgomery, James M. Mitchell Josiah Gorham, Charles K. Sawyer, aldermen; Andrew N. McDonald, city clerk; William Needham, marshal; Oscar A. DeLeuw, attorney; William G. Johnson, collector and assessor.

1872.—George M. McConnel, mayor; Michael H. Walsh, Leopold Weigand, Charles E. Ross, Henry R. Johnson, John M. Ewing, Michael Rapp, D. W. Fairbank, Dr. Clinton Fisher, aldermen; John N. Marsh, city clerk; William Needham, marshal; Edward Dunn, attorney; Bazzill Davenport, collector and assessor.

1873.—Matthew Stacy, mayor; Benjamin F. Gass, William S. Hurst, Charles E. Ross, John I. Chambers, Barton W. Simmons, William S. Richards Dr. Clinton Fisher, Andrew Jackson, aldermen; Benjamin R. Upham, city clerk; Francis M. Springer, marshal; George J. Dod, attorney; Bazzill Davenport, collector and assessor.

The county contests at the November hustings resulted in the election of the following:

1866—Sheriff, S. S. Moore, declared elected, but the office given Milton Mayfield after a contest; Coroner, Field Sample; Representative, Felix G. Farrell.

1867—Treasurer, George W. Fanning; Surveyor, W. S. McPherson.

1868 States Attorney, Wm. Brown; Senator, James M. Epler; Representatives, S. M. Palmer, Jno. Gordon; Circuit Clerk, George W. Clark; Sheriff, Isaac S. Sierer; Coroner, John H. Gruber.

1869 County Judge, Edward Scott; County Clerk, John Trabue; Treasurer, G. W. Fanning; School Superintendent, S. M. Martin; Surveyor, W. S. McPherson.

1870 Representatives, Newton Cloud, Wm. H. Barnes; Sheriff, Benjamin Pyatt; Coroner, Henry Lawler; Surveyor, C. C. Robbins.

1871—Treasurer, Wm. H. Wright; Surveyor, Charles B. Lewis.

1872—Senator, Wm. Brown; Representatives, J. W. Meacham, J. B. Nulton, John Gordon; Circuit Clerk, Joseph W. Caldwell; Sheriff, W. H. Broadwell; States Attorney, H. O. Cassell; Coroner, Michael Carney.

1873- County Judge, E. P. Kirby; County Clerk, Samuel M. Martin; Treasurer, W. H. Wright; School Superintendent, Henry Higgins; County Commissioners, Daniel Dietrick, John Virgin, J. H. Devore.

In 1869 the Jacksonville Southeastern Railway, then called the "Farmers' Road," was built from this city to the city of Waverly, eighteen miles, and in 1870 twelve miles more were built giving us direct and profitable rail connection with Virden and intermediate points. For a short line it was then one of the best, traversing some of the best farming sections in the state, and affording an outlet for the vast amount of grain and produce, as well as coal, for which this region is noted.

Jacksonville's most illustrious citizen, ex-governor, ex-senator Richard Yates died in St. Louis, on November 28, 1873, at the age of fifty five years. He had been viewing the Cairo & Fulton railroad, as one of its commissioners, having been appointed to that important position by the government. He had been to Little Rock, Arkansas, and was on his way home, when, becoming too weak to travel, he stopped to rest in St. Louis, where, in the midst of his many friends, he quietly passed away. His remains were brought home the next evening, and, after being viewed in the parlor of his own house by thousands, were carried to the grave, followed by an immense assembly.

Governor Yates' public career briefly resumed, shows: "Six years in the Legislature of Illinois, four years in the Congress of the United States, four years governor of Illinois, and six years senator of the United States; twenty years in political public life, with few men his superior, in any field of duty." He was born January 18, 1818, on the banks of the Ohio River, at Warsaw, Gallatin county, Kentucky. In 1831, his father removed to Illinois, and, after stopping at Springfield, settled at Island Grove, Sangamon county. After attending school awhile, Richard joined the family here. Subsequently, he entered Illinois College, at Jacksonville, where, in 1835, he graduated with first honors. He chose for his profession the law, and began at once its study with General John J. Hardin as instructor. Gifted with a fluent and ready oratory, he soon entered the arena of political life, and being an ardent admirer of Henry Clay, he joined the political party of his leader. In 1840, he engaged with great ardor in the "hard-cider campaign," for General Harrison. Two years after, he was elected to the legislature from this county, then a Democratic stronghold. He served four years here, and in 1850 was elected, after an exciting contest with Major Thomas L. Harris, to Congress. At the expiration of his term, he was re-elected, and coming into the political field the third time, was defeated by a small majority, owing to his decided stand against the repeal of the Missouri Compromise act, and his strong anti-slavery views, which, in a speech of great power and brilliant oratory, he advanced, and which gained for him a national reputation. Six years afterward, he was elected to the chair of State, and during the most critical period of the nation's history, held that important place. Here his true patriotism shone with a brilliancy and strength of will, and saved the State in the threatened crisis. He, like Governor Morton, of Indiana, earned the title of the "War Governor." The fate of the nation was involved in the destiny of the State. Governor Yates was equal to all emergencies; and when a Democratic House attempted to thwart his purposes and place the State where many of its members wanted it, he promptly squelched that body by his famous act of prorogation. His loyalty was as undoubted as true, and through all the long and bitter contest he was a close and intimate friend of President Lincoln, and one of his most earnest supporters.

Of the city's condition and prospects the *Journal* commented in April, 1867:

The characteristic feature of Jacksonville has ever been the universal interest which her citizens have felt in establishing and maintaining schools of learning of every grade. Besides the numerous private schools, the city can boast of three flourishing free schools, with the building for the fourth almost completed, three young ladies' seminaries, two commercial colleges, and the well-known Illinois College. Of the latter, as the oldest, we will speak first. It was the good fortune of the city to number among its earliest inhabitants men of intelligence and education, who, while they were rearing houses for their protection, were building school houses in which their children might be taught. The city was but three years old when the site for Illinois College was selected. * * * * *

The city has been known throughout the United States, and envied by the other places of our state, as the location of the benevolent institutions of Illinois. Upon three of the extreme limits of the corporation stand the immense buildings devoted to the noble work of healing, teaching, training and caring for the afflicted ones of the broad commonwealth of Illinois. In some respects they have been a real help to the place, bringing custom to the dealers and visitors to the city, while the officers of the various institutions have been a great addition to the *literati* of the community. * * *

Of the private residences of Jacksonville we might say much in praise, but want of space will forbid. Elegant mansions, the homes of the wealthy and learned, grace our streets and half disclose their beauties among the countless shade trees of the city. From year to year, as our houses have been erected, they have, fortunately, not been built closely together, but have been scattered over the whole of the town, thus giving to each one the advantage of large and pleasant site. The early planting of shade trees and the cultivation of them and shrubbery, have made very many fine homesteads delightful. * * * * *

In our city there are all conceivable kinds of business transacted, in as many varieties of houses or rooms. Jacksonville boasts of twenty-nine bakeries and groceries, has an even score of doctors; thirteen firms deal in boots and shoes alone; her guests are entertained at six hotels and twelve boarding houses; the members of her bar number fourteen, while the number of her bar-tenders are twice that; no wonder buildings can be rapidly put up, for there are seventeen boss carpenters in the city; the reading public are supplied from five book and stationery stores; there are fourteen dry goods establishments here, many of them extensive and attractive; ten live stock dealers have homes here; eight merchant tailors cut, fit and clothe the male portion of the community, while seven milliners get up duplicates of the famous "love of a bonnet;" right in the business portion of the city may be found seven first-class drug stores, many dealing largely in hardware; one flourishing house attends exclusively to the hardware and another to hide and leather business; two woolen factories, six insurance agencies, three agricultural houses, two auction stores, five barber shops, four billiard saloons, five tin shops, four brick yards, four meat markets, five carriage manufactories, three cigar and four stove manufactories, six wagon shops, four flour mills, five jewelry stores, three first-class livery stables, half a dozen saddler's shops, and a thousand (more or less) other establishments of different natures may be found in Jacksonville. Three fine cemeteries are now in use to receive the ashes of those citizens who are daily going to their long resting place. One is beautifully located on high wooded ground west of the city. It was opened for interments within a year, and will probably become the most highly ornamented of the three. Already it contains a costly and elaborate work of art commemorative of the greatest farmer of the world, our late fellow citizen, Jacob Strawn. This new burying ground, called the "Diamond Grove Cemetery," was purchased last year by the board of trustees of the town, and inaugurated with appropriate ceremonies. It has all been laid off regularly and will be handsomely fitted up by the various lot owners. The College Grave Yard has now been abandoned, the space allotted to it being filled and the situation of the land unfavorable to improvement and enlargement, many bodies and monuments have been moved from it to the new one. The East Grave Yard is the oldest cemetery in the city, situated a little over a mile from the center of the square. The yard is very full at present, and parts of it much neglected, yet it contains the graves of many honored men and women, among them Col. John J. Hardin whose remains were brought back to his home here from the battle field of Mexico. During the present year there will probably be much expended in improving both the "Diamond Grove" and East cemetery by private citizens and the corporation. * * * * * *

The business blocks of Jacksonville are not to be passed by unnoticed. Especially are those which have been erected within a year ornaments to the city, and monuments of architectural merit. The main business of the city has from its start concentrated around the court-house lawn and within a block of the public square. On the north side Messrs. Dayton & Adams, Hatfield, Price, and Chambers have each erected three story brick buildings, convenient and substantial structures which tower over the few of their humbler neighbors which remain. The west side also boasts of a block of three story brick stores occupied by seven different firms engaged in various occupations, also a fine structure owned and occupied by Messrs. Weil & Bro. which looks down upon the surrounding stores.

The erection of Strawn's Hall furnished our merchants with the finest business block on the square at that time which was speedily occupied.

Its nearest neighbor is the handsome marble block which is now receiving its finishing touches. The block is a stately structure of brick.

From the time that Jacksonville was incorporated as a town, she has had to undergo the annual ordeal of an election for town officers. The government of the place has heretofore been confided to the keeping of a board of trustees, five in number. These city fathers have very seldom been elected on strict party tickets, but the issue at stake has been license or anti-license, and the voice of our citizens has always in all these yearly balotings with but one solitary, sad, and not soon to be forgotten occasion, been strongly against legalizing the traffic in death dealing liquor. The continued triumphs of the "temperance tickets" in our town elections, have given Jacksonville a good name throughout the state, and her citizens have been quoted for sobriety and good order. However, whenever a party issue was made, and in all the state and presidential elections the town and precinct of Jacksonville have given rousing majorites for the nominees of the Republican party, ever since the party of freedom has been known by that title. The spring of 1860 was the one exception mentioned above, in which the license men carried the town. During the year following, the place was visited by a series of disastrous conflagrations, and as many of them were traceable to the liquor traffic, the sentiment of the community was much intensified against the license system. Our first municipal election under the new charter, was held on the first Monday of April, 1867. Two rival tickets were in the field. The regular republican nominees and a people's ticket made up from both parties, and generally understood to be a license ticket. The result is well-known—the triumphant choice of our future rulers of every candidate upon the Republican city ticket with the exception of the alderman of the first ward. * * * * * *

Jacksonville has never taken a remarkable interest in manufactures. Of late years, however, her capitalists have been investing more in that way.

Jacksonville Woolen Mills.—In the line of woolen products the factory of Messrs. Capps, McDonald & Co., has been enlarged and other buildings erected, until it is an immense establishment, employing numerous hands and turning off daily a large amount of goods, which would be creditable to any mills in the land.

Home Manufacturing Company.—The new woolen works of the Home Manufacturing Company are now also in operation. The stock company interested in it have carried the enterprise along briskly, erecting large and substantial buildings, employing the best of workmen, and producing flannels, cassimeres, jeans, etc., of unrivalled quality.

Foundries, etc. Farming implements of every description are furnished to the agriculturists of the county from the many shops of the city. Iron foundries are now in active operation, producing cast works of all patterns. Carriages, buggies and everything in that line, of superb style and the best of workmanship, are built in the shops of the city. The specimens of skill which emanate from the marble yards of Jacksonville in the shape of mantles and monuments are highly praiseworthy.

Banking Houses.—The city of Jacksonville now has four banking establishments, the First National, and three private houses. The former the only bank of issue, was organized under the national bank act of June 3rd, 1864, and opened for the transaction of business during the September following, with an authorized capital of $100,000.

As to the schools, before the incorporation, the town was divided into four school districts. Mr. Murray Martin, the school commissioner, had the oversight of all, while each was governed by an annually elected board of directors, three in number. Each school had its own principal, who was assisted by male and female teachers for each of the rooms in his or her school. Only three of the districts had separate school houses up to that time, but the fourth district, now the fourth ward, completed that spring a magnificent building, built in a grander scale than any of the others, furnished with an airy basement for a gymnasium and play ground in wet weather, in addition to all the conveniences of the other school houses.

The West Jacksonville District School, now second ward, corner of Fayette and West State streets, had five hundred and fifty pupils that year, and was under the charge of James L. Dyer, principal, with seven assistant preceptors. Directors, Messrs. I. L. Morrison, M. P. Ayers, E. P. Kirby.

Locust Grove District School, now third ward, on the north side of East College between Mauvaisterre and East streets, was superintended by Miss Rebecca Woods, an experienced teacher, with a faculty of four lady teachers under her. The number of pupils in attendance was two hundred. Messrs. W. Mathers, O. D. Fitzsimmons and A. C. Woods were the directors. The building was amply large.

Walnut Grove District School, first ward, had for its principal that year Mr. J. Warrick Prince, who had three assistant teachers. The board of directors consisted of Messrs. J. N. Marsh, S. Markoe and Frank Coulter. The school house stood on North street between Mauvaisterre and East streets. The number of scholars in attendance then is what the deponent knoweth not.

The Catholic Parochial School was the one carried on by the Roman Catholic denomination. The building was near the depot of the T. W. & W. R. R. One hundred and eighty-five pupils were attending. Rev. Joseph Costa, priest of the parish, was the principal. Two other instructors were employed to assist him.

With the incoming city council that year an entire change came over the face of school matters. The whole city was merged into one common school district, abandoning the former divisions altogether, under the management of a board of education, consisting of the mayor and one member from each ward, the latter appointed by the city council.

The present system of public schools in the city, has been in operation seventeen years. During this period they have advanced to the front rank, and are among the best in the State.

By 1867, the growth of the town had reached such proportions that a better form of government, and a better system of schools, became necessary. Under the city charter, granted that year, the present system of graded schools was adopted. The city was divided into four wards, and a school located in each. Mr. Israel Wilkinson was appointed superintendent, which office he held until 1869, when he was succeeded by Mr. J. M. Alcott, who held the office one year. He was followed by Mr. D. H. Harris, the immediate predecessor of the present superintendent, Prof. H. M. Hamill. Each ward maintains a separate district school, the grades in all being the same. The Washington High School is situated in the fourth ward. Its course of instruction is thorough and complete, and fits the pupil for the actual duties of life. Mr. Harris, in his report for the year 1877, gives an interesting resume of the schools for the past ten years, which we here append:

"Jacksonville has long been known as an educational center of great reputation, whose influence is felt far and wide. The early establishment of the public schools is due to the earnest efforts of two of our citizens—the late Gov. Duncan and Judge Wm. Thomas. The latter survives to witness the success of the cause which he so ably advocated.

"The honor of first popularizing the public schools in Jacksonville belongs to the well-known educator, Hon. Newton Bateman, who, for several years, was principal of the West Jacksonville school.

"Judge E. P. Kirby, of our city, immediately succeeded as principal of the same school, which he conducted for three years with eminent success; following him Michael Saunderson, Esq., nobly sustained the well-deserved reputation of the school for three years, when, in his valuable life-work, he fell at his post.

"Before the schools of Jacksonville were organized into a system under the present city charter, there were several independent schools, sustained in part by the general school fund of the State. A male teacher was employed as principal and superintendent of each of these district schools. The course of study in each of these schools therefore comprised not only the common branches, but also Latin, Greek, Natural Sciences, Higher English and Mathematics. The new school charter, in 1867, at once introduced a new regime which centralized the general supervision in one superintendent, and abolished the extravagant idea of sustaining four high schools of small classes by organizing one central high school for the accommodation of the entire city, which was found to be a great improvement in a pecuniary and educational point of view. The success of this system has led to a more economical expenditure by the gradual introduction of female principals into the ward schools. The new organization also led to a more careful and thorough classification of pupils, a more uniform course of study, resulting in a more efficient preparation of the pupils in the advanced studies."

The condition of the schools shows a steady progress and increasing efficiency of the public schools as an educational force in the community.

To meet a want, long and widely felt in this region, the Jacksonville Business College was founded by Prof. R. C. Crampton, in May, 1866. The college was located in Chambers' block, north side of public square, and was there successfully conducted for several years, sending forth hundreds of young men well qualified to act their part among the busy throngs of men in all the regions of the great West. Many of the youths who attended the college in the early years of its existence, are already numbered among the most successful business men of the State.

From the very first, the patronage of the college has been steadily increasing, and its popularity among men of business, more and more decided. Since the college was founded, it has instructed nearly three thousand students, and by them is honorably represented in the various industrial and commercial pursuits, all over this broad land, from Mexico to Maine.

The design of this college is to fit young men and women for the active duties of successful business life. The aim is not to send out mere book-keepers or clerks, but the course aims at symmetrical development, and is calculated to strengthen the mental power, and give a broad and substantial business training.

In the summer of 1869 the ownership of the Business College passed into the hands of the trustees of Illinois College, and for several years it occupied part of Whipple Academy building, a few blocks west of the public square.

As the principal of the Jacksonville Female Academy, Prof. Gilbert Thayer proved gifted in management and since his day, the institution has been entirely self-supporting, not in a single instance falling back, as it used frequently to do, on special subscriptions for its relief. Thus making it the duty and for the personal interest of the principal to manage the finances well has been an important step in the direction of permanent prosperity. We quote from Dr. Glover:

> Besides the worldly wisdom which Mr. Thayer brought to this work, he also contributed to it an engaging person, pleasing manners, fine social powers, the magnetism of enthusiastic purpose, by all which he impressed friends and drew to him strangers with remarkable facility. He took tours of observation in which he himself was as much the observed as the observer, and he seldom returned home without bringing with him a bevy of girls charmed by the beauty of his silver locks and more by the fascinations of his laughing eye and sparkling speech, and thus he laid not only Illinois, but Indiana, Missouri, Iowa and Kansas and more distant regions, under contribution to his purpose to build up Jacksonville Female Academy, and while making a good thing of it for the community, to make a good thing of it also for himself. The school was quite uniformly full as long as he continued in it, and the graduating classes much larger than they had ever been before. One hundred and thirty-one young ladies were added to the alumnæ during his period of service. It was also during his term that the eastern pediment of the building was erected at an expense of about $12,000. Prof. Thayer retired one year before the expiration of his lease, on account of ill-health. He now has charge of a female seminary at Morgan Park, near Chicago.

In 1872 Prof. W. D. Sanders established the Illinois Conservatory of Music, taking as his model the plan of the New England Conservatory of Music, which in turn received its origin in the conservatories in the old country. This institution is yet in successful operation, with a full corps of able and experienced teachers, who are justly appreciative of the responsibility resting upon them. Its founders and succeeding managers have undertaken to sustain an institution that shall be inferior to no other in the United States. From the beginning it has had a remarkable success. With a full corps of distinguished European and American professors, it offers the very best instruction in singing and on all the principal string and wind instruments, and in every department of theory and practice. Its violinists, its pianists, its organists, its cornetists and flutists, and its teachers of singing have been among the best. It receives pupils of every grade, from mere beginners to those already far advanced. Among its pupils are many who have been teachers, who come to perfect themselves in their art. Jacksonville may well be proud of such an institution. It is an honor to the city and to the State.

Connected with Illinois college is a preparatory school, known as Whipple Academy, taking its name from its founder, S. L. Whipple, who, in 1869, gave $10,000 to establish it. The building first used by the trustees for academic purposes, is the one now owned and occupied by Prof. George W. Brown for his Jacksonville Business College, and the Illinois College authorities have now erected and are using a large and well arranged brick building upon the college campus, for the accommodation of the academy students.

In February, 1870, the main building of the Illinois Female College was destroyed by fire; but it has been replaced by a building of superior architectural pretensions. On the resignation of Dr. Bastion in 1848, Rev. J. F. Jacques was appointed principal, which position he held with marked success until June, 1855. From this date till 1858, the position was filled successively by Rev. Reuben Andrus, D. D., and Rev. H. S. McCoy. In 1858, Rev. Charles Adams, D. D., was elected principal, and continued in that capacity until his resignation in 1868, when Rev. Wm. H. DeMotte, LL. D., was appointed to the vacancy. Prof. DeMotte continued in office until July, 1875, when he resigned to accept the position of Superintendent of the Wisconsin Deaf and Dumb Institution.

Jacksonville has never had much occasion to boast of her general manufacturing and wholesale interests. But those which she does sustain would reflect credit upon any city. The leading manufactory is known as the Jacksonville Woolen Mills, and was founded in 1839 by Mr. Joseph Capps, who removed from the State of Kentucky in the fall of 1838, locating in the town of Waverly, in this county, which place he reached about the middle of October of that year. Mr. Capps was a practical machinist, having learned the trade in the city of Louisville. On his arrival in Waverly he formed a co-partnership with the late Judge George Waller of Minnesota, for the purpose of carrying on a wool-carding and cloth finishing business, which business Mr. Waller had already established in a small way. During that winter he was engaged in building an engine and custom-carding machinery in the shops of his partner, and in the following spring he located permanently in Jacksonville, where he established what is now known as the "Jacksonville Woolen Mills." Having severed his connection with Mr. Waller in the summer of 1839, he devoted his time and energies thenceforward in building up his business which, at the time of his death had grown to large proportions. At first the business was confined to custom-carding alone, and shortly afterwards the fulling and finishing of home-made cloths was added. When we reflect that this enterprise was in the hands of a man who was not only capable of constructing his own machinery and building the steam engine to drive it, but also possessed in rare combination the requirements of a first-class business manager in every respect, it is not surprising the business of his choice prospered and attained rapid growth. In the year 1843 he associated with himself Mr. Ambrose Wetherbee as a partner in the business, which co-partnership lasted a number of years. A short time after the withdrawal of Mr. Wetherbee, Mr. L. C. Haskell became identified as a partner. The latter possessing some practical knowledge of the manufacture of woven fabrics, the firm decided to add spinning and weaving machinery, and in the year 1852 the *first piece of goods* in the history of the business was made and finished. At the expiration of a year Mr. Haskell withdrew, and in 1857 Mr. Capps' eldest son, Stephen R., who is now the senior member of the present firm and Mr. Wm. J. Metcalf became partners. The latter did not remain long in the business, when it was conducted under the firm name of Joseph Capps & Son. In 1862 the second son, Wm. E., was admitted, the firm name being known as Joseph Capps & Sons. In the year 1864 Mr. Alex. McDonald became a partner, and in the following year his brother Charles also, the latter assuming the superintendency of the mills. The Messrs. McDonald were extensive retail merchants in the city of Jacksonville, and Messrs. Capps became mutually interested also in that department of the business, the styles of the two firms being "Capps, McDonald & Co.," and "McDonald, Capps & Co.," respectively. The large store of the latter was situated on the site occupied at present by Messrs. Atwater & Pratt. During the year previous on account of the rapid increase of trade, it was determined to make extensive additions, both in machinery and buildings, and the present site of the mills was selected and a new mill projected. The old structure which stood on the premises now occupied by Mr. W. E. Capps as a dwelling place, was partially removed and most of the works transferred to the new buildings. The two firms as above constituted lasted but one year, when, on account of failing health, Mr. Alex. McDonald retired, his brother doing likewise soon after. The business again came into the entire control of Messrs. Capps & Sons, in whose hands it has ever since remained. The wisdom of an increase of the productive capacity, and the adoption of greater facilities as noted, was verified and sustained by the large and extended trade that was secured, and which, under prudent and safe management continued to spread as the years passed, until in the year 1872 it had become the largest manufacturing interest of the kind in this part of the western country. On March 10th of the last named year, the senior partner passed away. His untimely death, occurring as it did in the maturity of his plans and purposes for the further development of his business, did not, however, cripple or in anyway retard its onward progress, and to-day it stands a monument of the enterprise and pluck of a class of men whose individual success and welfare is the welfare of the community about them. There has been no further change in the firm and management since Mr. Capps' death, excepting that in 1878 Mr. Joseph L. Capps, his third son, was associated with his brothers, the *new* firm still bearing the *old* firm name of "Joseph Capps & Sons," thus perpetuating the name and memory of the founder in the wide circle of business connections throughout the country of the great west.

It is a very false impression that Jacksonville has nothing but educational, religious, literary or charitable institutions to boast of. The product of such an institution as our "City Mills" is a real source and justifiable cause of local pride, reflecting credit upon Jacksonville. Messrs. Fitzsimmons & Kreider, the well-known and enterprising proprietors, in order to meet the demands of increased business, have this year purchased the extensive warehouses, elevators and cribs of T. & F. Keener, to enable them to handle all classes of wheat and thus make better selections of grain for their milling. The capacity of the mills has also been again largely increased by the addition of the most improved roller mills, and another line of centrifugal machines, disintegrators, etc. These improvements necessitated increased capacity in motive power. Messrs. Fitzsimmons & Kreider have been in the flour-mill business together since 1876, a prospering period of eight years. Before 1876 both were engaged separately in the same business for several years. The City Mills, now in their control, has been in successful operation for thirty years.

In this chapter we have already made reference to the trial of Robinson, accused of the murder of Gen. McConnel. The tragedy itself occurred on the morning of the 9th of February, 1868. Mary Ryan, a domestic of the household, entered his office, which was also his bed-room, located in an L of his home on North Main street. She found the General lying on the floor upon his face in the midst of a pool of clotted blood. She testified that she had been in his room to make up his bed and that about ten minutes after leaving it, while up stairs she heard a loud sudden noise like a fall. Returning almost immediately, she found him murdered, and although it was broad daylight, no person was seen by any of the family to enter or leave the room. There was no evidence of a scuffle. The wounds were five in number, all in the head, the jaw bone was broken and the skull fractured in several places.

The general was in his usual health and had expected to go to Springfield that very day on professional business. The coroner's jury found that he came to his death "from and by reason of blows willfully and feloniously inflicted with some instrument unknown to the jury, *in the hands* of W. A. Robinson." This emphatic verdict was reached unanimously, fifteen minutes after the dismissal of the last witness. The accused was 28 years old, only resident here a short time, and was keeping a small grocery store. To raise means for this he had borrowed $420 in gold of Gen. McConnel, giving his note for the same. He was seen entering the General's premises that morning by W. H. Worrell, a milk-man, and the murdered man was evidently computing interest at the time of his death.

As to the deceased he has been already frequently referred to in these pages. He was born on the 15th of September, 1798, in Orange county in the western part of the State of New York, his boyhood's days were spent there and in Chemung county, near Elmira. At the early age of fifteen, he left the Empire State and his father's family for the great west - then so undeveloped, unpeopled, almost unknown. As early as 1815, he was in the boundaries of our own state, but not permanently settled until about 1820 or 1821. At that time, his home was in or near what is now Scott county. Soon after he removed to within the boundaries of what became the town of Jacksonville. Dwelling in this locality for almost fifty years, he had, of course, been deeply interested and identified with the growth of the place. A man of indomitable energy, of great endurance, addicted to no evil habits, always willing to contribute of the ample means which he acquired in his long residence here, he came to be one ever looked up to for advice in regard to matters pertaining to the interests of the place.

In his chosen profession of the law, he has been one of the most active and prominent members of the Morgan county bar.

In political life the General never swerved from his earliest attachments to the Democratic party, and worked so acceptably, so indefatigably, for the advancement of the principles which he advocated, that he well earned the *soubriquet* by which he was so universally known as the "wheel-horse of the Democracy." He has often represented his party in their national, State and county nominating conventions. For four or five years, during the administrations of Presidents Pierce and Buchanan, he filled the office of fifth auditor of the treasury. As early as 1838, he was a member of the lower house of the Illinois Legislature, and near the same time, served as commissioner of internal improvements.

A member of our general assembly for several successive terms, he became one of the most active participants in the deliberations of that body and the acknowledged leader of his party. His last service in political life was the filling of a term of two years in the State Senate, representing this district. His title of general was acquired, we believe, by his position in connection with our State militia, though he also served as a volunteer in the so-called "Black Hawk War."

During the darkened years of our country's history, when the pall of the rebellion and civil war hung over the land, the general was always found among the comparatively few of his party who followed in the lead of their lamented Douglas, and remained unflinchingly, a war Democrat, true to his country and to the real principles of his party.

Too far advanced in life to take an active part in military life, he nevertheless, with eloquent voice and stirring appeal, arrayed himself on the side of those who were sustaining the government in those trying hours.

The deceased left a widow and four children, all well advanced in life, to follow him to another world and mourn his loss while they survive him. Of the latter, one son, George, was an active Republican and prominent citizen, serving as alderman and mayor of the city. He is now the dramatic and musical editor of the Chicago *Times*. The other son, Edward, is a brilliant writer for the press, and now master in chancery. The two daughters are living in New York City, one the widow of the late Senator James McDougal, of California, the other the wife of his brother John. The only other child of the General, the talented lawyer and author, John L., preceded his father to the grave.

Returning again to the subject of manufactures, we feel that reference should be made to the long established flour-making industry now known as Morgan Roller Mills, now owned by Messrs. Scott, Hackett & Chambers. The mills are located on the banks of the Mauvaisterre, directly north of the city. They were first built in 1845 or '46 by Messrs. James Dunlap, Jonathan Neely and John Holland, all now deceased. In 1847 the building was destroyed by fire; Mr. Holland became sole proprietor and rebuilt the mills. In 1853 Messrs O. D. Fitzsimmons and Jonathan Neely bought interests. Three years later Messrs. Davenport & Fitzsimmons bought out Holland & Neely. In 1865 Mr. F., then owning the City Mills, purchased his partner's interest in the Morgan Mills and thus controlled both. In 1868 the latter property was sold to Mr. Mapes, and later became the property of the First National Bank through the failure of Mapes & Sons. Litigation regarding the title continued for several years. During this period, (in February, 1874) it passed into the hands of Messrs. Edward Scott & James H. Hackett, who in 1884 sold one-third interest to Mr. L. W. Chambers. In the fall of 1882, the mills were almost entirely rebuilt and supplied with modern machinery, necessary for the Hungarian system of gradual reduction.

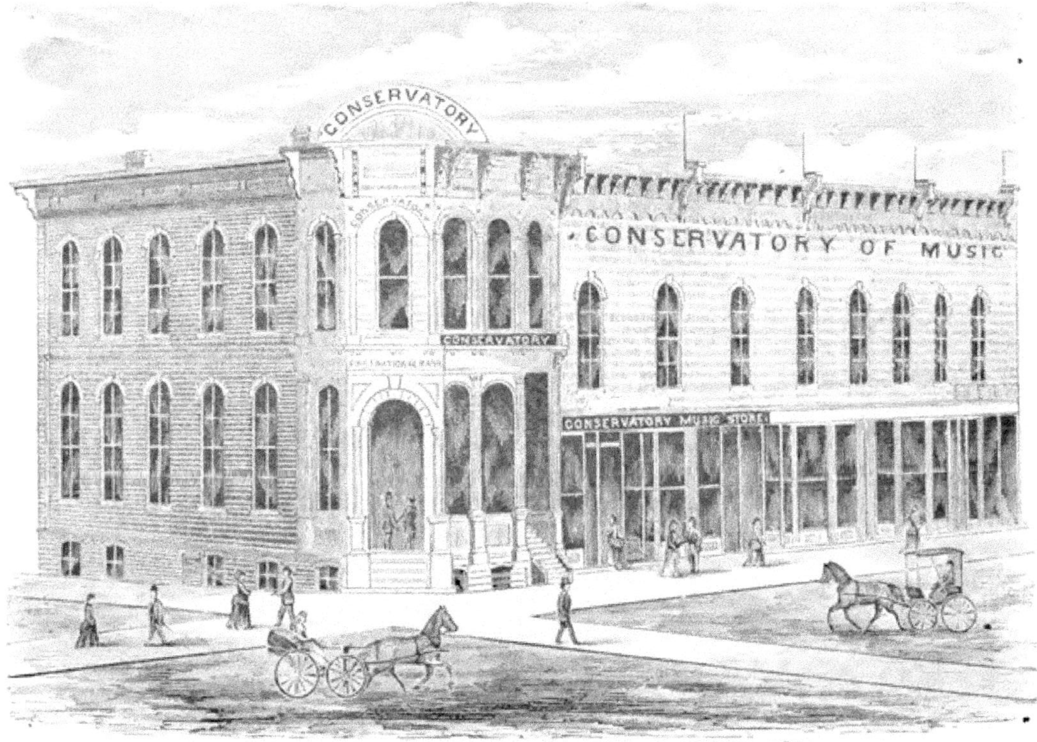

ILLINOIS CONSERVATORY OF MUSIC. FOUNDED 1872.

CHAPTER XI.—1874–'80.

A Glance at what Jacksonville was Ten Years Ago—A City of Churches, Colleges, Schools and Benevolent Institutions—Also a Business and Manufacturing Center of Present Prospective and Importance—Literary and Aesthetic Societies—Municipal Statistics—Public Improvements—A live Railroad Point, a good Stock Market, a Great Place for Marrying and a Place where some People die—The Original Garden of Eden, with all the Modern Improvements.

THE Chicago *Daily Tribune* of Jan. 6, 1875, editorially referred to our little city of ten years ago as follows, basing its comments upon the annual review published in the *Jacksonville Daily Journal:*

"Jacksonville, as everybody knows, is a city of State institutions, and, though not containing much more than 10,000 inhabitants, has many metropolitan features not usually found in places of greater pretentions. Its Insane Asylum contains 474 patients, and is one of the best conducted institutions in the country. The Deaf and Dumb Asylum has 341 pupils, who are taught reading and writing and the higher branches The Institution for the Education of the Blind has 107 pupils, and the Institution for the Education of the Feeble Minded Children has 103 inmates. In addition to the state asylum, there is the Jacksonville Surgical Infirmary, the Oak Lawn Retreat, or private asylum for the insane, and an Orphan's Home. It has musical and literary societies in a flourishing condition; a Free Public Library and Reading-Room; a Library Association—quite a distinct organization—with industrial schools and benevolent societies. There are seven public schools, with 1,500 pupils and 34 teachers; two private schools for boys and three for girls; 21 churches and two parochial schools. The city valuation for 1874 was: Real estate, $4,024,210; personal estate, $1,606,837; total, $6,-631,047. The city taxes for 1873 were at the rate of one and one half per cent. Park improvements for the year 1874 cost $9,768.45.

One of the important features of Jacksonville is the Union Stock-Yards, for the amount of business transacted in Jacksonville and the surrounding region is much greater than one would think. The number of cars of stock received and shipped by the railroads was $2,527. At the Stock-Yards the receipts for the year were: Cattle, 22,366; hogs, 16 723; sheep, 1,139; and horses and mules, 643. Jacksonville has also been at work adding to its buildings during the year, which are, according to *The Journal*, of a creditable description. In manufactures Jacksonville is still in its infancy, but *The Journal* is a pretty newsy paper, well filled with advertisements, which tell more perhaps than the year's exhibit on the fourth page. For a town of 10,000 inhabitants, Jacksonville can boast more business, life and enterprise, and back up its boast with facts and figures, than many a city of double its size.

This was a very comprehensive summary of the *Daily Journal's* review, but for the purpose of introducing more names, facts and figures, we quote more fully as follows:

"Jacksonville, a city of about 10,000 inhabitants, the county seat of Morgan county, is situated in the heart of the great corn-growing and stock-raising region of Central Illinois, about thirty five miles due west from the State Capital. The soil here is unsurpassed in richness and productiveness, and its cultivators, as a class, are prosperous and independent in circumstances. The city itself, as the result of the surrounding agricultural prosperity, and of the fact that its first settlers were imbued with the value of religious and educational advantages, has attained an importance and a reputation quite remarkable for a place of its size.

City valuation for 1874 is as follows: Real estate, $4,024,210; personal estate, $1,-606,837; total, $5,631,047. The city taxes for 1873 were at the rate of one and one-half per cent., and for last year will be only a little larger. This is very low compared with most of the cities around us, whose taxation rates from two to five per cent.

The total receipts of the city treasury from April 1st, 1874, to January 1st, 1875, were $172,189.33; total expenditures, $172,189.33, of which the principal were P., P. & J. R. R. bonds, $50,000; water works account, $28,593; streets and alleys, $16,165.15; park improvement, $8,468.45; extension Church street sewer, $3,907.99; street extension, $4,742.28; salaries, $5,668.32; police, $2,367.48; gas and gasoline, $5,874; board of health, $823 23; water expense, $2,350.26; teachers' salaries, $15,654; other school expenses, $5,418.

The number of marriages in the city last year were 318

The number of deaths about 180.

Jacksonville is yet in its infancy as a manufacturing town, but its infancy promises a sturdy manhood. The splendid system of water works now in successful operation has given a great impetus to manufacturing projects, and our list next year will be much extended. We mention now some of the more noticeable enterprises.

First among these stands the Jacksonville Woolen Mills, Joseph Capps' Sons, proprietors These mills manufacture largely of all sorts of woolen goods, yarns, &c., giving employment to a force of about one hundred persons. The proprietors ship largely to all parts of the country, doing an annual business of not less than $200,000.

A paper barrel factory, on a large scale is about to begin operations, some of the machinery having already arrived. This will form one of the most important manufacturing interests in this part of the State

The manufacture of fine carriages and buggies, and wagons of all kinds, light and heavy, is carried on, on a large scale, by W. S. Richards, Samuel Cobb, Hellenthal, Vogel & Co., J. W. Hall, and E. Keemer, R. Walton, Day & Dunavan, Philip Lee, H. D. Gouveia, largely manufacture wagons

J. L Padgett's Jacksonville Shirt Factory is a new institution, that has sprung into a surprising success. The business of manufacturing shirts, begun on a small scale, has now assumed wide proportions, and already manufactured goods are sent far and wide. A large force of hands are constantly employed to meet the demands made.

Another new and important manufacturing enterprise is that of C. H. Dunbrack & Co., who manufacture gents' furnishing goods. Their goods have a remarkable popularity, and are to-day sold from Iowa to Texas by agents. Orders come fast and thick. Large shipments have been made of late, some to the extreme south. The branches of work embrace almost every kind of gents' wear save heavy clothing. The enterprise is on an independent basis, sound and prosperous.

In the manufacture of fine candies of all kinds, and fine confectioneries, E. Hamilton & Son take the lead. Their arrangements are complete and their daily business very large.

The manufacture of cigars and of fine tobaccos in the city is immense. B Pyatt & Son have manufactured and sold during the year 415,600 cigars, an increase of 103,600 over 1873. Their sales of tobacco in other forms are fully as heavy. This firm is one of the most noted in the State.

Messrs. Myers & Knollenberg manufactured in 1874, 400,000 cigars, and their sales in other tobaccos will amount to as much as their cigar trade.

Romerman, the West State street tobacconist, has manufactured 200,000 cigars, and sold heavily of other tobaccos.

Flour is manufactured in large quantities and shipped to all parts of the country.

During the year just closed E. C. Kreider manufactured 12,800 barrels of flour, handling 64,000 bushels of wheat.

Messrs. Scott & Hackett manufactured 10,000 barrels of flour since April, when they began business.

Messrs. White & Shuff have manufactured 5,000 barrels of flour, and Messrs. Schoonover nearly as much more.

Other manufacturing interest might with propriety be mentioned, the coopers, the boot and shoe makers, harness makers, upholsterers, bottling establishments, where soda pop, beer, ale, cider, &c., are put up, collar makers, hoop skirt and hair makers.

Under the lead of our far sighted and public-spirited Mayor, Hon J. O King, supported by a progressive common council, many improvements have been inaugurated and carried through, and our municipal affairs are in a very favorable condition.

During the year the public square has been made attractive by a handsome iron fence and fountain, and by a complete system of brick walks, and in the coming spring and summer will be an ornament and a joy. The total cost of the improvement was $9,768.45.

An important improvement—the extension of Church street sewer a distance of 2,962 feet—has just been completed at a cost of $3,907.99.

A of number of street extensions have been carried through at a cost of $4,750.23, as follows: Mauvaisterre street, Versailles street, Clay avenue and Diamond street.

The expenditures for grading and draining streets, and building sidewalks and crossings for the eight months ending Nov. 30th, was $15,815. Several miles of brick walks have been laid at a cost of $3,306.34 The number of bricks used was 289,900. Three miles and six hundred and thirty-one feet of plank walks have been built since April 1st, for which 65,881 feet of pine plank, and 10,292 feet of oak lumber were used, making a total of 76,174 feet of lumber at a cost for material and labor of $1,563.23. Total cost brick and plank sidewalks $4,869.57

In the way of new buildings, public and private, for the year, there have been many marked improvements. Few years in the past have furnished more. Among the more noticeable private residences that have been completed are those of L. W. Chambers, a fine two story frame of modern design, on West State street; Prof. J. H. Woods, a splendid frame and one of the most capacious in the city, on West Lafayette street; Dr. Joshua Rhoads, corner Prairie and Reed streets, a fine frame of handsome design; Wm. E. Capps, a splendid brick, corner Westminster street and College avenue; Prof. R. C. Crampton, a frame residence on College hill; M. H. Carroll, a fine frame on South Main street; Abner Yates, an imposing frame, finished on East State street; A. N. McDonald, a fine frame on East State street; Major W. P. Callon, a costly frame on North Main street north of the city; Andrew Russel, a large and expensive frame residence on Mound avenue; Rev. Dr. Nevius, a large brick residence on West State street; Dr. Kellogg, a fine frame residence on College avenue; E. W. Bradley, fine frame residence on Diamond and Greenwood streets; James Scott, large frame on West North street, and many others, all adding to the beauty of the place that we would gladly speak of at length, but the list is long.

Many private residences in various parts of the city have been remodelled, added to and so improved in appearance that they seem as if entirely new, and certainly stranger eyes would so regard them.

Among the business houses erected, is Robert Buckthorpe's brick store building on East State street, 20 by 60 feet, two stories, with 14 feet ceilings, a neat building costing $4,000.

Among the public buildings that have been but recently completed, are the main building of the Institution for the Education of the Blind, a noble structure costing $75,000, a full and minute description of which has heretofore appeared

Though the corner stone of the fine new dormitory building of Illinois College on College Hill, was laid in 1873, most of the construction and the completion of the work were accomplished last year. The edifice is a handsome brick structure 100 feet by 50 feet, with three stories and basement, costing $21,000, though it has since been appraised by good judges, at $30.000 The building furnishes accommodations for 36 students, and is almost entirely paid for by the contributions of citizens of Jacksonville, alumni of the college and others

The dining hall and hospital building, and engine house, at the State Institution for Deaf and Dumb, the first a magnificent building completely adapted for the purposes for which it was built. A new and commodious school building is in course of erection, but for the present is left severely alone.

New building, such as an engine house, ice house, shop, house for produce, filter, &c., have been added to the State Hospital for Insane, while many internal improvements necessary and important have been made.

At the Institution for Feeble Minded Children, one or two minor but much needed frame buildings have been added.

The splendid new edifice of the Central Presbyterian church congregation was finished early in the year, and presents an imposing appearance. It is modest in style, but pleasing. With the tower and bell yet to be added, and the lot, it will have cost $33,000.

Grace M. E. church, one of the handsomest church edifices in the city, was dedicated to the worship of God, January 4, 1874 It cost $28,000. * * * * * * * *

Jacksonville has been remarkably favored in the location of State institutions, being the site of four of the largest and best regulated of the kind in the country, as follows:

Illinois Institution for the Education of the Blind—F. W. Phillips, M. D., superintendent.

Illinois Central Hospital for the Insane—H. F. Carriel, M D , superintendent.

Illinois Institution for the Education of Feeble Minded Children—C. T. Wilbur, M. D., superintendent.

Illinois Institution for the Education of the Deaf and Dumb—P. G. Gillett, L. L. D., principal.

The Insane Hospital has 474 patients, and is one of the best arranged institutions of the kind in the country. It is very pleasantly located about one mile south of the public square.

The Institution for the Education of the Deaf and Dumb, is located about one mile west of the public square and has 341 pupils.

The Institution for the Education of the Blind is located about three-quarters of a mile east of the public square, and has 107 pupils.

The Institution for the Education of Feeble Minded Children, is located one mile west of the square, on the property known as the Duncan estate, and has 103 pupils.

There are also three other benevolent institutions of note here, making seven in all.

The Jacksonville Surgical Infirmary is located on South Sandy street, three doors south of the public square, and is owned and managed by Dr. David Prince. It is supplied with large galvanic batteries, and all the apparatus appertaining to a thorough and complete adaptation of electricity as a theraupetical agency The establishment is also designed especially for the management of cures requiring surgical operations, and is supplied with ingenious apparatus for use in orthopedic and plastic surgery, in which operations Dr. Prince is regarded as a rarely prominent and successful

Oak Lawn Retreat is located about one mile and a half southeast of the public square, is a private hospital for the insane—arranged to accommodate about ten or twelve patients. It is managed by Dr. Andrew McFarland, for many years superintendent of the State Hospital for the Insane, and is remarkably successful in his treatment of the insane. It is delightfully located—being one of the pleasantest places in the city which is noted for its charming residences.

The Orphan's Home, on East State street, established by Mrs. Eliza Ayers, has tarted anew in its noble work under the charge of Rev. Dr. Passavant. * * * *

The following is a list of the numerous educational institutions in the city:

Illinois College—one of the oldest classical institutions in the west—Rev. J. M. Sturtevant, D. D., president.

Illinois Female College (Methodist) W. H. DeMotte, A. M., president.

Jacksonville Female Academy (Presbyterian) E. F. Bullard, A. M., principal.

Young Ladies' Athenaeum, Rev. W. D. Sanders, D. D., superintendent.

Illinois Conservatory of Music, Rev. W. D. Sanders, D. D., superintendent; Prof Pozuanski, musical director

Whipple Academy, (branch of Illinois College.)

Jacksonville Business College—This excellent and growing institution was founded in 1866 by Prof. R. C. Crampton. Its patronage has been steadily increasing from the first. During the term which has just closed, its attendance numbered over 130 students—both ladies and gentlemen. The course of study and business training is much more thorough than that found in many similar institutions. An evening school of great value to scores of young persons of our city is sustained for six months of the year. The principals, Prof. R. C. Crampton and G. W. Brown, have put forth every effort to make this the leading business college of the State and the west. Prof. W. R. Glen has charge of the penmanship department.

Parochial school (Catholic,) Sister J. Meber, principal

German Lutheran school—F. W. Knauch, principal. * * * * * * * * *

In respect to public schools, also, Jacksonville ranks very high. Under the charge of Prof. D. H. Harris, city superintendent, these institutions have reached a degree of thoroughness and excellence truly admirable. They number seven separate schools, with 34 teachers and about 1,500 pupils. The list is as follows:

Washington High School, Lewis J. Block, principal; First Ward School, Miss Hannah Tobey, principal; Second Ward School, Miss Mary A. Selby, principal; branch school (Second Ward) Miss Ellen Hammond, principal; Third Ward School, G. H. Littlefield, principal; branch school (Third Ward), Mrs. E. M Caldwell, principal; Fourth Ward school, M. S. Lincoln, principal; colored school, Mrs. F. C McLaughun, principal.

The literary tone given by the numerous institutions of learning extends in a marked degree into the society of the place, and a number of private and social organizations for purposes of culture—including many of our best citizens—are in flourishing existence. Among them we may barely mention The Jacksonville Literary Union, the Jacksonville Club, The Art Society, The Home Musical Club, The Dramatic Club, The Phi Sigma Literary Society, The Plato Club, The Sorosis, The Jacksonville Library Association, The Sigma Pi Society and the Phi Alpha Society at Illinois College; The Belle Lettres and Phi Nu Societies at Illinois Female College.

Among miscellaneous organizations may be named an Agricultural Society, Horticultural Society, a Poultry Association, a Trotting Association, a Turn Verein Society.

The Odd Fellows, the Masonic organization and Good Templars are represented by numerous bodies.

Within a year the Jacksonville Free Library and Reading Room has commenced a successful existence, and is doing much to raise and maintain the literary tone of the city.

The managers of the organization are Messrs. E. Wolcott, Dr. H. W. Milligan, F. G. Farrell, H. H. Hall, Mrs. Alex. McDonald, Mrs. Morris Collins, Miss Attilla Rawlings.

The trustees of the Jacksonville Library Association, an entirely distinct organization from the above, and which possesses a choice library of the higher order of works, are Messrs. H. W. Milligan, W. S Andras, E. P. Kirby, H. E. Dummer, J. H. Woods, T. J. Pitner, M. P. Ayers.

Among the private benevolent societies are the Industrial School for girls, Miss Maggie Catlin, principal; the Women's Benevolent Society; the Women's Educational Society, and various church benevolent societies. * * * * * * * * * * * *

Although hitherto chiefly noted as a delightful home and an educational center, Jacksonville has been steadily growing in business importance, and promises to become ere long a very important business and manufacturing center Situated in the heart of a magnificent region, with railroads running to all points of the compass, coal abundant and close at hand, and a splendid system of water works, affording an unfailing supply of water, and moreover possessing the advantage of the presence of an abundance of capital, it needs only increased energy and enterprise to double the population and business of our city in a few years. And to this our citizens are awakening A new era, we believe, has dawned upon Jacksonville, and our next annual review, we think, will show a great increase in our prosperity as a city. * * * * * * * * *

While the year has not been one of great growth or unusual business, our city can compare favorably, in that respect, with other places in the west, and indeed in passing through the "hard times" has shown itself and its citizens to be established on an exceptionally safe and solid basis. There are few cities in the west where so much wealth is concentrated in proportion to their size, and very few which contain so many attractions as places of residence and such natural advantages for growth in business and manufactures and general prosperity. * * * * * * * * * *

The amount of business transacted in live stock, particularly in cattle, in Jacksonville and the surrounding region, is far greater than most persons imagine. The number of cars of stock received and shipped by the railroads during the year is 2,527—representing, probably, over 100,000 animals.

The shipments of stock over the Peoria, Pekin & Jacksonville railroad for the year 1874 were: Cattle, 490 cars, or about 6,850 head; hogs, 358 cars, or about 21,500 head; sheep, horses and mules scattering

The Chicago & Alton railroad shipments of various classes of freight, and also receipts of stock for the year. Wheat, 1,353 bushels; corn, 29 505 bushels; rye, 5 790 bushels; barley 1,834 bushels; potatoes, 5 534 bushels; iron, 85,616 pounds; hides, 28-020 pounds; merchandise and sundries, 3 890,271 pounds; flour, 3,701 barrels; whisky, 1,829 barrels; lard, 151 barrels; salt, 185 barrels; ice, 3,073 tons. Cars of stock received 1,049; do shipped, 833; cars coal received (12 tons per car), 272; do sand received, 109; do lumber received, 140; do lumber shipped, 130; collected on freight received, $91,200; chargeson freight forwarded, $44 000.

Toledo, Wabash & Western railroad—395 cars of cattle, or 6,320 head, were received on the road at this point during the year; during the same term six hundred cars of grain were forwarded, and 600 cars of coal received: charges for freight received, amount to $120,000; tickets sold $48,000.

The receipts at this point of the Jacksonville Northwestern & Southeastern railroad were: Hogs, 177 cars, or 10,600 head; cattle, 225 cars, or 3,600 head, one thousand cars of coal from Virden, averaging 300 bushels each car, or a total of 300,000 bushels.

Continuing our record of the criminal cases involving human life, which came up in our courts during this period—1874 to 1880, we find that Julius H. Elmore was indicted at the January term, 1875, of the circuit court, for the murder of Claiborn Coker on the 24th of December, 1874, by cutting him in the neck with a knife. He was found not guilty by the jury.

Robert Mayes was indicted at the May term of the circuit court, 1875, for the murder of his wife, Mary Mayes, on the 5th of June, 1876, at Meredosia, by hitting her over the head with a brick, and then throwing her into the cellar of his house. The trial took place in August, 1876. This was a bad case, and the jury found the defendant guilty of murder, and sentenced him to the penitentiary for a period of 22 years.

Bion Shaw was indicted at the August term, 1876, by the circuit court of Cass county for the killing of John Davis on the 10th of August, 1876, by shooting him with a pistol. A change of venue was taken to this county and a trial had in May, 1877. The defendant was found guilty of manslaughter and sent to the penitentiary for one year.

William T. Hannas, better known as "Tobe" Hannas, was indicted in May, 1878, for the shooting and killing of William Baker and Clarence Hubbard, at the Baptist (colored) church in Jacksonville on April 14th, 1878. This case created much excitement in Jacksonville, and public opinion ran high against the defendant. The jury found him guilty and sentenced him to the penitentiary for a period of twenty years. He was afterwards transferred to the Insane Hospital where he died.

Samuel W. Mathews was indicted at May term, 1878, for the murder of his father, Richard Mathews, on May 20th, 1878, by shooting him with a pistol. Trial in May, 1879. The jury found defendant guilty of manslaughter and he was given one year in Joliet.

John Angelo and Theodore Angelo were indicted in August, 1878, for the murder of Isaac Hammill. A trial was had and John Angelo was declared to be not guilty, insane, and the boy Theodore, sent to the reform school. Theodore's case was reversed by the supreme court, brought back, dismissed and his discharge granted.

Albert DeFrates was indicted in May, 1879, for the killing of Antonio DeFrates on the 25th of February, 1879, by shooting him with a musket. Trial was had and the defendant was found not guilty.

Charles Van Wey was indicted by the grand jury in May, 1880, for the killing of Ira Kimball at the depot in Chapin on the night of the 28th of February, 1880, by shooting him with a revolver. The trial took place May 20th, 1881, the defendant being found guilty of manslaughter and sentenced to one year in the penitentiary.

In the spring of 1874, the Christian churches of this city, united in a series of evangelistic meetings under the leadership for two weeks of E. P. Hammond and afterwards continued for several months under the conduct of the pastors. The result of this effort was the most thorough religious awakening the city had experienced for years if not the most thorough ever witnessed. The result was particularly noticeable amongst the young men, many of whom were born into the kingdom for the first time, and many others set to work, who, although connected with the churches, had hitherto been inactive. By this revival the young men were inspired with a strong desire for associated work for their fellows. In response to a call on the 12th of June, 1874, at the Illinois Female College, a meeting for re-organizing the city Y. M. C. A. was held. The former organization was ignored and all present, forty-three in number, were considered the founders of the society. The constitution and by-laws of the old association were adopted; and officers to serve until November 1st, were elected. The choice for president fell on Dr. H. A. Gilman, who was successively re-elected to the same position until Nov. 1st, 1877.

The first religious work undertaken was the young people's meeting, held in the First Presbyterian and Central Presbyterian churches at different times. The attendance at these meetings was very large; sometimes as many as 400 or 500. Tracts and religious papers have been circulated in large quantities. In the winter of 1875–'76, a cheap restaurant, or as it was commonly called a "soup house," was carried on to meet a pressing demand. Beginning in August, 1875, the Association paper *Work* was published for two years; this was a strong help in educating the people in the plans and purposes of the society, informing them from mouth to mouth of what was being done and making known the wants and desires. Healthful lectures and entertainments have been furnished from time to time. The headquarters of the association for seven years were any place that would temporarily accommodate.

The list of the churches of the city in the year 1874, shows the following denominational summary:

Baptist, 2; Congregational, 1; Catholic, 1; Christian, 2; Episcopal, 1; Lutheran, 2; Free Congregational, 1; Methodist, 7; Presbyterian, 5. Total 22.

The pastors of the leading churches were: L. M. Glover, First Presbyterian; C. W Garoutte, Christian; L. Washington, Baptist; P. C. Cooper, African Methodist Episcopal; R. Lennington, Portuguese; W. W. Harsha, Central Presbyterian; J. W. Sinnock, Brooklyn; E. N. Pires, Portuguese; Earl Cranston, Grace; W. H. Savage, Congregational; A. J. McCoy, Centenary M. E.; Jos. Cross, Trinity Episcopal J. A. Beagle, Soule Chapel; Wm. Winter, German M. E.; R. W. Allen, Unity.

The M. E. preachers of these six years were:

Centenary—Geo. Stevens, 1874–'75–'76; D. W. English, 1877–'78; Horace Reed, 1879–'80.

Grace—I. Crook, 1874–'75; R. M. Barns, 1877–'79.

Brooklyn—W. H. H. Moore, 1875–'77 W. F. T. Spruill, 1878–'80.

Presiding Elder—W. F. Short, 1873–'75; W. H. Webster, 1876; W. S. Prentice, 1877–'79

The new church edifice [illegible] the C[illegible] Presbyterian congregation on corner of Ch[illegible] and West State street at a cost of $25,000, or with the lot $33,000, was dedicated to Almighty God on Sabbath, April 19th, 1874. The sermon was preached by Rev. N. L. Rice, D. D., from Romans, 3d chapter, 28th verse: "Therefore we conclude that a man is justified by faith without the deeds of the law."

There were present and taking part in the exercises the following clergymen of the city: Rev. R. W. Allen, Rev. Geo. C. Wood, Rev. Wm. D. Sanders, D. D., Rev. H. V. D. Nevius, D. D., and Rev. I. W. Ward, of the Presbyterian, and Rev. Earl Cranston of the Methodist Episcopal and Rev. J. G. White of the Cumberland Presbyterian church.

The architects were Messrs. Dennis & Sutton, of Springfield, Ill., whose plans were followed throughout with a few slight variations. Mr. Thomas Waddell, a member of the church, was the efficient superintendent of the whole, and the carpenter in charge of the woodwork. Messrs. Mount & Engles had the contract for the brickwork and plastering. Mr. Peter Compton, also a member of the church, had the painting and glazing. The frescoing was done by Shubert & Koenig, of Chicago. The chairs for the lecture room, and pulpit and platform chairs (gothic) were obtained through Mr. Wm. Branson, from Henry Closterman, of Cincinnati. The pulpit and the comfortable pews were made by Mr. Hugh Wilson, and the cushions by Mr. Henry Higgins, both of this city. The beautiful communion table was the donation of one of the younger members, Mr. H. P. Huntsinger.

In 1875, Trinity church premises were surrounded by a neat and substantial iron fence, and in 1876 the interior of the church was greatly improved and an elegant pipe organ of twenty-six stops put in. In 1878 the membership was 200.

The following will show the number of scholars in the Protestant Sabbath schools of the city, as prepared and read at the county Sabbath school convention at Murrayville, in 1875, by Charles M. Eames, county Sabbath-school statistician:

Presbyterian—First	275
" Central	104
" Westminster	117
" First Portuguese	193
" Second Portuguese	160
Methodist—Centenary	411
" Grace	300
" Brooklyn	199
" Soule Chapel	164
" African	186
" German	78
Congregational	222
Baptist—First	140
" Mt. Emory	75
Christian—Church of Christ	200
" South Main street	148
Episcopal—Trinity	86
Zion Lutheran—German	35
Total	3,053

Rev. Eli Corwin, D. D., was the pastor of the Congregationalists from 1876 to 1880, succeeding Rev. W. H. Savage.

In June of the year 1880, the Jacksonville Female Academy celebrated its semi-centennial with appropriate and very interesting exercises. From Dr. Glover's historical discourse upon that occasion we have liberally quoted for this book. We extract further, as follows:

> The number of graduates of the Academy up to this time is 329, not including many who, previous to the year 1845, went forth from the Institution, well educated but without any official testimonials of that fact. This mother institution is proud of her children, their goodly number, their worthy character, their standing as educated women, their excellent influence over all the wide field of their dispersion, the good they have done, or are doing, as wives, mothers, teachers, members of Christian society,

and helpers in very desirable work. As a whole, we have no reason to be ashamed of the record they have made, or are now making. The Academy has a treasure in them of increasing value, a treasure well secured, especially in the case of those who have already exchanged the cross for the crown.

As the mother institution of the great Northwest, Jacksonville Female Academy, on this semi-centennial occasion, looks kindly upon the numerous enterprises with similar object that have sprung up around her, and sends cordial greeting to them all. At the same time, she is free to confess that, as it is her honor to be the first in point of time, so it is her purpose to be the best in point of character and worth. *Prima inter pares.* Though admitting others to social and official equality, she claims for herself primacy, in the aspects named.

Prof. E. F. Bullard, A. M., the present incumbent, entered upon his duties as principal in 1874. He had succeeded Prof. Thayer in an institution at Keesville, N. Y., and was warmly recommended by him as a suitable person to take charge of this Academy. Prof. Bullard was unanimously elected to the position he fills with such satisfaction to the trustees and patrons of the school.

Upon the retirement of Dr. Sturtevant from the presidency of Illinois College, in 1876, the management of the institution was in the excellent hands of Rufus C. Crampton, LL. D., senior professor, who was continued as acting president until Prof. Edward A. Tanner was chosen as president, by the unanimous vote of the trustees.

In 1878 the college had not yet completed its first half century. The best of our American colleges have not been the creation of a day. They have had their origin with the communities in which they were founded. They have often struggled for existence while material prosperity was being developed around them, until accumulated wealth should flow into them. This college is no exception to the rule. With the struggles of the past the friends of the college are now concerned no further than to know that they are safely passed, and that future prosperity seems well assured. Aside from grounds, buildings, and other appliances, the invested endowment funds were then about $110,000, with from $10,000 to $15,000 available in the future.

The present faculty consists of ten earnest, faithful men, each of marked ability and experience in his department, fully alive to the increasing demands of the times upon those who would be found worthy to represent the higher culture.

As to the Young Ladies' Athenæum, (see cut page 170,) Prof. Sanders continued as superintendent up to the close of the school year, June, 1878, when the alumnæ numbered 103.

Prof. Rider succeeded as superintendent in September, 1878, continuing until February, 1879, when he retired, under a cloud, and Prof. Sanders took up the management again, holding it until September, 1880, when Prof. Elmore Chase assumed the superintendence. By the graduation of the class of 1880, in June of that year, the alumnæ were increased to 125.

In 1876 the number of students in the Jacksonville Business College had become so great that enlarged facilities became an absolute necessity, since which the college has been conducted upon an enlarged plan, occupying the entire building on Kosciusko street, with its commodious halls, recitation rooms and office.

Prof. G. W. Brown, who has been connected with the college since 1866, first as instructor, but later as managing principal, purchased the institution, including its building and grounds. The rooms were enlarged and improved, new and valuable features added to the course of study, and every effort put forth to make this institution, in the strictest sense, a business college, which shall thoroughly train its students for the practical affairs of life.

No business college in America has a better array of talent in its faculty of instructors and lecturers than this. The departments of the college are: 1, The English training school; 2, the theoretical business department; 3, the actual business department; 4, the special penmanship department; 5, the telegraphic department. Each department is in charge of a specially qualified teacher, by which arrangement the highest grade of instruction is insured in all parts of the course of study.

The course is short, practical and reasonable. It is just what every man needs and will use, no matter what his calling or professson is to be.

In the number, experience and ability of its teachers, in the excellence of its course of study, in the healthfulness and beauty of its location, and in its moderate expenses, this college is equal to any in the land.

The annual catalogue issued in 1878, showed an enrollment of two hundred and fifty students for the year just closed. During the four years, 1875-'78, the institution graduated more than one hundred and fifty students, representing ten different states.

The thirteenth year of the college began September 2, 1878.

The faculty for 1876 and 1877 were R. C. Crampton, A. M., and G. W. Brown, Principals. I. J. Woodworth, superintendent of theoretical department, teacher of book-keeping, correspondence and business penmanship. C. B. Reynolds superintendent of the English training school, and teacher of the English branches. H. B. Chicken, superintendent of the special penmanship department, and the teacher of plain and ornamental penmanship. J. M. Sturtevant, D. D., LL. D., lecturer on political economy. H. K. Jones, A. M., M. D., lecturer on anatomy and physiology. J. M. North, Esq., member of Morgan county bar, lecturer on commercial law.

In July, 1875, Rev. W. F. Short, presiding elder of the Jacksonville district of the Illinois Conference, for a number of years, was appointed to the vacancy occasioned by the resignation of Rev. W. H. DeMotte, principal of Illinois Female College, and still fills the office.

There were graduated from the college, up to 1878, about three hundred and twenty young ladies. The school continued in a very prosperous condition, a credit to its founders, some of whom are still living, and may well feel proud of this noble institution of learning. The course of study is as extensive and thorough as that usually pursued in first-class schools for young women, embracing all the branches of a solid and ornamental education. It is so arranged that the student will have three studies each term, which, with her other college and society duties, is as much literary work as should be attempted. This arrangement will give every one sufficient time to devote to some of the ornamental branches, as instrumental and vocal music, drawing, painting, wax work, or other branches of art. Every young lady should give attention to this part of polite education, both for the pleasure and profit to herself and her friends.

In order to meet the demands in the department of music, a corporation has been formed, under the statute relating thereto, under the name of The Illinois Academy of Music and Art. A course of musical study has been arranged similar to that of like institutions.

The rooms devoted to this department (fifteen in number), are of good size and convenient location, under the same roof with the literary department; and the pianos and organs are sufficient in number and quality to meet the demands of a large class. Musical recitals are frequently given in the chapel of the college.

In 1878 the faculty of the college consisted of the following persons: Rev. W. F. Short, A. M., president, professor of mental, moral and political sciences; Miss Mary S. Pegram, preceptress, teacher of mathematics and astronomy; Miss Mary A. McDonald, teacher of Latin and modern languages; James B. Smith, professor of natural sciences; Miss Lottie D. Short, teacher of preparatory department. Department of Music, A. E. Wimmerstedt, director, professor of instrumental and vocal music, and harmony and composition; Mrs. Marion Phillips Wimmerstedt, teacher of instrumental and vocal music; Mrs. Kate Murdock Smith, teacher of instrumental and vocal music. Art, Mrs. Mary S. Vigus, teacher of painting and drawing. Matron, Mrs. Sarah B. Short.

Our free graded public school system by this time was a success in every particular, and received honorable mention at the Vienna exposition of 1874. During the year 1875, our schools furnished instruction to about 1,700 pupils. Here were found scholars of the higher walks of life, seeking knowledge at the same fount as those of the most humble positions, all sharing the same privileges. The colored pupils have the same favors extended to them as children of white skins; thus are the foundations laid for permanent intelligence, which must ever be one of the main pillars of this great and glorious republic. The schools are all graded, from the primary to the high school department, as each pupil is examined upon his introduction and assigned to the grade he or she is best fitted for.

Of Journalistic changes from 1874 to 1880 Mr. Ensley Moore writes in 1881 as follows:

Mr. Glover sold his interest to Mr. H. R. Hobart, of Chicago, in April, 1874, Capt. Chapin remaining in the firm. Mr. Wm. L. Fay became foreman of the news room under Chapin & Glover, a place he still fills in a creditable manner. L. B. Glover then went to Chicago, and, in connection with Major George M. McConnel and John M. Dandy, started the *Saturday Evening Herald*, of which Glover & Dandy are now the proprietors.

Horace R. Hobart was an experienced newspaper man of metropolitan views and independence. As editor and manager, he made the *Journal* more of a literary sheet, and also took an active part in local politics on some occasions. He improved the appearance of his paper, changing the weekly to an eight page form, and put it on a good business basis. George N. Loomis was his local editor.

Hon. Milton F. Simmons, formerly of Mexico, Mo., bought out Mr. Hobart in April, 1875, and Mr. Simmons became editor, Loomis continuing as local.

H. R. Hobart returned to Chicago, where he found a good thing in the *Railway Age* of which he is now an editor, and he is also a "city father" of Hyde Park.

As the history of Jacksonville covered by this chapter and since includes several important business, editorial and location changes in the *Journal*—the only daily paper then published—we may be pardoned if we occupy space enough in these records to refer to them.

On the first of March, 1876, the writer purchased a half interest in the *Journal* of Messrs Chapin & Simmons, the proprietors, Capt. Chapin retiring. The latter part of the same month he took charge of the city editorial department, succeeding the popular "local" Mr. George N. Loomis, now of the Duluth (Minn.) *Tribune*.

From the date of this change in the business the *Journal* has been in regular receipt of the associated press reports, a feature of the paper greatly appreciated by the community. The office of the paper remained in the McDonald block, on North Main street, until July, 1877, when a removal was made to the Mathers building, on East State street, one block from the square. Simmons & Eames continued as publishers until October 1st, 1878, when we bought out the interest of Mr. Simmons, to enable him to buy into the Springfield *Journal*, in company with Paul Selby and Horace Chapin both ex-*Journalists*. Having purchased new material, an enlarged sheet was issued under the new management, October 3. The subscription list and business of the office generally is growing continually and its prospect for enlargement and increasing influence was never more flattering. The daily is published every morning in the week except Monday—the weekly on Wednesday. The encouragement received from the business community has been very great.

At first we associated with us in the editorial work Hon. Judge Moses, lately of Winchester, who attended to the political and general departments, H. H. Palmer, Esq., in the local, Prof. J. H. Woods in the literary, Prof. J. B. Smith in the musical departments, J. S. Hambaugh as general solicitor, Wm. Fay, Esq., foreman of the news room and Robert A. Bradbury, foreman of job-room.

Since then Prof. H. A. Allen in the editorial, George N. Loomis, Hiram H. Palmer, Richard Yates Carl Black, and Samuel W. Nichols in the local, and Prof. James B. Smith in the business departments, have been devoting their talents and time to the interests of the *Journal's* readers and patrons.

In 1874, the Jacksonville *Enterprise* was established as a weekly paper by James S. Hambaugh, who, in 1875, started a daily paper. After the *Sentinel* and *Enterprise* offices were purchased by T. D. Price & Co., in May, 1876, the offices were united under the name of *Illinois Courier*, the paper being published daily and weekly until January, 1877, when the daily was suspendedand a tri-weekly edition substituted.

The firm of T. D. Price & Co., as publishers of the *Courier*, was composed of T. D. Price, M. N. Price, H. L. Clay and G. E. Doying, all practical printers--each giving personal attention to its business--Mr. Clay as editor, Mr. Doying as manager. The office is in Ayers' block, on West State street, in the business center of the city. In all respects the office is fully equipped and equal to all demands upon it.

In 1876 the Jacksonville Microscopical Society was organized for scientific study with the aid of the microscope.

Its numbers include Drs. Black, D. Prince, A. E. Prince, H. K. Jones, C. G. Jones, Frost, Freeman, Milligan, Pitner, Prof. Storrs, Mr. Bleuler, Prof. Hamill Miss Alice Rhoads, Miss Fuller and Mrs. H. W. Milligan.

Eleven of these members have instruments which have cost, with their objects from one hundred to eight hundred dollars.

At each meeting of the society some member announces a subject which he will introduce in an essay at the succeeding meeting. The other members prepare specimens illustrative of this subject, and show them at the next meeting under their respective instruments. The society occasionally holds a semi-public exhibition of the "infinitely little" through its instruments. The Free Reading Room, the Female Academy and Illinois College has each invited and enjoyed exhibitions of this society within its halls. It is doubtful if there is in the state of Illinois, outside of Chicago, a microscopical society so active and so thoroughly equipped as this.

The U. S. census of 1880 gave Morgan county a population of 32,520, Jacksonville precinct 14,831, the city proper 10,938. By wards as follows: 1st, 2,343; 2d, 2,171; 3d, 2,913; 4th, 3,501.

On the 16th of March, 1874, the Womans' Christian Temperance Union, of Jacksonville, was organized and the society is still meeting regularly and doing all it can to uplift the fallen. The first officers were Mrs. Lucy Washington, president; Mrs. Emily Bancroft, secretary; Miss Jennie Hockenhull, treasurer. A year later the president and secretary were re-elected and the following vice presidents chosen: Mesdames Glover, North, Craig, Gilman, Russell, Orear, DeMotte, Pierson and Capps.

The city officials of the years named were:

1874. Joseph O. King, mayor; William P. Callon, V. Edward Higgins, Philip Lee, Ensley Moore, Henry C. Stewart, William Hackman, Abram Wood, Andrew W. Jackson, aldermen; Benjamin R. Upham, city clerk; James S. Hurst, marshal; James N. Brown, attorney; Bazzill Davenport, collector and assessor.

1875. Wesley Mathers, mayor; V. Edward Higgins, William P. Callon, S. Henry Thompson, Edward S. Greenleaf, Emanuel Hamilton, Abraham R. Gregory, Abram Wood, Joseph Tomlinson, aldermen; Benjamin R. Upham, city clerk; Charles O. Sperry, marshal; Robert D. Russell, attorney; Bazzill Davenport, collector and assessor.

1876. E. S. Greenleaf, mayor; L. S. Olmstead, C. Widmayer, James Scott, W. C. Carter, A. R. Gregory, T. J. Bronson, G. S. Russel, Geo. Hayden, alderman; B. R. Upham, city clerk; C. O. Sperry, marshal; John G. Morrison, attorney.

1877. E. S. Greenleaf, mayor; G. W. Hobbs, N. Kitner, V. E. Higgins, James Scott, J. P. Willard, W. S. Snyder, G. S. Russel, Geo. Hayden, aldermen; Henry W. Hunt, city clerk; C. O. Sperry, marshal; Robert D. Russell, attorney; John A. Schaub, street commissioner.

1878. S. H. Thompson, mayor; Nathaniel Kitner, John H. Myers, John Hopper, Michael H. Carroll, W. S. Snyder, John R. Loar, Geo. Hayden, D. B. Smith, aldermen; Henry W. Hunt, city clerk; David Schoonover, marshal; John A. Bellatti, attorney; William E. Veitch, treasurer.

1879. H. C. Stewart, mayor; F. F. Schmalz, Chas. Widmayer, John Hopper, Wm. E. Capps, B. W. Simmons, John R. Loar, Geo. Hayden, Abram Wood, aldermen; Henry W. Hunt, city clerk; John Pyatt, marshal; Wm. A. Crawley, attorney; B. F. Beesley, treasurer.

1880. John R. Loar, mayor; Chas. Widmayer, M. H. Walsh, W. E. Capps, W. H. Thompson, J. M. Goodrick, W. C. Wright, Geo. Hayden, Abram Wood, aldermen;

John W. Melton, city clerk; John Pyatt, marshal; C. Harry Dummer, attorney; B. F. Beesley, treasurer.

The county officers were elected as follows:

1874.—Senator, Chas. D. Hodges; Representative, John Gordon, A. J. Thompson, Sam Wood; Sheriff, Irvin Dunlap; Coroner, Theodore Allen; County Commissioner, Daniel Dietrick.

1875.—Treasurer, W. H. Wright; Surveyor, W. H. Rowe; County Commissioner, James H. Devore.

1876.—State's Attorney, James N. Brown; Circuit Clerk, John N. Marsh; Sheriff, Irvin Dunlap; Coroner, Philip Braun; Commissioner, John Virgin.

1877.—County Judge, E. P. Kirby; County Clerk, B. R. Upham; Treasurer, W. H. Wright; School Superintendent, Henry Higgins, Commissioner, David H. Lollis; Surveyor, W. H. Rowe.

1878.—Sheriff, Irvin Dunlap; Coroner, Daniel Riley; Commissioner, M. S. Kennedy; States Attorney, E. L. McDonald; Senator, W. P. Callon; Representative, Richardson Vasey.

1879.—Treasurer, W. H. Wright; Commissioner, John H. Mathews.

1880.—Circuit Clerk, John N. Marsh; Sheriff, W. H. Hinrichsen; Coroner, Daniel Riley; Commissioner, Charles Heinz; States Attorney, E. L. McDonald; Representative, Oliver Coultas.

The number of arrests, great variety of offenses and amount of fines collected in 1879 show an efficiency in our police force highly commendable, and the general verdict is that Marshal Pyatt was deserving and had faithful officers. The number of arrests for all causes from April 17 to November 30, was 215.

Fines and costs collected on above	$737.57
For violations of Sunday liquor law (10 arrests,) fines collected	275.00
Gambling houses (5 arrested,) fines collected	175.00

This is the official statement of the business of the Jacksonville postoffice for the twelve months ending Nov. 20th, 1879:

Letters mailed	378,196
Letters received	410,072
Postal cards mailed	160,396
Postal cards received	72,710
Pieces second class matter mailed	106,750
" third " " "	45,084
" fourth " " "	4,004

REGISTERED BUSINESS.

Letters sent	1,062
Letters received	1,932

MONEY ORDER BUSINESS.

Orders issued, 6,165, amounting to	$50,381.00
" paid, 8,510, "	55,391.24

In 1879 the schools had an enrollment of about 2,000 pupils. These were enrolled in the eight buildings, as follows:

High School—Prof. L. J. Block, Principal	115
Seventh Grade—Miss Lyde Kent, "	70
First Ward—Miss Hannah Tobey, "	310
" " Branch,	50
Second Ward—Miss M. A. Selby, "	380
" " Branch,	165
Third Ward—Prof. J. B. Smith,	450
" " Branch,	40
Fourth Ward,	260

The average cost of tuition of each pupil, that year, including High School, if computed on the whole expenditure, was $18.46; if computed upon a basis excluding expenditure for permanent investment, it was $12.40 for each pupil.

The introduction of such an illuminating power as coal-gas into any community is a matter worthy of especial place in historic data. For nearly forty years Jacksonville had nothing better than the tallow dip, the sperm candle or the coal-oil lamp.

In 1852 or '53, a charter was obtained for speculative purposes by foreign capitalists. The solidity of the document was conditioned upon stock subscriptions amounting to $5,000 on which $250 must be paid in to the treasurer. These speculators held their charter for several years insisting upon the subscription by our citizens of $30,000. This amount was not forthcoming and the charter was about to lapse, when some one in the city discovered that these outsiders had given a draft to cover the paid up capital required, but it had never been cashed as they had not made it payable to any one who could draw the money. Messrs. J. O. King, M. P. Ayers and others who were deeply interested in having such a forward step taken, were instrumental in having the stock books re-opened. Just before they were closed, Mr. King appeared and subscribed for $5,000 worth of stock for himself and Mr. Ayers, and paid down the $250. Another year or so was consumed in futile efforts to form a stock company. Finally a Mr. Edward Gwynn, from Cincinnati, Ohio, came here and took hold of the matter, agreeing to erect the necessary works, furnish land for same, lay necessary service pipes, &c., for $45,000. Also to receive his pay as follows: $20,000 in bonds of the company, $10,000 in stock, and the remaining $15,000 in cash. The bargain was sealed and the works constructed, costing about $52,000, additional bonds being issued for the surplus $7,000. After the works were in successful operation, Mr. Gwynn disposed of all his bonds and stock that he had not hypothecated in construction, to Mr. Nimrod Deweese. The street lamps were first lighted Jan. 9, 1858, and private residences during the same month. The Jacksonville Gas-light & Coke Co. started off with a debt of $28,000, with eighty-three consumers of gas, besides the city, which used twenty street lamps. The works did not pay running expenses for years, hence, of course there were no dividends, and not even any meetings of the directors. It soon became necessary to replace and rebuild everything connected with the business except the street pipes, because of the imperfect original construction by the contractor. It was not until 1866 that dividends were paid and these in stock. The efforts of Mr. King, Mr. Ayers and others were purely disinterested and public spirited. Mr. King was induced to give up his business in the lumber firm of Massey, King, Neely & Co. to become superintendent, and has faithfully served the company as superintendent since 1858—an uninterrupted period of twenty-six years. Consumers have increased and semi-annual cash dividends have been declared for several years, but these have grown less for the last year or two on account of reduced price of gas. It started here at $3.50; in war time got up to $5.00 and meter rent and now is furnished through seventeen miles of service pipe to 400 consumers at $2.00 per thousand feet, cash. The dividends of 1884 were less than six per cent per annum. In 1883, the company spent $10,000 in improvements in order to be able to produce gas at the reduced rate.

The same gentlemen and others like them who might be named, were as anxious that Jacksonville should have the advantages of a water supply as of gas-light. A Mr. Deiley who came to this city from Philadelphia on gas business, was induced to make an examination of the country surrounding Jacksonville. He declared that there would be no trouble in procuring an abundant supply. Messrs. J. O. King, S. W. Nichols and R. C. Crampton made a survey for the reservoirs, &c. Mr. Diley went home and prepared full plans and made a bid for constructing the works. His figures were $170,000, but called for larger pipe than were needed, stand pipe, two Duplex engines, &c.

Mr. King and others went around among their fellow-citizens procuring their signatures to a petition for an election for and against an appropriation by the city council of $150,000 for water works construction. The city fathers called the election in June,

1869, but its requirement was a majority of all votes cast at the last previous election, which was on a presidential election year, viz: 1868.

There was much opposition to the project, excitement over it and wild talk to the effect that it would cost the tax-payers a half million dollars. The opposers had no idea that the required votes "for" could be obtained, but a few enterprising spirits, Messrs. D. B. Smith, S. W. Nichols, J. O. King, Dr. Bibb and others made a "still hunt," got carriages and drew out so large a vote of the friends that the measure carried by fifty or sixty majority. It was two or three years, however, before the works were built. The city issued ten per cent bonds, having twenty years to run, to pay the contractor, and in 1876 refunded them at eight per cent.

The city water works were completed and put in operation January 20th, 1875, being nearly five and one-half years after the ordinance was passed by the city council authorizing the appropriation.

The works, as constructed, consisted of an impounding reservoir, capacity 65,000,000 gallons; distributing reservoir, capacity 2,500,000 gallons; two medium working pumps, one with a capacity of pumping 600 gallons, the other 280 gallons, per minute; eight and one-third miles of pipe and sixty-six hydrants, the cost of construction being $150,000, including land, right of way, &c., &c. They afford every facility and convenience for the prevention of an extensive conflagration in the business portion of the city. The high elevation of the distributing reservoir dispenses with the use of fire engines in time of a conflagration; the only auxiliary required being a bountiful supply of hose attached to the hydrants, the force of water being sufficient to throw a stream to the height of eighty feet or more.

For further reference, cost, &c., see page 179.

The year 1879 passed away famous, locally, for its remarkable weather. It was a season never-to-be-forgotten for its scarcity of water. The drouth continued without a noticeable intermission from the opening of spring until the close of Autumn. The exact measurement of the water-fall within those nine months we are not aware of, but it is sufficient to say that there was only an occasional shower—not enough to keep the dust laid.

For the first time since their erection the water works were put to a very severe test. A long and unexpected drouth met us with an increased demand for water. Without discussing the cause of failure, we know the fact—the water supply was insufficient to withstand the terrible drouth.

During this period the older secret benevolent orders—I. O. O. F. and A. F. and A. M.—reached their height of membership and means and were meeting in elegantly furnished lodge rooms, asylums, &c.

Four new organizations, having as special features mutual insurance, were introduced, viz: A. O. U. W., I. O. M. A., R. T. of T. and K. of H.

The Ancient Order of United Workmen was founded at Meadville, Pa., in November, 1868. The local lodge "Athens" No. 19, was instituted on the 19th day of October, 1876. There have been only two deaths of members in this city, Jonathan Gill and John H. Myers; in each case the beneficiary certificates being paid within twenty days from death. Athens lodge has a nice and suitable lodge room, properly furnished, in the third story of the Marble Block, where its regular meetings are held on Thursday evening of each week. This lodge has a membership of 90, and has been honored by the election of Hon. E. M. Sanford to the position of Grand Master Workman of the State and Grand Representative to the Supreme Grand Lodge, and H. H. Palmer to the office of Grand Recorder for two years. No society could be more successful than this lodge has been.

Among the various organizations in the nature of both a brotherhood and a beneficiary institution, one of the best is the Knights of Honor. This institution has for its main feature a cheap and safe mutual insurance. The heirs of any deceased member are paid $2,000, which is made up by an assessment on the other members in the state.

This order founded what is called Royal Lodge, No. 828, in this city, in 1876. On the charter we find the following names: J. K. Sharpe, F. M. Doan, H. H. Palmer, Frank Hine, W. A. Alcott, C. E. Flack, H. L. Clay, J. S. Hambaugh, W. B. Elledge, A. W. Cadman, John N. Ward, A. J. Ward, W. J. Moore and F. L. Sharpe. Among the first officers elected were H. H. Palmer, P. Dictator; J. H. Sharpe, Dictator, and H. L. Clay, Reporter. There were in 1881 thirty-three active working members in this lodge, who had influence sufficient in the Grand Lodge to secure the meeting of that body in Jacksonville in 1882.

Among the various organizations founded for mutual insurance one of the newest is called the Independent Order of Mutual Aid. This organization gives to the representatives of a deceased member $2,000 and all dues previously paid. This amount is paid by a pro rata assessment on the other members. On February 7, 1879, a lodge of this order was established in this city, called Morgan Lodge No. 28. The charter members of this body were as follows: F. A. Stevens, C. G. Brown, N. W. Reid, C. L. Hastings, F. A. Mosely, J. S. Hambaugh, G. W. Clark, E. Woodman, A. W. Cadman, Hugh Barr, G. E. Mathews, G. E. Doying, J. F. Hackman, Neil Matheson, Royal Oakes, T. J. Mosely, D. W. Rawlings, Clinton Fisher, F. C. Taylor, J. A. Goltra, M. N. Price, J. M. Ewing, T. Brennan, C. W. Stout, W. H. Worrell, C. M. Eames, S. O. Barr, Charles Henry, Henry Bretherick, M. H. Carroll, John Rottger, W. M. Phillips, W. C. Ward, T. C. Michaels, J. Ellerts, E. Duncan, J. S. Barlow and H. A. Gilman.

The Royal Templars of Temperance is the latest fraternity to find a foot-hold in our city. The order was organized in Buffalo, N. Y., February 3, 1877, with only a membership of seven men and three women. There are now over 400 Councils and about 20,000 members. The order is a strictly total abstinence organization, as no person can pass its threshold and obtain its benefits who will not sign and faithfully maintain a pledge of total abstinence. The most rigid medical examination is required for beneficiary membership, every medical examination being carefully reviewed by the chief medical examiner before a certificate can be issued. The benefit to active members is limited to $2,000 in case of death or $1,000 in case of total disability for life; and to ladies $1,000 in case of death and $500 in case of permanent disability. The admission of ladies lends a social charm to the Council meetings which any similar beneficiary order does not possess.

Among the charter members of Crystal Council, No. 41, which was instituted by J. G. Shea, of Decatur, January 22, 1880, were Rev. Eli Corwin, D. D., and wife, Prof. E. F. Bullard, Rev. Horace Read, Mr. and Mrs. J. H. Hackett, H. H. Palmer, L. A. Patterson, Mr. and Mrs. Robert Buckthorpe, Mr. and Mrs. C. M. Eames, Dr. and Mrs. J. A. Dougherty, S. Tefft Walker and Miss Kate R. Cassell.

To preserve the names of the christian women, of Jacksonville, most active in religious and charitable labors at this period we give the names of the officers of the Women's Christian Association for the year beginning May 4, 1876: President, Mrs. E. J. Bancroft; Vice presidents, Mrs. I. L. Morrison and Mrs. P. Dummer; Recording Secretary, Mrs. Clara Lippincott; Treasurer, Mrs. J. W. Lathrop.

Standing Committees. *Finance*, Mesdames Delia Wadsworth, A. J. Link J. S. Morse, W. N. Ross; *Mission Work*, Miss E. F. Ryder, Mesdames L. M. Glover, E. L. Reed, A. Hartt, E. J. Bancroft; *Industrial School*, Miss M. E. Catlin, Mesdames T. G. Taylor, M. J. Harriott; *Visiting*, Mesdames Leanna Orear, C. Schermerhorn, Ellen Ennis, C. Chadwick, Morris Collins, H. A. Gilman

On Saturday, June 30th, 1877, the Presbyterians celebrated the fiftieth anniversary of their first church in Morgan county. The speakers of the occasion were Drs. Glover, Harsha and Allen, the city pastors of this faith and Revs. Lamb, Allen and Corwin of sister churches. The twelve members of 1827 had grown to fourteen churches in the half century, viz: Manchester, Winchester, Murrayville, Unity, Pisgah, Providence, Zion and Virginia. In Jacksonville three Portuguese churches—the First, Second and Independent church, and three English speaking—the Westminster, First and Central.

nd in Beardstown, the German church. Altogether they had a membership of 1,600 with 1,500 children in the Sabbath-schools.

At this time, speaking for the Baptist brethren, Rev. M. T. Lamb reported 13 churches of that denomination in existence in Morgan, representing a membership of 1,000, or 1 to every 30 of population. In Jacksonville there were, he said, between 350 and 400 including the colored brethren, who outnumbered the white Baptists.

We present below a table showing the assessed values of the different species of property in Morgan county for the years 1875 and 1876, together with many other interesting facts and figures worthy of attention and study:

	1875.			1876.		
	No.	Av. Val.	As. Val.	No.	Av. Val.	As. Val.
Horses, all ages	6,438	$ 60.17	$ 387,392	6,059	$ 58.02	$ 351,542
Cattle, all ages	17,279	19.34	332,670	17,298	18.27	318,000
Mules and asses, all ages	976	62.51	61,035	1,019	65.74	73,570
Sheep, all ages	7,586	1.91	14,482	6,743	2.26	15,284
Hogs, all ages	23,737	3.05	72,681	19,427	3.50	68,060
Steam engines, including boilers	10	545.00	5,450	9	614.44	5,800
Fire or burglar proof safes	18	300.00	5,400	22	251.63	5,385
Carriages, wagons, etc	2,508	37.07	92,983	2,347	33.38	78,346
Sewing and knitting machines	1,116	21.15	23,611	1,103	22.35	24,661
Watches and clocks	922	8.05	7,427	904	7.52	6,799
Piano Fortes	233	111.60	26,005	251	106.65	26,771
Melodeons and Organs	122	16.05	2,075	67	47.16	3,160
Annuities and Royalties			1,330			
Total assessed value of enumerated property			1,042,311			967,268

UNENUMERATED PROPERTY.

	1875	1876
Merchandise	$ 273,955	$ 270,467
Materials and manufacturers' articles	12,470	11,425
Agricultural tools, implements and machinery	33,356	34,671
Moneys of banks, bankers, etc	76,080	61,960
Credits of banks, bankers, etc	19,500	18,572
Credits of others than bankers, etc	735,587	
Bonds and stocks	5,875	4,146
Household and office property	136,904	144,089
Shares of Stock, State and National Banks	300,000	300,000
Total assessed value of unenumerated property	$1,593,747	$1,645,162
Total assessed value of personal property	2,636,057	2,622,430

RAILROAD PROPERTY.

	1875	1876
Total assessment	$ 20,275	$ 20,731
Real estate, lands; total assessed value	7,419,790	7,212,898
Real estate, town property; total assessed value	3,008,175	2,736,859
Total value of all taxable property assessed in county	$13,084,538	$12,592,218

ACRES IN CULTIVATION.

	1875	1876
Wheat	9,087	11,300
Corn	79,693	81,200
Oats	8,367	
Meadows	27,570	28,180
Other field products	11,300	30,493
Acres in enclosed pasture	133,766	131,280
In orchard	3,470	3,530
In woodland	79,972	77,868

To show what it cost yearly, about this time, to run this county, we record the following, taken from the county clerk's report for 1880. It includes the total expense for that year. It is about $30,000 less than the expenses of the previous year:

Charity	$ 1,812.56
Paupers	1,293.17
Roads	20,244.70
Bridges	9,340.80
Supervising roads	731.75
Road viewers	120.00
County farm (current expenses)	5,211.76
County farm repairs	66.45
County farm permanent improvements	233.28
Salaries	9,156.45
Stationery and printing	2,259.92
Court house	1,909.13
Jail	1,706.10
Criminals	1,426.25
Elections	683.57
Inquests	168.10
Miscellaneous	1,247.10
Debt and interest	9,940.17
Insurance	525.00

Wolf scalps	$145.00
Attorneys fees	1,625.00
Grand jury	64.35
Per diem	669.48
State Institutions	701.06
Interest coupons on bonds	8,000.00
Jury warrants, circuit court	3,348.50
Jury warrants, county court	669.80
Total, 1880	$86,637.05

The Illinois Central Hospital for the Insane, located in our city, is not only the oldest in the state, but the number of patients it cares for is the largest. On the 30th of September, 1880, it had 633. The admissions up to October 1, 1882—the close of the biennial period—were 514. The number discharged during the period was as follows: Recovered, 141, or 27 per cent.; improved, 178; unimproved, 86; "eloped"—the Jacksonville euphemism for "escaped"—7; died, 95, or 8 per cent. The whole number under treatment during the period was 1,147; remaining September 30, 1882, 639; remaining to date 631; daily average presence, 639. The number of recoveries in the cases of those deranged for a period of three months and less prior to their admission was 70 per cent.—a fact which speaks volumes in favor of the management.

In 1878, at the Illinois Institution for the Education of Deaf Mutes the number of pupils in actual attendance was four hundred and twenty-six. The value of the property is estimated to be $325,000.

The present prosperity of the institution is owing in no small degree to the untiring labors of the present superintendent, Dr. Gillett. The State Board of Charities in their report to Governor Beveridge, say: "With the advent of Mr. Phillip G. Gillett, from Indiana, to the superintendency, in 1857, the institution entered upon a new career of vigorous growth and expansion. His energetic spirit has driven the school, the public, and even the Legislature before him; when this has been impossible, he has sometimes gone in advance, himself, and waited for the rest to come up." Asbury University, in Indiana, in 1871, conferred on Mr. Gillett the title LL. D. The institution has grown to be an honor to the State of Illinois, and occupies a position second to none in this country.

Dr. Rhoads, owing to failing health, resigned his position as Superintendent of the Blind Asylum in 1874, and F. W. Phillips, M. D., for many years a prominent minister in the Methodist Episcopal Church, was appointed to the vacancy. The school continues to prosper. There were in 1876, 120 pupils in attendance. Additions and improvements have been made from time to time, as necessity demanded. It is hoped by the friends of the institution, that the east wing will before many years be erected. When this is completed, Illinois will have furnished ample provision for all this class of unfortunates, within her borders. The inventory and appraisement of the buildings, grounds and property belonging to the institution, on the 30th of September, 1876, was $167,558.91.

Dr. Rhoads continued as principal of the institution through a period of twenty-four years; during which time, many improvements were made, and the institution brought to the front rank.

Dr. F. W. Phillips the present superintendent, speaking of Dr. Rhoads, says:

"Since my last report, my predecessor, Dr. Joshua Rhoads, has died. His health, feeble at the time of his resignation, continued to fail until February 1, 1876, when death relieved him of his sufferings. A graduate of the Pennsylvania University of Medicine, he was engaged in the active practice of his profession for a number of years. He was principal of the Pennsylvania Institution for the blind for four years. In 1850, he was elected principal of this institution, which position he occupied for twenty-four years. Possessed of a good mind, which was well cultivated, he was qualified both by nature and habit, for the work to which he gave so much of his life. Methodical, earnest, and in love with his work, the institution was well conducted and successful under his administration. At the time of his death he had entered upon his seventieth year."

CHAPTER XII.—1881-'84.

The Present Condition and Prospects—City and County Officials—Churches and Schools—Criminal—Meteorology of 1883, Including the Disastrous Liter Tornado—Realty and Personal Property Values—Manufactures—Public Improvements.

AS WE reach the present prosperous era in our city's history we find the work of glancing over the whole field in a single chapter as difficult as it is delightful. The condensation necessary in such summarizing will destroy all attempts at descriptive writing and all enlivening details, confining us to statistics and briefest possible statements, although the period covered is less than three years, or only one-half the time embraced in the other divisions of this historic view of Jacksonville.

The city government from April 1880 to 1881 was as follows: John R. Loar, mayor; J. W. Melton, city clerk; C. Harry Dummer, city attorney; John Pyatt, city marshal; J. F. Nagle, street commissioner; William H. Beastall, keeper city prison; Dr. C. G. Brown, health warden.

Aldermen—M. H. Walsh, Charles Widmayer, W. E. Capps, W. H. Thompson, J. M. Goodrick, W. C. Wright, George Hayden and Abram Wood.

From April, 1881 to 1882, it was: John R. Loar, mayor; J. W. Melton, city clerk; George J. Dod, city attorney; B. F. Beesley, treasurer; Peter Rabbitt, city marshal; Arch. Norris, street commissioner; Lee G. Minter, keeper city prison; Dr. C. G. Brown, health warden.

Aldermen—M. H. Walsh, Charles Widmayer, Phillip Lee, Jonathan Neely, W. C. Wright, D. M. Simmons, Abram Wood, Dr. C. K. Sawyer.

From April, 1882 to 1883, it was: Charles Widmayer, mayor; George E. Sybrant, city clerk; Peter Rabbitt, marshal; Frank I. McDonald, treasurer; C. A. Barnes, city attorney; John F. Nagle, street commissioner; Lee Minter, keeper city prison; Dr. W. H. H. King, health warden.

Aldermen—William Eppinger, James J. Murphy, Fred L. Sharpe, John E. Bradbury, George Jameson, James Montgomery, W. Chauncey Carter, Felix G. Farrell.

From April, 1883 to 1884, it was: Edward S. Greenleaf, mayor; George E. Sybrant, clerk; Peter Rabbitt, marshal; John A. Ayers, treasurer; C. H. Dummer, attorney; Lewis R. Mitchell, street commisioner; Lee Minter, keeper city prison; Dr. Morris H. Goodrick, health warden.

Aldermen—William Eppinger, James J. Murphy, Robert D. Russell, William A. Oliver, George Jameson, Wesley Snyder, John W. Hall, W. Chauncey Carter.

From April, 1884 to 1885, it is: Joseph Tomlinson, mayor, (Rep.); George E. Sybrant, clerk, (Rep.); Charles E. Goodrick, marshal, (Rep.); D. M. Simmons, street commissioner, (Rep.); John A. Ayers, treasurer, (Rep.); C. H. Dummer, attorney, (Rep.)

Aldermen—W. P. Callon, (Dem.,) Wm. Eppinger, (Dem.,) M. H. Carroll, (Dem.,) John Hopper, (Rep.,) W. Snyder, (Rep.,) Thomas Rapp, (Rep.,) John W. Hall, (Rep.,) W. C. Carter, (Rep.)

Fire department James Mitchell, chief; Charles Meade, assistant. Health warden, Dr. T. M. Cullimore. Sextons, Diamond Grove cemetery, E. R. Walters; Jacksonville cemetery, Caleb Letton. Policemen, E. M. Allen, John Holian, Joseph Vieria, James Rutledge and Isaac Hicks. Board of Education, 1st ward George W. Smith (Dem.,) 2d ward Ensley Moore, (Rep.,) 3d ward Thomas J. Bronson, (Dem.,) 4th ward Julian P. Lippincott, (Rep.) Superintendent of Public Instruction, Prof. H. M. Hamill, (Dem.)

Board of Water Commissioners, Felix G. Farrell, (Dem.,) W. Chauncey Carter, (Rep.,) Alex. Platt, (Rep.;) superintendent, D. C. Fry, (Rep.,) engineer, Alex. Armstrong, (Rep.)

It will be observed that the dominant political party of the nation, from 1860 to 1884, have complete control of all branches of the municipal government. On the other hand turning to the list of county officials we find the reins in Democratic hands.

1881–'82.—Sheriff and collector, W. H. Hinrichsen; assessor and treasurer, W. H. Wright; circuit clerk and recorder, John N. Marsh; clerk of county court, Benjamin R. Upham; superintendent of schools, C. M. Sevier; Surveyor, James Cain; Coroner Daniel Riley; commissioners, M. S. Kennedy, Charles Heinz, John H. Matthews.

1883–'84—Representatives, I. L. Morrison, (R.,) E. M. Kinman, (D.) Sheriff, W. C. Wright, (D.) Treasurer, Irvin Dunlap, (D.) County Clerk, B. R. Upham, (R.) County Judge, M. T. Layman, (R.) School Superintendent, C. M. Sevier, (D.) Coroner, A. H. Hocking, (D.) Commissioners, Job W. English, (D.,) M. S. Kennedy, (D.,) Charles Heinz, (D.)

First Presbyterian church burned in 1861 and the brick building, taking its place, having been dedicated January 6, 1867, was burned in 1883. Rev. L. M. Glover, for a third of a century, was the faithful and beloved pastor of this church, and passed from earthly scenes mourned and regretted by all regardless of church bias or sectarian creed. The Rev. J. R. Sutherland D. D., was the pastor for 1882–'84, resigning his charge June 22, 1884, to accept a call to Rockford. This people were for a second time made homeless through fire on the 26th of September, 1883. The work of rebuilding began in July, 1884, upon what was known as the Dr. Cassell property corner of West State and North Church streets, where, at present writing, a very handsome brick edifice is rapidly rising. No steps have been taken towards filling the vacant pulpit.

Since January 1881, Rev. H. E. Butler has been pastor of the Congregational church with a growing church strongly attached to him.

The M. E. preachers have been as follows:

Brooklyn—George B. Wolfe, 1881–'82; D. Gay, 1883; James Leaton, 1884.

Centenary—Horace Read, 1881; M. D. Hawes, 1882–'83–'84.

Grace—W. H. Webster, 1880–'82; W. N. McElroy, 1883–'84.

Presiding elder, George Stevens, 1880–'83; J. A. Kumler, 1884.

As to the latest criminal cases affecting human life:

George Hutchinson was indicted for the murder of Miss McNamara by assisting in performing an abortion, was indicted by the grand jury and plead guilty to manslaughter May 15th, 1882, being given 18 months in the penitentiary.

Matheson Munday was indicted in Greene county for the murder of James Sheriffs, but brought his case here by change of venue. McDonald and King prosecuted and English and Carr defended. A trial was had in May 26th, 1883; the defendant being found guilty and sentenced to Joliet for 14 years. This was a bad case and created much excitement in Greene county.

George W. Cooper was the last person to be indicted and tried for murder, his trial taking place November term of court 1883. He was charged with the murder of John Stewart. E. L. McDonald, states attorney, prosecuting, and Wilson and Epler defending. The jury found the defendant not guilty.

By a general review of the homicide trials of the sixty years under consideration in this work we find that 43 persons have been charged with murder in Morgan county. We are glad to state that none of the accused persons were women. Of the 43 indicted 13 were found "not guilty," and eight cases were stricken from the docket. The highest penalty was death, though the escape of the prisoner prevented an execution. The next most severe sentence was that of Isaac Berry, who was sent up for life. The other periods run thus: one for 22 years; one for 21; two for 20; three for 15; one for 14; two for 10; one for 8; three for 5; one for 2; one for 18 months; and three for 1 year. Of these the average sentence is ten years and one month. Include in the average those who were acquitted and the average punishment for all indicted is about five years in the penitentiary. In conclusion, we might say that Morgan county, considering its population, is much below most of the other counties in the state, in the number of indictments for murder, that have been found, and that the average sentence is above the general average punishment. We can only hope, that this list will not be added to, in many years.

To the people of Illinois there is, perhaps, nothing of more importance than the public schools. They have grown into a vast agency- an agency that is attracting much attention in the country. Illinois is spending yearly from $7,000,000 to $8,000,000 for the maintenance of her public school system. The general verdict in intelligent circles is that it is money well spent.

Hon. James P. Slade, the State Superintendent of Public Instruction, and his assistants, were long and busily engaged recently in revising and reviewing the reports of county superintendents for the year 1881. The report from this county, prepared by Prof. Henry Higgins, shows up as follows:

Persons under twenty-one		16,137
Persons between sixteen and twenty-one		10,338
Public Schools		110
Pupils enrolled		6,882
Teachers employed		186
New school houses		4
Illiteracy—Persons in the county between the ages of 12 and 21 unable to read and write		8
FINANCIAL EXHIBIT—RECEIPTS.		
Amount received during the year		$133,976.23
Amount expended	$87,917.03	
Loan of dist. funds	65.00—	87,982.03
Balance		$ 45,994.20
Amount paid teachers		60,323.51

The present system of public schools has been in operation eighteen years. They have constantly advanced until now they have reached the front rank of any in the state. They have been under the most complete and thorough system and governed in the most satisfactory manner. They have always held first rank for their thoroughness and good scholarship, and have been a great blessing to the county. .

A special meeting of the trustees of Illinois College was held in this city on Monday, March 6th, 1882, to take into consideration the question of filling the office of president of the college, rendered vacant by the resignation of Dr. J. M. Sturtevant. The meeting was fully attended, all the trustees being present except two, and by a hearty and unanimous vote, Rev. E. A. Tanner, D. D., the professor of Latin language and literature in the college, was elected president, to assume the duties of the office, at the close of that scholastic year. Of the appointment the *Journal*, at the time, said:

> Prof. Tanner is a graduate of Illinois College, of the class of 1857, and has been engaged in teaching ever since his graduation, with more than ordinary success. In 1861 he was appointed Professor of the Latin Language and Literature, in the Pacific University of Oregon, a position which he held until 1865, when he was elected to the same chair in Illinois College, which he still holds. While teaching in Pacific University Professor Tanner also studied theology and was ordained as a minister of the Congregational church.
>
> During his residence in Jacksonville he has often filled the pulpit in various churches in this and other cities, and his success as a pulpit orator has been co-extensive with his experience. We venture to predict that Prof. Tanner will meet the demands of the presidential office as fully, and with as much credit to himself and those who have chosen him to this office, as he has hitherto met the demands made upon him as student, professor and preacher. We cannot ask that he should do more.

Throughout its history, like all other western institutions of learning, the college has found its current expenses largely exceeding its income, and to balance its yearly accounts, has felt forced to borrow from its principal. This has prevented its unproductive property and endowment funds from increasing as rapidly as might have been expected by those unacquainted with the situation. The trustees have, however, recently adopted a rule to which they will rigidly adhere, namely: "The current expenses of the college shall be kept within its income." This principle is vital to the prosperity of the institution. Had there been no "Illinois" there would be in Jacksonville few, probably none, of the female seminaries and state institutions. Its location here brought the others in its train, by directing public attention throughout the state to this place, as a center best suited to foster the interests of liberal learning and christian philanthropy. Silent forces generated here have contributed not a little to the higher civilization which is our delight. Strong men drawn this way by the college, directly or indirectly, have developed all these resources, material and immaterial. Of its four hundred graduates not a few have occupied, and still occupy, important positions in different parts of the republic, while thousands of others, who have passed a shorter period within these halls of learning, have aided greatly in elevating the standard of good citizenship throughout the country. In short, Illinois College has been a better maker of history than of money.

The resources of the college, in 1884, are as follows:

Interest bearing notes secured on real estate	$ 75,000
Interest bearing subscription notes	20,000
Farm yielding fair rent	6,000
Farm taken on mortgage, probably yielding income next year	1,000
City lots yielding no income	3,000
Subscription notes, soon productive	17,000
Site	60,000
Buildings, libraries and apparatus	75,000
Total	$250,000

The college is free from debt, and we consider this a fair valuation; but, to use figures easily remembered, you may call the clean assets a quarter of a million, half in productive and half in unproductive property. The income from endowments is about $7,500; that from term bills about $4,500, total, $12,000, the amount of current expenses.

Whipple Academy is the preparatory school of Illinois College, and it is under the control of the same board of trust, and instruction is given by the same corps of teachers.

The college library numbers about 10,000 volumes. An extensive collection of mechanical apparatus for the illustration of the principles of chemistry and physic, has also been added to the college equipment.

The two literary societies—Sigma Pi and Phi Alpha—each possess valuable libraries and convenient halls.

Of Illinois College now at its highest point of prosperity with grounds and buildings in best of condition, it should be mentioned that the members of faculty are the following:

Edward A. Tanner, D. D., president and professor of the Latin language and literature.

Julian M. Sturtevant, D. D., LL. D., professor of mental science and science of government, and instructor in political economy, moral philosophy and evidences of Christianity.

Rufus C. Crampton, LL. D., Hitchcock professor of mathematics and astronomy.

Henry E. Storrs, A. M., PH. D., Hitchcock professor of natural sciences and instructor in German.

Harvey W. Milligan, A. M., M. D., professor of history and English literature.

Edward B. Clapp, A. M. Collins professor of the Greek language and literature.

Harold W. Johnston, A. M., instructor in Latin.

Lieut. N. H. Barnes, U. S. N., instructor in natural sciences and mathematics.

Joseph R. Harker, principal of Whipple Academy.

During the past few years the Jacksonville Female Academy has made rapid and substantial gains in all that renders an institution of learning valuable to its patrons. Its friends are justly proud of its record of fifty-four years of successful work. This, in itself, with all its associations and memories, is a rich endowment for any institution.

The present standing of the academy in excellence of appointments and instruction, healthfulness and beauty of location, stability and independence of character has given it deserved command of a large and discriminating patronage.

The school year 1883-'84 was the most happy and successful in the history of the institution. The entire capacity of the building was filled from the opening of the year, and many applicants declined for want of room. The excellence of instruction, the high character of pupils in attendance, the spirit of earnestness that pervaded all departments, the general good health and freedom from all forms of interruption, have secured results highly satisfactory to all connected with the institution.

The institution is provided with a good library and reading room, furnished with the best periodicals of the day, to which the pupils have daily access.

The government of the school is in the hands of the principal; it is designed to be mild and genial, but watchful and strict in the enforcement of all wholesome rules of study and propriety. It aims to secure a prompt and cheerful obedience to rightful authority; to lead pupils to act from right principle, and to discipline to truth and honesty in all the relations of life. This year a new building was erected, running directly south of chapel, fifty-four feet in length by forty wide, with first story joined to walls of main building. The basement room of the new building is divided north and south into two divisions, the east division devoted to music rooms, the west division entire—forty-four feet in length by sixteen wide devoted to play room and gymnasium. This room is furnished with apparatus for physical exercise, and in care of a teacher skilled in this department. It will also afford abundant room for roller skating.

The south wall of first story of main building has been removed, and the chapel enlarged by an extension of ten feet south. The first floor, in addition to extension of chapel, is divided into an entry-way and cloak room on each corner, east and west, a hall running through center north and south, with two large recitation rooms on each side.

The second and third floors of new building are twelve large rooms for young ladies, with spacious closets framed into the walls.

There is also an extension of the study and reading room, and an extension for bath rooms, closets and water pipes, all outside of main walls of both buildings. The total improvements aggregated a cost of $12,000.

The whole establishment, including new and present buildings, is now heated with steam. A new and complete system of ventilation has been introduced in connection with the steam heat, which secures for the institution perfect sanitary regulation, and all that can be desired for convenience, comfort and safety.

With these improvements completed, the academy is one of the best equipped institutions in the country for the education of young ladies.

The Illinois Female College has been in successful operation since 1847, under the auspices of the Methodist Episcopal denomination. The location of this institution—in a town favorably known throughout the west for its social and literary advantages, for the absence of most of the vices of larger cities and the presence of many virtues—is an item worthy of consideration with those having daughters to educate.

Though this college has been partially destroyed by fire at three different times, yet at present it is entirely free from financial embarrassment; this and the foregoing advantages should entitle it to the confidence of the entire community.

Rev. W. F Short is the worthy president of the board of instruction at this time. The accommodations of the Illinois Female College are as full and satisfactory as those of any school of like grade in the west. The teachers have been selected, not alone for their high qualifications as educators, but also for their worth as christian ladies. It has its classical, scientific and musical departments, and is arranged on the President's Home plan, with his family and the teachers living in the college, and having charge not only of the intellectual, but of the social and religious instruction of the students. The college has, without interruption, continued its prosperous career till its graduates number *four hundred and forty-three;* and several thousand others have received partial education within its halls, many of whom are the first women in the church, in society, and in usefulness in the communities where they reside.

The buildings are commodious and substantial, and are equipped with the most modern facilities and appointments, such as suitable and completely furnished rooms, gas-light, water -hot and cold, &c., &c. There is hardly another school building in the west that combines equal advantages for comfort, health and safety.

The president and teachers reside in the college, and exercise constant watchfulness over the deportment, application and health of the pupils.

Mrs. Sarah B. Short, wife of the president, has entire charge of the household department, and possesses the highest adaptation to the position of matron; and, having had experience in rearing daughters to womanhood, she is capable of that motherly and christian sympathy and counsel which young ladies constantly require.

The Phi Nu and Belles-Lettres Societies are an important feature of the college. They are sustained with great vigor and usefulness.

The reading room receives a large number of the best American and foreign weekly, monthly and quarterly publications, and furnishes an agreeable recreation from the routine of study.

To meet the demand for competent and trained teachers, as also, the necessities of young ladies whose circumstances will not allow them to complete the collegiate or English course, a normal course has been arranged, which includes such branches as will prepare them for teaching in the public schools of the State. Multitudes of students, who received their education in this institution, rank among the best educators in the country. Provision has been made for lectures and attendance at teachers' institutes, for the benefit of those in this department.

The Young Ladies' Athenaeum continued under the charge of Prof. Elmore Chase from Sept. 1880 until Dec. 1884, when its care was transferred to three lady teachers owing to the superintendent's financial inability to further continue the management. During the school year 1883-'84, a large brick addition was made to the building for an art studio, this department of the school, under the accomplished artist, Prof. A. T. VanLaer, being in a flourishing condition. The lady teachers having charge of it at present and since Prof. Chase's retirement, are Misses Merrill, Stickney and Fairbank.

The Illinois Conservatory of Music continued under the care of its founder from its opening in September, 1872, as already noted, until June, 1883, when Prof. Sanders had it incorporated with a board of directors, which board was duly organized by the election of Hon. Edward P. Kirby as president, and Rev. J. D. Easter, D. D. and Ph. D. as secretary, and Mr. B. F. Beesley as treasurer. The board elected Prof. Elmore Chase as superintendent, and Prof. J. S. Barlow as musical director. This management continued for the one school year that is until June, 1884, when Prof. Chase retired. The Conservatory is now under the sole business management as well as musical direction of Prof. Barlow with Professors Nutting and Rivaz, Mrs. Annie Smith and Misses Stella Prince and Kate Sawyer as the faculty. Among the many graduates of the Conservatory we might mention: Mrs. Marian Phillips Wimmerstedt, Mrs. Mary Berdan Tiffany, Mrs. Jennie Marsh Dunlap, Mrs. Annie Thompson Brown, Mrs. Ida Alexander Capps, Mrs. Virginia Rutledge Warren, Mrs. Virgie Gordon Vasey, Mrs. Kate Detrich Sterrett, Miss May Beesley, Miss Allie Thompson, Miss Mabelle Ewing, Miss Emma Meek, Miss Ellen Billings, Miss Carrie Whittlesey, Mrs. Fanny Rees Pierce, Mrs. Lillie Tipton Collin, Mrs. Effie DonCarlos Thompson, Miss Annie Tarbell, Miss Kate Sawyer, Miss Emma Rider, Miss Stella Prince, Miss Kate Rider, Mrs. Nellie Loar Pendleton, Mrs. Fanny McCoy Brown, Mrs. Constance Barlow Smith, Miss Jennie Nutting and Mrs. Hattie Nutting Burnham.

The coming to this country in 1846 of a band of Portuguese colonists has already been noticed in Chapter VII. They have increased quite rapidly, so that there are now about 5,000 in Morgan, Sangamon, Cass, Menard and adjoining counties. We are unable to ascertain the number of families in this county who were of the original colony. The number is, however, very small. Among them are the Vasconcellos, Vieria and DeFrates families. The number of families sprung from them is very large. Many have removed here from other points where they first located. The total Portuguese population in this immediate vicinity is almost 1,200. The first ship load from Madeira comprised 200 souls and the second 500. From this mere handful of exiles has grown the important and extensive element of our population which our Portuguese citizens comprise to-day.

They have a secret organization of a benevolent character which has a system of sick and death benefits, similar to those of most secret benevolent societies. It was organized in Springfield as the Grande Sociedade Lusitania. This organization became the parent lodge of the order and established another lodge in Jacksonville, August 2d, 1880, which became known as the Grande Sociedade Philanthropica. The two lodges have held a celebration each year since those in 1881 and '83 being in Springfield, in 1882 and '84 in Jacksonville. The order is made up of good, sound, reliable and industrious men the very flower of the Portuguese manhood of the two communities and is in a prosperous condition. Its membership is not large but its influence is great and its charitable acts are many. The order is very popular and its celebrations are always well attended and very successful. The imposing appearance made by their processions each year, as with music sounding and banners waving, the members of the order, clothed in suitable regalia, march steadily onward is noticeable. Two magnificent banners are carried in the processions, one by each society.

The year 1883 was marked by two storms that will be long remembered. The ice storm of Feb. 5th and the tornado of May 18th.

On the 3d of February a storm of unusual severity was noted approaching from the northwest. It swept down the water-shed of the Missouri river spreading from the mountains to the great lakes, increasing in intensity as it came—blocking all the northwestern railroads with snow, causing great delay of trains. The cold was intense. When the storm center had reached the region of Omaha, with its southern wing stretching far down toward the Gulf of Mexico, it made the usual curve to the east and northeast. The great whirl of winds being from right to left (against the hands of the watch) the warmer air from the region of the Gulf was drawn into the storm area, and great modification of the character of the storm resulted. Very soon after reaching this point on the 5th of the February, the snow, which prevailed in the regions west and north ceased, giving place to, first a kind of hard balled snow gradually changing to fine dry sleet and then to a mixture of sleet and rain which froze solid as fast as it fell. It froze fast to everything. Every tree became a mass of ice, every twig an icicle. Many fine trees were broken down by the mass of ice.

As the storm swept on eastward it continued to be modified by the whirl of the south winds until it become a driving rain which melted down the ten or twelve inches of snow which then covered the ground in Indiana, Ohio, and Western Pennsylvania, producing the greatest floods ever known in the Ohio river. The details of this terrible flood, however, are still fresh in the mind of the reader.

Here in Jacksonville and vicinity, the storm, though damaging trees, telephone and telegraph wires, was a thing of beauty. Every tree and shrub was brilliant with ice hanging in every conceivable form. No description can do justice to the scene. This continued for nearly a week before there was sufficient thaw or wind to make the ice drop from the trees. The telephone wires of the city were nearly all broken down by the weight of the ice and that means of communication almost entirely destroyed for the time. The telegraph was in but little better condition and the railroads were blocked by the ice on the track. We are told that an engineer on the O. & M. road found his engine blocked in Cass county. Gathering the train men to clear the rails in front of him, he found, after digging awhile, that the wheels were several feet to one side of the rails. His locomotive had actually been running on top of the crust of ice. This field of ice, however, was not of very great extent—it seems not to have been more than 100 miles across it in any direction. Jacksonville was very near its center.

In April, May and June of that year there were a number of lines of tornadoes developed in different parts of the west. Two of these passed over this region.

On the 17th of May, a storm center passed down the eastern slope of the Rocky

Mountains and spread out into a long belt of low barometer extending from Yankton to the Gulf of Mexico. On the morning of the 18th the center of this long belt of low barometer changed its movement to the northeast passing to the north of an area of high barometer which lay over the Gulf and Middle States. During the day this entire belt of low barometer passed around to the northeast and in this rapid movement a line of tornadoes was developed extending from Springfield, Missouri, almost to Chicago. Almost directly in this line then occurred no less than fifteen distinct tornadoes within a space of about five hours. Jacksonville lay directly in the line, and two of the tornado tracks passed near by. One about eight miles to the southeast, the other about five miles to the northwest. These are now known as the Greasy Prairie and the Literberry tornadoes, and will be long remembered by our citizens. They were each first-class specimens of the western tornado.

The Greasy Prairie tornado first touched the ground in Greene county, a few miles east of Roodhouse, in section 21, township 12 north, range 11 west, and swept in a great curve to the northeast, the concavity of the curve being to the northwest, and left the ground in section 21, township 14 north, range 9 west, in Morgan county, forming a path 19 miles in length through a region of country most of which was thickly settled. Although no village was struck, the destruction of property was very great, and how the people escaped with so little loss of life seems quite mysterious, when looking over the ruins of their dwellings. There were 41 dwellings destroyed or badly wrecked, and about the same number of barns and outhouses. Five persons were killed and fifteen seriously hurt. A considerable number of families found shelter in out door cellars, and we may say in passing, the out door cellar has proved to be a perfectly safe retreat. A number of families who were not provided with such cellars resorted to thickets of underbrush. All of these came out safely. In this tornado all injuries happened to those who remained indoors. In some places this tornado spread out about one mile wide; in other parts it was much narrower but not often less than one-fourth of a mile. It was very irregular in outline and in its effects. It sometimes happened that a part of a house would be left standing while everything else about was torn to fragments for a quarter of a mile on either side, and occasionally there was a point of destruction that seemed to be to one side of the storm's track--out of its course. This tornado, although much larger, and, on the whole, doing much more damage to property, seemed to lack the compactness, certainty of movement and terrific force of the Literberry tornado. The cloud accompanying it seems to have been continually changing its form, so much so that no two observers of it give the same description of what they saw. The time of the tornado was definitely fixed as it entered Greasy Prairie. Mr. A. S. Gunn had very carefully corrected his clock the same day at noon. The part of the house in which this clock sat was thrown out of plumb so that the clock stopped. This showed the time to be 6:15 p. m.

The Literberry tornado is especially memorable from the fact that it struck and almost totally destroyed the village of Literberry. It first touched the ground in section 36, township 16 north, range 11 west, in Morgan county, at about 8 o'clock p. m. Passed into Cass county about the center of the south line of section 31, township 17 north, range 9 west. It left Cass county and entered Menard county from section 33, township 18 north, range 8 west, having pursued almost a straight course a distance of twenty miles and how much farther we do not know. In its course it struck and destroyed nine dwellings, one church and one schoolhouse outside of Literberry, thirteen dwellings, two churches, eight business houses, one depot, five freight cars and several large corncribs, besides barns and out houses in Literberry. A few other buildings were injured but not seriously.

This tornado was very compact and perfect in outline throughout its course. Its power was irresistible; everything that lay in its path was literally made into kindling wood. To say houses were destroyed but partially expresses it. They were torn to splinters. Even the fence posts were generally torn out of the ground or broken down.

The large grain scales at Literberry were not simply destroyed, but the heavy irons were taken out of the pit and carried away or broken up. The cloud accompanying it was always definite in outline, a cone with its apex on the ground and base upward during most of its course. Different observers agree substantially in their descriptions of it.

In all, four tornadoes have been known to touch Morgan county in former years. Two of these, which passed to the south of this city, are well remembered. One May 29th, 1859, and one May 7th, 1880. Another passed close to the site of Literberry, (about three-quarters of a mile northwest) and passed through Little Indian creek timber, in May 1845. It destroyed a log stable in Morgan county, the old Walnut Grove schoolhouse and the cabin of Mr. Beard in Cass county. Its path through the timber could be seen for many years. Perhaps some of our older citizens may remember it. The fourth tornado was near the same region. It seems to have been a small affair, at least we have been unable to learn anything very definite about it. This makes six tornadoes in, say, sixty years, an average of one in ten years.

January and February, 1883, were very cold; giving our ice men abundant opportunity to harvest a crop of fine ice. The sleighing was good almost continuously up to the 15th of February, at which time a great thaw set in causing floods which did much damage to bridges and the like. At the beginning of the thaw there was about one foot of snow and ice on the ground. The spring was wet and cold, interfering with early planting so that as a rule our farmers were much belated with their farm work. The temperature mild. There were very few days uncomfortably warm. There was enough rain interspersed to prevent the drying up of the streams. The fall season was unusually wet, delaying the ripening of the late corn; at the same time the first frosts came early, doing great injury. There was more injury done in this county by frost that year than before for thirty years. The winter up to December 15th, 1883, was unusually mild: there was not enough ice to afford skating, even for the small boys.

	TEMPERATURE.			RAIN FALL INCHES.			Mean number of times in three daily observations, the wind is found blowing from the								
	Mean	Maximum.	Minimum.	Mean.	Maximum.	Minimum.	North	Northeast	East	Southeast	South	Southwest	West	Northwest	Calm
January	27.3	64	-20	1.46	3.19	.07	12.5	6.3	1.5	10.5	24.6	10.5	12.5	12.5	1.0
February	32.1	64	-4	2.81	5.85	.39	8.5	4.7	8.0	9.0	16.0	9.5	13.0	16.[illegible]	1.2
March	42.3	76	7	2.93	4.45	1.83	12.0	9.5	8.5	12.0	5.5	5.7	6.0	24.7	3.0
April	52.2	82	20	3.35	4.79	1.99	13.5	6.4	9.0	8.0	19.4	8.2	7.0	17.5	1.5
May	68.3	89	35	3.91	5.92	1.35	7.5	9.6	14.0	10.0	30.6	11.0	3.0	6.5	1.0
June	72.9	94	47	4.95	8.70	2.47	9.5	8.0	11.0	7.0	21.5	15.5	12.5	3.5	1.5
July	79.9	101	58	2.87	6.77	1.52	9.3	9.0	8.8	5.2	17.5	20.5	9.4	10.0	3.0
August	76.2	97	52	3.19	4.57	1.80	12.5	11.5	6.5	12.3	23.0	10.3	6.6	5.5	4.3
September	64.2	91	38	2.14	3.21	.84	10.7	6.3	4.0	9.5	24.5	7.2	7.0	16.0	1.3
October	56.5	88	23	2.16	5.22	.28	11.5	7.2	2.7	11.0	25.6	13.0	8.5	13.5	3.2
November	40.7	76	6	2.79	6.12	1.13	6.0	1.5	4.3	8.5	25.4	13.0	10.0	18.0	3.0
December	27	62	-14	1.68	2.88	1.10	7.5	5.0	8.0	8.0	17.0	5.5	16.0	22.0	3.0
Annual	53.5	85	49	34.2	37.8	30.4	131	85	86	111	250	129	112	166	27
							REDUCED TO DAYS								
							43	28	28	37	83	43	37	55	9

We present above a tabulated report of the weather in this region taken from five years' observations. These observations were not all made in Jacksonville, but were near enough to represent quite perfectly the weather here. In the temperature columns we give first the mean temperature for five years as computed from the daily observations. Second the maximum temperature as ascertained by the self registering thermometer. Third the minimum temperature as ascertained by the self registering thermometer. These last show the highest temperature observed in the month in any one of the five years and the lowest observed in any one month. In the next column we give the rainfall in the same way. In the succeeding columns we give the direction of the wind, or rather the number of times it was observed blowing from the eight principal points of the compass, or points nearest these in three observations daily. A study of this will show the great variability of our winds contrasting strongly with points north and south as may be seen by the following statement of the same class of observations.

Direction of wind—	North.	Northeast.	East.	Southeast	South.	Southwest.	West.	Northwest	Calm.
Jacksonville, Fla..	58	342	105	156	93	176	39	67	42
Marquette, Mich....	106	69	59	91	110	168	178	271	25

During the year 1882, real estate transactions in Morgan county were quite brisk. The entry book in the county recorder's office shows that 2,061 instruments were filed for record, with 1,994 during 1881, and 1,805 during 1880. Those best posted in real estate matters, think the prices of city property were at the top, during that year. In farm lands the prices and number of transfers were in 1882 about as in 1881. The fair crops, with high prices of the last two years, gave a boom to farm lands, and they now reached the top value for some time to come. Fancy farm lands sold from $75 to $95 an acre; while the general price for the best farms ran from $60 to $75. The barren and bottom lands brought from $30 to $45. We think this showing cannot be beat in any county in the state. In fact, Morgan county is the garden spot of Illinois. In the county there are 353,352 acres of farm land, which is worth an average of at least $40 an acre, or $13,634,080. The amount of loans placed on the farm land of the county is much smaller than for many previous years. Most of the loans are those made in taking up and reducing former ones. The good crops have done much in the last few years in reducing the farm indebtedness of the county. The best informed place the amount of money now loaned on Morgan county farm land at $1,000,000.

In the city of Jacksonville, outside of the city school property and the state institutions, there is estimated to be $580,000 worth of church, school and charitable property that is exempt from taxation.

As an item of interest we will state that the railroads passing through this county paid taxes here in 1881, as follows:

Chicago & Alton Railroad	$ 7,289.84
Wabash, St. Louis & Pacific Railroad	5,355.70
Jacksonville Southeastern Railroad	2,341.45
Chicago, Burlington & Quincy Railroad	2,159.50
Peoria, Pekin & Jacksonville Railroad	1,120.10
Total	$17,266.59

The assessment of personal and real property, in the county in 1882, furnishes many interesting facts. In Morgan county there are said to be 6,657 horses, worth $311,015, an average of $46.72 a head. Of cattle there are 16,017 head, worth only $306,885 or $19.16 each. There are 1,015 mules, worth $50,932 or $50.18 each. Of sheep 12,650 are given, worth $1.94 each, or $24,541. Hogs appear 24,360 in number, worth $75,028 or $3.08 each. Only 13 steam engines are given, worth $5,330, an average of $410 each. Fire and burglar proof safes only count up 37 in number, averaging $180.16 each. There are only 12 billiard or pigeon hole tables, averaging $70 each. Of carriages and wagons 2,515 are listed, worth $22.18 each. Of watches and clocks 930 are given, worth on an average $6.15 each. Sewing machines are given as 1,260, valued at only $10 each. Our people not loving music, only gave in 256 pianos, worth on an average of $115. 30. There are also 102 organs, averaging $51.06 each.

The total valuation of agricultural implements is placed at $35,360. No gold and silver-plated ware or diamonds and jewelry appear, and it is therefore safe to presume there are none in the county. No bonds and stocks appear, while the money on hand is placed at $659,916. As a matter of praise to the county, we state that no saloon or eating-house property appears. Household and office property is given at $121,760; grain at $39,650; stock in national banks at $100,000.

Of improved lands there are 293,140 acres, valued at $6,273,196, or $21.40 an acre. Of unimproved there are 60,212 acres, valued at $307,809, or an average of $5.11. Of improved city lots there are 3,570, averaging $599.32 each, and 1,920 unimproved lots valued at $56.58 each. The total value of all property assessed in the county is given at $11,007,592. Of course the valuation is placed low, one-third its real value, and the assessor probably failed to get or the taxpayer to give all the personal property.

H. H. Palmer, city editor of the daily *Journal*, retired in the summer of 1881, to take editorial charge of the Roodhouse *Journal*. Judge Moses had been succeeded as political writer by Captain N. C. A. Rayhouser, formerly of the Lafayette, Indiana, *Journal*. This department was next conducted by Mr. Eames in person. In the city editor's place was soon found Mr. Richard Yates, whose nose for news and swift pencil took in the daily situation. He was succeeded by Mr. Carl Black, and Mr. Eames as general editor by Prof. H. A. Allen. In September, 1884, Messrs. Eames and Yates did the editorial writing, and in November, 1884, Mr. Yates resumed his law practice, and Mr. H. H. Palmer became "ye local," again to be succeeded after a few weeks by Samuel W. Nichols.

March 1st, 1883, the tri-weekly *Courier* became a daily again and has so continued to date, with Messrs. George L. Doying and William H. Hinrichsen as editors and proprietors. The *Courier* under their management is vastly superior as a newspaper to any of its predecessors.

In 1881, two new secret orders were established in the city. During the meeting of the Grand Lodge of Knights of Honor, in this city, on the 3d of September, 1881, many of our citizens had their attention called to this order for the first time. The more they learned about it the better pleased with its system they became. To accommodate these a new lodge was instituted here on November 10, 1881, called Lyceum Lodge, No. 2,602. The credit of working up and founding this new lodge is due mainly to Mr. H. L. Clay, now deceased. Twenty-two citizens of prominence composed the charter members of this lodge. Prof. E. F. Bullard was chosen past dictator; Dr. W. F. Short, dictator, and E. M. Kinman reporter. Later it was consolidated with Royal Lodge.

Athens Chapter, No. 52, Order of the Eastern Star, was organized in the Masonic Temple, Jacksonville, on May 24, 1881, by Brother J. M. Burch and Sister Lina N. Young, officers of the Grand Chapter of Illinois. As a charter members we find Mr. and Mrs. J. T. Bronson, Mr. and Mrs. W. H. Worrell, Mr. and Mrs. N. Metheson, Mr. and Mrs. E. Keemer, Mr. and Mrs. W. M. Starr, Mr. and Mrs. H. A. Mayor, Mr. and Mrs. F. G. Hocking, W. N. Ross and Hiram Ennis. This society occupies the same relation to Masonry that the Rebekah Lodges do to Odd Fellowship. This lodge has now 24 members, and its meetings are made exceedingly pleasant.

There are now in full membership in Ridgely Encampment, No. 9, I. O. O. F., 165 members. Up to this date 27 deaths have occurred among members. The fees for membership are $10 for initiation, yearly dues $4.00 and $1.00 assessments on the death of each member. As benefits, the sum of $2.50 per week sick benefits are paid, and $1.00 per member to the personal representatives of a deceased member.

There have been 439 persons initiated as members of Urania, who are now classified as follows:

Active members	220
Dropped (for non-payment of dues)	149
Withdrawn	46
Died	20
Expelled	4
Total	439

The active membership can be classified, as regards rank, in the order as follows:

Past Grands	28
Degree of Faith	107
Degree of Brotherly Love	8
Degree of Friendship	27
Initiatory	50
Total	220

From 1837 to 1881, this lodge has expended for charitable purposes the following amounts, and who can estimate the good done and suffering prevented thereby?

Funeral benefits	$ 4,160 00
Sick benefits	7,140 00
Widows relief	2,293.48
Orphans relief	514.08
Total	$14,107.45

The assets on hand July 1, 1881, were $5,583.94, a sufficient guarantee that all benefits will be paid.

In 1881 the J. S. E. R. R. was extended 24 miles, from Virden to Litchfield. The next year it was continued on to Smithboro, 82 miles from Jacksonville, and in 1883 Centralia 29 miles further, was reached, and new territory opened up and railroad connections made south and east.

The following is a true and correct statement of the valuations of property listed for taxation in Morgan county as taken from the records of the county clerk, for the year 1883, and the taxes charged:

CLASS OF PROPERTY.	Corrected valuation..	Equaliz'd per cent. Add....	Equaliz'd per cent. Deduct.	Equaliz'd valuation.
Personal	$2,159,253	...	30	$1,511,498
Lands	6,551,326	...	17	5 437,602
Lots	2,314,982	...	30	1,620,487
Railroad Property { Class C, Personal	....	...	...	932
Class D, Lands	....	...	...	....
Class D, Lots	....	...	...	....
Class A, Track	....	...	...	524,296
Class B, Rolling stock	....	...	...	126,146
Gas Company and Western Union Telegraph Company	....	...	...	22,800
Totals	....		....	$9,243,761

KIND OF TAX.	Value	Rate...	Amount of tax.	Total ....
State tax of 1883	$9,243,761	$ .32	$29,580 03	
Forfeited, 1882			532.67	$30,112.70
Jacksonville city bonds	2,084,418	.44	9,171.43	
Forfeited in 1882			289.38	9,460.81
Morgan county bonds	9,243,761	.06	5,546.25	
Forfeited in 1882			20.91	5,567.16
Waverly bonds	166,184	1.90	3,157 49	3,157.49
Forfeited in 1882				
County	9 243,760	.75	69,328.20	
Forfeited in 1882			959.12	70,287.32
Dog tax				1,409.00
Road tax	No levy.			
Jacksonville	2,084,418	2.20	45,857.19	
Forfeited in 1882			3,808.19	49,665 38
Waverly	166,184	.85	1,412.56	1,412.56
Franklin	41,272	.25	103 18	103.18
Murrayville	43,080	.59	254.17	254 17
Lynnville	29,119	63	177.14	177.14
Drainage				355.84

The following statistics from the assessor's books returned to the county clerk, give the relative amounts and value of the personal property of Morgan county in 1883

	Number..	Assessed value......
Horses	6,531	$ 298,536
Cattle	16,638	330,563
Mules and asses	1,002	48,700
Sheep	10,814	22,796
Hogs	22,689	73,277
Steam engines including boilers	24	10,015
Fire or burglar-proof safes	52	5,580
Billiard, pigeon-hole, bagatelle or other similar tables	7	179
Carriages and wagons	2,637	74,845
Watches and clocks	1,251	9,165
Sewing and knitting machines	1,470	14,524
Pianofortes	286	29,050
Melodeons and organs	295	12,640
Total value		$1,629,745

VALUES OF UNENCUMBERED PROPERTY.

Merchandise	$259,445
Manufactured articles	9,110
Manufactured tools, implements and machinery	2,180
Agricultural implements	42,418
Gold and silver plate, and plate ware	195
Moneys of banks, bankers, brokers, etc	50,803
Other moneys	369,676
Property of corporations	5,000
Property of saloons and eating houses	1,020
Household property	151,380
Investments in R. E	2,400
Grain of all kinds	25,588
Shares of stock of State and National Banks	109,000
All other personal property	1,808
Total assessed value	1,259,283
Total assessed value of personal property	2,160,523
Railroad property assessed in the county as personal property	1,330

REAL ESTATE LANDS

	Number of Acres.	Assessed Value.
Improved lands	296,130	$ 6,257,812
Unimproved lands	57,222	293,600
Totals	353,352	$ 6,551,412

TOWN AND CITY LOTS

	Number of Lots.	Assessed Value.
Improved lots	3,620	$ 2,222,529
Unimproved lots	1,890	106,974
Totals	5,510	$ 2,329,503
Total assessed value of all taxable property in Morgan county		$11,041,475

NUMBER OF ACRES IN CULTIVATION.

Wheat	37,296
Corn	158,784
Oats	42,013
Meadows	30,181
Other field products	8,011
Number of acres inclosed in pasture	56,086
Number of acres inclosed in orchard	3,790
Number of acres inclosed in woodland	57,232

Jacksonville to-day, January, 1885, contains twenty church organizations, viz:

German Evangelical Lutheran Salem, Rev. Edward Beck.

Mt. Zion (colored) Church, Rev. A. L. Stewart, pastor. No church edifice.

BAPTIST—First, West State near West; B. F. Simpson, pastor. Mt. Emory (African), Rev. J. O. Bonner, pastor.

METHODIST—Brooklyn M. E., Rev. James Leaton, D D., pastor. Grace M. E., Rev. W. N. McElroy, D. D., pastor. Centenary M. E., Rev. M. D. Hawes, pastor. German M. E., Rev. H. Ellerbeck, pastor. African M. E., Rev. Mr. Jackson, pastor.

PRESBYTERIAN—Central, Rev. A. B. Morey, pastor. First, no pastor; no church edifice; worship with Central congregation. Westminster, Rev. Samuel M. Morton, pastor. First Portuguese, no pastor. Second Portuguese, Rev. C. B. Barton, pastor Central Portuguese, Rev. E. N. Pires, pastor.

CHRISTIAN—Church of Christ, Rev. A. N. Gilbert, pastor. Christian (colored), Rev. W. S. Hancock, paster, no church edifice.

CONGREGATIONAL, Rev. H. E. Butler, pastor.

EPISCOPAL—Holy Trinity, Rev. J. D. Easter, rector.

ROMAN CATHOLIC—Church of Our Savior, Rev. T. Hickey, pastor.

Of these twenty all but two have pastors and all but three have edifices for worship. Some of these churches are among the finest in the West.

In addition to all other railroad facilities referred to elsewhere, the city is likely to have another Western connection. On March 17th, last, the articles of association for the organization of the Quincy, Jacksonville & Eastern Railway Company were filed in the county recorder's office. The articles set out the name of the corporation thereby created and organized as above, and the purpose and object of the said corporation shall be to build, construct, own and operate a railroad through the counties of Adams, Pike, Scott and Morgan to Jacksonville. Isaac L. Morrison, Lewis S. Olmsted and William D. Sanders are the Jacksonville incorporators

THE FOLLOWING IS THE OLD SETTLERS NECROLOGICAL RECORD FOR 1883-'84.

Date of death	NAME.	Age	Res in Co.	Nativity
September 29	Herbert Carpenter	41	41	Illinois
October 3	John Walker	60	56	Kentucky
December 4	William Richardson	69	52	England
July 13	James B Spires	46	46	Illinois
July 8	John A J Carson	67	57	Virginia
July 5	Morris J. Olive	37	37	Illinois
August 27	Mrs. Mary Reid	72	35	Virginia
July 3	Mrs. Polly Embree	73	33	Kentucky
August 10	Mrs. Anna Ainsworth	70	30	England
August 15	Mrs. Harriet Moore	45	45	Illinois
August 16	Talma Smith	48	42	Kentucky
August 10	Mrs. Sarah Litton	77	58	Kentucky
August 8	Mrs. Eliza J. Stringham	58	44	Massachusetts
May 11	John W. Goltra	71	49	New Jersey
May 14	Stephen Sutton	69	47	New Jersey
June 21	Jonathan Neely	74	42	Pennsylvania
February 23	John M. Cole	64	29	New Jersey
June 27	Joseph Liter	65	50	Kentucky
June 17	Mrs. Hannah S. Vasey	78	36	England
June 8	John Gledhill	38	38	Illinois
March 4	T. J. Weatherford	51	51	Illinois
March 16	William Wright	73	52	Kentucky
March 6	Samuel McKean	63	33	Scotland
August 1	John C. Pfeil	63	45	Germany
August 27	Mrs. B. F. Gass	65	50	Kentucky
August 29	John D. Keedy	50	46	Maryland
October 6	Thomas C. Huckstep	78	50	Virginia
July 4	Mrs May Ann Hall	43	40	England
December 7	Mrs. Mary Jacinto	65	36	Maderia
December 8	Edward Weil	57	26	Germany
December 18	Leroy Shulty	44	30	Ohio
December 20	Mrs. Mary Fuster	62	60	New York
December 28	Thomas Rountree	60	40	Kentucky
October 18	Morris H. Worcester	34	34	Illinois
October 14	B. F. Rynearson	41	40	Missouri
October 14	Mrs. Mary Stevenson	72	50	Ohio
October 23	Mrs. Maria Hussey	86	35	New York
November 5	Mrs. Ellen Miles	46	33	New York
November 10	Mrs. Chastina Simmons	48	30	Ohio
November 18	Henry W. Hunt	42	42	Illinois
November 22	Miss Cornelia Trask	45	24	Connecticut
November 29	Mrs. Priscilla J. Hurst	78	54	Kentucky
September 23	George Hess	52	35	Germany
November 11	Cyrus J. Tond	58	45	Pennsylvania
February 12	Mrs. Ann Alexander	89	44	Ireland
December —	Isaac N. West	45	3-	Ohio
September 5	John Mapes	72	53	Missouri
September 10	William S. Andras	80	49	England
September 12	Jairus Kibbe	55	40	Connecticut
September 15	Mrs. Elizabeth Berry	75	51	Tennessee
September 24	Ebenezer T. Miller	84	65	Kentucky
September 25	Mrs. Sarah P. Hurst	79	54	Kentucky
May 24	Joseph W. King	75	45	Connecticut
March 8	Peter Kirkman	70	50	Kentucky
April 2	Mrs. Elizabeth E. Scott	48	48	Illinois
May 7	Joseph G. Hayden	74	50	Virginia
April 5	James H. Mack	43	43	Illinois
April 9	Mary F. Henderson	65	44	Kentucky
April 7	Mrs. Hannah Fairbank	86	50	Connecticut
April 11	Mrs. Sarah A. Myers	39	39	Illinois
April 28	John H. Bohn	38	33	North Carolina
April 20	Mrs. Helen V. Stout	67	45	New Jersey
March 26	John Edgar Ward	35	35	Illinois
March 28	Mrs. Hulda Carey	75	40	Virginia
March 25	James Burnes	40	40	Ireland
March 21	Richardson Vasey	41	35	England
March 4	John W. King	49	43	Massachusetts
March 5	George B. Daniels	45	45	Illinois
January 16	Ida Vasconcellos	69	33	Maderia
February 1	Mrs. Joaquin Smith	36	35	Maderia
January 17	Mrs. Eva H. Craven	47	47	Illinois
January 31	Richard Jordan	52	—	Illinois
January 12	Mrs Visenia Smith	47	35	Maderia
March 6	Samuel McKean	63	33	Scotland
February 17	Albert Price	35	35	Illinois
February 10	Miss Mary F. Allen	32	18	Illinois
December 16	Robert P. Macken	42	42	Illinois
September 14	Mrs. Hannah Edwards	35	35	Illinois
September 18	Mrs. Mary Killiam	61	54	Kentucky

The State of Illinois has in the city three large institutions, the Central Hospital for the Insane, the Institution for the Education of the Deaf and Dumb, and the Institution for the Education of the Blind. Dr. H. F. Carriel has charge of the Hospital for the Insane, Dr. P. G. Gillett that of the Deaf and Dumb Institution, and Rev. F. W. Phillips that of the Blind, all gentlemen who are entirely competent to fulfill the duties of the high positions which they have attained. These institutions now (1884) contain about 1,300 inmates, officers, teachers, attendants, pupils and patients divided as follows: Blind, 168; Insane, 633; Deaf and Dumb, 586.

The principal buildings are the Court House, Opera House, City Hospital, Y. M. C. A. Hall, Sanitarium, Oak Lawn Retreat for Insane, State Institutions for Blind, Deaf and Dumb, and Insane, Dunlap House, Rataichak Hotel, Illinois College, Jacksonville Female Academy, Illinois Female College, Young Ladies' Athenæum, Conservatory of Music, Jacksonville Business College, Washington High School and five public school houses. It has always been an educational center for the west, and so numerous are its schools and so high the grade of scholarship that it has been dubbed "The Athens of the West." It is equally proud of its other well deserved name of the "New Haven of Illinois," on account of the gigantic size and great number of beautiful elms shading its principal streets. The city is lighted with gas—streets and houses. It has never had any rapid growth in population nor done much in the manufacturing line, yet now possesses a very large woolen mill, three brick yards, two carriage manufactories, four flouring mills and some smaller industries.

A street railway line furnishes easy communication through the two principal streets (State and Main) from depots to State institutions at western and southern city limits. No running stream furnishes water power but an excellent system of reservoirs supplies water abundantly for city and fire department use. There are no city steam fire engines but four paid hose companies and a hook and ladder brigade. The churches number over a score, including all the leading sects and many handsome and commodious buildings. The Y. M. C. A. has a fine building—the best of its kind in the State outside of Chicago and owned by the association—and takes charge of a Public Library and Free Reading Room. Illinois College and its literary societies have three other libraries. A Library Association and the Deaf and Dumb Institution also possess large book collections.

With the growth of our city has grown our capacity to entertain travelers, whether brought to our place by business or pleasure. Our hotels are constantly being beautified and enlarged, and passing into hands that understand their business. The patronage annually received by our leading hotels from commercial travelers alone is a big thing in itself. Take the Rataichak Hotel, on East State street, just completed, as an example. It is a large and elegant building, which not only adds much to the general appearance of that part of the city, but is one of the permanent kind of enterprises that we like to see built up and encouraged in our community. It will doubtless prove a paying investment.

The hardware, stove and furniture trade has assumed large proportions in our city within the last few years. Small rooms and meagre stocks have been supplanted by commodious buildings and assortments rivaling in size those of metropolitan establishments. There is very little jobbing, but the retailers have customers that come from great distances, and the Jacksonville market supplies a large territory.

The principal shipments are horses, cattle, sheep, hogs, flour and walnut logs. Besides the Opera House there are three public halls, seating altogether 1,650 persons. The assessed valuation of real and personal property in 1882 was $2,827,320, reduced by the State Board of Equalization to $1,979,224. The total bonded indebtedness is now only $154,500.

There is nothing in the entire catalogue of a city's advantages so positive to advance its commercial growth, and to raise it in the scale of mercantile importance among cities, as its communications with the outside world. In this respect, Jacksonville is not wanting, but has the necessary railroad advantages, to meet the requirements of all kinds of business. The extension of the Jacksonville Southeastern to Centralia, recently, has its many advantages, and will eventually result in the bringing of a considerable amount of business to the city from the southeast, that has heretofore been going elsewhere, while another avenue for competition on freights has been added. Through the great Wabash line, Jacksonville has an outlet for traffic east and west, and by the Peoria branch, north; while the Chicago & Alton gives direct transportation north, south and southwest. The sharp competition waged between these great corporations, the C. & A. and the Wabash has the beneficial result of cheapening transportation; hence no inland city of the size of Jacksonville, possesses such advantages in this respect.

The soil of the vicinity is a rich black loam, with an almost unbroken level surface and only enough timber land to supply home consumption of wood. Two daily newspapers, with weekly editions, one Republican (*Journal*. Weekly established in 1831, Daily in 1866,) and one Democratic (*Courier*) are published, besides two college newspapers. There are three job printing offices Hon. John Gordon is postmaster. The city is now entitled to free mail delivery and expects soon to have the carrier system. The United States and Pacific Express and Western Union Telegraph Companies have offices. There are five solid banking and saving institutions. Three of these have capital as follows: Jacksonville National, $260,000; First National, $200,000; Central Savings, $100,000, and two private concerns. M. P. Ayers & Co., and Hockenhull, King & Elliott, which do not publish amount of capital, but do a very large business.

Jacksonville has often been famed for good "turnouts." Her smooth and well shaded streets are splendid boulevards for pleasure driving, and hence a taste for fine equipages has been cultivated. Of course many cannot afford the luxury of a team of their own, and hence livery and feed stables have sprung up, wherein all classes of vehicles and horses for driving, wedding or funeral purposes, can be procured.

In its proper place mention should have been made of the Young Men's Christian Association, which for years has had a good organization here, and which lately has completed a very handsome edifice on Morgan street, devoted to the fulfillment of the aims and objects for which the association was organized. A public library and reading room find a home within the walls of the Association building, and are open day and evening to all who are desirous of availing themselves of the benefits there to be found.

The health of the city has always been remarkable, the average death-rate being much lower than in the majority of cities of the west. The U. S. census statistics puts Jacksonville in the front rank in point of health.

With its admirable Fire Department, in connection with the abundant and convenient supply of water, a disastrous fire is almost impossible.

With its well officered and equipped Military Company, the Morgan Cadets, it vies with neighbor cities in promoting and fostering this strong arm of security and defense, a well-ordered and drilled militia. The number of brave boys in blue who volunteered to stem the tide of treason in our late civil war, of which Jacksonville and Morgan county furnished their full share, shows how fully we could rely on them in any hour of danger.

The initiatory steps in the matter of paving the principal streets with the best of hard burned brick, have proven most conclusively that Jacksonvillians are awakening to a most important sense of duty they owe to themselves and the business interests of the community and the enterprise will now be pushed forward until the principal avenues for travel in our city are put in the best possible condition.

At no time in the history of Jacksonville, now 58 years old, have her various interests been in a more satisfactory condition than at present, and it is with a considerable degree of pride that she shows the world the onward march of progress and the prosperity that has attended the efforts of her business community the past few years.

With some 13,000 inhabitants, her situation, surroundings, growth, improvements and prospects, she is the peerless inland city of the west. Her position is commanding and beautiful; her broad streets and avenues are finely shaded; her palatial dwellings are set in commodious lawns, dotted with evergreens and flowers; her numerous public buildings are costly and rich in architectural finish; her halls and business houses are solid, roomy and convenient. Gas works, water works and street cars, are in successful operation; railroads lead out in six different directions. While noted for the three State benevolent institutions which are elegantly situated within the city limits, giving her a State-wide reputation, the city is no less renowned for her schools, academies and colleges, the seat of learning and art.

In the political world it has exerted its full share of influence in moulding public opinion and laws, resulting in the rapid advancement of our State to its present enviable position. It has furnished a Secretary of State, five Judges of the Circuit and one of the Supreme Court a State Superintendent of schools, two Governors, two members of Congress and a United States Senator; in each case, men of distinguished ability, who have reflected honor upon their State and Nation.

In the religious world, her church-going population is comfortably accommodated in some twenty different houses of worship, costing all the way from $2,000 up to $10,000, $20,000 and $40,000 each; and while our city suffered the loss of the finest one of these church buildings, the First Presbyterian, in a recent fire, we have every assurance that it will be rebuilt at no distant day—possibly more elegant and tasty in appearance than before. Every shade of religious belief can find a home, as there are all kinds to choose from.

In addition to the work of benevolence carried on in our churches, our citizens are characterized for their activity and liberality in this direction through societies. We have our Free Masons and Odd Fellows, United Workmen, Knights of Honor, Royal Templars, Y. M. C. A., the Woman's Christian Association, the Orphan's Home, City Hospital, Woman's Christian Temperance Union, and other worthy organizations. Great and good work is being effected by all these organizations.

Her citizens are also widely celebrated for the attention paid to music and the arts. There is perhaps no city in the State with so many pianos, musical instruments and able teachers of music, in proportion to the inhabitants. Her reputation in this regard has attracted pupils from all portions of the west to receive the benefit of the training and instruction of her competent professors. Culture is indispensable to progress, and that city which is not fully abreast of the times in all the varied requirements of art and learning, will surely fall behind in the race for assured success.

In her numerous literary and scientific clubs, her citizens find time to exercise their minds and improve their taste. D.D.'s, L.L. D.'s, A. M.'s, M.D.'s and gentlemen with no titles to their names, all take a part and bear their portion of the labor, and share equally in the enjoyment of its result. The ability to contribute is only exceeded by the desire to excel in literary attainments. The ladies, not to be behind, as they never are indeed, in any good work, have their Sorosis, P. E. O., and other societies, which afford them ample room for discussion, for composition and general improvement.

In addition to the educational establishments already spoken of, there are four ward schools and a High School appertaining to Jacksonville proper, which are under the supervision of a school board, which has ample power in the selection of the city superintendent of schools, the principals and subordinate teachers in the ward schools, as well as in determining the course of study to be pursued in each.

Jacksonville has never been famous for the amount of capital and enterprise invested in manufacturing, yet this division of commerce is growing upon us, and few realize the number of men now employed by our city manufacturers, and the number of families supported by home industries. Take the tobacco trade alone. Three large establishments, and several smaller ones are constantly turning out man's favorite weed in its various shapes, employing many hands and paying a large revenue to the government.

The addition of an extensive tile factory, in 1883, to our manufacturing interests, is one of great importance, and it should be the duty of every resident to use his or her influence—let it be great or small—to induce other like institutions to settle among us. We need more manufactories.

The Woolen Mills of Capps & Sons, continues to be the chief manufacturing establishment of the city, carrying on a business of half a million annually.

Two very large and two small flour mills do a very large business in that line, and manufacture the very best flour in the western market.

Business stability is a fact that can easily be verified by the records. There have been fewer business failures in our city and county, the past ten or twenty years, than in any other section of the State. This speaks volumes for the management of our financial and business institutions, and the ability to maintain themselves under all circumstances in a prudent and careful manner. These are extremely encouraging facts, that go to show that the business interests of Jacksonville and Morgan county are on a solid basis, and that speculation and involvement in debt have not been indulged in to the same extent as in other localities. With these facts before them, our citizens should feel greatly stimulated and become aroused to renewed efforts in the extension of their business.

Jacksonville has a grand future before her. With no city of its size within 33 miles on the east, 80 miles on the south or west, or north, she can command the trade of the intervening country—the most beautiful and productive of any in our glorious State. To do this there must be enterprise, liberality, intelligent concentration and universal interest among all her citizens. Manufactures will be increased, the jobbing and retail trade enlarged, and every facility afforded for active growth and expansion.

The Central Presbyterian church, after the departure to Belleview College of Dr. Harsha, gave a unanimous call to Rev. A. B. Morey, of Cincinnati, Ohio, who accepted and is now ministering most acceptably to them as well as to the First church which has continued to worship with them since September, 1883.

The election of November 4, 1884, resulted in a complete Democratic victory for county and national tickets. Hon. Edward L. McDonald, states attorney, was elected as Representative to the General Assembly and he took his seat in that body January 7th, 1885. Mr. Charles A. Barnes was elected states attorney, Mr. John N. Marsh re-elected circuit clerk, D H. Sorrells was elected county commissioner, John R. Knollenberg coroner and T. D. Richardson surveyor. At this election the county again failed to give the requisite majority to the proposition to adopt township organization.

On May 21, 1883, the hardest frosts and freeze ever known in the county occurred in the night. Everything in the way of vegetables that had come up was killed, potatoes, beans and corn especially suffered. On the 22d there was another frost finishing the destruction of the little still undamaged. All grapes and tomatoes were destroyed.

The Jacksonville Historical Society was formed Tuesday, August 5th, 1884, and the following officers were elected: Dr. Hiram K. Jones, president; Dr. H. W. Milligan, secretary; Samuel W. Nichols, historian; and the following managers, Messrs. M. P. Ayers, W. F. Short, Henry H. Hall, Mesdames Edward Scott and Edward P. Kirby, and the president and secretary. The society meets monthly and has already had interesting papers read before it by Prof. Turner, Mr. and Mrs. J. H. Bancroft and Dr. Milligan.

January 5th, 1884, is said to have been the coldest day for fifteen years in this locality. Mercury ranged from 30 to 35 degrees below zero in Jacksonville.

On pages 185 and 195 we gave a few figures as to the city's schools. We can now present later ones: For the year ending June 30th, 1883, the average attendance of pupils was 1,288; the number enrolled 1,750. The average number attending was probably not less then 1,400. There were 35 teachers employed, including the principal, giving an average of 40 pupils to each teacher. The salaries were: 28 at $45 per month.

$405 per year; 2 at $50 per month, $450 per year; 1 at $60 per month, $540 per year; 4 at $70 per month, $630 per year; 1 at $1,200 per year.

Certainly no less than thirty-five teachers were necessary to teach 1,400 children, and when 1,500 were present the hands of the teachers were full. The salaries of the teaching force amounted to $17,168.

Janitors (four main buildings and four branches)	$ 1,215.00
Fuel	1,000.00
Insurance (premium on $20,000 three years)	200.00
Salaries of members of board	300.00
Interest	2,500.00
Repairs	1,000.00
Stationery	300.00
Contingent	200.00
For the year ending June 30, 1883, the entire expenses of the schools amounted to	.$23,495.58

For the school year ending June 30, 1884, $2,864 was expended under the head of building, including putting in of steam into the first ward, $2,077.79 under the head of repairs $317.03 for furniture, $1,178 for fuel, and $2,549.15 for interest, the first two items being unusually large, yet the tuition in our public schools amounts to an outlay of $20 per pupil, or exactly one-half that charged by private institutions of high grade.

The amount of annual revenue is about as follows:

Tax gross levy		$20,000.00
Shrinkage as follows:—Cost of collecting two per cent	$400	
Uncollectable taxes, not less than	400	800.00
		$19,200.00
County superintendent		3,300.00
Interest on township fund		400.00
Total		$22,900.00
That is to say the expenses inevitable without reducing schools exceeds the revenue about		$913.00

A comparative exhibit of attendance and expenses for the years 1874, 1879 and 1884, a period of ten years, is appended. The figures are taken from the records of each school year, closing in August:

	Pupils Enrolled.		
	1874	1879	1884
High School	87	126	134
Seventh Grade	39	76	89
First Ward	340	405	363
Second Ward	373	451	421
Third Ward	346	507	521
Fourth Ward	327	303	283
Colored School	152	discontinued.	
Total	1664	1868	1811

Total expense account for 1874, $34,957.21; for 1879, $34 508.20; for 1884, $29,426.13.

In the comparison of expenditures, the items of building, repairs, furniture, &c., are all included.

Eighteen-Eighty-Four was a prosperous year to the Art Association, which now numbers over fifty members. The meetings have been well attended and interesting. The subjects considered have been: The History of Architecture, What an Art Association may do, Japanese Art, Modeling in Clay (a lecture by Prof. E. A. Spring,) A Utilitarian View of Art, American Wood Engraving, The Old and New in Art, The French Artist, French Sculpture.

There was a larger attendance at the art exhibition than ever before with one exception, and the association had reason to be proud of what they had to exhibit. The net proceeds were $80 and the sale of pictures amounted to over $300. The society has made important additions to their library and have purchased two valuable pictures one by Wm. Sartain and the other by Kiefer. Dr. Prince has presented them with a valuable collection of autotypes. They have also received a charcoal study from Prof. Van Laer.

The present officers are: Prof. J. H. Woods, president; Mrs. M. J. Dewees, Miss M. E. Morse, vice presidents; Mr. H. H. Hall, treasurer; Miss L. E. Sturtevant, secretary; Mrs. M. D. Wolcott, Mrs. M. L. D. Keiser, Mrs. David Prince, Dr. T. J. Pitner, additional trustees.

The painting and charcoal club is a sturdy infant which has recently come into existence, but is likely to be heard from in a most artistic manner in the future. Like all model children it will be seen rather than heard.

The meetings of the Microscopical Society are held on the first Saturday of each month, and continue throughout the year. Dr. Black has been president this year—1884.

The subjects studied and illustrated by home-made specimens are "Badena Musca Comestica," "The Nose," "The Tongue," "Phylloxera," "A grain of corn," "The Heart," "Texture and Color of Corollas," "Plant Hairs," "Stomoxys Calatrans." The society met with the Horticultural Society Nov. 1st, 1884, and exhibited specimens in the interest of horticulture. Probably the best work done this year is that in illustration of the sprouting of a grain of corn from the first to the seventeenth day after planting, by Dr. Black.

The Horticultural Society was formed in 1868 and has met regularly once per month. The greatly distinguishing feature of the year has been the increased interest taken in the meetings both by members and outsiders who attend, and this interest has manifested itself in the greater display of fruits, flowers and plants at each meeting, which proves that more attention is being devoted to the cultivation and care of all horticultural products, and more especially house plants. A union meeting of this society n connection with the Microscopical Society in November was one of the most interesting and instructive meetings of the year. The present officers are Hon. Edward Scott, president; A. L. Hay, secretary; Miss M. E. Catlin, treasurer.

The Young Men's Catholic Benevolent Association was organized in November, 1878, with twenty-three members, and has now sixty-five. Its officers are: President, M. H. Murray; vice-president, Geo. Buhre; secretary, O. Weisenburg; financial secretary, Ed. Keating; treasurer, M. S. Harmon.

The Ancient Order of Hibernians was organized September 18, 1883, which have increased to ninety-five. Its officers are:

John Boylan, president; Chas. Develin, vice-president; E. A. Cosgriff, recording secretary; W. A. Carroll, financial secretary; M. McGinnis, treasurer; Den. J. McCarty, door-keeper; M. S. Harmon, grand marshal; John Develin, sergeant-at-arms.

Both the above societies are for benevolent purposes, paying weekly benefits to sick and needy members. They report an usually prosperous year.

The Turnverein was organized February 3d, 1858, with seven members, Ph. Braun, H. Lomb, L. Weil, Nat. Neuman, Fred. Fries, M. Rosenbach and H. Fitzenberger. They first met in a barber shop under the Park House, afterward in a hall on a lot now owned by Mrs. Fay. The membership increased until the war, when by volunteering it was reduced to six. After the war it grew again and in time removed to its present quarters on North Main street, which it bought for $6,500, and improved at a cost of $3,000. The present membership is thirty. Meetings occur the first Sunday of each month. Officers are elected in June and December. This society belongs to the National "Bund" and has for its object the relief of needy and distressed members as well as the practice of gymnastics. Its present officers are: President, A. Miller; vice president, L. Leurig; treasurer, H. Engel; treasurer of sick fund, John Schafer; secretary, Ph. Schultz; teacher of gymnastics, Wm. Kempf; warden, H. Brune.

Our colored citizens have their fraternal lodges in our city. Among them are the Knights of Tabor and Daughters of the Tabernacle which have kept on in the even tenor of their way, trying to render assistance to the needy and elevate the race with which they are identified, and to exalt the principle of the great brotherhood of man, thus becoming a power for good. This is an auxiliary branch of the grand body, and will no doubt be well represented in the grand session, to be held in the city of Louisville, Ky., this year.

Also Fame Lodge, No. 2206, G. U. O. O. F., which was organized August 25th, 1881, by H. Gorum, D. Hudson and Isham Hicks, in Hatfield's Hall, on the northwest corner of the square. Also the Household of Ruth, No. 291, G. U. O. O. F., which was organized April 28th, 1883, by R. S. Donalson and C. L. Wilson, of Quincy.

During the year 1884, the Ancient Order of United Workmen leased the room over Jebb Bros'. jewelry store, known as Music Hall, and remodelled the same, taking out the old stage, &c., and now have one of the most comfortable secret society halls in the city. There were twelve assessments during the year. The increase in membership has been limited for this year owing to the political campaign.

The Royal Templars paid fifteen assessments and gained one member.

The year 1884 for the Knights of Honor, was uneventful. They continued to do and receive good according to the principles of the order. W. A. Oliver is now dictator.

The various Masonic lodges have met and labored for the benefit of their members and their dependent ones, doing good in truly scriptural way. The various bodies are Hospitaler Commandery, No. 31, Knights Templar, Jacksonville Chapter, No. 3, Royal Arch Masons, Harmony Lodge, No. 3, A. F. and A. Masons, Jacksonville Lodge, No. 690, A. F. and A. Masons, the Order of the Eastern Star and a lodge of Ancient York Masons.

The noble order of Odd Fellows had a prosperous year as its merits well deserve. We are enabled to present the following statistics:

Illini—Members 243, accessions during the year 11, sick benefits paid $527, paid widows and orphans $464, donations $42. Sick benefits are $5 per week. The lodge pays to widows of deceased members an assessment of $2 per member at the time of death and a quarterly allowance for five years afterward.

Ridgely Encampment, No. 9, I. O. O. F., paid for the relief of sick brothers in 1884, $160. Increase in membership very light, owing to a political campaign; membership 156.

Urania Lodge, No. 243, I. O. O. F., paid for relief of sick brothers $610; paid for relief of widows of deceased brothers $160; paid for education of orphans of deceased brothers $105; donated to needy brothers $40; paid funeral benefits $480; total relief for the year $1,395. The receipts for the year to December 1st, were $2,038.90. The lodge has a capital of about $6,000. The membership is 220.

The Illinois Institution for the Education of the Deaf and Dumb is increasing in usefulness under the able management of Dr. P. G. Gillett, who has been at its head so long. It has at present 503 pupils, one superintendent, twenty-eight teachers, three matrons, three clerks, one physician, four supervisors, two attendants, two engineers, two firemen, one baker, four cooks and thirty-six other employes. All the improved methods of teaching are employed, including the wonderful art of articulation, in addition to which the pupils are instructed in gardening, cabinet making, printing and many other useful and beautiful arts.

During the past year the Central Hospital for the Insane has gone on increasing its facilities for usefulness. Numerous additions have been made to the shops, stables and other out houses, while the great work has been the new and commodious detached building, especially designed for the treatment of incurables. This is to cost, when completed, $135,000 and will be a model structure of its kind when ready for occupation, which will probably be sometime during the coming year. There were in the institution, December 30th, a total of 633 patients, 315 males and 318 females, with a daily average of 629 for the preceding two years. There have been admitted during the past two years 480 patients and 486 discharged. Of these the gratifying number of 326 went away recovered and improved. Since the organization of the hospital 7,630 patients have been treated. Great credit is due the present superintendent for his remarkably efficient management of this vast concern.

The Institution for the Education of the Blind has just passed through an unusually prosperous year. The work which was done in its various departments was thorough, and accomplished good results. The school has been better attended this year than ever before, the roll showing an attendance of 168, 106 male and 62 female pupils.

These pupils represent seventy-five counties of the state. The graduating class numbered three young ladies and was composed of Joanna Gibbons and Alice Roberts of Madison county and Minnie McCrea of Will county. Certificates of proficiency from the mechanical department were given to William Appel, and James Hennessey of Cook county, John Jennings of Logan county, John D. Marvin of DuPage county, Fritz Schrage of Adams, and George D. Williams of McHenry county. These young men have mastered the trades taught in the workshops of the institution, and are now trying to support themselves. The health of the inmates has been good. The corps of instructors in the literary department consists of Misses Harriet Reed, Frances McGinnis, Lizzie B. Simpson, Annie H. Martin, Lulu Nichols and Mrs. Mary H. Burr; in the musical department Miss Susie A. Draper, Prof. T. D. Nutting, Mrs. Katie Smith Dummer and Mrs. Annie Smith; in the mechanical department Byron B. Gray and William H. Smith; in the domestic department Mrs. L. J. Phillips; and in the organizing and financial department Julian P. Lippincott treasurer, and F. W. Phillips superintendent. And at this time the institution is better prepared to do its work than ever before.

The Oak Lawn Retreat for the Insane, founded in 1872 by Dr. Andrew McFarland, for the past few years has been a success, for three hundred patients have been admitted. The grounds consist of sixty acres of land in the southeastern part of the city, laid out as only can be done by taste and money. The building has all the modern improvements. The great success this institution has had in the past few years is a pride to Jacksonville people. At present thirty patients are at this institution, and applications are often refused for want of room

The City Hospital continues its beneficent labors, the faithful, self-denying sisters remaining at their posts without any remitting of their work. About fifty-five unfortunates were received and cared for during the year 1884, most of whom have been sent away cured or much improved. The entertainment for the benefit of the institution given in February, 1884, when nearly a thousand dollars was realized, furnished most acceptable help at a time when it was much needed. To Drs. Passavant and W. H. H. King the beneficiaries of the hospital are under a lasting debt of gratitude for their cheerful, self-denying labors.

The Jacksonville Lyceum was organized October 25th, under the auspices of the Young Men's Christian Association. The object of the organization is for the social intercourse and intellectual development of the young men who may become its members.

The Anti-Horse Stealing Society under the able management of Alderman W. C. Carter, continues to be a terror to all evil-doers who would get a ride at the expense of honest men. The assessments have been small the past year, but the members have had the satisfaction of feeling that their valuable animals were in a measure protected.

Among the literary societies of Jacksonville is one, composed of the younger professional men, literati and merchants, called "The Round Table." During 1884 it held twenty-four meetings and discussed all conceivable subjects. The membership of the club is limited to twenty, the present number being sixteen During the year the club has lost one member, Frank I. McDonald, by death, and two, R. D. Russell and John G. Morrison, by reason of their removal from town; and within the same period, W. J. Bryan, J. R. Harker and Richard Yates have become members.

The Benefit Building Association, established in 1872, and its newer rival the Building and Loan Association, continue on in their good work.

The Young Men's Christian Association received and expended about $2,500 in 1884. It has maintained its regular weekly prayer meetings, lyceum and reading room, besides doing a great deal of missionary work. Its visitors have been many hundreds, and the books, papers and periodicals always to be found there, have been read by a large number of persons. Their building and its furnishing cost $14,000.

The most important event in the history of the Congregational church during the past twelve months was the celebration of its fiftieth birthday during the month of

December, 1883. An historical discourse was delivered by Dr. Sturtevant and the next day Rev. T. M. Post, D. D., a former pastor, preached to the people with whom he had once labored. Two evening services were held, in one of which the pastors of the other churches participated, and in the other special mention was made of some of the early members. The anniversary of the Sunday-school was also observed. The church and Sunday-school have sustained the loss of Mr. R. D. Russell, whose absence causes a vacancy not easily filled. Mr. Durfee and family have also removed to California. There have been fifteen accessions during the year and nine admissions by letter.

During the past year the Brooklyn M. E. church has parted with its former diligent pastor, Rev. David Gay, and has been exceptionally favored by receiving in his stead Rev. James Leaton, D. D. The present membership is 125, with the same number in the Sunday-school. There have been twenty accessions, two deaths and six baptisms of children. Improvements on the building, including a $300 bell, have been made at an expense of $1,200. For some time there has been a small debt owed by the church but it was recently discharged.

At the Christian church, on East State street, a most successful meeting was held in the month of March, 1884, by Prof. W. F. Black, of Tuscola, Ill., resulting in 140 additions. The present membership of the church is about 450. During the summer the church was without a settled pastor for some months. Elder A. N. Gilbert, of Maysville, Ky., accepted a call from the church and entered upon his duties the 1st of October. Elder Gilbert's popularity as a preacher is becoming known in the community and his audiences are increasing every week.

At the Church of Our Savior, Roman Catholic, from January 1st, 1884 to December, 1884, there were 58 baptisms, 34 funerals and 21 marriages. May 25, 1884, 114 persons received the Sacrament of Confirmation at the hands of Right Rev. P. J. Baltes, bishop of the diocese of Alton. There are 298 children enrolled at the Catholic school who are instructed by the Sisters of St. Dominic. Mother Josephine is superioress of the Dominican Sisters here and this is the mother house for the diocese of Alton. There are now branches from the mother house Jerseyville, Carrollton, Mt. Sterling and Beardstown. The school here is in a large three story brick building, containing four spacious rooms and two smaller class rooms. A fine hall occupies the top story, in which the society attached to the church meets and exhibitions are held.

The church has a seating accommodation for 800 persons. There is also standing room on the floor of the church and a large gallery. Two masses are celebrated every Sunday. The first at 8 and the second 10 o'clock a. m. At one of the masses all the seating space is occupied, and some persons are standing and many in the gallery. At the other mass the church is more than three-fourths full. Catechism at 2 and vespers at 3 o'clock p. m. The congregation owes only a little over $3,000.

There are two societies of ladies attached to the church. One the Altar Society, the other the Young Ladies' Sodality of the Blessed Virgin. Their object is to help one another by mutual prayer, and to supply the sacred vestments used at divine service. Besides the Young Men's Catholic Benevolent Society, and the Ancient Order of Hibernians, there is also attached to the church an Orphan Society, whose holy object is to provide for the orphans of the parish and get them good homes.

In a paragraph relating to the *Daily Journal*, on page 174 of this book, we discover, after that form has gone to press, that through carelessness we have not done full justice to the shrewd business management and editorial abilities of our old playmate, L. B. Glover, now of Chicago. The advertising, the business and the editorial departments of this office, and not the job-office only, were built up under his control. Perhaps there has been no equal period in the history of this paper, when it was developed more in every direction than from 1869 to 1874. He was young and inexperienced and of course made mistakes, but the business was built up in every department, the office was well equipped and the paper made itself felt in a number of important interests. One was the establishment of the city water works, another a high license campaign that reduced the number of saloons from 35 to 26. The advertising patronage more than doubled during his part-ownership.

Of all the business enterprises of our city, there are none more worthy of mention, than are the manufacturing interests, and we are only sorry that we have not more of them in our community. One of the most thriving of these is the Star Planing Mills, located on the northeast corner of West and Court streets. This institution was started two years ago by Messrs. Mathers, Buckingham & Ziegler, and ever since steam was first started in their engine, business has been booming with them. Their machinery is all of the most modern make—the very best that is now in use, and with the large force of skilled workmen they are enabled to turn out an immense amount of work in a day, and that too of a superior quality. The principal work turned out by these gentle man consists of sash, doors, blinds, frames, mouldings, stairs, railing, posts, balusters, scroll sawing, wood-turning, etc. While the work is turned out rapidly, all is first-class.

A similar establishment of long-standing and large business is that of Hugh Wilson, Esq., one of our most enterprising citizens and a leading contractor for the erection of buildings. His Steam Planing Mills, on North Main street, is a large brick building and one of the valuable institutions of the city.

In 1884, as in all other years, the angel of death was reaping among the sheaves of this field. Among those who have left us we note the names of Mrs. Jonas Scott, J. H. Self, Mrs. Hannah Fairbank, Mrs. Mary Henderson, John Goltra, Stephen Sutton, Wm. Wright, Sr., Joseph W. King, J. Neely, Judge James Berdan, Mrs. Ann Alexander, John S. Russel, Dr. Grant and of those formerly identified with this community, J. A. Willard, Mrs. Naomi Pierson, John Flack, Rev. C. G. Selleck and others; nor has the dark angel been content with calling away the aged, but many in the prime of life have been summoned as well. Loving hearts have been called on to part with John W. King, Frank I. McDonald, Miss Mary F. Allen, Hon. Richardson Vasey, Mrs. John N. Marsh and many beside.

The principal work of our city fathers in addition to their routine duties the past year has been the paving of a part of the square and short distances on East and West State streets and West Court street. It is to be regretted that the tax voted to pave the remainder of the square could not be legally levied, but we must endeavor to be grateful for the crust in the absence of the whole loaf.

Nearly 100,000,000 gallons of water have been raised for thirsty consumers, an amount which is liable to be increased in future years.

CENTENARY M. E. CHURCH ERECTED 1867

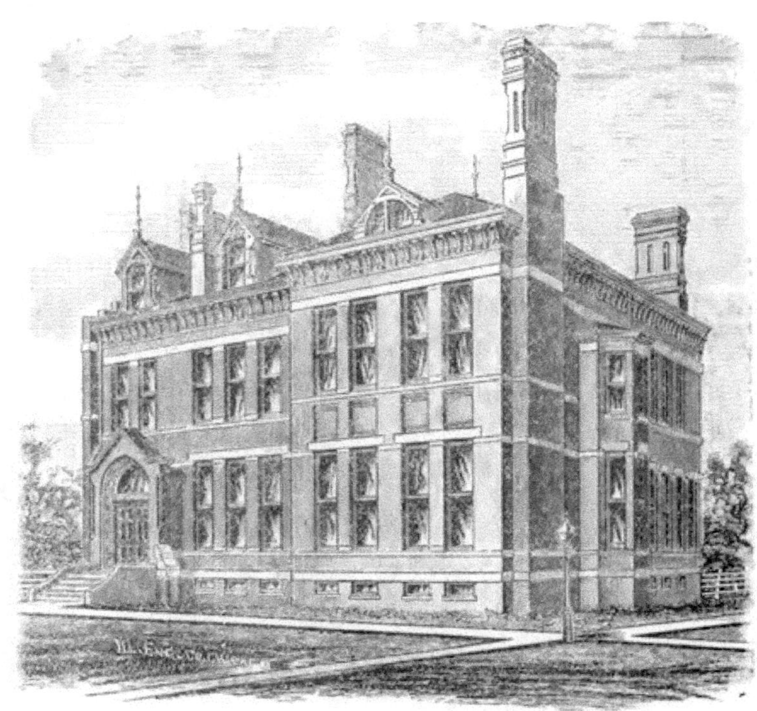

YOUNG MEN'S CHRISTIAN ASSOCIATION BUILDING.

Dedicated October 13th, 1881. Dimensions 60 by 60 feet. Cost $14,000.

CHAPTER XIII.

Composed of a Series of Appendices—The Kelloggs and their Cabin—Postal Facilities in the Thirties—David Manchester's Life—Death of Dr. Willard with a Sketch of his Life—Reminiscences of 1837 by Miss Fayerweather—First things by Anderson Foreman—History of the Baptist Church—Roll of Honor of Old Settlers—The Pioneer Sewing Society—Its Benevolent Work—The Jacksonville Library—Mere Mention Graphic Sketch of Judge John Leeper—Coming West Fifty Years Ago—A few Manufacturing Interests—School Matters in 1833—Correction of Errors, by Dr. Sturtevant and the Compiler.

OWING to the placing in the compiler's hands of documents and letters relating to periods of local history after the chapters covering the same time had gone to press he is moved to close the volume with a salmagundi chapter, consisting of a series of disconnected articles or collections of items as follows:

First.—THE KELLOGGS' CABIN IN 1819 AND THE SUBSEQUENT HISTORY OF THESE PIONEERS.

We are permitted to make the following extracts from a private letter to Mr. Timothy Chamberlain, written from Golete, Santa Barbara county, California, by Florentine Erwin Kellogg, a grandson of Elisha Kellogg, who, with his brother Seymour, built the first white man's home in Morgan:

You ask me to pen some of my early remembrances of times, persons and things, connected with the early settlement of our family in Morgan county, Ill., as my father and uncle were the first to settle in Morgan county. I was quite young then, but still I remember very well some of the earliest settlers, who came in soon after the families of my father and uncle, who were the first. They left the State of New York in the spring of 1818, and came down the rivers, Albany and Ohio, in a flat boat of their own construction, with their families and their few earthly goods; and after many weeks of hardships and dangers were landed at Shawneetown, near where the Ohio joins the Mississippi. Here we bought four yoke of oxen and two wagons, and went to a small town called Carmi.

We stopped at this place until the spring of the next year, when we again started north. After many delays and stops at several places we finally came to a halt in what is now Morgan county. About the 1st of September, 1819, we encamped on the head of Mauvaisterre creek about ten miles east of the city of Jacksonville, that is where it now is, but it did not look much like a city at that time. Our nearest neighbors were thirty miles away upon Spring creek, near Springfield, where Sangamon county now is. While occupying our first camp in Morgan county, one afternoon about 3 o'clock, while my father and uncle were out looking for a suitable place to build a house, we saw the prairie fire coming with great rapidity towards the camp. That morning my father had burned off a small piece of ground, about an acre in size, just to please the children, and into this my mother, aunt and the children carried the goods of our camp, and then rolled in the two wagons, just in time to escape the flames which encircled us on all sides, and for a time almost suffocated us with smoke. Very soon after the fire had passed away my father and uncle came hurrying to camp, almost frantic with apprehension for what might have been the fate of the families, but found us all safe, though somewhat frightened. The near approach of winter made us hurry up a cabin, and soon we were as comfortable as circumstances would permit. Away from neighbors and far from any place where we could get anything to supply our many wants, we had to go ninety miles down to Edwardsville for corn, and then take it home and pound it in the hominy block; then boil and eat it, with water for sauce and little else. Only once in a while our Indian neighbors would give us a piece of meat. My father and uncle were not hunters. If they had been we could have lived much better; and they did not even have a gun, save a small shotgun, with which we sometimes succeeded in getting squirrels, and they were a luxury in more ways than one. The squirrel made nice food and the skin was seized upon by the nearest of the children and drawn over the foot, where it did good service as both stockings and shoes, as we had no others. During this winter there came to our house three men: one was Dr. Roe, who is supposed by some to be the first settler of Morgan county; but he was later by nearly one year than my father; one was Thomas Beard, who afterwards settled where Beardstown now is, the other was Billy Robinson, the old bee and deer hunter. These were the first white men we saw after we settled here. One year afterwards my father sold his property to Mr. Slattern and moved three miles northwest of where Jacksonville now is. Here my uncle also settled. About this time or a little later, there came others and settled not far away. James Deaton and Abram Johnson, and still later Judge Aaron Wilson and Isaac Reeve, who had the first blacksmith shop that I can remember. Geo. Hackett came and put up a small store. James Deaton built a small horse mill to run with a raw-hide band twisted around the spindle. We now entered upon an era of comfort, and thought we were able to have a school. My father, I think, taught the first school in the county; we also had a Sunday school at Uncle Jimmy Deaton's. Stephen Corban, John Carpenter, Mr. Hibbard, Moses Carlock, Benjamin Spartzen and others now came in; also Adam Allison and the Holidays. About this time Jacksonville came into being as a town; with Rearick, Rockwell, Cobbs, Carson, Taylor and others. The first nurse was Mrs. Carson; I remember she was a lady with kind feelings.

Our first article of export from Morgan county was cotton. My father and uncle made a large canoe, or perogue as they were called, and ran the freight down to St. Louis, all joining together. About this time the lead mines of Galena were beginning to attract attention and my father started in the midst of winter, with his team loaded with feed, and drove the first team ever driven to Galena; and eventually sold out his place in Morgan to a man by the name of Isaac Dial. Finally in the spring of 1832 he moved up to Jo Daviess county, again on the frontier, twelve miles from the nearest neighbors. Here I lived for thirteen years; the place became thickly settled, I was a man grown and married the daughter of Elias Williams, of old Morgan county.

My father died and again I felt the pioneer spirit stir me for a newer country. And in 1846, or 38 years ago, I left Illinois for the still farther west. I started with two teams of oxen and a double buggy to carry my wife and babies. After braving the wild, mountainous country, filled with wild beasts and still wilder Indians, for seven months I finally reached Napa Valley, Cal. Again I was in a country wild enough to rejoice the heart of any true pioneer; here I found nature in her primitive grandeur and beauty; and unlike my father and uncle when they came to Illinois, when I came to California I did not come without my trusty hunting rifle and with the hunter knowledge to use it. It was my living here. It brought me my meat, shoes and clothes for a long time. The mountains were full of elk, deer, grizzly bears and other game and I enjoyed this hunter's paradise for many years. Every Saturday I went to the mountains to get my supply of meat for the ensuing week. I have killed seventy-five grizzly bears, and deer without number; have seen elk by the thousand in droves and as many as 154 deer at one sight in one place. So you see I consider myself a pioneer in the fullest sense. But this is now the most thickly settled country in which I ever lived and I can scarcely tell where to turn to find another new country to go to. I expect I shall have to be content nere the balance of my life. My health is excellent; I can still do my share in the hunt. Last year in one of our hunts we got nine deer and one bear. But I must stop, though I have not told you a tithe of my frontier experience. I would like to attend one of the Old Settlers' meetings, but hardly expect that of all things; I don't see it clear to do so now, and so I will bid you good-bye, asking to be kindly remembered.

Second—MAIL FACILITIES IN 1832. MEMORIAL TO CONGRESS ON THE SUBJECT.

The following article taken from the *Illinois Patriot*, formerly published in Jacksonville, of the date of February 23d, 1832, is of interest in itself, and gives a vivid suggestion of the growth of the state and the wonderfully increased means and facilities of communication since that period:

The following letter was received by a gentleman of this town

QUINCY, February 23d, 1832.

SIR:—The undersigned, a committee of correspondence appointed by a meeting of the citizens of Quincy, take the liberty to enclose to you a copy of their proceedings, hoping that your citizens cannot fail to perceive the interest they have in co-operating with us. We understand that the inhabitants of Jacksonville have petitioned the postmaster general upon the same subject. But believing as we do that he has no power to establish such mail routes as these, we thought it better to apply at once to the press. We respectfully request that you will procure the enclosed copy to be inserted in the paper in your town, and that you will use your influence to get up a public meeting in Jacksonville to take into consideration the propriety of petitioning Congress on the same subject. If it shall be inconvenient for you to bestow your personal attention upon this matter, we request that you will at least interest some of your personal friends to take the matter in hand. We have the honor to be your obedient servants.

JAMES H. RALSTON,
THOMAS FORD,
ROBERT TILSON.

A meeting of the citizens of Quincy was held on the 11th day of February, 1832, when Adolphus F. Hubbard was appointed chairman and William G. Flood secretary. On motion

Resolved, That the chairman appoint a committee of fifteen members to draft a memorial to Congress on the subject of the mails to and from this place.

Whereupon the chairman appointed Thomas Ford, —— Williams, Robert Tilson, Earl Pierce, O. H. Browning, Levi Wells, George Taylor, W. G. Flood, J. H. Ralston, E. L. Pierson, J. M. Higbee, Arthur Anderson, H. H. Snow, E. S. Freeman and D. G. Whitney. On motion

Ordered, That this meeting adjourn until the 13th inst., at 2 o'clock.

MONDAY, February 13.

The meeting convened pursuant to adjournment and Thomas Ford, from the committee appointed on Saturday, reported the following memorial:

To the Honorable Senate and House of Representatives of the United States Congress assembled:

Your memorialists, citizens of the town of Quincy, state of Illinois, in public meeting convened, respectfully represent:

That the transportation of the mail to and from this place is arranged in a manner exceedingly inconvenient. That there is no direct mail to or from any place, but Montebell and others, two of the least considerable points with which we have communication. The great mail from Vandalia, by which alone we receive our eastern and most of our southern intelligence, is so arranged as to come by Springfield, Jacksonville, Carrollton and Atlas, making a distance of two hundred and forty miles. The distance on a straight line, by Hillsboro and Jacksonville, is only one hundred and sixty miles, and the mail might be transported on that route in four days; whereas on the route now established nine days are required.

Your memorialists further represent that the town of Quincy has lately grown into considerable importance, and is improving with unusual rapidity. It contains about eight hundred inhabitants, is the seat of justice of a county containing upwards of three thousand, and is the principal place of deposit for a large district of country. Also a land office where considerable business transacted. The town of Rushville contains about six hundred inhabitants, and is about forty-six miles east of this. With that place we have no mail communication except by way of Atlas, Gilead, Carrollton, Jacksonville, Job's and Beardstown, making a circuit of two hundred miles and requiring near two weeks to accomplish the route. With Lewiston, Peoria and Galesburg we have no communication except by a route equally inconvenient and circuitous.

Your memorialists further represent that the town of Palmyra, in the state of Missouri, is situated eighteen miles west. To that place there is no mail except by way of Atlas, Louisiana and New London, making a circuit of more than a hundred miles, and requiring ten days for transportation. Our principal commercial intercourse is with the city of St. Louis, from which place the mail is brought by way of Bowling Green, New London, Palmyra, Louisiana and Atlas. At the latter place it is permitted to remain six days before it is conveyed to Quincy. By establishing a route from Palmyra here, we would receive intelligence from St. Louis and the greater part of Missouri, seven days sooner than by the present arrangement.

Your memorialists represent that the arrangement of the mails for the military tract in the state of Illinois is a real grievance to all its inhabitants, requiring the speedy interposition of Congress. That the country north of the Illinois River is organized into eleven counties, and by a reference to the late census, it will be perceived that it contained in 1830 seventeen thousand. This whole region is nearly destitute of mail privileges. The alterations herein suggested could be made, not only without injury, but with profit to the post office department, inasmuch as the revenue of the single office at Quincy amounts to four hundred dollars annually, and would much increase if we enjoyed more facilities of mail communication.

We earnestly solicit the attention of congress to the subject of this memorial, and therefore pray your honorable bodies will establish a mail route from this place direct to Vandalia by way of Jacksonville and Hillsboro; also a route to Peoria by way of Rushville and Lewiston; and a route to Palmyra in Missouri. On motion,

Resolved, That the memorial be adopted.

Resolved, That James H. Ralston, Thomas Ford and Robert Tilson be a committee of correspondence, and that they open a correspondence with citizens of such places as may be interested in the objects of the meeting.

Resolved, That the proceedings of this meeting be signed by the chairman and secretary, and a copy thereof be transmitted to each of our members of congress.

ADOLPHUS F. HUBBARD, Chairman.
WILLIAM G. FLOOD, Secretary.

Now, in Jacksonville, there are more than a dozen daily mails received and forwarded. During the twelve months, ending March 31, 1878, the number of mails received daily, was fifteen, the same number being dispatched. Number of letters mailed during same time, 510,000, and the number received was 540,000. The receipts from the sale of stamps and envelopes was $16,000; number of money orders issued being 4,940, amounting to $45,000; number of money orders paid 7,890, amounting to $65,000. The number of letters registered was 875.

As to the business of the Jacksonville postoffice for the year 1884 we are indebted to Postmaster Gordon for the following information: Number of money orders issued 10,681, postal notes 1,500; money order business, paying and receiving, amounts to an average of about $500 per diem. The receipts for stamps and envelopes $18,000. Number of mails received daily 13, and sent out 15; pieces of mail matter letters and papers going out *over one million*. Letters and packages sent out as registered matter 1,610. Number received or handled in transit 2,701. Total number handled 4,311

Third—ONE OF THE EARLY SETTLERS—DAVID MANCHESTER.

One of the county's earliest settlers, David Manchester, was born by the side of Lake George, in Warren county, N. Y., in 1798. As soon as he was old enough he engaged in the lumber business and often went to Quebec, Canada, with lumber and brought back groceries, etc. When about twenty-one years old he left home and went to Fort Du Quoin, in Pennsylvania, bought a skift and rowed alone to Shawnetown then went on foot from there to St. Louis and worked in a liverystable four months for $5 per month, when he came to this county with less than one dollar, and settled where he now lives. Times were hard then; provision scarce and no money in the country. He split over 500 rails for a pair of shoes, very poor ones at that. The leather was tanned in a trough, and the hair not one-half removed, and to get clothes he raised cotton which he took to Beardstown and traded for cloth.

They suffered very much in the winter of 1830 from the deep snow. It commenced snowing in November and snowed steadily forty days and nights in succession. They were forced to dig the corn out of the snow and dry it by the fire when they took it to Hall's Mill, where they had it ground. The only road they had was a sort of Indian trail and once when he and his brother-in-law had been to mill, his horse stepped from the path, and it was several hours before they could get him back, and get home; and they were nearly frozen when they got home. He was a fifer in the war of 1812 under General Strong, and Captain Spencer, thirty days, saw the battle of Plattsburg and thinks that our victory was owing to a quarrel between two English Generals; was through the Black Hawk War and was chief musician of Colonel Ewing's spy battallion with Captain Lindsay, and discharged from service by Major Anderson of Ft. Sumpter fame. While in this campaign he often saw Gen. Taylor, Jefferson Davis and A. Lincoln and was under the the immediate command of Gen. Atkinson. Enlisted as musician under Gen. Hardin to go to the Mexican War. Went as far as Alton and was taken sick, and sent back to Jacksonville where he was discharged, but was in the campaign against the Mormons. At the time he came here there were very few white people here, and the Indians were encamped all around here but they were friendly.

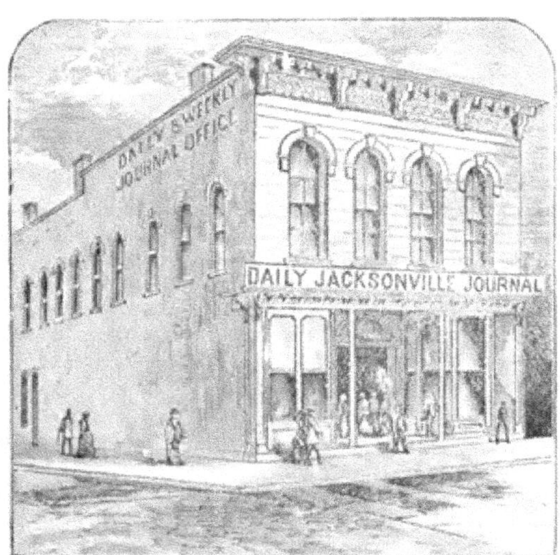

THE JOURNAL OFFICE, 1877-'85. See page 201.

EAST STATE STREET.

Fourth.—A PIONEER ABOLITIONIST OF MORGAN. SKETCH OF MR. WILLARD'S LIFE.

In September, 1884, the venerable J. A. Willard died at the advanced age of 91 years at the home of his son Samuel Willard, M. D., in Chicago. Mr. Willard will be remembered by many of the early settlers of this county as one, who, with his son above mentioned, stood up so fearlessly for the cause of human rights in the perilous times described in Chapter VIII.

Mr. Willard had a varied career during his life, but leaves a fragrant memory. Coming from Vermont at an early day he first located at Carrollton, Ill., but soon after went to Alton. While there he made the acquaintance of the sainted Lovejoy and at one time defended him with his gun from a furious mob. Soon after 1837 he removed to this place and engaged in the dry goods business, keeping up his efforts in the cause of freedom.

In 1843, while assisting a fugitive slave to escape, he was arrested and hardly treated, narrowly escaping the vengeance of the mob. He waived trial, carrying his case to the Supreme Court, and losing it there. Nothing daunted he continued to be a station agent of the "underground railroad," where he did good service in helping fugitive slaves to escape. He became so disgusted with the indifference and opposition of the church in the cause of human rights that he withdrew in 1840, and never renewed his membership. In 1845 he removed to Quincy, returning to Alton in 1850. Under Buckmaster he became clerk of the penitentiary. In 1864 he quit active work, and moved to Springfield, busying himself with his garden and poultry. In 1871 he came to Chicago and lived with his son till his death. He lost his wife in October, 1875. At the first appearance of spiritualism he began to take an interest in that phenomenon, and in his last years he was as energetic in spiritualism as he had been in the church. He passed away full of hope, rejoicing to go, feeling that his warfare was accomplished and his work done.

Dr. Thomas of Chicago, at the funeral, referred to the services of Mr. Willard in the cause of the oppressed negro, when to do so was to court social ostracism. A man of that calibre could not be forced to say he believed what he did not belie~e. Grand old Lyman Beecher was of the same stock. He would not change a chapter in his history had he the power. He stood with the Lovejoys, the Lincolns, Garrisons and Phillipses.

Fifth.—SOME REMINISCENCES OF EARLY TIMES BY MARY JANE FAYERWEATHER.

JACKSONVILLE, OCT. 6th, 1884.

Sir:—I have thought you might be interested in the following statement for your History of Jacksonville: I came to Jacksonville in June, 1837. At my home in the east, not far from New York City, I had some greenhouse plants. Desiring to bring them with me to my new home, I employed a skillful gardener to pack them. Of the geraniums there were the rose, beefsteak, nutmeg, silverleaf, horseshoe, &c.; the passion flower, coral honeysuckle, calacanthus or sweet-shrub, mountain daisy, &c., were in the collection. I was told by friends that called, these were the first greenhouse plants brought to Jacksonville. I did not bring the flower-pots, and thoroughly hunted at all the stores in the town for them and could not find one, I believed it was true; the best I could do was to purchase some "milk crocks," and with a gimlet pierce a hole in the bottom and use pie plates for saucers. The plants all lived and thrived finely. In the next two years I am unable to tell how many slips I cut and gave away. A young lady friend from the Jacksonville Academy, dubbed the rose geranium the "Patriarch." The coral honeysuckle and calacanthus in Dr. Sturtevant's yard are descendants from some of the original plants. In hunting for flower pots I was informed several times that there was a pottery in Winchester, if I would send an order describing the article I wanted, I might receive some in a month or so. We also brought a colored girl, about 12 years old, who was bound to my sister, (now Mrs. J. H. Chamberlain,) who, with my brother, James R. Fayerweather, was laid under bonds of $1,000 that she should never become an expense to the State of Illinois. The girl died in 1845.

Sixth.—FIRST THINGS IN JACKSONVILLE, ACCORDING TO MR. ANDERSON FOREMAN.

John Eads first blacksmith.
John Handy first carpenter.
Joseph Meeker first tin-shop.
Richard Nelson first rope walk.
Tolbert Hite the first shoe shop.
Orsen Cobbs the first tailor shop.
Frank Reed the first silver-smith.
Mr. Hardwick the first bake shop.
Murray McConnel the first lawyer.
George Rearick kept the first store.
Thomas Carson kept the first tavern.
Mr. Terry first Windsor chair maker.
Caleb Breech the first carriage shop.
George Hackett had the first tan-yard.
The first blacksmith—Isaac Reeve, Sr.
Samuel Vanpelt made the first pumps.
John Henry kept the first cabinet shop.
Andy Newcomb first spinning wheel wright.
Sinclair & March manufactured spun cotton.
John P. Wilkinson built the first brick house.
Parkinson & Miller first wool-carding machine.
Thomas J. Starr first stationed Methodist minister.
The first school teacher—Judge Wm. Thomas, 1826.
The first ground was broken for cultivation in 1820.
James V. Hedenberg first manufactured linseed oil.
Smiley H. Henderson took out first license to sell whisky.
The first female born here was Mrs. Ellen Conn *nee* Rearick.
The first male born in Jacksonville was Archibald W. Carson.
The first man to plant a crop of corn was John Reeves in 1824.
The first sermon was preached by Rev. John Glanville in 1822.
The first church was organized in 1822 in Father Jordan's cabin.
The first circuit court was held by Judge Reynolds in April, 1823.
The first male child born in the city and now living here Wm. Rockwell.
The first white settlers in the county—Seymour and Elisha Kellogg, 1819.
The first marriage in Jacksonville was John Smith to Deborah Thornton.
The first to die in county was Isaac Fort Roe; first in the city Daniel Ditson.
Lorenzo Dow preached on the ground where the Rataichak Hotel now stands, in 1830.

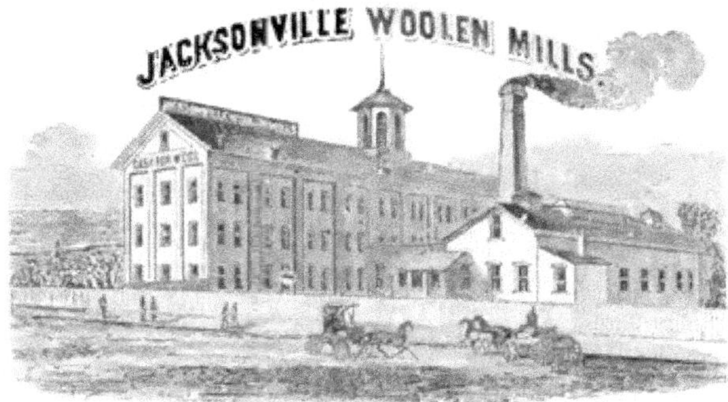

WOOLEN MILLS OF JOS. CAPPS & SONS. See pages 187-8.

Seventh.—HISTORY OF THE FIRST BAPTIST CHURCH OF JACKSONVILLE FROM 1841 TO 1884.

The Jacksonville Baptist Church was constituted June 1st, 1841, at the house of M. C. Goltra, lately deceased, who was one of its constituent members. Rev. Alvin Bailey served as pastor for six years, from its organization; the first two and a half years of which he preached two Sabbaths each month, after that every Sabbath. Its first house of worship was dedicated in 1845.

Rev. W. F. Boyakin assumed pastoral care of the church Jan. 1st, 1849, remaining with the church for one year. In June, 1851, Rev. A. J. Bingham took charge of the church and continued a year and a half. During his ministry, Rev. Jacob Knapp held a protracted meeting of six weeks, as the result of which, nearly one hundred persons united with the church, few of whom proved to be permanent members.

On the 1st of April, 1854, Rev. G. W. Pendleton entered upon his labor as pastor of the church, and continued until 1858, when W. S. Goodno became pastor, serving two years. Dedicated new house of worship at a cost of $15,000, April 9 1858. In 1862, Rev. W. T. Nelson, and in 1863, Rev. Wm. G. Pratt served as pastor, one year each. In 1865, S. A. Kingsberry settled as pastor and continued to serve the church for three years. In May, 1868, Rev. Wm. Green entered upon the pastorate of the church and remained two years. Rev. S. Washington became pastor of the church, November, 1869, and served five years, until 1874. Rev. Hugh S. Marshall served as pastor from October, 1875, to October, 1876. Rev. M. T. Lamb served as pastor from 1877, to July 10, 1879. Rev. C. C. Pierce supplied the church from Oct. 1st, 1879, until February, 1883, when he resigned as pastor. Rev. B. F. Simpson was his successor until 1884.

Eighth—PERSONALITIES—PRESIDENT BATEMAN, MISSIONARY EDDY.

Jacksonville was honored in 1860 and again in 1862 and 1864 by the election of Prof. Bateman as State Superintendent of Public Instruction. His boyhood and early manhood had been spent here, where he was graduated from Illinois College, and where he was principal of one of the public schools and temporarily of the Jacksonville Female Academy.

Newton Bateman, LL. D., for eight years Superintendent of Public Instruction, did more than any other man for our noble system of public schools, and is now the second of the graduates of Illinois College to become president of Knox College. But space will not permit even the mere mention of names to show how much the college has done to make Illinois what it is. The good work already accomplished would amply repay its friends for all their labors and self-sacrifice in its behalf.

William Eddy, son of a former pastor in the First Presbyterian Church, is now Rev. Wm. Eddy, D. D., professor of the college in Beiroot, Syria, and editor of a paper there; and his son, William King Eddy, is also a missionary of the Presbyterian board in Sidon, Syria. his daughter, Harriet M. Eddy, a teacher of the girls school there.

William Ireland also of Jacksonville has been in Africa, as missionary of the American board, a long time.

Ninth—Roll of Honor—Half Century or More in Morgan.

The following named present residents of Morgan county have lived here for a half century or more, the figures attached to their names indicating the year of their arrival or birth here. There are many more names, and we should have been glad to have had them sent in, in order that the list might be made complete.

J. T. Taylor, 1833.
A. J. Ausemus, 1842.
Sarah J. Anderson, 1831.
William Gordon, 1832.
J. C. Spires, 1830.
J. S. Wenkle, 1830.
Ellen McClusky, 1832.
Mrs. Fannie Hunt, 1831.
Howard Turley, 1830.
C. Ferguson, 1832.
R. Y. Park, 1831.
Mrs. S. E. F. Barnes, 1830.
G. Gainer, 1830.
Mrs. S. E. Johnson, 1831.
Mrs. Wm. Hamilton, 1831.
Frank Patterson, 1830.
Spencer Taylor.
William D. Humphrey.
Col. George M. Chambers.
Isaac D. Rawlings.
James S. Anderson, 1830.
Mrs. George Richards.
Mrs. Cornelius Hook.
Mrs. John Lawson.
Smiley H. Henderson.
Mrs. Eliza B. Ayers.
Mrs. Joseph Cassell.
B. F. Gass, 1833.
James H. Lurton, 1832.
A. C. Patterson, 1830.
Judge H. G. Whitlock, 1831.
William Groves, 1830.
Mrs. P. W. Vail, 1825.
Mrs. Mary Barr, 1830.
M. C. Pond, 1831.
Stephen S. Tunnel, 1830.
George W. Hackett, 1833.
John T. Henry, 1830.
J. H. Self, 1831.
James Wood, 1827.
L. D. Graham, 1830.
Mrs. W. A. Park, 1831.
Joseph Fry, 1831.
John W. Lathrop, 1830.
Marshal P. Ayers, 1830.
Mrs. Matthew Ashelby, 1832.
Mrs. Mary Campbell.
John Jordan.
Rev. Charles B. Barton.
Timothy Chamberlain.
Anderson Foreman.
Mrs. S. Wiswall.
Mrs. E. T. Miller.
Mrs. Robert Cassell.
Mrs. C. B. Barton.
Mrs. John Gorham.
Mrs. Dr. M. M. L. Reed.
Mrs. Hiram Smedley.
Mrs. Rachel King, 1831.
Mrs. E. Lawson, 1833.
David M. Simmons, 1830.
Rev. J. M. Sturtevant, 1829.
James P. Young, 1830.
Mrs. Mary Hinrichsen, 1825.
Eliza J. Johnson, 1832.
Mrs. V. H. Ferguson, 1833.
Henry Rudisil, 1833.
Mary A. Langley, 1832.
John L. Dawson, 1832.
David M. Bryant, 1833.
W. T. Spires, 1831.
Samuel Sinclair, 1833.
William H. Wright, 1832.
Thomas M. Angelo, 1831.
Henry M. Park, 1831.
Augustus E. Ayers, 1830.
J. W. Graham, 1833.
Capt. Wm. Patterson, 1829.
Ira Mapes.
Robert T. Cassell.
Stephen H. Reed.
Prof. J. B. Turner, 1833.
Mrs. George D. Rearick.
Mrs. Benjamin Humphrey.
Mrs. George M. Chambers.
Mrs. Susan Rapp.
Mrs. Joseph Capps.
Judge William Thomas, 1826.
Rev. Peter Akers, 1832.
John R. Loar, 1833.
Milton Mayfield, 1830.
F. M. Springer, 1833.
Matthew Stacy.

SULKY PLOW WORKS AND THOMPSON'S FOUNDRY

Tenth—WOMENS' WORK.—A PIONEER BENEVOLENT AND INDUSTRIAL ASSOCIATION.

(Official Records.)

As the Jacksonville Sewing Society was the first organization of the ladies in Jacksonville, and as most of the efforts, that have succeeded, have *originated* in and through the sewing society, it is proposed that a regular history of the events, as they occurred, be written and embodied for preservation in the fourteenth report of the Jacksonville Sewing Society.

It may be thought that so trifling and common an occurrence as the formation of a sewing society, is not worth the mention and detail here given to it, also the account here given of the formation of other societies: but we would ask you to remember that this organization has claims that none other in the state of Illinois can have. We believe it to be the first female organization; we know it to be the first that exerted any influence on the state, and extended has that influence been in favor of education, female enterprise, and active efforts.

A notice having been given by the Rev. J. M. Ellis, the Jacksonville Sewing Society was organized the 10th day of August, 1830, in the log school house in the southeast quarter of town, the only meeting house in the place. Materials of different kinds, collars, infant dresses, handsome needle-work, partly done, were brought from Philadelphia, the remains of a sewing society there, and was the commencement of the sewing society here.

Present at the formation. Mesdames Ellis, Taylor, Hackett, Ayers, Misses R. Barton, Leonard.

The two objects recognized in the constitution, viz: "To assist in the building of a Presbyterian Church," and the education of "poor and pious youth." (The second object being changed some years after to "the cause of education,") were not the prominent objects for which the society was formed. It was designed as a central point, where we might plan and purpose and agree to execute.

The antagonist of all that is good knowing our designs, that we were laying foundations for the future, that would defeat his purposes, and a sewing society being a new thing to many, we were subjected to much ridicule from the gentleman here, and also from the editor of the Springfield paper; but the name of John P. Wilkinson should stand here, as one who at the first suggestion, encouraged and aided, and whose last social hours were spent with us. This ridicule soon passed away, and these gentlemen became regular attendants at our meetings. This society was truly Catholic in its spirit. October 1st, 1831, we find the following resolution: "That the funds of the society be appropriated yearly to the payment of the tuition bills, of the six beneficiaries now in Illinois College." One of these was a Baptist, another the lamented Borien of the M. E. church. This was the first responsibility assumed by the ladies, only one year after the formation of the society, we pledged ourselves, for the time of four or five years, for the tuition bills of the six beneficiaries then in Illinois College. This was not presumptuously done, *we* knew, *we* felt our weakness, and the opposition and ridicule, that we might have to contend with; but we designed to test a principle for future operations. May we not go forward trusting in God, was the question, and when the resolution was offered by one whose voice was soon heard no more among us, Mrs. Julia Wolcott, the response was unanimous, we will; we did go forward, and fulfilled our pledge. One of the six was soon rejected by the American Education Society. We then divided equally: Mr. Borien did not go through, we then added room-rent to tuition bills, for the remaining four who graduated.

December of 1831, a resolution was passed by the sewing society, to address letters to the different towns, Hillsboro, Edwardsville, Collinsville on the subject of education, in behalf of the American Education Society, see letter No. I, and we presume it is not saying too much, to say that it was the first time that the claims of that society had been presented. St. Louis also was written to. The question may here be asked, why those towns so distant and those with which we have now so much intercourse passed by? Those towns with which we have now so much intercourse were not. An unbroken prairie excepting Carrollton lay between us and St. Louis, only a house where the town of Manchester, Jerseyville, Monticello and Alton are now located; Springfield on the east much older than Jacksonville, Quincy on the west somewhat older, Rushville an infant town on the north; here we must stop, as much of the northern part of the state was in possession of the Indians, and the Indian War, the following summer, all of us who were here at that time well remember.

As the avails of the Jacksonville Sewing Society, eight hundred dollars paid to Illinois College for the students, one hundred and ninety-two dollars for female education, thirty-six dollars for furniture for Jacksonville Presbyterian Church, total one thousand and twenty-eight dollars, was always pledged to students or objects named and specified, consequently what was done for other students and the cause of education, was not reported to the sewing society, and was the result of individual effort.

The first subscription made by the ladies in Jacksonville, was a few months after the formation of this sewing society, a paper was passed and each lady subscribed one dollar for an infant school apparatus, the expense to us was sixteen dollars and seventy-five cents, a donation being obtained in Philadelphia to make it complete, a school was for a long time successfully taught here.

November, 1831.—The agent of the American Bible Society, Rev. Solomon Hardy, one of the first ministers in the state, suggested to a member of the sewing society, the propriety of forming a female Bible society, which he did, and having presented the subject, they agreed to meet at the residence of J. P. Wilkinson, for the purpose of forming a society. The Jacksonville Female Bible Society was then organized, whose efficient operations have been continued until the present time. See annual report.

In 1832, a Juvenile Sewing Society was formed by Mrs. C. Baldwin, which continued until they were no longer juvenile. As the ladies through whose influence these things had thus far progressed, looked over the unbroken prairies, on the north, south, east and west, it took no prophetic eye, emigration pouring in as it then was, to see the use of town and cities as they now are, or rather have been, and as those ladies, whose motive and object in coming to the west was simply to do good, were so scattered in consequence of the sparseness of the towns as they then were, it was thought advisable, by consultation at the sewing society, to get together at college commencement, all the ladies from abroad and confer with them, on the formation of an association, the object of which should be to devise plans of usefulness, adapted to a new and rising state. After conference with the ladies they met at the house of Rev. J. M. Ellis, August, 1832, and there formed an association for said object, present Mesdames Baldwin, Ayers, Misses Abiah Chapin, Laura Hitchcock, Elizabeth Wolcott. The plan of usefulness devised, was the Female Education Society, by Mrs. C. Baldwin, and after much consultation was formed in 1833, in the Female Academy, standing on the lot owned by the Jacksonville Presbyterian Church, present Mesdames Baldwin, Ayers, Misses S. Crocker, A. Ellis, Fowler, C. Leonard. For the operations of this society, see printed reports.

June, 1833, by conference with ladies at sewing society the Maternal Association was formed at the house of Rev. J. M. Ellis, as it is now, see records.

May, 1834.—"Trustees having been elected in 1831 for a Female Academy," they commenced building the east wing, so embarrassed were they for funds, that they were roofing a one-story building, a delay of twelve hours was asked for by a lady, with proposals for a second story, when she received the amount of four hundred dollars which was pledged to the trustees in behalf of the ladies. In consequence of the change a second contract was made, and the whole amount paid for second story by the ladies, was five hundred and eighty-eight dollars; two hundred and twenty was collected in Jacksonville from the ladies, and thirty from students in Illinois College; forty-two was received by Mrs. Baldwin from the east, by Mrs. Crocker from the east twenty-five, the remaining two hundred and seventy-one dollars by Mrs. Beecher from the east. Expended for beds and pillows, $156; for bedding and table cloths, $40.75; a donation of

Expended for beds and pillows, $107; for bedding and table-cloths, $40.65; a donation of apparatus, $36; Paid for second story, $588; for apparatus, $60. Total, $831.65.

February 18th, 1837, the Sewing Society resolved that the funds for that year be appropriated to the improvement of the lot of the Female Academy; also painting and white-washing the building; the expense of which was one hundred and twelve dollars. A resolution the same year was passed to pay fifty dollars for rent owed by the trustees, as they had no funds. Total for that year $162. Whole amount paid by the ladies $1,002.65.

1835.—When the ladies in New York pledged themselves to the American Tract Society for a given amount; we received a circular from them; a subscription was taken at the Sewing Society, the amount of $70 forwarded to New York.

1836.—A circular received, subscription taken at the Sewing Society—the amount of $80 forwarded to New York.

1835.—The first class graduated in Illinois College, two in number, these studied law; one had been assisted by the Sewing Society through college course.

1836.—Second class, four in number, three of these had been assisted through preparatory and college course by the Sewing Society; they designed themselves for the ministry. Assistance was offered to one of the class for the three, to cancel their debts, which were heavy, that they might pursue their theological studies if assistance could be obtained. Twenty dollars was given each one of them to defray their expenses to Lane Seminary—clothing, bedding and books to the amount of $100—a pledge also given that the debt of $180 should be paid to college within one year; one of these was carried through Lane Seminary, amounting in all to $460.

1838.—Fourth class, one of these, being needy, received the amount of $25 through Miss Phebe Adams.

1840.—Sixth class—six of these being destitute, were ready to pursue their theological course if assistance could be given them. One received a new suit of clothing, cost $40; another $40 cash; five $25 cash each to defray their expenses to the seminary; clothing to the amount of $200, in all $405.

In 1840-'41 assistance was given by the Sewing Society to three of this class. See minutes of Sewing Society. 1843.—Two of this class received cash $82, clothing to the amount of $30, in all $112. Total $1,002.

It should here be distinctly stated that this is but a part of what has been done by individuals not reported to any organization for the students of Illinois College. It must be but a small proportion as all stated above, with the exception of the $25 by Miss P. Adams has passed through the hands of one individual, and had been preserved—very much has been indefinitely known to the writer, but as no statement could be made with a certainty of its being correct, prefer that none should be made.

Dec. 1844, an invitation was given to the ladies of the Jacksonville Presbyterian Church, to meet at the house of David B. Ayers to confer on matters of interest to the church. Present, Mesdames Fairbank, Mayhew, Buckley, Eames, Kerr, Ayers, Ayers and Miss E. Adams.

The object of the meeting was stated, that it had appeared in the providence of God, that the time had come for us to arise and assist in building a house for the Lord; that the house that we now occupied could not be used much longer. *Comfortable*, it never had been, as it was built of unseasoned timber and designed only for a temporary building, (1830.) fourteen years ago. The floor soon shrunk, and the half-inch opening between the boards of the floor had always made it cold and uncomfortable, but so much better were we provided for than others all over the state, (as the house when built was the largest and best Presbyterian Church in the state) that whenever the question was asked, "Ought we not to do something for ourselves?" The reply has been, Not while our house will answer and others have none. We believe that time has now come, as the sun has so shrunk the whole house that no fire can warm it. The question had been asked of those who were disinterested at a distance, "Does the Lord require this at our hands?" The reply was, "A more acceptable offering you could not make." The question was still asked of one deeply interested in benevolent objects, "What if the benevolent, systematic operations of the church be encroached upon by so doing?" The reply "Build, and you will do more three years hence than you ever have done; and if you do not build, three years hence you will do less." It was also stated that when the subject was suggested to one whose name we may now mention, Hon. Joseph Duncan, he immediately proposed that Mrs. D. should be one of five ladies to pay the sum of two hundred dollars. So deeply interested, and so highly did he approve of the undertaking, and to his advice and co-operation, more than any other one, we are indebted for the present effort, although in three short weeks he was numbered with the dead. It was asked, "in what way it was proposed to raise money?" as it had been said that it must be done in some way, so as not to offend any other object or interest. The answer was, "By our own labor and self-denial, over and above what we have been giving and doing for other objects."

January 2d, 1844.—Mrs. Barton, chairman of the meeting, Emily J. Adams, secretary, the following preamble and resolution was unanimously adopted.

After much consultation, advice and prayer, the ladies of the Jacksonville Presbyterian Church have unanimously decided that they can with "singleness of eye," for the honor and glory of God, assist in the erection of a house to be called by his name, believing as we do that he requires this obligation at our hands. Therefore,

Resolved, That we pledge ourselves to assist in the building of a church by our own efforts, labor and self-denial to the amount of $2,000.

Amount reported to the Jacksonville Sewing Society for one year by committee, to take charge of the fund $900.07.

Eleventh.—HISTORY OF BETHEL A. M. E. CHURCH. PREPARED BY SAMUEL W. NICHOLS.

In the year 1846, Philip Ward, of Bloomington, found a number of faithful souls in this place who were extremely desirous of worshiping God according to the rules and doctrines of the African Methodist Church, and accordingly in November of that year a formal organization was effected. The first meeting was held in a house owned by Rev. A. W. Jackson, situated on the lot now owned by him, but then inhabited by Franklin Davis,one of the first members. The little band consisted of Franklin Davis and wife, Chloe Hayden, Abby Allen and Judge Allen.

In the little room in which the organization first saw the light of the day, they continued to meet for two years, after which they held service in the Mt. Emory Baptist Church for the succeeding two years, when the room could be obtained. For one year Rev. Philip Ward rode a circuit consisting of Bloomington, Springfield, Alton and Jacksonville. The next conference year Rev. William Johnson occupied the field, but the year after Philip Ward was again in charge. The little band continued to increase in number under the faithful labors of these early pioneers, who sought nothing but the salvation of souls.

In 1850 a heroic effort was made to get the building enclosed and finished and when the members of the church had exhausted their means, the citizens of the town were asked to aid the enterprise. One of the best contributions was $20 worth of lumber from Judge Brown, which in those days meant considerable. The women aided in getting up suppers and festivals. By strenuous efforts the building was completed and dedicated before time for conference. Never did a happier congregation assemble for the worship of God than the little band which gathered in this humble edifice, nor did more fervent prayers or gladder songs of praise ever ascend to the throne of grace from the worshiping throngs in lofty cathedrals and sumptuous churches, than those which went up from this little room on Grove street This house of worship continued to be used until its destruction by fire March 3, 1868. By the strenuous efforts of Lafayette Allen, W. A. Hubbard, J. Duke, H. Givens, S. Bolden and some other friends, funds were secured to erect the walls of the present building and furnish roof, windows and doors. The work could go no farther for lack of funds and the old church building on East State street was sold and must be torn down. Late one Saturday evening S. W. Nichols bought some seats which had been removed from the opera house, and getting Henry Reed to bring his team they were hauled to the church and services held there the next day, and though enclosed by bare brick walls with naked rafters overhead, the church and Sunday school were nevertheless at home, and thanking God, took courage.

The destruction of the records renders statistics out of the question, but it is safe to say that hundreds have been brought to Christ through the instrumentality of this organization and that it has done important work for the good of the community. The present condition of the society will be shown by the following statistics taken from the minutes of the last quarterly conference:

Members 127, books in Sunday school library 125, pastor's salary last year $610, Sunday school collections $54.60, trustee's collections for three months $100.53.

Twelfth.—THE JACKSONVILLE LIBRARY—A VALUABLE ORGANIZATION AND BOOK COLLECTION.

Thirteen years ago a few persons, desiring the benefits of literature without unnecessary expense, pooled their money, to the amount from each person of five dollars per year, and expended it for books. These were placed in charge of Hon. S. M. Martin as librarian, in his office of superintendent of schools in the court house. The books purchased were solid in character, including history, biography, science, literature, philosophy, politics and religion. Poetry and novels were unknown to their shelves. An objection by any member in committee of the whole, was fatal to the purchase of any book. No book could be bought unless there was money to pay for it in the hands of the treasurer, and unless an order for payment had been voted by the association and signed by the president and secretary. Three American reviews and the five British reprints were also taken by the society.

This experiment was a success. At the end of the year, the members were ready to make the association permanent. The contributions were increased to ten dollars per year from each member. The number of members was increased to twenty-one. The association was chartered under the law of the state. The management was committed to a board of seven trustees elected annually by the share-holders. Messrs. Andras, Dummer, Ayers, Kirby, Martin, Milligan and Woods constituted the first board of trustees. The first two were re-elected annually as long as they lived.

To Judge Dummer the association is mainly indebted for its admirable Constitution and By-Laws, under which success became easier than failure. More than to any one else, the stock holders are under obligations to the late president of the board, Mr. Wm. S. Andras, for his wise oversight of its concerns and for the sum, $1,000, which he gave to be expended for additions to the library.

Messrs. Ayers, Kirby, Milligan and Woods have been members of the board of trustees from the beginning. The other present members are J. C. Andras, Bullard and Elliott.

The officers of the board are: president, M. P. Ayers; secretary and librarian, J. H. Woods; treasurer, H. W. Milligan.

The stock of the association is divided into fifty-eight shares, held by twenty-nine stock-holders. Each share represents a par value of sixty-seven dollars.

The regular annual income of the library is two hundred and ninety dollars; made up by an annual assessment of five dollars on each share of stock, together with the fees paid by readers, who may enjoy the privileges of the library for five dollars a year.

The association has a room for the library, and for an occasional Literary Social in the second story of Ayers' Bank, where, on every Saturday afternoon, book-lovers do congregate.

The present number of volumes catalogued is twenty-one hundred and fifty. From the manner in which the books are selected, one might suppose that the library was a very choice selection, and the supposition would be strictly in accordance with fact.

Thirteenth.—ONE OF THE FIRST, SKETCH OF THE LIFE AND CHARACTER OF JUDGE JOHN LEEPER, WHO CAME TO MORGAN COUNTY IN 1823.

John Leeper, or Judge Leeper, as he was called, one of the early settlers of Morgan county, and whose residence was near where Jacksonville now stands, a man of some note in his day, deserves more than passing notice by any who undertake to write a satisfactory history of early days in this county.

He was born in Cumberland county, Pennsylvania, August 23d, 1786. His father, James Leeper, was brought from County Down, Ireland, by his father, Allen Leeper, when he was but a child seven years old. They were of Scotch origin, and Presbyterians, and fled from Scotland to Ireland in the days of religious persecution.

In an early day James Leeper moved from Pennsylvania to Georgia, where John Leeper was married at the age of twenty to Fidelia McCord, who was but sixteen. They were married October 28th, 1806. In the year 1809 he moved with his wife and two children to Bradford county, Tennessee, and grubbed out a farm in the cane and cedar woods on Rock Creek, near Duck River. Here Mr Leeper remained until the spring of 1816, when being pervaded by a desire to find a better country, and one in which there was no human slavery an institution he was bitterly opposed to from principle-- he started, with his wife and six children, on the 5th of April, 1816, for Illinois territory, arriving at Edwardsville the 25th of May. Remaining here a few days, he moved on into Bond county, and located four miles south of Greenville on Beaver Creek. On the first Sabbath after their arrival here—other emigrants being along with Mr. Leeper—they drew their wagons up in a circle and herein worshipped the God of their fathers, and called the place Bethel.

Mr. Leeper proceeded to open up a farm near this place, and also built a mill, and set about building up good society by organizing the church and the school. In 1823 he moved to Morgan county, arriving the second day of November, and bought the cabin then owned by Thomas Arnett, one mile southeast of the public square in the present city of Jacksonville. At that time there was no house in sight in any direction. Here, by the help of his wife and ten children, Mr. Leeper soon made a large farm, planted ten acres of orchard, built a large two-story double log house, and a large Pennsylvania barn. Said barn was built in 1827, and is still standing at this writing (1884) as an old landmark in the southeast part of the city.

Morgan county at this time was a wilderness of uncultivated land; but very soon emigration began to come in from the east and the south, and the lands were taken up rapidly. The city of Jacksonville was laid out in 1825. The church and the school soon became a felt want. A school was opened in a log house, built about 200 yards south of the southeast corner of the public square, and the Hon. Judge William Thomas was the first teacher. This was about the year 1827. A Presbyterian church was organized June 30, 1827, in Judge Leeper's barn, the Rev. John Brich presiding at the organization. Mr. Leeper and wife, and ten others constituted the church. John Leeper and William C. Posey were elected ruling elders. The only surviving member of the original church is Mrs. Polly Mears, now 82 years old, and living in Greenville, Bond county.

In the years 1828-'29 the idea of building Illinois College began to be agitated. Mr. Leeper being a man of some wealth and feeling much interested in any movement having a tendency to improve the country and elevate humanity, pushed this enterprise forward, delivering on the ground the brick for the first building. The first day of January, 1830, school began in this building with nine students. They were Alvin M. Dixon, James P. Stuart, Merrill and Hampton Rattan, Samuel R. and Chatham H. Simms, Rollin Mears, Charles B. Barton and William Miller.

Mr. Leeper was elected a member of the legislature in 1827. He was a Whig in politics, of the Adams school, and his house was a kind of headquarters of the politicians of those times. He also kept a kind of ministers hotel, where all of every denomination felt free to come, and very often preaching meetings were held in his house before there was any church or school house. His horses and carriages were always ready for the conveyance of those who traveled to and from their appointments in this way, and his teams were ever at hand to haul wood to the poor and to the preacher. Mr Mr. Leeper had a farm of nearly 400 acres; but large as it was, he felt it was not sufficient for the support of his growing family—being the father of fourteen children. In October, 1831, he moved to Putnam county, Ill., and opened up another large farm; and two years after built mills on Bureau creek, which supplied flour and lumber and carding for this new country for many miles around. He died the 14th of December 1835, from an injury he received while working at his mills. Thus ended a most useful and active life, beloved and esteemed by all who knew him. Ex-President Sturtevant thus speaks of this good man, in an historical address delivered in Jacksonville in 1855: "John Leeper was a man whose strict integrity, enlarged public spirit, unaffected piety and comprehensive charity is worthy to be held in remembrance. His removal from this community was a great loss. It was considered a privilege, in early days, to hold meetings in Judge Leeper's barn."

Fourteenth COMING WEST FIFTY YEARS AGO—FROM NEW YORK TO JACKSONVILLE IN 1834. READ BEFORE THE JACKSONVILLE HISTORICAL SOCIETY, DECEMBER 4, 1884, BY JOSEPH H. BANCROFT, ESQ.

Fifty years ago, when Gen. Jackson was President and Webster, Clay, Calhoun and Benton ornamented the Senate, the tide of emigration was sweeping towards the West. Then a young man, struck by the wave, like Cassius M. Clay as he was standing on the bank of the troubled Tiber—he into the river, I into a steamboat—I was an emigrant. "Then the glorious thoughts which, now to speak, would bring the blood into my cheeks, passed o'er me." I thought of—a governor, a member of Congress, perchance a justice of the peace. But the highest flights of fancy, the highest aspirations of my ambitions, imagination's utmost stretch, in wonder died away without even suggesting the possibility of being called on to narrate the incidents of that eventful journey before an historical society in the Athens of the West. This was before Mr Greeley gave his advice to the young man, so often quoted. It was a raw and gusty day in March, in 1834; the parting words were said, we took the boat for New York, glided quickly down the Connecticut and entered Long Island Sound, which seemed to be holding high carnival with the elements. The "raging waves dashed high on bleak New England's shore" that night. The torrents roared and we did buffet it. Our gallant steamer, with lusty screws dashing them aside and stemming it with heart of controversy, out-rode the storm, passed safely through Hell Gate and landed us safely at the wharf in New York, then a thriving city of about 200,000 inhabitants, who were just introducing gas for illuminating purposes. The storm continued all the next day with unabated fury, and but few persons were seen on the streets. Here we met Mr. E. Wolcott, a leading merchant of this place, and we journeyed together. The day following we steamed down the bay to Amboy, where we first discovered a railroad, a fair description of which I am quite sure would bring tears to the eyes of Brother Morse. We were five hours in getting under way, and were conveyed about thirty miles to a point on the Delaware, whence a steamer took us to Philadelphia. We found comfortable quarters at Mrs. Yohie's celebrated hotel on Chestnut street. Next morning we took stage for Reading, where we spent the Sabbath. Monday morning found us packed inside of a stage coach, having capacity for twelve passengers inside, and every seat was occupied, all bound for Pittsburg, having the Alleghany mountains to pass—and who that has ever made that trip in Winter has forgotten Sideling hill? As we were nearing that place, one of the passengers entertained us with his previous experience. The stage was overturned, and rolled down an embankment sixty feet high and lodged in the branches of a sturdy oak.

In due time the dreaded place was reached, and our driver shouted, "Hold on to the upper side," and cracking his long whip, the horses flew and the passengers, with beating hearts and bated breath, held with all their might to the upper side.

At the end of three days' and nights' continuous travel we reached Pittsburg, somewhat tired. Here we found two boats taking in cargoes, for St. Louis and intermediate ports, both of which, we were assured, would leave that day, and selecting the one we liked best, went on board. The night passed and we were at the wharf, and so on until the third day the boat was loaded, and we were gliding down the beautiful Ohio. We stopped at most of the landings, spent a day and night at Cincinnati and Louisville, where we lost much time in getting through the canal. Our boat had a large number of passengers, among whom were about the usual number of gamblers who plied their vocation through the night, and money was freely wagered. After leaving Louisville we made but few stops till we rounded into the turbid waters of the Mississippi.

Passing the Grand Chain and the Graveyard, we saw three steamboats which had been wrecked by snags and sawyers in that dangerous locality, which place has since been made comparatively safe and is no longer a terror to navigators of the Mississippi. Reaching St. Louis on the second day from Cairo, we found a city of about 6,000 inhabitants, and here for the first time met the institution of negro slavery. There were still standing many of the old French residences, which gave it the appearance of a foreign city. Here we found an old schoolmate, who had been a resident about two years, from whom we learned much about the city and the people. I remember that a short walk west from Main street brought us into a timbered region, probably where Fourth street is now situated. After waiting two days for a boat going up the Illinois river, without success, we took the stage for Jacksonville. On the way we were several times advised by our driver to get out and walk over some place where he thought it dangerous to ride. We reached here, having been three weeks on the way, and found a small place with a population of about 600, it having been greatly reduced by the prevalence of Asiatic cholera during the previous year. Of all the men who were then in business here, I can think of but two who are now living, and out of all the then residents but few are with us.

The old United States Bank furnished the entire circulation of paper money in this state—not a bank within its borders; no railways in existence; no telegraph; letter postage twenty-five cents.

AYERS' BLOCK, WEST STATE STREET, IN 1884.

Occupied by D. B. & H. B. Smith, Geo. H. Huntoon, E. C. Simms, Jenkinson Bro. and the Daily Courier.

Fifteenth.—A FEW MANUFACTURING ENTERPRISES.—SOME DEFUNCT AND OTHERS STILL IN EXISTENCE.

There should be due reference made in such a work as this to all efforts to promote industrial or manufacturing interests whether they have been financial successes or not. The Shirt Manufactory of J. L. Padgett & Co., the Broom Factory of C. H. Dunbrack, the Home Woolen Mills, the Jacksonville Car and Manufacturing Co., and the Jacksonville Sulky Plow Works are among the number. All but the last are now defunct. As to the Home Mills the inopportune time of the fire alone smothered the scheme.

A company for the manufacture of woolen goods was organized in 1865, with a paid up capital of $100,000. This was entirely invested in four acres of land adjacent to the brook in the southern part of the city, in a large and convenient building, in a tenement block on South West Street and in necessary mill machinery. The incorporators were Messrs. A. E. and M. P. Ayers, George M. McConnel, John Gordon, William T. Beekman, William Richardson and Henry Staley. Mr. Beekman was elected president, and McConnel secretary. The mills started with from 60 to 70 employes and a good trade. The mill itself is said to have been the best constructed in the West. In January, 1873, by the carelessness of a spinner, who allowed threads to be ignited in a gas jet, burning in the early morning, and then to fall upon an oil-soaked floor, it was totally destroyed by fire, and the loss was so heavy upon the stockholders, coming at the very outset in their investment, that they have never rebuilt. They still hold the ownership of the land and the Factory Block.

As to the Car Works, this enterprise was started in 1872, the company being incorporated in March, 1873, by stock subscribers with a paid up capital of $40,000. The most active promoters and original stockholders were E. C. Kreider, (president,) Wm. E. Veitch, (secretary and treasurer,) Joseph O. King, A. C. Wadsworth, Dr. David Prince, Edward S. Greenleaf, John A. Ayers and others. Five acres of land in the southeastern part of the city, on the line of the Jacksonville Southeastern Railroad, were purchased, the needed building was erected, tools and machinery purchased and the "Jacksonville Car Works" were in running order by August, 1873. A small contract was filled, then the panic came on and the works shut down temporarily. Later an attempt was made to manufacture agricultural implements, in the building, under the management of Joseph N. Taylor. This venture proved unsuccessful and was soon abandoned. The floating indebtedness of the company became quite large, but was taken up by a few gentlemen who secured themselves by a second mortgage under which the property had to be sold. It was bought in by the mortgagees and held until a sale was consummated with Mr. T. C. Dutro, of St. Louis, Mo., at a price which gave them no profit. Dutro organized the "Jacksonville Car Company," enlarged the capacity from two to ten cars per diem, by additions to building and machinery, and operated it for a number of years, building many flat, box and stock cars. This company in turn became involved, got an extension of time on their paper, but finally were foreclosed under mortgage held by the bank and individual creditors, all in Jacksonville, and thus the matter stands to-day.

One other enterprise deserves mention, the Jacksonville Sulky Plow Works, with a paid up capital of $20,000 was organized in January, 1881. The original stockholders were Mr. A. C. Wadsworth, (president,) Dr. H. F. Carriel, (vice-president,) Mr. James H. Hackett, (secretary and manager,) Mr. William E. Veitch, (treasurer,) Messrs. S. B. Gray, William D. Mathers and Mortimer Cahill. The company purchased the property near the junction depot, known as the Russell & Akers foundry, added buildings, machinery, stock, etc., and proceeded to manufacture and wholesale a certain patented sulky attachment for plows, harrows, etc. Their manufacture to date amounts to 1,500, none of which have been retailed, but sales have been throughout Illinois and Missouri. Price $40. The works do not run continuously, and shut down last summer (1884.) Some changes are contemplated before re-opening. A part of their building is now rented and occupied by A. C. Thompson, iron founder and moulder. See cut page 243

Sixteenth—EXTRACTS FROM THE "PATRIOT"—SCHOOL MATTERS IN 1833.

In a copy of the *Illinois Patriot*, published in this city February 1833, we find the following: "The new *school house* at Linnville will be opened for Divine worship to-morrow, when sermons will be preached as follows: At 11 o'clock a. m., by Rev. E. Beecher; at 1:30 p. m., by the Rev. W. Spencer."

We also find communication from (then) Prof. Sturtevant, dated January 17, 1833, copied from the *Illinois Herald*, then edited by Brooks, from which we extract as follows:

SIR:—In your paper of the 12th inst. is a paragraph purporting to be an extract from a letter from some person in this town I observe with mingled emotions of indignation and regret, some statements fitted, and I fear designed, to throw contempt upon the institution in which I have the honor to be instructor. I should have allowed the matter to pass by in merited neglect, but for two reasons—first, because, as the person principally referred to in the above named letter is said to be a "Professor" in the college in this place, and as I am at present the only instructor in the institution to whom that appellation is appropriate—it bears the appearance of a personal attack on me; and such to a considerabl eextent must be the impression on the community—though I am persuaded the writer should not so have intended it. And second, because, though it is not my custom to turn aside to reply to every ill-natured remark which may be made in a passion, about the literary institution of which I was the first instructor—and of which I am now and ever will be a devoted friend, while it adheres to the enlightened, liberal and truly republican principles upon which it is founded, yet there is a point beyond which the friends of this institution will not endure in silence the propagation of the most malignant slanders through the newspapers, but will avail themselves of that public vindication, which the unquestionable soundness of their principles will always render easy. That point in the present case has been already reached, and we shall vindicate ourselves, lest we prove traitors to that good cause—the cause of education—which we are laboring with our whole strength to promote. Suffer me, therefore, to request that you will insert this communication in your paper without delay—and I make this request the more freely, as it is over my proper name, and I am therefore personally responsible for the statements which it contains.

The letter above referred to relates to certain transactions which took place in the Court House in this town on New Year's eve. A meeting of citizens had been called at that place on that evening, to take into consideration the expediency of forming a "Peace Society." Such societies have been in existence in different parts of the United States and Great Britain for many years; and as they are all formed on the same principles, there is fortunately no difficulty in obtaining "exact" information on the subject.

A Peace Society is a voluntary association of individuals, for the purpose of promoting the general prevalence of peace among the nations of the earth. Its only means for effecting this object is by operating on public opinion; and this again it seeks to move only by free discussion, and the circulation of facts illustrative of the evils of war. It neither inculcates on its members nor requires of them anything in the least inconsistent with the justice and necessity of defensive war, but enrolls among its members those who strenuously maintain both. Such is a Peace Society. The writer, whose words you extract, says "The Presbyterians were about to form some kind of society." Here I must correct a little. The Presbyterians here are not in the habit of doing such things as a party—we ever assume the right individually of thinking for ourselves, and acting according to our own private judgment. And in this case we differ in opinion many thinking a Peace Society a very good thing, and many others thinking it of little or no use Not *one* of the Presbyterian "clerical gentlemen" of the town and vicinity was present at the meeting. The chairman, one of the oldest settlers, and most respected citizens of this county, was never suspected of being a Presbyterian; and would not, I presume, feel himself flattered by being placed at the head of a Presbyterian movement. The secretary is a highly respected clergyman of the Methodist Church. * * * *

Seventeenth—A FEW GENERAL REMARKS BY DR. ANDREW MCFARLAND, AS PUBLISHED IN THE DAILY JOURNAL, IN 1875.

From its first settlement, Jacksonville has been pre-eminently favored in numbering among its inhabitants men of great public spirit, combined with large insight of the future. They left a stamp which can never be effaced save through a most unpardonable negligence. Their influence and efforts drew to it colleges, seminaries, and State institutions of a high philanthropic character these last an especial compliment to the intelligence and standing of this community in the State. They showed their appreciation of learning, in prompt efforts to promote a good system of common school education in the State, and well filled and well supported churches have always been proof of their regard for religious interests. Indeed, from the very first, Jacksonville took a position usually left till wealth and leisure give time for such undertakings. In all they did this large foresight is now seen. Wide and well-shaded streets, ample sidewalks and tasteful, well-ornamented dwellings, became an early characteristic, and are now a distinguishing beauty. The city at once attracts the attention of strangers of taste, who never leave it without encomiums upon its rare beauty.

* * * * * * * * * *

Of the topography of Jacksonville, as the seat of a flourishing city, hardly too much can be said. It is, indeed, "beautiful for situation." Lying upon a gentle elevation, mostly sloping to the east and south, both the soil and aspect have the essentials of complete salubrity. However populous it may become, it can never be sickly, if even common provision for drainage is made. There are no swamps, stagnant waters, or other sources of noxious exhalation anywhere in its vicinity. These malarious diseases are seldom met; and the mosquito, save in occasional seasons, rarely puts in an appearance. The streets of the city have yet some of the faults incident to all rich soils in wet weather. But pedestrians have nothing to complain of from the excellent sidewalks, extending far into the suburbs of the city; and pavements, in due season, will remove the evil.

As before mentioned, strangers invariably comment on the luxuriance of the shade-trees and ornamental shrubbery with which Jacksonville abounds. The early taste that promoted this feature of the city was greatly aided by the soil itself. Every kind of tree tolerated by the climate, whether evergreen or deciduous, finds a congenial soil here. It is a field where the landscape artist has everything ready to his hand, and some specimens of this most delightful art in the city deserve especial mention, if such mention did not seem invidious. When larger lots are taken up in the suburbs of the city, where an enlarged taste may have full scope, we hope to see elegant homes that may vie with those in the environs of Boston and Philadelphia.

The crying evil of Jacksonville, up to a recent period, had been a scarcity of water for extensive requirements. Important interests for a time suffered from this deficiency. After much discussion of plans and ways and means, active measures were set on foot in 1873, which resulted in a most satisfactory accomplishment of the object, so that is believed that the city will be abundantly supplied for all coming time. The supply it gained, by surface impounding, and from the area of rain fall at command, is practically inexaustible. Except in the highest parts of the city, the water is carried into the upper parts of dwellings by its pressure a feat of untold value in its use. Being essentially a rain water, it is soft, free from chemical impurities, sufficiently clear for all mechanical purposes, and, by infiltration, absolutely so. The general plan of the water-works was suggested by E. S. Chesbrough, Esq., the eminent hydraulic engineer of Chicago. But large credit is due the water commissioners and resident engineers in their employ, for carrying to completion, under the estimated cost, and contrary to the experience of most of our sister cities and the predictions of many at home—this most eventful undertaking. We venture the assertion that never, since

Moses took his celebrated water-works contract on Mt. Horeb, has any similar job been done so cheaply, expeditiously and substantially.

In its communication with the outer world, by means of railroads, Jacksonville has nothing further, in reason, to desire. No less than six radiating lines fix their center at this point. Several of these again branch within a short distance, forming a network so extensive that every considerable town in any direction is readily reached, while several competing lines connect with the larger cities. These enterprises have left no drawback whatever on the city, in the shape of taxes in aid of their construction. In the beginning of this article it was pointed out that the progress of any people in material and intellectual advancement is greatly influenced by its food supply. It is not claimed that Jacksonville has any special pre-eminence over many other places in the same latitude. But it is certain that it is surpassed by none. The great staples of living, meat and grain, ought to reach here their very lowest minimum of cost. The greatest wheat-producers and cattle-breeders on the continent have long been found in the immediate vicinity. The great multiplication of institutions has gradually created a home market which for variety can nowhere be excelled. Here could fully be realized the wish of the great Henry of France, that every peasant in his dominion might have a capon in his dinner-pot whenever he desired. This abundance of the good things of life does away, in the greatest number, with anxiety as to the mere means of living, and affords thought for things higher and beyond. Where abundance does not run into an unworthy and useless luxury, it leads in this higher direction. And we hope and believe that it is this very thing that has contributed much to give Jacksonville its present enviable reputation.

From the foregoing summary the characteristics of Jacksonville as a city may readily be gathered. Most favorably situated as to climate and topography; suffering from neither extreme of heat or cold; favored by the State in a large inpouring of money at unfailing periods; having the example of many eminent and useful citizens now gone to their rest, and feeling as we trust, the spur of others yet living, who are their not unworthy successsors, there should and may be a yet greater future. The post is not the superstructure, but merely the foundation. That the State has done so much by establishing here so many of her enduring charities, is well. But also these must be supplemented by a large measure of individual enterprise, or stagnation may follow, for all that has gone before. And as a field of judicious enterprise, there is none superior. Cheap fuel, free water, abundant labor, and ready communication, supply all the conditions of a varied and most successful system of manufactories.

THE DUNLAP HOUSE, WEST STATE STREET, JACKSONVILLE, ILLINOIS.

REMODELED AND RE-OPENED IN 1880, BY CAPT. ALEX. SMITH.

Eighteenth.—PLACES FOR EATING AND SLEEPING, 1885.

The hotel accommodations of any city form quite an important feature of its prosperity, especially in these days when so large a proportion of the commercial business is transacted by traveling men. The "Dunlap" after prolonged litigation passed from the hands of the founder Col. James Dunlap and in the summer of 1880 Capt. Alex. Smith purchased it of the Northwestern Mutual Life Insurance Company. Both he and his wife were experienced in hostelry business and have made a success of the hotel (see cut on page 257) from that time to the present. At the time of the transfer it was closed for three months for changes, repairs and improvements. The building was repainted inside and outside, handsomely repapered, furnished, many conveniences added and the house almost entirely remodeled at a cost of over ten thousand dollars. It was opened for business again September 22d, 1880. With the exception of ten months, in 1882 and 1883, when Meserve & Kittredge were the temporary lessees, Cap. Smith has been the landlord as well as proprietor. The house has seventy-five sleeping apartments for guests, besides all the other rooms such as office, reading-room, parlors, halls, dining-room, billiard-hall, sample-rooms, and bedrooms for help.

In November, 1883, Mr. Smith also became the owner of the Park Hotel, (see cut page 247,) purchasing it at master-in-chancery sale. It is the successor of the old Mansion House, and located on the north side of the public square. Since passing into his control it has been used solely as an apartment house with restaurant attached, the latter run by lessees.

The last addition to the hotels of the city was built in 1883, by Anton Rataichak, and named after him—the Rataichak Hotel. He is sole proprietor and landlord with Daniel Williams, Esq., as office clerk. The building is a plain, but substantial three story brick, located on East State street in the same block as the *Journal* office. Ground occupied by the hotel 60x180, sleeping rooms number sixty-one, besides parlors, halls and usual hotel apartments. The steam-heating, water-closet and general plumbing and ventilating arrangements are especially commendable, and the new candidate for public favor is being well patronized.

The other large hotel of the city is the Southern, located on West College Ave., two blocks southwest of the square. It was built by Elijah Cobb. The successive managers have been Messrs. Cobb, Hume, Aspinwall, Irland (formerly of the Park House) and the present landlord A. H. Hocking, ex-county coroner, who has been "mine host" since September, 1876, The property is now owned by Mr. Julius E. Strawn. It was at one time known as the Avenue House.

Among the smaller hotels are:

The Metropolitan, at the Junction, Mrs. E Sweeney, proprietress; established fourteen years; accommodates fifty or more guests; over 4,000 registered in a year.

The Northeastern House, corner East and Court streets, Mrs. J. F. Dew, proprietress; accommodations for fifty or sixty; established seven years; over 3,000 registered in 1884.

Transit House, North Main and Washington streets, Mrs. Mary E. Faul, proprietress; established three years; accommodates twenty-five guests.

Morgan House, North Main street, Mrs. M. Guthrie, proprietress; established eight years; accommodates twenty-five guests.

Central House, No. 231 North Main street, Mrs. D. Moss, proprietress; accommodates thirty guests; established seven years.

European Restaurant and boarding house, northeast corner of public square, established October, 1884, Mrs. Philip Braun, proprietress.

Hilligass' Restaurant and boarding house, north side East State Street, Capt. B. F. Hilligass, proprietor.

Nineteenth.—MERE MENTION OF VARIOUS MATTERS OF INTEREST.

To conclude this chapter we shall briefly refer to a few local events which have been omitted in the preceding pages covering their time.

In the early part of the year 1837, there was in existence in this community an organization "for the purpose of affording relief to the sick and disabled members thereof, and to the widows and orphans of deceased members, and for the promotion of literature, science and the mechanic arts, and for no other purpose whatever." It had its constitution and by-laws, and was regularly incorporated, the above quotation being from its charter which was granted February 28, 1837. Hon. Newton Cloud, being speaker of the house at that time, and Governor Duncan, also of this county, signing it. The first president was William W. Happy, the secretary was Calvin Goudy and among the directors were Stephen Sutton, Michael Rapp, John Holland and John W. Goltra—all now deceased. Among the members the following are still living: William Branson, Anderson Foreman, Cornelius Goltra, Benjamin F. Gass, W. D. Humphrey, Lewis Hatfield, Samuel S. Cobbs, Josiah M. Lucas and Matthew Stacy.

Our well-known citizen Prof. J. B. Turner has twice been a candidate for congressional honors from this district, not as an office seeker but as representative of political principles. In November, 1868, he was the candidate of the Republican party for a seat in the lower house of the forty-first congress of the United States, and received 17,290 votes as against 21,420 for the late Judge Albert G. Burr. In 1874 he ran as an Independent candidate for the forty-fourth congress. His support was 2,417, with 9,027 for Simpson, (Rep.) and 10,623 for Wm. M. Springer, (Dem.) Consequently Mr. Springer was duly declared elected and has represented this district from that day to this, being re-elected for his sixth two-year term November 4, 1884.

November, 1855, witnessed the publication of the *Jacksonville Hatchet*, by William T. Davis. The paper was devoted to wit, humor, fancy, news, etc. It contained four pages of four columns each,and had no advertisements. The paper contains some of the standard jokes that are still current in the city. We are glad we have found their source. By the way, how many people now living in Jacksonville remember the *Hatchet?* It was before the time of most of the boys.

For a change Jacksonville tried the saloon license plan in 1861, but in April, 1862, there was an anti-license triumph again and the next year the same ticket and cause prevailed.

The cause of education and religion hereabouts lost one of its pioneer and noblest exponents in April, 1863, in the death of "Father Adams"—teacher, colporteur and Sunday-school missionary.

In June, 1862, the annual convention of the State Sunday-school Association was held in our city.

Near the close of the War for the Union, January, 1864, Morgan county's quotas for the army had been 1,757 and she was duly credited upon the muster rolls of Illinois and Missouri with 1,883 recruits or an excess over all demands of 126. In September, 1864, there was a draft of 110 men, and in April, 1865, ten more were drafted from this city. So near was our cup of patriotism full to the brim.

The Chicago & Alton, or as it was then called the St. Louis, Jacksonville & Chicago, Railroad was completed northward as far as Mason City, in August, 1867.

In the summer of that year Col. G. P. Smith, of the *Journal*, engineered through a very enjoyable editorial excursion along the line of the Union Pacific Railway, then being laid, as far as the base of the Rocky Mountains. Ralph Reynolds, Ed. C. Simms, D. B. Smith, C. M. Eames and others, from Jacksonville, were of the party.

A local sensation of December, 1867, was the so-called legislative investigation *in re* Mrs. Packard versus Dr. McFarland, of the Insane Hospital.

The year 1868 witnessed the laying of corner-stones of two of the largest buildings in the city, the Court House and the "Church of Our Savior," (Roman Catholic) also the organization of our city's great convenience the street railway company. In Sep tember at a special city election the vote for license was 400, for prohibition 507, for railroad subscription 814 against 99. October and November of that year saw the *Daily Union* in existence, in Jacksonville, with William T. Davis as editor, and I. J. Ketcham and H. J. Atkins as its backers.

Water works election, June 17, 1869, for the subscription 674 votes, against the proposition 61. In October, 1871, the water works were voted.

The Jacksonville Southeastern, then called the Farmers' road, was completed to Franklin and Waverly during December, 1870, and the same month the street railway was opened.

In 1871 there were twenty-five licensed dram-shops in Jacksonville, and saloons have been regulated by this system every year except one. The license fee grew much larger in 1884, rising from $400 per annum to $550 and then to $800.

The Jacksonville Library Association was incorporated and library opened, in the Court House, in October, 1871.

In December, 1873, occurred the funeral of ex-Governor and ex-Senator Yates.

For the second time the Illinois State Sunday-school Association held its annual mass convention in Jacksonville, in May, 1876. The presence of the great evangelists, Moody and Sankey, drew thousands to the meetings.

In December, 1877, the Murphy Blue Ribbon Temperance Movement reached the city and county. At the close of the year the pledge signers numbered 5,000 and were increased in spring of 1878 to 6,200 in Jacksonville, and 12,000 in Morgan county.

In the year 1877, on the 19th of October, it commenced raining and continued to rain, more or less, every day up to December 27th. On Christmas day fish worms were crawling on the sidewalks and the streets almost impassible for teams Scarcely any person came into the city except by rail. Business almost suspended. Deep mud and more or less rain continued until the middle of March, 1878.

At the annual meeting of the Old Settlers' Association of Morgan county, held in August, 1884. Mr. Chamberlain, the secretary, read the following resolution which was adopted:

RESOLUTION.—William Richardson, one of our vice-presidents, was called to the Spirit Land, December 4th, 1883. In the death of William Richardson this society has lost one of its most efficient workers, as well as most social members, ever ready to do all he could for the profit or pleasure of this association and to make our reunions happy gatherings, long to be remembered. We miss his cheerful presence and mourn his sudden departure, yet feel assured that he has but changed homes from one where sickness and age blight fond hopes to that pure existence where immortal youth and endless happiness is his portion. May his mantle fall upon another as worthy.

This was unanimously adopted.

The first order of business of the afternoon session was the election of officers. Only two changes were made. J. H. Tureman was elected in the place of William Richardson as director and Rev. John Sargent was elected chaplain instead of Rev. E. Roach. The officers are now as follows:

President, M. P. Ayers; Vice-Presidents, Anderson Foreman, Charles Samples, Huram Reeve, J. H. Tureman and William Stevenson; Secretary, T. Chamberlain; Treasurer, John Robertson; Marshal, Charles Sample; Chaplain, Rev. John Sargent; Executive Committee, M. P. Ayers, Huram Reeve, A. J. Thompson, Charles French, Zachary W. Gattan and J. H. Tureman; Finance Committee, Bazzill Davenport, Charles French and Henry Johnson.

In June, 1884, occurred a most singular freak of nature in the shape of a tremendous hail storm a few miles west of the city. The storm extended over but a narrow strip of territory, but with great violence. In one field containing a depression in the center, a heavy rain following the hail washed the latter down the declivity on both sides until it was piled up to a depth of from one to four feet. After a lapse of twenty-four hours S. W. Nichols secured two negatives of what was left of the fallen ice, prints from which have been given to the Historical Society. They show masses of hailstones as large as a man's body, and a heap as large as the pile of stones which marked the resting place of the disobedient Absalom.

The most recent institution of a secret society in this city was in August, 1884—a local lodge of the Order of Knights and Ladies of Honor. This is a fraternal institution of both social and beneficiary character, an offspring of the Knights of Honor, but a distinctly separate organization. In Jacksonville there were eighty charter members of both sexes. Crystal Lodge meets semi-monthly. J. W. Bowen, protector; George W. Fox, secretary; Fred L. Sharpe, treasurer; Lew H. Pratt, financial secretary. The lodge meets in Osborne's Hall, northeast corner of the square.

Twentieth.—ERRATA, BY DR. J. M. STURTEVANT.

To C. M. EAMES:

Dear Sir:—The following errors seem to me to be important:

Page 55, you speak of an interview between "Dr. John Todd, of Springfield, Judge Lockwood, of Jacksonville, dining with Rev. T. Lippincott, etc." Hon. Samuel D. Lockwood was not then a resident of Jacksonville, but of Edwardsville, holding an official position in the United States Land Office at that place. Mr Lippincott was not then a minister of the gospel, but a clerk in Judge Lockwood's office, though already known as an able writer and an enlightened Christian patriot. The proposition that he should accompany Mr. Ellis in an exploring tour in the region then known as "the Sangamon Country" came from Judge Lockwood and was backed up by a gift of $25, to pay expenses and other valuable assistance in aid of the journey. Judge Lockwood did not become a resident of Jacksonville till the winter of 1829-'30.

On the same page you say "Rev. Julian M. Sturtevant came from New Haven with assurances of $1,000 more." It should read, Rev. Theron Baldwin, and Rev. Julian M. Sturtevant, arrived here in November, 1829, with assurances from the young men at Yale College of $10,000 more.

Page 60, 25th line from bottom, "country" should be "county."

Page 68, 4th line from the bottom, "chiefly in the State," should be "chiefly from friends of the cause at the East."

Page 69, 4th line from the top, the impression is made of but *one* graduate. The first graduating class was composed of two, Jonathan E. Spilman, now a Presbyterian minister in southern Illinois, and Richard Yates.

Page 88. James G. Edwards came to Jacksonville in November, 1829. Never had any connection with the college. He was a printer by trade, and came to Jacksonville purely to establish a paper. Capt. John Henry must be mistaken as to there having been a printing press or paper in Jacksonville previous to Mr. Edwards.

I regret to say that in what has been published relative to the history of the college sufficient honor has not been accorded to Hon. S. D. Lockwood. This is to some extent true in respect to what I myself have published. It has not resulted, however, from any want of appreciation of his services or lack of affectionate reverence for his character. It has resulted from the fact that when I wrote he was still among the living. I never can feel the same freedom in eulogising the living as I do in honoring the dead. It may be a false delicacy, but I must confess to the fact of having been influenced by it. Full justice never *can* be done to the grand services which Judge Lockwood rendered to the college during his long connection with it, from the first conception of the idea of founding it till his death.

J. M. STURTEVANT.

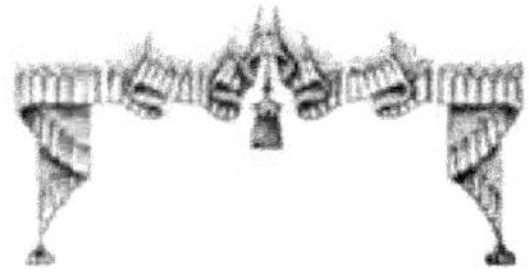

Twenty-first.—CORRECTIONS AND ADDITIONS, BY THE EDITOR.

Page 10, six lines from bottom, "Kellogg" should be Kellogg's.

Page 14, thirteenth line from top, for "Kettner" read Keltner.

Page 40, last line, "Marsh's" Point should be Mark's.

Page 57, Rev. J. M. Ellis was installed 1830 not "1828."

Page 71. The Diamond Grove Baptist Church is still in existence, hence was not "short lived."

Page 72, twenty-eighth line from top, for *H.* P. Melendy read *S.* P.

Page 85. This description of the quick freeze was not by Mr. Lathrop, but some unknown old citizen.

Page 88, twelve lines from bottom, Mr. Edwards remained in Jacksonville six years or more, not "two" as stated.

Page 96, eleventh line from bottom, for Carrollton read Manchester.

Page 97, town trustee William *B.* Warren, not "William *P.*"

Page 125, sixth line from top, "1840" should be 1850.

Page 173. The first "Christian" Church here was organized in October, 1832, by elders Barton W. Stone and Josephus Hewitt, with eighty-six members.

Twenty-second.—AUTHORITIES CONSULTED OR USED.

The compiler of "Historic Morgan" would acknowledge his indebtedness, for valuable data for this work to the following:

Dr. L. M. Glover's sermons 1873, 1877 and 1880, historical discourses upon twenty-fifth and fiftieth anniversaries of First Presbyterian church and Jacksonville Female Academy.

Dr. W. W. Harsha's historical sermon 1864, at dedication of Central Presbyterian church.

Dr. J. M. Sturtevant's historical address, twenty-fifth anniversary of Illinois College and fiftieth anniversary of Congregational church, October, 1883.

Judge William Thomas' communications to *Journal* during past twenty-five years.

J. W. Graham's "Jacksonville Illustrated" in *Potter's American Monthly*, Oct., 1878.

Messrs. Huram Reeve, Timothy Chamberlain, Anderson Foreman, Keeling Berry and Rev. William Clark—conversations and documents.

Charles A. Barnes' History of the Secret Societies of Jacksonville, in the *Daily Journal* December 15, 1881.

Samuel W. Nichols' interviews with anti-slavery pioneers and underground railroad conductors, in *Daily Journal*, 1884.

History of Morgan county, 1878, Donnelley, Loyd & Co., Chicago, publishers.

First annual report of Woman's Christian Temperance Union, of Jacksonville.

Recollections of old times, in *Daily Courier*, 1883, by Anderson Foreman, J. W. Lathrop, James S. Anderson and Col. George M. Chambers.

J. R. Bailey's articles on Early Days, in files of *Weekly Sentinel*.

Historical Sketch of Cass county, by Hon. J. Henry Shaw, of Beardstown.

History of Cass county, 1882, edited by William Henry Perrin; O. L. Baskin & Co., Chicago, publishers.

R. W. Ranson's Descriptions of State Institutions as printed in *Chicago Tribune*, November, 1883.

Ensley Moore's "Local Epitomes," 1830, 1840, 1850 and 1860, as published in the *Daily Journal* in 1879.

Rev. J. M. Ellis' diary in *Presbytery Reporter*, Alton.

Gen. Murray McConnel's Sketch of Jacksonville, in Nixon's Directory.

Capt. John Henry's Scrap Book, in Y. M. C. A. Reading room.

Mrs. Joseph H. Bancroft's History of Ladies' Education Society, fiftieth anniversary, October 6, 1883.

Dr. G. V. Black's Meteorological Articles, in *Jacksonville Daily Journal*.

Twenty-third. THE NEW CENTENARY.—ELECTRIC LIGHTS.—TOBACCO FACTORIES.

The new Centenary (formerly East Charge) M. E. church (see view on page 233) was dedicated and occupied in November, 1868, but the movement for the erection started in 1866, the centennial year of American Methodism, when the name was changed. Rev. Alex. Semple, the pastor, undertook the work of securing the subscriptions for the amount thought to be necessary, viz: $25,000. He succeeded in the laudable work and the lot was purchased and foundation laid that year. The building was not completed ready for use until November, 1868, costing about $40,000. Underwood, of Chicago, was the builder of all except the towers and spire and the interior finish of the auditorium which was the work of Hugh Wilson, Esq., of this city.

In January, 1884, an effort was made by outside parties to introduce the Vanderpoele Electric Light into the city by the formation of a local joint stock company. This venture failed, but Mr. George H. Huntoon, of our city, took up the matter and sixty-eight subscriptions for lights were obtained, thirty-three to be used every night and the others once a week. With this much encouragement the plant was put in—a forty light dynamo being attached to the engine at the Car Works. The first exhibition of the lights was May 3d, 1884, a very satisfactory Park and store illumination being made. The lights put into the places of business and hotels, etc., some forty in number, were used several months, but the power was found to be too weak and the lights consequently not satisfactory. It was, therefore, impossible to sell stock in the enterprise and so it rests *in statu quo.*

The cigar and tobacco manufacturing industry has hardly been referred to in our work, but should have been as it represents a good deal of capital and the employment of many men. We have not succeeded in obtaining any statistics as to the annual manufacture, but the following are the principal factories: Benjamin Pyatt & Sons, Henry H. Knollenberg, Gotthelf & Kahn, Cassell Bros., Scott & Duckett, and Joseph Keeney.

In 1884, the veterans of the War for the Union organized a local branch of the well known patriotic order—the Grand Army of the Republic. It was named and numbered Mat. Starr Post, No. 378. Present officers: Capt. Philip Lee, commander; Henry Hoover, adjutant.

Twenty-fourth.—EXTRACTS FROM A LETTER FROM AN OLD MORGANIAN.

GRAND ISLAND, Nebraska, December 24, 1884.

Mr. Editor:—Seeing of late in the *Journal* invitations to early settlers of Morgan county to forward any reminiscences that might aid you in your forthcoming history of the county and city, I thought of sending a few items, if it were not that much more interesting matter will fill the book. True, I feel as much or more interest in the subject than those still with you. Old people are apt to live much in the past, reconnoitering the paths of early life. I came and settled with my father and family at the head of Big Sandy in 1830—before the deep snow, when the spring mornings boomed with the prairie chicken and night was hideous with howling wolves. Sheep were scarce. I am now past seventy-four, the only one remaining of my father's family; the rest, all except my youngest sister, have their resting place in your county; I was thirty years in Morgan, except three years in Springfield, the years 1835, 1836 and 1837. Then I spent twenty years in Urbana, Champaign county. Then, as all my children, except the doctor at Arcadia, had taken Greeley's advice, I followed in the wake, stopping not until I rounded the last part of the United States at the mouth of the Columbia, and there for thirteen months, within the ocean roar, paddling on the tide water, and trapesing through the mountain trails amongst those old monarchs of the forest on Louis and Clarke, some of them sixteen feet in diameter. Well, now I'm here to try and encourage your noble enterprise. I was conversant with nearly every one of the old folks lately noticed in your columns, and many others, many of whom have taken their leave. Happy to know some of my particular friends still linger, among them Judge William Thomas, Dr. Akers, Col. Chambers, Uncle Johny Jordan and Huram Reeve. * * * * I knew your father and grandfather well, for ten years during my residence in Jacksonville, 1847 to 1857; knew your old veteran stock man and financier, Jacob Strawn, for thirty years. I might give some rather amusing anecdotes connected with our dealings. The only fault he ever found with me he said that I was too honest. It didn't shock my nerves and we didn't quarrel about it. * *

WILLIAM CRAIG.

ODD FELLOWS' BLOCK, NORTH SIDE SQUARE, JACKSONVILLE, ILLINOIS

Twenty-Fifth.—THE ILLINOIS COLLEGE ALUMNI ASSOCIATION—THE OLDEST SOCIO-LITERARY SOCIETY IN THE STATE—A RECORD OF OVER HALF A CENTURY.

At the annual "commencement" exercises, held in June, 1879, Illinois College celebrated its fiftieth anniversary, and a part of the exercises were under the special charge of its Alumni Society. On June 4th the exercises were held in the college chapel, Hon. Newton Bateman being president of the occasion, Mr. Epler, secretary, and M. P. Ayers, Esq., toast-master. Ex-President Sturtevant delivered a lengthy address, historical of the college, and Rev. Thos. K. Beecher, of Elmira N. Y., delivered an eloquent speech to the Alumni—an unusual number of whom were present.

The society deserves more than passing notice from Illinoisans, and as no full historical sketch of it has ever been published, we lay it before our readers, who will note that the portions quoted are from the society record.

"At a meeting of the Alumni of Illinois College, held at the office of Richard Yates, Esq., on the 19th of September, 1839. Richard Yates was called to the chair and Joseph N. Porter was appointed secretary. The object of the meeting was made known by Mr. Chairman, and on motion of Mr. Blood it was

"*Resolved*, That this meeting appoint two persons, each with an alternate, to pronounce an oration and poem before the Alumni, on Thursday evening after the next annual commencement of Illinois College.

"T. E. Spilman, Esq., was appointed to deliver the oration, and R. Yates his alternate; R. Mears to deliver a poem, and Robt. W. Patterson his alternate. On motion of J. P. Stewart, a committee of three was chosen to make arrangements for the occasion, consisting of Messrs. Patterson, Blood and Goudy, and on motion the chairman was added to said committee A committee was appointed to purchase a blank book for keeping the record of the association, and the names, residence, etc., of the Alumni, to be left in keeping of the chairman. On motion, the meeting adjourned.

"In 1840 Richard Yates was chosen president of the association, and Calvin Goudy secretary for the ensuing year. J. Park Stewart was chosen orator, and A. M. Dixon alternate; R. Goudy, jr., poet, and J. Chandler alternate. On motion of Mr. Blood it was ordered that the meetings of the Alumni be hereafter opened with prayer."

Yates was re-elected president in 1841, with Wm. Coffin as secretary. In 1842 Richard Yates was re-elected, with Wm. P. Bradley secretary. The society made its first necrological record, that of Robert Goudy, M. D. The secretary was instructed to correspond with graduates of other colleges, with a view to union with them. The society had been disappointed by their orators failing to appear, until June 30, 1842, when Rev. C. E. Blood delivered an address, and Rev. Rollin Mears a poem, in the Methodist Episcopal Church. Yates was re-elected president in 1843, with R. Mears, secretary, and Rev. Wm. Holmes delivered an address.

The society met at the house of D. B. Ayers, Esq., in 1844, when Samuel Willard was chosen president, with M. P. Ayers secretary. In 1845 the day of meeting fixed upon was that preceding commencement, and it was decided to have a vice-president, "to supply the place of the president in his absence," and to act on the committee of arrangements. The committee were ordered to provide an annual dinner, at which each member should offer a sentiment, and it was

"*Resolved*, fourth, That, as Alumni of Illinois College, we feel a deep and abiding interest in the prosperity of the institution, and that we believe that its success is intimately connected with the future standing and advancement of Illinois."

The appointment of Prof. J. M. Sturtevant president of the college was endorsed, after which Mr. Ayers was chosen president; Wm. Coffin, vice-president, and W. H. Starr secretary for the next year. Rev. Wm Coffin was chosen president, Chauncey Carter, vice-president, and J. B. Shaw, secretary, in 1846. The deaths of Rev. G. W. Pyle and J K. Morse Esq., were reported. In 1847, Rev. C. E. Blood, president, J. B. Shaw, vice-president, and M. P. Ayers, secretary, were chosen; N. Bateman was constituted poet for the next year, and the society passed resolutions regretting the resignation of Prof. J. B. Turner. The society met in the Presbyterian Church in 1848, re-electing Messrs. Blood and Ayers, and making R. S. Kendall vice-president. Richard Yates was selected to preside in 1849, with M. P. Ayers vice-president, and A. L. Harrington, secretary. M. P. Ayers was made president; J. B. Shaw, vice-president, and Harrington, secretary, again, in 1850. The same were chosen again in 1851, except Jas. W. English, vice-president.

Prof. Sturtevant invited the society to hold its next reunion at his residence, which was agreed to, and the annual addresses for the next year were dispensed with. An annual fee of fifty cents was ordered paid. Newton Bateman was chosen president in 1852; Cyrus Epler, vice-president, and J. W. English, secretary. R. Yates was chosen orator and H. K. Jones, alternate, for the next year. Bateman, Epler and English were re-elected in 1853; and in 1854 Bateman was re-elected, with M. P. Ayers, vice-president, and Thos. W. Smith, secretary. These latter were re-elected in 1855, and the death of Edward Ruggles was announced. Bateman, Ayers and Smith were again elected in 1856, and the name of Rollin Mears was reported in the necrology. The same officers were elected in 1857. J. D. Whitney, Daniel Brown and Edward Geyer died that year. M. P. Ayers, Esq., introduced resolutions congratulating the Alumni upon the increased encouragement afforded by liberal subscriptions to Illinois College.

No meeting is recorded in 1858, but in 1859 Hon. Cyrus Epler was elected president, Rev. Chas. B. Barton, vice-president, and Thos. W. Smith, Esq., again secretary. M. P. Ayers, John H. Wood, N. W. Branson, E. Dayton, and E. B. Eno were appointed a committee to reorganize the annual reunion, with Messrs. N. Bateman, R. M. Tunnel and E. P. Kirby in charge of the literary section of the plan.

In 1860 the society met in the Congregational Church, and N. Bateman was chosen president; Jas. W. English, vice-president, and E. P. Kirby secretary. Rev. G. C. Noyes was chosen orator, and Rev. J. M. Sturtevant, jr., poet.

June 21st a literary and gustatory reunion was held at the college building, and it was quite a success. The same officers were elected in 1861. Bateman, English and Kirby were again re-elected in 1862, Richard Yates being elected orator and Henry M. Post poet. The death of Prof. W. W. Happy was announced.

No meeting was held until June, 1866, when Dr. Samuel Willard was chosen president. Rev. J. M. Sturtevant, Jr., vice-president, and E. P. Kirby, secretary. Bateman and R. Wolcott were appointed orator and poet, and a number of class secretaries elected.

The incumbent officers were re-elected in 1867, and some reports received from class secretaries.

In 1868 the officers were re-elected, E. W. Blatchford was chosen orator, and F. V. L. Eno, poet.

Prof. E. A. Tanner succeeded E. P. Kirby as secretary, and the other officers were re-elected in 1869. The death of Lieut.-Col. Frank Adams was announced. N. Bateman, president; H. K. Jones, vice-president, with E. A. Tanner, secretary, were chosen in 1870. A dollar fee was decided upon for the annual levy.

A committee was appointed to secure representation in the college government, consisting of Dr. H. K. Jones, Rev. J. M. Sturtevant, Jr., N. W. Branson, Esq. At the annual meeting, in 1871, a committee was appointed to publish an alumni register. The trustees of Illinois College agreed to give the society three trusteeships and an alumni professorship, provided the society raised an endowment fund of $25,000. The association re-elected its officers. Rev. James McLaughlin, Dr. E. Dayton and William Gallagher Esq., were on the necrological roll.

In 1872, the meeting was held in Strawn's Opera House. A balance was reported in the treasury, and the officers were re-elected.

Rev. T. K. Beecher was chosen orator, and Hon. F. V. L. Eno, poet. Rev. Eugene Strode's death was reported.

Hon. N. Bateman, president, and H. K. Jones, M. D., vice president, were re-elected, and Ensley Moore chosen secretary and treasurer in 1873, and the latter has held this position ever since.

Judge J. T. Morton was chosen orator and E. H. Bristow, Esq., poet. The necrology consisted of John S. Howell, J. Warren Sturtevant, John D. Fry, James D. Masters.

No meeting was held in 1874 but in 1875 the society met in the Opera House, the same officers being re-elected.

Dr. H K. Jones and Judge E. P. Kirby, on behalf of the trustees of Illinois College, announced that hereafter the alumni might nominate three trustees of Illinois College, as vacancies might occur, each such trustee to serve five years. The offer was accepted by the alumni association, and it selected five names to be voted on as the candidate for 1876.

Richard Yates, John H. McClintock and A. J. Ellison were among the dead for the previous year.

In 1876, the secretary announced that Julius E. Strawn, Esq., had been chosen first alumni trustee. R. S. Kendall and Frederick Brown had died. Messrs. N. Bateman, H. K. Jones and Ensley Moore were re-elected officers.

The same officers were re-elected in 1877, and it was moved that hereafter the two literary societies and this association hold their respective reunions tri-ennially, instead of annually. The motion was passed and a committee appointed to confer with the Sigma Pi and Phi Alpha societies, consisting of Messrs. W. D. Wood, E. L. McDonald and J. E. Strawn. Calvin Goudy, M. D., was the only brother who died during the year. Resolutions were adopted upon the recent death of Prof. Samuel Adams, M. D., long time connected with the college and loved by all.

In June, 1878, Bateman, Jones and Moore were chosen officers, and a committee appointed on semi-centennial celebration of Illinois College. Hon. N. Bateman, H. K. Jones, M. D., Ensley Moore, T. J. Pitner, M. D., and E. L. McDonald were charged with this duty. The death of Lieut. Wm. L. English, 7th regiment, U. S A., was reported.

Messrs. M. P. Ayers, Carl Epler and J. P. Lippincott were appointed to raise funds and arrange for a monument to Dr. Adams, and five persons were nominated for alumni trustees for 1879.

At the great meeting held in 1879 it was announced that M. P. Ayers, Esq., had been chosen alumni trustee. The same officers were again selected for the ensuing year, and the committee on Dr. Adams' monument reported.

Dr. H. K. Jones was elected president in 1883, and E. L. McDonald, vice-president, at the same time. Both were re-elected in 1884.

This completes the official record of the organization, but its members have written their names high on the scroll of fame all through our land, and others have given their lives to Christianizing other lands, where they have labored for years.

Richard Yates, war governor; Newton Bateman, the great educator; E. W. Blatchford and the Ayers brothers, prominent business men; Hons. James M. Epler, Wm. P. Callon, H. S. Van Eaton, N. W. Branson, Judge J. T. C. Flagg, of Missouri; Hon. J. P. Garlick, of Oregon; the Goudy brothers, of Illinois; Chas. E. Lippincott, argonaut to California in 1849, hero in the war and twice state auditor; Rev. Dr. R. W. Patterson, the brothers Thomas W., John A., and D. B. Smith, of Jacksonville; Fairbank, Atkinson and Bergen, foreign missionaries; Judge E. P. Kirby, Hon. J. M. Lansden, Judges C. Epler and Lyman Lacey, Col. A. C. Matthews, James E. Munroe and J. Scott Stevens, of Chicago; Hons J. N. Carter, W. H. Govert, W. H. Collins, Q. E. Browning and Ed. L. McDonald; Rev. Dr. W. S. Curtis, Judge Morton, of Kansas; Dr. Samuel Willard, of Chicago; Dr. H. K. Jones, the Platonic philosopher; Gov. Wm. Jayne, Paul Selby, the editor; and President Tanner, are but representatives of the large and increasing brotherhood, who love old Illinois College, as their Alma Mater, and have honored our great state.

Twenty-Sixth—A FEW MORE ITEMS PERTAINING TO THE YEARS 1854–9, GLEANED FROM "WEEKLY SENTINEL" FILES BY MRS. M. T. BAILEY.

The amount of expenditure for the Illinois State Hospital for the Insane, at Jacksonville, was, according to the treasurer's fourth biennial report, ending November 30, 1854, $100,680.93, leaving a balance on hand of $4,015.66. From December 1, 1852, to the above date, 340 patients had been admitted into the institution.

In 1855 a bill was presented to the Legislature to incorporate the Morgan county Agricultural and Mechanical Association, and to amend the charter of Jacksonville.

In February, 1855 a snow storm prevailed all over the northern and middle portions of the Union and kept Jacksonville waiting for news for several weeks.

In 1846 an act was passed by the Nineteenth General Assembly of Illinois, to incorporate the Jacksonville Gas Light and Coke Company; also an act to incorporate the Jacksonville & Savanna Railroad Company.

In April and May, 1855, a portion of the pupils of the Blind Institution gave concerts at Decatur, Clinton, Bloomington, Carlinville, Lower Alton and Upper Alton, for the purpose of extending a knowledge of the institution and to induce the blind to apply for admission.

In May 1855, a terrible cyclone swept through the central part of Morgan county, killing stock and people and destroying property.

In the election in Illinois in 1855 for and against prohibition, Morgan county gave a majority of fifty-five for prohibition.

The first Morgan County Fair held at Jacksonville was opened on Tuesday, October 23, 1855, but owing to the unfavorable weather there was no exhibition until the day following. A heavy, driving snow from the north, accompanied by a chilly wind, made the fair-ground anything but a comfortable locality. One shed capable of sheltering some twenty head of cattle had been erected. The balance of the stock were exposed to the storm.

In August, 1855, the marshal's tables showed the population of Jacksonville to be 5,500. In 1850 Morgan county had 16,064 inhabitants; in 1855, 17,755.

On March 28, 1855, the officers of the Circuit Court of Morgan county and the Grand Jury passed resolutions complimenting the retiring judge, Hon. D. M. Woodson, earnestly requesting that he be a candidate for re-election.

Illinois Female College was attended in its first year by 117 pupils; seven years later by 283.

On the night of October 25, 1855, a fire broke out south of the square in Jacksonville, destroying a whole block. Thirty-nine business men shared in the loss, which aggregated $65,000. Seven horses and one man were burned in a livery stable.

In 1855 Hon. Newton Cloud was appointed temporary principal of the Illinois Deaf and Dumb Institute, and in April 1856 Mr. Edward Peet, of New York, was appointed principal.

In March, 1856 Mr. Clayton, junior editor of the *Journal*, retired from the editorial chair and Mr. Selby conducted the *Journal* alone. At that time there were three papers published in the city, *Sentinel*, *Journal* and *Constitutionalist*.

On the night of the 15th of April, 1856, a hurricane passed over the county, south and southeast of Jacksonville, uprooting trees and destroying property in the same path of the noted hurricanes which destroyed life and property in 1859 and 1880.

In 1856 a campaign sheet, called *Buchanan Banner* was published by Wm. T. Davis, who had shortly before published the Jacksonville *Hatchet*.

Lots one mile south of the public square, in Lurton and Kedsie's addition to Jacksonville were sold in November, 1856, at auction, bringing from $300 to $690, being lots of two acres each.

During the month of November, 1856, there were shipped from Jacksonville 29,604½ bushels of wheat; hogs, 3,700 head. From July 1, 1856, to January 21, 1857, 151,387¾ bushels of wheat were shipped; hogs, 22,876 head.

In the Hospital for the Insane, December 1st, 1854, there were 166 patients, and in 1856, 214.

In 1855 the municipal revenue of Jacksonville was $4,800.25, the salaries of town officers amounted to $875, liquors bought by the corporation $1,428.70. In the beginning of the year 1857 the city charter was advocated, Hon. Cyrus Epler warmly advocating the change, also the necessary appropriations to increase the size, furnish and properly heat and light the Insane and Deaf and Dumb Institutions. The charter referred to was voted upon by the people Monday, March 9th, and voted down by a majority of 198.

In 1857, Mr. J. T. Springer commenced the practice of law in Morgan county.

In January 1859, Rev. L. M. Glover commenced a series of free lectures in the Presbyterian Church; subject: Europe, Asia and Africa.

In 1844 a tract of eighty acres lying northwest of the square brought at public sale $10.12½ per acre. Two other twenty acre lots brought $17 and $20 per acre. In 1848 twenty acres east of the above was bought for $13.34 per acre, worth in 1857 $41.00 per acre. Sixteen acres, north of railroad, sold in 1850 for $37.50 per acre, re-sold in 1855 for $100 per acre, again in 1859 for $400 per acre. In 1843 the State Bank sold for its notes, worth fifty cents on the dollar, forty acres east of Beardstown street, for $14.50 per acre, re-sold in 1857 for $150 per acre. In 1854 twenty acres were bought for fair ground at $100 per acre, sold in 1858 for $296 per acre. Off the same tract in 1857 twenty acres at $300 per acre. In 1847 a lot was purchased adjoining railroad for $27, sold in 1856 for $2,500.

In May 18th, 1857, a letter from Waverly says: We have four churches, about fifteen business houses, two flour mills, several carriage manufactories, two monument or grave-stone manufactories, five physicians and about nine hundred inhabitants. There is one good hotel, kept by Joseph Challen, and a fine livery stable kept by J. W. Meachem & Co., is filled with good horses, among which are "Andrew Hamet" raised by Dr. Warfield, of Lexington, Ky., "Ned Forest" a Penna draft horse and "Illinois" a small pacer.

August 21st, 1857, Mr. John Hockenhull bought a lot on the east side of the square in Jacksonville for $10,125, or $150 per foot. This was known as the Congregational Church property; that society bought a lot on College Avenue and built the same year a brick edifice.

In 1858 there were in the county asylum for the poor thirty-three inmates.

The Baptist Church was dedicated April 7th, 1858.

July, 1858, the lot on which Strawn's Opera House stands was bought for $225 per foot. The two adjoining lots on the west of the above sold the same day for $175 per foot.

On Friday evening, February 3rd, 1859, Hon. Abraham Lincoln lectured before one of the literary societies of Illinois College; subject: Discoveries and Inventions. When Prof. Sturtevant was soliciting aid for Illinois College he approached Jacob Strawn, who immediately put down his name for five hundred dollars and paid it soon after.

July 15th, 1869, the thermometer stood 135.

November 14th, 1859, the *Journal* office with all its material, presses, accounts and *Journal* files of many years was destroyed by fire. Wm. H. Collins was then proprietor.

The Congregational Church, on College Avenue, was dedicated Sunday, December 4th, 1859. The discourse was delivered by Rev. T. M. Post, of St. Louis.

From January 1st, 1859, to January 1st, 1860, there were eighty-eight deaths in the town of Jacksonville.

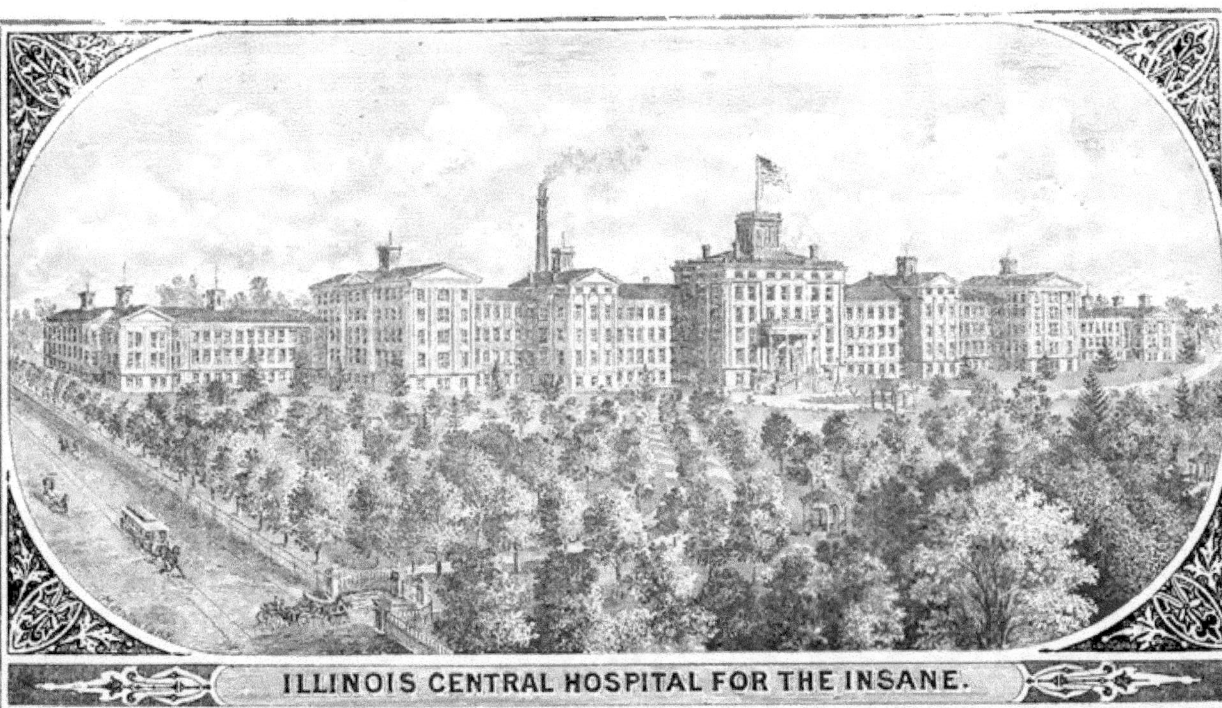

ILLINOIS CENTRAL HOSPITAL FOR THE INSANE.

CHAPTER XIV.

Cass County Since the Separation from Morgan—Its Officials and Legislators—Laying off of Towns—Modern Virginia—Its Officers, Schools, Opera House, Etc.—Sketches of Old Settlers—"The Three Mile Contest"—Population Growth.

THE separation of Cass from old Morgan occurred in 1837. The first county seat was Beardstown; then Virginia had the honor. In 1843 Beardstown secured it again and kept it until 1872, when Virginia again received the prize and still retains it.

The following are the names of the resident representatives of Cass county in the Legislature, from the separation until the present date:

William Holmes, for the years 1838-'40; Amos S West, 1840-'42; David Epler, 1842-'44; John W. Pratt, 1842-'46; Francis Arenz, 1844-'46; Edward W. Turner, 1846-'48; Richard S. Thomas, 1848-'50; Cyrus Wright, 1852-'54; Samuel Christy, 1856-'58; Henry E. Dummer, senator, 1860-'64; Frederick Rearick, 1860-'62; James M. Epler, 1862-'64; James M. Epler, 1866-'68; James M. Epler, senator, 1868-'72; Wm. W. Easley, 1870-'74; John F. Snyder, 1878-'80; John W. Savage, 1878-'80; J. Henry Shaw, 1880-'82; H. C. Thompson, 1882-'84; T. L. Matthews, 1882-J. Henry Shaw, 1884-'85.

The principal officers of Cass county since its formation, are as follows:

County Commissioners—Joshua P. Crow, Amos Bonney, Geo. F. Miller, elected August 7, 1837. Joshua P. Crow, Amos Bonney, Isaac C. Spence, elected August 6, 1838. Amos Bonney, John C. Scott, elected August 3, 1840, for three years; Marcus Chandler, for two years. John C. Scott, Marcus Chandler, W. J. DeHaven, elected. August, 1841; John C. Scott, W. J. DeHaven Robert Leeper, elected August, 1842; John C. Scott, W. J. DeHaven, Henry McHenry, elected December 26, 1842; W. J. DeHaven, Henry McHenry, Jesse B. Pence, elected August 7, 1843; Henry McHenry, J. B. Pence, Geo. B. Thompson, elected August, 1844; J. B. Pence, George B. Thompson, Wm. McHenry, elected first Monday of August, 1845; G. B. Thompson, Wm. McHenry, Henry McHenry, elected first Monday of August, 1846. Wm. McHenry, Henry McHenry, Geo. H. Nolte, elected first Monday of August, 1847. Henry McHenry, Geo. H. Nolte, Geo. W. Weaver elected first Monday of August, 1848.

County Court, established 1849—James Shaw, judge; Wm. Taylor, associate; Thomas Plaster, associate; elected November 6, 1849. James Shaw, judge; Thomas Plaster, associate; Jacob Ward, associate; elected May 19, 1851. John A. Arenz, judge; Isaac Epler, associate; Sylvester Paddock, associate; elected November, 1853. John A. Arenz, judge; Sylvester Paddock, associate; John M. Short, associate; elected November, 1855. H. C. Havekluft, judge; Wm. McHenry, associate; G. W. Shawen, associate; elected November, 1857. F. H. Rearick, judge; Wm. McHenry, associate; G. W. Shawen, elected November, 1861. John A. Arenz, judge; Jennings G. Mathis, associate; Samuel Smith, associate; elected November, 1865. Alexander Huffman, judge, Andrew Struble, associate; Jeptha Plaster, associate; elected November, 1869. F. H Rearick, judge; Andrew Struble, associate; Jeptha Plaster, associate; elected February 24, 1872. John W. Savage, judge; elected November, 1873. Jacob W. Rearick, judge, elected November, 1877. Darius N. Walker, judge, elected November, 1882.

County Commissioners—Wm. Campbell, John H. Malone, Robt. Fielden, elected November, 1873. Wm. Campbell, John H. Malone, Luke Dunn, elected November,

1875. John H. Malone, Luke Dunn, Robert Crum, elected in 1876. Luke Dunn, Robert Crum, Robert Clark, elected in 1877. Robert Crum, Robert Clark, Thomas Knight, elected in 1878. Robert Clark, Thomas Knight, Robert Crum, re-elected in 1879. Thomas Knight, Robert Crum, Lewis C. Hackman, elected in 1880. Robert Crum, Lewis C. Hackman, Luke Dunn, re-elected in 1881. Faulkner W. Gerdis, elected in 1882. Lewis C. Hackman, re-elected in 1883. George A. Beard (to fill vacancy), elected April, 1884. Henry Gann, elected November, 1884.

Probate Justices—1837 to 1849—Jno. S. Wilbourne, elected August 7, 1837; Joshua P. Crow, 1839; Alexander Huffman, 1841; H. E. Dummer, 1843; Hulett Clark, 1847; H. E. Dummer, May 13, 1849.

Sheriffs—Lemon Plaster, elected August 7, 1837; John Savage, 1841; Joseph M. McLean, 1848; J. B. Fulks, November, 1850; Wm. Pitner, 1852; James Taylor, 1854; James A. Dick, 1856; Francis H. Rearick, 1858; James Taylor, 1860; Charles E. Yeck, 1862; James A. Dick, 1864; Charles E. Yeck, 1866; Thomas Chapman, 1868; Horace Cowan, 1870; George Volkmar, 1872; Wm. Epler, 1874; A. H. Seilschott, 1876; A. H. Seilschott, elected November, 1878; re-elected in 1880 and 1882.

Clerks of County Commissioners' Court—John M. Pratt, elected in 1837; H. H. Carpenter, 1845; Lewis F. Sanders, 1847; re-elected in 1849 as county clerk.

Clerks of County Court—Allen J. Hill, 1857; James B. Black, 1873; James Frank Robinson, 1883.

Clerks of the Circuit Court—Nathaniel B. Thompson, appointed by the judge in 1837. James Berry and Reddick Horn, appointed by the judge; date of appointment not known. Thos. R. Sanders, elected in 1848; Silvester Emmons, 1852; James Taylor, 1856; Henry Phillips, 1860; C. F. Diffenbacher, 1868; Albert F. Arenz, 1872; Thomas V. Finney, 1876; Finis E. Downing, 1880; re-elecced in 1884.

Superintendents of Public Instruction—Richard S. Thomas, 1845; John B. Shaw, 1849; Frank Hollenger, 1857; James K. Vandemark, 1861; Harvey Tate, 1869; John Gore, 1873; Allen J. Hill, 1877; Andrew L. Anderson, 1882.

State's Attorneys—Linus C. Chandler, elected in 1872; Arthur A. Leeper, 1876; Reuben R. Hewitt, 1880; re-elected in 1884.

County Assessors and Treasurers—Thomas Wilbourne, Isaac W. Overall, Wm. W. Babb, 1837-'38; Wm. H. Helms, 1838-'39; Robert G. Gaines, 1839-'47; John Craig, 1847-'51; Martin F. Higgins, 1851-'53; Phineas T. Underwood, 1853-'57; Frank A. Hammer, 1857-'59; David C. Dilley, 1859-71; Philip H. Bailey, 1871-'73; John L. Cire, 1873-'81; John Rahn, 1881; Henry Quigg, 1882.

By the plots, surveys and legal instruments on file in the Recorder's office, we learn that places were laid out into town lots, before the separation, as follows: Beardstown, September 9, 1829; Princeton, February 19, 1833; Richmond, March 2, 1833; Virginia, May 17, 18, 19, 1836; Philadelphia, July 11, 1836.

Princeton, on "Jersey Prairie," was laid off by John G. Bergen. Richmond was in the northeast part of the county, but is now out of existence. Johnston Shelton was the surveyor of Virginia in 1836, as well as of Jacksonville in 1825—eleven years before.

Since the separate existence of Cass, several other towns have been duly laid off, viz: Monroe (since vacated), Lancaster, May 6, 1837; Arenzville, February 17, 1840, Chandlerville, April 29, 1848; Ashland, July, 1857; Newmanville, April 6, 1859. In the latter case, Rev. Wm. Clark owned the land, and will sell no lots without a provision in the deeds prohibiting the sale of liquor. This excellent provision is also insisted

---

NOTE.—Thomas Wilbourne was elected Treasurer August 7, 1837, and afterward resigned, and Isaac W. Overall was elected December 16, 1837, to fill the vacancy, and took possession of the office and entered upon its duties, but his election was contested by Wm. W. Babb, and Babb was declared the rightful incumbent. Martin F. Higgins was re-elected Assessor and Treasurer November 8th, but died shortly afterward, and Phineas T. Underwood was elected to fill the vacancy, and re-elected in 1855. John L. Cire died during his last term of office, and John Rahn was appointed by the County Commissioners to fill the vacancy, and he was elected by the people November 1881, to fill a constitutional interim of one year. Faulkner W. Gerdis died February 26, 1884.

upon by Mr. William C. Stevenson, in the sale of Little Indian property. Francis Arenz was the founder of the town bearing his name and Archibald, Job and Alexander Beard laid out Philadelphia as School Trustees.

The compiler of this volume gave himself the pleasure, a few days since, of visiting the city of Virginia. The courteous treatment received from merchants, bankers, editors, county officers and old settlers was worthy of this sincere acknowledgment of obligation. The little municipality did not seem to be feeling the hard times any more than sister cities of much larger pretensions, and her business men were hopeful and evidently enterprising. The burg's biggest item of the day was the formal dedication of the new opera "house that Jack (Tureman) built," and that Charlie Tinney, of the *Gazette*, with more than the average newspaper man's enterprise, has done so much to secure for his home. After trying the road from the depot to the square, both on foot and in the 'bus, we were decidedly of the opinion that if Bro. Beatty, of the *Enquirer*, wants to get even with his rival in the way of public benefits, he should secure the dedication of a street railroad for Virginia. After newspapers and an opera house, the next "long-felt want" is a street raiload or well-paved highways.

At his old stand in the drug store we found our old friend, Mr. Will Wood, busy in the calendar, almanac, pill and cigar business. He finds time, too, for his share of Sunday-School work. Here we met the bibliopole and naturalist of the community, Dr. Snyder, who was prompt to volunteer words of encouragement, and an order for "Historic Morgan."

In the court house we found quite a number of friends and much assistance. Circuit Clerk F. E. Downing obligingly searched the records for us for dates of the laying out of the various towns of the county. The present county officials are D. N. Walker, county judge; J. F. Robinson, county clerk; Finis E. Downing, circuit clerk; Henry Quigg, treasurer; A. H. Sielschott, sheriff; R. R. Hewitt, state's attorney; A. L. Anderson, school superintendent; Joseph Wilson, surveyor; George L. Warlow, master in chancery. Under their management "Little Cass" seems to be waxing fat and prospering.

The city of Virginia we found to be governed by the following officials: Mayor, Ernest P. Widmayer (a former Jacksonvillian and brother of its ex-mayor); clerk, George Kelly (absent, but ruling by proxy in the person of S. W. Bailey); attorney, A. A. Leeper; marshal, Thomas Finn; aldermen, L. R. Simmons, Morrison Graves, C. I. Haskell, Joseph F. Cherry, R. W. Rabourn, W. W. Bishop—two from each of the three wards into which the city is divided.

There are three school buildings in Virginia, all located in one school district, and managed by three directors, viz: J. N. Gridley, D. G. Smith, A. A. Leeper. The instructors in their employ are: Prof. J. F. McCullough, superintendent; Samuel B. Rach and R. P. Anderson, assistants, and the following teachers: Misses Rachael Berry, Harmonia Tate, Adelia Snyder, Belle Rodgers, Marie Way, Jessie Wilson, and Mr. George Schafer. As far as we could learn the schools are well governed and attended, the pupils making very satisfactory progress. With a population of 1,800 Virginia sends 475 pupils to her schools.

The saloon license system prevails here, the fee being $720 per annum.

In the Circuit Court room we found Hon. Richard W. Mills, so well known and whose aged mother, now living near Arcadia, in Morgan county, was among the earliest settlers of this part of the state. Mills was trying a case before Esquire Keeling Berry, who addressed the last Old Settler's meeting so interestingly, and whose mind as to old-time matters in Morgan and Cass is as clear as that of a man forty years younger. He gave us much valuable information as to the pioneers and customs of log cabin days. Before we write of a few others of the first settlers of Cass we should speak of this old-timer and his recollections. He remembers making the first purchase in the first store in Virginia—three pairs of shoes for his father's family—of Mr. Oliver, while the goods were being unpacked from the shipping-boxes.

Mr. Berry informs us that he came to Morgan county in 1833, in the fall of the year, from East Virginia, with his parents, two brothers and four sisters. One brother was already out here. The family traveled 900 miles to reach their new home. The men and boys footed it nearly the whole way. They settled one mile east of Little Indian station, where his parents lived until their deaths in 1857 and 1861.

Mr. Berry, Sr., had bought 130 acres of land, thirty-five under cultivation. Keeling had but little opportunity of education, not attending school more than eleven months in his life-time. The boy was thoughtful and studious, and gained knowledge by night-study at home. In his twenty-second year he began teaching in a log school-house, one-fourth of a mile west of Little Indian, on what is now Henderson Massey's farm, and there the identical old school house continues to stand to this day. Young Berry continued there as teacher for three terms, in the years 1839 and 1840. Since then he has followed the same occupation, up to 1876, in Cass or Macon county. In politics he has always been identified with the Whig or Republican party. In 1856, in Macon county, he was quite an active campaigner for Fremont. In 1867, as one of the commission he adjudicated the county seat contest. It was one of the hottest ever known in the State. The result was that the court house remained in Beardstown. In November, 1872, there was another warm contest and vote on the same subject, but a fairer vote. Virginia triumphed. Beardstown contested, but lost. A change of site cannot now be made until a three-fifths majority for a change can be obtained, which is not likely. It might be mentioned in this connection that in one of these county seat elections Virginia returned a poll-book with 2,820 votes recorded, when at any preceding election she had never polled over 750. Mr. Keeling Berry continued to make his home on a farm until he moved into Virginia in January, 1868. He was county surveyor for one term, not being physically able to work on a farm. Now he is filling for the third term the office of justice of the peace.

In writing of the pioneer settlers of old Morgan, now Cass, we are reminded that there is a class often neglected by local historians that deserves the highest praise for heroic endurance, self-sacrificing labor, and that permeating influence upon a community that tended to mould and elevate character more than any others. We refer to the devoted Christian women who came in the prime of life, with husbands and children, from homes of comfort, to these unsettled regions where they toiled for their families and labored and prayed for the advancement of the morals of the new settlements. At all hours of the day or night they went at the call of Philanthropy to care for the sick, to relieve the needy, to comfort the afflicted and even to bury the dead. There were no professional nurses or physicians, homes were widely separated and the calls of distress would often cause the women to ride many miles in the night-time, over lonely prairie roads or forest paths. Many lives were doubtless saved by their prompt response and timely attention. "Mother" Redman, of Sugar Grove, Cass county, now gone to her reward, is mentioned as living an especially useful life in this respect. Undoubtedly many others deserve strong praise for similar services. Among the older settlers of Morgan county is Maria [widow of George] Cunningham. She reached this county in the spring of 1825, with the family of her father—Allen Q. Lindsey. They settled two miles south of Princeton, and she was married in 1835. Since then she has not lived farther from Virginia than four miles. Her father was a justice of the peace; so was one of her brothers. Her brother Allen is said to have precipitated the Black Hawk war. Being then a boatman on the Illinois river, he was attacked by the Indians and defended himself vigorously with firearms. The Lindsey family were prominent and public spirited, exerting themselves to wisely shape society. They were Kentuckians of much refinement and general knowledge, always active in politics, although not office seekers. Their views were of the Clay-Whig school.

Mrs. Elizabeth Hopkins is another living witness of early times hereabouts. In the fall of 1825 she removed from Clark county, Ind., to what is now the southern part of Cass county. The next year they made a home and settled in Sugar Grove, in the southeast part of Cass, some four miles from Virginia. Her husband, Henry (now deceased), without help, improved 100 acres of prairie and lived on that farm forty-nine years, raising to maturity a family of eleven children. Mr. and Mrs. Hopkins saw this region grow from nothing to as prosperous and thrifty a community as the county affords. Their home was a preaching-place for the Methodist ministry from the first up to 1840. They always had a hearty welcome for the itinerant preachers, some of whom, when stopping there, went out into the field to help their host reap the harvest.

Another Indianian to locate in the now Cass part of Morgan was James Garner, who came into "Panther Grove," six miles southeast of Virginia, in 1831. He is well remembered by early settlers as a Methodist preacher, of but limited education, yet he was one whom all loved to hear, and he exercised as much influence, perhaps, as any other man in the county in his time, for the moral improvement of its inhabitants. It is said of him that after plowing all the week he would consider his horse as needing rest too much to be used on the Sabbath so he would walk three or four miles to meet his appointments. He died in 1863.

Among the present residents of Virginia, known and respected by all, is the Rev. William (commonly called "Uncle Billy") Clark. His father, Thomas, brought him and four other children out to Morgan in April, 1827, and the family settled in North Grove, some four miles west of the present site of Virginia, where they farmed it until 1833, but soon returned. William began preaching in 1839 in Iowa, but returned to Cass in '40, when he was twenty-three years of age, and has been preaching the Gospel in or near his old home from that day to this, as a circuit rider of the Methodist Episcopal church. Now-a-days he only preaches occasionally.

Mr. Clark furnishes us with the following account of himself:

I was born in Franklin county, Tennessee, January 17, 1817. My father, Thomas Clark, was born in Pennsylvania, and my mother in East Tennessee. They came to Madison county, Illinois, in 1826. In April, 1827, they came to Morgan county, now Cass. They settled in North Grove, four miles west of the present site of Virginia. The family consisted of father, mother and seven children. Our first school teacher was Joshua P. Crow, in 1827, who taught several terms at the Bridgewater school house, a log cabin in that neighborhood. The county then abounded in wild game including deer and turkeys, without number. The people were remarkable for their industry, honesty, frugality and sociability and were much on an equality—none rich, but few wealthy. Had no churches but their log cabins. The old Baptists were the most numerous among the early settlers in this section. The first Methodist meetings in the neighborhood were held at my uncle William Clark's, on the farm now owned by Edward Davis. The first circuit preachers were Joseph Talkington and Isaac House. The first burial in the Clark grave yard was a child of Mr. Norton. The first Methodist class organized was at the house of William Myers, on the Tureman farm, consisting of five members—William M. Clark, his wife and daughter, Mrs. Myers and my mother. The people gave more attention to the gospel in those days than now.

We saw the deep snow in 1830. It fell early in December and remained until spring, and was about three feet deep on a level. Nearly all the game was destroyed by reason of the snow that winter. It was never so plenty afterwards.

I will name a few of the families living in this part of the county in that early day, as far as my knowledge goes: Matthews, Bridgewater, Ruby, Davis, Hoffman, Williams, Crow, Bowyer, Savage, Summers, Case, Wiggins, Hamby, Bristow, Gilpin, Rev. Levi Springer, Rev. Reddick Horn, Myers, Tureman, Haynes, my uncle William M. Clark and my father's family.

We had no two-horse wagons or stoves; the old wooden mould barshare and shovel plow was the order of that day. One great difficulty we labored under was lack of mills. We had to go from three to twenty-five miles to get a little corn ground. In company with an uncle I had to wait three days and nights at uncle Jimmy Sims' horse mill, near Arcadia, to get grinding done. In 1829, I rode sixteen miles to get a single letter out of the postoffice in Jacksonville; the postage was twenty-five cents in those days. Jacksonville was but a small village when I first saw it, in 1827, and Beardstown was scarcely begun. In the spring of 1831 the big snow went off with such a rush that it raised the streams unusually high. Uncle Tommy Beard, the founder of Beardstown, brought his ferryboat out to the slough on this side and ferried the folks across the slough to get to town. The first steam flouring mill was built by Knapp & Pouge, in Beardstown. I think it was built in 1828, and was the first steam engine I ever saw.

After five years residence in this neighborhood my father moved eleven miles eastward of Jacksonville, to near the head of the Mauvaisterre, on the Vandalia road. Big Indian Creek in that day was flush enough with water to run mills and several were built on it, and so with other streams, but matters have greatly changed. In the fall of 1833, there occurred a strange phenonema, on the night of the 13th of November—the apparent falling of the stars, raining like hail from the clouds, which created some alarm among the people. This year, 1833, the cholera visited Jacksonville in a fearful manner, carrying off about one hundred of its inhabitants, and laid the town in mourning. My father left Morgan county that fall and went into Schuyler county, where he remained two years, and then went to Iowa Territory and remained there until May, 1840, and then returned to Cass county and settled in the old neighborhood where he first settled in 1827, not far from the present site of Virginia, and remained in the county until his death, which occurred August 16, 1852, and my mother died August 2, 1866. They are both buried, with other members of the family, at the old burying ground in North Grove, four miles west of Virginia.

I was converted while living in Iowa, September 28, 1837, and was licensed to preach in the M. E. church, November 30, 1839. I traveled the circuits about four years in all. I have been a local preacher or minister in said church ever since. I have been a resident of Morgan and Cass counties fifty-one years—farming mostly for a livelihood. I have seen nearly all the first settlers pass away and new ones take their place and have marked the many changes and improvements that have taken place in the last half century. As time has rolled on and improvements have been made, such as railroads and telegraphs, the facilities have become much greater for the development of the resources of the world and also the speedy communication to and from all parts of the habitable globe And schools and churches have so increased that society ought to have been more refined, elevated and christianized ere this. But with all these advantages the world seems to be no better, but worse. Why is this? We answer, because man is a fallen and depraved being, and to materially change his life he needs the converting grace of God. It is not frequent, to say the least, for anyone to find himself so near the same spot at the end of fifty-eight years, as the writer. And he will say of himself that he has led an active and laborious life, wholly abstaining from the use of all intoxicants and tobacco; that he has enjoyed good general health, and finds in the midst of the evils of this wicked world many good things to be thankful for, and as a Christian, "having promise of the life that now is and of that which is to come;" and is comfortably situated, with his kind companion in their quiet home, in the decline of life, in the beautiful little city of Virginia, the county seat of Cass.

Mr. John H. Tureman, one of the wealthy farmers of Cass, now lives in the neighborhood where Mr. Clark settled. He was born there in 1828 and has made it his life home. He has just made himself "a reputation and a name" in Virginia by erecting an opera house at a cost of $17,000. His mother-in-law, Mrs. Elizabeth Davis, now over eighty years of age, is also still in that neighborhood, being the only person now living there who has been there since 1828. But to return to the Clarks. Circuit court was in session when they came through Jacksonville in 1827, from Madison county, enroute to North Grove. Jacksonville was then a village of 300 or 400 inhabitants, and court was being held in a log cabin. William remembers that in 1829 they heard of a letter in the postoffice at Jacksonville for his father from his (William's) brother on the

Okaw. So he rode on horseback sixteen miles to get the letter, paid the required twenty-five cents postage and returned home with it. He used to go eighteen miles to a horse power mill for grinding and even farther—twenty-five miles—to Exeter to a water power mill.

Mr. Clark says the first school teacher in Cass was Joshua P. Crow, who in 1828 taught the young idea how to shoot in a log cabin, some three and one-half miles west of Virginia, called the Bridgewater school house. The first burying ground was near-by and this is now called after the Clarks. The first burial was that of a child of Mr. Norton in 1826. The first frame meeting house in Virginia was built by the Protestant Methodists in 1836. In those circuit-riding days there were no frame houses; log cabins were the homes, the school houses and the churches. Preaching was heard in private houses or school cabins. The Baptists were the prevailing denomination. The first M. E. circuit preaching was in 1828 by Revs. Isaac House and Joseph Talkington, who organized the first Methodist church in Cass. Mrs. Clark, whose maiden name was Glover, came from Pope to Madison, then to Morgan, settling in the neighborhood of the Clarks and Turemans.

We have recorded the statement that Mr. Crow was the first school teacher in this part of old Morgan. The second is said to have been Daniel Corbey who taught in Sugar Grove, and the third, John Biddlecombe, who wielded the birch in his neighborhood. Mr. William Holmes was teacher, according to Mr. Keeling Berry, as early as 1830, using one of the abandoned cabins in Sugar Grove.

The first tannery erected in Cass county, and in fact in this part of Illinois, was by Andrew Cunningham, who is still living, but out of business.

Among the Kentuckians who came in 1837 was John Biddlecombe, from Logan county. He came as a Missionary Baptist preacher, a man of much piety and very useful. He was one of the early day teachers of the regions of "The Narrows" and died only a few years ago loved and respected by all who knew him.

There came with him a brother-in-law from the same county and like him both teacher and preacher—Benjamin Corbey. He was of the Cumberland Presbyterian faith and probably the ablest minister of the gospel in this section at that time. His power was not in his fine education but in his ability to win the love of all with whom he came in contact. It is reported of him that he did more than any man in his time to spread the influence of his denomination. He died many years ago.

Still another settler came from Logan county, Kentucky. Coming to Morgan about the same time was Reddick Horn, a prominent Protestant Methodist. He and Corbey founded a church and did much to mould sympathy in the neighborhood of the present Virginia.

Thomas J. Cosner came from Indiana in 1843 and located four miles from Virginia. Some three weeks after his arrival the nag he had come on from Indiana was stolen and he was left without a particle of property. For ten years or more he was a farm laborer by the month, at a time when wages were only $10 per month. Now by frugality, honesty and industry he has accumulated farm property aggregating about three-fourths of a section worth $60 per acre. In all he is probably worth to-day about $30,000 and now lives in the city, and owns one building on the square, of Virginia.

Z. W. Gatton was born in Allen county, Kentucky, but came to Illinois with his father in September, 1824, locating within a quarter of a mile of Little Indian on a farm then all raw prairie. He put twenty acres under cultivation the first year. The family remained there a few years and then moved to Beardstown. Their house was headquarters of traveling M. E. preachers. After Z. W. became grown he went to Ottawa for one winter and Beardstown for four years. Now he is living just outside the city limits of Virginia, has been there over twenty years. He recollects the deep snow and quick freeze of 1831 and 1836; was living in Beardstown; had gone to his father's, where were two cabins some ten feet apart. He walked across in slush and back in fifteen minutes *on ice*. He carried a petition, after having circulated it, to Vandalia for the separation of Cass from Morgan.

His father and Judge Thomas, of our city, were well acquainted and particular friends in Kentucky before either came to Illinois, to meet again in Morgan county. Mr. Gatton recollects the cholera year, 1833, and how bad the scare was in Beardstown. Nurses could not be obtained and men had to give up their business to nurse the sick and care for the dead and dying. And not one of these volunteer nurses caught the disease.

The earliest white settler of Cass county, of whom we find any knowledge, was old Eli Cox. He settled in the eastern part of what is now Cass county, in the year 1816, stopping at a grove at the head of a creek, which have since been known as Cox's Grove and Cox's Creek. At that early date there was not a white man in all this part of the state. The United States government had not even stretched a surveyor's chain over the land, neither section nor township had been laid off. This man Cox, being, perhaps, a trapper and hunter and accustomed to look carefully at his surroundings, saw at a glance the great advantages of the prairie for farming and grazing purposes, and conclud- to make himself a permanent home here. He staked out a claim and after remaining on it for a time left it; returned in 1819, built a cabin and commenced permanent improvements, and lived there until his death which occurred in 1880, or 1881. Of the early history of Mr. Cox little, or nothing, is known to the writer, although well acquainted with him since 1836, he never on any occasion referred to his early life or the place of his birth. He was an honest, industrious man, strictly upright and honest in all his dealings, but mingled very little in society, and those who knew him best held him in the highest esteem. During his long years of residence in the old cabin, he married and raised a large family and also accumulated property and money to the amount of thirty or forty thousand dollars.

Mrs. Cox died in 1866 or 1867, after which time the old man lived alone till a short time before his death, his children having grown up and left him.

He always kept about his cabin a considerable sum of money, and two attempts were made to rob him, in both of which he was most brutally treated; the first time by choking and beating, and the second by burning the old man till he gave up some of his money. We are sorry to say that none of the perpetrators were ever discovered.

Perhaps right here we should recall the

"THREE MILE STRIP"

contest. It appears, from Judge Shaw's statements, that from January, 1837 to 1843, there was growing "a feeling of dissatisfaction among the people of the southern half of township XVII, and other parts of Morgan, with Jacksonville." By act of the Legislature, two votes were taken; one in August 1843, on a proposition to divide Morgan into two counties—Morgan and Benton. This proposition failed of the requisite number of votes, and "Benton" county was not created. In May, 1845, those living in the four precincts forming the "three mile strip"—the northern tier of precincts—voted for and against being attached to Cass county, and through the votes and influence of Arenzville, the majority for taking the territory from Morgan was 168. There was considerable of a contest before the Legislature in getting this election ordered; Morgan then had four representatives in the Legislature, all Whigs. Among them was Francis Arenz, a resident on the "strip," and John W. Pratt, who, in two terms, did much to gain for Cass this valuable political and cultivable territory. So close was the Legislature at this time as between Whigs and Democrats that it was urged as an argument that this loss of territory to Morgan would change it from Whig to Democratic control and that change would transfer the majority in the House from one party to another.

Cass county had a population in 1860 of 11,325. For the next ten years there was very little change, so that in 1870 there were only 11,580 reported by the census gatherers

In 1880 she came up nicely, however, showing 14,493 residents. The first census ever taken was in 1840—total population 2,981. In 1850 she had grown to 7,253.

Circuit Clerk Downing informed us that the first entry in a criminal case in Cass county was for a change of venue in a murder case. Messrs. Gatton & Berry told us more about this cause. It was a very deliberate murder, a Mr. Fowl in Philadelphia, being shot with a revolver, by Nathaniel Graves. The murderer was tried at the May term and sentenced to be hung, but broke jail before sentence was executed, and escaped to his native State, Kentucky. There have been quite a number of murder trials in Cass since the separation, but never a conviction where the punishment was more than a fine, except in the case of a German living near Chandlerville, convicted of wife-murder and sentenced to Joliet for life. He is still there, in the State penitentiary.

THE FIRST FRAME HOUSE

built in Virginia was by Dr. H. H. Hall, father of Henry H. Hall, Esq., of Jacksonville. He was not only the founder and first house-builder, but first merchant and the ruling spirit of the place up to the day of his death, in 1847. He first visited the West in 1831, when he entered several hundred acres of land, upon a portion of which Virginia now stands. In 1835 he moved to this State from the Old Dominion, and settled upon his land already entered. He laid out and named the town of Virginia in 1836, making sales of quite a number of lots that year. He opened the first store in the village, employing as a clerk Charlie Oliver, afterwards a prominent merchant himself. In 1838 Dr. Hall made an addition of fifteen acres of public grounds, donating them to the county. Of the first frame houses in Virginia, both built by Dr. Hall, one is now occupied by John Berryhill as a residence and the other, built for a store, is now used for a dwelling, being located two blocks from the square and occupied and owned by the Misses Suffern.

POSTSCRIPT. FINAL CORRECTION OF ERRORS.

Page 82. Twenty-sixth line from top, 1822 should read 1832.
Page 253. Fourteenth line from bottom, for "bank" read banks.
Page 255. Twenty-second line from top, for "*these* malarious diseases" read *thus*.
Page 256. Eighth line from bottom for "feat" read fact.
Page 223. The figures "633" cover patients only and to include all inmates should be 746, making the total 1,500 instead of "1,300."

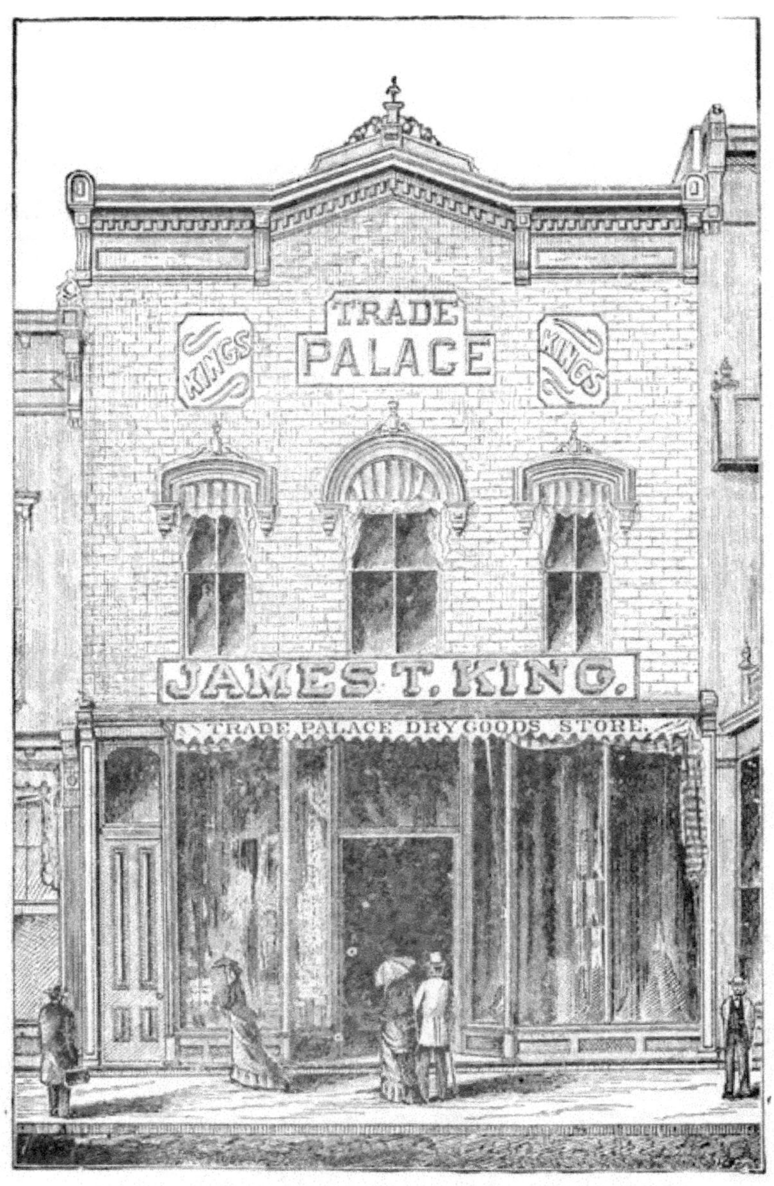

J. T. KING'S STORE, EAST SIDE SQUARE, JACKSONVILLE.

CHAPTER XV.

Biographical Sketches, with some Portraits of Prominent Citizens of Morgan County, including many now numbered with the dead. The Pioneers, the Cattle Kings, the Educators, the State Officials, the Politicians and the Business Men, such as Strawn, Alexander, King, Smith, Gillett, Carriel, Phillips, Bullard, Morrison, Duncan, Kirby, Tanner, Bailey, Yates, Glover, Turner, Thomas, Sturtevant, Morse, Short, Sanders, Moore, Tomlinson, Munroe, et al.

HON. JOSEPH O. KING has been frequently mentioned in the preceding pages of this volume. We have tried to give him due credit for his activity in prominent local institutions and interests.

Mr. King was born in Enfield, Connecticut, in 1814, and came West in 1838. His home was made in this city at that time, and here has he remained, in active and honored social, business and political life until the present date. Mrs. King, who has been called to heavenly rest, was always a favorite in the social, musical and religious circles of the city, and ever ready to identify herself with that which was pure, elevating and philanthropic. Two sons (Edw. J. and William M.) and two daughters (Miss Mary and Mrs. Emma Dwight) have survived their mother and cheer the declining years of their father the subject of this brief sketch.

Mr. King has held many offices of trust in the Town Board of Trustees, City Council, and as Mayor for one term. Upon arriving in Jacksonville, he first engaged in the drug and hardware business, afterwards was interested in the dry goods, lumber and milling trade. For the last twenty-five years of his life he has been Superintendent of the City Gas Light and Coke Company. It was through his activity and zeal that the ball was started which located here the State institutions for the blind and insane and gave the city its gas-light and water privileges.

For further information as to his useful life here, see pages 107, 109, 114, 118, 121, 123, 135, 136, 145, 148, 193, 202, 204, 205, 253 of this volume.

JACOB STRAWN, SR., agriculturist and stock dealer, was born in Somerset county, Pennsylvania, May 30th, 1800, descending from English and Welsh ancestry. His paternal ancestor came over in the ship which brought William Penn.

His father, Isaiah Strawn, had four sons and two daughters, and Jacob, the subject of this sketch, was the youngest of the family. These children were early initiated into the mysteries of farming, in which business the Strawn family in its various branches has since become so distinguished.

Jacob Strawn inherited an unusual share of the hardy vigor and energy of his ancestors, and early manifested those tastes and facilities for agricultural and business pursuits for which in later life he became quite remarkable. He was born of the soil, and had for it a kind of filial regard. He took to farming naturally and from a love of the employment. It was the bent of his mind. But his special inclination was to the handling of cattle. When but ten years of age he had ideas of stock-raising, and began operations in that line, which foreshadowed the talent and success subsequently evinced in the same. These native tendencies were but little stimulated or modified by advantages of education, which at that time and in the rural region where his boyhood was spent were very limited. In the year 1817 the family removed to Licking county, Ohio, where they renewed the business of farming, but on a much larger scale.

Two years later, at the age of nineteen, Jacob was married to Matilda Green, a daughter of a Baptist minister in the neighborhood. He was soon settled on a farm of his own, not far from his father's, and at once began to breed and deal in cattle and horses, and was so successful in this line of business that in a few years he was worth several thousand dollars. But desiring to extend his operations beyond what was possible on a comparatively small tract of land in Ohio, he turned his eye towards the rich and cheap prairies of Illinois, and in 1831 settled in Morgan county, four miles southwest from Jacksonville, on the large farm for so long the homestead and still the property of the family. A that time he was probably worth from six to eight thousand dollars. In the December following his wife died; she had borne him seven children, of whom three sons are living and largely engaged in agricultural pursuits.

In July, 1832, he married Phœbe Gates, daughter of Samuel Gates, of Greene county, Illinois. By his second marriage he had five sons and one daughter, of whom three sons survive, and are owners of large agricultural estates, settled upon them by their father some years previous to his decease.

His settlement in Illinois marks an era in western farming, but especially in stock-raising. Once firmly fixed on his vast farm, exceeding eight thousand acres of rich and beautiful land, in a few years he had it all under fence and a large portion of it under cultivation. From time to time he added to his estates large tracts of valuable land in other places in furtherance of his vast plan of stock-feeding, and with a view of supplying the great markets of the East, South and West. His vast herds were often seen passing from one of these farms to another. No one thought of competing with him in this business; no one could well do so, for if any had the necessary funds, they had not the required genius for enterprises of such a character. They had not the generalship which combines such numerous operations and successfully directs them to a single end.

It is related that to defeat a formidable combination to break down his trade in St. Louis he sent out agents upon every road leading to that city with positive instructions to purchase every drove on the way thither, and so well was this movement conducted that for a time, ample enough to show his capacity to cope with any such clique, he held a complete monopoly of the trade. None of his great success was due to chance, or what is called good fortune; but it was all the legitimate result of wise foresight, prudent management, and a most untiring industry, while not a little was due to a ceaseless activity, both of mind and body, which few men would be capable of, whatever their talent or disposition might be. He had wonderful physical endurance. He did not spend much time in bed, or in the house, but a great deal in the saddle, night and day, when gathering and directing the movements of his vast herds. His business was his pleasure; he got much of his sleep and rest on horseback. Certain maxims, which he published for the benefit of others, were the secret of his own prosperity. Some of them sound like Benjamin Franklin's and are worthy to be placed with them; for instance these: "When you wake up do not roll over but roll out," "I am satisfied that getting up early, industry, and regular habits are the best medicines ever prescribed for health," "Study your interests closely, and don't spend any time in electing presidents, senators, and other small officers or talk of hard times when spending your time in town whittling on store boxes, etc.." "Take your time and make your calculations; don't do things in a hurry, but do them at the right time, and keep your mind as well as your body employed."

It is well known that he made no professions of piety. Yet he believed religion important and necessary. He had faults peculiar to a person of powerful passions and strange eccentricities, but his life was an example of many worthy qualities and deeds. In uprightness he was severe; in honesty unquestioned. He had a high sense of honor. His word he held sacred. His promptitude in meeting promises was proverbial. He came to time in making payments, and required those who owed him to do the same. Yet he was kind as well as just; he was slow to take advantages of any person's necessities or misfortunes. He had no sympathy for the lazy, but he was a friend to the industrious poor; he had a warm heart for the laboring class, and he did not coldly turn away from any well authenticated tale of sorrow.

During the late war he was strong for the Union cause, and generous in his expressions of regard for our soldiers in the hospital and the field. At one time he contributed ten thousand dollars to aid the Christian Commission. Other citizens of the county giving a like amount at the same time. He was also instrumental in sending fifty milch cows to Vicksburg for the relief of the wounded and suffering troops at that place.

He was a true patriot, and his habits were marked by extreme simplicity, as became the greatest farmer of the republic. He made no show of dress or equipage. He thought more of well tilled fields and handsome stock than of all personal adornment. He hated all show and sham, but admired all substantial worth. He had the strong temptations of opulence and passion, but he was remarkably free from the vices which often spring up in the midst of such influences. The young, especially, may profit from his example of industry, frugality, honesty, and strict temperance. In principle and habit he was a thorough total abstinence man, never using intoxicating liquor in any shape, and not furnishing it for laborers or for guests. He could not endure men about him who indulged in strong drink. Tobacco also he discarded as both unnecessary and injurious. He could not bear the presence or enjoy the company of persons given to any bad principles, vulgar habits, or low vices.

After a life of almost unexampled activity, and of very unusual success in accomplishing the worldly objects at which he aimed, he died suddenly at his home, August 23d, 1865, from a disease to which for many years he had been subject. His funeral was largely attended, and on the 17th of September following, a commemorative discourse was delivered by Rev. L. M. Glover, D. D., the pastor of the family, in Strawn's Hall, Jacksonville. Mr. Strawn is buried in the beautiful "Diamond Grove Cemetery," an expensive and worthy monument marking the spot. The Strawn mansion is occupied by tenants of his surviving widow, who is spending the latter portion of her busy life in a home of elegant ease and hospitality located on West College Avenue, Jacksonville. His sons Julius E., Isaiah and Gates are also residents of the city at the present time.

JOHN ADAMS, LL. D., was born on the 18th of September, 1772, in Colchester, Connecticut; he was, consequently, four years old when the Declaration of Independence was declared. He was born when these United States were colonies, under George III. He saw the Federal Government at its beginning, witnessed its growth and prosperity for nearly three-quarters of a century; voted at every Presidential election from Washington to Lincoln, inclusive.

He had a strong and vigorous constitution, which had much to do with the results of his long and remarkable life.

He received a liberal education, entering Yale College in the year 1791, at the age of nineteen. He graduated with a sound scholarship; to the culture and knowledge there acquired, he added that of constant study and mental action, to the end of life.

When he left college, he intended to study law, but the sickness of his mother, to whom he was devoted changed his plans, and he commenced the business of teaching in 1795, which occupation he followed for forty-eight years. He was principal of literary institutions in Canterbury, Colchester, and Plainfield, Conn. In 1810 he was invited to become Principal of Phillips Academy, at Andover, Massachusetts; an institution designed to prepare young men for college. Eleven hundred and nineteen pupils were admitted under his administration.

In 1837, Mr. Adams, having resigned his situation at Andover, turned his face towards the Western country, locating in Jacksonville, taking charge of the Female Academy, until 1843, when he resigned, having placed the institution on a firm and substantial basis.

His pupils from these different institutions, numbering some 4,000, are scattered over this and other countries, occupying places of honor and usefulness.

He was a lover of children and youth and possessed the rare art of winning their confidence and love. At the age of seventy he engaged in the Sunday-School work, and organized in destitute places 322 schools, embracing more than 16,000 scholars. He was the first one who gave life and zeal to this work in this region of country. He was for a long time Superintendent of the Sunday-School connected with the First Presbyterian Church in this city, and for a quarter of a century a member of the Session

He received the title of Doctor of Laws from his Alma Mater, but was universally greeted by one dearer to him than any other, "Father Adams."

He was of an equable and happy disposition. A combination of personal and social qualities gave him access to many hearts. He was a daily student of the Bible; a sincere and earnest Christian, a bright, cheerful, happy man. He lived a long and honored life, and died. April 24, 1863 in the 91st year of his age.

The Trustees of Phillips Academy requested that his remains should be borne to New England, and laid by the side of those men who, in their early days, were banded together to establish literary and benevolent institutions, which should bless not only the States bordering the Atlantic, but be felt throughout the world. The first religious newspaper, the Bible and Tract Societies, Foreign Missions, and other kindred associations were born on that hill, and consecrated to God. But his last request was that he might be laid beneath the prairie sod of his much loved and adopted home. No tall or costly shaft, but the simple epitaph, "A lover of children, a teacher of youth, be inscribed upon the granite which should mark his last resting place

---

CAPT. ALEXANDER SMITH, proprietor of the Dunlap House, was born in Eaton, Ohio, June 27, 1844. He emigrated to Atlanta, Ill., in 1859.

He enlisted as a private soldier in Company E, 7th Illinois Infantry, April 17, 1861, to serve three months. The company was the first in Camp Yates, at Springfield, under the Governor's call for troops. It was stationed, during its term of enlistment, at Alton, Cairo and Mound City. He was very apt in learning military duty, so much so that at the organization of the company for the three years service he was unanimously elected first lieutenant of the company, though not quite seventeen years old, and on the 12th of March, 1862, before reaching his eighteenth year, he was promoted to the captaincy for gallantry at the siege of Fort Donaldson. He was mustered out of the service at the termination of the war, at Louisville, Ky., in 1865, after having served continuously for over four years and seven months, and participated in all the great battles, marches and sieges in which the Army of the Tennessee took part, from Belmont, Donaldson, Shiloh Seige of Corinth, Battle of Corinth, Altoona Pass, Atlanta, March to the Sea Bentonville, N. C., (last battle of the war), to the final great event of the war, the grand review at Washington. At the battle of Altoona Pass (Ga.), the company which he had the honor to command lost, in a square stand-up fight, the unprecedented number of sixteen men killed outright, two mortally wounded, a loss said to have never been equalled during the war, in one company.

Capt. Smith returned to Illinois at the close of the war, and for four years was clerk of the Essex House, at Mattoon. He came to Jacksonville in 1869, and was clerk of the Dunlap House till 1874; clerk of the Park Hotel till 1875; manager of the Dunlap House, 1876; proprietor of the Park Hotel from 1876 to 1880; owner and proprietor of the Dunlap House and Park Hotel since and now.

J. R. BAILEY, editor and publisher the founder of the Jacksonville *Sentinel*, and its editor and publisher from January 1855, to January, 1872 seventeen years—was a native of Bucks county, Pennsylvania. He was of Protestant Irish descent; his ancestors emigrated from the north of Ireland during an early period in the first settlement of the colony of Pennsylvania. They bought a tract of land on the banks of the Delaware river, some thirty miles above Philadelphia, of the London Land Company, on which they settled, and on part of which some of their descendents yet reside. Here the subject of this sketch was born, in May, 1818. In 1824 his father sold his farm and moved with his family to the city of Philadelphia. At the age of fourteen years he found it necessary to quit school and engage in the active business of life. He first served two years at the printing business, in a small German and English office. At this time buckskin balls were in use for inking the type, and he remembers working at one time on the old wooden press used by Benjamin Franklin during his publishing career in Philadelphia, since on exhibition at the Patent Office at Washington. It came about in this way: The Franklin press had fallen into the hands of Mr. Ramage, the veteran Philadelphia press maker, who had it stored away. The Ramage press in the office needed repairing, and while this was being done, the old wooden Franklin press was loaned to the office as a substitute. The frame was like that of an ordinary country loom; the bed of stone and the platen a block of wood, just half the size of the bed, requiring two impressions to a full form. Tiring of the printing office, young Bailey, at the age of sixteen years, commenced to learn the carpenter trade, and in company with his brother, Judge J. S. Bailey, of Macomb, Ill., he worked at that business two more years. Desiring, however, a vocation giving him more outdoor exercise, and seeing an opportunity to better his condition by moving farther West, Mr. Bailey made up his mind to such a move. After his marriage to Miss Ann Henderson, a young lady from New Jersey, he removed to Iowa, and commenced the work of building up a home on his claim, the land not yet being in market. At that day the country was very new, the entire territory being in possession of the Indians, with the exception of a narrow strip along the Mississippi river, known as the Black Hawk Purchase. All supplies had to come from the east side of the Mississippi, and the first settlers underwent many hardships, Mr. Bailey having to shoulder his full share of the exposure and hardship of a frontier life. Not yet twenty-three years old, and unaccustomed to the use of the pioneer's ax and maul, he found making rails and building log cabins heavy work; but he persevered until his farm was fenced and broken and the land paid for. During the first year of his settlement, Mr. Bailey began to take an active part in politics: was elected a justice of the peace, and in 1844 he received the Democratic nomination for Representative in the Territorial Legislature. In the meantime the Indian title to the lands west to the Missouri river had been extinguished by purchase, and a number of new counties had been laid out and settled. Wapello, the new county west of Jefferson, became attached for legislative purposes, the district thus formed to be represented by one Member of the Council and one Representative. The Democrats of Wapello claimed the Representative, and Mr. Bailey voluntarily retired from the canvass to give place to another. During the next two years a State constitution was formed, and Iowa became a State. In the fall of 1846 Mr. Bailey was nominated by the Democrats of Jefferson county, again a district by itself—for Representative to the first State Legislature. He was elected, and thus participated in setting the wheels of the new State government in motion, serving during the sessions of 1847–'48. Both these sessions were characterized by stormy excitement over the election of the first United States Senators, and the Legislature failed to elect until the session of 1849. During this period he began to exercise his talents as writer, contributing articles of a political character to the local press, and hence his attention became directed to the publishing business. In 1852 Mr. Bailey sold his farm and removed to Mt. Sterling, Brown county, Ill. Here he commenced his carreer as editor and publisher, by investing in a newspaper office that had been established by John Bigler, who went to California in 1849, and afterward became Governor of that State. The paper was called the *Prairie Pioneer*, but the name was afterward changed to *Chronotype*. While publishing this sheet, Mr. Bailey was appointed postmaster under Mr. Pierce's administration, and held the office three years, resigning when he removed to Jacksonville, in the winter of 1855. Since that time the history of J. R. Bailey has been intimately blended with the history of Morgan county, there having been few matters of public interest in which, as a journalist, he has not taken an active part. He was an active member of the Illinois Press Association: was one of the committee that drafted its constitution, and was twice elected treasurer of the association.

During 1854 he suffered domestic misfortune in the loss of his wife and two children. During the fall of 1861 he was united in marriage to Miss Mary T. Williams, a lady of some local literary reputation.

About this time the long agitation of the slavery question culminated in the Southern rebellion, and during the continuance of that war Mr. Bailey was of the class of Democratic editors who advocated a vigorous prosecution of the war for the purpose of crushing out the rebellion, and in this he was sustained by the leading men of his party in the county. As before stated, Mr. Bailey established the Jacksonville *Sentinel* in 1855, and published it as editor and proprietor for seventeen years--embracing a period of long-continued high political excitement and full of historical incidents. Such long-continued, active labors began to impair his health, and in 1872 his eyesight so far failed that he was unable to read or write, even with the aid of the strongest glasses. Having no sons of an age to assist him, he disposed of the *Sentinel* establishment to other parties, and resided on his farm near Jacksonville, living a retired and quiet life until his death, August 19, 1880, from cancer of the mouth.

The remains of Mr. Bailey were interred in Jacksonville cemetery, August 20th, with the impressive burial service of the Independent Order of Odd Fellows, of which fraternity he was for many years an active member in good standing.

Eight children survived him, including Mrs. J. H. Hackett, Mrs. Reeves, and Mrs. D. H. Hall, of this city.

At a meeting of the representatives of the press of Jacksonville, at the *Journal* editorial rooms, to take same action in relation to his death, the following resolutions were adopted:

WHEREAS, The press fraternity of Jacksonville are called upon to mourn the death of Mr. James R. Bailey, the founder and publisher of the Illinois *Sentinel* (now *Courier*) in 1855; and

WHEREAS, In the death of this pioneer of journalism in this city, it being the first recorded of the kind in our midst, it is fitting that this meeting of those now and heretofore connected with the publishing enterprises of the city, should bear willing testimony to his many virtues as an editor and publisher. Therefore,

Resolved, That we recognize in the character of our departed friend and predecessor a man worthy of his calling, a forceful writer, conservative in his views, but firm in his purpose to serve the public interests in his day, ever faithful as one who sought the public good, and labored most industriously for the achievement of just ends.

Resolved, That the members of the press of this city hereby tender their heartfelt sympathy to the widow and bereaved friends and commend them to the consolation to be drawn from the example of uprightness manifested in the life of him who has been called to his reward.

Signed—C. M. Eames, H. L. Clay, N. C. A. Rayhouser, J. S. Hambaugh, Jos. J. Ironmonger, M. N. Price, Geo. E. Doying, Ensley Moore, Geo. N. Loomis, J. Aug. Fay, G. W. Fanning.

JOHN T. ALEXANDER, stock-raiser, was born September 15, 1820, in Western Virginia, and when but six years old removed to Ohio with his father, who engaged in agricultural pursuits. He enjoyed in his youth but few opportunities for securing an education, and was engaged in roughing it through the continuous labors incidental to a farm in a newly opened country. When thirteen years of age he began to assist his father, then an extensive drover, in sending his cattle to the Eastern market, and from that period until reaching his twentieth year he passed his time in driving his father's herds from Ohio, over the Alleghanies, to Philadelphia, Baltimore, New York, and Boston. His father, then suffering severe reverses in fortune, he determined to go farther West and commence life upon his own account. He traveled to St. Louis, where he was soon employed, at a moderate salary, by a firm which at that time transacted the largest live-stock business in that section of the country. His employers, discovering the unusual precision of his judgment in estimating and averaging the weight of cattle, detailed him to travel into the interior to make purchases, and he served them faithfully and satisfactorily for many months in this capacity. He then ended his service with them and, on a small scale, suitable to his limited means, commenced to fatten cattle for the markets on his own account. For three years he was thus occupied, gradually increasing his herd, until it reached such proportions that he felt justified in setting out as a drover. He accordingly took 250 head of fat cattle to Boston, occupying the entire summer in driving them to that market, and sold them at a price that yielded him a handsome profit.

For three years he continued in this line of business, and then concluded to establish a large stock farm. In 1848 he made his first purchase, buying a tract of land in Morgan county, Illinois, for $3 per acre, which is now worth $100 per acre. This tract, which lies ten miles from Jacksonville, on the Toledo, Wabash & Western railroad, soon became, under his management, one of the most valuable stock-farms in the State. He made it the site of his residence, and by gradual additions enlarged his possessions in this section, until they covered 6,000 acres. Soon after his original purchase in 1848, he stocked his farm with cattle, purchased mainly in Missouri, and within a few years was the owner of the largest herds in the State. By judicious purchases and sales he acquired a very large fortune, part of which he unfortunately lost in the years 1854-'55, by reason of the great expense of keeping his stock, occasioned by the severe droughts, which killed the crops, and the unusual decline in prices. In 1856 he was remarkably successful in all his ventures, clearing in that year $60,000. In 1859 he fattened 15,000 head of choice cattle, for which he obtained a ready sale in the large Eastern cities; but the closing of this year's operations indicated, what very few suspected, that his losses overbalanced the value of his entire estate. Upon the breaking out of the rebellion, great inducements were offered stock-raisers by the heavy decline in prices in Missouri, occasioned by the insecure tenure of all personal property. By taking advantage of this opportunity for cheap purchases, Mr. Alexander completely retrieved his lost fortune, and at the close of the rebellion was a millionaire. He subsequently bought the "Sullivant" farm, of 20,000 acres, afterwards called "Broad Lands," situated on the Toledo, Wabash & Western Railroad, in Champaign county, Illinois, in order to have all the necessary facilities for handling vast herds of cattle. He experienced, soon after, many reverses, losing many cattle by Spanish fever, and large sums of money by the repudiation of certain railroad contracts for shipments. His losses in one year aggregated $350,000. These misfortunes produced a crisis in his affairs, and by a failure to sell his "Broad Lands," for which the agreements had been partially drawn up, he was compelled to assign his entire estate for the benefit of his creditors. Notwithstanding the fact that his liabilities exceeded $1,200,000, his estate paid his creditors dollar for dollar. His estate now includes the "home" farm of 6,000 acres, composed of the most arable land in the State, 2,000 acres of which are yearly planted with corn. The remaining 4,000 acres are used for the pasturage of a herd of from 2,000 to 3,000 cattle, and this stock is regarded as the finest in the West. He required, at one time, for his farm labor forty yoke of oxen and eighty horses and mules.

He was a man of large means and of generous impulses. He was tall and commanding in appearance, sanguine in temperament and unassuming in manner. He was the possessor of fine social qualities, and conscientious in all his business transactions. These traits secured for him the respect of the entire community, and the confidence of merchants throughout the country.

At the age ot twenty-four he was married to Miss Mary Deweese. They had a family of eight children, five of whom are still living, to mourn the loss of their loved father.

Mr. Alexander's last trip to the East was made some three weeks before his death, August 22, 1876. The very day after reaching New York he was violently attacked with chronic diarrhœa, a disease from which he had suffered before, in fact was not free from trouble with it when he left home. He became better and started upon his return. By the time he reached Detroit the malady returned with renewed and prostrating severity He telegraphed his son William, who was at home, to come to him. He did so, remaining with his father until he felt able to renew his journey, which was after a rest of six days in Detroit. The physician there said his condition was a precarious one, but a change for the better came and he thought himself able to bear the journey. The invalid was attacked again at Danville, so that by the time he reached his home near Alexander Station, ten miles east of Jacksonville, he was in a very enfeebled condition. This was upon Friday, August 18th, and he grew rapidly worse until on Sunday there remained no hope of his recovery, and Monday evening, at 11 o'clock, he succumbed to the great destroyer. His wife and children John T., William H., Lizzie, Lou (the bride of a few weeks previous), and Annie—and many other relatives were at his bedside.

The widow and sons still occupy the old homestead and home farm, at Alexander.

JOSEPH W. KING was born in Hartford, Conn., in the year 1808. When he was eight years old his father died. He, with his mother, went to Westfield Mass., and remained there till his education was finished, then returned to his native city and learned the jeweler's business; after that he established himself in his former home in Massachusetts.

In 1833 he was married to Miss Abbie E. Hamilton, who still survives. Some years after, indications of failing health induced him to try the effect of a warmer climate. He spent three years in the South, most of the time in Mobile. Not wishing to make his home there, and feeling that the climate had not benefitted him as he had hoped, and being advised by his physicians to go to a prairie country, and spend much of his time in outdoor employment, he came to Jacksonville in 1838, and established the jewelry business; and here was his home for the remainder of his life.

Mr. King was a genial, warm-hearted man, a kind husband, an excellent neighbor, generous to a large extent. He took a lively interest in all schemes to invite business enterprise here and contributed liberally to further all such efforts. His hand was always open and his means freely given to aid the soldiers during the war.

In politics he was an old Clay Whig, till in 1856 he was appointed a delegate to the State Convention which formed the republican party in this State, to which he always adhered.

It was the good fortune of some of our citizens to be with him at the convention which nominated Mr. Lincoln for President, and they will never forget his enthusiasm on that occasion.

Mr. King was appointed one of the Trustees of the Soldiers' Orphans' Home, and was selected as treasurer of the Board, which he held during the entire period of its construction.

Early in the year 1884 he was deeply affected by the death of his only son, John, a young man in the prime of his manhood, to whom he had fondly looked as the stay and support of his advancing years. The severity of the stroke was more than his physical organization could bear, and yielding to an attack of fever, he passed away, and we laid him in our beautiful cemetery in May, 1884; a few months only intervening between the burial and the golden wedding celebration

All deeply sympathized with the bereaved family, where "his place is vacant at the table, his footsteps no longer heard in the hall;" they miss his friendly greeting on the streets, his animated and enthusiastic expressions relating to current events, and a large circle of friends are saddened with the thought that they shall see his face no more. See pages 119, 125, 132, 151, 232, 288.

COL. JOHN W. KING, only child of Joseph W. and Abby, dropped from life's ranks ere the march was ended. In the strength and beauty of his manhood, he faded away. God's finger touched him and he slept.

In 1839, a fair, curly-headed boy of four years came with his parents from Westfield, Massachusetts. From childhood to youth and then to manhood, John King made this his home. He was of a happy, frolicsome disposition when young; genial and social in after years. His attachments were strong and his friends numerous.

He attended the public schools of this city, also Illinois College for a time, and also Mr. Wyman's school in St. Louis.

In 1859 he entered into partnership with his father in the jewelry business.

At the first call for three months troops in 1861, he entered Company B, 10th Regiment of Infantry, but was soon after promoted to the captaincy. At the expiration of three months he returned home. At the next call for three months troops, he formed a company and entered the 68th Regiment, and went to Alexandria, Virginia. He was sent up the James river with rebel prisoners in exchange for Union soldiers. He soon after returned home. He ranked as colonel on Gov. Yates' staff, which position he held during that administration

In 1869 he went to Chicago and remained one year; he then entered the revenue service for a short time in this place.

He married, in 1872, Miss Eva Lillian Atwood, of Alton, a descendent of one of our best New England families. She, with her only son, survives.

He afterwards entered into partnership with others in the jewelry business, but for the last few years was alone.

He was a member of a number of secret orders; held a position in the Knights of Honor, and in the Grand Army of the Republic, and was once an active Mason and Odd Fellow.

He was fond of reading and had laid the foundation for a large and valuable library. His home was his delight. A loving husband and son, a devoted and fond father.

For some time before his death he had been interested in books which related to the life beyond, and on the mystery we call death. At the funeral of a young friend, one week previous to his sickness, he expressed satisfaction at the remarks uttered, and standing over the casket said, "This is not death, but life."

For some months he was a sufferer, though not complaining. One night he returned from business in great pain; laid down to rest, never again rising to attend to business. For three weeks he alternated between hope and fear; all that love and care could bestow was lavished upon him, but of no avail—he gradually failed. He conversed but little, but bright visions floated before him, and waving his hand as forms of beauty, exquisite flowers and attractive children passed, he would exclaim "How beautiful!"

On the afternoon of the 3d of March 1884, the last word was spoken, the last fond look was given, the hand clasped in his was dropped, the eye closed, and John King went to sleep; he slept on, unconscious of the loved ones bending over him, until, the next afternoon, as the sun was setting, leaving only its faded light, he passed away. See pages 159, 232, 289.

REV. WILLIAM HENRY MILBURN, lecturer, better known as the "blind man eloquent," was born in Philadelphia, Pennsylvania, on September 25, 1826. His father was a merchant, but meeting with reverses, removed to Jacksonville, Ill., in 1838. William was an active, robust boy, possessed of perfect faculties, both bodily and mental, but at the age of five met with an accident which resulted in his blindness. He was playing with another lad in an open lot, engaged in throwing at a mark, when his companion, in lifting his hand to cast a piece of iron hoop or something of the kind, inadvertently struck the edge of it into Milburn's eye. From this accident, however, the eye recovered without injury to vision, except that the scar formed a slight protuberance which interfered with the sight downward, but not direct or upward. This protuberance the physician decided to burn off with caustic, an operation which, twice repeated, was hard for the boy to bear. He begged for relief, and at last resisted, declaring that he could not endure it. Upon this the physician seized him in his arms, forced the caustic upon the wound, and in the struggle both eyes of the poor boy were dashed with it. As a remedy he was confined in a dark room, and both eyes were kept bathed with a solution of lead for two years, during which time the pupils became permeated with depositions of lead, and light was shut out, with the exception of the left upper corner of the right eye, through which narrow aperture objects were visible. By placing a narrow shade over the eye, the hand convexly shaped beneath it, and leaning the body forward at an angle of forty-five degrees, Milburn was able to read; seeing, however, only one letter at a time. By this slow process, and by the aid of friends who read to him, he was obliged to get his education. Cut off from most sports, he became absorbed in reading, and day after day would sit in the constrained posture necessary to see, poring over books often twelve hours out of the twenty-four. His constitution was so good, that he did not suffer under his confinement and unnatural attitude until he was nineteen years of age, when a senior in college; then his health suddenly gave way, and it was discovered that he had a slight curvature of the spine and some internal organic disease. He left college and joined the Illinois Conference as a traveling preacher, on September 26, 1843, on his twentieth birthday. Before being regularly recognized by the Conference, in the spring and summer of 1843, he traversed a region of 1,000 miles in extent, preaching every Saturday and Sunday, and three or four times during the week, always in company with his theological instructor, his text-book and his seminary course.

In September 1845, he moved East by order of the Conference, to present the cause of education and collect funds for the establishment of Methodist schools and colleges. On his journey he found himself on board of an Ohio river steamer, on which were 300 passengers. From the number of days the passengers had been together Mr. Milburn had become well informed of their character, and he found that most prominent among the gentlemen were a number of Members of Congress, on their way to Washington. These gentlemen had attracted his attention on account of their exceptional habits. On Sunday morning Mr. Milburn was invited to preach. He consented, and in due time began Divine service. The Members of Congress were among the congregation, and by common consent had possession of the chairs nearest to the preacher. Mr. Milburn gave an address suitable to the occasion, full of eloquence and pathos, and was listened to throughout with intense interest. At the conclusion he stopped short, and turning his face, now beaming with fervent zeal, towards the "honorable gentlemen," he said: "Among the passengers on this steamer are a number of Members of Congress. From their position they should be exemplars of good morals and dignified conduct; but from what I have heard of them, they are not so. The union of these States, if dependent on such guardians, would be unsafe, and all the high hopes I have of the future of my country would be dashed to the ground. These gentlemen, for days past, have made the air heavy with profane conversation, have been constant patrons of the bar and encouragers of intemperance; nay, more, the night, which should be devoted to rest, has been dedicated to the horrid vices of gambling, profanity and drunkenness. And," continued Mr. Milburn, with the solemnity of a man who spoke as if by inspiration, "there is but one chance of salvation for these sinners in high places, and that is to humbly repent of their sins, call on the Savior for forgiveness, and reform their lives."

As might be supposed, language so bold from a delicate stripling, scarcely twenty two years of age, had a startling effect, and made a deep impression on the gentlemen particularly addressed.

After Mr. Milburn had returned to his state-room, a gentleman entered and said that he came with a message from the Members of Congress; that they had listened to his remarks, and in consideration of his boldness and eloquence, they desired him to accept a purse of money which they had made up among themselves, and also their best wishes for his success and happiness in life. Furthermore, they offered to make him Chaplain to Congress at the approaching session—a promise which they fulfilled.

And thus Mr. Milburn, at the age of twenty-two, entered upon the duties of his new and responsible position, the youngest man who has ever opened his mouth in either house of Congress. This election to the office of Chaplain to Congress, so honorably conferred, brought him before the nation, and his name became familiar in every part of the Union. His health still being delicate, in the year 1847 he went South, for the advantage of a mild climate, and took charge of a church in Alabama. For six years he labored industriously in Montgomery and Mobile, and in four years of that time preached 1,500 times and traveled over 60,000 miles.

In December, 1853, he was re-elected Chaplain to Congress, which post he held till March, 1855.

During the summer of the last-named year, he prepared a course of lectures, entitled "Sketches of the Early History and Settlements of the Mississippi Valley," which were first delivered before the Lowell Institute, at Boston, in December; and afterwards published by Derby & Jackson, New York. The same firm also published "Rifle, Axe and Saddle-bags," in 1856, and "Ten Years of Preacher Life," in 1857.

In 1857 Mr. Milburn went to Europe and remained about six months. He was everywhere cordially received, both by Wesleyan and Church of England people, and preached and lectured wherever he went.

In the spring of 1868 he again went to Europe, for the purpose of having his eye operated upon by the celebrated oculist Von Graefe, of Berlin. The operation took place, but no increase of vision resulted therefrom. He is now unable to see any object, and has but a dim perception of light.

In 1865, for personal reasons, he joined the Episcopal Church, and in 1871, these reasons having ceased, he returned to the Methodists.

For the past thirty years he has been largely engaged in lecturing; he has spoken from Maine to California, from Minnesota to Louisiana. He speaks, on an average, seven times a week for nine months of the year, and travels 30,000 miles. His health is now superb; and, from present indications, he has before him many years of activity and usefulness.

His parents were both well known and honored citizens of Jacksonville to the time of their deaths. His brother Nicholas is still a resident of our city and, although crippled by a railroad accident, is actively engaged in business, as agent for coal companies.

JOSEPH TOMLINSON, our present efficient Mayor, is a native of Bridgton, New Jersey. At the age of eighteen years he lost his father, after which he removed to Philadelphia, Pa., and at the age of 21 commenced business for himself. His capital being limited and, in a large city, his success not as great as he desired, he disposed of his interest in the business and in the spring of 1855 moved to Jacksonville, where he has resided ever since with the exception of one year, which he spent in Aurora.

Mr. Tomlinson commenced business in this city in a very humble way, but by his perseverance, business qualities and sterling integrity has succeeded in building up a large, and, we think, lucrative business. He takes rank to-day with our leading business men. In 1875 Mr Tomlinson was elected from the Fourth Ward to represent it in the City Council, making an efficient and useful member of the same. In the spring of 1884 he was selected by the Republicans of the city as a candidate for Mayor, and after a spirited and closely contested election, by the zeal of his party, his fitness for the position and his personal popularity his election was secured, and he was duly installed in the office. He has discharged the duties of the same with signal ability and universal satisfaction. Mr. Tomlinson, though an earnest Republican, is not a bitter partisan. His ambition and desire seems to be to encourage and advance every enterprise that has for its object and aim the general prosperity of the city and the benefit of his fellowmen.

The subject of this sketch is an active member of Grace M. E. Church, of our city, a pronounced and consistent temperance man, a worthy and useful citizen. He was married in the city of Philadelphia, in the year 1852, to Miss Eliza Jane Apple, of said city, and by their marriage there have been three sons and one daughter, all of them living and numbered among our highly respected young people. The daughter is the wife of Dr. T. Van Welsh, a prominent druggist of our city. Mr. Tomlinson has our best wishes for his future welfare and success. See also pages 202, 209.

ENSLEY MOORE is to-day one of the most prominent of the young men of our city, and identified with its best religious, literary and political interests. He was born in Springfield, Ill., April 16, 1846, but taken to Perry, Pike county, a year or two later, whence he removed to Jacksonville in July, 1857. His early education was in the West District School (now Second Ward, for which ward he is the school board member) under Principals Bateman, Tunnel and Kirby, having the personal instruction of the two latter From Illinois College, where he was one of the most active members of "Sigma Pi," he graduated in June, 1868. For several months after his graduation he was travelling and visiting in the East. In April, 1869, he accepted the place of local editor for the *Daily Journal* then in its infancy, (Chapin & Glover, proprietors.) This arrangement was but temporary, however, yet Mr. Moore's journalistic propensities and abilities soon found him employment on *The Independent*, the new weekly of Messrs. Ironmonger and Funk, during the years 1869 '70. A part of the time he was associate editor. A year later he was the monied partner in the bookbinding business of Moeller & Moore. In October, 1873, he was married to Miss Clara, daughter of the late Rev. George I. King, D. D., of Jerseyville. By this marriage there have been four children, three of whom, William, Walter, Maggie K., and an infant, are living in their happy West State street home.

Mr. Moore has always been a zealous Republican and active in city and county politics. He was elected an alderman for the Second Ward in 1874, and returned as elected in 1882, but "counted out." In 1881, was chosen by the city council as water commissioner, and in 1883 elected Member of the Board of Education from the Second Ward.

He has long been a member of the Westminster Presbyterian Church, and has served as trustee of the same since 1870, being treasurer of the board about one-half this time. The Sabbath School of the church was under his superintendency during the years 1881 to 1884. See pages 85, 108, 125, 151, 156, 174, 201, 202, 209, 262, 267, of this book.

REV. FRANKLIN W. PHILLIPS, M. D., Superintendent of the Institution for the Blind, was born November 5, 1827, on Lulbegrud creek, Montgomery county, Kentucky, and is the son of the late Rev. Wm. Phillips, and grandson of John Phillips, formerly of Dorchester county, Maryland. His parents both died in Cincinnati, Ohio, and he then became an inmate of the household of an uncle living in Paris, Indiana, where he remained about three and one-half years. He returned to Cincinnati in 1840, and was an interested looker-on during the "log cabin and hard cider campaign" of that year.

In the fall of 1840 he entered Woodward College, now Woodward High School, of which Dr. B. P. Aydelotte was President, and Dr. Joseph Ray, Professor of Mathematics. He left college without graduating; and, to prepare himself for active life, served an apprenticeship of four years with G. W. Townley & Bro., house-carpenters. But having made a profession of religion, in February, 1845, his mind was directed to the ministry, and he immediately set about a preparation for that work. In September, 1848, he was received into the Kentucky Conference of the Methodist Episcopal Church South.

After eight years of active labor in the ministry, he was compelled to desist and located in 1856. Having studied medicine, he attended lectures in the Kentucky School of Medicine," at Louisville, and engaged in the practice thereof, first at Livermore, on Green River, and afterwards in Todd county, not far from the Tennessee line, where he established a good business. Here he remained until near the close of the war, when he yielded to the pressure of circumstances and sought peace and quiet by removing to Illinois, arriving at Carlinville in December, 1864.

His original intention was to establish himself as a physician, but the way seemed hedged up, and finding his health improved, he re-entered the ministry in connection with the Illinois Annual Conference of the Methodist Episcopal Church. In this work he has spent two years in Mattoon, four in Jacksonville, three in Springfield, and one year on the Danville District.

In June, 1874, he was elected Superintendent of the Illinois Institution for the education of the Blind, which position he still retains.

He was married in October, 1853, to Miss Lucy J., daughter of Rev. Richard J. Dungan, of Maxville, Kentucky, and has a family of three sons, two of whom reside in Kansas, and one in Illinois.

For further reference to Dr. Phillips' life here see pages 111, 171, 173, 175, 194, 208, 223, 230 of this volume. See page 294.

REV. FRANKLIN W. PHILLIPS, M. D.

SUPERINTENDENT OF ILLINOIS INSTITUTION FOR THE EDUCATION OF THE BLIND,

JACKSONVILLE, ILLINOIS.

OLD TIME ENGRAVING—CAMPAIGN CARTOON OF 1840. The above cut made by Mr. J. O. King, of this city and still preserved at the JOURNAL OFFICE, was an imitation of a similar one published in the democratic paper to represent the trap by which the whig party was to be caught. This cut was published in the *Illinoisan* with a mate showing the dead-fall sprung and *Martin Van Buren* caught in it

THE PIONEER'S LOG CABIN.

The following poem was written by one of the modest old settlers of Sangamon and read at the annual reunion in 1884 held on the spot where the first cabin in that county was built. "President Matheny—The first move toward civilization was the log cabin which"

Was a house of logs unhewed,
That bore the marks of workmen rude.
The logs were "notched" and "saddled" down.
By "corner men" "round after round,"
On the first "round" the joists were laid
And "flattened" as the floor was made,
When up about six feet or more,
The logs were cut out for the "door"
With the "falling axe" the work was done,
Few other tools were used or known.
A smooth split piece then "fac'd" the "eends"
Secured by season'd hickory pins.
Then above this a "round" or two
Built on, a "*loft*" tho' somewhat low.
Next came "eend" plates extending out
Beyond each corner about one foot,
And next the "ribs" a pole full length
Straight, and just large enough for strength.
Now "gable logs" slop'd at each end
Were built till the "ridge pole" was gain'd
And then around all take a sight
To see how near the "pitch" is right.
And if the "ribs" are straight and true,
The next thing is the "roof" you know—
Clapboards "broke joint" are laid along
And then a "weight pole" straight and strong,
Rests on a "beater" made to "scotch"
Each end by resting in a "notch"
Cut near the end of the "eend plate,"
'Gainst which rests all the coming weight.
Another course "broke joint" comes next,
The end butt to the weight pole fixed,
Course after course thus neatly fitted
With "weight poles" on, the roof completed.
And next the "fire-place" is made,
Full four feet high and eight feet wide,
The logs cut out, then split and framed
Just like a cabin. At the end
A wall within this wooden square,
Of stone and clay, layer after layer.
Some two feet thick the "back walls" stood,
The "jams" were less, but strong and good.
On this the chimney, wide below,
But narrowing as it upward grew.
It was not made of stone or bricks,
But built in layers of mud and sticks,
Until it reach'd the topmost roof,
And more of it was "plumb" enough.
We should have mentioned, but forgot,
That it was plaster'd in and out.
A clapboard paddle was the tool
Then used for plastering, as a rule.

The Pioneer's Log Cabin.

The hearth was made of native soil
And pounded with an "injun maul"
Then by the hearth—under the floor
With a loose "puncheon" for a door,
A hold was dug in which a "hun"
Was made to keep the "taters" in.
The next work was to lay the floor
And make a "shutter" for the door,
The puncheons, mostly made of lind,
Some edges thick some edges thin.
This came, of course, as they were riven
And made the floor somewhat uneven.
By hewing off the rough edge bevel
Down to the thin, the floor was level.
Next came a floor up overhead
On which to have an extra bed.
The joists were poles, the bark peeled off,
The floor of clapboards like the roof
A ladder rear'd up for the guest
Would bring him to his cozy nest.
But to remain aloft while there
Requir'd his utmost skill and care.
(A visitor once rose to dress
And mix'd the breakfast in a mess
The clapboard slipp'd and he fell through,
Clapboards and all were brought to view
Table and tea and meat and bread
Were substituted for a bed.
Frightened and fill'd with grief and pain
He hied him to his bed again.)
The door was framed with wondrous skill
And make to suit the maker's will,
Of clapboards shav'd and jointed too,
Sav'd from the pile the straight and true;
Tho' rough and strong, open or shut,
You ever found *the latch string out*.
A box behind this door was made,
In which to keep the corn for bread;
Now comes the "chinking" of the cracks,
With pieces driven with an ax,
At angle plac'd, leaning one way,
And wedged and pounded in to stay.
Then came the "daubing," well mixed mud
With the same paddle made of wood.
Inside and out the work goes on,
The cracks all filled, the cabin's done.
The last man in the settlement
Is fixed to leave his wagon tent,
At the back end he bores some holes
In which to "fix" some hickory poles,
The other ends he rests secure
Upon a pole braced from the floor
The first named in this bedroom set
"Tumbles to the racket" well, you bet,
And now to rest his weary head,
Washes his feet and goes to bed.

Aug. 5th, 1884. 1817—O. S

PHILIP GOODE GILLETT, A. M., LL. D.

SUPERINTENDENT OF ILLINOIS INSTITUTION FOR THE EDUCATION OF THE DEAF & DUMB.

JACKSONVILLE, ILLINOIS.

PHILIP GOODE GILLETT, A. M., LL. D., Superintendent of the Illinois Institution for the Education of the Deaf and Dumb, was born in Madison, Indiana, March 24, 1833, his father being Samuel Trumbull Gillett, a descendent of Jonathan Gillett, who emigrated from England and settled at Dorchester, Massachusetts, in 1630. His mother's family (the Goodes) were among the founders of the first settlements on the James river, Virginia.

His father was early connected with the United States Navy, and during his attachment to the Mediterranean squadron visited the Holy Land, where he received religious impressions which changed the tenor of his life. He resigned from the service and enrolled himself as an itinerant of the Methodist Episcopal Church, and for forty-five years, up to the present time, has faithfully pursued this higher calling.

His son Philip was educated at Indiana Asbury University, Greencastle, Indiana, where he graduated in 1852. He accepted the offer of a position in the Indiana Institution for the Education of the Deaf and Dumb, and entered upon its duties in October, 1852. In April, 1856, he was selected as Principal of the Illinois Institution for the Education of the Deaf and Dumb, located at Jacksonville, and upon his arrival he found it disorganized, its faculty broken, and the entire fabric under a cloud of embarrassments. Out of this general wreck, by skill and undaunted labor, he re-erected the institution upon a sounder basis, secured new and better buildings, established a wholesome discipline, and adopted a course of study which was most adapted to the peculiar needs of the unfortunates for whose benefit the institution was intended. It has, under Dr. Gillett's management, become the largest and one of the completest of its kind in the world. The State annually grants it a liberal support, and the last report of an examining committee of the Legislature was of the most favorable character, and flattering in its tribute to the talent and energy of its Superintendent, whose efforts of pen and voice have been directed towards arousing popular sympathy for the inmates of the institution.

He was President of the International Sabbath-School Convention, which, in 1872, held its triennial meeting at Indianapolis, and was twice selected as a member of the International Committee, whose duty it is to designate a seven years' course of study in the Sacred Scriptures.

In 1865 he succeeded in establishing, by legislative aid, an experimental school for the education of feeble-minded children, and became its Superintendent, serving without compensation.

He has been an active Sabbath-School worker, and was one of a few gentlemen who secured the adoption of a general system of county associations of Sabbath-Schools. In 1871 his *alma mater*, Indiana Asbury University, conferred on him the honorary degree of LL. D.

He was married, May 2, 1854, to Ellen M. Phipps, daughter of the late Isaac N. Phipps, a prominent citizen of Indianapolis. He is the father of four children, one of whom, Mrs. Chas. K. Cole, resides in Helena, Montana; another, Charles P. Gillett, is Dr. Gillett's assistant, while the third, Miss Alma, is a member of the faculty of the Institution for the Deaf and Dumb, and the fourth, Frederick P., is a student of Illinois College.

For reference to Dr. Gillett's work here, in connection with the institution for Deaf Mutes, see pages 129, 131, 151, 194, 208, 223 and 229 of "Historic Morgan." See also full-page cut on page 298.

JOSHUA RHOADS, M. D. Dr Joshua Rhoads was descended from an old Quaker family of Pennsylvania whose founder Adam Rhoads, came from England about 1682. Joshua Rhoads was the son of Joseph and Naomi Rhoads and was born at Philadelphia, September 14th, 1806. In his early years he attended Westown Boarding School, and the boarding school of the well known educator, John Gummere, at Burlington, N. J., studied medicine with Dr. Joseph Parrish, of Philadelphia, and afterwards graduated with honor at the University of Pennsylvania obtaining the degree of M. D. Princeton College also conferred upon him the degree of Master of Arts.

He was married in 1833 to Rosanna, daughter of Barclay and Mary Ivins, of Penn's Manor, Bucks county, Pennsylvania. Their family consisted of eight children, but three daughters alone survive.

For ten years he devoted himself to the practice of his profession as a physician, but from his peculiar organization, the anxiety and responsibility incident to his calling, so undermined his health, that he was obliged to abandon it. He then turned his attention to teaching and after several years experience as principal of some of the prominent schools of Philadelphia, in 1839, he was elected principal of the Pennsylvania Institution for the Blind, thus entering upon the work to which he gave the best years of his life—the instruction of those deprived of sight.

This position he filled for some years to the satisfaction of the trustees. In 1850, a committee of the trustees of the Illinois Institution for the Blind, then in its infancy, visited the East in search of a superintendent with experience and ability to whom they would be willing to entrust its interests. As he enjoyed the confidence and esteem of some of the most eminent teachers of the blind in the United States, they invited him to preside over the institution which has since become one of our noblest state charities. At that time the institution had only been founded two years, numbered twenty-three pupils, and occupied a rented building wholly inadequate to the necessities of the school. Owing to the liberality of the state, however, a suitable building was in process of erection, which in due time afforded the much needed facilities for the education of the blind. The curriculum of the school was extended, the department of music advanced to a higher standard, the library enlarged, new trades and modes of handicraft introduced.

Of an eminently practical turn of mind, and inclined to be conservative in his views, Dr. Rhoads was always glad to avail himself of anything that promised to be a *real* improvement in the methods of instruction, and at the time he was connected with the Pennsylvania Institution invented a system of raising maps for the blind, that was far superior to any then in use. He also visited other institutions in this country, examined the workings of the institutions of France and England as far as practicable from published records, translating from French authors such hints as he thought would aid him in advancing the cause. The institution grew and prospered until the new building was crowded with eighty-eight pupils, when in April, 1869, it was destroyed by fire originating in a defective flue. Owing to the kindness of citizens of Jacksonville, combined with the energy and promptness of Dr. Rhoads and the trustees, the school was not disbanded until the summer vacation, and by the next January a wing was erected in which seventy pupils could be accommodated.

One of the kindliest, and most benevolent of men, he desired that the institution should be a home to the pupils during the time of their stay, as well as a school, and his government of them was truly paternal—his generous sympathy being always freely given to those so much in need of it. In all the care and anxiety that devolved upon him while holding this important trust, he was aided and sustained by his wife, who brought her heart, her energy, rare judgment and fine executive abilities to the work. He was a member of the "Religious Society of Friends," to whose early training he may have owed in part, some of the conscientiousness, the love for humanity, and sympathy for the poor and oppressed that distinguished him through life. His consideration for others was unbounded, and it could be said of him with truth

"To do him any wrong, was to beget
A kindness from him, for his heart was rich,
Of such fine mould, that if you sowed therein
The seed of Hate, it blossom'd Charity."

For almost a quarter of a century, his life, his hopes and aims were identified with the history of this institution and in all that time through various changes in the Board of Trustees composed of men of different political opinions, he had the confidence and undivided support of every Board under whom he served. In 1874, the retiring Board of Trustees consisting of Matthew Stacy, E. B. Hawley and W. H. Grimshaw, who had been in the most intimate relations to the institution for many years and were familiar with everything connected with its management, passed resolutions expressing their satisfaction with the condition of the institution and their confidence in the "zeal, integrity and devotion to duty" of its officers. He had the happiness to live to see the institution occupying the position of one of the best in the country, the buildings ready to receive more pupils, and retired to private life in 1874. In the spring of that year he was taken with a violent attack of illness, from which he rallied, but never entirely recovered, and passed away in the utmost peace February 1st, 1876. In the community that had so long been his home, and where he had labored so efficiently to ameliorate the condition of the unfortunate, he was respected by high and low, rich and poor. After his death the leading citizens testified in a public meeting to his worth as a private citizen and as chief executive of the institution over which he had so long presided, and in one of the resolutions adopted, stated that "the fidelity and economy with which during his administration the state benefactions had been applied, furnished an example unsurpassed by any similar institution in the country." See pages 111, 123, 126, 208.

JOHN P. WILKINSON was born December 14th, 1790, in New Kent county, Virginia, and emigrated to Kentucky, in Todd county, of that state. He married Mary Harlan in 1827, and in 1828 removed to this place which he had selected as a permanent home. Mr. Wilkinson was a merchant, and as such, was long and favorably known in Morgan county. Prompt, honest and liberal in his dealings he enjoyed in a high degree the confidence of those with whom he transacted business and his example salutary anywhere and at any time, was particularly so in the early period of our local history. It is, however, in social life that we especially love to contemplate the character of Mr. Wilkinson. In the early days of our town and county, no man paid more (nor as much) attention to strangers, who thought of settling amongst us, as he. He gave them information as to property and location, furnished them facilities for examining the country, tendered them the hospitalities of his house, and thus, and otherwise, induced many valuable persons to settle in this community. Kind in his feelings, pleasant in his manners, courteous in his deportment, those who visited Jacksonville in primitive times remember Mr. Wilkinson with pleasure.

He was a man of great public spirit. No one had a truer conception than he, of the superiority of his obligation to society or those due to his individual interests. With him the controlling idea was not, will this contribute to my ease, and advance my fortune? But will it promote the greater, wider, higher object of social life. Of comprehensive views, he was the fast friend of our literary institutions. Liberal in his public benefactions, he was especially so to Illinois College, and the Jacksonville Female Academy, of each of these institutions he was a trustee from their origin, to his death, and the office of trustee with him was no sinecure. He did what so few men are willing to do, he gave them his time, his thought, his watchful care and insight. For a long time he also gratuitously served the college as treasurer, and in many ways endeared his name and memory to those who were connected with the valuable institution in its early struggles, and those who now preside over it would doubtless recognize its present peace and prosperity, as, in some measure, the results of his benefactions, and self-sacrificing labors. Mr. Wilkinson made profession of religion in 1830, and was received into the Presbyterian Church by President Sturtevant. His walk and conversation thereafter, was such as became a follower of Jesus Christ. Mr. Wilkinson was one of the building committee of the church this same year. Equally removed from as much criticism on the one hand, and levity on the other, he was a fine specimen of an unaffected, genial, hopeful, Christian gentleman. In December, 1841, Mr. Wilkinson was taken ill while in St. Louis on business, and died at the Planters' House. He left no children, but his adopted son Rev. George Harlan, whom he educated, survived him until November 21st, 1858. Mrs. Wilkinson was a woman of stirring worth, she was a sister of Mr. Levi Harlan, of Winchester; they were deprived of their parents early in life by accident, both being drowned with their three youngest children while crossing James River, Virginia, in a skiff. No one knew how it happened, but supposed her father must have dropped one of his oars, and thus was swept over a mill dam near by. Mrs. Wilkinson left alone in the world became a very self-reliant woman, and took a very serious view of life, which at times made her seem almost severe, but this was not true of her. She was particular and exact, but gentle and thoughtful, full of good deeds to the sick and unfortunate. Let not her memory perish from our midst, but be ever cherished as a noble example of a self-denying christian. Also see pages 45, 51, 57, 241, 244, 245.

ERASTUS FRANKLIN BULLARD, A. M., Principal of the Jacksonville Female Academy, Jacksonville, Ill., is a native of Jay, Essex county, New York. In early boyhood he was subjected to all the privations and hardships incident to a rugged country life and indigent circumstances. When he was but six years old his father died, leaving a widowed mother and a large family of children to fight the battle of life as best they could. From the age of fourteen, he was left dependent upon his own resources. His opportunities for early education were limited, and it was not until he had made a trial of several years of farm life that he began to realize the need and appreciate the benefits of something better in education. In view of fitting for college, he began teaching in the country schools during the winter and prosecuting his studies during the spring and autumn. In September, 1860, he entered the Freshman class in the University of Vermont, and although frequently interrupted by ill health and pecuniary embarrassments, he was graduated with honors in the regular course, four years after.

On leaving college, in 1864, he was called to the Principalship of Royalton Academy, Royalton, Vermont, in which position he remained for two years. In 1866 he returned to his native county in New York, and was shortly after elected, on the Republican ticket, to the office of School Commissioner for Essex county, which position he held for three consecutive years. In the fall of 1869 he assumed the principalship and superintendence of the public schools of Keeseville, New York. He remained in this position five years and until his election as Principal of the Jacksonville Female Academy, in 1874.

Prof. Bullard is now completing the eleventh year of his management of the Academy, already a longer term than any of his predecessors remained in the position. By his judicious management and rare executive ability, he has placed the institution upon an independent basis and raised it to a rank second to none in the West, in its standards of discipline and scholarship.

Professor Bullard is a widower, having one child, a daughter, who has made her home from infancy with her grand parents, in Burlington, Vermont. He has attained high rank as an educator and as a business man. He is a gentleman of literary tastes and scholarly attainments, loyal in his friendships, active in good works and a public spirited citizen. His familiar features are given by our artist. For further reference to his life and work in Jacksonville, see pages 195, 199, 206, 219.

DR. ~~WILLIAM~~ *Thomas* MUNROE,

OF RUSHVILLE, SCHUYLER COUNTY, ILL.

THOMAS MUNROE, M. D.—The propriety of introducing some faces and names not, at first, recalled by younger readers of this work may be questioned; but it must be remembered that history treats rather of the past than of to-day; that things done, instead of doing, are recorded by the historian.

The subject of this sketch, "Doctor Munroe," as he was known to many of our oldest and best citizens, needs only naming to place an honorable man, an honored citizen and a Christian gentleman before the recollecting mind.

Although many years have passed since Dr. Munroe left Jacksonville as a residence, yet we doubt if any of the earlier settlers are recalled with pleasanter thoughts than he, by those who had the good fortune to know him. As a physician here, his practice must have brought him into tender ties with many families before the writer of these words had come upon the scene of action. At this time a wealthy resident of Rushville, this State, the doctor has revisited our city occasionally of late years, and was present, last, at the Commencement of Illinois College, in 1882, when his youngest son, William was graduated.

But, to proceed to the biographical sketch: Thomas Munroe, son of John and Ann Munroe, was born in Annapolis, Maryland, January 4, 1807. His grandfather, William Munroe, was one of 135 men, residing in and near Annapolis, who, in 1774, signed a protest against certain acts of the Colonial Government, then under British rule, and when the war broke out, the next year, he espoused the cause of the Colonies against King George.

Dr. Munroe was educated at St. John's College, Annapolis, taking the full classical course, finishing in 1826; he studied medicine at that place, attended lectures at the University of Maryland, at Baltimore; received his medical degree in 1829, practiced at Baltimore several years. He came to this State in December, 1835, practiced at Jacksonville until 1843, and then settled in Rushville. Here (Rushville) he was in steady practice till 1862, when he was appointed Surgeon of the 119th Regt. Ill. Vols., which was attached to the 16th Army Corps, and he remained in the service until June, 1864, when his health broke down in the Red River Expedition, and he resigned.

Dr. Munroe was married, in 1841, to Miss Annie Hinman, of Utica, New York, daughter of Major Benjamin Hinman, who was an officer in the Revolutionary War and some time aid to Gen. Greene. They have six children: Thomas, educated at Bloomington (Ill.) University, is successfully engaged in the lumber business, at Muskegon, Michigan; James Edward, a graduate of Illinois College, is practicing law in Chicago; Mary E., Hinman, Charles G., and William, also a graduate of Illinois College, are residing in Rushville.

James E. Munroe, referred to above, was graduated from Illinois College, with the highest record of his class, in 1868, and was married, in 1876, to Miss Kate B. Smith, daughter of the late D. A. Smith, of Jacksonville.

In 1875 Dr. Munroe was appointed United States Examining Surgeon for Pensions.

Soon after his location in Jacksonville, in 1835, he formed a professional partnership with Dr. Shirley and subsequently with Dr. English.

John J. Hardin, Stephen A. Douglas, Wm. Thomas, Wm. Brown, Joseph Duncan, Richard Yates, and Murray McConnel were leading men, some in politics and some in law.

About the spring of 1836 Douglas returned from teaching a school at Winchester, and soon outran all competitors in the Democratic county convention and was nominated and elected to the Legislature. This was the beginning of his political career.

Hon. Richard Yates was a young man during the time of Dr. Munroe's residence here, and at Mr. Yates's marriage, his friend, the doctor, was a groomsman.

Dr. Munroe is a member of the Methodist Episcopal Church, in which he is greatly respected, and has been the continued recipient of trust and honor at the hands of his co-religionists.

Our portrait, made from a very striking likeness just taken, places before the younger citizens a man whom those acquainted with love and respect; a man whose silvered hair, whitened by over three score and ten years, is emblematic of the purity of his life, and whose later years show that the end of a man who follows a Christian life "is peace."

HON. SAMUEL DRAKE LOCKWOOD was born in Poundridge, Westchester county, New York, on the second day of August, 1789.

When he was ten years old his father died, and his mother was left with three small children, and with but slender means for their support. By this event his plans for a liberal education were broken up and he was thrown very much upon his own resources.

In 1803 he went to Waterford, New York, to live with his uncle, Francis Drake, a lawyer in that place, and remained in his family as errand boy and law-student until February, 1811, when he was licensed to practice law, and opened an office in Batavia, New York. The next year he removed to Auburn, and continued in the practice of law there till the fall of 1818, holding during a part of that time the office of Master in Chancery. At that time his constitution (never very strong) seemed so broken down by disease and constant application to business that his physician advised him to give up his profession and engage in some out-door employment as the only way of regaining even his former degree of health.

This advice, together with the glowing accounts of the great "far West" then prevalent, induced him to change his residence and seek his future home in the new State of Illinois. On October 19th of that year, in company with the late William H. Brown and others, he started on his Western trip.

At Olean Point, New York, they purchased a flat-boat, on which they floated down the Allegheny and Ohio rivers to Shawneetown, reaching that place on December 15th, and making the trip in fifty-seven days.

After remaining a few days in Shawneetown, Lockwood and Brown started for Kaskaskia on foot, a walk of 120 miles. The next year Mr. Brown was appointed Clerk of the United States District Court, and their arrangement for a law partnership being thus broken up, Mr. Lockwood removed to Carmi as a more favorable point for the practice of his profession.

At the second session of the Illinois Legislature, which was held at Vandalia in 1821, Mr. Lockwood was elected Attorney General of the State, and his acceptance of this office rendering another change of residence necessary, he chose Edwardsville for his future home.

In 1823 he was, very unexpectedly to himself, nominated by Gov. Cole to the office of Secretary of State, but soon after accepting that office he was greatly surprised by receiving from President Monroe a commission appointing him Receiver of Public Monies at the land office in Edwardsville. This commission was, in itself, as undesired as it was unsought, but the Secretary of State's salary was small and payable in depreciated currency, while that of Receiver was liberal and payable in gold, and had attached to it a percentage on receipts. These considerations induced him to resign the office of Secretary and accept that of Receiver.

At the next session of the State Legislature, 1824 '85, he was, against his expressed wishes, elected Judge of the Supreme Court, which office he accepted and held until the State constitution of 1848 went into operation, under which new judges were elected by the people.

In 1826 he was married to Miss Mary Virginia Nash, of St. Louis county, Missouri, the amiable and excellent wife who survived him a few years and whom all friends so long loved and admired.

In 1829 he removed from Edwardsville to Jacksonville, and in 1853 from that place to Batavia, Kane county, where he died. He was sent from Morgan county to the Constitutional Convention of 1848, and in that convention was Chairman of the Committee on Executive. To him is due the recognition of Deity in the preamble of the constitution adopted by this convention.

In 1851 he was appointed, by the Legislature, Trustee of the Land Department of the Illinois Central Railroad, which office he held at the time of his death.

The position which he held in the history of our State is indicated by the offices which were conferred upon him. Having a natural distaste for everything like office-seeking, and never putting himself forward for official position, still he was kept in offices of high position and trust for over fifty years.

In the anti-slavery controversy over the question of a State Convention, in 1823, he took an active part and contributed materially to the support and editorial efficiency of the Edwardsville *Spectator*, one of the two papers that took decided ground for freedom in this State.

Though never an active partisan, he was fully identified with the Whig party till 1855, when he, with most of that party, helped to form the Republican party. Many of the offices which he held were conferred upon him by administrations with which he was not in political sympathy.

In Governor Ford's history of Illinois are found the following notices of Judge Lockwood: "In 1820 was fought the first and last duel in Illinois. One of the parties fell, mortally wounded; the other was tried and convicted of murder, and suffered the extreme penalty of the law by hanging. Judge Lockwood was then the attorney of the State and prosecuted in the case. To his talents and success as a prosecutor the people are indebted for this early precedent and example, which did more than is generally known to prevent the barbarous practice of dueling from being introduced into the State."

"In 1826-7 Judges Lockwood and Smith presented to the Legislature a revision of the laws of the State, prepared by them in accordance with the instructions of the preceding Legislature, and these laws have been standard laws in every revision since."

In his chapter on a somewhat bitter controversy that occurred between the executive and judicial departments of the State in 1840, Governor Ford says: "It is due to truth to say that Judges Wilson and Lockwood were in every respect amiable and accomplished gentlemen, and commanded the esteem and respect of all good men for the purity of their conduct and their probity in official station."

"Judge Lockwood was an excellent lawyer, a man of sound judgment, and his face indicated uncommon purity, modesty and intelligence, together with energy and strong determination. His face was the true index of his character."

Any account of Judge Lockwood's services to the State which should fail to notice his connection with its educational, benevolent and religious interests would come far short of doing him justice. As early as his residence in Auburn, he was so identified with the religious interests there as to be appointed one of the trustees of the Presbyterian Church.

In 1815 was formed the Cayuga County Bible Society, the first organized in the State of New York, two years before the organization of the American Bible Society, and Judge Lockwood's name appeared as one of the originators and directors of that organization. Of the twenty-four first directors of that society, he was the last survivor. The stand he thus took, as illustrated by these incidents, he maintained through life.

His influence and liberality were extended toward promoting the scheme which resulted in the establishment of Illinois College, and it is believed that without his labors in Jacksonville's behalf, the institution would have been located elsewhere—in all probability in Southern Illinois. Most of the settlers of the State were then in that section. Judge Lockwood was one of the first in the State to propose and advocate such an institution, and he advised those who were interested with him in the matter not to decide until they had seen some of the beautiful country around Jacksonville; and on this advice, Revs. Thomas Lippincott and John M. Ellis were sent to spy out the country, Judge Lockwood furnishing a horse, and paying the traveling expenses of one of the party. The result was, the location of the college on the tract of land he had a few months before secured for his own homestead. Judge Lockwood was one of the Trustees of this institution from its organization until 1868, when he resigned, as his failing health would not allow his attending the meetings of the Board. A part of the time he was President of the Board. So, too, he was always a staunch friend and promoter of the interests of the Jacksonville Female Academy, at one time, with a few others, saving it from suspension by liberality and personal exertions. He presided at the first meeting held to establish it, and was an honored member of the first Board of Trustees, holding the same connection until his death in 1874.

Judge Lockwood took an active part in organizing and locating the State Asylums for the Deaf and Dumb, the Blind and the Insane—and was on the first Board of Trustees of each.

In every place where he resided in the State his influence was indeed a strong, steady and reliable power for good, always on the side of freedom, temperance, morality, and the mainspring of them all—Christianity.

For the last twenty-one years of his life Judge Lockwood resided in Batavia, in honored old age enjoying his quiet home on the banks of the Fox river, and rejoicing in everything tending to advance the material or moral prosperity of the State he had loved so long and served so faithfully.

On the 23d of April, 1874, he passed away in a death as quiet and peaceful as his life had been.

For further reference to his life and labors, see pages 18, 40, 47, 53, 55, 56, 69, 110, 118, 120, 123, 126, 127, 138, 261.

JUDGE EDWARD P. KIRBY was born October 28, 1834, in Putnam county, Illinois, and is the eldest son of the late Rev. William and Hannah (Wolcott) Kirby. Rev. William Kirby was one of the founders and first professors of Illinois College; but owing to failing health, he was obliged to relinquish the latter position. He died December 20, 1852, leaving a family of six children, the care and support of whom devolved on the oldest son.

Judge Kirby was educated at Illinois College, and graduated therefrom in 1854.

In the autumn of that year he went to St. Louis, where he taught a private school for three years. On his return to Jacksonville, he became the successor of Hon. Newton Bateman in the principalship of the West Jacksonville District School.

He commenced the study of law in 1863, and was admitted to practice in the following year. In 1865 he commenced the compilation of the Land Titles of Morgan County, Ill., which he subsequently completed and still owns.

In 1873 he was elected Judge of the County Court of Morgan county, by the Republicans, for with that party he has been identified ever since its formation.

He was married in 1862 to Julia S., daughter of the late Governor Duncan, of Jacksonville.

He is now in partnership with the Hon. William Brown, in the practice of law and the abstract-of-titles business, with a large and remunerative patronage.

Mr. Kirby has also filled the honorary positions of Trustees of Illinois College and Illinois Central Hospital for the Insane.

See pages 126, 144, 156, 176, 181, 185, 195, 203, 214, 226, 266, 287.

DR. HENRY F. CARRIEL,

Superintendent of the Illinois Central Hospital for the Insane.

DR. HENRY F. CARRIEL now Superintendent of the Illinois Central Hospital for the Insane, was born in Charlestown, N. H. He passed his boyhood chiefly upon his father's farm, but his father dying when he was nine and his mother when he was sixteen years of age, he was thus early thrown upon his own resources.

His education was obtained at the district school, at Marlow Academy, N. H., and Wesleyan Seminary, Vt. After preparing for the Sophomore year in college, failing health compelled him to relinquish study, and this circumstance probably turned his attention to medicine.

In the year 1853 he commenced the study of medicine with Dr. E. A. Knight, of Springfield, Vt. He attended his first course of medical lectures at Woodstock, Vt.; his second course at Pittsfield, Mass., and his last course at the College of Physicians and Surgeons, New York city, where he graduated in the spring of 1857.

In April, 1857, he accepted the appointment of Assistant Physician in the New Jersey State Lunatic Asylum, which position he filled until 1870, a period of thirteen years.

Dr. Carriel, in 1866, feeling the need of rest and recreation and being desirous of informing himself of the mode of management of the insane in other countries, went to Europe and visited some thirty hospitals and asylums for the insane in England, Scotland, Ireland and France; observing particularly the per capita costs for buildings, mode of care and general management.

In June 1870 he received, unsolicited, the appointment of Superintendent of the Illinois Central Hospital for the Insane, and on the morning of July 1st arrived in Jacksonville to enter upon the duties of his position. Since that to the present time, he has applied himself assiduously to the duties of his position, and his administration is justly receiving the cordial support, commendation and approval of the people of the State.

During the time Dr. Carriel has been in charge, the institution has been doubled in capacity, and the entire building has been renovated, ventilated and vastly improved till to-day it will compare favorably with any institution in the country for conveniences, home-like comforts and medical appliances. As an organizer he has few equals and no superiors; everything under his care moves with the precision of machinery; he has shown marked ability in planning and erecting hospital buildings, and the State has good reason to be proud of the results of his attention to the smallest details of work committed to his care.

He was married May 6, 1862, to Miss Mary C., only daughter of Dr. H. A. Buttolph; married his second wife, Miss Mary L., only daughter of Prof. J. B. Turner, May 6th 1875.

Dr. Carriel has seven children—six sons and one daughter.

See pages 176, 177, 194, 223, 253.

WILLIAM FLETCHER SHORT, D. D., was born in Butler county, Ohio, November 9, 1829. His father, Rev. Daniel Short, came, with his family, to Morgan county, in 1834. He was widely known and greatly respected as an earnest, able and useful preacher of the Methodist Episcopal Church through Central Illinois.

Dr. Short was brought up on a farm, where he experienced all the privations and hardships of those early times.

At about the age of twenty, feeling himself called to the ministry, he determined to seek a collegiate education. He accordingly entered McKendree College, and pursued the course of study to the senior year. He then entered the Illinois Wesleyan University at Bloomington and graduated in 1854. Before his graduation he accepted a call to the charge of the Missouri Conference Seminary, located at Jackson. At the end of two and a half years he resigned, to enter the active pastorate in this State. The several charges filled were: Island Grove, two years; Williamsville, two years; Waverly, two years; Winchester, two years; Carlinville, three years; Hillsboro, one year; Grace Church, three years; Presiding Elder of Jacksonville District four years.

In July of 1875 he was elected President of Illinois Female College, which position he still holds.

His administration of affairs as head of this important and flourishing educational institution has been marked by a wise Christian policy, an elevation of the standard of scholarship, the establishment of home-like government and the employment of a higher grade of talent in the art and musical departments. The result, of course, has shown itself in increased patronage and a broadened and higher reputation for the school.

The degree of Doctor of Divinity was conferred by Ohio Wesleyan University.

As a citizen, Dr. Short has always been public-spirited, and a favorite in social and religious circles and holds high rank in the Masonic organization.

In August, 1854 he was married to Miss Sarah B. Laning, of Petersburg. Three daughters and one son are living; one son having died while Dr. Short was pastor of Grace Church.

HON. RICHARD YATES, Lawyer, War Governor of Illinois, and United States Senator, was born in Warsaw, Gallatin county, Illinois, January 18th, 1818, and when thirteen years of age removed with his father to Springfield, in the same state. His preliminary education was obtained in Illinois College, at Jacksonville, from which institution he was graduated with the class of 1838.

He afterward studied law under the instructions of Colonel J. J. Hardin, who fell in the war with Mexico. Entering upon the practice of his profession, became a successful participant in political affairs, and from 1842 to 1849 represented his district in the Illinois Legislature. In 1850 he received the congressional nomination at the Whig convention, was elected a member of the Thirty-second Congress, and on taking his seat in that body was found to be its youngest member. At the next election, notwithstanding the political change in his district at the county elections, he was again chosen as a member of the Thirty-third Congress, but two years subsequently failed to secure a re-election. While a member of the House he became an earnest opponent of the slave power and of the repeal of the Missouri Compromise; evinced great ability and entire fearlessness in his words and actions, and in numerous ways was importantly instrumental in advancing the interests of the anti-slavery cause. In 1860 he was nominated by the Republican party as a candidate for Governor, and after a very exciting canvass was triumphantly elected. During the war of the rebellion he was an efficient and indefatigable supporter of the United States government, and, by his well directed energy and activity in providing fresh relays of needed troops, acquired an enviable position in the ranks of the "War Governors."

April 23d, 1861, he issued a proclamation to convene the Legislature at Springfield for the purpose of enacting such laws and adopting such measures as were deemed necessary for the organization and equipment of the militia of the state, and also for the raising of such money and other means as were required to preserve the Union and enforce the laws.

In May, 1861, he conferred upon Ulysses S. Grant, then engaged at Springfield in the organization of the volunteer troops of Illinois, the Colonelcy of the 21st Regiment Illinois Infantry.

May 20th, 1862, he issued a proclamation calling for recruits to fill up the volunteer regiments from Illinois, and on the following July 11th published a letter to the President of the United States urging the employment of all available means to crush the rebellion and prevent the overturning of the constitution. On one occasion he paid an unusual, but merited, compliment to Mrs. Reynolds, wife of Lieut. Reynolds, of Company A. of the 17th Illinois Regiment, of Peoria. She had accompanied her husband through the greater part of the campaign in which that regiment had participated, and was present at the battle of Pittsburg Landing, where she ministered with tireless heroism to the wants of the dying and wounded. Upon hearing of her praiseworthy conduct he presented her with a commission as major in the army, the document conferring the honor being made out with all due formality, and having attached to it the great seal of the state.

June 8th, 1863, he adjourned the Legis-

Your friend
Richd Yates

lature of Illinois, "fully believing that the interests of the state will be best subserved by a speedy adjournment, the past history of the present Assembly holding out no reasonable hope of beneficent results to the citizens of the state or the army in the field from its farther continuance."

In June of the same year, upon receiving a letter from a town in the southern part of the state, in which the writer complained that traitors in his town had cut down the American flag, and demanded his advice as to what measures should be taken, he promptly wrote the querist as follows: "Whenever you raise the flag on your own soil, or on the public property of the state or country, or at any public celebration, from honest love to that flag, and patriotic devotion to the country which it symbolizes, and any traitor dares to lay his unhallowed hand upon it to tear it down, then I say shoot him down as you would a dog, and I will pardon you the offence." His whole course during the war was such as to win for him a popularity second only to that enjoyed by, perhaps, two other citizens of the state, and to cause his name to be a grateful remembrance to the whole country.

His term of office expired with the year 1864, and March 5th, 1865, he took his seat in the United States Senate, having been elected as the successor of Richard A. Richardson, Democrat. At the second session of the Thirty-ninth Congress, when the bill regulating suffrage in the District of Columbia was brought under consideration, in his speech following that of Mr. Cowan, of Pennsylvania, he expressed his views in strong, terse, and logical language, saying among other things: "I am for universal suffrage. I am not for qualified suffrage; I am not for property suffrage; I am not for intelligent suffrage, as it is termed, but I am for universal suffrage. That is my doctrine. * * * * *

The question of negro suffrage is now an imperative necessity that the negro should possess it for his own protection; a necessity that he should possess it that the nation may preserve its power, its strength, and its unity. We have now negro suffrage for the District of Columbia, and I say I believe we have won it for all the states, and before the 4th of March, 1869—before this administration shall close—I hope that the negro in all the loyal states will be clothed with the right of suffrage. That they will be in the ten rebel states I cannot doubt, for patriotism, liberty, justice and humanity demand it.

He served actively and prominently until the expiration of his term, March 3d, 1871, returning subsequently to Illinois, when he resumed the practice of his profession. In March, 1873, he was appointed a Government Director of the Union Pacific Railroad, in which office he continued until his decease, which occurred at St. Louis, November 27th, 1873.

The family of the distinguished deceased are still numbered among our honored citizens, Mrs. Yates, his widow, occupying the old homestead on East State street, Jacksonville. With her are the two sons, Henry and Richard, Jr.—(the latter a brilliant and popular practitioner-at-law, now holding the office of city attorney)—and one daughter, Mrs. Thomas Woodman.

See pages 64, 89, 102, 103, 114, 117, 123, 125, 127, 130 to 136, 156, 158, 181, 182, 261, 265, 266, 267, also steel plate engraving on opposite page.

PRESIDENT EDWARD A. TANNER, D.D., was born November 29, 1837, at Waverly, Illinois. He is the youngest child of Jos. A. and Orra S. Tanner, who are old settlers in Morgan county, though formerly from Warren, Connecticut. The ancestors of the family were English. His parents removed to Morgan county about 1834, and located on a farm, where the subject of this sketch spent his boyhood.

He entered Illinois College at the age of fifteen and graduated therefrom in 1857, receiving the degree of A. B., and, three years after, the degree of A. M. was conferred upon him, after the delivery of the master's oration.

After finishing his collegiate course, he taught in the public schools of Waverly and Jacksonville for a period of three years. He was called, in 1861, to the professorship of Latin in Pacific University, Oregon, and filled that position four years. In the meantime, having studied theology he was licensed to preach by the Congregational Association of Oregon in 1864. In 1865 he was appointed Professor of Latin in Illinois College, which position he held until 1882, when he was promoted to the presidency of the institution. He has also officiated four years as Chaplain of Illinois Central Hospital for the Insane, at Jacksonville. As an eminent educator, Dr. Tanner holds a front rank in the state, and received the degree of D. D. from his *alma mater*, in 1880, being a scholar of fine classical culture and solid erudition.

He was married June 27, 1861, to Miss Marian L. Brown, a lady of charming social qualities and earnest religious character, a daughter of Dr. I. H. Brown, of Waverly. Her parents were formerly from Connecticut. President Tanner and lady have had a family of six children, one of whom is deceased.

In politics the Professor is a Republican. He is a devoted son of "Illinois College" and still fills with greatest of credit the presidency. His earnest labors in the financial interest of the college have brought thousands of dollars into its treasury.

CHARLES M. MORSE, was born July 21st, 1820, in Wilton, Maine, and is a son of Col. Charles Morse. His education was obtained chiefly at the village school, supplemented by an attendance, during four terms, at a higher academy, and frequently interrupted by ill-health.

His father was a farmer and miller, but as the son was physically unable to perform much labor, very little was required of him. A remark made by the father to a friend, and accidentally overheard by the son, created a great impression on his mind, insomuch that it very materially determined his future course of action. "Charles," he said, "cannot work with his brothers, but we can always depend upon him for closing the gates—he don't leave things half done."

When seventeen years old, he entered the post office at Augusta, the capital city of the state, where he served four years, and where, for weeks together, he had sole charge of the office. Although he differed politically with the postmaster, he never lost the latter's confidence and esteem, who refused to displace him at the behest of party managers, to make way for a party favorite. Shortly after arriving at manhood, he married and returned to his native town, where he assisted his father in the management of his business, and ultimately succeeded to it, on the death of his parent in 1845. Immediately upon his return to Wilton, he was elected Town Clerk, which, with other town offices, he held for seven years, when he was chosen a representative in the State Legislature. In 1850, he entered the office of the treasurer of the Maine Central (then the A. and K.) Railroad Company, and, excepting four months, was connected with that corporation for over fifteen years, serving in various capacities, from Fireman to Superintendent, the longest period being as General Ticket Agent and Cashier, nearly the entire earnings of the company passing through his hands. His services as Superintendent covered three years at two different times. In 1866 he became Superintendent of the St. Louis, Jacksonville & Chicago Railroad; and in 1868, when that line was leased to the Chicago & Alton Railroad Company, he was appointed to the position of Superintendent of a Division, embracing 190 miles of road and is now Freight Division Superintendent of the C. & A. with headquarters at Jacksonville.

He is a man of fine literary attainments, although he makes no claim to scholarship. He is interested in inaugurating and sustaining all literary and art enterprises in this city. He is fond of books, possessing a library of choice works, numbering nearly one thousand volumes, and is a lover of antiquarian research.

He takes great interest in all matters pertaining to the welfare of the community in which he resides; and is, in short, a useful, worthy and honorable citizen.

As a Freemason Col. Morse ranks high and never allows himself to grow rusty. He has not only been Eminent Commander of Hospitaler Commandery, Knights Templar, of this city, but has risen to the exalted honors of Grand Commander of the Illinois Grand Commandery, Knights Templar.

One who knows our Frater well says of him, that his big-hearted and broad liberality is only limited by the length of his purse. That wherever he has lived and whatever his official and social duties might be, he was always trying to help somebody do better and to be better. To which we who know him Masonically will heartily say, Amen.

"With malice towards none, with charity for all, with firmness in the right, as God gives us to see the right."

He was brought to Masonic Light in Waterville Lodge, No. 33, in Maine, where he received the third degree March 21, 1853, and afterwards served as Master. July 10, 1856, in Jerusalem Chapter, at Gardiner, in the same State, he accomplished the journey over the rough road which pertains to the R. A. Chapter; and at Bangor, in St. John's Commandery, No. 3, on June 13, 1861, he participated for the first time in the solemn service attending the reception into the Templar Order.

It is a little remarkable that in his thirty-five years' railroad experience, while traveling much of the time, he was never in an accident where a human being was materially injured, or resulting in any considerable destruction of property.

Mr. Morse is not a member of any church, but is a regular attendant (Congregationalist). He traces his genealogy, on the paternal side, through the Morses and Lelands, back to the "Pilgrims," 1630-50, and on the maternal side, through the Scotch-Irish Scales and Mathes, to about 1680.

His excellent wife and three daughters, Mrs. John G. Loomis, Mrs. Alfred Sturtevant and Miss Mattie, are numbered among our citizens, while one son, Charles, is in the Providence Savings Bank, in St. Louis.

JONATHAN BALDWIN TURNER.—Few if any among present residents of Jacksonville are better known. He was born at Templeton, Mass., Dec. 7th, 1805. His ancestors were among the emigrants on the Mayflower. He studied at Yale, in which university he took a high rank, and where his determined energy and vigorous mind gave early promise of a useful and illustrious future. In October 1835, he married Rhodolphia S. Kibbe, and in succeeding years became the father of seven children. He accepted the situation of teacher in various schools in Massachusetts, and at New Haven, Connecticut, before his graduation, and won the encomiums of his associates and the love of his pupils.

He came to Illinois as teacher in Illinois College in 1832 and was soon after chosen one of the Professors in that institution, holding the position for fifteen years, when failing health, and what was then deemed over-zealous resistance to slavery and sectarianism, compelled his resignation. He was deeply interested in educational problems, and as early as 1833 delivered in the state a series of lectures for the purpose of arousing popular sentiment in favor of a broad and permanent system of common schools. While thus philanthropically engaged, during college vacations, on horseback and on foot through this then sparsely settled commonwealth, on the vast timberless prairies, he concluded that they would remain undeveloped so long as the people were without the means of enclosing their farms. This led him to the study of some device as a substitute for timber for fences. In his experiments at this public labor he exhausted his means and effects, and was repaid by the silly jeers of the incredulous. He tried various plants with little success for a long time, until he found the Osage Orange; and this for a considerable period was always spoken of as "Professor Turner's Folly," but at length, by the force of successful experiments, incredulity was compelled to admit the great benefits of his discovery.

He interested himself in the advancement of agriculture, and was one of the originators of the modern methods for planting corn by machinery and for the extensive use of machinery in the general cultivation of the ground. He was restlessly active, contributing, to various magazines and journals, papers on "Microscopic Insects," "Fungoid growths and Diseases of Plants and Trees," on "The Preparation and Rotation of Crops," on "The Analysis of Soils," and on kindred subjects, they were filled with practical suggestions of incalculable value to his fellow-men. His political discussions have at all times attracted the attention and study of statesmen. Daniel Webster pronounced his essay on "Currency" one of the ablest papers he had ever read on that subject. His "Mormonism in All Ages," published in this country, and reproduced in Europe, was one of the keenest expositions of the character of a community which has so long defied civil and military power. His numerous lectures, speeches, essays and papers against all modes of slavery and sectarianism and party drill, whether in church or in state, and his persistent defense of the absolute freedom of the individual man as against all unjust corporate power, are equally pointed and characteristic.

As a lecturer and essayist he was voluminous, and widely varied in his productions; and his discourses on "Practical Education," "The Three Races of Men," "The Ocean Currents and Open Sea at the Poles," "Meteorology," "Practical Culture," "Metaphysical Analysis," "On Matter, Force and Spirit," have been printed and distributed by the State Natural History, Horticultural and Agricultural and other societies and periodicals. He was among the earliest advocates in Illinois of a United States Agricultural Bureau; and in 1851 produced a series of lectures and papers on the necessity for educating the working classes by means of schools and universities endowed by the State, which led to the endowment of our national system of industrial institutions.

He was a strong advocate of a State Normal School. He is a man of broad church views, and abhors close sectarianism. His life-long study has been that of ameliorating the condition of the working classes through the medium of technical and variously graded industrial schools. His various labors have secured to his enjoyment a comfortable fortune, and though he has retired from the more active duties of life, he exhibits the same deep interest in the questions which from early age employed his thoughts. He is regarded in most honorable esteem by his fellow-citizens; and is solaced in his declining years by witnessing the fruits of those institutions which, in labor prompted by the true spirit of philanthropy, he aided in founding.

For some time past he has almost wholly withdrawn from all private business and all public effort to devote his time more exclusively to a renewed and thorough reexamination and review of the real groundwork and basis of those great religious, social, civil, philosophical and educational questions which have so much engrossed the public mind and his own past life.

Although four score years of age he is still in such health as to be, in active home life and to mingle with his fellow-citizens upon all public occasions He has survived his beloved wife, but occupies the old home on West College Avenue, in our city. With him is his youngest son—Frederick C., and his wife, *nee* Alexander. His daughter Mrs. Dr. H. F Carriel is also among our citizens. His sons, Wm. and Rodolphus, have departed this life, others —John, Charles and Howard are living useful lives in different parts of this land.

Prof. Turner and his most intimate friends feel that eventually if not now his writings on religious subjects, will be deemed by far the most important of all his publications. This series of books which he claims "have been passed in utter silence by the settled policy of the sects, Catholic, Protestant and Mormon," is as follows:

(I.) "Mormonism in all ages" written and published in the vacation of 1842.

(II.) "Christ's Creed and Charter of the Kingdom of the Heavens" published in 1847 in which the author says he applys the "same principles to all ecclesiastical sects. Here I hit the near ox, as well as the off ox" The entire edition was sold and read.

(III) "Christs Words," as related to Philosophy, Law and Religion, and every human or social need—a book of over four hundred pages, now out of print.

The last mentioned is now called for more than the others and more than when written.

See pages 81, 85, 99, 102, 133, 136, 137, 138, 139, 148, 157, 178, 226, 243, 259, 266, 309.

REV. WILLIAM COFFIN, A. M., at one time in the faculty of Illinois College, is well remembered by many of the present citizens of Jacksonville although his home has been in Batavia, Kane county, for the last thirty years. Of genial disposition, versatile talents, attractive social qualities and with wife and children that any man might be happy with and proud of, it is not to be wondered at that he has made a host of friends, here and elsewhere. As preacher in the pulpit, professor in the chair, banker in the counting room, *pater familias* in the quiet Christian home, or friend in social circles, he has ever been honored and loved. He was born in Wiscassett, Maine, on the 19th of January, 1822, and at the age of fourteen, in 1836, he came to Jacksonville, with his father's family. Here his education was continued and he was graduated from Illinois College five years later, viz: in 1841. Three years after this he was a member of the faculty filling the chair of Mathematics, Natural Philosophy and Astronomy in his *Alma Mater* from 1844 to 1852. In 1847 he was most happily united in marriage with a lovely Christian woman, now gone to her Heavenly reward Mary E. Lockwood, eldest daughter of the late Judge Samuel D. Lockwood, whose life and labors have been fully mentioned already in these pages. Of the children by this marriage, Lockwood is married and living in Chicago, William, also married, is in active business life, Charlie was graduated from Yale with honors and is now in Chicago, Nellie is filling well her station as a pastor's wife in Rochester, Minn., Frank was suddenly taken from earth last year, John and Mattie, the two youngest, are at home. Their beloved mother was taken from them in 1877. Mr. Coffin was married again in 1883, to Miss Sophia M. Sawyer, with whom he is living in Batavia at the present time.

We are glad to be able to give the readers of Historic Morgan, through an artist's skill, a glance at the face so familiar to old time residents of Jacksonville.

See page 277.

JOSHUA MOORE.—There are lives, so unostentatious and independent that those living about them fail to realize at the time, the good if not the great work accomplished by them. Joshua Moore's life was an exemplification of this class. He was a dweller in this county about 1835, at Beardstown, before the separation of Cass county, and at Naples a few years later, just about the time, if not before, Scott county was set off from Morgan. But it was after July 9 1857, that, having purchased what was known as "Mr. Owsley's" house, Mr. Moore took up his final residence in this city and county. We note hereafter, from an article appearing as leading editorial in the Daily Journal, of Oct. 2nd, 1871, the following obituary:

As previously announced in the *Journal*, on Thursday morning last at 10 o'clock, Joshua Moore, Esq., an old and respected citizen of Jacksonville, depart this life. Long cherished as one of the most reliable and exemplary residents of Jacksonville, it is appropriate at this time to give a brief sketch of his life.

Mr. Moore was born August 5th, 1807, near Mt. Holly, N. J.

His parents and only sister died when he was quite young, and he then went to an uncle's and remained with him till of age. Having means left him he was desirous of entering business, and soon after becoming of age, went to Philadelphia to acquire a knowledge of business, acting in the capacity of clerk in the dry goods trade. In a short time, however, he started on his own account, remaining in Philadelphia some time. In

1832 he came west, as far as Logansport, Indiana, for his health, making the distance partly in a "Dearborn" and partly on horse back. Returning to Philadelphia, and resuming business he came to St. Louis in 1835. Remaining there a short time he came to Beardstown, in this state, where he engaged in business. Afterward he returned to St. Louis, and engaged in the same line there, for a short time; removing thence to Naples, Ill, where he remained till about 1843. In 1840 he was married to Miss Margaret McMackin, of this city. During his residence in Naples, Hon. Mark L. Delahay, of Kansas, was in his employ as clerk; as were also Hons. R. Mooers, Thomas Hollowbush and Judge Moses. In 1843 Mr. Moore removed to Perry, keeping his establishment in Naples. He prosecuted his business successfully in both places, and won for himself many warm friends.

In 1850 he joined the Presbyterian church, at Perry, and contributed largely to its support. He was elected elder and trustee, and was always looked up to as an irreproachable christian.

In 1858 he removed to Jacksonville, intending to retire from business, which he did in 1865.

Mr. M. became a member of Dr. Glover's church after removing to this city, but joined the Westminster church in 1864, where he was elected a trustee and an elder. In 1860 he was elected trustee of Illinois College.

During the war he manifested the warmest interest in the cause of the Union, and gave his money freely for the support of the sick and wounded. He also as a matter of duty, invested largely in government bonds, and has been a liberal donor to all the educational institutions of this city, as well as to all its public enterprizes.

During the past three years ill health has prevented him being his former self; but the last few months had been very encouraging as to his complete recovery.

All hopes, however, have proved delusive, and to-day the community mourns the loss of an upright man and a good citizen. Though gone from our midst, the memory of his kindly spirit and christian graces will remain as a bright example to all who have come within the circle of his influence.

WILLIAM D. SANDERS is a native of Huron county, Ohio, and the son of Dr. Moses C. Sanders, a distinguished physician and surgeon. He prepared for an academic career at Huron Institute, Milan, Ohio, and in 1841 entered the Western Reserve College, at Hudson, and received its degree in 1845. During the three years immediately following his graduation, he was Principal of the Richfield Academy, in Summit county, Ohio. In 1848 he entered the Hudson Theological Seminary, completing its course of study in 1851.

During this period there occurred a crisis in the financial affairs of this institution, which threatened its complete ruin, and in this emergency he was importuned by both trustees and faculty to lead a forlorn hope for its rescue. He was absent from the institution in this generous service over a year, and in this time executed a plan which rescued the college from great peril, and added over one hundred thousand dollars to its resources. Upon the ending of his studies in this institution, he was married, in Cleveland, Ohio, to Cornelia R. Smith, and soon after was ordained to the ministry by the Presbytery of Portage, and took charge of a church in Ravenna, Ohio. Here he labored for three years with very remarkable success, and was then called to the chair of Rhetoric, Elocution and English Literature, in Illinois College, at Jacksonville, Illinois.

He entered upon the duties of this professorship in the autumn of 1854, and performed them with enthusiasm and fidelity for the protracted period of fifteen years. While thus laboring, he was called upon to aid the institution in its embarrassed financial situation, and though the work was an exceedingly grave and difficult one, his efforts were quite successful. Upon his resignation of his professorship in 1869, an appropriate tribute to his talents, his culture, and his generous services was paid him by the trustees of the college.

During the Civil War, his allegiance to the Government was never in doubt, and one of the most eloquent of patriotic appeals was pronounced by him in Strawn's Opera House, to the Hardin and Union Guards, on the Sabbath preceding their departure for the field. Among other oratorical efforts which gave him great celebrity were his welcomes to General McClernand in 1862, to General Benjamin Grierson in 1863, his oration at Carlinville in the same year, and his discourse at Quincy, upon the fall of Richmond.

His name, however, will perhaps be perpetuated longer as that of the founder of institutions of learning, than from any other cause. He was the originator of the "Young Ladies' Athenæum," a school established in 1864, which enjoyed for the twenty-one years of its existence the patronage of some of our wealthiest and most intelligent families, and which under his superintendency occupied a large field of usefulness. The "Illinois Conservatory of Music" is also the offspring of his untiring energy. Its faculty has embraced many of the finest of European and American professors in both theory and practice, and comprehends a scale of instruction in vocal and instrumental music which can elsewhere be scarcely equalled. Professor Sanders is also the founder and actuary of "The Central Illinois Loan Agency," by which millions of eastern capital have been invested in Illinois, Missouri and Kansas, and the business now flowing in the channels it has created has grown into immense proportions. Its principal office is at Jacksonville, branch offices being located at various points in Missouri and Kansas.

Besides all the multiform labors growing out of his intimate connection with these educational and financial institutions, Dr. Sanders has been often called to the assistance of the church, and has repeatedly filled the pulpits of Jacksonville. For eight years he was the regular supply of the church at Pisgah. At various times he has received calls to the pastorate of churches in Chicago, Cincinnati, and elsewhere, but has been compelled to decline them. It may be readily inferred that, in founding and fostering so many important institutions, he is in the fortunate possession of rare powers of mind and body. He has a keen faculty for organization, and wrings success out of every enterprise in which he sets out.

His entire career is an exemplification of remarkable power of concentrating thought and of indomitable persistence. He is a man of strong convictions, frank utterance, warm impulses, and ceaseless vigilance over the welfare of the interests with which he is identified. Although now over fifty years of age, and despite his arduous and ceaseless labors he is in the enjoyment of excellent health and mental vigor. He has had five children all but one of whom are living and two of these are college graduates. His oldest son William B., is in an active law-practice in Cleveland, Ohio. The others—Mrs. Nellie Elliott and her brothers Charles and Clarence are residents of our own city.

See pages 155, 156, 186, 195, 199, 214, 221.

HON. CYRUS EPLER, one of the three judges of the seventh judicial circuit, was born in Charleston, Clark county, Indiana, November 12th, 1825. He pursued his law studies in the office of Brown & Yates, at Jacksonville, Illinois, in the year 1848, and after an absence of two years continued his studies for one year alone in Jacksonville. In 1853 he commenced the practice of law as states attorney, having been admitted to the bar in 1852, at Jacksonville, Illinois. Judge Epler was elected States Attorney in November, 1852, in the first judicial district, and was elected a member of the lower house of the general assembly of the State of Illinois, in the year 1857, and re-elected in 1859, thus serving two terms. He also held the office of master of chancery for Morgan county from 1867 to 1873, a term of six years.

In 1873 he was elected judge for a term of six years, and re-elected in 1879 and 1885 to the same position and for the same terms. Judge Epler has given very general satisfaction upon the bench, his decisions having heretofore been regarded as those of a man who seeks to arrive at conclusions which the fact and the law will sustain. During his entire professional life his home has been in this county and city. Here he has, besides carving for himself an enviable name as a citizen and jurist, reared a family, and some of these arriving at years of maturity are filling places of trust and usefulness in this and other cities. His oldest son Carl, is now City Attorney of Quincy, the second, Ernest is assistant physician in a Cook county hospital.

See pages 117, 129, 130, 148, 295, 296, 269

HON. JOSEPH DUNCAN,

OF JACKSONVILLE.

SIXTH GOVERNOR OF THE STATE OF ILLINOIS, 1834–38.

HON. JOSEPH DUNCAN, soldier, statesman, member of congress and governor of Illinois, was born, in February, 1794, at Paris, Bourbon county, Kentucky, and was the youngest son of Major Joseph Duncan, a native of Virginia, who removed to Kentucky at an early period of its settlement, where he died during the childhood of his youngest son. The latter was, in consequence of this event, called at a very tender age to share with his widowed mother the responsibilities of her bereaved family.

In this situation he was distinguished for firmness and steadiness of purpose beyond his years, and for those kind, deep, and generous social affections which characterized his whole life.

Thus his life passed on with little of incident to give it peculiarity, other than his superior skill in all the athletic sports of boyhood, until he reached the age of sixteen. At this period he received a commission in the United States army, in which he remained until the close of the last war with Great Britain. Notwithstanding his extreme youth, he discharged the duty of a soldier with such vigor and fidelity as to merit and receive through the remainder of his life the thanks of his country. It were enough for his military reputation to name him as one of the intrepid band of between one and two hundred men, who, in the battle of Sandusky, repulsed with tremendous havoc the combined British and Indian forces, amounting to ten times their own number, and as having commanded, in that splendid affair, notwithstanding his youth, a post of pre-eminent responsibility. For the great services performed on this occasion his grateful country conferred on him, and on each of his associates in the command, a gold mounted sword as a testimonial to them, and their children after them, that their country is not unmindful of those who nobly peril their lives in her defence. At another time, with a handful of men under his command, he penetrated one hundred and fifty miles into the interior of upper Canada, and there, enduring all the rigors of a northern winter, watched the movements of the enemy within twenty miles of his camp, and crossed Lake Erie from Malden to Sandusky in an open yawl, accompanied by only three men.

Again, he made a journey of fifty miles through forests, across streams, and amidst hostile Indians, where an Indian guide refused to accompany him, in order to execute the orders of his superiors in command. When peace was declared he retired from the army and for a time devoted himself to agricultural pursuits in his native state. In 1818 he removed to Jackson county, Illinois; and so highly was his military character esteemed that he early received the appointment of Major-General of the militia; and he rendered important military service, in the spring of 1831, in the first outbreak of the "Black Hawk War." In 1823 he was elected to the senate of Illinois from Jackson county for four years. The part of his labors in that body from which he derived the most satisfaction was the bill he introduced, and which was passed, to establish a system of common schools for the state.

Though the law soon became unpopular and was repealed, it was a noble conception and reflected a lasting honor on the name of its originator.

In 1826, one year before the expiration of his term, he was elected as the only representative of the state in the United States Congress, and was re-elected constantly until 1834. One year prior to the expiration of his last congressional term he was elected governor of Illinois. During all the political storms that raged throughout the state and nation he enjoyed the reputation of being an honest man.

He was neither selfish nor malignant; and was not the personal enemy of his political opponents, nor did he bear them aught of malice. His character as a public man was marked by enthusiastic patriotism, an intuitive and generally accurate discernment of the character and motives of those around him, a Napoleon-like rapidity in arranging his plans, and a high degree of energy in their execution. He exercised great honesty of purpose in the formation of his opinions, and a bold and manly frankness in avowing and advocating them.

Attachment to the cause of education marked the whole course of his life both as a citizen and as a public man; and to it he freely and liberally contributed his time, money, personal services and official influence. To Illinois College his services were most valuable, his donations were liberal, and the amount of time and personal attention which he gratuitously devoted to the object was probably greater than the public were aware of.

From 1835 until his death he was a member of its board of trustees, and of the prudential committee, by which the details of the board are generally transacted. He was a member of the Presbyterian church, and was ever distinguished for his reverential deportment in public worship, and for those marks of respect and kindness which he was accustomed to bestow on the ministers of religion. He was a friend to universal humanity. His affections were limited by no sectional, sectarian or party lines; but were ready to embrace true worth, and honor true virtue wherever found.

To raise the money to pay for the land for the State Deaf and Dumb Institution, in February, 1839, Gov. Duncan prepared a subscription paper which he headed with $50, and then secured from others the balance of about $1000, with a part of which the present site, of about six acres, was purchased from the Hon. S. D. Lockwood and David A. Smith, Esq. The balance was subsequently expended in improving the grounds. Gov. Duncan was chosen the first President of the Board of Trustees and remained as such until the time of his death. He died January 15th, 1844, after a short illness, leaving a wife. Three sons died in infancy or early childhood. One son is still living in Chicago. Three daughters are numbered with the silent majority and two estimable daughters survive both father and mother—Mrs. Mary Putnam, of Davenport, Iowa, and Mrs. Julia S. Kirby, of this city.

His estimable wife survived him many years, continuing her residence in Jacksonville and growing dearer from year to year to those who knew her but to love her for her true christian worth.

See pages 47, 53, 58, 70, 74, 78, 79, 80, 97, 100, 110, 247, 259.

JULIAN MONSON STURTEVANT was born at Warren, Litchfield county, Connecticut, July 26, 1805, his parents having been Warren Sturtevant and Lucy Tanner, both natives of the same place. He is a descendant of Samuel Sturtevant, who was a farmer in the old Plymouth colony, in 1643. During his childhood, his father removed to what is now Summit county, Ohio, and in the winter following this migration, which occured late in 1816, the little household was domiciled in a log cabin, in the heart of what was then an almost interminable forest of Northern Ohio.

Here he spent his youth, obtaining, in the interim of the seasons of farm labor, a good common school education, and here was developed a strong inclination for the work of the Christian ministry.

In his thirteenth year, then ambitious for a collegiate education, he commenced the study of the Latin language with his brother, whose desires were kindred with his own, and together they labored diligently, with the limited means placed at their disposal for self-culture. Thus he obtained a very good preparatory standing for a college course, and before his seventeenth year was thoroughly acquainted with the Æneid, Georgics and Bucolics of Virgil, with the works of Sallust and Cæsar, the orations of Cicero, and the more important productions of literature, during the Augustan age, of ancient Rome.

In the summer of 1822, in company with his elder brother and Elizur Wright, since not unknown to fame, he went to New Haven and was enrolled among the Freshmen of Yale. By careful attention to his studies, by making the most of all the advantages afforded him, he graduated with distinction, in 1826, and in a class of 101 was regarded as one of its best scholars.

Upon his graduation, he assumed the office of Principal in an academy at New Canaan, Connecticut, and retained it for nearly two years, when he entered the Theological Department of Yale. While prosecuting his studies here, he joined an association of his fellow-students, whose object was the selection of some State in the Mississippi Valley, where all should seek their homes; where they might unite their efforts for the founding of churches, schools and a college, and the fostering of all institutions which tended to develop a Christian civilization. Their Eastern friends readily contributed to aid them in this noble mission, and, after considerable correspondence, Illinois was selected as their future home and field of labor. This State was then in its infancy, having in 1830 less than 160,000 inhabitants.

In 1830 Dr. Sturtevant married Elizabeth Maria Fayerweather, of New Canaan, Connecticut, and soon after, accompanied by his wife and his life-long friend, Rev. Theron Baldwin, he emigated to Illinois. In December of that year, he and his associates organized the Board of Trustees of Illinois College, at Jacksonville, and he was selected to open the institution for the reception of pupils.

On the morning of January 4th, 1831, in an unfinished building, the southern half of what is now known as the Library, he met *nine* students as its first matriculants, and the institution was inaugurated. One year after, Rev. Edward Beecher being selected as President of the college, he was chosen Professor of Mathematics and Natural Philosophy, holding that position until 1844, when he was elected to succeed Rev. Mr. Beecher in the Presidency of the institution. Since then he has confined his instruction to mental and moral science, resigning the Presidency in 1876.

In 1885, after serving Illinois College since its founding in 1829, 14 years as professor, 32 years as President, and 9 years as ex-President, President Sturtevant, at the ripe age of 80, retired from the institution. We congratulate him on his long and beneficent public career. With intellect still vigorous and bright, may he enjoy many years of rest and peace in this community, with the highest interests of which he has been so closely connected for more than half a century.

In 1840 Dr. Sturtevant's wife died. He subsequently married her younger sister, Hannah R. Fayerweather, who still survives. Three of his sons have been graduated from Illinois College, one of whom—Dr. Julian M., Jr.—is now a Congregational pastor, in Cleveland, Ohio; and one—Alfred H.—was for some time a tutor in the institution, and now is farming. The third—Warren—died at the age of thirty-seven.

Dr. Sturtevant has written voluminously for the newspapers and periodicals, and his articles in the religious weeklies, *The Advance*, *Independent*, *The Congregationalist*, *The New Englander* (quarterly), and others, show him to be a writer of no ordinary culture. His style is smooth and fluent; his reasoning is clear and powerful; his descriptions the choicest specimens of word-painting. He has also made two most scholarly and valuable contributions to library literature in his published volumes entitled "Sect" and "Economics."

In 1863 he visited England and Continental Europe, and as this was during the Rebellion, he had frequent opportunities for ascertaining, with much precision, the character of foreign sentiment regarding the North and South. Upon his return, he delivered and finally published a lecture on "British feeling and Its Causes." This discourse was published in England, at the instance of Richard Cobden.

Many years ago he received the degree of D. D., from the University of Missouri and the degree of LL. D., from Iowa College.

See pages 55, 56, 60, 68, 69, 70, 74, 75, 77, 81, 84, 91, 110, 114, 126, 148, 156, 195, 199, 200, 211, 212, 231, 240, 243, 251, 254, 261. 262, 265, 269, 301.

EDWARD L. McDONALD, a member of one of Jacksonville's oldest families, was of the manor born October 28th, 1849. His early education was obtained at the west district school, Jacksonville. He attended the Jacksonville Business College as well, and obtained the first scholarship issued by that college. Afterwards he entered Wabash College, Crawfordsville, Indiana, in the fall of 1866, but remained there only part of the year, being called home on account of the sickness of his father, Alexander McDonald. He entered Illinois College in the fall of 1867, but not continuing the course there, he became engaged in the dry goods business as clerk. At the expiration of one year he resumed his studies at Illinois College, and remained until the graduation of his class in 1871. The following year he commenced the study of law with Judge Cyrus Epler, and after the latter's election as judge, pursued the reading of law in the office of Henry Stryker, Jr. He also attended law lectures at Michigan University, Ann Arbor, Michigan, for two terms, and graduated there in the class of 1874, being class orator.

He entered upon the practice of law in this city, in partnership with his brother Frederick A., now County Judge in Washington Territory. He was also for awhile in partnership with Judge Wm. Thomas.

Throughout his life he has been active in politics, taking the Democratic view of all questions, yet he has always been a fair minded and conscientious man. He has been honored by his fellow partisans by many places of trust in the management of party affairs and has acceptably served his county as States Attorney and this legislative district as Representative in the 34th General Assembly, being elected to that body in November, 1884, receiving 5,621 votes, a larger number than his Democratic colleague or Republican opponent. He is a married man now, with a family of four children. His church connections like those of his parents have always been Presbyterian and he is now a member of the State Street Presbyterian Church.

See pages 208, 210, 226, 267.

HON. EDWARD SCOTT was born in Yorkshire, England, May 10, 1828. He is the son of Zachariah and Elizabeth Scott, who emigrated to and settled in Morgan county, four miles west of Jacksonville, in December, 1830. On Christmas day of that year the "deep snow," so frequently spoken of by the old settlers, commenced falling. Mr. Scott had a family of five children, of which the subject of this sketch is the youngest. He died July 2, 1846, at his residence, on section 20, township 15, range 11, where he entered land, on which he resided until he died His wife died, also, in June, 1847. Mr. Scott and his wife were members of the Episcopal Church.

The subject of this sketch received his education in Morgan county. He followed farming until 1847. He was next engaged for two years in completing his education. He engaged in a clerkship with Mr. T. C. Routt, in 1849, which he followed for three years. He established himself in mercantile business in Jacksonville, in 1852, which he continued until September 15, 1857 The next year he was appointed Deputy Sheriff, and continued in that office two years In February, 1864, he was engaged in the firm of Lambert & Scott, in a wholesale and retail grocery business, which he continued until the fall of 1869, when he was elected County Judge.

Judge Scott is now engaged in banking and milling, being a large stockholder and President of the First National Bank, Jacksonville, and active member of the firm of Scott, Hackett & Chambers, proprietors of Morgan Mills.

He has been politically, thus far through life, a Democrat. He warmly sustained the flag of our country during the rebellion, by voluntarily putting a man in his place, and other acts of patriotism.

As the character of Judge Scott is so well known, we will simply say that he is one of the pioneer citizens of Morgan county, and stands conspicuous among the reliable business men of the community in which he has lived, and won the esteem of a large circle of friends by his many virtues and noble qualities as a citizen.

See pages 65, 108, 180, 181, 190, 226, 228.

JOHN N. MARSH is a native of Sullivan county, New York, and was born November 20, 1823. He is the youngest child of S. N. Marsh, who was a lumber dealer.

The subject of our sketch received his early education in the schools of Monticello, New York. After leaving school he taught for a period of three years. He then engaged in mercantile pursuits at Bridgeville, New York. He continued in that business, at that place, for three years.

In the fall of 1846 he was married to Miss Thirza N. Ketchum, daughter of Dr. Alex. Ketchum, of Bridgeville. New York. Mr. and Mrs. Marsh have had a family of eight children, three boys and five girls.

In the spring of 1855 Mr. Marsh removed to Lanesborough, Pennsylvania, where he resided five years, and in the fall of 1860 settled in Jacksonville, Illinois, where for five years he was engaged in the boot and shoe business. He was then appointed Assistant Assessor of Internal Revenue, under Johnson's administration, and held that office nearly two years.

Mr. Marsh has given his family a good education in our city, and was so interested in school matters as to be selected as one of the directors of the Walnut Grove District (now First Ward) school, in 1867.

In April, 1872, he was elected City Clerk of Jacksonville, as the "People's" candidate

He is now filling, in an acceptable way, the important office of Circuit Clerk and Recorder, having been elected thereto, on the Democratic ticket, in 1876, and successively re-elected in 1880 and 1884.

See pages 181, 185, 203, 210, 226.

WILLIAM THOMAS.—No present citizen of Jacksonville was, probably, so closely identified with early times here. He was born November 22, 1802, in what was then Warren, but is now Allen county, Kentucky. His parents were natives of Virginia, who in their infancy removed with their parents, to Kentucky, soon after the Indian wars, and married in 1800. They settled in the woods, where they opened a farm, on which they resided for over fifty years.

His education included only the rudimentary branches, and was obtained in the rude log cabins of that early day. When he was but eighteen years of age, his father, who was then Sheriff of the county, appointed him his deputy; his duties being confined to serving notices, summoning witnesses, and collecting taxes. At the expiration of his father's official term, he was made Deputy Clerk of the County Court of Allen county, receiving, in lieu of salary, his board and clothing. He remained in that position about two years, when he accepted a similar place in the county of Warren, at a salary of $200, and there he continued, also, for a year and a half. While attending to the duties of these offices, he became familiar with the forms of deeds, mortgages and other instruments used in the proceedings of courts; also with the modes of proceeding and rules of decisions upon important questions of practice. On leaving the Clerk's office, his friends advised him to study and follow the profession of the law. At this time Hon. James T. Moorehead, of Bowling Green, who was afterwards Governor of the State, and a United States Senator, tendered him the use of his office and library free of charge, while his father proposed to board him and wait for his pay from the fees he should receive after his admission to practice. He accepted these kind offers, and his law-license was issued July 5, 1823, when he engaged in professional duties with Counsellor Moorehead, who had a large practice in Logan county, as attorney for a bank located at Bowling Green, to attend to which Lawyer Thomas went to Russellville, where he remained over a year in that service. In December, 1824, he returned to Bowling Green, and entered the office of the Hon. Joseph R. Underwood, to assist the latter in his professional engagements, and continued with him, at a small salary, until September, 1826, when he removed to Illinois, and located at Jacksonville, where he has ever since resided. During his first winter here he taught school, and in the spring and fall of 1827 he attended all the courts in the First Judicial Circuit, composed of nine counties, and was fortunate enough to find some clients.

In the summer of 1827 he volunteered as a private in the mounted militia, called out by Governor Edwards, to protect the miners and settlers of Jo. Daviess county against threatened incursions of the Winnebago Indians. He was appointed quarter-master-seargant, and ultimately filled the post of commissary to the troops. During the winter of 1828-29, he attended the Legislature, then sitting at Vandalia, and he reported the proceedings for the only newspaper printed at the seat of government. During this same session the First Judicial Circuit was divided, and a new circuit was created north of the Illinois river. He received the appointment of

State's Attorney, and attended the courts thereof in 1829, when he resigned. On March 25, 1830, he was married to Catherine Scott, of Morgan county, Illinois, a native of Litchfield, New York. In 1831 he was appointed School Commissioner of Morgan County, by which he was authorized to sell the school-lands of the several townships, and secure the money arising from the sales. He resigned this office early in 1835. He participated in the Black Hawk war: first in the spring of 1831, in the brigade under General Joseph Duncan, and a year later under General Samuel Whitesides, and filled the position of quarter-master and commissary on both of those occasions.

He was elected to the State Senate for four years, and took his seat in December, 1834. That body then consisted of twenty-four members, of whom but two others—Cyrus Edwards, of Alton, and Richard Taylor, of Chicago—besides himself survive. The leading question pending during that winter was the construction of the Illinois & Michigan Canal, and after some time had been passed in discussing it, a loan of $500,000 was authorized, though subsequent legislation was required to effect this. Beside several other bills of minor importance, Senator Thomas was the author of the following general laws: 1. The seven years' limitation law in regard to actions and suits against parties having possession of lands with a connected title in law or equity. 2. The act (and the first on that subject) authorizing religious societies to hold in perpetuity ground whereon to build houses of worship, and to bury the dead. 3. The act vesting trustees of incorporated towns or cities with power to declare what should be considered nuisances, and to provide for their abatement. 4. The act to provide for the distribution and application of the interest on the school, college and seminary funds. 5. The act to provide for the security of the school-funds. At this session provision was made for the appointment of State's Attorneys by the Legislature, which he opposed as being unconstitutional, these offices having been previously filled by the Governor and Senate.

The Legislature convened again, under the call of the Governor, in December, 1835, the chief objects being to provide for work on the canal, and for appointing the representation for the succeeding five years.

At the session of 1836-7 Senator Thomas was appointed chairman of the committee on the canal and canal lands, and so continued until he left the Senate, in March, 1839. During this session (of 1836-37) an effort was made to change the canal from Ottawa to Joliet, to a slack-water navigation, but it did not succeed. He made a report against the change, and in favor of the "deep cut." He prepared all the bills for acts relating to the canal and canal lands, that were passed from December, 1836, to March, 1839. He was opposed to the system of internal improvements adopted in 1836-37. He prepared and introduced the bill for the "Act to amend the several laws in relation to common schools," approved March 4, 1837, by which, for the first time, provision was made for the organization of a system of common schools throughout the State. In the session of 1838-39, his time was mostly occupied in preparing and acting upon bills relating to the canal. At this session an act was passed incorporating the Deaf and Dumb Institution, of which he was made one of the trustees, and was continued as a member of the board until 1869, when he was appointed a member of the Board of State Charities, which position, owing to infirmity, he resigned during the following summer. In March, 1839, he was elected Circuit Judge of the First Judicial Circuit, by the Legislature. He was elected to the lower branch of the State Legislature in 1846. During the first week of the session of 1846-47 he proposed and introduced a bill for an act incorporating a Retreat for the Insane—the first movement in the Legislature on that subject—with provisions for the care of that unfortunate class. This bill passed the House and had been read, and referred to a committee in the Senate, when Miss Dix arrived at the seat of government, on her mission to petition the Legislature to make provision for the care of the insane of the State. She objected to this bill because it made no appropriation of funds; and she, with the committee, decided to propose and introduce a new bill in the Senate. Accordingly, with the assistance of Miss Dix, the Hon. Charles Constable, of the Senate, prepared the bill, which was finally passed; and Judge Thomas was made a trustee of the institution. When Miss Dix reached Springfield, he was the only member of the Legislature with whom she had any acquaintance; he therefore introduced her to the members. He remained a trustee of this Retreat until after the purchase of the site and the walls of the building were ready for the reception of the roof, when he resigned. He was elected and served as a delegate in the Constitutional Convention of 1847. He was one of the parties who paid the expenses of maintaining a School for the Blind for nearly a year previous to the meeting of the Legislature in January, 1849; and he was the author of the bill creating and incorporating the Institution for the Blind, which was passed without a change. He prepared the bill which was enacted in March, 1845, incorporating the Sangamon & Morgan Railway Company, and authorizing the sale to that company of the railroad from Springfield to the Illinois river. He also prepared, and secured the passage of the acts under which the road was extended eastward from Springfield to the State line.

He was a member of the Legislature during the session of 1851–52, and the subsequent called session. He was charged with being the author of the bill for the "Act to establish a general system of banking," passed in 1851; but the charge was false. At the request of the committee he revised the bill, arranged the sections, and proposed several amendments, all of which were adopted. He prepared all the bills required at this session in relation to the State institutions located at Jacksonville. At the subsequent called session he proposed the bill for the obtaining of the right-of-way for roads, which was passed without any substantial change.

During the two sessions he was placed on numerous committees. Upon most of them he acted, and his time was constantly occupied in reading bills and in preparing, suggesting and reporting amendments. He uniformly opposed special legislation, especially acts authorizing executors, administrators and guardians to sell real estate of infants, acts granting divorces, acts granting ferry-licenses, and acts for all purposes that could be compassed by application to the courts.

The present "Illinois Female College" was originally incorporated as the "Illinois Annual Conference Female Academy," intended to be established and sustained by the voluntary contributions of the preachers, members and friends of the Methodist Episcopal Church. He was appointed one of the trustees, and contributed very liberally towards the same. He continued a trustee until the institution was changed to a college, and until a large debt had been contracted (for which the trustees were personally responsible), in enlarging the building and providing boarding and rooms for pupils coming from distant points. As all of his time was required in attending to private and public engagements, he proposed to resign his place as trustee; and to avoid the implication that this proposition was with a view to escape responsibility for liabilities, he advanced $1,000 to the board, which was supposed to be a liberal part in case the trustees should be required to meet the liabilities out of their private means. In 1861 the west wing was burned, and this so reduced the capacity of the building to accommodate boarders, that no revenue could be expected from that source; and therefore the trustees decided at once to meet the indebtedness, which amounted to over $30,000, or to abandon the college. He now paid what was admitted to be more than his *pro rata* part of the amount; and it was said that, but for his liberality, the debt could not have been paid. Although this may be true, the same remark would apply to several of the preachers, who paid as much, if not more than he did, in proportion to their means.

Following the payment of this indebtedness, he was one of several who contributed about $6,000 for rebuilding the west wing. He then insured the building for $5,000, and the trustees did the same for $30,000. In less than three years the main building was burned. He charged the institution the cost of the insurance, and gave the college the balance of what was paid him on his policy. In addition he donated $1,000 to pay for heating the main building with steam, which, being rebuilt, he again insured it, and in less than two years it met a similar fate. He donated, as in the first instance, the balance accruing to him, amounting, altogether, to about $7,000, but has not reinsured since the rebuilding of the main edifice. He proposed to resign his position as trustee, in 1874, but the Conference were unwilling to accept. His term of office expired in 1875, and he determined not to accept a reappointment.

In the spring of 1861 he was appointed, by the Governor and Senate, a member of the Board of Army Auditors. In the following summer he was deputed to go to Washington to obtain funds from the United States, to pay war-accounts, and succeeded in obtaining $450,000. He had the accounts in such form, that Secretary Chase, without occupying more than twenty minutes' time, gave the order for the money. On applying at the Treasurer's office, he discovered that the treasury-notes which he expected to receive were not printed, and twenty days elapsed before they were delivered to him. He continued in the office of Auditor until the spring of 1862, when he resigned, having examined upwards of $2,000,000 of accounts.

Judge Thomas long since gave up the practice of his profession by reason of advancing years and consequent infirmities; but, happily married in his old age, to Mrs. Leanna Orear, still occupies with her and other relatives, a delightful home on West College avenue.

See pages 14, 15, 43, 45, 48, 50, 53, 57, 58, 63, 65, 80, 81, 87, 97, 101, 102, 110, 114, 115, 118, 119, 120, 121, 123, 127, 175, 241, 243, 250, 262, 263, 278.

ISAAC L. MORRISON has been a resident of the city of Jacksonville since June, 1851. He is a native of Kentucky. He was admitted to the bar in his native State, and has made the practice of the law his business from the time of his admission to the bar.

In politics he is Republican. He was a delegate to the Republican Convention which assembled at Bloomington, Ill., in 1856. He attended the Republican Convention at Baltimore, in 1864, as a delegate, and served as a member of the Executive Republican State Central Committee for that year. In 1877, 1879 and 1883 he was a member of the House of Representatives in the State Legislature and served as Chairman of the Committee on Judiciary in the Thirtieth and Thirty-Second General Assemblies. In 1880 he was the Republican candidate for Congress in this district. The district being largely Democratic, he perhaps had no expectation of being elected. However, he made an active canvass, and reduced the Democratic majority about 900 votes and ran ahead of the State and national tickets.

REV. LIVINGSTON M. GLOVER, D. D., was born February 21st, 1819, in the the township of Phelps, Ontario county, New York, and was the son of Philander and Ruhamah Glover, who removed from Massachusetts to the "Genesee country" in 1800. He is descended from English ancestry, traceable back to Saxon times, when the name was written Gelofre. Several persons of the name have been distinguished in the fatherland; as, Robert Glover, who perished at the stake in 1555, in the reign of "bloody Mary," and Richard Glover, an eminent poet, merchant, and member of Parliament, born in London in 1712, and who died in 1785 in that city, author of an epic called "Leonidas," also of several tragedies.

About the year 1640, two brothers, John and Henry Glover, emigrated to America, and settled in New England, near Boston. From the latter of these the Rev. Dr. Glover was descended; and his immediate ancestors were residents of Conway, Mass.

After passing a third of a century in New York State, his father removed, in 1833, to the then Territory of Michigan, and settled on Lodi Plains, near Ann Arbor. Thither his son Livingston accompanied him, and up to the age of seventeen was reared on a farm, following the plow, etc., but without any special fondness for an agricultural life, as his tastes, from early childhood, strongly inclined him to letters, study, and public life. Stories are narrated of his stopping the team in the harvest field, and of his mounting a stump to exercise his gifts in declamation. When other boys of his age were at play, he was engaged in writing articles for the village paper; so that his father early predicted the uselessness of inducing him to follow in his footsteps, as an agriculturalist.

About the year 1834 a "Manual Labor School"—then very common and a furore throughout the country—was established in Ann Arbor, very near the site of the present university. He was enrolled among its first pupils, and for a year or more pursued the studies preparatory to a college course, laboring four hours per day on the "school farm" in payment for board.

In the autumn of 1836 he entered the Western Reserve College at Hudson, Ohio, from which institution he was graduated at the commencement in 1840. After leaving college, he at once connected himself with the Lane Theological Seminary, Cincinnati, studying for the ministry, to which he had devoted himself at the time of his conversion in 1836, although previous to that date his preferences led him in the direction of the law and of political life.

Having passed two years in theological study, he was licensed to preach the gospel, and in October, 1842, took charge of the Presbyterian church of Lodi, Michigan, where his first profession of faith had been made. He continued at that place for six years, making proof of his ministry in a wide-spread country congregation, and among a people who had known him from boyhood, enjoying their confidence, and being very successful in his ministrations, proving somewhat of an exception to the rule that "a prophet is not without honor, save in his own country."

In the autumn of 1848 he received, very unexpectedly, a call from the First Presbyterian Church of Jacksonville, Illinois which against the wishes of his people he deemed it his duty to accept. He took charge of that important congregation in October, 1848, and continued to serve this congregation as beloved pastor for the term of thirty-two years.

In October, 1873, the quarter-centennial of the pastorate was observed with appropriate and interesting ceremonies. His pastoral charge was of longer duration than any other of this denomination in the State, and perhaps in the West.

He received, in 1864, the honorary degree of Doctor of Divinity from Centre College, Kentucky. As a theologian, he had few equals in the country, and was a most influential and useful clergyman and citizen. He was a man of broad, liberal and Christian views. Dr. Glover thoroughly identified himself with the educational and benevolent interests of this place. For eighteen years he was a member and Secretary of the Board of Trustees of Illinois College. At the time of his death he was President of the Board of Trustees of the Jacksonville Female Academy, and also President of the Board of Directors of "Oak Lawn Retreat," a private institution at Jacksonville for the insane. He took a firm and advanced stand in the temperance reform, and in all kindred causes.

In the course of his ministry he published more than thirty discourses, ordinary and special, generally at the request of his people or of the community. In addition to these, he gave numerous articles on various subjects to the religious and secular papers. Through the same medium he published many poems of a moral and religious character, and, for the most part, lyrical in form.

He has twice gone abroad: in 1858, he travelled through Europe, and as far East as Syria and Egypt, and again in 1873, by appointment of the Presbyterian General Assembly of the United States, he went as a delegate to the Assembly of the Free Church of Scotland, meeting in Edinburgh. At that time, he made an extensive tour through the British Isles.

He was identified with Illinois during a period of wonderful development and saw the humble village of Jacksonville expand into a beautiful and thriving city of 10,000 inhabitants.

He was married in 1843, to Marcia A., daughter of Professor Rufus Nutting, of the Western Reserve College. As the fruit of this remarkably happy union there were five children all of whom survived him and are living to day: Mrs. Mary Mitchell of Springfield, Lymnn Beecher of Chicago, Mrs. Mattie Higginson of Humboldt, Kansas, John Adams of Indianapolis, Ind., and William Brown of Humboldt, Kansas. Dr. Glover's beloved wife, mother and brother are still residents of this city, honored for their own sakes as well as for the memory of his consecrated Christian life, which terminated after weeks of great suffering from disease, on Thursday, July 15th, 1880 The entire community felt the loss incurred in his transfer to "the better land" and joined their sympathies and tears with the afflicted family and the stricken church of his loving care as the mortal remains were lain to rest in the beautiful Diamond Grove Cemetery.

See also pages 55, 57, 61, 69, 71, 94, 115, 116, 125, 130, 153, 154, 156, 173, 186, 197, 198, 206, 210, 262, 269, 283.

HENRY CUTHBERT TUNISON was born in Tazewell county, Illinois, on February 5th, A. D. 1855. Removed with his parents to Greene county, Illinois, when less than one year old. His boyhood was spent on the farm formerly owned by his father, Isaac C. Tunison, part of which is within the limits of the city of Roodhouse. His present place of residence is Jacksonville, Morgan county, Illinois. He was married on March 23d, 1876, near Manchester, Illinois, to Miss Kate R. Murray. In 1868, at the age of thirteen, he began business for himself as a canvasser. Soon after he became an employer, sending out, over a limited territory, a few sub-agents. Later he became a publisher of atlases, maps and charts. To-day his name is a household word in every part of the United States, Canada and the Maritime Provinces, and his trade extends into British Columbia, Old Mexico, the Bermudas and the West Indies. He has traveled in every state and territory of the United States, also in foreign lands, and is the proprietor, to-day, of wholesale Atlas, Map and Chart houses in the following cities: New York City; London, Canada; Chicago, Illinois; Cincinnati, O.; Atlanta, Georgia; Jacksonville, Ill.; Kansas City, Mo.; and San Francisco, Cal.,—and contemplates establishing a house in London, England.

JOHN J. HARDIN, eldest child of Martin D. and Elizabeth Hardin, was born January 5, 1810. His father, a distinguished lawyer of Kentucky, died October 8, 1823, John then being thirteen years old. Upon his mother, as sole executrix of his father's will until he should be twenty-one years of age, devolved the care of the family and the management of the estate, The latter was so embarrassed by security debts, amounting to nearly $50,000, that Henry Clay and other friends of the family advised her to surrender it to the creditors and free herself from the perplexities connected with its settlement. Of firm and resolute purpose, and with a will to discharge any liability of her deceased husband, and educate her children, she said, "Gentlemen, give me time, and I will pay all." Time was granted; and, applying herself to the task, she managed the estate with so much discretion and ability, that she paid all of the liabilities against it, supported and educated her children, and provided for their advancement in life

John, who early manifested that determined purpose and energy of character which was impressed upon him by the example of his mother, received a liberal education and was bred to the law, under the late Chief Justice Boyle. The Chief Justice resided about five miles from Harrodsburgh Springs, and employed a portion of his leisure in the instruction of a few law-students, who boarded in the families in the neighborhood and repaired weekly to his library for examination. In 1829 John J. Hardin boarded in the family of Mrs. Smith, whose daughter, Sarah, he afterwards married. Judge Wm. Brown, of Jacksonville, studied law with the Chief Justice at the same time, and became the warm friend of Hardin for life.

Hardin's professional studies completed, his active temperament led him at once to seek out a theatre upon which he should act his part in the drama of life.

He explored Illinois; and, captivated with its beauty, settled in Jacksonville in 1830. In the January following, he returned to Kentucky and was married. Possessing a correct judgment of human nature, an ardent temperament, uncommon tact, energy, perseverance, he made his mark wherever he moved, and soon stood in the front rank of his profession. As an advocate, notwithstanding an occasional hesitancy of speech, he was always heard with attention. He selected the strong points of his case with discretion and sustained them with great force of argument.

At times the strong passions and sympathies were stirred up, and he became persuasive and eloquent. A plain, blunt man when his indignation was aroused, woe to the man who, either before the jury or the people, felt the heavy stroke of his "meat-axe oratory."

In 1832 he was appointed State's Attorney for this circuit, and for years discharged the duties of the office with faithfulness to the public interests.

At the session of 1839 O. H. Browning, of Adams, and Wm. Thomas, of Morgan, of the Senate, and John J. Hardin, of the House of Representatives, procured the enactment of a law founding the Deaf and Dumb Institute, in this place. In time the Insane Asylum and the Institution for the Blind were also located here.

Social in his habits, warm hearted and free in his intercourse with the people, bold and fearless in the promulgation and advocacy of his political opinions; and withal *public spirited*, he soon became a leader in politics. How successfully he maintained the strife, against large odds, is well remembered by friend and foe.

In 1836, 1838 and 1840, he was returned as a member of the House of Representatives of the General Assembly, from Morgan county.

In 1843 he was chosen to represent this district in Congress, which he did with honesty, vigor and patriotism.

Possessing a taste for military life, Col. Hardin passed from one grade to another in the militia until he was appointed to the high office of Major General. He participated with honor in the Black Hawk war, and was selected by Gov. Thos. Ford as a man eminently to be relied upon in the settlement of the Mormon disturbance in Hancock county.

In 1847, the United States entered into war with Mexico, without deciding the question of the justice or injustice of that war. Thousands differed with the government, yet when the call was made for volunteers, John J. Hardin, then Major General of the Illinois Militia, was the first to appeal to his fellow citizens to rally around the national flag. His appeal was promptly responded to, and Gen. Hardin was elected colonel of the First Regiment of Illinois Volunteers. In training his undisciplined troops, in providing for their wants, in cheering them on the march, in watching over them in camp, he discharged successfully the duties of his arduous command.

On the 21st of February, 1847, General Taylor, who commanded our army in Mexico, being satisfied that the Mexicans, under Santa Anna, were upon the forward march, broke up his camp at Agua and fell back to the strong mountain pass, a little in front of Buena Vista. The road at this point becomes a narrow defile, the valley on its right being rendered quite impracticable for artillery by a succession of rugged ridges, extending far back towards the mountains which bound the valleys. "The features of the ground were such as to nearly paralyze the artillery and cavalry of the enemy, while his infantry would not derive all the advantage of his numerical superiority. In this well-selected position, Gen. Taylor, at the head of 5,000 effective men, chiefly volunteers, prepared to receive the enemy—22,000 strong, and composed of the flower of the Mexican nation. In the order of battle Capt. Washington and battery was posted to command the road, while the First and Second Illinois Regiments, under Cols. Hardin and Bissell, and the Second Kentucky, under Col. McKee, occupied the crest of the ridges on the left and in the rear." At 11 o'clock on the 22d, the American army was summoned to surrender at discretion, and the usual defiance returned. The battle of Buena Vista began in earnest on the morning of the 23d of February, and continued all day. Towards evening the enemy were driven from the field and the Americans were victorious, but not without great loss of life—264 killed, 450 wounded, 26 missing, on the American side; Mexican loss estimated, killed and wounded, 2,000 men. The commanding general, in his official report, remarks: "In the last conflict we had the misfortune to sustain a very heavy loss—Col. Hardin, First Illinois; Col. McKee and Lieut.-Col. Clay, Second Kentucky Regiments fell, while gallantly leading their commands." He further adds, "No loss falls more heavily on the army than that of Col. Hardin.

Thus ends the life of Col. John J. Hardin. His career was brilliant, and his star went down ere it had reached its zenith. He left three children—Ellen, now the widow of M. T. Walworth, of Saratoga; Gen. Martin D. Hardin, a lawyer of Chicago, who lost his arm in defense of his country in our late war, and Lemuel Smith Hardin, who lost an arm in the Southern army and lives in Kentucky.

Col. Hardin we have seen as a statesman and warrior. He was also a Christian for years, and elected, just before leaving for the Mexican war, an elder in the Presbyterian Church. He entertained sound religious principles and hoped for salvation only through the Atonement of Christ.

Col. Hardin's services for the community and country are referred to on pages 44, 45, 50, 53, 63, 70, 74, 78, 79, 80, 89, 100, 103, 110, 111, 117, 119, 120, 121, 127, 129, 162, 182, 239, 328.

HON. WM. BROWN, one of the older attorneys in practice and senior member of the firm of Brown & Kirby, was born in Booneville, Mo., September 20th, 1840, and is a graduate of Illinois College. He read law at Booneville, Mo., under the direction of Judge Wash. Adams, late Chief Justice of the Supreme Court of Missouri, and was admitted to the bar in 1861. Mr. Brown was elected City Clerk and Attorney of Jacksonville in 1862, and re-elected to the same position in 1863. In 1864 he was elected State's Attorney of the counties of Morgan, Scott, Greene, Jersey and Calhoun, and in 1868 was re-elected as State's Attorney in same circuit. In 1872 he resigned, and was appointed County Attorney, by Judge Scott, for term ending December 1872. He was elected in November, 1872, State Senator for the 30th district, composed of the counties of Morgan and Greene, and from 1872 to 1874, was chairman of the Democratic State Central Committee. Mr. Brown is justly regarded as one of the most prominent members of the bar, with a large and lucrative practice. He has been identified with the politics of the State for many years, and often favorably spoken of by his party friends in connection with the highest offices of the State. As a practitioner he is justly regarded as one of the ablest and most brilliant in the West, interests of the largest of railroad and other corporations being placed in his care.

Mr. Brown has been happily married twice, first to Miss Clara, daughter of David Robb, Esq., and secondly to Miss Eliza Martin. Three promising children by the first marriage—Miss Kate and Masters William and Lloyd—survive their mother and there is also one child by the second union.

See pages 179, 181, 248.

JOSHUA MOORE,

OF JACKSONVILLE.

For Biographical Sketch see pages 315-16.

DAVID B. AYERS.—Among the men who early became identified with the moral and intellectual welfare of Jacksonville and Morgan county, no one has left a more desirable record than the subject of this biography. The great aim of his life, like that of His whom he humbly sought to imitate, was to do good. He was active and energetic among the few pioneers of the Sabbath School work of his time. His history shows conclusively, that for nearly half a century of life, he fully comprehended its importance. He has left to the world a brilliant record of his faith, shown by his untiring zeal and energy in this work. As one of the original trustees of the Jacksonville Female Academy, which position he occupied till his death, he exhibited his love and devotion to the cause of education.

One of the channels of his benevolence was furnishing finances, aid and encouragement to young men who were striving to obtain an education. These private acts of his beneficence are still treasured up in grateful hearts living to-day.

David B. Ayers was born November 21, 1798, in Newark, New Jersey. He was the son of David and Abigail Ayers, and removed to Philadelphia, where he engaged in the sale of drugs and medicines. Here the subject of this sketch was educated, and was married November 1, 1821, to Miss Eliza, daughter of Daniel and Mary Freytag. He continued his business in the sale of drugs until 1830, when with his family, he settled in the village of Jacksonville, where he established, on East State street, near the Public Square, the first drug store in Morgan county, which was doubtless the first in the state.

He erected a building on the corner of West State street and the square, which he moved into in 1832 and occupied for many years. The site is now covered by the elegant banking house of M. P. Ayers & Co. He soon added books to his trade, which was the first stock of importance in that line in the county. As agent of Mr. John Grigg, of Philadelphia, assisted by others, he sold 125,000 acres of land, in various counties in Illinois. In the sale of these lands he was actively engaged, his two sons becoming his successors in his former mercantile interests. He finished his earthly record September 26, 1850. He was an earnest Christian, and a useful and highly respected citizen. Mr. Ayers and his family (as his parents before him) were active members of the Presbyterian church. His mother, after a residence of eighteen years in Morgan county, died at the advanced age of ninety-four years. His wife is still living in Jacksonville. Mr. Ayers has not only bequeathed to posterity the example of a well spent life, but has left representatives who are among the business men of the county, interested largely in the financial and manufacturing interests, with which, for over forty years, they have been identified.

JAMES H. LURTON was born in Scott county, Kentucky, March 21, 1813. He was the fourth child of Dr. William Lurton, who had a family of nine children, six of whom are now living. Dr. Lurton was a prominent physician of Kentucky. He removed to Morgan county in 1833, where he resided till his death in 1839. James H., came to Morgan county in October, 1831, and located on what is known as Jersey Prairie. He was Deputy Sheriff for three years, under Alexander Dunlap. In 1833 he was appointed by the county court, Collector of Morgan county, which position he filled about four years. He was then elected Assessor and Collector, which office he filled for several consecutive terms. One fact worthy of record is, that Mr. Lurton was never defeated for any office in the county; i. e. when he had the vote of the county for a county office. He resigned his office in 1850, and engaged in merchandising, in Jacksonville, which business he continued until 1862. He was elected in 1861, Collector and Treasurer of the county, which position he filled with ability till 1869. He was married at the age of 39 to Miss Mary Stribling, daughter of Rev. W. C. Stribling. By this union they have had a family of nine children, eight of whom are still living. His oldest daughter is the wife of Dr. G. B. Sarchette, a gentleman of French origin, who is now residing at Terre Haute, Indiana. His oldest son,

William S., is married and resides near his father and is largely and actively engaged in the ice trade.

Mr. Lurton has given all his children the advantages of a good education. He became early in life identified with the Democratic party. Mr. Lurton, when he became a citizen of Morgan county, had but little capital, but by persevering energy and strict adherence to business has amassed sufficient to make him comfortable. He is one of the early citizens of the county whom the people have thoroughly tested and as an advocate of their interests, he has never been found wanting. He has done much, by his energy and capital, to develop and improve the county, in which for over forty years he has been an active public man, and a respected and useful citizen. The people have reposed in him the utmost confidence by conferring upon him many posts of honor and trust.

E. S. HINRICHSEN was born in the Grand Duchy of Mechlinberg, on the 29th of April, 1815, and was educated in the mercantile line of business. After attending the usual common schools of the country, he was a clerk of the city of Laarge for three years. He next entered a large wholesale establishment in the city of Hamburg. He was also supercargo of a vessel for nearly three years, and made two trips to the Mediterranean, one to Sumatra, and one to South America. After the latter voyage he was shipwrecked on the Louisiana coast, and finally landed on the Unhappy Islands. He then went up the Mississippi river, then up the Ohio, and came to Pennsylvania. He then made two trips to New Orleans, on the river, and next engaged in railroading, under Thad. Stevens—afterwards the great commoner—on the Harrisburg & Gettysburg railway. This road was called the "Thad. Stevens tape-worm," owing to its peculiar grade and curves.

When Mr. Hinrichsen first came to Pennsylvania, he discovered the oil which of late has made Oil Creek so famous. He had some analyzed by a chemist at Pittsburg, who pronounced it excellent for wheel-grease. It was called at the time, "American Rock Oil." He did not understand the nature of the same, and thus let the golden opportunity of making a fortune slip through his hands, not knowing that the oil could be obtained in large quantities by boring. At that time, any of the land could be purchased for eighteen and three-fourths cents per acre. Mr. H. was the first man in the country to have oil analyzed, and was the predecessor of those speculating parties, who almost coined gold out of the wild and inhospitable soil of the oil regions. There is much credit due Mr. H., for first introducing to the chemist this far-famed petroleum.

Mr. H. started for the West in 1840, and arrived in Illinois in the latter part of March of the some year. After a close examination of the State, he settled in Franklin, Morgan county, about seven miles south of where Alexander is now situated. Here he established himself in the mercantile business. He remained in this line of trade until 1852. He laid out Franklin, now known as Orleans, in 1852, and established his brother in the general merchandise business, but the style of the firm was in the name of the subject of this sketch. In 1853 he sold his store at Franklin, and purchased a farm three miles north of that place. He was also station-agent at Orleans, and grain-buyer. In 1856 he purchased over 100,000 bushels of wheat. Not being able to obtain sufficient ground for building purposes at Orleans, in 1857 he laid out the present town of Alexander. This place ever since has been the home of Mr. Hinrichsen. He was the stock-agent of the Great Western (now W. St. L. & P.) railroad, in 1857. He held that position, to the satisfaction of all parties concerned, till 1867, when the consolidated Toledo, Wabash & Western railway appointed him general stock-agent for the road, with the single exception of the city of St. Louis. The position was a great compliment to the business skill and management of the subject of this article. That he was worthy the confidence placed in him by the officers of this great corporation, is evident from the long series of years in which he was in their employ.

As to the domestic relations of Mr. H.,

we would state that he was married in 1845, to Miss Anna Wyatt, daughter of William Wyatt, Esq., of Franklin precinct. He was among the first pioneers of Morgan county, and is regarded as among its most prominent citizens. Six children are the result of his marriage,—three boys and three girls. The oldest son—Wm. H.—is now thirty-five years of age, and the popular editor and part owner of the *Illinois Courier*.

We have given a terse and brief sketch of the life of Mr. H., so full of striking and interesting events. What he is today is due to his remarkable business adaptability, his knowledge of men, and that instinctive love of order—a peculiar characteristic of great railroad men. Withal, he is a kind, affectionate neighbor, hospitable to strangers, and an advocate of the right. His generosity is only equalled by his urbanity. He is popular among all acquaintances, and is recognized as a first-class business man.

GEORGE W. SMITH, Attorney, was born in Danville, Boyle county, Kentucky, November 19th, 1837, and came with his parents to Jacksonville, March 8th, 1841. He was educated at private schools, and attended the school under the charge of President Newton Bateman, during the years 1856-'57, and also was a student in Illinois College in the years 1858-'59. In 1868 he was elected City Marshal, of the city of Jacksonville, for one term. He pursued his law studies in the law office of Judge Cyrus Epler in the years 1863-'64, and again read law in the winter of 1868-'69. He was admitted to the bar by the Supreme Court of this State. In April, 1877, Mr. Smith was elected a member of the City Board of Education from the First Ward, and re-elected to the same position, and for the same length of term, in 1879, '81, '83 and '85. Mr. Smith has followed his profession closely since he began practice, and is quite active in politics, figuring prominently in all local Democratic caucuses and conventions.

Mr. Smith was a volunteer soldier in the Union army, serving as a private in Company A, 68th Regiment, Illinois volunteer infantry. This was under a three months call in June, 1862, and in May, 1864, he re-enlisted for one hundred days service in the 133d Illinois volunteer infantry regiment, being Captain of Company B, until mustered out September 24, 1864.

JUDGE SAMUEL WOOD was born in Madison county, Kentucky, October 16, 1813. He is the oldest son of Richard Wood, who was a native of Amherst county, Virginia, and who emigrated to Madison county, Kentucky, in 1806. He was married to Miss Celia Gregory, several years before he left Virginia. He had, by this union, ten children, four of whom died in youth; the others, in after life, became citizens of Morgan county. They were, in the order of their birth: Nancy (deceased), former wife of Andrew Samples, now residing near Waverly; Jane (deceased), former wife of Robert Hardin, of California; Polly, present wife of Nathan Moore, of La Plata, Missouri; Samuel the subject of this sketch, residing on section 16, township 14, range 9; James, of Labette county, Kansas; Rebecca (deceased), former wife of James Antyl, of Morgan county, Illinois. Mr. Wood's first wife died in Madison county Illinois, in November, 1819. He was again married in 1821, to Mrs. Hessie Conlee. He settled on section 9, township 14, range 9, in March, 1826. Mr. Wood was one of the pioneers of Morgan county who, by practical industry and a moral life, was an ornament to the early community in which he lived, and a blessing to his family. His wife died in September, 1861, and he June 20, 1865. They were both esteemed for their many virtues.

The subject of this sketch first settled on section 16, in the township where he now resides. He purchased, entirely on credit, forty acres, in 1837, which he has from time to time, increased until, at the present, he has nearly 3,000 acres of land, being the largest improved farm in the county.

Although Judge Wood had but a small financial capital, with which to begin life, yet he possessed that which was more valuable, viz., an enduring basis of moral principles, with an energy untiring and persistent, which, combined, have not only made him a good farmer, but a useful citizen. He is strictly a self-made man. His education is practical, and he possesses those business qualifications which insure success. His citizenship outranks the State, as he became a citizen of Illinois one year before it was admitted into the Union. He has devoted an active and industrious life, thus far, to developing a county and State which take pride in claiming him as one of their prominent and useful citizens.

He was married January 5, 1831, to Mrs. Martha Smith, relict of Harvey Smith, by which union he had eight children, in the following order of birth, viz.: James, born March 16, 1833, residing two miles east of his father; Elizabeth, born September 24, 1835, who died July 27, 1844; David, born April 4, 1838, residing three miles east of his father; Milton, born September 4, 1839, residing five miles west of Springfield; Iven, born February 24, 1841, residing near his father; George, born December 9, 1842, also residing near his father; Julia A., born June 17, 1847, wife of James B. Beekman; and Richard S., born October 20, 1851.

Judge Wood and his wife are still living, in the enjoyment of mental and physical strength almost unimpaired by age, and they may still remain for years, a blessing to their family, and to the community of which, for so many years, they have been active and useful members.

Mr. Wood was elected Commissioner of the County Court, in November 1869, which position he filled with ability, and satisfactorily to his fellow citizens. He, like his father before him, has made farming and stock-growing a specialty, yet his activity and zeal as a Democrat and worth as a citizen caused him to receive nomination and election as a member of the House of Representatives, in 1874, where he served his constituents in a most creditable manner. At the close of his legislative term he returned to his farm home, and has since been content to remain in quiet rural employment

See pages 51 and 203.

NEWTON BATEMAN was born July 27, 1822. His father, Bergen Bateman moved to Illinois in 1833, taking with him, among his children, one of the brightest natives of that New Jersey town of Fairfield. This youth, in his seventeenth year, was permitted to prepare himself for college. He had no teacher, and there was no room in his father's house in which he could study; but near the house stood an old elm tree, eleven feet in diameter. He tried it, found it hollow, with an ax cut a door in the side of it, removed some of the dead wood, put down a carpet, made a rough table and stool, built a fire in front of the door, and commenced the study of the Latin Grammar. He made the preparation for college in four months, and entered the Freshman class of Illinois College, in September, 1840, and was graduated in the class of 1843. From 1868 to 1876, he served as one of the Board of Trustees of the college.

In 1850 he was Principal of the West District (now Second Ward) School, of Jacksonville. During the years of 1856-58 he was County Commissioner of Schools for Morgan county, and for part of the time in charge of the public schools of the city. He was re-elected County Commissioner without opposition. After devoting seven years to this work, he resigned, and became Principal of the Jacksonville Female Academy, in 1858; but he was elected, before the close of the year, State Superintendent of Public Instruction. In the meantime he had taken a foremost and toilsome part for three years, in the successful effort to establish the Normal University. Five times he was elected State Superintendent, for two years each; and every time, except one, by a larger majority than any other man on the successful Republican ticket with him. He published, near the end of each term, a masterly volume in the form of a report, and the volumes of the series have placed him in the front rank of educational writers. It is believed that the reports of no other State Superintendent except Horace Mann, have ever received so widespread and profound attention and study in this country.

During the years 1862-64 he had charge

of the correspondence of the Provost Marshal General of the state, and kept thirty-five clerks busy in this work. He then resumed the State Superintendency of Public Instruction. He was appointed, by the National Association of Superintendents, to be one of the committee of three to ask Congress to establish the Bureau of Education; and the committee were charged to prepare a bill for the purpose. He went to Washington on this business in 1867, and the law now in force is essentially the committee's draft. He sometimes has made an hundred public addresses a year, and he rarely repeats one more than five times. He makes good use of his native language and of a persuasive eloquence. In 1847 he was elected President of Knox College, and has since successfully filled that office, showing himself well worthy of his degree of Doctor of Laws.

See pages 108, 127, 130, 153, 185, 242, 265, 266, 267.

In closing this series of biographical sketches the compiler begs the indulgence of space sufficient to copy the following from Jeriah Bonham's "Fifty Years' Recollections," Peoria.

"Charles M. Eames was born at Jacksonville, November 6th, 1845, son of T. Dwight and A. M. Eames, of that city. He early entered the schools, but from the fact of having delicate health never completed his education fully. He entered the freshman class of Illinois College in September, 1863, and did his first journalistic work as a county fair reporter in October, 1866, and was the Jacksonville reporter for the Chicago *Republican* and Springfield *Journal* in 1868, and later, in the same year, was city editor of the Quincy *Whig* for six months. After practicing the journalistic profession he, for a while, gave it up and engaged in the wholesale and retail book and stationery business in Jacksonville for eight years.

In 1876 he bought Horace Chapin's half interest in the *Daily* and *Weekly Journal*, and in 1878 bought the other half interest of M. F. Simmons, and filled successively the positions of city editor, news editor, political editor and business manager. At present he is sole proprietor and managing editor, devoting most of his time to the business. He was married November 14, 1876, to Carrie M. Hall, of Wallingford, Conn., and four children has been the result of this marriage—Hattie, Beverly, Charlie and Susie.

Mr. Eames is active in sustaining the benevolent efforts of the following orders: He became an Odd Fellow in 1868, a Good Templar in 1866, a Mason in 1871, a Knight Templar in 1881, and a Royal Templar of Temperance in 1880. He gave his first presidential vote for Grant in 1868, and voted for every republican candidate since. In 1880 he was a member of the republican city, county, state and national conventions, and in the latter voted with the "306." Mr. Eames is very active in all the religious and benevolent works of the churches; has been a delegate to the Presbytery, Synod and General Assembly of the Presbyterian church, with which denomination he has been connected since 1863. He has been Ruling Elder since 1879, and Sunday School Superintendent since 1871; was State Sunday School Statistical Secretary from 1880-'82, and District Sunday School President for four years.

For a man that does not enjoy first class health Mr. Eames performs an immense amount of labor, so many duties requiring his attention that he is obliged to economize his time very closely to fill all the responsibilities he has assumed."

GENERAL INDEX.

A.

B.

C.

D.

E.

F.

G.

H.

I.

J.

K.

L.

M.

N.

O.

P.

Q.

R.

S.

T.

U.

V.

W.

Y.

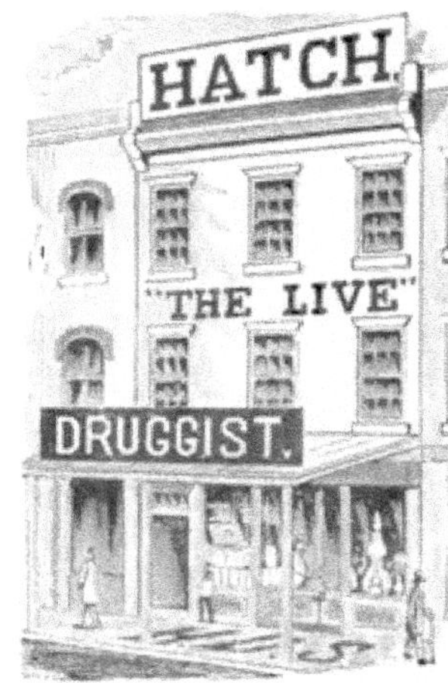

Two West Side Stores, 1885.

Interior View of the Jacksonville Business College, 1885.

INDIVIDUAL INDEX.

A.

B.

C.

D.

E.

F.

G.

H.

I.

J.

K.

N.

O.

P.

LIST OF PORTRAITS.

LIST OF ILLUSTRATIONS.

www.ingramcontent.com/pod-product-compliance
Lightning Source LLC
Chambersburg PA
CBHW030912270326
41929CB00008B/663